Manual of
Forensic Taphonomy

Manual of
Forensic
Taphonomy

Edited by
James T. Pokines
Steven A. Symes

CRC Press
Taylor & Francis Group
Boca Raton London New York

CRC Press is an imprint of the
Taylor & Francis Group, an **informa** business

CRC Press
Taylor & Francis Group
6000 Broken Sound Parkway NW, Suite 300
Boca Raton, FL 33487-2742

Printed on acid-free paper
Version Date: 20130722

Printed and bound in India by Replika Press Pvt. Ltd.

International Standard Book Number-13: 978-1-4398-7841-5 (Hardback)

Library of Congress Cataloging-in-Publication Data

Manual of forensic taphonomy / [edited by] James Pokines, Steven A. Symes.
    pages cm
    "A CRC title."
    Includes bibliographical references and index.
    ISBN 978-1-4398-7841-5 (hardcover : alk. paper)
    1. Forensic taphonomy. 2. Postmortem changes. 3. Crime scene searches. I. Pokines, James T. II. Symes, Steve A.

RA1063.47.M36 2014
614'.1--dc23   2013027839

Visit the Taylor & Francis Web site at
http://www.taylorandfrancis.com

and the CRC Press Web site at
http://www.crcpress.com

For Ted Rathbun, scholar and friend.

Contents

Preface

The recognition of the importance of taphonomy to forensic anthropological analysis has grown greatly in the past two decades due to the work of multiple researchers to whom this volume owes a great debt. As a subdiscipline, however, forensic taphonomy still lags behind other types of basic forensic anthropological analysis, including pathology, trauma, and determination of biological parameters (sex, age, stature, etc.) in terms of comparative data and codification of observations and terminology. The greater codification of taphonomic observations and their interpretations is also becoming more necessary professionally. This change is due to the requirements placed upon the field of forensic anthropology through the recent findings of the National Academy of Sciences, mandating the establishment of best practices and increased professional certification for forensic laboratories and individual practitioners.

This volume addresses the many taphonomic alterations to bone and related taphonomic processes that are common to cases of forensic interest. It also addresses the many taphonomic processes that commonly occur in cases that may need to be ruled out as being of forensic interest. These taphonomic processes include the effects of varying burial environment, animal scavenging and transport, fluvial transport, human transport, cultural modification, marine environments, subaerial weathering, fire, and recovery methods used in collecting the remains. In addition, background information is presented concerning the inherent variations in survivability of different bones or portions thereof, degradation of DNA in different environments, and the processes of and organisms involved in soft-tissue decomposition, which results in skeletonization. Effects to the bones described and explained include microscopic alterations, color changes, macroscopic physical damage of multiple types (including cracking, erosion, and consumption), and bone loss through dispersal away from the location of initial body deposition. The methods that can be employed to determine the timing of taphonomic damage (perimortem vs. postmortem) are also presented, as well as checklists for the collection of microscopic and macroscopic taphonomic data.

While information is lost through these destructive alterations, information is also gained through accurate analysis and interpretation of the changes imprinted upon osseous remains, allowing, in many cases, the determination of the causal agency or agencies involved. These observations in turn can be used to demarcate taphonomic suites of characteristics, which are often combined with other lines of evidence and can indicate a probable set of forces or processes that altered a set of skeletal remains. Alterations to bones are rarely singular in their origin, with the overlapping markers of multiple taphonomic processes being typical. We hope that this volume will aid greatly in sorting out among the multiple alterations to bones involved in complicated taphonomic histories.

The information that can be derived from these taphonomic observations falls into three categories: the depositional contexts to which the remains were exposed (what kind of environments), temporal information regarding the absolute timing of events (how long the remains have been exposed to those environments), and perimortem versus postmortem timing of taphonomic alterations (the relative timing of events and processes that altered the remains). These data greatly affect the interpretation of osseous remains gathered from potential crime scenes and are in many cases the major determinant of what type of case a forensic anthropologist is dealing with: an actual crime scene with alteration or transport of remains deliberately caused by humans; a death not caused by criminal acts, which is followed by animal scavenging, dispersal, and other largely natural processes; or a historical or archaeological burial, which must be ruled out as being a crime scene and referred to another government agency. Taphonomic analysis therefore is analogous to a type of triage, where the type of skeletal case and its ultimate disposition are decided by the changes that have occurred to the skeletal remains. This analysis of course is greatly aided by knowledge of the recovery context and associated artifacts, and both types of data should be used when determining the chain of events that occurred between the time of death and the time when the remains were recovered.

The focus of the volume therefore is upon the recognition of taphonomic characteristics and the discrimination between osseous alterations with similar appearances but dissimilar origins. It is hoped that the information presented here will be useful to students and nonspecialists and will serve as a reference manual for professionals.

Editors

James T. Pokines, PhD, D-ABFA, is an assistant professor in the Forensic Anthropology Program, Department of Anatomy and Neurobiology, Boston University of Medicine. Prior to this, he served for 12 years at the Central Identification Laboratory in Hawaii as a forensic anthropologist and forensic archaeologist. Dr. Pokines received his BA in anthropology and archaeology from Cornell University, his MA and PhD in anthropology from the University of Chicago, and his ABFA board certification in forensic anthropology in 2003. His research includes taphonomy, vertebrate osteology, zooarchaeology, and paleoecology, and he has ongoing osteological research projects in the Bolivian and Peruvian Andes (Tiwanaku sites); Tell Timai in the Nile Delta, Egypt; and the Paleolithic of northern Jordan. He is also the Forensic Anthropologist for the Commonwealth of Massachusetts, Office of the Chief Medical Examiner, Boston.

Steven A. Symes, PhD, D-ABFA, is a US forensic anthropologist best known for his expertise in interpreting trauma to bone and a leading authority on saw and knife mark analysis. With 30 years experience, he has assisted federal, state, local, and non-US authorities in the identification, analysis, and documentation of those suspected to be victims of trauma. A sought-after consultant in criminal cases, Dr. Symes has been qualified as an expert for both the prosecution and defense, testifying specifically on forensic tool mark and fracture pattern interpretation in bone, as well as blunt force, ballistic, burned, and healing trauma in bone. Because of his specialty in criminal dismemberment and mutilation, he has worked a number of serial homicides and has provided analysis of cut marks in nearly 200 dismemberment cases and approximately 400 knife wound cases. Dr. Symes is one of about 100 forensic anthropologists certified by the American Board of Forensic Anthropology. He has lectured, consulted, or testified on trauma cases, among them high-profile human rights cases, in the United States, Canada, Mexico, Peru, Argentina, Chile, El Salvador, Colombia, Indonesia, Cyprus, Kosovo, and numerous areas in Europe and Southern Africa. In addition, he has authored more than 50 publications and delivered over 100 papers, lectures, and workshops on a variety of forensic anthropology topics on bone trauma.

Contributors

Joan E. Baker
Defense Prisoner of War/Missing Personnel Office
Department of Defense Pentagon
Washington, District of Columbia

Stephanie E. Baker
Centre for Anthropological Research (CFAR)
Faculty of Humanities
University of Johannesburg
Johannesburg, South Africa

David O. Carter
Laboratory of Forensic Taphonomy
Division of Natural Sciences and Mathematics
Chaminade University of Honolulu
Honolulu, Hawaii

Derek Congram
Central Identification Laboratory
Joint POW/MIA Accounting Command
Joint Base Pearl Harbor-Hickam, Hawaii

Franklin E. Damann
Anatomical Division
National Museum of Health and Medicine
Silver Spring, Maryland

Tosha L. Dupras
Department of Anthropology
University of Central Florida
Orlando, Florida

Thomas Evans
Department of Earth Sciences
Montana State University
Bozeman, Montana

Nicholas D. Higgs
Marine Institute
Plymouth University
Plymouth, United Kingdom

Miranda M.E. Jans
Central Identification Laboratory
Joint POW/MIA Accounting Command
Joint Base Pearl Harbor-Hickam, Hawaii

Christine A. Junod
Forensic Anthropology Program
Department of Anatomy and Neurobiology
School of Medicine
Boston University
Boston, Massachusetts

Natalie Keough
Department of Anatomy
Faculty of Health Sciences
School of Medicine
University of Pretoria
Pretoria, South Africa

Alexandra R. Klales
Department of Anthropology
University of Manitoba
Winnipeg, Manitoba, Canada

Ericka N. L'Abbé
Department of Anatomy
Faculty of Health Sciences
School of Medicine
University of Pretoria
Pretoria, South Africa

Marcelle LaCroix
Forensic Anthropology Program
Department of Anatomy and Neurobiology
School of Medicine
Boston University
Boston, Massachusetts

Krista E. Latham
Department of Biology and Anthropology
University of Indianapolis
Indianapolis, Indiana

R. Lee Lyman
Department of Anthropology
University of Missouri
Columbia, Missouri

Megan E. Madonna
Department of Biology and Anthropology
University of Indianapolis
Indianapolis, Indiana

Diana Messer
Department of Applied Forensic Science
Mercyhurst University
Erie, Pennsylvania

Josephine M. Paolello
Department of Anthropology
University of Hawai'i at Manoa
Honolulu, Hawaii

James T. Pokines
Forensic Anthropology Program
Department of Anatomy and Neurobiology
School of Medicine
Boston University
and
Office of the Chief Medical Examiner
Commonwealth of Massachusetts
Boston, Massachusetts

John J. Schultz
Department of Anthropology
University of Central Florida
Orlando, Florida

Amy Stromquist
Department of Applied Forensic Science
Mercyhurst University
Erie, Pennsylvania

Kyra E. Stull
Department of Anatomy
Faculty of Health Sciences
School of Medicine
University of Pretoria
Pretoria, South Africa

Steven A. Symes
Department of Applied Forensic Science
Mercyhurst University
Erie, Pennsylvania

Taylor Yuzwa
Department of Applied Forensic Science
Mercyhurst University
Erie, Pennsylvania

Introduction

Collection of Macroscopic Osseous Taphonomic Data and the Recognition of Taphonomic Suites of Characteristics

1

JAMES T. POKINES

Contents

> And we don't know just where our bones will rest
> To dust I guess; forgotten and absorbed into the earth below
> —**Smashing Pumpkins, *1979***

Goals of This Volume

Why does one so rarely have a complete human skeleton to examine? This question is of maddening frequency and considerable importance in forensic anthropology, since it tempers in so many ways what other information may be read from a set of remains (Ubelaker 1997). The fundamental questions in any forensic skeletal analysis include the determination of human vs. nonhuman, the minimum number of individuals, age at death, sex, stature, ancestry, perimortem trauma, antemortem trauma, osseous pathology, and odontology. These analyses together are used to form the biological profiles of the individuals present, which in turn narrow the identification of those remains or in some cases lead to their positive identification. The patterns of perimortem and antemortem trauma may aid other medicolegal specialists in the determination of the cause of death and manner of death. All of these other analyses become incrementally more difficult or impossible with the fragmentation, general surface degradation, and loss of skeletal elements. Whether these bones were made unavailable for analysis through their actual destruction or through their nonrecovery due to dispersal by water, gravity, carnivores, or the lack of a suitable archaeological field system, the overall effect is the same regarding the information lost. These analytical problems parallel those of other disciplines, including the field of biological anthropology as a whole, zooarchaeology, and vertebrate paleontology, where taphonomic changes often lead to information loss.

Taphonomic processes affecting skeletal remains leave behind alterations, macroscopic (Lyman 1994; Micozzi 1991) and microscopic (Nielsen-Marsh and Hedges 2000; see Chapter 2, this volume), which can be "read" and interpreted. Indeed, the patterning of present versus missing skeletal elements can be interpreted as well (Chapter 4). The aim of this volume is to categorize these alterations to skeletal remains, illustrate and explain their significance, and demonstrate how to differentiate among them where possible. These observations may then be combined into higher-order patterns to aid forensic investigators in determining what happened to those remains in the interval from death to analysis. Moreover, it is rare that a single type of alteration has affected a set of skeletal remains, and the overlapping markers of multiple types of skeletal alteration are typically left upon them. Since these processes affect other vertebrates in similar manners, this volume will be of use to other disciplines, and information derived from these other disciplines is also presented here.

While this volume is primarily focused upon large vertebrate and specifically human skeletal remains, it synthesizes data from human (Berryman et al. 1991, 1997; Nawrocki 1995; Rogers 2005; Schultz et al. 2003), ethological (Patterson 1996; Peterson 1977; Pobiner 2007), geological/paleontological (Behrensmeyer 1991; Martin 1999; Voorhies 1969), paleoanthropological (Brain 1980, 1981; Hill 1980; Shipman 1981), archaeological artifactual (Odell and Cowan 1987), and zooarchaeological (Binford 1981; Binford and Bertram 1977; Fisher 1996; Lyman 1994, 2008; Payne 1983) studies. Apart from the similarities in postmortem changes between humans and other large vertebrates (Micozzi 1991), studies utilizing nonhuman fauna have the benefit of typically much larger sample sizes (Behrensmeyer 1991) to add to forensic taphonomic discussions as well as the greater availability for experimental analyses. Indeed, pigs (*Sus scrofa*) are the most common analog used for humans in forensic experiments of all kinds, given their overlapping characteristics with humans (range of adult body mass, subcutaneous fat stores, skin thickness, hair covering, and omnivorous diets) and the ubiquity of purpose-bred pigs for experimentation in university settings. Nonhuman remains can be left exposed outdoors to natural forces with fewer strictures on their placement or (often justifiable) concern of the public, and often for longer durations. Human remains from decomposition studies also are usually expected to yield at the end of soft-tissue decomposition a largely intact human skeleton for subsequent research and teaching, so most highly destructive taphonomic processes affecting osseous remains directly (large vertebrate scavenging and dispersal, extensive subaerial weathering, acidic soil corrosion, thermal alteration, abrasion, cracking from drying, etc.) are actively avoided. It is also important to note that zooarchaeological samples can be typically two orders or more of magnitude larger than human samples from the same broad depositional setting (with some exceptions mostly coming from cemetery settings) or modern observational studies of humans.

While this volume covers differentiation between perimortem trauma vs. postmortem damage (Chapter 13), broad treatment of human-induced perimortem trauma (gunshot wound, blunt force trauma, etc.) is too large and varied a topic to cover effectively in this volume. It is logical to group this type of trauma under the broader category of taphonomy, if one views human-induced damage to bone as another specialized type of taphonomic alteration. Like other types of taphonomic alteration, human-induced trauma may begin at the time of death or continue into the postmortem interval (PMI) through dismemberment and burial (Chapter 5) of remains. Human transportation of remains in both wartime and homicide settings is covered in Chapter 10, and human ritual and anatomical collection taphonomic characteristics are covered in Chapter 8. The effects of archaeological recovery upon remains recovered are discussed in Chapter 17.

Taphonomy

The study of these changes in biological remains from the time of death until their recovery and analysis is of course referred to as *taphonomy*. The term taphonomy was coined by Efremov (1940) in his famous article, defining it as "the science of burial." This first interest in taphonomic changes in organisms emerged among geologists and paleontologists, curious about why and how the fossils they found were preserved, and how observations of processes ongoing today would explain what had gone on in the past. Though preceded by other early geologists, James Hutton in his *The Theory of the Earth* (1788) first published the principle of *uniformitarianism*: the Earth's sedimentary rocks were accumulated by the same processes of sediment deposition visible in contemporary rivers and seas. This concept is applied throughout taphonomic investigations, where observations of bone-altering processes today are applied to the past. While taphonomy as a named discipline dates only from Efremov's work, earlier investigations into that specific topic exist. As early as 1823, Buckland (1823:93) had noted that "the bones of various birds, of moles, water-rats, mice" had been accumulated in limestone caves by the "agency of hawks," while fish bones had been accumulated in the same sites by gulls. This relationship between the type of osseous remains recovered and the species that had fed upon them, dispersed them, or in some cases reconcentrated them was to become central in twentieth and twenty-first century investigations of taphonomy. The early geologist Charles Lyell (1830–33:II:219–227) discussed how animal remains could accumulate in the deposits of caves and fissures by their acting as natural pit traps over long periods. In this manner, he noted that these remains often became associated with those of humans. In terms of direct alteration of bones themselves, Wedl (1864) examined postmortem microscopic changes to bone and found taphonomic changes in the form of microtunneling (Wedl tunnels) damage (see Chapter 2). Examining more specifically the decomposition and potential long-term preservation of vertebrate remains, Johannes Weigelt, a German professor of geology and paleontology, published *Rezente Wirbeltierleichen und ihre paläobiologische Bedeutung* (Recent Vertebrate Carcasses and Their Paleobiological Implications) in 1927, where he examined naturally occurring death assemblages such as the mass kills of large ungulates and their subsequent bone deposition (Weigelt 1989 [1927]). The direct link between observations of contemporary natural processes and their use in interpretation of events of the past is the core of this research, just as is common in more recent studies in forensic taphonomy including observations of animal behavior and natural physical forces such as marine transport affecting human remains (Haglund and Sorg 1997, 2002). Paleontologists, however, also have the unique problem of attempting to understand the ecological relationships of species with no modern analogs, an aspect explored in Shotwell's (1955) seminal early paper that presented a method for interpreting the paleoecological abundance of mammalian taxa within an assemblage and the biases affecting bone preservation. More actualistic experimental approaches to taphonomy came in the ensuing decades, including the early work of Voorhies (1969) in the use of water flume experiments to study the transport potential of large vertebrate remains to interpret remains from paleontological sites. By the 1970s, taphonomic research integrated into the analysis of biological remains became the norm (Behrensmeyer 1978; Binford and Bertram 1977; Miller 1969, 1975).

Forensic Taphonomy

Forensic taphonomy is more a descriptive term than a practical boundary, given the profuse overlap in taphonomic analytical techniques, data collected, interpretations, and goals with those of other anthropological and paleontological fields. A forensic anthropologist estimates the age of a recent human skeleton in much the same manner that a biological anthropologist estimates the age of a human skeleton from an excavation of an ancient (pre-Inka) Tiwanaku site in the Andes, citing many of the same standard sources, such as Buikstra and Ubelaker (1994) for basic biological profile data and Galloway (1999) for perimortem trauma. As stated previously, there are also wide areas of overlap with vertebrate zooarchaeology and paleontology (Behrensmeyer 1991), where, for example, much of the early data regarding weathering (Behrensmeyer 1978) still cited (Buikstra and Ubelaker 1994) in biological/forensic anthropology comes.

Forensic taphonomy is also the least quantified analytical subfield of forensic anthropology, perhaps due in part to this overlap with and reliance upon other disciplines, but also due to a lack of basic research in some areas, especially regarding human (or other species acting as proxy) skeletal degradation across a range of environments over prolonged periods. Also lacking is a comprehensive comparison of common taphonomic observations, the sets of environmental circumstances that caused them, and the places where confusion may occur when making observations and interpreting them. Forensic taphonomy also has some problems relatively unique to itself and the parameters under which it operates.

Time Frames Involved

Forensic anthropology concerns itself with a generally briefer time frame than other disciplines of biological anthropology or archaeology, and much shorter time frames than geology and paleontology (Pokines 2009). Many crime scenes or potential crime scenes are on the order of hours to days old before they are reported to and investigated by law enforcement. The PMI may increase to years in the case of remains such as those discovered in sealed homes, where the decedent's death went unnoticed or unreported. The interval also is increased for remains hidden in more rural locations that prevented their discovery (Haglund 1997a) or massive crime scenes such as the World Trade Center that yielded previously undiscovered osseous remains years later simply because it took so long to process the scene to recover them (Sledzik et al. 2009). Mass burials investigated for evidence of war crimes are typically on the order of years or decades old. This delay is typical, since the conflict that produced them often takes years or more to be resolved and allow outside aid agencies into an area (where their data collection may produce evidence indicting members of current or recent governments). Deeper into the PMI, historical burials are (by definition) decades or centuries old. These often must be investigated as if they are of forensic interest until determined otherwise, and the disturbance or looting of historical graves may be of law enforcement interest. Sites of archaeological or paleontological interest are usually not mistaken for those of forensic interest, but sometimes must be treated as pertaining to the latter category until proven otherwise (e.g., the famous cases of the Kennewick Man in the United States or the Bronze Age Ice Man in the Italian Alps).

All of these temporal categories share the early PMI, where decomposition, consumption, and most dispersal occur. Study of this subdiscipline of taphonomy is sometimes termed *necrology* (Behrensmeyer and Kidwell 1985), where the initial changes following death and the loss of soft tissue are examined. A bone encountered during these earlier stages, with more associated soft tissue attached externally or contained internally, is of higher resource potential to other species coexisting in the depositional environment. Most destructive processes affecting skeletal remains occur during the early phases after death, when the bone is attached to or contains more nutrients: if the bone can survive beyond the initial mortality incident, the numerous changes that may occur in the next few years, and be deposited in a location favorable to long-term preservation, its chances for survival into the historical, archaeological, and paleontological periods with potential for later discovery become much greater. The taphonomic subdiscipline of *biostratinomy* examines the processes prior to and leading up to burial, including transport, dispersal, and sedimentation, which is followed temporally by *diagenesis*, the chemical changes occurring to a bone after burial (Behrensmeyer and Kidwell 1985). The vast majority of bones, of course, do not survive to reach the processes examined in studies of biostratinomy or diagenesis, or the surface of the Earth would be covered in bone. While it is difficult to survey the surface or excavate in most terrestrial environments and not locate some kind of bone from the local vertebrate fauna, that same bone likely would not survive in a recognizable state decades or centuries later. Exceptions occur in some artificial environments, including some cemeteries or grander burial environments such as extensive Old World urban catacombs or Egyptian monuments. They also occur in some natural environments, such as where burial in undisturbed sediments occurred quickly or especially in limestone caves where their neutral to low alkaline pH sediments and overall protective environment greatly increase bones chances for surviving into the paleontological time range (Brain 1981).

Osseous analysts studying these older PMIs are equally as curious about the very early PMI (relative to those remains, i.e., the events immediately following the death of a species millions of years ago) as are forensic anthropologists investigating contemporary human decomposition. All bones must survive this phase (necrological) to reach the later phases (biostratinomic and diagenetic), and the early phase often determines if the bone survives at all and if the bone makes it into a depositional setting where it can be preserved for later discovery. In terms of vertebrate taphonomy, these disciplines have much more in common than not. One must also note that in many settings, other large vertebrates besides humans (including other hominins) pass through the same or very similar phases of taphonomic alteration, so the examination of zooarchaeological specimens is highly relevant to forensic taphonomy. Cross-pollination between these disciplines therefore is very productive, both in terms of past research and future joint research.

Other Problems in Forensic Taphonomic Analysis

Forensic anthropologists do not always perform their own field recovery of skeletal remains. They are often given remains by others associated with law enforcement and asked to reconstruct what may have happened to these remains during the PMI and to estimate the PMI itself. In these cases, the forensic anthropologist essentially must read the taphonomic history from the remains, with no other initial sources of information. This may be in some cases because the information is neither known nor suspected. Whether voluntary or involuntary, this procedure is known as *blind analysis* and also applies to the other portions of the biological profile (age, sex, ancestry, etc.). In some cases, forensic anthropologists are expected to perform voluntarily a blind analysis and deliberately have been given no information on the taphonomic history of the remains or suspected identity/ biological parameters; that is, the suspected identity of the individual and the general provenance of the remains are known, but these are not disclosed to the skeletal analyst until after he or she performs the analysis. This procedure is standard in many forensic anthropology laboratories, especially where a larger analytical staff is present and multiple layers can be placed between the person who makes initial contact with the external agency or internal branch supplying the remains.

Information Loss, Information Gain

One may believe that taphonomy is nothing but a series of statements of bad news (Stiner 1994). As indicated earlier, taphonomic processes reduce the portions of a biological profile that can be generated and in particular lead to a loss of individuating characteristics of a skeleton. Especially susceptible to destructive processes are the physical characteristics of the pubic bones and the midfacial area, with all their potential information regarding age, ancestry, and sex. Epiphyses and metaphyses (especially unfused ones) are easily destroyed and with them their information regarding developmental age. Similarly, long bones and other elements useful for the determination of stature can no longer be measured after the relatively fragile epiphyses have been eroded. Sternal rib ends, with their potential aging information, stand very little chance of survival in most depositional settings. General surface erosion throughout the skeleton makes complete measurements impossible, again causing a loss of potential metrical information to estimate sex and ancestry. Teeth, while often the most durable part of the skeleton, are not immune to damage and loss: single-rooted teeth often fall out of the maxilla and mandible after the loss of soft tissue and are not recovered in the field, and anterior teeth are particularly prone to thermal destruction as a body burns. Tooth roots also erode and with them eruption stage data. Elements already damaged and scattered by perimortem trauma (gunshot wound, high speed impact, etc.) are even more susceptible to further postmortem damage, especially the perimortem fracture surfaces with their distinctive characteristics (Ubelaker and Adams 1995). It is easy to see taphonomic changes as wholly negative processes.

Taphonomic analysis is filled with other caveats. Bones do not have to pass through a singular taphonomic trajectory and in practical experience almost never do. Consider a common forensic scenario where an individual is shot and the body is dumped in the woods. The initial lethal trauma may have damaged some of the bones. The remains next may be partially eaten and dispersed by canids and smaller scavengers or decomposers, with some elements consumed or dispersed for hundreds of meters and tooth marks left behind on the surviving remains (Carson et al. 2000; Haglund 1997a; Willey and Snyder 1989). Decomposition of soft tissues may proceed rapidly and deter scavenging carnivores until it subsides. The surviving skeletal remains may lie on the surface for several years and variably undergo subaerial weathering (Behrensmeyer 1978) on their exposed surfaces and acidic topsoil erosion and staining on their contact surfaces (Gordon and Buikstra 1981; White and Hannus 1983). Once the bones are dry and weathered, rodents such as porcupines (*Erethizon dorsatum*), squirrels (Sciuridae), and rats (*Rattus* spp.) may gnaw on them and transport them from where they were deposited by previous scavengers (Haglund 1997b). Gravity and water also may disperse the remains downhill or downstream, with differential innate transportability affecting how far different elements are transported and dispersed (Voorhies 1969). The slow buildup of decomposing leaf litter may partially bury some elements (Pokines 2009), making them much more difficult to locate even when otherwise exposed on the surface. They also may become commingled with unrelated remains, likely of nonhuman large vertebrate species dying in the vicinity. The original set of skeletal remains, if any are discovered after all of this destruction and movement, may display overlapping traces of some or all of these taphonomic processes. It is the task of the forensic anthropologist to sort out these conflicting signals and place them in correct temporal order to reconstruct the postmortem history backward from the recovered remains to their original living source. The collection and analysis of all of this data are akin to the diagnosis of perimortem skeletal trauma or pathological conditions in bone, where all changes in bone differing from their living, healthy states must be examined, and even then a single diagnosis may not be possible.

Taphonomic processes also *add* information (Behrensmeyer and Kidwell 1985). In the example given earlier, each process has left traces upon the bone. The perimortem fracturing or other damage caused during the homicide may still be visible. Scavengers, including large mammals and rodents, leave their tooth marks behind and disperse (and reconcentrate) bone in ways that are sometimes patterned, allowing these changes to be distinguished from human activity. Weathering of bone has been studied for decades (Behrensmeyer 1978; Miller 1975), and this gradual process of bleaching and cracking can be distinguished from broadly similar changes such as cremation/calcination as well as give some indication of the PMI. Loss of bone may be understood by comparisons with known survivability rates (i.e., a femur midshaft is far more likely to survive long term than a sternum, due to the greater density of the former's cortical bone) and natural processes that delete bone. Bones therefore in many cases record their postmortem history by the alterations caused to them, be these cut marks, surface cracking and bleaching, adhering fauna, mineralization, marks from plant roots, algae growth, adherent sediments, thermal alteration, overall patterns of recovery, the loss of cortical surface and epiphyses in patterned areas, or with retained tooth markings. These types of alterations are divided into three broad categories, based upon the information gained: contextual, temporal (absolute timing of events), and perimortem vs. postmortem (relative timing of events).

Contextual Information

Contextual taphonomic information concerns what forces have acted upon and altered those remains, and what it indicates about the life history of those remains between the time of death and the time of analysis. These include both macroscopic and microscopic alterations to bone. These may indicate depositional context: in what environment(s) did skeletal remains spend the majority of their time, or at least enough time so that the environment could leave visible alterations on bone (or destroy or disperse bone to such a degree that it was not recovered at all)? Examples of depositional context include multiple types of burial (primary, secondary, coffin, etc.) and their multiple subtypes vs. surface deposition of remains. The actions of biological agencies, such as plants, fungi, and vertebrate and invertebrate scavengers, are also affected greatly by the context of the remains during the PMI and therefore may be indicators of that context. Context may also extend to different types of artificial alteration to bone, such as reburial, storage, and alteration for cultural purposes (trophy-keeping, scientific study, etc.). Multiple types of contextual information also may apply, as in remains that have undergone multiple taphonomic processes in multiple environments due to their dispersal.

Transport is another major aspect of contextual information: how and to where bones got moved/dispersed after death, from their initial point of deposition to their recovered location, and if reconcentration in a different location occurred through a human or natural agency (water, scavengers, etc.). Water transport of whole decomposing bodies or of individual skeletal elements is a frequent cause of bone transport (Chapters 6 and 7), as is bone carrying by large carnivores and other vertebrate taxa (Chapter 9). Understanding differential movement of disarticulated skeletal elements by these forces is also crucial for understanding the context of what remains are recovered and what remains are missing from a scene. This must be contrasted with what elements were likely destroyed by different forces, as modified by the inherent survivability of different elements due to their structural properties (Chapter 4). A bone lost from a scene due to dispersal easily may be misinterpreted as a bone lost due to its actual destruction, so potential transport of skeletal elements must be an integral part of contextual taphonomic analysis.

The process of contextual taphonomic analysis also includes assembling data and interpreting those data that are relevant to the manner of death (i.e., homicide, suicide, accidental, natural, or undetermined) and the cause of death (the original underlying medical condition that initiates the lethal chain of events that culminated in death), although these final determinations are in the realm of medical examiners and coroners. Any type of damage or alteration to bone may be relevant to these determinations, if only to rule out some type of taphonomic alteration as having a mundane, postmortem natural cause instead of a perimortem, human-induced one (see "Perimortem vs. Postmortem Alteration" section). The role of forensic taphonomy in these cases often lies in the elimination of multiple scenarios, especially where these indicate that nothing of legal interest occurred. These scenarios can include that an otherwise unidentified bone is likely non-human in origin due to its taphonomic state (fresh, butchered, cooked, etc.). Cases such as these often form the bulk of casework in a medical examiner's office, so their efficient processing allows more time to be devoted to cases of forensic interest.

Temporal

Some taphonomic changes aid in the estimation of the PMI, as we learn more about the timing of alterations to bone from multiple sources. These include subaerial weathering (exposure causing drying, bleaching, and eventual flaking, *sensu* Behrensmeyer 1978). This type of temporal information is examined in Chapter 11. This category also includes more general indicators of the PMI, such as the stages of decomposition during the early PMI (Chapter 3) and how they lead to skeletonization and disarticulation, plant growth through bones, or large carnivore consumption and scattering. All of this temporal information is used to estimate the amount of time that has elapsed between the death of the individual(s) in question and the recovery of remains. This is an important part of the identification process, since it may greatly help narrow the range of possible identities for a given set of remains, thus amounting to an indirect form of individualization.

Temporal information is also integral to the establishment of the order of taphonomic changes as they occur (or co-occur) on a set of remains. Noting that perimortem sawn surfaces are weathered and stained and have adherent algae (all of which take, at a minimum, months to develop in most environments) to the same degree as the surrounding un-sawn bone surfaces is crucial in determining the likely perimortem origin of that sawing. Similarly, noting prior markers of burial on remains now disarticulated and scattered on the surface indicates the chain of events as they occurred (burial first, then scattering) and some of the possible agencies involved (inhumation by humans, followed by accidental exhumation by burrowing animals, active scavenging, or water erosion). The margins of the sawn surface of the remains in this example then may be gnawed upon by rodents (see Chapter 9), which would be determined under analysis as having occurred later in the temporal chain of taphonomic events. Other taphonomic clues, however, may establish the temporal chain of these changes to bone, or these events may be estimated and placed in order based upon known behavior of other species or typical taphonomic arcs in a given environment.

Temporal information also may separate remains of forensic interest from those that are not. If remains pertain to historical/archaeological or paleontological time frames, they are by definition not of legal interest. Within the United States, these often include Native American remains, the unearthing of which represents a different kind of legal matter regarding the disturbance of remains and the damaging of archaeological sites. Multiple skeletal taphonomic alterations may indicate that bones are not of a recent homicide victim but more likely from an eroding grave or disturbed mausoleum in a historical cemetery or other source. Certainly, remains of this nature will be of interest to other government agencies charged with their study and preservation (typically, state historical offices/commissions), and these should be alerted as a part of the forensic anthropological analysis when this final determination of temporal age has been made and reported to the other law enforcement/medicolegal agencies involved. Similarly, modern cemetery remains often find their way into forensic investigations, and determining their origins from this context removes them from consideration as the result of recent homicide.

Perimortem vs. Postmortem Alteration

Another important forensic taphonomic analytical category is the differentiation of human from natural alteration of bone (Fisher 1996; Miller 1969; Morlan 1984). Again, human alteration to bone (perimortem trauma) is of specific interest to forensic anthropologists, given that the reconstruction of the events surrounding death is one of the main reasons that their analytical skills are sought by law enforcement agencies. Acts of violence may leave traces upon bone, which may be obscured or destroyed by later, unrelated taphonomic processes, or other postmortem forces may cause damage to bone, which can be mistaken for perimortem trauma. More precisely, taphonomic analysis often focuses upon the differentiation between perimortem trauma from *pseudotrauma* (postmortem damage to a bone that superficially or more deeply appears to be perimortem in origin). Naturally, the presence of such postmortem alteration to bone, if misdiagnosed as perimortem trauma, can result in serious legal ramifications for that case. This type of analysis (Chapter 13) includes differentiation between sharp force trauma vs. postmortem marking on bone (incidental scratches, carnivore tooth marks, etc.); blunt force trauma vs. postmortem sources of bone breakage (animal gnawing, weakening through decomposition and postmortem erosion, etc.); and thermal alteration to fresh bone vs. dry, already skeletonized bone (Chapter 14). This type of analysis is also restricted by a relative dearth of studies involving exactly how long the perimortem interval extends (Ubelaker and Adams 1995; Wheatley 2008), especially regarding how long do bones have to age after death before they no longer fracture in the same manner as in a living or recently deceased individual (Chapters 13 and 14).

"Natural" alteration, however, also may include details of death information of significance to law enforcement. Death by wild animal attack is an obvious example, and this predation upon a human may lead to both perimortem trauma from the initial fatal attack damaging bone and to subsequent postmortem alteration as feeding on the deceased person proceeds and remains are dispersed. Death from accidental falls from height or drowning also have a high natural component, in the sense that the primary agency of death was a part of the natural world (sudden impact into hard surfaces or water) and as such may have had the largest amount of influence over immediate (massive perimortem blunt force trauma) or later (water transport and feeding by marine species) taphonomic changes to those remains. As difficult as it may be to study and codify the full range of taphonomic variation caused in various natural environments, it is less difficult than to study and codify the full range of human behavior causing death of other human beings through all types of homicide, including psychosis-induced interpersonal violence, neglect, abuse, deliberate withholding of life-giving aid, war, terrorism, and genocide directed at civilian populations. The motivations for these types of acts may be difficult to comprehend, but the actions used to hide evidence of them may follow clear, rational patterns (Chapter 10).

One must also note that some taphonomic changes can occur in an identical manner regardless of their ultimate origin being a criminal act of killing a person or subsequent efforts to dispose of the remains vs. these events having an accidental, suicidal, or unrelated natural origin. Bones burned in a brush fire, whether that fire was intentionally set to hide evidence of a crime or started by a random lightning strike or tossed cigarette, are going to burn in a manner indiscernible from each other. Wolves finding a fresh body in a forest often feed on it in a manner that is later taphonomically indistinguishable from a person that the wolves have killed themselves. Falls from great height, such as off of tall bridges, may result in the same trauma pattern if the individual fell accidentally or was pushed off. The intent of the organism in most cases (and certainly any natural force) is neutral in terms of the taphonomic changes that it causes, the major exception to this rule being human action (Chapter 10).

Taphonomic Suites of Characteristics

The practical aim of this volume is to present a system to organize the gathering of macroscopic and microscopic taphonomic observations common to forensic anthropology cases, to interpret and explain those observations and how they vary, and to recognize these alterations on bone and distinguish them from each other. Suites of these taphonomic characteristics sometimes may form a *taphonomic signature*, defined as a suite of observations, often combined with other lines of evidence, which can indicate a unique set of forces, taphonomic history event, or process that altered a set of skeletal remains. Unambiguous signatures, however, are rare in taphonomic analysis for multiple reasons. Some alterations to bone are too indistinct or their traces are too easily removed by subsequent taphonomic degradation to be detected by the time the bone can be analyzed (Fernández-Jalvo and Andrews 2003). It will also be made clear that these suites of taphonomic changes are usually overlapping on the same set of skeletal remains; that is, it is rare that just a single type of taphonomic alteration from one wholly unambiguous cause is present on a bone. In addition, some suites of taphonomic alterations are obvious subsets of other related processes, and some suites of taphonomic alterations can themselves be combined into higher-order groupings in order to explain broader patterns of postmortem processes.

Some taphonomic suites of characteristics are very basic and require little elaboration. Without thinking much about it, archaeologists and biological anthropologists recognize the characteristics of a primary burial or secondary burial, and how they overlap with each other. A primary burial is usually characterized by articulation of skeletal elements, a largely complete skeleton, soil staining and/or adherence, plant root damage and invasion, erosion (in acidic soil) of cortical surfaces, and a lack of weathering. A secondary burial may have most of these characteristics, but with disarticulation of the skeletal elements, loss of smaller skeletal elements, and other markers of having been transported and reburied (postmortem breakage, ritual treatment, etc.) likely in a much smaller grave. Other suites of taphonomic characteristics are more complex, atypical, or specialized, can be ascribed to more than one possible cause, or frequently co-occur with other types of alteration.

Data Collection for Common Taphonomic Alterations to Bones

Appendices A (macroscopic) and B (microscopic) present checklists for the gathering of taphonomic data. These taphonomic alterations and the processes that cause them are covered in the following Chapters 2 through 17. Recovery contexts include common forensic scenarios or those potentially mistaken for forensic scenarios. These include multiple burial types (primary and secondary, coffin, and multiple subtypes based upon differences in substrate including bog, ice, and forest); human interventions including plowing, cremation, dismemberment, curation, anatomical preparation, and ritual utilization; the effects of multiple types of animal scavenging (large mammals, rodents, birds, and termites); and other depositional contexts greatly impacting osseous remains (freshwater and saltwater, and surface exposure).

Other Lines of Evidence

Other lines of evidence beyond osseous remains viewed in isolation may be just as vital in the determination of their origin as the taphonomic alterations that they accumulated prior to their examination in a laboratory. These always must be taken into consideration. For example, excavating a set of remains that appears to be of prehistoric origin might be reinterpreted if modern artifacts are found in association with those remains. Was it mixing of burial fill contaminated with later artifacts? Was the determination of prehistoric origin in error? Was a lack of a larger assemblage of modern artifacts not recovered due to a recent body being stripped prior to burial, in order to decrease the chances of later identification? The reverse situation (recent remains being mistaken for those of historic or prehistoric origin) can occur if older artifacts get mixed, unnoticed, with burial fill. Similarly, the clear recovery context of the remains may be known to the forensic anthropologist examining them, as that person may have done the excavating. In cases like these, each known recovery scene becomes a natural laboratory for taphonomic changes to human remains, and the forensic anthropologist is then in the position to gather additional data regarding that particular environment. Given that a large portion of what has been determined about taphonomic changes occurring to human remains has been achieved by the slow accumulation of data from individual forensic case studies (Haglund and Sorg 1997, 2002) combined with actualistic experimental results, this source of data should be collected whenever possible (Chapter 17).

Other forms of naturally caused alterations are also important in determining the taphonomic history of human remains. The signs that carnivores, rodents, and other scavengers (see Chapter 9) may leave at a scene include damage to soft tissue and artifacts, tracks in the ground, fur, and feces, all of which are important clues to the origins of taphonomic changes to a set of skeletal remains. Some species, especially smaller wild species, household pets, or domesticated farm animals, still may be present at a scene (Steadman and Worne 2007). Exclusion of some taphonomic forces, such as weathering from buried remains or wild carnivore scavenging from remains found in a sealed building, is also an obvious source of information to narrow down the possibilities encompassing the total life history of a set of skeletal remains.

The physical characteristics of a grave itself are also important clues as to the postmortem history of the remains contained within. The collection and analysis of this type of data are termed *geotaphonomy* (Hochrein 2002). Hochrein (2002) categorizes six types of evidence regarding the burial environment itself: (1) stratification, the juxtaposition of layers within the burial feature and the temporal/formation information that may be derived from them; (2) tool marks left in the walls of the feature that may indicate the types of implements used to excavate and fill it; (3) bioturbation, the movement of sediments and the jumbling of the objects contained within them by burrowing species and plant growth; (4) sedimentation, the natural buildup of sediments within the feature; (5) compression/depression of sediments and other burial contents subsiding and causing a lowering of its surface; and (6) internal compaction, the rare occurrence of individuals buried alive leaving impressions in sediments. Hochrein (2002) stresses the need for careful excavation techniques in conjunction with beginning excavations with the assumption that such evidence may exist. Forensic archaeological excavation destroys geotaphonomic evidence as it proceeds, and the evidence cannot be collected after the fact. Geotaphonomic data may answer questions such as the nature of the original burial (a hastily improvised grave or one that was carefully excavated with heavy tools), the sequence of events occurring when the body was deposited, the identification of natural forces changing spatial relationships of objects later in the PMI, and potential information regarding the PMI. These can be combined with taphonomic data derived from direct alteration to bone and other sources. For example, the dispersal of small elements on the surface and their displacement within a grave (spatial recovery data), combined with the detection of rodent burrows through the burial fill (geotaphonomic data) and marks of rodent gnawing on some skeletal elements (osseous taphonomic data), give a clearer picture of the likely postmortem events of the partial disturbance, movement, and surface alteration that have occurred. However mundane this scenario, the combined evidence for it makes it easier to reject competing scenarios, including perimortem trauma or postmortem dismemberment.

Future Forensic Taphonomic Research

In all forensic taphonomic analyses (and educational programs), one of the primary goals should be the separation of natural processes from artificial (i.e., human actions of legal relevance), so a clear understanding of natural processes and the inherent physical and chemical properties of bone is necessary. Indeed, it is the author's opinion that a natural explanation for all forensic taphonomic alterations should be the default until proven false. These natural processes and properties that must be considered first include the normal progression of decomposition (Chapter 3), the inherent differences in the durability of skeletal elements (Chapter 4), environmental degradation of bone through chemical and biological factors (Chapter 5), water transportation and damage (Chapter 6), chemical and biological processes in marine environments (Chapter 7), animal gnawing and dispersal (Chapters 9 and 16), environmental exposure and mineral diagenesis (Chapters 11 and 12), thermal alteration (Chapter 14), and how these processes may affect bone on a microscopic (Chapter 2) and organic molecular (Chapter 15) level and the potential to derive aging and DNA data from bone. Similarly, taphonomic alterations left by human actions that have an origin unrelated to forensic matters also must be eliminated from contention, including nonclandestine burial (Chapter 5), incidental marking on bone including from excavation (Chapter 17), and deliberate alteration of bones for anatomical teaching or ritual reasons (Chapter 8). Only then can interpretations of human actions of direct forensic interest be accepted with confidence, including such processes as the deliberate movement of remains (Chapter 10) and perimortem trauma (Chapter 13).

In concordance with this need for training in natural processes, taphonomy is amenable to actualistic, small-scale research projects and as such meshes well with the parameters of student research, both at the master's and doctorate levels. Given the ongoing expansion in the field of forensics and the number of programs with outdoor research facilities, taphonomic projects of all kinds lend themselves well to student research in terms of need and practical budgetary limitations. Longer-term research also is needed. Many questions in forensic taphonomy relate to the PMI and how bone changes over the course of decades. Experimental designs to determine the characteristics of bone recovered from a variety of microenvironments—including fleshed bodies at the base of mass burials, surface exposure in primary forest, frozen conditions, and defleshed burial in acidic soil—need to span many years or decades of observation to determine the changing bone characteristics, as has been undertaken in the United Kingdom (Armour-Chelu and Andrews 1996).

The author also recommends that the influx of nonhuman remains into medical examiner offices be examined, however cursorily, for their taphonomic alterations. This source of data gives the analyst typically a much larger sample of large vertebrate remains from the same jurisdiction than the human remains received from the same natural settings and likely remains with a longer temporal span of deposition. These remains are essentially a free source of data about the common taphonomic processes occurring in that region, and taphonomic alterations from these processes likely will be encountered on subsequent human remains recovered.

Forensic taphonomy would be better served by de-emphasis of the word "forensic" in favor of the word "taphonomy," in the sense that the processes that we observe over the short-term (forensic) interval are also relevant to other researchers in the fields of zoo-archaeology, paleoanthropology, and paleontology and frequently examined by them. (Since it is not possible to operate an actualistic taphonomic experiment that proceeds for millennia or longer, researchers from these disciplines necessarily rely upon experiments involving taphonomic processes over the short term, using the uniformitarian principle, to extrapolate processes that may have happened in the unreachable past.) It is of primary concern to these other disciplines in what contexts, how many, and in what states bones survive this initial deposition period (roughly equal to the forensic interval), since surviving this gamut before final deposition in a more protected setting (in caves or sediments) is how the majority of bones are preserved to become part of the archaeological and paleontological record (Brain 1980, 1981; Hill 1980). The majority of bone destruction and dispersal takes place relatively early during the PMI (often within the first month and certainly within the first year), and the majority of bones do not survive past this early postmortem phase. Slower but persistent processes of destruction make it unlikely that the remaining bone will still be identifiable, if lying exposed, within a few decades. Burial in benign soil can greatly slow bone destruction, but acidic soils can degrade bone until only unanalyzable residue remains (Gordon and Buikstra 1981). All researchers in taphonomy therefore have as a primary concern the initial changes occurring immediately after death, which this volume will examine.

Acknowledgments

Thanks go to April Nowell and Steve Symes for their review of an earlier draft of this chapter and to Brianne Charles for her kind editorial assistance. Thanks also go to the many contributors to this volume from which this summary is drawn.

References

Armour-Chelu, M. and P. Andrews (1996) Surface modification of bone from Overton Down, Wiltshire. In *The Experimental Earthwork Project 1960–1992*, eds. M. Bell, P. J. Fowler, and S. W. Hillson, pp. 178–185. Council for British Archaeology, York, U.K.
Behrensmeyer, A. K. (1978) Taphonomic and ecologic information from bone weathering. *Palaeobiology* 4:150–162.
Behrensmeyer, A. K. (1991) Terrestrial vertebrate accumulations. In *Taphonomy: Releasing the Data Locked in the Fossil Record*, eds. P. A. Allison and D. E. G. Briggs, pp. 291–335. Springer, Dordrecht, the Netherlands.
Behrensmeyer, A. K. and S. M. Kidwell (1985) Taphonomy's contributions to paleobiology. *Paleobiology* 11:105–119.
Berryman, H. E., W. M. Bass, S. A. Symes, and O. C. Smith (1991) Recognition of cemetery remains in the forensic setting. *Journal of Forensic Sciences* 36:230–237.

Berryman, H. E., W. M. Bass, S. A. Symes, and O. C. Smith (1997) Recognition of cemetery remains in the forensic setting. In *Forensic Taphonomy: The Postmortem Fate of Human Remains*, eds. W. D. Haglund and M. H. Sorg, pp. 165–170. CRC Press, Boca Raton, FL.

Binford, L. R. (1981) *Bones: Ancient Men and Modern Myths*. Academic Press, New York.

Binford, L. R. and J. B. Bertram (1977) Bone frequencies and attritional processes. In *For Theory Building in Archaeology*, ed. L. R. Binford, pp. 77–153. Academic Press, New York.

Brain, C. K. (1980) Some criteria for the recognition of bone-collecting agencies in African caves. In *Fossils in the Making: Vertebrate Taphonomy and Paleoecology*, eds. A. K. Behrensmeyer and A. P. Hill, pp. 107–130. University of Chicago Press, Chicago, IL.

Brain, C. K. (1981) *The Hunters or the Hunted? An Introduction to African Cave Taphonomy*. University of Chicago Press, Chicago, IL.

Buckland, W. (1823) *Reliquiae Diluvianae, or, Observations on the Organic Remains Contained in Caves, Fissures, and Diluvial Gravel, and on Other Geological Phenomena, Attesting to the Action of an Universal Deluge*. John Murray, London, U.K.

Buikstra, J. E. and D. H. Ubelaker (eds.) (1994) *Standards for Data Collection from Human Skeletal Remains*. Arkansas Archeological Survey Research Series No. 44, Fayetteville, AR.

Carson, E. A., V. H. Stefan, and J. F. Powell (2000) Skeletal manifestations of bear scavenging. *Journal of Forensic Sciences* 45:515–526.

Efremov, J. A. (1940) Taphonomy: New branch of paleontology. *Pan-American Geologist* 74:81–93.

Fernández-Jalvo, Y. and P. Andrews (2003) Experimental effects of water abrasion on bone fragments. *Journal of Taphonomy* 1:147–163.

Fisher (1996) Bone surface modifications in zooarchaeology. *Journal of Archaeological Method and Theory* 2:7–68.

Galloway, A. (ed.) (1999) *Broken Bones: Anthropological Analysis of Blunt Force Trauma*. Charles C Thomas, Springfield, IL.

Gordon, C. G. and J. E. Buikstra (1981) Soil pH, bone preservation, and sampling bias at mortuary sites. *American Antiquity* 46:566–571.

Haglund, W. D. (1997a) Dogs and coyotes: Postmortem involvement with human remains. In *Forensic Taphonomy: The Postmortem Fate of Human Remains*, eds. W. D. Haglund and M. H. Sorg, pp. 367–381. CRC Press, Boca Raton, FL.

Haglund, W. D. (1997b) Rodents and human remains. In *Forensic Taphonomy: The Postmortem Fate of Human Remains*, eds. W. D. Haglund and M. H. Sorg, pp. 405–414. CRC Press, Boca Raton, FL.

Haglund, W. D. and M. H. Sorg (eds.) (1997) *Forensic Taphonomy: The Postmortem Fate of Human Remains*. CRC Press, Boca Raton, FL.

Haglund, W. D. and M. H. Sorg (eds.) (2002) *Advances in Forensic Taphonomy: Method, Theory, and Archaeological Perspectives*. CRC Press, Boca Raton, FL.

Hochrein, M. J. (2002) An autopsy of the grave: Recognizing, collecting, and preserving forensic geotaphonomic evidence. In *Advances in Forensic Taphonomy: Method, Theory, and Archaeological Perspectives*, eds. W. D. Haglund and M. H. Sorg, pp. 45–70. CRC Press, Boca Raton, FL.

Hill, A. P. (1980) Early postmortem damage to the remains of some contemporary East African mammals. In *Fossils in the Making: Vertebrate Taphonomy and Paleoecology*, eds. A. K. Behrensmeyer and A. P. Hill, pp. 131–155. University of Chicago Press, Chicago, IL.

Hutton, J. (1788) *The Theory of the Earth; Or, an Investigation of the Laws Observable in the Composition, Dissolution, and Restoration of Land upon the Globe*. Transactions of the Royal Society of Edinburgh, Vol. 1, Edinburgh, Scotland.

Lyell, C. (1830–33) *Principles of Geology* (Vol. 3). J. Murray, London, U.K.

Lyman, R. L. (1994) *Vertebrate Taphonomy*. Cambridge University Press, Cambridge, U.K.

Lyman, R. L. (2008) *Quantitative Paleozoology*. Cambridge University Press, Cambridge, U.K.

Martin, R. E. (1999) *Taphonomy: A Process Approach*. Cambridge University Press, Cambridge, U.K.

Micozzi, M. S. (1991) *Postmortem Change in Human and Animal Remains: A Systematic Approach*. Charles C Thomas, Springfield, IL.

Miller, G. J. (1969) A study of cuts, grooves, and other marks on recent and fossil bones. 1. Animal tooth marks. *Tebiwa* 12:9–19.

Miller, G. J. (1975) A study of cuts, grooves, and other marks on recent and fossil bones. 2. Weathering cracks, fractures, splinters, and other similar natural phenomena. In *Lithic Technology: Making and Using Stone Tools*, ed. E. H. Swanson, Jr., pp. 211–226. Aldine, Chicago, IL.

Morlan, R. E. (1984) Toward the definition of criteria for the recognition of artificial bone alterations. *Quaternary Research* 22:160–171.

Nawrocki, S. P. (1995) Taphonomic processes in historic cemeteries. In *Bodies of Evidence: Reconstructing History through Skeletal Analysis*, ed. A. Grauer, pp. 49–66. Wiley-Liss, New York.

Nielsen-Marsh, C. M. and R. E. M. Hedges (2000) Patterns of diagenesis in bone I: The effects of site environments. *Journal of Archaeological Science* 27:1139–1150.

Odell, G. H. and F. Cowan (1987) Estimating tillage effects on artifact distributions. *American Antiquity* 52:456–484.

Patterson, J. H. (1996) *The Man-Eating Lions of Tsavo*. Field Museum, Chicago, IL.

Payne, S. B. (1983) Bones from cave sites: Who ate what? In *Animals and Archaeology: 1. Hunters and Their Prey*, eds. J. Clutton-Brock and C. Grigson, pp. 149–162. BAR International Series 163, Oxford, U.K.

Peterson, R. O. (1977) *Wolf Ecology and Prey Relationships on Isle Royale*. U.S. National Park Service Scientific Monograph Series No. 11, Washington, DC.

Pobiner, B. L. (2007) *Hominin-Carnivore Interactions: Evidence from Modern Carnivore Bone Modification and Early Pleistocene Archaeofaunas (Koobi Fora, Kenya; Olduvai Gorge, Tanzania)*. Unpublished PhD Dissertation, Department of Anthropology, Rutgers University, Newark, NJ.

Pokines, J. T. (2009) Forensic recoveries of U.S. war dead and the effects of taphonomy and other site-altering processes. In *Hard Evidence: Case Studies in Forensic Anthropology* (2nd edn.), ed. D. W. Steadman, pp. 141–154. Prentice Hall, Upper Saddle River, NJ.

Rogers, T. L. (2005) Recognition of cemetery remains in a forensic context. *Journal of Forensic Sciences* 50:5–11.

Schultz, J., M. Williamson, S. P. Nawrocki, A. Falsetti, and M. Warren (2003) A taphonomic profile to aid in the recognition of human remains from historic and/or cemetery contexts. *Florida Anthropologist* 56:141–147.

Shipman, P. (1981) *Life History of a Fossil: An Introduction to Taphonomy and Paleoecology*. Harvard University Press, Cambridge, MA.

Shotwell, J. A. (1955) An approach to the paleoecology of mammals. *Ecology* 36:327–337.

Sledzik, P. S., D. Dirkmaat, R. W. Mann, T. D. Holland, A. Zelson Mundorff, B. J. Adams, C. M. Crowder, and F. DePaolo (2009) Disaster victim recovery and identification: Forensic anthropology in the aftermath of September 11. In *Hard Evidence: Case Studies in Forensic Anthropology* (2nd edn.), ed. D. W. Steadman, pp. 289–302. Prentice Hall, Upper Saddle River, NJ.

Steadman, D. W. and H. Worne (2007) Canine scavenging of human remains in an indoor setting. *Forensic Science International* 173:78–82.

Stiner, M. C. (1994) *Honor among Thieves: A Zooarchaeological Study of Neandertal Ecology*. Princeton University Press, Princeton, NJ.

Ubelaker, D. H. (1997) Taphonomic applications in forensic anthropology. In *Forensic Taphonomy: The Postmortem Fate of Human Remains*, eds. W. D. Haglund and M. H. Sorg, pp. 77–90. CRC Press, Boca Raton, FL.

Ubelaker, D. H. and B. J. Adams (1995) Differentiation of perimortem and postmortem trauma using taphonomic indicators. *Journal of Forensic Sciences* 40:509–512.

Voorhies, M. R. (1969) *Taphonomy and Population Dynamics of an Early Pliocene Vertebrate Fauna, Knox County, Nebraska*. University of Wyoming Contributions to Geology, Special Paper No. 1. Laramie, WY.

Wedl, C. (1864) Ueber einen Zahnbein und Knochen keimenden Pilz. *Sitzungsbericht der Mathematische Naturwissenschaftliche Classe der Kaiserliche Akademie der Wissenschaften Wien* Band L. Kl(1) 50:171–193.

Weigelt, J. (1989 [1927]) *Recent Vertebrate Carcasses and Their Paleobiological Implications*. Reprint edition, translated by J. Schaefer. University of Chicago Press, Chicago, IL.

Wheatley, B. P. (2008) Perimortem or postmortem bone fractures? An experimental study of fracture patterns in deer femora. *Journal of Forensic Sciences* 53:69–72.

White, E. M. and L. A. Hannus (1983) Chemical weathering of bone in archaeological soils. *American Antiquity* 48:316–322.

Willey, P. and L. M. Snyder (1989) Canid modification of human remains: Implications for time-since-death estimations. *Journal of Forensic Sciences* 34:894–901.

Microscopic Destruction of Bone

2

MIRANDA M.E. JANS

Contents

> He that unburied lies wants not his hearse,
> For unto him a tomb's the Universe.
>
> **—Sir Thomas Browne, *Religio Medici* (1642)**

Introduction

Skeletal remains are an important resource for biological characteristics of humans and animals in forensic, archaeological, and paleontological settings. Bone is an intricate composite material, containing organic and inorganic components, and a multitude of factors influence its preservation from the moment of death to its recovery and analysis. Bone components (collagen and mineral) initially offer each other mutual protection from degradation, accounting for bone's great preservation potential (Trueman and Martill 2002), but these components are eventually affected by diagenetic processes. *Diagenesis* in bone is defined as postmortem alterations in the physical, chemical, and microstructural composition of bone following its deposition in the environment.

After skeletonization, bones and teeth often survive for a considerable period. Depending on environmental circumstances, this can range between mere decades to millions of years in the case of fossilized remains. Alteration of bones in the burial environment has been studied in detail within archaeological contexts. Smith et al. (2007) identify four main diagenetic pathways: accelerated collagen hydrolysis, bioerosion, dissolution, and fossilization (Nielsen-Marsh et al. 2007; Smith et al. 2007). Environmental parameters influence degradation of bone, such as rapidly fluctuating water levels and acid soils in a burial site (Nielsen-Marsh et al. 2007). From several studies, it appears that alteration can occur early postmortem (Bell et al. 1996; Hedges et al. 1995; Yoshino et al. 1991), making it relevant to the forensic time frame.

Histology, the study of (thin sections of) tissues and cells using microscopy, is a technique often successfully applied in the case of fragmented and/or burned skeletal remains to identify species (Cuijpers 2006, 2009; Hillier and Bell 2007) and biological age at death (Cuijpers and Schutkowsky 1993). Moreover, bone histology has a long history of use in taphonomic research, which probably started with the research by Wedl on bioerosion of bones and teeth (Wedl 1864). A basic knowledge of degradation features is necessary to distinguish diagenesis from pathology. Additionally, using histology, different degradation mechanisms can be identified, and bone quality can be (semi) quantified (Garland 1989; Hedges et al. 1995; Jans 2008; Jans et al. 2002), which makes it useful in archaeological heritage management studies. It has been established as an often-used approach in determining bone preservation in the Netherlands (Van Heeringen et al. 2004). Currently, histology is investigated for its potential in sample selection for biomolecular analyses of archaeological material, as there appears to be a relation between bone microstructural and biomolecular preservation (e.g., Gilbert et al. 2005; Haynes et al. 2002). As such, it is also relevant to forensic taphonomic analysis. The succession of putrefactive stages is well characterized (see Chapter 3, this volume), as are the sequences of different invertebrates that colonize the body postmortem. This serves the purpose of estimating an accurate postmortem interval (PMI), one of the first questions to arise when remains have been located. Similar possibilities exist for histology, focusing, for example, on the sequence of events that marks the processes of skeletonization. The macroscopical preservation of bone is unfortunately not very informative regarding its microstructural or molecular preservation (Garland 1993; Stout 1978). Histology is a technique that is available in most osteological laboratories and can be performed without expensive equipment (Maat et al. 2000), making it suitable as a quick screening or research technique. Important research questions range from determining the rate of decay in different environments to resolving early postmortem history or sample quality evaluation. So far, the effects of taphonomic events have been primarily studied for bone or its components in the framework of archaeological heritage management or in laboratory situations (see, for example, Nielsen-Marsh and Hedges [1997] and Smith et al. [2007]).

The usual view on bone taphonomic processes affecting skeletal remains is that they result in the loss of information on different levels and therefore need to be identified to avoid bias or false interpretation. However, detailed knowledge of taphonomic features or signatures also adds valuable information on the sequence of taphonomic events (Turner-Walker and Jans 2008). In this chapter, the potential of histology in the research of taphonomy will be reviewed. Studying these signatures (see Appendix B) in more detail could improve identification of early postmortem history and lead to more accurate estimates of the PMI.

Preparation of Thin Sections and Analysis

Many osteological laboratories will have bone thin-sectioning facilities available. Such facilities can include dedicated hard tissue microtomes, which cut bone after embedding in an epoxy resin into semi-thin sections (30–80 μm) (e.g., Van der Lubbe et al. 1988). Other methods are based on cutting slivers of bone (±300 μm), which are then mechanically ground to the desired thickness (e.g., Tersigni 2007). If no sectioning equipment is available, Frost's rapid manual method as proposed by Maat et al. (2000) is a useful alternative. Briefly, a sample of bone of ±3 mm thick is cut from cortical bone using a Dremel tool or hack saw; this sample is then manually ground using 220-grit abrasive paper (available in most hardware stores), with water for lubrication (Maat et al. 2000, 2001). The finished, polished semi-thin section (50–80 μm) is mounted on a glass slide and is ready for analysis using a (polarized) light microscope. Thin section samples prepared for diagenetic research can, of course, also be used for histological age determination or species identification (if taken from suitable bones).

Sections can be evaluated using normal and polarized light microscopy. In addition to light microscopy, high-resolution scanning electron microscopy (SEM), backscattered electron scanning microscopy (BSE-SEM), and energy dispersive x-ray spectroscopy (EDS) can be used to explore bone alteration in higher resolution and obtain information on the presence of different elements and mineral density (e.g., Hollund et al. 2012). Uncovered thin sections prepared for light microscopy or, preferably, the embedded bone blocks remaining after sectioning, are suitable samples for BSE-SEM. To facilitate quantification of alteration and comparison to other possible measurements, a few methods are available that will be described here. The presence or absence of microbial alteration is (semi) quantified using the *Oxford Histological Index* (OHI; Hedges et al. 1995; Millard 2001). The OHI is a scale of six categories ranging from 5 (pristine bone) to 0 (no original bone left). Turner-Walker and Syversen (2002) have developed a method quantifying microbial (bacterial) alteration using BSE-SEM and digital image analysis. This method results in a *Bioerosion Index* (BI), which offers information on the percentage of original bone matrix destroyed by bacterial alteration. This method is more precise than the OHI but has the disadvantage of being more time-consuming as well as analyzing a relatively small portion of the bone.

Using the description of bioerosion morphology by Hackett (1981), it is possible to discern different types of *microscopical focal destructions* (MFD), which are attributed to bacterial or fungal action; indeed, histology and SEM are the only methods that can differentiate between bacterial and fungal alterations. In some cases, the microorganisms themselves are present and visible in the bone, although these may be different from the organisms that caused the alteration. In most archaeological cases, alteration happened early in the diagenetic history of the bone, and direct evidence of the organisms causing the alteration will have disappeared, save for—perhaps exceptional—cases where fossilized bacteria were found (Baud and Lacotte 1984; Jackes et al. 2001; Pesquero et al. 2010).

Microscopic cracking of the bone microstructure is hard to quantify, as it is often irregularly spread across the bone microstructure, and there are multiple types of cracking with different causes. The amount of micro-fissures in bone can be quantified as a percentage of cracked and noncracked bone *basic structural units* (e.g., osteons; in non-Haversian bone, a grid is used) as described in Jans et al. (2002). Other types of diagenetic change, such as *inclusion* of foreign material in the natural bone pores, *infiltration* of foreign material into the bone matrix (common examples are humic factors or metallic ions), or a decrease in natural *birefringence* of the bone matrix, can also be observed and (semi) quantified with histology (Jans et al. 2002). The intensity of birefringence of the bone matrix when observed with polarized light can be expressed, for example, as a scale ranging from 1 (comparable to fresh bone), to 0.5 (reduced intensity), to 0 (no birefringence present).

Bioerosion

Microbial alteration is an important pathway for bone degradation (Jans et al. 2004; Smith et al. 2007). *Microbioerosion* of bone (and teeth) has been the focus of several publications over the span of more than 140 years. Microbioerosion in bone can be caused by a range of organisms: fungi (Marchiafava et al. 1974; Wedl 1864), bacteria (Baud and Lacotte 1984; Hackett 1981; Jackes et al. 2001), or microorganisms in aquatic environments (Bell and Elkerton 2008; Bell et al. 1996; Davis 1997; Pesquero et al. 2010). The morphology of microbial alterations has been described and illustrated in detail by Bell and Elkerton (2008), Davis (1997), Hackett (1981), Pesquero et al. (2010), and Turner-Walker et al. (2002). There are three morphological types of bacterial MFD (Hackett 1981): *linear longitudinal, budded,* and *lamellate.* Bacteria produce MFD with a relatively intricate morphology, reorganizing the bone mineral rather than removing it (Jackes et al. 2001). All types of MFD consist of a localized grainy, porous area on the light microscopical level, often surrounded by a hypermineralized cuff (Figure 2.1) ranging in diameter from approximately 10 to 60 μm. High-resolution imaging by BSE-SEM and pore size analysis using mercury intrusion porosimetry (HgIP) reveal that the grainy ultra-structure of bacterial alteration consists of small, connected 0.5–1.0 μm spongiform pores (Jackes et al. 2001; Turner-Walker et al. 2002). Yoshino et al. (1991) found (remains of) bacteria and remains of collagen fibrils in these micropores or vacuoles. They assumed that the spongiform porosity is produced by bacteria and the growth of bacteria, and the extension of tunnels is stopped by deposition of waste products and dissolved mineral (Yoshino et al. 1991).

Bacterial alteration as viewed in transversal thin sections of bone usually originates from the vascular (Haversian) canals and proceeds by "packing" or filling up of osteons until no original microstructure is left (Hackett 1981). Where there is a cementing line, for example, surrounding an osteon, this line initially serves as a barrier for further bacterial

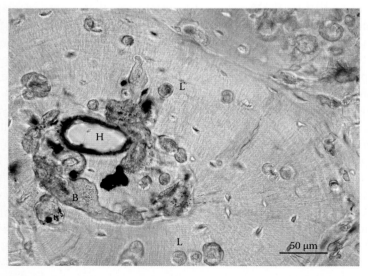

Figure 2.1 Micrograph of a transversal thin section of a human femur (about 60 years postmortem, North Korea, Korean War). Two different types of bacterial tunneling are present: linear longitudinal (L) and budded (B) tunneling. H: Haversian canal.

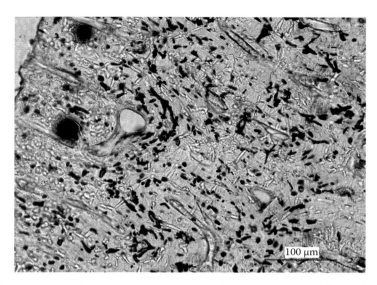

Figure 2.2 Micrograph of a transversal thin section of an animal bone (unknown PMI, Vietnam War). Wedl tunneling is present in much of the microstructure. Some tunnels appear dark due to enclosed air in the section.

tunneling (Hackett 1981). Bacterial alteration normally occurs early postmortem, probably in the first decades after death (Hedges et al. 1995; Jans et al. 2004; Yoshino et al. 1991). The earliest documented find of MFD is 7 months postmortem; however, this sample was recovered from a predator scat and may not be representative (Bell et al. 1996). Yoshino et al. (1991) found bacterial MFD in bone as soon as 5 years postmortem. The anatomical arrangement, along with the early postmortem occurrence and the predominance of bacterial alteration in bones derived from graves, indicates that bacterial alteration is perhaps initiated during putrefaction, while soil bacteria may become involved only in later stages of decay (Child 1995; Jans et al. 2004).

The first description of fungal alteration of mineralized tissue dates from 1864, when Wedl found branching tunnels approximately 8 μm in diameter in sections of teeth exposed to untreated well water and in fossil reptile teeth. Hackett (1981) named those tunnels, caused by fungi, after Wedl (Figure 2.2). Marchiafava et al. (1974) succeeded in identifying a bone-boring fungus and identified tunneling in bone in an experimental setting. Trueman and Martill (2002) identified a second type of *Wedl tunnel*, characterized by a much smaller diameter (Figure 2.3). This thin microtunneling, or Wedl type 2, was associated in another study to acidic soil environments (Fernández-Jalvo et al. 2010), although in that case it was mostly found in superficial areas in bone. According to Marchiafava et al. (1974), bioerosion by fungi is the result of absorption of solubilized organic and mineral bone components, where substances that attack bone are present inside and outside the fungal membranes. Saprophytic fungi are obligatory aerobic (Carlisle et al. 2001); thus, the presence of fungal alteration of bone is a reliable indicator of the presence of oxygen at the time of the alteration in the burial environment.

In aquatic environments, typical forms of bioerosion have been found by Bell and Elkerton (2008; cyanobacteria), Davis (1997; algae, fungi, and/or cyanobacteria), and Pesquero et al. (2010; bacteria). Bioerosion in shallow marine as well as freshwater

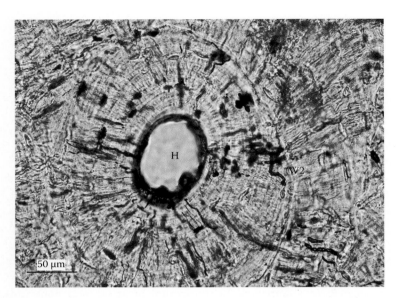

Figure 2.3 Micrograph of a transversal thin section of a human femur (about 65 years postmortem; Palau, WWII). Small branching tunnels are present (W2).

environments is an important diagenetic pathway and occurs soon after deposition (Davis 1997). In an experimental bone deposition study in Southern Florida in freshwater and marine locations, bioerosion by endolithic cyanobacteria and algae was found on exposed bird bones within 4–15 days (Davis 1997). Superficial borings (about 250 μm in diameter) that meandered parallel to the bone surface were also found in these bones (Davis 1997). This newly described type of bioerosion was named *Hackett tunneling* and is likely caused by cyanobacteria and/or algae (Davis 1997). In this study, it became clear that in these aquatic environments, when bioerosion could occur, it almost always did. Rapid covering with sediment inhibited the process (Davis 1997). MFD caused by cyanobacteria in marine contexts consist of peripheral microborings (similar to the Wedl type) affecting the outer compact layer of the bone, apparently only at light-exposed areas of the bone (Bell and Elkerton 2008; Davis 1997). Slightly different types of MFD recently have been found by Pesquero et al. (2010) in a lacustrine Miocene site in Spain, where the MFD have a hypermineralized rim and contain internal microspheres, which are probably the fossilized remains of bacteria.

From the earlier discussion, it becomes clear that early taphonomic conditions influence type and extent of bioerosion. Archaeological studies of bioerosion patterns recording the taphonomic history of bone show promising results. In a study on the preservation of skeletal remains from a Bronze Age site in Cladh Hallan, Scotland, the lack of significant bacterial alteration of bones of a particular skeleton was combined with other data, including a discrepancy in the ^{14}C dating and a different burial context as compared to other skeletal material from that site (Parker Pearson et al. 2005). The collection of anomalies suggested postmortem manipulation, most likely artificial mummification due to the arrested character of the decay of the body (Parker Pearson et al. 2005). Microbial alteration causes loss of information present in archaeological bone, but characterizing the diverse spectrum of bioerosion will open up pathways to obtaining more accurate taphonomic histories.

Taphonomic Signatures

Once remains are buried or inhumed, the burial environment will affect the preservation of bone. On both the microscopic and macroscopic scales, bone diagenesis will cause recognizable site-specific features. An important factor influencing the preservation of bone is of course soil pH (Gordon and Buikstra 1981; Nielsen-Marsh et al. 2007). Soils described as corrosive for bone preservation are generally acidic (pH < 6), aerated, and well-drained, reducing the capacity for local buffering (Nielsen-Marsh et al. 2007). These circumstances result in poor preservation of bone due to leaching of the bone mineral, which in turn will expose the organic components of bone to further alteration. Additionally, these circumstances will exacerbate preexisting microbial damage by collapsing the spongiform pores (Nielsen-Marsh et al. 2007). Corrosive damage results in *generalized destruction* of the microstructure—a loss of recognizable features—and dissociation of the bone (flaking, Figure 2.4) (Garland 1989). Conversely, a rapid, nonbiologically mediated collagen loss, probably due to alternate wetting–drying cycles or a strongly alkaline environment, can cause extensive cracking of the bone microstructure as well as loss of natural birefringence (Nielsen-Marsh et al. 2007; Smith et al. 2002).

Bone is a porous material, and, as such, soil components or metals from artifacts can infiltrate the bone matrix (infiltrations) as well as infill the natural bone pores (inclusions) (Garland 1989). In some cases, infiltration of material like copper or humic acids can contribute to the structural, if not biomolecular, preservation of bone by inhibiting the actions of microorganisms (Janaway 1987; Nicholson 1998). In many cases, such infiltration will interfere with biomolecular studies, such as ^{14}C dating (Van Klinken and Hedges 1995). Adipocere, as a product of saponification of fats present in bone, can sometimes be preserved in bone pores and the medullar cavity. It is visible as birefringent, almost crystalline structures of variable size (Figure 2.5).

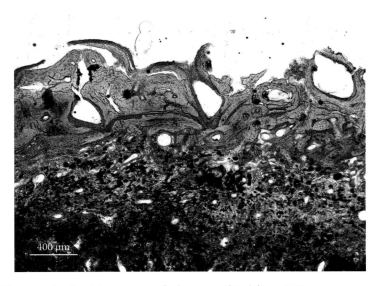

Figure 2.4 Micrograph of a thin section of a human tibia (about 200 years postmortem, United States). Extreme microbial alteration is present on the inside of the bone, with generalized destruction leading to flaking of the outer layers of bone.

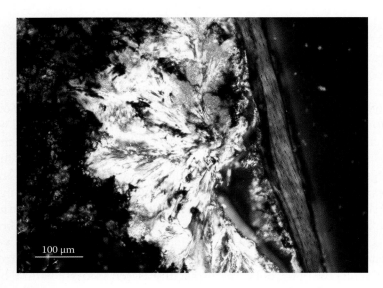

100 µm

Figure 2.5 Micrograph of a thin section of a human femur (about 65 years postmortem, Papua New Guinea, WWII) showing a thin trabecula of bone with adipocere (polarized light).

Several minerals are strong indicators for local conditions in the burial environment. For example, the presence of vivianite (Figure 2.6) is indicative of a reducing, anoxic environment (Mann et al. 1998; see also Chapter 12, this volume). Framboidal pyrite can form only in anoxic conditions; when exposed to oxygen, it will corrode (Turner-Walker 1999; Turner-Walker and Jans 2008). Framboidal pyrite formation is mediated by sulfate-reducing bacteria in anoxic conditions and is often found in marine environments where sulfate is abundant (Turner-Walker 1999). Changes in the oxygen content in the burial

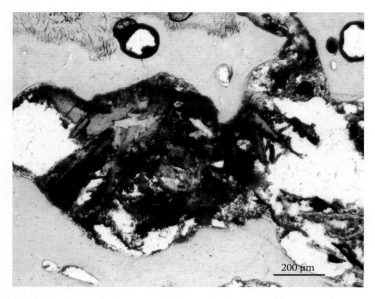

200 µm

Figure 2.6 Micrograph of a thin section of animal cortical bone (Neolithic, the Netherlands). In a damaged area of the bone, blue crystals (vivianite) are present.

environment can cause oxidation of the pyrite, leading to (localized) acidification and damage to the bone structure (Turner-Walker 1998).

Although morphology and color are diagnostic in microscopy, SEM-EDS is a very useful technique to identify exactly the composition of inclusions and infiltrations. Knowledge and identification of these inclusions are important, because they not only can inform on the (micro)environment of buried bone but can also mimic biological structures (Kaye et al. 2008). Turner-Walker and Jans (2008) as well as Hollund et al. (2012) related certain characteristic diagenetic signatures in bone to sequences of taphonomic events in selected, well-documented archaeological sites. The environmental taphonomic signatures in bone can thus inform on changing environmental conditions or illustrate local stratigraphic conditions (Turner-Walker and Jans 2008; Wilkin et al. 1996).

Temperature

Alteration of the bone material by (extreme) temperatures has been described abundantly in the literature with a focus mainly on color changes but also on cracking and fragmentation patterns (Schmidt and Symes 2008). On the macroscopical level, color changes are a well-established indicator of thermal exposure. These color data are important, as time of heat exposure and temperature will alter the bone and can cause significant loss of information (see Chapter 14, this volume). However, color as an indicator for specific temperatures/durations of exposure is problematic in histology, as color intensity and hue are influenced by light source, section thickness, and perception of the researcher (Hanson and Cain 2007). Bone heated while fully fleshed and for the purpose of food preparation (cooking, roasting, etc.) does not show histological change as described by several previous studies (Hanson and Cain 2007; Roberts et al. 2002). Transmission electron microscopy analysis of structural changes in collagen fibers can be used to detect low-level heating as described by Koon et al. (2003). This method has proven reliable in sorting cooked and noncooked archaeological bone (Koon et al. 2008).

In addition to color change and incorporation of carbon (which is again lost with increasing temperatures), another histological indicator of thermal alteration is cracks emanating from the Haversian canals (Brain 1993; Hanson and Cain 2007). In the study by Hanson and Cain (2007), other types of cracks were found; however, as these were also present in unburned archaeological bone, it is unclear whether they were perhaps caused by (later) diagenetic processes (Figure 2.7). Although these types of cracks could in some cases confuse the interpretation of microstructure in species determination studies, generally they are of little influence on the interpretation of bone histology (Cuijpers 2006).

Few studies have been performed on the effect of freezing or freezing–thawing cycles on bone histology. Tersigni (2007) investigated the effect of freezing on bone segments but found no statistically significant effect or trend (e.g., change in size of Haversian canals or osteocyte lacunae). However, using SEM, cracks were found originating from the Haversian canals that were not found in unfrozen samples. These are somewhat smaller than the cracks caused by heating, as discussed earlier. A possible explanation for these cracks is ice expansion in the bone pores, affecting the structural integrity of the surrounding bone matrix. In the case of fresh bone with adhering soft tissue, this could be expansion of moisture in the blood vessels permeating the bone (Tersigni 2007). From the results of this study, it does not appear that freezing damage would impair histological analysis of

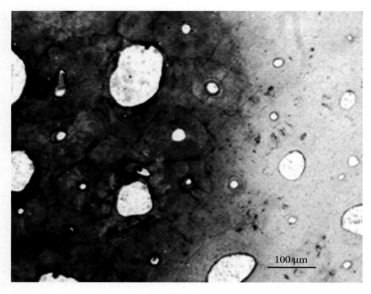

100 µm

Figure 2.7 Micrograph of a thin section of cortical animal bone (Neolithic, the Netherlands). The bone was partially burned, and the burned area in the section shows cracking and a difference in color compared to the unburned area.

the sample, but it is also hard to recognize, as the signature is similar to thermal alteration and other diagenetic changes.

Case Studies

Swifterbant, the Netherlands

Swifterbant (Flevoland, the Netherlands) is a unique early Neolithic Dutch site discovered in the 1960s, and excavation of part of the site yielded a wealth of archaeological material including human burials (Huisman et al. 2008, 2009). The burial environment at Swifterbant currently is changing due to lowering of the groundwater table for agricultural activities. During an excavation in 2005, bone samples were taken while environmental parameters were monitored to assess whether the rate or mechanism of degradation had changed (Huisman et al. 2008). In a case with such a long taphonomic history, it is essential to determine the timing of the decay signatures that are present, as the local burial environment (e.g., ground water level and quality) will have varied in the past.

The 15 Swifterbant bone samples all consist of fragmented animal bone and tooth remains found in the site refuse layer. Two samples were burned (Figure 2.7). Thin sections were prepared by impregnating small samples and fragments with Concresive EP2055 (BASF). After hardening, they were cut and then ground with a diamond grinding wheel on a Jacobson 618 grinding machine. The sections were mounted on glass slides using Araldite D and Hardener REN HY 956 (Huntsman) and finally ground to a thickness of 30–50 µm. Of the 15 samples, 2 show fungal tunneling (Table 2.1). None of the samples show bacterial alteration. Five samples contain well-preserved framboidal pyrite crystals. In one of the samples, a vivianite crystal is present (Figure 2.6). Most samples lack any birefringence.

Table 2.1   Histological Analysis of the Swifterbant Bone Remains

Sample	OHI	Fungal	Bacterial	Cracking (%)	Birefringence
56110	1	1	0	0	0
56109	5	0	0	20	0
56107	5	0	0	No data	0.5
56108	4	1	0	No data	0
56102	5	0	0	10	0.5
56103	5	0	0	75	0
56104	5	0	0	20	0
56105	5	0	0	20	0
56106	5	0	0	20	0
56111	5	0	0	40	0
56112	5	0	0	20	0
56113	5	0	0	10	0
56114	5	0	0	10	0
56115	5	0	0	10	0.5
56116	5	0	0	40	0.5

Fungal alteration of the bone (and teeth) likely occurred early in the site's history. The presence of unoxidized framboidal pyrite indicates that at least locally the environment remained reducing and anoxic, making it unsuitable for fungal activity. However, if the circumstances were to change, the presence of pyrite may cause additional preservation problems, as oxidation of pyrite results in the formation of sulfuric acid. This acid formation should be buffered by the relatively high concentration of calcium present in this burial environment (Huisman et al. 2008). Much of the cracking (certainly in the case of the burned bone) probably took place earlier in the burial history of the bones. Many of the cracks are filled in with soil material and pyrite. As too little is known of the stratigraphic history of these samples, or the site history, it is impossible to say exactly when this happened. The lack of birefringence is probably caused by the long postmortem period, allowing for, among other factors, significant collagen decay due to hydrolysis. To ensure the preservation of the important archaeological heritage at Swifterbant, it is essential that environmental parameters are monitored closely as further environmental change may challenge the buffering capacity for preservation exhibited by this rich site.

Anthropological Research Facility, University of Tennessee

Several studies suggest that normally, bacterial degradation takes place within the first 100 years postmortem, most possibly during putrefaction (Child 1995; Hedges et al. 1995; Jans et al. 2004; Yoshino et al. 1991). The Anthropological Research Facility (ARF) of the University of Tennessee is located in Knoxville and has generated a great deal of data relevant to this question (see Chapter 3, this volume). After degradation, bones are usually harvested to become part of the Bass forensic anthropological collection (Klippel and Synstelien 2007). The facility provides a unique opportunity to study decay and monitor the depositional environment in great detail. To investigate histological bone preservation in the early postmortem time frame, 14 bone samples were taken from the ARF and were evaluated using thin section histology in 2007.

Ribs (11th or 12th) were taken from 14 bodies decomposed at different locations on the ARF terrain. Care was taken to sample remains in different stages of decay to represent a spectrum of degradation, and the PMI of the remains ranged from 10 days to 4 years. Overall, the rate of macroscopical decay was fairly quick, showing advanced decomposition stages and partial skeletonization within a few weeks postmortem, and after 1 year, all samples were either mummified or skeletonized. After describing and photographing the remains, any remaining soft tissue and debris were removed, and the bone was put in a polystyrene bag and stored in a cool and dark place until it could be frozen at −20°C.

From the ribs, samples were taken for histology using a Dremel tool. Histological sections were prepared manually according to the improved Frost's technique. After grinding, the section was cleaned in distilled water and dried overnight between layers of tissue paper. The section was mounted on a glass slide using Permount (Fisher Scientific) and was ready for analysis using normal transmitted light and polarized light microscopy.

Histologically, the samples were very well preserved (see Table 2.2). The only observable diagenetic feature was the presence of adipocere, which was included in the bone pores, even in samples where macroscopically no adipocere was present. The amount of adipocere present in a bone section decreased with increasing PMI. There was no adipocere visible in both 4 year old samples, while samples exposed between 12 and 24 months showed generally intermediate amounts of adipocere (only some present in scattered Haversian canals or osteocyte lacunae). All but two samples younger than 12 months showed large amounts of adipocere (present in Haversian canals, osteocyte lacunae, and medullary area). Sample N, for example, had been exposed for only 10 days but had been completely skeletonized by invertebrate activity, so presumably there had not been enough time for adipocere formation.

Table 2.2   Description of Samples

Sample	OHI	PMI (Months)	Adipocere
A	5	49	0
B	5	46	0
C	5	25	0.5
D	5	23	0.5
E	5	12	0.5
F	5	18	0.5
G	5	12	0.5
H	5	12	1
I	5	10	0.5
J	5	8	1
K	5	7	1
L	5	2	1
M	5	1	1
N	5	1	0

Note: All samples taken consisted of ribs (number 11 or 12).

The lack of microbial alteration is surprising and has several possible explanations. One possibility is that the microbes responsible for (initial) bone alteration are anaerobic, and decay in an oxygen-rich environment simply is too fast for a prolonged anaerobic putrefaction stage such as would occur in coffin burial. Most, if not all, human samples from the study by Jans et al. (2004) were inhumed, many of those in coffins. Moreover, some of the bodies, especially those deposited in summer, skeletonize exceptionally quickly. The skeletons are not protected from small vertebrate scavengers or invertebrates, which results in a rapid removal of soft tissue and organics. The remains appear to be in advanced decomposition stages, and skeletonization occurs within weeks to a month of deposition (in summer), before significant bacterial degradation can take place. After the fast putrefaction, the bones dry out quickly, inhibiting further bacterial action. More research is clearly needed, comparing early decay of surface-exposed remains to buried remains in varying circumstances.

Conclusions and Future Research

Diagenetic alteration can destroy bone microstructure, which interferes with (histological) analyses such as age or species determination (e.g., Cuijpers 2006). Knowledge of the different types of alteration is essential to avoid confusion with pathological changes in bone (Bell 1990). Decomposition can affect bone quality extensively, impeding biomolecular analyses. Histology is a technique for quick sample evaluations, aiding in sample selection, possibly even identifying well-preserved areas within a single bone. Additionally, precisely because peri- and postmortem events leave behind recognizable signatures in bone microstructure, taphonomical histories can be reconstructed. Not only is material from the environment included in natural bone pores, formation of different minerals is useful as indicators of (past) microenvironmental conditions. In addition, different types of bioerosion are indicative for burial or deposition in different (aquatic) environments or for the presence of oxygen in the environment (fungi). The presence or absence of bacterial alteration of bone has been linked in archaeological studies to early postmortem treatment of the remains (fragmentation, defleshing, or complete burial).

All the existing data notwithstanding, further research is clearly needed on this topic. Experiments, consisting of degradation of specific material in controlled or well-characterized environments, are needed to bring this study forward from a field based on observation of trends and patterns of alteration in different burial environments. The sequence, rate, and cause of taphonomic signatures can be firmly established only when factors influencing preservation are isolated using experimental control or detailed observation of the burial environment throughout the experiment. Identifying specific (sequences of) bioeroding microorganisms for PMI determination will require experimental approaches such as practiced in the ARF or as showcased in the Neuadd experimental burials (Fernández-Jalvo et al. 2010) and the experimental bird bone deposition by Davis (1997). Experiments must include different (micro)environments as well as different climates. The focus of such studies could, for example, be on differences in bioerosion in defleshed, exposed, or buried material. Similar experiments would be necessary to establish detailed knowledge of the speed of diagenetic processes in different environments, important in archaeological heritage management as well as PMI determination. Useful information on the rate of diagenesis already has been obtained by comparing the preservation of archaeological bones excavated from the same site but deposited at different points in time (e.g., Van Heeringen et al. 2004). Additionally, in a similar recent study, it became very clear that diagenesis continues even when bone is in storage and can result in significant and fast loss of (molecular) information (Pruvost et al. 2007). As much material from ongoing and past taphonomic studies is potentially available in the original experimental settings or in storage, relevant samples for analysis may be obtained with relatively little investment.

Acknowledgments

The Forensic Anthropology Center (University of Tennessee) and the Dutch State Service for Cultural Heritage are gratefully acknowledged for providing samples. Wynanda Koot (VU University Amsterdam) is thanked for preparing thin sections (Swifterbant). I especially would like to thank the following individuals for their invaluable contributions and discussions: Hege Hollund (VU University Amsterdam), Dr. Franklin Damann (National Museum of Health and Medicine, Washington, DC), Audrey Meehan (JPAC-CIL), and Dr. Hans Huisman (State Service for Cultural Heritage, Amersfoort, the Netherlands).

References

Baud, C. A. and D. Lacotte (1984) Étude au microscope électronique à transmission de la colonisation bactérienne de l'os mort. *Comptes Rendus de l'Académie des Sciences* 298:507–510.

Bell, L. S. (1990) Paleopathology and diagenesis: A SEM evaluation of structural changes using backscattered electron imaging. *Journal of Archaeological Science* 17:85–102.

Bell, L. S. and A. Elkerton (2008) Unique marine taphonomy in human skeletal material recovered from the medieval warship Mary Rose. *International Journal of Osteoarchaeology* 18:523–535.

Bell, L. S., M. F. Skinner, and S. J. Jones (1996) The speed of postmortem change to the human skeleton and its taphonomic significance. *Forensic Science International* 82:129–140.

Brain, C. K. (1993) The occurrence of burnt bones at Swartkrans and their implications for the control of fire by early hominids. In *Swartkrans: A Cave's Chronicle of Early Man*, ed. C. K. Brain, pp. 229–242. Transvaal Museum, Pretoria, South Africa.

Carlisle, M. J., S. C. Watkinson, and G. W. Gooday (2001) *The Fungi*. Academic Press, New York.

Child, A. M. (1995) Towards an understanding of the microbial decomposition of archaeological bone in the burial environment. *Journal of Archaeological Science* 22:165–174.

Cuijpers, A. F. G. M. (2006) Histological identification of bone fragments in archaeology: Telling humans apart from horses and cattle. *International Journal of Osteoarchaeology* 16:465–480.

Cuijpers, A. F. G. M. (2009) The application of bone histology for species identification in archaeology; with a photo catalogue. *Geoarchaeological and Bioarchaeological Studies* 12. Institute for Geo and Bioarchaeology, Vrije Universiteit, Amsterdam, the Netherlands.

Cuijpers, A. G. F. M. and H. Schutkowsky (1993) Histological age determination of the cremated human bones from the urnfields of Deventer-'t Bramelt and Markelo Friezenberg. *Helinium* XXXIII 1:99–107.

Davis, P. G. (1997) Bioerosion of bird bones. *International Journal of Osteoarchaeology* 7:388–401.

Fernández-Jalvo, Y., P. Andrews, D. Pesquero, C. Smith, D. Marín-Monfort, B. Sánchez, E. Geigl, and A. Alonso (2010) Early bone diagenesis in temperate environments. Part I: Surface features and histology. *Palaeogeography, Palaeoclimatology, Palaeoecology* 288:62–81.

Garland, A. N. (1989) Microscopical analysis of fossil bone. *Applied Geochemistry* 4:215–229.

Garland, A. N. (1993) A histological study of archaeological bone decomposition. In *Histology of Ancient Human Bone: Methods and Diagnosis*, eds. G. Grupe and A. N. Garland, pp. 109–126. Springer, Berlin, Germany.

Gilbert, M. T. P., L. Rudbeck, E. Willerslev, A. J. Hansen, C. Smith, K. Penkman, K. Prangenberg et al. (2005) Biochemical and physical correlates of DNA contamination in archaeological bones and teeth. *Journal of Archaeological Science* 32:785–793.

Gordon, C. C. and J. E. Buikstra (1981) Soil pH, bone preservation, and sampling bias at mortuary sites. *American Antiquity* 46:566–571.

Hackett, C. J. (1981) Microscopical focal destruction (tunnels) in exhumed human bones. *Medicine, Science and the Law* 21:243–265.

Hanson, M. and C. R. Cain (2007) Examining histology to identify burned bone. *Journal of Archaeological Science* 34:1902–1913.

Haynes, S., J. B. Searle, A. Bretman, and K. M. Dobney (2002) Bone preservation and ancient DNA: The application of screening methods for predicting DNA survival. *Journal of Archaeological Science* 29:585–592.

Hedges, R. E. M., A. R. Millard, and A. W. G. Pike (1995) Measurements and relationships of diagenetic alteration of bone from three archaeological sites. *Journal of Archaeological Science* 22:201–209.

Hillier, M. L. and L. S. Bell (2007) Differentiating human bone from animal bone: A review of histological methods. *Journal of Forensic Sciences* 52:249–263.

Hollund, H. I., M. M. E. Jans, M. J. Collins, H. Kars, I. Joosten, and S. M. Kars (2012) What happened here? Bone histology as a tool in decoding the post-mortem histories of archaeological bone from Castricum, the Netherlands. *International Journal of Osteoarchaeology* 22:537–548.

Huisman, D. J., A. G. Jongmans, and D. C. M. Raemaekers (2009) Investigating Neolithic land use in Swifterbant (NL) using micromorphological techniques. *CATENA* 78:185–197.

Huisman, D. J., A. Smit, M. M. E. Jans, W. Prummel, A. G. F. M. Cuijpers, and J. H. M. Peeters (2008) Het bodemmilieu op de archeologische vindplaatsen bij Swifterbant (provincie Flevoland): Bedreigingen en mogelijkheden voor in situ behoud. *Rapportage Archeologische Monumentenzorg* 163. RACM, Amersfoort, the Netherlands.

Jackes, M., R. Sherburne, D. Lubell, C. Barker, and M. Wayman (2001) Destruction of the microstructure in archaeological bone: A case study from Portugal. *International Journal of Osteoarchaeology* 11:387–399.

Janaway, R. C. (1987) The preservation of organic materials in association with metal artefacts deposited in inhumation graves. In *Death, Decay and Reconstruction. Approaches to Archaeology and Forensic Science*, eds. A. Boddington, A. N. Garland, and R. C. Janaway. Manchester University Press, Manchester, U.K.

Jans M. M. E. (2008) Micro-bioerosion of bone: A review. In *Current Developments in Bioerosion*, eds. L. Tapanila and M. Wisshak. Erlangen Earth Science Conferences, Springer Verlag, Berlin, Germany.

Jans, M. M. E., H. Kars, C. M. Nielsen-Marsh, C. I. Smith, A. G. Nord, P. Arthur, and N. Earl (2002) In situ preservation of archaeological bone. A histological study within a multidisciplinary approach. *Archaeometry* 44:343–352.

Jans, M. M. E., C. M. Nielsen-Marsh, C. I. Smith, M. J. Collins, and H. Kars (2004) Characterisation of microbial attack on archaeological bone. *Journal of Archaeological Science* 31:87–95.

Kaye, T. G., G. Gaugler, and Z. Sawlowicz (2008) Dinosaurian soft tissues interpreted as bacterial biofilms. *PLoS ONE* 3:e2808.

Klippel, W. E. and J. A. Synstelien (2007) Rodents as taphonomic agents: Bone gnawing by brown rats and gray squirrels. *Journal of Forensic Sciences* 52:765–773.

Koon, H. E. C., R. A. Nicholson, and M. J. Collins (2003) A practical approach to the identification of low temperature heated bone using TEM. *Journal of Archaeological Science* 30:1393–1399.

Koon, H. E. C., T. P. O'Connor, and M. J. Collins (2008) Sorting the butchered from the boiled. *Journal of Archaeological Science* 37:62–67.

Maat, G. J. R., R. P. M. Van den Bos, and M. J. Aarents (2000) Manual for the preparation of ground sections for the microscopy of bone tissue. *Barge's Anthropologica*. Leiden University Medical Centre, Leiden, the Netherlands.

Maat, G. J. R., R. P. M. Van Den Bos, and M. J. Aarents (2001) Manual preparation of ground sections for the microscopy of bone tissue: Update and modification of Frost's 'rapid manual method'. *International Journal of Osteoarchaeology* 11:366–374.

Mann, R. W., M. E. Feather, C. S. Tumosa, T. D. Holland, and K. N. Schneider (1998) A blue encrustation found on skeletal remains of Americans missing in action in Vietnam. *Forensic Science International* 97:79–86.

Marchiafava, V., E. Bonucci, and A. Ascenzi (1974) Fungal osteoclasia: A model of dead bone resorption. *Calcified Tissue Research* 14:195–210.

Millard, A. R. (2001) The deterioration of bone. In *Handbook of Archaeological Science*, eds. A. M. Pollard and D. R. Brothwell, pp. 637–647. Wiley, New York.

Nicholson, R. A. (1998) Bone degradation in a compost heap. *Journal of Archaeological Science* 25:393–403.

Nielsen-Marsh, C. M. and R. E. M. Hedges (1997) Dissolution experiments on modern and diagenetically altered bone and the effect on the infrared splitting factor. *Bulletin de la Société Géologique de France* 168:485–490.

Nielsen-Marsh, C. M., C. I. Smith, M. M. E. Jans, A. Nord, H. Kars, and M. J. Collins (2007) Bone diagenesis in the European Holocene II: Taphonomic and environmental considerations. *Journal of Archaeological Science* 34:1523–1531.

Parker Pearson, M., A. Chamberlain, O. Craig, P. Marshall, J. Mulville, H. Smith, C. Chenery, M. Collins, G. Cook, G. Craig, J. Evans, J. Hiller, J-L. Montgomery, G. Taylor, and T. Wess (2005) Evidence for mummification in Bronze Age Britain. *Antiquity* 79:529–546.

Pesquero, M. D., C. Ascaso, Y. Fernández-Jalvo, and L. Alcalá (2010) A new taphonomic bioerosion in a Miocene lakeshore environment. *Palaeogeography, Palaeoclimatology, Palaeoecology* 295:192–198.

Pruvost, M., R. Schwarz, V. Bessa Correia, S. Champlot, S. Braguier, N. Morel, Y. Fernández-Jalvo, Th. Grange, and E-M. Geigl (2007) Freshly excavated fossil bones are best for amplification of ancient DNA. *Proceedings of the National Academy of Sciences of the United States of America* 104:739–744.

Roberts, J. P., C. I. Smith, A. M. Millard, and M. J. Collins (2002) The taphonomy of cooked bone: Characterising boiling and its physico-chemical effects. *Archaeometry* 44:485–494.

Schmidt, C. W. and S. A. Symes (eds.) (2008) *The Analysis of Burned Human Remains*. Academic Press, London, U.K.

Smith, C. I., C. M. Nielsen-Marsh, M. M. E. Jans, P. Arthur, A. G. Nord, and M. J. Collins (2002) The strange case of Apigliano: Early fossilisation of Medieval bone in Southern Italy. *Archaeometry* 44:405–416.

Smith, C. I., C. M. Nielsen-Marsh, M. M. E. Jans, and M. J. Collins (2007) Bone diagenesis in the European Holocene I: Patterns and mechanisms. *Journal of Archaeological Science* 34:1485–1493.

Stout, S. D. (1978) Histological structure and its preservation in ancient bone. *Current Anthropology* 19:601–604.

Tersigni, M. A. (2007) Frozen human bone: A microscopic investigation. *Journal of Forensic Sciences* 52:16–20.

Trueman, C. N. and D. M. Martill (2002) The long-term survival of bone: The role of bioerosion. *Archaeometry* 44:371–382.

Turner-Walker, G. (1998) The West Runton fossil elephant: A pre-conservation evaluation of its condition, chemistry and burial environment. *The Conservator* 22:26–35.

Turner-Walker, G. (1999) Pyrite and bone diagenesis in terrestrial sediments: Evidence from the West Runton freshwater bed. *Bulletin of the Geological Society of Norfolk* 48:3–26.

Turner-Walker, G. and M. M. E. Jans (2008) Reconstructing taphonomic histories using histological analysis. *Palaeogeography, Palaeoclimatology, Palaeoecology* 266:227–235.

Turner-Walker, G., C. M. Nielsen-Marsh, U. Syversen, H. Kars, and M. J. Collins (2002) Sub-micron spongiform porosity is the major ultra-structural alteration occurring in archaeological bone. *International Journal of Osteoarchaeology* 12:407–414.

Turner-Walker, G. and U. Syversen (2002) Quantifying histological changes in archaeological bones using BSE-SEM image analysis. *Archaeometry* 44:461–468.

Van Der Lubbe, H. B. M., C. P. A. T. Klein, and K. De Groot (1988) A simple method for preparing thin (10 μm) histological sections of undecalcified plastic embedded bone with implants. *Stain Technology* 63:171–176.

Van Heeringen, R. M., G. Mauro, and A. Smit (eds.) (2004) A pilot study on the monitoring of the physical quality of three archaeological sites on the UNESCO Monument of Schokland, province of Flevoland, the Netherlands. *Nederlandse Archeologische Rapporten* 26, Rijksdienst voor het Oudheidkundig Bodemonderzoek, Amersfoort, the Netherlands.

Van Klinken, G. J. and R. E. M. Hedges (1995) Experiments on collagen-humic interactions: Speed of humic uptake, and effects of diverse chemical treatments. *Journal of Archaeological Science* 22:263–270.

Wedl, C. (1864) Ueber einen Zahnbein und Knochen keimenden Pilz. *Sitzungsbericht der Mathematische Naturwissenschaftliche Classe der Kaiserliche Akademie der Wissenschaften Wien* Band L. K1 (1) 50:171–193.

Wilkin, R. T., H. L. Barnes, and S. L. Brantley (1996) The size distribution of framboidal pyrite in modern sediments: An indicator of redox conditions. *Geochimica et Cosmochimica Acta* 60:3897–3912.

Yoshino, M., T. Kimijima, S. Miyasaka, H. Sato, and S. Seta (1991) Microscopical study on time since death in skeletal remains. *Forensic Science International* 49:143–158.

Human Decomposition Ecology and Postmortem Microbiology* 3

FRANKLIN E. DAMANN
DAVID O. CARTER

Contents

Introduction

Decomposition is the mobilization of nutrients bound to once-living organisms into the surrounding ecosystem so that they may become recycled as living biomass (Swift et al. 1979), be released into the atmosphere and soil, or become preserved as inorganic constituents of fossilization (Behrensmeyer 1984). Human decomposition is no exception to this process and lies at the center of a complex web of cultural, physicochemical, and biological reactions. The extent of preservation/destruction of a corpse is a function of the surrounding decomposer populations, the quality of the resource being decomposed, and the cultural and environmental modulators, all of which combine to form a unique and yet ephemeral decompositional environment (Carter et al. 2007).

This chapter reviews the general patterns of human decomposition and various factors that affect the rate of decomposition, while paying particular attention to the role played by microbes. In general, human decomposition follows a pattern that includes an early and relatively short period of heightened taphonomic activity from multiple trophic levels, which is followed by a longer period of less taphonomic activity. In other words, the rapid loss of the nutrient-rich soft tissue gives way to the generally nutrient-deprived skeleton for subsequent and generally slower diagenetic processes.

---

* The views expressed are those of the author and should not be construed to represent the U.S. government.

The traditional paradigm of decomposition and nutrient cycling comes from reviews of litter decay in soil science and basic ecology texts (Burges 1967; Paul 2007; Ricklefs 1997; Swift et al. 1979), while less attention had been placed on functions inherent to carcass decay (Putman 1978a,b), and only recently has awareness of carcass enrichment of gravesoils and its relationship to microbiology and ecosystem function increased (Benninger et al. 2008; Carter et al. 2007, 2010; Damann 2010; Damann et al. 2012; Dent et al. 2004; Hopkins et al. 2000; Towne 2000).

In general terms of organic decomposition, biological modification in the terrestrial landscape is accomplished primarily by edaphic fungi and bacteria. Their activity accounts for approximately 90% of the mobilization of carbon and nitrogen in an ecosystem (Swift et al. 1979); in fact, decomposition is second only to photosynthesis for the cycling of nutrients and energy (McGuire and Treseder 2010). It is no wonder that "microbes are essential in the decay and recycling of materials important to life (e.g., carbon and nitrogen) by transforming the detritus of human society" (Prostgate 2000:244).

Carter et al. (2007) explored the notion of a corpse as a rich source of nutrients and energy. In doing so, they reported on the contribution that carcass decomposition has on the terrestrial landscape by creating a heterogeneous hub of activity marked by an increase in carbon, nitrogen, and water (Carter et al. 2007). They suggested that this hub of activity is its own localized ecosystem that is bound in both time and space. Recent studies on the microbial communities associated with decomposing corpses in terrestrial (Damann 2010; Howard et al. 2010; Parkinson 2009; Parkinson et al. 2009) and aquatic ecosystems (Dickson et al. 2011) have identified patterns and shifting community profiles associated with macroscopic tissue change, as the microbial community is selected for by the quality of the resource being decomposed (Moorhead and Sinsabaugh 2006).

Microbially mediated decomposition of organic material occurs primarily by catalysis, where complex macromolecules are broken down into simpler organic structures. For example, lipids are decomposed to long-chain and short-chain fatty acids. The resulting short-chain fatty acids are water soluble and are easily leached into the surrounding environment (Vass et al. 1992). In the presence of increased moisture, the micro- and macronutrients leached from the body will be used by a growing community of local edaphic heterotrophic microorganisms, provided appropriate physicochemical conditions exist within the surrounding soil matrix.

At a site of carcass decomposition, the movement of carbon and energy occurs through consumption by grazers and scavengers and the leaching of organic and inorganic compounds (Putman 1978a,b). The consumption of a corpse is dominated by primary and secondary consumers, originating from multiple trophic levels (c.f. Haglund 1997a,b; Klippel and Synstelien 2007; Rodriguez and Bass 1983) that obtain nutrients from the corpse and release carbon as carbon dioxide through respiration.

Human Decomposition

Decomposition begins at the moment of death. Perper (1993) defined death as the irreversible cessation of the brain, respiratory, and circulatory abilities, causing internal biochemical reactions in response to the depletion of oxygen in tissues. Once the systems of normal living have stopped functioning, the internal biological mechanisms that require oxygen for energy production have ceased, and the multiple decomposition processes that take place after death ensue.

For convenience, those who study cadaver decomposition superimpose a categorical-ordinal scale based on observable patterns of gross-tissue change (Megyesi et al. 2005; Payne 1965; Reed 1958). Clark et al. (1997) provide an overview of stages and modulators of human decomposition. This pattern begins with a fresh corpse that undergoes discoloration and bloating to decay, skeletonization, and eventual disarticulation and bone diagenesis. This pattern demonstrates the continuum of human decomposition, where a complete cadaver becomes reincorporated within the landscape or it becomes sequestered within the biogeochemical footprint (e.g., fossilized remains).

General Patterns of Human Decomposition

Fresh (Autolysis)

Under natural conditions, which are defined here by exclusion of desiccation and/or freezing, a body will begin to decompose soon after death. The processes that take place in the moments immediately following death initiate a complex series of biochemical reactions, affecting the entire microcosm of organic components, which manifest in cellular destruction by a body's own enzymes.

The cessation of the circulatory system causes a loss of oxygen transport throughout the body. Without oxygen, the central metabolic pathway fails to produce adenosine triphosphate (ATP) (Love and Marks 2003; Powers 2005). Because of the living cell's high demand for oxygen, autolysis first occurs in areas that demand high-energy output, such as tissue with high concentrations of mitochondria (Clark et al. 1997; Gill-King 1997). Without oxygen, the mitochondria swell, causing the cell and internal cellular organelles to rupture in a process similar to cellular apoptosis (Evans 1963). Similarly, the death of a cell initiates the rupture of the lipoprotein membranes of lysosomes that are packed with high concentrations of cellular enzymes (lipases, proteases, DNAses, etc.) that break down enteric protein, lipids, carbohydrates, and DNA (Evans 1963). Consequently, membrane pumps fail, releasing calcium ions and destroying cell membranes, effectively ending cell-to-cell adhesion. Internal biochemical changes initiate the macroscopic changes of algor mortis, livor mortis, and rigor mortis (the mortis triad), which typically occur within the first 24 h after death (Clark et al. 1997).

Mortis Triad

Algor mortis is the modification of body temperature from the normal average of 37°C (98.6°F) to ambient temperature. Traditionally, a cooling rate of 1.5°F per hour is accepted, but the correlation is not exactly linear, as there tends to be a moment of heat retention immediately after death, followed by a quicker decline, and then a plateau is reached (Clark et al. 1997). There are many intrinsic and extrinsic factors that affect the rate of cooling, but as a time since death estimator, it is generally applicable within the first 10–12 h postmortem (Dix and Graham 2000; Henβge and Madea 2004).

Intravascular concentration and hemolysis of blood cells result in *livor mortis* or lividity (Perper 1993). As a direct result of gravity, the low-lying body tissues develop a reddish-purple appearance as a subcutaneous pool of degraded blood forms. When a body is discovered supine, lividity appears on the back, buttocks, and calves, and may become visible as soon as 20 min after death (Perper 1993). In this example, pallor would be present in the areas of the body that are in direct contact with the surface on which the body is lying. Similarly, blanching of the pooled blood occurs when pressure is applied to the areas of lividity (Love and Marks 2003). Lividity becomes fixed when blanching of the pooled blood is no longer possible. Fixation may occur approximately 8–12 h after death (Di Maio and Di Maio 2001; Payne-James et al. 2003).

Rigor mortis results from a decrease in cellular ATP and pH, and the presence of calcium ions (Perper 1993). In combination with the low pH and the proper amount of free calcium ions, chemical bridges are formed, binding the contractile units of actin and myosin, thus giving the muscle a rigid and hard appearance (Perper 1993), which is similar, but not identical to contractile activity (Dix and Graham 2000). Rigor may initiate by 2–6 h postmortem and may persist for 1–2 days (Clark 1997; Krompecher 2002; Perper 1993).

Without protection from the intestinal mucosa and normal homeostatic mechanisms, autolysis initiates the breakdown of normal biological structure and function. The combination of depleted oxygen and the activity of enzymes during autolysis facilitates destruction of proteins and entire organ systems. The first organs to decompose include those of the alimentary system (e.g., pancreas, intestines, and stomach), given the high concentrations of lytic enzyme, while the prostate and uterus are typically the last of the soft tissue organs to decompose (Di Maio and Di Maio 2001).

The breakdown of the alimentary system permits initial microbial proliferation and transmigration across internal mucosa, allowing microbes to move passively through the body's circulatory and lymphatic systems (Kellerman et al. 1976; Melvin et al. 1984). Enteric heterotrophic microbes metabolize organic macromolecules such as lipids, proteins, amino acids, and nucleic acids, selectively using them to meet their own metabolic demands (Child 1995).

Bloat and Active Decay (Putrefaction)

Autolysis also initiates putrefaction of a corpse, which is marked by the widespread breakdown of biomolecular components and subsequent destruction and liquefaction of soft tissue by enteric obligate and facultative anaerobic microorganisms. Evans (1963) noted that during decomposition, the bacteria transition from the aerobic groups, exemplified by the coliform–staphylococcal–proteus varieties, to the anaerobic groups in which the Clostridia predominate. Melvin et al. (1984) and Carter et al. (2007) identified a similar trend and suggested that the destruction of soft tissue is caused by enteric obligate and facultative bacteria from the phyla Actinobacteria, Firmicutes, and Proteobacteria. This includes bacteria from the genera *Clostridium, Bacteroides, Staphylococcus,* and the Enterobacteriaceae family, those bacteria observed by Micozzi (1986). Recently, Howard et al. (2010) observed species from the genera *Acinetobacter, Arthrobacter, Bacillus, Brevibacterium, Kurthia, Pseudomonas,* and *Serratia* in gravesoils of swine (*Sus scrofa domesticus*) carcasses. From skin swabs taken during bloat and putrefaction, Sidrim et al. (2010) identified fungi of the *Aspergillus, Penicillium,* and *Candida* genera, while Carter and Tibbett (2003) reported the presence of several strains of Ascomycetes, Deuteromycetes, and saprotrophic Basidiomycetes as early-stage decomposers recovered from gravesoils.

During putrefaction, a hypoxic internal environment promotes anaerobic metabolism and the transmigration from the gastrointestinal tract to surrounding tissue systems. For example, the amino acid arginine is present in many foods of the human diet, and when in the gut, enzymes of *Enterococcus faecalis* convert arginine to ornithine, enabling *Escherichia coli* only then to convert ornithine to putrescine (Wilson 2008). Gill-King (1997) reported that the foul-smelling compounds of putrescine and cadaverine that are present during putrefaction result from the decarboxylation of amino acids. Therefore, this naturally occurring process in the living body is only elevated during putrefaction due to a loss of homeostatic mechanisms and the postmortem bacterial transmigration from the gut to the surrounding tissues.

As a result of increased microbially mediated decomposition, the skin will undergo a series of color changes, first appearing paler, and then green to dark brown (Love and Marks 2003). The dark brown to black coloration appears from the drying of tissue and typically appears first at the head, around the nose and ears (Love and Marks 2003). The earlier transition to a green discoloration first appears near the right anterior abdominal wall. The buildup of biliary acids causes this color change, which is the result of newly formed sulfa-hemoglobin complexes from reduced sulfur- and iron-containing compounds (Clark et al. 1997; Gill-King 1997). In fact, a high concentration of sulfate-reducing organisms of the bacterial order Desulfarcales was identified in gravesoils associated with elevated levels of human decomposition at the University of Tennessee Anthropology Research Facility (Damann 2010).

The increased anaerobic microbial activity accompanies increased levels of carbon dioxide and other volatile compounds that become trapped in the face and neck, abdominal cavity, and scrotum, causing swelling and bloating (Vass et al. 1992). Two volatile fatty acids have been identified emanating from the body during the bloat stage; they are the three-carbon propionic acid and the four-carbon butyric acid, both of which are the products of anaerobic fermentation (Vass et al. 1992).

Externally, the processes associated with increased bloat and pressure cause blistering and skin slip along the neck and abdomen (Love and Marks 2003). Additional areas of skin slip occur at the hands and feet, which result from the lack of cell-to-cell adhesion within the epidermis. Additional macroscopic change includes the appearance of a ferrous sulfide complex at the skin surface. A black precipitant is sequestered in the capillaries near the skin surface of a decomposing corpse (Love and Marks 2003). Gill-King (1997) explains that during putrefaction sulfur-containing amino acids are reduced by the desulfhydrase, producing hydrogen sulfide, pyruvic acid, and ammonia. In the presence of iron released during intravascular hemolysis, hydrogen sulfide forms ferrous sulfide (Gill-King 1997). Microbially mediated fermentation will persist until oxygen replenishes the system. The rupturing of orifices from putrefactive processes is one example of how oxygen replenishes the system (Gill-King 1997; Micozzi 1991). Replenishing the decomposing corpse with oxygen initiates the transition to late-stage decomposition, which is associated with aerobic metabolism and involves skeletonization and diagenesis.

Advanced Decay and Skeletal Remains

In the terrestrial setting, skeletal exposure typically originates with the head and face and is often advanced by insect (maggot) activity. Other early sites of skeletal exposure may include areas of traumatic lesions (Mann et al. 1990; Rodriguez 1997). Furthermore, scavenging accelerates skeletonization and may promote disarticulation and bone loss (Haglund 1997a,b; Klippel and Synstelien 2007; Willey and Snyder 1989; see also Chapter 9, this volume). The last portions of soft tissue to remain are the dense connective tissues of joint surfaces (Stewart 1979).

Once exposed, the skeleton interacts directly with the environment, as it is no longer protected by internal viscera and skin. During late-stage decomposition, at the advanced or dry-remains stages, microbially mediated decay persists in facilitating the recycling of the organic phase and the inorganic nutrients bound within the bone matrix (i.e.,

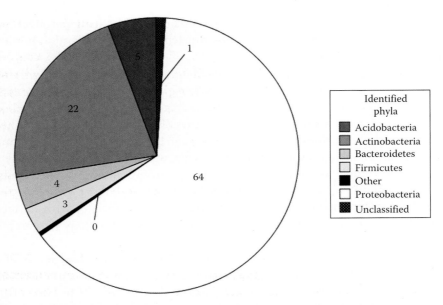

Figure 3.1 Percent distribution of bacterial phyla recovered from a human bone 4 years post-mortem. The sample consists of 12,193 aligned and classified bacterial sequences.

calcium and phosphorus) into the environment (Vass et al. 1992). In fact, recent investigation by one of the authors (FED) into the presence of eubacteria in skeletal remains identified 12,193 bacterial DNA sequences by pyrosequencing from a human rib that was exposed on the surface at the University of Tennessee Anthropology Research Facility for 48 months. Taxonomic classification was achieved using the Ribosomal Database Project 10.0 following Wang et al. (2007), which classified all sequences into seven different phyla (Figure 3.1). *Sphingomonas, Streptomyces, Ochrobactrum, Actinoplanes, Pseudomonas,* and *Clostridium* contributed 51% of the identified genera from this sample. This work is a preliminary investigation of what bacterial organisms are present in bone during late-stage decomposition in this environment. There has yet to be a clear determination about whether these organisms are directly related to the microbially mediated destruction of bone or if their presence is purely opportunistic. For a review of taphonomic effects due to microbial bioerosion of the skeleton, see Jans (this volume, Chapter 2).

Factors Affecting the Rate of Human Decomposition

In the terrestrial landscape, natural human decomposition follows a sigmoidal curve, indicating rapid mass loss followed by periods of less change (Carter et al. 2007), which contrasts with the decomposition rates of plants and fecal material where percent mass loss is more linear over time (Coleman et al. 2004; Olson 1963; Putman 1983). Natural decomposition, however, is often the exception rather than the rule, since cadaver decomposition lies at the nexus of four influential modulators that include (1) the quality of the resource being decomposed, (2) cultural determinants, (3) environmental determinants, and (4) the potential decomposer community. Each modulator contains a suite of possible factors that affect preservation/destruction, as well as the rate of decomposition. These four categories are similar to those of Jenny's (1941) five ecological state factors that regulate soil formation, which is a function of climate, topography, potential biota, parent material, and time.

In this model, only cultural influence is absent, but it may be reasonably included within the framework of potential biota.

Resource Quality

Resource quality is inversely proportional to the ratio of carbon and nitrogen, where the amount of carbon is expressed per single nitrogen atom; a high ratio indicates a poor-quality resource and vice versa. A high-quality resource implies increased availability of carbon and nitrogen mobilization in the ecosystem (Swift et al. 1979). For example, plant material contains a carbon:nitrogen ratio of 100:1, whereas cow manure contains a ratio of 18:1 (Carter et al. 2007). In this example, cow manure is the higher-quality resource. For a human cadaver, the carbon:nitrogen ratio is approximately 5.5:1 (Carter et al. 2007), creating the expectation that the rate of decomposition is greater for a human cadaver than plant material in the same environment. This interpretation is consistent with percent mass loss curves for the rate of decomposition between cadavers and plants (Carter et al. 2007). However, intra-species variation also contributes to the decomposition rate, as not all members of the same species enter the burial environment in a similar manner. Factors that an individual organism contributes to accelerating or decelerating the rate of decomposition have been identified previously and include the presence or absence of clothing (Aturaliya and Lukasewycz 1999; Mann et al. 1990) and an individual's age, mass (Hewadikaram and Goff 1991; Spicka et al. 2011), and health status (Campobasso et al. 2001; Mann et al. 1990).

Cultural Determinants

Culturally distinct human behavior is a significant modulator in the decomposition rates of a cadaver (Evans 1963; Holland et al. 1997; Sledzik 1998). Through various cultural practices that the living does to the dead, such as mortuary and interment practices, the natural processes of decomposition are affected. In Western cultures, certain post-death practices affect the condition of the corpse. These may include, but are not limited to, autopsy and organ removal, embalming, anatomical preparation, burning, and/or disarticulation by criminal or traumatic mechanisms (see Chapter 5, this volume).

Interment practices vary from deliberate exposure to burial where the corpse may be wrapped in plastic; submerged in water, buried in a sealed casket or wooden box, or wrapped in cloth and placed in dirt; or a concrete burial vault above or below ground. Burial may occur at various depths, or there may be no burial at all, with the remains left on the surface to decompose. Containment of the body in clothing, vault, casket, or plastic tarp contributes to the variation inherent to the decay/preservation dichotomy. Jans et al. (2004) noted that animal remains buried intact displayed greater signs of bioerosion at the microscopic level than those that were disarticulated prior to burial, suggesting the early postmortem transmigration from the gastrointestinal tract as a primary mechanism of bacterial dissemination and subsequent erosion of bone.

Environmental Determinants

Potentially the most recognized factors controlling the rate of human decomposition are variations in the environment, which either decompose biological materials completely or suspend their decomposition through freezing (Micozzi 1991), desiccation (Evans 1963; Galloway 1997; Galloway et al. 1989), or adipocere formation by hydrolysis and saponification of adipose tissue (c.f. Forbes et al. 2003, 2004, 2005; Mant 1987). Environmental factors that create varied ecological niches include, but are not limited to, temperature, moisture, seasonality, altitude, latitude, air circulation, burial depth, soil type, vegetation, topography, exposure to direct sunlight, and placement in water. Of these, temperature is typically regarded as the most significant in that it is a prime mover of all biological activity and biochemical reactions (Hopkins 2008; Mann et al. 1990).

There is a positive correlation of temperature to biological and chemical reaction rates over the mesophilic interval of 15°C and 35°C. This relationship was defined by van't Hoff (1884) as the Q_{10} temperature coefficient and is the factor by which a rate increases in a biochemical system with every 10°C increase in temperature (Moorhead and Sinsabaugh 2006; Tibbett et al. 2004). By increasing temperature and physiological reactions, the diffusion of soluble substrates in soil is also accelerated. Vass et al. (1992) and Megyesi et al. (2005) drew on the basic importance of temperature for driving biological reactions and applied Edwards et al.'s (1987) concept of accumulated degree days (ADD) to standardize decomposition rates across variable temperature regimes.

Moisture, too, can have a significant effect on the rate of human decomposition. Because the human body contains a significant amount of water, it begins to desiccate at death. A corpse can desiccate rapidly; great effort is invested in preventing embalmed cadavers from desiccating (C. A. Wacker, pers. comm.). Thus, the deposition of a body in an arid environment can lead to a high level of desiccation but relatively little decomposition. A lack of moisture retards microbial activity (Carter et al. 2010) and inhibits maggot activity, because they require moist soft tissue.

Moisture also can significantly affect the rate of cadaver decomposition following burial in soil due to its role in gas diffusion through the soil profile (Carter et al. 2010). Soil pore space (the space between soil particles) contains moisture and air. A negative correlation exists between soil moisture content and the rate of gas diffusion because gas diffuses slower in water than in air. As a result, the burial of a corpse in a soil with high moisture content can slow the rate of decomposition, because the gravesoil will become dominated by anaerobic metabolism; this process is more inefficient than aerobic metabolism. Gravesoil with high moisture content is also conducive to adipocere formation, which can help to preserve a corpse for several years (Forbes 2008).

Additional environmental considerations include soil pH and redox potential. In a terrestrial setting, acidic soil dissolves the mineral components of bone (Gordon and Buikstra 1981) and promotes leaching, allowing additional destruction by microorganisms and the release of volatile compounds (Vass et al. 1992, 2002, 2004, 2008). Soil pH affects nutrient availability and microbial metabolism. Soil-dwelling microorganism activity is highest when pH is near neutral. Child (1995) indicates that burial sites with highly positive redox potentials will facilitate oxidation of structural macromolecules, such as those of collagen fibrils.

Potential Decomposer Community

The final category of factors that contribute to variation in decomposition rates considered in this chapter is the available biological agents that use a cadaver as a resource for acquiring essential nutrients and minerals (Carter et al. 2007; McGuire and Treseder 2010; Swift et al. 1979). Many of the taphonomic agents that consume a cadaver have been identified and studied from the perspective of their specific taphonomic effects (c.f. Catts and Haskell 1990; Haglund and Sorg 1997). Potential biological consumers of a corpse include, but are not limited to, bacteria, fungi, nematodes, diptera, coleoptera, hymenoptera, decapods, murids, suids, canids, felids, ursids, cathartids, hyaenids, and hominids. McGuire and Treseder (2010) point out that potential biota are not just those organisms occupying the niche where the cadaver is placed but also taxa that can potentially colonize the area via dispersal, migration, or germination.

Conclusions

Decomposition is a complex series of biological and physicochemical processes that are directly linked to the surrounding ecological niche and which functions to recycle nutrients and energy. As demonstrated, the decomposition of a human is no exception. At death and subsequent deposition, the body becomes a nutrient-rich resource that is reincorporated into the landscape as living biomass. Integral to the processes of decomposition of the human are the same ecological state factors that govern the formation of soil from parent material (bedrock, alluvial sediments, etc.) and include climate, topography, potential biota, and time (Jenny 1941).

In order to realize the full potential of decomposition ecology to the forensic sciences, additional taphonomic research is certainly required. Both experimental and evidenced-based data collection should continue to be employed to identify patterns of change in the physicochemical (e.g., soil pH, total carbon, nitrogen, moisture content, ninhydrin-reactive nitrogen, and volatile fatty acids) and biological (e.g., bacteria, fungi, and nematodes) constituents of gravesoils, in addition to descriptive gross observations and plotting of daily mean temperatures currently undertaken in most master's theses. The methods of collection, recording, and analysis of such information should be standardized to facilitate comparison between and among the various recovery sites and decomposition facilities across the United States.

Postmortem microbiology is a particularly nascent field. Next-generation sequencing allows us to characterize microbial communities that were previously not culturable. For example, we now understand that while human bacterial community structure often shows minimal variability during an adult lifespan, it can vary significantly between individuals due to factors such as diet and environment (Costello et al. 2009). This observation indicates that an individual can house a personalized microbial community. This, in turn, may result in a personalized postmortem microbiology, which could explain some of the significant variation associated with cadaver decomposition (c.f. Shirley et al. 2011). Understanding the general modulators of decomposition such as these and their effect on the rate of human decomposition is important for furthering our understanding of the observable patterns of how humans decompose and how those patterns and changes in the landscape may be used to locate clandestine graves better and estimate time since death.

References

Aturaliya, S. and A. Lukasewycz (1999) Experimental forensic and bioanthropological aspects of soft tissue taphonomy: 1. Factors influencing postmortem tissue desiccation rate. *Journal of Forensic Sciences* 44:893–896.

Behrensmeyer, A. K. (1984) Taphonomy and the fossil record. *American Scientist* 72:558–566.

Benninger, L. A., D. O. Carter, and S. Forbes (2008) The biochemical alteration of soil beneath a decomposing corpse. *Forensic Science International* 180:70–75.

Burges, A. (1967) The decomposition of organic matter in the soil. In *Soil Biology* eds. A. Burges and F. Raw, pp. 479–492. Academic Press, New York.

Campobasso, C. P., G. D. Vella, and F. Introna (2001) Factors affecting decomposition and Diptera colonization. *Forensic Science International* 120:18–27.

Carter, D. O. and M. Tibbett (2003) Taphonomic mycota: Fungi with forensic potential. *Journal of Forensic Sciences* 48:168–171.

Carter, D. O., D. Yellowlees, and M. Tibbett (2007) Cadaver decomposition in terrestrial ecosystems. *Naturwissenschaften* 94:12–24.

Carter, D. O., D. Yellowlees, and M. Tibbett (2010) Moisture can be the dominant environmental parameter governing cadaver decomposition in soil. *Forensic Science International* 200:60–66.

Catts, E. P. and N. H. Haskell (1990) *Entomology and Death: A Procedural Guide.* Joyce's Print Shop, Clemson, SC.

Child, A. M. (1995) Towards an understanding of the microbial decomposition of archaeological bone in the burial environment. *Journal of Archaeological Science* 22:165–174.

Clark, M. A., M. B. Worrell, and J. E. Pless (1997) Postmortem changes in soft tissues. In *Forensic Taphonomy: The Postmortem Fate of Human Remains* eds. W. D. Haglund and M. H. Sorg, pp. 151–164. CRC Press, Boca Raton, FL.

Coleman, D. C., D. A. Crossley, Jr., and P. F. Hendrix (2004) *Fundamentals of Soil Ecology* (2nd edn.) Academic Press, Amsterdam, the Netherlands.

Costello, E. K., C. L. Lauber, M. Hamaday, N. Fierer, J. I. Gordon, and R. Knight (2009) Bacterial community variation in human body habitats across space and time. *Science* 326:1694–1697.

Damann, F. E. (2010) *Human Decomposition Ecology at the University of Tennessee Anthropology Research Center.* Unpublished Ph.D. Dissertation, University of Tennessee, Knoxville, TN.

Damann, F. E., A. Tanittaisong, and D. O. Carter (2012) Potential carcass enrichment of the University of Tennessee Anthropology Research Facility: A baseline survey of edaphic features. *Forensic Science International* 222:4–10.

Dent, B. B., S. L. Forbes, and B. H. Stuart (2004) Review of human decomposition processes in soil. *Environmental Geology* 45:576–585.

Di Maio, D. J. and V. J. M. Di Maio (2001) *Forensic Pathology* (2nd edn.). CRC Press, Boca Raton, FL.

Dickson, G. C, R. T. M. Poulter, E. W. Mass, P. K. Probert, and E. W. Kieser (2011) Marine bacterial succession as a potential indicator of postmortem submersion interval. *Forensic Science International* 209:1–10.

Dix, J. and M. Graham (2000) *Time of Death, Decomposition and Identification: An Atlas.* CRC Press, Boca Raton, FL.

Edwards, R., B. Chaney, and M. Bergman (1987) *Pest & Crop Newsletter* Vol. 2, pp. 5–6.

Evans, W. E. D. (1963) *The Chemistry of Death.* Charles C Thomas, Springfield, IL.

Forbes, S. L. (2008) Decomposition chemistry in a burial environment. In *Soil Analysis in Forensic Taphonomy: Chemical and Biological Effects of Buried Human Remains* eds. M. Tibbett and D. O. Carter, pp. 203–224. CRC Press, Boca Raton, FL.

Forbes, S. L., B. B. Dent, and B. H. Stuart (2005) The effect of soil type on adipocere formation. *Forensic Science International* 154:35–43.

Forbes, S. L., J. Keegan, B. H. Stuart, and D. B. Dent (2003) A gas chromatography-mass spectrometry method for the detection of adipocere in gravesoils. *European Journal of Science and Technology* 105:761–768.

Forbes, S. L., B. H. Stuart, I. R. Dadour, and B. B. Dent (2004) A preliminary investigation of the stages of adipocere formation. *Journal of Forensic Sciences* 49:566–574.

Galloway, A. (1997) The process of decomposition: A model from the Arizona-Sonoran desert. In *Forensic Taphonomy: The Postmortem Fate of Human Remains* eds. W. D. Haglund and M. H. Sorg, pp. 139–150. CRC Press, Boca Raton, FL.

Galloway, A., W. H. Birkby, A. M. Jones, T. H. Henry, and B. O. Parks (1989) Decay rates of human remains in an arid environment. *Journal of Forensic Sciences* 34:607–616.

Gill-King, H. (1997) Chemical and ultrastructural aspects of decomposition. In *Forensic Taphonomy: The Postmortem Fate of Human Remains* eds. W. D. Haglund and M. H. Sorg, pp. 93–108. CRC Press, Boca Raton, FL.

Gordon, C. C. and J. E. Buikstra (1981) Soil pH, bone preservation, and sampling bias at mortuary sites. *American Antiquity* 46:566–571.

Haglund, W. D. (1997a) Dogs and coyotes: Postmortem involvement with human remains. In *Forensic Taphonomy: The Postmortem Fate of Human Remains* eds. W. D. Haglund and M. H. Sorg, pp. 367–381. CRC Press, Boca Raton, FL.

Haglund, W. D. (1997b) Rodents and human remains. In *Forensic Taphonomy: The Postmortem Fate of Human Remains* ed. W. D. Haglund and M. H. Sorg, pp. 405–414. CRC Press, Boca Raton, FL.

Haglund, W. D. and M. H. Sorg (1997) *Forensic Taphonomy: The Postmortem Fate of Human Remains.* CRC Press, Boca Raton, FL.

Henßge, C. and B. Madea (2004) Estimation of the time since death in the early post-mortem period. *Forensic Science International* 144:167–175.

Hewadikaram, K. A. and M. L. Goff (1991) Effect of carcass size on rate of decomposition and arthropod succession patterns. *American Journal of Forensic Medicine and Pathology* 12:235–240.

Holland, T. D., B. E. Anderson, and R. W. Mann (1997) Human variables in the postmortem alteration of human bone: Examples from U.S. war casualties. In *Forensic Taphonomy: The Postmortem Fate of Human Remains* eds. W. D. Haglund and M. H. Sorg, pp. 263–274. CRC Press, Boca Raton, FL.

Hopkins, D. W. (2008) The role of soil organisms in terrestrial decomposition. In *Soil Analysis in Forensic Taphonomy: Chemical and Biological Effects of Buried Human Remains* eds. M. Tibbett and D. O. Carter, pp. 53–66. CRC Press, Boca Raton, FL.

Hopkins, D. W., P. E. J. Wiltshire, and D. B. Turner (2000) Microbial characteristics of soils from graves: An investigation at the interface of soil microbiology and forensic science. *Applied Soil Ecology* 14:283–288.

Howard, G. T., B. Duos, and E. J. Watson-Horzelski (2010) Characterization of the soil microbial community associated with the decomposition of a swine carcass. *International Biodeterioration and Biodegradation* 64:300–304.

Jans, M. M. E., C. M. Nielsen-Marsh, C. I. Smith, M. J. Collins, and H. Kars (2004) Characterisation of microbial attack on archaeological bone. *Journal of Archaeological Science* 31:87–95.

Jenny, H. (1941) *Factors of Soil Formation: A System of Quantitative Pedology.* McGraw-Hill, New York.

Kellerman, G. D., B. G. Waterman, and L. F. Scharfenberger (1976) Demonstration in vitro of postmortem bacterial transmigration. *American Journal of Clinical Pathology* 66:911–915.

Klippel, W. E. and J. A. Synstelien (2007) Rodents as taphonomic agents: Bone gnawing by brown rats and gray squirrels. *Journal of Forensic Sciences* 52:765–773.

Krompecher, T. (2002) Rigor mortis: Estimation of the time since death by evaluation of cadaveric rigidity. In *Estimation of Time Since Death in the Early Postmortem Interval* ed. B. Knight, pp. 144–160. Hodder Arnold, London, U.K.

Love, J. C. and M. Marks (2003) Taphonomy and time: Estimating the postmortem interval. In *Hard Evidence: Case Studies in Forensic Anthropology* ed. D. W. Steadman, pp. 160–175. Prentice Hall, Upper Saddle River, NJ.

Mann, R. W., W. M. Bass, and L. Meadows (1990) Time since death and decomposition of the human body: Variables and observations in case and experimental field studies. *Journal of Forensic Sciences* 35:103–111.

Mant, A. K. (1987) Knowledge acquired from post-war exhumations. In *Death, Decay and Reconstruction: Approaches to Archaeology and Forensic Science* eds. A. Boddington, A. N. Garland, and C. Janaway, pp. 65–78. Manchester University Press, Manchester, U.K.

McGuire, K. L. and K. K. Treseder (2010) Microbial communities and their relevance for ecosystem models: Decomposition as a case study. *Soil Biology and Biochemistry* 42:529–535.

Megyesi, M. S., S. P. Nawrocki, and N. H. Haskell (2005) Using accumulated degree-days to estimate the postmortem interval from decomposed human remains. *Journal of Forensic Sciences* 50:618–626.

Melvin, J. R., Jr., L. S. Cronholm, L. R. Simson, and A. M. Isaacs (1984) Bacterial transmigration as an indicator of time of death. *Journal of Forensic Sciences* 29:412–417.

Micozzi, M. S. (1986) Experimental study of postmortem change under field conditions: Effects of freezing, thawing, and mechanical injury. *Journal of Forensic Sciences* 31:953–961.

Micozzi, M. S. (1991) *Postmortem Change in Human and Animal Remains*. Charles C Thomas, Springfield, IL.

Moorhead, D. L. and R. L. Sinsabaugh (2006) A theoretical model of litter decay and microbial interaction. *Ecological Monographs* 76:151–174.

Olson, J. S. (1963) Energy storage and the balance of producers and decomposers in ecological systems. *Ecology* 44:322–331.

Parkinson, R. A. (2009) *Bacterial Communities Associated with Human Decomposition*. Unpublished Ph.D. Dissertation, Victoria University of Wellington, Wellington, New Zealand.

Parkinson, R. A., K. R. Dias, J. Horswell, P. Greenwood, N. Banning, M. Tibbett and A. A. Vass (2009) Microbial community analysis of human decomposition in soil. In *Criminal and Environmental Soil Forensics* eds. K. Ritz, L. A. Dawson, and D. Miller, pp. 379–394. Springer, New York.

Paul, E. A. (2007) *Soil Microbiology, Ecology, and Biochemistry* (3rd edn.). Academic Press: Amsterdam, the Netherlands.

Payne, J. A. (1965) A summer carrion study of the baby pig *Sus scrofa* Linnaeus. *Ecology* 46:592–602.

Payne-James, J., A. Busuttil, and W. Smock (2003) *Forensic Medicine: Clinical and Pathological Aspects*. Greenwich Medical Media, San Francisco, CA.

Perper, J. (1993) Time of death and changes after death: Part 1: Anatomical considerations. In *Medicolegal Investigation of Death: Guidelines for the Application of Pathology to Crime Investigation* (3rd edn.) ed. W. U. Spitz, pp. 14–49. Charles C Thomas, Springfield, IL.

Powers, R. H. (2005) The decomposition of human remains: A biochemical perspective. In *Forensic Medicine of the Lower Extremity: Human Identification and Trauma Analysis of the Thigh, Leg, and Foot* eds. J. Rich, D. E. Dean, and R. H. Powers, pp. 3–15. Humana Press, Totowa, NJ.

Prostgate, J. (2000) *Microbes and Man* (4th edn.) Cambridge University Press, Cambridge, U.K.

Putman, R. J. (1978a) Patterns of carbon dioxide evolution from decaying carrion. Decomposition of small mammal carrion in temperate systems 1. *Oikos* 31:47–57.

Putman, R. J. (1978b) Flow of energy and organic matter from a carcass during decomposition. Decomposition of small mammal carrion in temperate systems 2. *Oikos* 31:58–68.

Putman, R. J. (1983) *Carrion and Dung: The Decomposition of Animal Wastes*. The Institute of Biology's Studies in Biology, No. 165. Edward Arnold, London, U.K.

Reed, H. B. (1958) A study of dog carcass communities in Tennessee, with special reference to the insects. *American Midland Naturalist* 59:213–245.

Ricklefs, R. E. (1997) *The Economy of Nature* (4th edn.). W. H. Freeman and Company, New York.

Rodriguez, W. C. (1997) Decomposition of buried and submerged bodies. In *Forensic Taphonomy: The Postmortem Fate of Human Remains* eds. W. D. Haglund and M. H. Sorg, pp. 459–468. CRC Press, Boca Raton, FL.

Rodriguez, W. C., and W. M. Bass (1983) Insect activity and its relationship to decay rates of human cadavers in east Tennessee. *Journal of Forensic Sciences* 28:423–432.

Sledzik, P. S. (1998) Forensic taphonomy: Postmortem decomposition and decay. In *Forensic Osteology: Advances in the Identification of Human Remains* (2nd edn.) ed. K. J. Reichs, pp. 109–119. Charles C Thomas, Springfield, IL.

Shirley N. R., R. J. Wilson, and L. Meadows-Jantz (2011) Cadaver use at the University of Tennessee's Anthropological Research Facility. *Clinical Anatomy* 24:372–380.

Sidrim, J. J. C., R. E. Moreira Filho, R. A. Cordeiro, M. F. G. Rocha, E. P. Caetano, A. J. Monteiro, and R. S. N. Brilhante (2010) Fungal microbiota dynamics as a postmortem investigation tool: Focus on *Aspergillus*, *Penicillium* and *Candida* species. *Journal of Applied Microbiology* 108:1751–1756.

Spicka, A. R., R. Johnson, J. Bushing, L. G. Higley, and D. O. Carter (2011) Carcass mass can influ-ence rate of decomposition and release of ninhydrin-reactive nitrogen into gravesoil. *Forensic Science International* 209:80–85.

Stewart, T. D. (1979) *Essentials of Forensic Anthropology: Especially as Developed in the United States.* Charles C. Thomas, Springfield, IL.

Swift, M. J., O. W. Heal, and J. M. Anderson (1979) *Decomposition in Terrestrial Ecosystems.* Blackwell Scientific, Oxford, U.K.

Tibbett, M., D. O. Carter, T. Haslam, R. Major, and R. Haslam (2004) A laboratory incubation method for determining the rate of microbiological degradation of skeletal muscle tissue in soil. *Journal of Forensic Sciences* 49:560–565.

Towne, E. G. (2000) Prairie vegetation and soil nutrient responses to ungulate carcasses. *Oecologia* 122:232–239.

Van't Hoff, J. H. (1884) *Etudes de Dynamique Chemique.* Frederik Muller and Co., Amsterdam, the Netherlands.

Vass, A. A., S.-A. Barshick, G. Sega, J. Caton, J. T. Skeen, J. C. Love, and J. A. Synstelien (2002) Decomposition chemistry of human remains: A new methodology for determining the post-mortem interval. *Journal of Forensic Sciences* 47:542–553.

Vass, A. A., W. M. Bass, J. D. Wolt, J. E. Foss, and J. T. Ammons (1992) Time since death determinations of human cadavers using soil solution. *Journal of Forensic Sciences* 37:1236–1253.

Vass, A. A., R. R. Smith, C. V. Thompson, M. N. Burnett, N. Dulgerian, and B. A. Eckenrode (2008) Odor analysis of decomposing buried human remains. *Journal of Forensic Sciences* 53:384–391.

Vass, A. A., R. R. Smith, C. V. Thompson, M. N. Burnett, D. A. Wolf, J. A. Synstelien, N. Dulgerian, and B. A. Eckenrode (2004) Decompositional odor analysis database. *Journal of Forensic Sciences* 49:760–769.

Wang, Q., G. M. Garrity, J. M. Tiedje, and J. R. Cole (2007) Naïve Bayesian classifier for rapid assignment of rRNA sequences into the new bacterial taxonomy. *Applied and Environmental Microbiology* 73:5261–5267.

Willey, P. and L. M. Snyder (1989) Canid modification of human remains: Implications for time-since death estimation. *Journal of Forensic Sciences* 34:894–901.

Wilson, M. (2008) *Bacteriology of Humans: An Ecological Perspective.* Blackwell, Malden, MA.

Bone Density and Bone Attrition

4

R. LEE LYMAN

Contents

Introduction

Physical anthropologists have long studied the density of human bones as a reflection of activity and other variables (references in Galloway et al. 1997; Willey et al. 1997), but seldom have they considered it as an intrinsic property of bones that has a significant mediating influence on a variety of taphonomic processes. Thus, the great majority of the literature on bone density as a taphonomically and forensically significant variable concerns nonhuman animal bones. In this chapter, I first briefly review the history of considerations of bone density in taphonomic contexts. Then, I turn to definitions of density as a generic property; this is necessary, because several different properties that more or less closely approximate the density of bone have been measured, but all have been called "density." Part of the reason that different properties have been measured is revealed by a consideration of how density has been measured in ungulate and other skeletons. Historical review of the techniques used to measure density reveals strengths and weaknesses of the several techniques, provides guidance about how density might be measured in the future, and underscores why certain density values for human skeletal parts are better than others for taphonomic/forensic purposes. Subsequent to the historical review, I turn briefly to how to quantify bone frequencies in order to determine if some skeletal parts have survived attritional processes better than other parts. This leads to a consideration of how past researchers have analytically detected density-mediated attrition in particular collections. Then I present data on the density of human bones and work through examples of analytical techniques using real data. The discussion is concluded with a few thoughts on the future.

Throughout, I use the term *taphonomy* and its derivatives as a synonym for forensics; both concern answering the generic question "Why are these particular bones here and in this condition, rather than some other bones over there in a different condition?" The term *skeletal element* is used to signify a discrete, anatomically complete unit of the skeleton such as a cervical vertebra or tibia. The term *skeletal part* is used as a generic term for a skeletal element or portion thereof, such as the distal half of a tibia or the distal condyle of a humerus.

History

Nearly 200 years ago, geologist William Buckland (1823:37–38) noted that a hyena quickly destroyed and devoured the proximal end of a tibia, then cracked the diaphysis open and consumed the exposed marrow, but "left untouched the [distal end], which contains no marrow, and is very hard." Archaeologist Karl von Adolph Morlot (1861:300) later noted that "nearly all the cartilaginous and more or less soft parts of [deer] bones [had] been subtracted" from a collection of ancient bones as a result of carnivore gnawing. Paleontologist Boyd Dawkins (1869:207) subsequently remarked that the "stone-like molars of the Mammoth would survive the destruction of all traces of the bones of the smaller mammals," and also quoted Buckland (1823) a few years later (Dawkins 1874:281–283). Finally, archaeologist Sir John Lubbock (1913:321) noted that less dense skeletal parts contained more blood, marrow, and grease and thus were more nutritious and more prone to destruction by bone-gnawing carnivores than skeletal parts of greater density. Thus, it has long been known by observant natural historians that bones of greater density—typically measured as a ratio of mass to volume—tend to survive the ravages of time better than skeletal parts of lesser density. That ancient knowledge is of an ordinal scale (i.e., it is of the greater than–less than sort), and that sufficed in the nineteenth century. It would not do in the twentieth century when quantification became a hallmark of many fields of inquiry that claimed to have the status of a science (however, science might be defined beyond the necessary condition of involving empirical phenomena).

   Although it was known early in the nineteenth century that the structural density of skeletal parts mediated carnivore attrition—the soft or low-density parts were destroyed, the hard or high-density parts survived gnawing—no one bothered to measure the mass-to-volume ratio of the individual parts of a skeleton and to thereby generate numerical values of density. Similarly, the fact that density seemed to mediate attritional processes did not get much attention for the first few decades of the twentieth century. Vertebrate paleontologist Dale Guthrie (1967) mentioned density as a potentially important variable that influenced the frequencies of skeletal parts of Alaskan Pleistocene mammals, but he did not measure bone density. Paleontologist and archaeologist C. K. Brain (1967) noted that modern domestic dogs (*Canis familiaris*) and humans tend to destroy skeletal parts by gnawing, preferentially consuming the softer, nonfully ossified and unfused epiphyseal ends of long bones, and neither destroying nor eating the more completely ossified and fused epiphyseal ends of long bones of domestic goats (*Capra hircus*). Two years later, he measured a kind of density (see next section) of goat bones (Brain 1969). That same year, paleontologist Michael Voorhies (1969) suggested that the density of anatomically complete skeletal elements influenced their transportability by fluvial processes, but he did not measure bone density. That topic—differential fluvial transport of bones based on their density—would be taken up by Anna Behrensmeyer a few years later (1975); she measured the density of the bones of several nonhuman animal taxa for her study of Plio–Pleistocene hominid fossil and paleontological loci in eastern Africa.

Paleontologists tended to focus on fluvial transport as mediated by the density of a skeletal part (e.g., Boaz and Behrensmeyer 1976) and the related "settling velocity" of skeletal parts (Korth 1979) [low-density parts are more readily transported by water and settle in water slower than high-density parts], whereas archaeologists focused on the damage and attrition caused by carnivore gnawing as mediated by the density of a skeletal part (e.g., Binford and Bertram 1977; Elkin 1995; Kreutzer 1992; Lyman 1984). By and large, the majority of the latter studies examined the density of ungulate bones, though eventually bones of smaller mammals (Lyman et al. 1992; Pavao and Stahl 1999), fish (Butler and Chatters 1994), and birds (e.g., Dirrigl 2001) were examined. We now have density data for more than three dozen taxa (Table 4.1). Although some early research on bone density as a significant taphonomic property concerned human bones (Boaz and Behrensmeyer 1976), that research was not expanded upon in a taphonomic framework until the 1990s (e.g., Galloway et al. 1997; Willey et al. 1997). Because the latter research is particularly pertinent in the context of this chapter, I reserve discussion of it until later.

What Is "Density"?

As noted earlier, the generic definition of density is a mass to volume ratio, such that

$$D = \frac{M}{V}$$

where
    D is the density
    M is the mass
    V is the volume

There are two recognized kinds of density with respect to solids that are porous. *True density* is the mass to volume ratio without pore space included in the measurement of volume; *bulk density* is the mass to volume ratio with pore space included in the measurement of volume. Thus,

$$D_t = \frac{M}{V_s}$$

and

$$D_b = \frac{M}{V_t}$$

where
    M is mass
    D_t is true density
    V_s is volume of the solid material only (pore space excluded)
    D_b is bulk density
    V_t is total volume of the substance including pore space (Lyman 1984)

Table 4.1   Taxa with Bone Density Data (Chronological Order)

Taxon	Source(s)
Domestic goat (*Capra hircus*)	Brain (1969), Lam et al. (1998)
Domestic sheep (*Ovis aries*)	Behrensmeyer (1975), Binford and Bertram (1977), Lyman (1984), Ioannidou (2003), Symmons (2005)
Reedbuck (*Redunca* sp.)	Behrensmeyer (1975)
Forest hog (*Hylochoerus* sp.)	Behrensmeyer (1975)
Topi (*Damaliscus* sp.)	Behrensmeyer (1975)
Zebra (*Equus* sp.)	Behrensmeyer (1975), Lam et al. (1999)
Hippo (*Hippopotamus* sp.)	Behrensmeyer (1975)
Human (*Homo sapiens*)	Boaz and Behrensmeyer (1976), Galloway et al. (1997)
Caribou (*Rangifer tarandus*)	Binford and Bertram (1977), Lam et al. (1999)
Deer (*Odocoileus* spp.)	Lyman (1984)
Pronghorn (*Antilocapra americana*)	Lyman (1984)
Bison (*Bison bison*)	Kreutzer (1992)
Phocid seals (*Phoca* sp.)	Chambers (1992)
Marmot (*Marmota* sp.)	Lyman et al. (1992)
Cod (*Gadus* sp.)	Nicholson (1992)
Chinook salmon (*Oncorhynchus tshawytscha*)	Butler and Chatters (1994)
Guanaco (*Lama guanicoe*)	Elkin (1995), Gutiérrez et al. (2010)
Vicuña (*Lama vicugna*)	Elkin (1995)
Llama (*Lama glama*)	Stahl (1999)
Alpaca (*Lama pacos*)	Stahl (1999)
Wildebeest (*Connochaetes taurinus*)	Lam et al. (1999)
Domestic rabbit (*Oryctolagus cuniculus*)	Pavao and Stahl (1999)
Eastern cottontail (*Sylvilagus floridanus*)	Pavao and Stahl (1999)
Snowshoe hare (*Lepus canadensis*)	Pavao and Stahl (1999)
Black-tailed jackrabbit (*Lepus californicus*)	Pavao and Stahl (1999)
Turkey (*Meleagris gallopavo*)	Dirrigl (2001)
Baboon (*Papio cynocephalus*)	Pickering and Carlson (2002), Carlson and Pickering (2004)
Lesser Rhea (*Pterocnemia pennata*)	Cruz and Elkin (2003)
Pig (*Sus scrofa*)	Ioannidou (2003)
Cattle (*Bos taurus*)	Ioannidou (2003)
Domestic dog (*Canis familiaris*), Wolf (*Canis lupus*), Coyote (*Canis latrans*), Red fox (*Vulpes vulpes*), Swift fox (*Vulpes velox*)	Novecosky and Popkin (2005)
Double-crested cormorant (*Phalacrocorax auritus*); Ducks (*Anas* spp.); Canada goose (*Branta canadensis*); Common merganser (*Mergus merganser*)	Broughton et al. (2007)

The property known as *specific gravity* (SG) is also relevant here. It is a temperature-dependent measure of the ratio of the mass of a volume of a material to the mass of an equal volume of a standard substance, usually water. The equation describing SG is

$$SG = \frac{D_{te}}{D_w}$$

where
  D_{te} is the density of the study material at temperature te
  D_w is the density of water

SG is the basis for the well-known relationship that at one atmosphere of pressure and 4°C, 1 g of distilled water has a volume of 1 cc.

Most taphonomists have not produced measures that approximate SG or true density. Instead, they have produced measures that approximate bulk density. This is useful for two reasons. First, it is appropriate to measure bulk density, because bone tissue itself (minus pore space) is mostly composed of hydroxyapatite $[Ca_{10}(PO_4)_6(OH)_2]$, which has a true density of 3.1–3.2 g/cc (Shipman 1981:25). Bone tissue itself is reported to have a density between 1.9 g/cc (Cameron et al. 1999:96) and 2.0 g/cc (Currey 1984:90). Second, from a taphonomic perspective, it is correct to measure bulk density, because it seems to be the porous structure of bone tissue that actually influences the susceptibility of the tissue to taphonomic processes. As Hill (1980) noted, the ratio of trabecular to cortical bone influences the ability of a skeletal part to withstand taphonomic processes, and Shipman (1981:25) similarly noted that the ratio of spongy to compact bone—what she referred to as the "composition" of the tissue sample, in preference to the ambiguity of "density"—influences how well a skeletal part withstands taphonomic processes. Nevertheless, throughout the remainder of this chapter, I use the term *density*, and by it I mean an approximation of bulk density. Approximation is an appropriate qualifier because of the techniques used to measure density.

How Has Density Been Measured?

Often, the term *density* is used uncritically in the taphonomy literature to describe some unspecified form of mass-to-volume relationship. This uncritical usage became clear when it was found that early measurements of the "density" of skeletal parts tended not to correlate well with one another (Lyman 1984). As shown in Table 4.2, those early measurements were rather different even at an ordinal scale. Possible reasons for this were suggested to involve differences in the individual skeletons measured, but what quickly became apparent on close reading of the literature was the fact that the researchers involved used different measurement protocols. Brain (1969) measured what he called "specific gravity." The measurement protocol he used suggests that the property was a sort of hybrid of true and bulk density, because temperature, mass, and volume were neither rigorously controlled nor consistently measured. Behrensmeyer (1975) also measured a hybrid of true and bulk densities, because temperature and pore volume were neither rigorously controlled nor consistently measured. Binford and Bertram (1977) measured bulk density, but it was only approximate, because their efforts to include pore space volume differentially influenced measures of skeletal part volume (Lyman 1984). All of these

**Table 4.2   Early Measurements of Bone "Density"
of Ungulates (Sheep and Goat)**

Skeletal Part	Brain (1969)	Behrensmeyer (1975)	Binford and Bertram (1977)
P humerus	0.58	1.26	0.78
D humerus	0.97	1.75	1.33
P radius—ulna	1.10	1.64	1.32
D radius—ulna	0.97	1.59	1.14
P femur	0.75	1.47	1.17
D femur	0.72	1.42	1.16[a]
P tibia	0.82	1.32	1.11[a]
D tibia	1.17	1.64	1.24

[a] Binford, L. R., *Bones: Ancient Men and Modern Myths,* Academic Press, New York, 1981.

Note: P, Proximal; D, Distal.

early researchers measured the mass of a specimen (sometimes wet, sometimes dry) and used water displacement to measure the volume of a specimen. They all also apparently measured proximal and distal halves of long bones, but this was seldom explicit in the published literature. If they in fact measured such long bone halves, they were mixing varied amounts of (epiphyseal) trabecular bone tissue and (diaphyseal) laminar bone tissue in one unit. This would serve to obscure any causal relationship between a skeletal part's potential to withstand attritional processes because of its (bulk) density and the part's actual survival of density-mediated attrition.

Lyman (1984) used single-beam photon densitometry to measure the density of multiple locations (typically five or six) on most bones making up ungulate skeletons. This was an explicit acknowledgment of the fact that not only do different bones or skeletal elements of a body have different densities, but bone density (particularly, bulk density, as defined earlier) varies more or less continuously across each kind of skeletal element, much as Buckland (1823) recognized that proximal tibia were readily destroyed whereas distal tibia often survived carnivore ravaging. Lyman (1984) took measurements of bone density (in 1980–1981) using a (now primitive) technology that had been developed to monitor the postmenopausal loss of bone mineral in vivo among women. The single-beam photon densitometer provided a g/cm reading based on the diameter of the photon beam (1/8 in.) and the distance across what Lyman (1984) termed a scan site. (The densitometer projected the photon beam through the bone by passing slowly under the specimen; a detector above determined the amount of photons that passed through the specimen. Fewer photons meant more bone tissue.) The scan distance across a specimen was determined by photon beam attrition, and the machine provided that distance along with an overall g/cm measurement of bone tissue.

Lyman converted the machine-provided measurements (g/cm and scan distance) to g/cc by measuring the maximum external thickness of the skeletal part at the position of the scan; he referred to the derived measure as "volume density" (Lyman 1984). Using the third dimension measured as Lyman did simplified the shape of the skeletal part to a cube and also implied that the cube was internally homogenous (i.e., that bone tissue and pore space were both homogenously distributed throughout, instead of, for example, tube-like for long bone diaphyses), imparting a degree of error to the resulting measurements of density. Nevertheless, the results were sufficiently robust to explain much variation in bone survivorship in a number of collections of prehistoric ungulate remains that clearly had been influenced by destructive processes such as gnawing carnivores (in light of tooth marks on the bone specimens).

Subsequent researchers also used photon densitometry but measured bone thickness at several positions or used other techniques to derive a multidimensional estimate of volume (Elkin 1995; Kreutzer 1992; Lyman et al. 1992; Pavao and Stahl 1999; Pickering and Carlson 2002; Stahl 1999). This refined the accuracy of the measurements, but none of these researchers accounted for the medullary cavity of long bones, effectively producing measurements of density that assumed a homogenous structure in cross section, when in fact it was heterogeneous. To resolve this issue, Lam and colleagues (Lam et al. 1998, 1999, 2003; Lam and Pearson 2005) used computed tomography, a technique that, like photon densitometry, depends on attenuation of a photon beam projected through a tissue sample. Again, the more bone mineral encountered by the photon beam, the fewer photons pass through to be detected. The significant difference between the two techniques is that while photon densitometry uses a single (or double, see the following) beam passed through a sample in one direction, computed tomography records photon beam attenuation from multiple directions and constructs a detailed cross-sectional image of the scanned sample (Cann 1988; see also Novecosky and Popkin 2005). Cautious use of photon densitometry values can, nevertheless, provide insight into whether a collection of bones has undergone density-mediated attritional taphonomic processes (Carlson and Pickering 2004). Some researchers have used dual-energy x-ray absorptiometry (Ioannidou 2003; Pickering and Carlson 2002). Again, the most serious weakness attending this technique is measurement of the volume of the specimen under study, and again, some find it less satisfactory than photon densitometry (Symmons 2004, 2005).

Bone Frequencies and Survivorship

How does one determine frequencies of skeletal parts if one is interested in detecting density-mediated attrition? Note that I said "determine frequencies" rather than "tally frequencies." A tally is simply a summed enumeration of each individual part. However, if one wishes to know if one skeletal part is better represented (i.e., survived taphonomic attritional processes better) than another part, then simply saying there are more ribs than thoracic vertebrae will not do. This is so because there are twice as many ribs (lefts plus rights) as there are thoracic vertebrae per skeleton. The quantitative protocol typically followed takes advantage of the fact that different bone types (ignoring left–right distinctions) have different frequencies in a body (one cranium, seven cervical vertebrae, two humeri, etc.), and it also takes advantage of the fact that we know how many of each bone type are necessary to make up one complete skeleton. Therefore, simplistically, 3 humeri represent 1.5 bodies, and if we know that 3 bodies were at one time present, then the %survivorship of humeri is the equivalent of 50, even if all three humeri are left elements. The implicit assumption is that all skeletal parts of a kind (e.g., humeri) have equivalent survival potential regardless of side. Similarly, vertebrate taphonomists typically assume that all vertebrae of each category (cervical, thoracic, lumbar, sacral, and caudal) have equivalent survival potential, but different categories have different survival potential. The only exception to this assumption is that C1 (atlas) and C2 (axis) are often treated individually.

It is critical to make the quantitative protocol clear. First, one determines categories of skeletal parts for tallying; these can be anatomically complete skeletal elements such as ribs, femora, and tibiae, but often long bones are tallied by proximal and distal halves, such as proximal femora and distal tibiae. Finer distinctions of portions of individual skeletal elements can also be made (as in the examples on human remains presented later). Then, one may tally up the number of identified specimens (NISP) per category of skeletal part. If a category is the distal half of the tibia, then any specimen that represents in whole or in part that category represents a tally of 1 for that category. The analyst, however, must determine the minimum number of skeletal parts per category, typically in zooarchaeology labeled the MNE or minimum number of elements (Lyman 1994a,b, 2008). The MNE is a minimum because it represents the smallest possible number of skeletal parts necessary to account for the specimens or NISP of a skeletal part category. For example, assume we have seven fragments (NISP) of proximal left tibiae. Two (A and B) of those fragments represent the proximal articulation and refit one another (like a jigsaw puzzle), a third specimen (C) represents a portion of the diaphysis that does not anatomically overlap A or B, and the other four specimens (D, E, F, G) are all anatomically complete proximal halves of left tibiae. These seven (=NISP) specimens represent a minimum of five (=MNE) proximal left tibiae. It is a minimum because specimens A and B anatomically overlap (are redundant with) specimens D, E, F, and G. Specimen C, however, overlaps specimens D, E, F, and G, but does not overlap specimens A and B and thus *could* be part of the same particular element as A and B. Thus, the true number of proximal left tibiae could be five, or it could be six; by convention, the minimum is used for analysis.

The preceding concerns the determination of NISP and MNE. What about survivorship? If there is an MNE of four proximal right tibiae along with the MNE of five left tibia described in the preceding paragraph, then the minimum number of animal units (MAU) or survivorship [the two are mathematically identical (Lyman 1994a)] is 4.5 (=[4+5]/2). MAU is derived by dividing the total MNE for a skeletal part category by the number of times that category occurs in a single complete skeleton. The division norms (or normalizes) the MNE counts to the standard of a carcass [see Lyman (2008) for extended discussion].

Single-element and multi-element skeletal portions are treated the same way. Say, for example, fragments of the skull represent an MNE of 4 skulls; divide that MNE by 1 to determine the MAU of skulls. On the other hand, let us say that we have 45 NISP of ribs, and those specimens represent an MNE of 20 ribs. Divide 20 by 26 (the number of left + right ribs in a single ungulate) to derive a value of 0.769 MAU (or survivorship) of ribs. Norming the MNE values to MAU values is unnecessary if, for example, only paired long bones are considered, because in that case, all MNE values would be divided by two.

Once MAU values are available for all skeletal categories (parts such as distal humeri and multi-element portions such as thoracic vertebrae), those values can be transformed to % survivorship (also known as % MAU) values. This transformation is done by individually dividing the MAU value for each skeletal part by the maximum observed MAU in the assemblage. For example, if the maximum MAU is for distal humeri and it is 20, then divide the MAU of all skeletal parts and portions, including distal humeri, by 20 (and multiply the result by 100) to determine the % survivorship. A maximum MAU of 20 distal humeri in a collection indicates that there should be (we would expect) an MAU of 20 proximal humeri (or 40 MNE), 140 cervical vertebrae, 10 skulls, etc., if all parts of every skeleton were present and had survived destructive taphonomic processes equally. If the observed values of those skeletal portions are less than the expected values, then some parts are not represented for any of a myriad of reasons, including the fact that perhaps they did not survive density-mediated attritional processes because they were of relatively low density. The variable %survivorship and its mathematical equivalent % MAU are useful for the comparison of samples of disparate sizes to facilitate detection of similarities and differences between abundances of skeletal parts in two or more collections. They need not be calculated if only one collection is examined. As the following examples indicate, tallies of MNE suffice when all categories of skeletal parts occur with equal frequency in a skeleton (e.g., humeri, tibia, and femora); determine MAU if the included kinds of skeletal parts vary in frequency in a carcass (e.g., cervical vertebrae, humeri, and ribs).

How to Determine Attrition

Brain (1967, 1969) noted two things about the relationship between the density and what he referred to as the "survival" of skeletal parts in a collection of domestic goat bones gnawed by dogs and humans. First, unfused ends of goat long bones were infrequent relative to fused ends in the collection of more than 2000 NISP, where a *specimen* is a skeletal element (an anatomically complete bone) or a fragment thereof (Grayson 1984; Lyman 2008). Second, what Brain termed the "specific gravity" of the long bone ends that fused ontogenetically early in life tended to be greater than the SG of ends that fused ontogenetically late in life (Brain 1969). He showed this in several ways; one was a table of the data, reproduced here as Table 4.3, and another involved a graphical representation of the relationship, reproduced here in modified form as Figure 4.1. Brain (1969) also constructed histograms of the frequencies of skeletal parts of goats, ordering the parts from most frequent to least frequent, noting that parts with larger SG values tended to be more frequent than those with smaller SG values (see also Brain 1976). Brain (1969, 1976) did not calculate

Table 4.3   Observations on the Relationship between Ontogenetic Age When Epiphysis Fuses, Specific Gravity, and Bone Frequencies (Normed to % Survival)

Skeletal Part	%Survival	Specific Gravity	Age at Fusion (Months)
P humerus	0.0	0.58	17
D humerus	64.0	0.97	4
P radius—ulna	50.8	1.10	4
D radius—ulna	17.2	0.97	21
P femur	14.1	0.75	18
D femur	7.0	0.72	20
P tibia	10.1	0.82	25
D tibia	56.3	1.17	15

Source: Brain, C. K., *Scientific Papers of the Namib Desert Research Station,* 39, 13, 1969.

Note: P, Proximal; D, Distal.

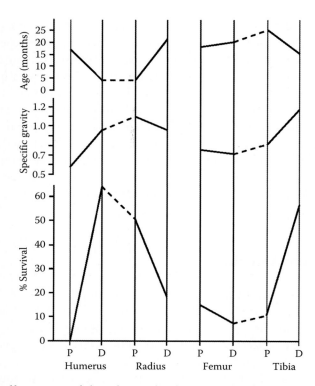

Figure 4.1 Brain's illustration of the relationship between the age (in months) when an epiphysis fused, the specific gravity of a skeletal part, and the %survival of skeletal parts in a collection of goat bones. (After Brain, C.K., *Scientific Papers of the Namib Desert Research Station*, 39, 13, 1969; Brain, C.K., Some principles in the interpretation of bone accumulations associated with man, In *Human Origins: Louis Leakey and the East African Evidence*, eds. G. Ll. Isaac and E.R. McCown, W.A. Benjamin, Menlo Park, CA, pp. 97–116, 1976.)

correlation coefficients between any of the pairs of variables, but his interpretation of the relationships between the variable pairs was spot on. Spearman's rank-order correlation coefficient between the SG values he determined and survivorship is positive and significant ($rho = .874$, $p = .007$), and while the correlation between age at fusion and survivorship is not significant, it is an inverse relationship ($rho = -.599$, $p = .13$), just as Brain suspected.

Binford and Bertram (1977) presented data in a plethora of tables and figures that showed the frequencies of skeletal parts in several collections of ungulate bones. It was Binford's Figure 3.16 (Binford and Bertram 1977:138) that clearly illustrated, in the form of a bivariate scatter plot, the direct relationship between the surviving frequencies of skeletal parts and bone density. A version of that figure is shown in Figure 4.2. Binford computed a polynomial regression to describe the relationship between the two variables; the simple linear correlation coefficient was significant ($r = .863$, $p < .0001$), as was the rank-order correlation coefficient ($rho = .907$, $p < .0001$). Binford did not later use this sort of bivariate plot; instead he (Binford 1981:219) developed a different type of graph that could quickly provide an indication of density-mediated destruction. Referred to as "bone-destruction graphs" (Lyman 1994c:401), these graphs are rapidly constructed, because the analyst can include as many or as few data points as desired. Each plotted point requires two calculations— the frequency of the high-density end of a long bone and the frequency of the low-density end of that long bone. Frequencies are normalized to a scale of 0–100. The quick way

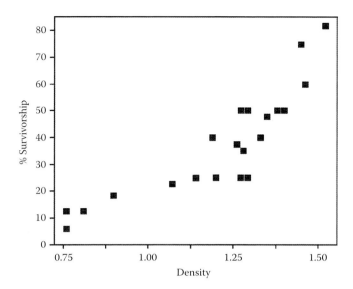

Figure 4.2 Binford's bivariate scatter plot of the density of caribou (*Rangifer tarandus*) skeletal parts and the frequency of skeletal parts in a collection of caribou bones that had been gnawed by dogs. (After Binford, L.R. and J.B. Bertram, Bone frequencies and attritional processes, In *For Theory Building in Archaeology*, ed. L.R. Binford, Academic Press, New York, pp. 77–153, 1977.)

to accomplish this task when the skeletal remains are from artiodactyls is to determine frequencies of relatively low-density proximal humeri, proximal tibiae, and distal radii, and frequencies of relatively high-density distal humeri, distal tibiae, and proximal radii. Those frequencies are presented in Table 4.3 for Brain's (1969) data and are plotted on the destruction graph in Figure 4.3. That plot suggests, not surprisingly, that the represented set of goat bones has undergone some degree of density-mediated attrition. If the destruction graph produces an ambiguous result, then all skeletal parts for which frequency data and density data are available can be plotted in a bivariate scatter plot like that in Figure 4.2 and a correlation coefficient calculated. Spearman's rank order correlation coefficient (*rho*) (as opposed to Pearson's correlation coefficient, *r*) is recommended, because (a) skeletal part abundance data tend to be at best ordinal scale (Grayson 1984; Lyman 2008), and (b) differences in density of skeletal parts are likely at best ordinal scale as well given variation in individual age, sex, genotype, nutrition, and health status (Lyman 1984).

Binford (1984:87) used a single destruction graph in a later analysis. Lyman (1984) merely listed correlation coefficients between %survivorship and bone density values under the presumption that a statistically significant (positive) coefficient indicated density-mediated attrition had taken place. He continued that pattern in later analyses (e.g., Lyman 1993, 1994a). Some followed this analytical strategy (e.g., Ioannidou 2003; Kreutzer 1992; Pavao and Stahl 1999). Others published not only correlation coefficients but also bivariate scatter plots that showed the relationship between the density and the frequency of multiple kinds of skeletal parts (e.g., Bartram and Marean 1999; Cruz and Elkin 2003; Dirrigl 2001; Klein 1989; Pickering and Carlson 2002). Most recently, Bever (2004) showed that identical correlation coefficients could be obtained from quite different relationships between frequencies of skeletal parts and their respective densities. He therefore suggested that the analyst both build a scatter plot and calculate a correlation coefficient. That way, one could determine both what kind of relationship existed (by the form of the scatter of points) and if that relationship was

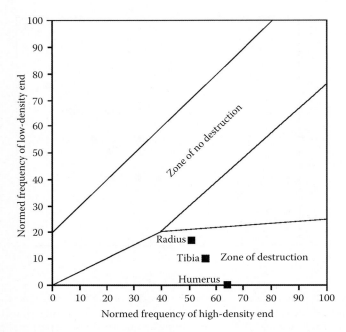

Figure 4.3 Binford's destruction graph with frequencies of proximal and distal humeri, radii, and tibiae of goats in Brain's (1969) sample. Data from Table 4.1. (Graph design from Binford, L.R., *Bones: Ancient Men and Modern Myths*, Academic Press, New York, 1981.)

significant (by the correlation coefficient). Today, taphonomists would argue that the analyst also should examine individual bone specimens for evidence of density-mediated attritional agents such as carnivore gnawing damage to assist with interpreting what the frequencies of skeletal parts actually reflect with respect to their taphonomic history.

Human Bone Density

As indicated earlier, there are limited data on the density of human skeletal parts determined for the purposes of taphonomy. Boaz and Behrensmeyer (1976) produced measurements of human skeletal parts that seem to approximate bulk density. They found a significant inverse correlation ($r = -.63$, $p < .001$) between the bulk density of a skeletal part and its velocity of transport in flowing water. That is, parts of high density moved slowly whereas parts of low density moved more rapidly. Boaz and Behrensmeyer's (1976) density data were, however, based on unprovenienced prehistoric human remains that were poor proxies for fresh bone, the remains were few in number, and density was estimated based on volumes derived from water displacement and was done in such a manner as to be likely not replicable. To generate what are arguably the most sophisticated data thus far published on the density of human skeletal parts, Galloway et al. (1997) used single-beam photon absorptiometry and measured multiple loci on the six major long bones of multiple modern human skeletons. The majority of the bone portions scanned with the photon densitometer were located at a set percentage of an element's total length from the distal end; these are shown in Figure 4.4. To produce a measure of density that took into account the cross-section shape of the bone at each scan site, Galloway et al. (1997) measured the circumference of each scan site, divided

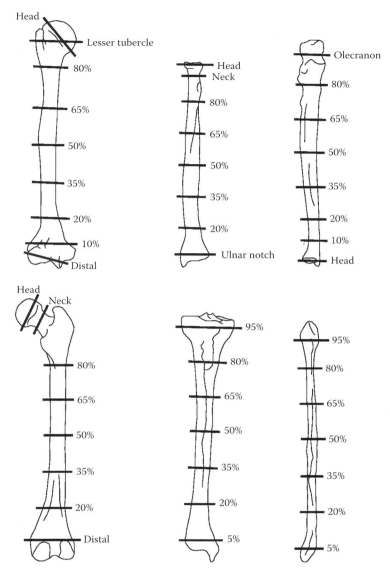

Figure 4.4 Scan site locations on human long bones where density was measured. (Redrawn from Galloway, A. et al., Human bone mineral densities and survival of bone elements: A contemporary sample, In *Forensic Taphonomy: The Postmortem Fate of Human Remains*, eds. W.D. Haglund and M.H. Sorg, CRC Press, Boca Raton, FL, pp. 295–317, 1997.)

that value by 3.14 (π) to obtain an approximate diameter of the scan site, and then divided the bone mineral content of each scan site (provided by the densitometer) by the diameter. They found that this measure of density, which they termed bone mineral density by circumference (BMDc), provided a good predictor of bone survivorship in the prehistoric collection of human remains that they examined. It was in fact better than the value of density calculated following Lyman's (1984) protocol, although BMDc still assumes a uniform structure or amount of bone tissue throughout the scan site—the problem later addressed by computed tomography (Lam et al. 2003; Lam and Pearson 2005).

Galloway et al. (1997) and Willey et al. (1997) originally presented their bone density data for 22 male and 8 female, left and right elements, of adult Caucasians. They provided me with their original raw data per skeleton, and following the protocol of taphonomists who have examined nonhuman skeletons, I calculated mean BMDc values for each scan site on the six limb/long bones regardless of side or sex (Table 4.4). Galloway et al. (1997) found that scan sites of right elements displayed greater densities than left elements within each sex, that scan sites of male elements displayed greater densities than female elements, and that scan sites of African American skeletons were denser than those in Caucasian skeletons. However, overall, correlations between scan sites across sides, sexes, and races were relatively strong and statistically significant. This suggests that we can use Caucasian skeletons (the most frequent skeletal type measured) as a general model indicating the density-mediated survival potential of one skeletal part relative to another, regardless of the side, sex, or race of those parts. That is, if the right distal humerus is denser than the right proximal humerus among male Caucasians, we can assume that the left distal humerus is denser than the left proximal humerus among female African Americans and other race–sex categories as well. How well, then, do the density data in Table 4.4 explain frequencies of skeletal parts in a collection of imperfectly preserved human skeletons?

Unfortunately, few studies of large collections of human skeletal remains provide frequencies of skeletal parts in a form conducive to analysis (e.g., Turner and Turner 1999; White 1992). Willey et al. (1997) provide just such data for Crow Creek, a fourteenth-century collection of remains of about 500 individual American Indians who were massacred. The archaeological site is a prehistoric village located in south-central South Dakota. The MNE values of all but two scan sites shown in Figure 4.4 are provided by Willey et al. (1997) and listed in Table 4.5. There is no need to calculate MAU values in this case, because all tallied skeletal parts (scan sites) would be divided by two. There is also no need to norm the frequency values to %MAU (or %MNE for that matter), because this need only be done when two assemblages of widely disparate sizes are compared (see "Bone Frequencies and Survivorship" section).

Following the precedents set in studies of density-mediated attrition among ungulate remains, there are several kinds of analysis that can be performed with the Crow Creek data. As indicated earlier, a quick way to determine if density-mediated attrition has affected an assemblage would be to construct a destruction graph like that in Figure 4.3. To construct such a graph for the Crow Creek remains, I chose one high-density scan site and one low-density scan site for each long bone in Figure 4.4 with the exception of the fibula. Frequencies of each were normed to the scan site with the greatest value in order to plot the data on the destruction graph. For illustrative purposes, the data used are summarized in Table 4.6, and the resulting destruction graph is shown in Figure 4.5. That graph suggests that indeed the Crow Creek remains have undergone some density-mediated attrition, though the results are more ambiguous than one might hope. The graph suggests that the radius and ulna have undergone density-mediated destruction, though this may be a function of the small sample size for these elements. The humerus and femur may have undergone minor destruction, and apparently the tibia did not undergo any significant destruction. In just such a case, one should turn to a different technique for assessing whether the attrition of a collection was density-mediated or not.

Another way to determine if the Crow Creek materials have been subjected to density-mediated attrition is to construct a scatter plot of the BMDc of each of the 45 scan sites

Table 4.4 Summary Density Data for Human Long Bones by Scan Site

Scan Site	Mean ± SD	NSP Measured
Humerus head	0.832 ± 0.177	54
Humerus tubercle	0.704 ± 0.176	54
Humerus 80%	0.867 ± 0.182	56
Humerus 65%	1.107 ± 0.277	56
Humerus 50%	1.228 ± 0.328	56
Humerus 35%	1.246 ± 0.307	56
Humerus 20%	1.270 ± 0.297	56
Humerus 10%	0.925 ± 0.251	56
Humerus distal	0.847 ± 0.216	56
Radius head	0.717 ± 0.229	53
Radius neck	0.581 ± 0.136	58
Radius 80%	0.780 ± 0.195	58
Radius 65%	0.849 ± 0.180	58
Radius 50%	0.910 ± 0.177	58
Radius 35%	0.895 ± 0.176	58
Radius 20%	0.749 ± 0.148	58
Radius ulnar notch	0.561 ± 0.137	55
Ulna olecranon	0.704 ± 0.192	55
Ulna 80%	0.975 ± 0.214	55
Ulna 65%	0.996 ± 0.181	55
Ulna 50%	0.884 ± 0.212	55
Ulna 35%	0.833 ± 0.164	55
Ulna 20%	0.658 ± 0.142	55
Ulna 10%	0.420 ± 0.103	54
Ulnar head	0.417 ± 0.092	54
Femur head	1.024 ± 0.337	50
Femur neck	0.870 ± 0.284	51
Femur 80%	1.617 ± 0.379	50
Femur 65%	1.810 ± 0.319	50
Femur 50%	1.717 ± 0.314	50
Femur 35%	1.512 ± 0.320	49
Femur 20%	1.171 ± 0.270	50
Femur distal	0.999 ± 0.298	48
Tibia 95%	0.811 ± 0.286	45
Tibia 80%	0.982 ± 0.343	46
Tibia 65%	1.226 ± 0.371	46
Tibia 50%	1.320 ± 0.373	46
Tibia 35%	1.272 ± 0.359	46
Tibia 20%	0.940 ± 0.341	46
Tibia 5%	0.761 ± 0.282	42
Fibula 95%	0.362 ± 0.117	44
Fibula 80%	0.591 ± 0.150	50
Fibula 65%	0.717 ± 0.183	50

(*continued*)

Table 4.4   (continued) Summary Density Data for Human Long Bones by Scan Site

Scan Site	Mean ± SD	NSP Measured
Fibula 50%	0.735 ± 0.191	50
Fibula 35%	0.748 ± 0.160	50
Fibula 20%	0.821 ± 0.107	40
Fibula 5%	0.561 ± 0.171	47

Note: All Caucasian adults (22 Males, 8 Females); Both lefts and rights included.

Table 4.5   Frequency (MNE) of Each Scan Site among American Indian Long Bones at the Crow Creek Site

Scan Site	MNE	Scan Site	MNE
Humerus head and tubercle	170	Femur head and neck	496
Humerus 80%	288.5	Femur 80%	569.5
Humerus 65%	310.5	Femur 65%	555
Humerus 50%	322	Femur 50%	554.5
Humerus 35%	329.5	Femur 35%	545.5
Humerus 20%	340.5	Femur 20%	522
Humerus 10%	150.5	Femur distal	311
Humerus distal	250	Tibia 95%	288.5
Radius head	145	Tibia 80%	405
Radius neck	150.5	Tibia 65%	427.5
Radius 80%	175.5	Tibia 50%	432
Radius 65%	176	Tibia 35%	425
Radius 50%	163	Tibia 20%	409.5
Radius 35%	163	Tibia 5%	342.5
Radius 20%	135	Fibula 95%	165
Radius ulnar notch	53.5	Fibula 80%	214.5
Ulna olecranon	160.5	Fibula 65%	224.5
Ulna 80%	201	Fibula 50%	236
Ulna 65%	206	Fibula 35%	229
Ulna 50%	183	Fibula 20%	210.5
Ulna 35%	183	Fibula 5%	155
Ulna 20%	138		
Ulna 10%	57.5		
Ulnar head	38		

Source: Willey, P. et al., *Am. J. Phys. Anthropol.,* 104, 513, 1997.

(the independent variable, on the x axis) against its MNE frequency (the dependent variable, on the y axis). Just such a plot is shown in Figure 4.6. The scatter plot implies that the two variables are correlated, that the relationship is direct and linear, and therefore that the Crow Creek remains have undergone density-mediated attrition of some sort, though the identity of the responsible taphonomic agent is unclear. Finally, calculation of a rank-order correlation coefficient (Spearman's *rho* = .806, $p < .0001$) and overlaying the simple best-fit regression line

Table 4.6   Frequency (MNE) of Scan Sites Selected for the Construction of a Destruction Graph

Scan Site	MNE	Normed (%) MNE
Humerus head	170	29.8
Humerus 20%	340.5	59.8
Radius 80%	175.5	30.8
Radius ulnar notch	53.5	9.4
Ulna 80%	201	35.3
Ulna head	38	6.7
Femur 80%	569.5	100.0
Femur distal	311	54.6
Tibia 65%	427.5	75.1
Tibia 5%	342.5	60.1

Note: Normed (%)MNE = [MNE/569.5]100.

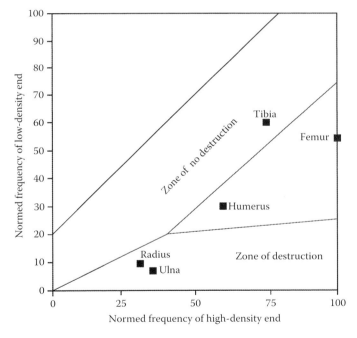

Figure 4.5 Destruction graph for the American Indian remains from Crow Creek. Data from Table 4.6.

confirm our subjective interpretation based on the scatter plot of the relationship between the two variables. As Willey et al. (1997) report, given gnawing damage to some of the human remains, it is likely that consumption by scavenging carnivores is the responsible taphonomic process. Although it is beyond the scope of this discussion, I suspect that differential recovery, in particular the failure to recover small pieces such as the distal ulna (ulnar head) and parts of the fibula, has contributed to the observed frequencies of skeletal parts.

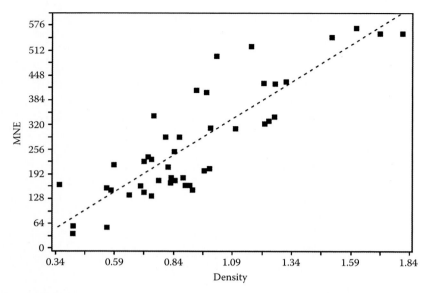

Figure 4.6 Bivariate scatter plot of the density of 45 scan sites on human long bones against MNE frequencies of American Indian remains from Crow Creek. Data from Table 4.5.

Discussion

There are two interrelated reasons to be concerned about variability in the density of skeletal parts, regardless of the taxon. First, many taphonomic processes—carnivore attrition, chemical alteration, fluvial transport, settling in fluid media, and the like—are mediated by the density of a skeletal part (Lyman 1994c). Second, we know of what a complete skeleton of an individual is composed—for a mammal, a cranium, seven cervical vertebrae, a left scapula, right scapula, left humerus, right humerus, left radius, etc.—and thus we can immediately determine if we have something less than (or more than) a single (or multiple) complete skeleton(s) lying on the laboratory table. Together, these two facts mean that we can begin to surmise the preservational condition of a collection of skeletal remains based on its inventory. If certain parts are missing, for example, those known to be of low structural density, then we have immediate insight into the general taphonomic history of the materials comprising the collection. It cannot be overemphasized, however, that the discovery of a significant statistical correlation between skeletal part frequencies and part density does not indicate which particular density-mediated taphonomic process (or even if there was one) influenced the collection. Inference of the taphonomic agent(s) involved requires other sorts of observations, such as if (and how many) specimens display evidence of carnivore gnawing, if specimens appear to be abraded, or if specimens have a corroded appearance, and the like.

Biological interpretations of collections of human remains, whether archaeologically or forensically derived, demand knowledge of which skeletal parts are missing. For example, interpretations of ontogenetic age at death of individuals could be biased if no dentitions are available. Knowing *which* particular parts are missing indicates what sorts of questions can be answered with the materials at hand. Knowing *why* particular skeletal parts are missing provides indications of taphonomic history and forensic history, and contributes to building warranting arguments for answering some kinds of questions but not others. The universal influence of the density of a skeletal part as a property that mediates many taphonomic processes makes it indispensable to bioarchaeological, zooarchaeological, and forensic research.

Conclusion (or on the Future)

Brain (1967) originally noted that long bones—both the diaphyses and the epiphyses—with unfused epiphyses tend to not survive ravaging by bone-gnawing carnivores as well as long bones with fused epiphyses. This has been thought to relate to the fact that ossification and calcification increase with ontogenetic age; that is, density increases with increased age (at least to some middle age, after which it may decrease). Recent research on domestic sheep (*Ovis aries*) suggests that although unfused long bone ends tend to be less dense than fused ends, the relationship is neither rigid nor consistent across the skeleton (Symmons 2005). Further, no statistically significant relationship was found between increasing age and density (Symmons 2005). However, work with domestic pig (*Sus scrofa*) bones indicates that skeletal parts of younger individuals are less dense than those of older individuals (Ioannidou 2003). Results for South American camelids also suggest, but do not conclusively demonstrate, that bones of younger individuals are more prone to destruction than bones of older individuals (Izeta 2005). It seems, then, that the nature of the relationship between ontogenetic age and density of skeletal parts will need to be determined for each population of each species.

The density data gathered by Galloway et al. (1997) and Willey et al. (1997) and summarized in Table 4.5 are presently the best available on human bones. This is so for two reasons. First, the data in Table 4.5 involve averages; each value incorporates sexual and some ontogenetic or age variation (though all were adults in the sense of having fused epiphyses) within a single race. Second, multiple scan sites per skeletal element (seven or eight per element) are included, giving statistical power to any test using those data to detect density-mediated attrition. Only one other study of human bone has used photon densitometry to derive measures of density (Suby and Guichón 2004), but they measured only one skeleton and three or fewer scan sites per skeletal element. Their data for limb bones correlate well with those in Table 4.5 (Pearson's $r = .839$, $p < .0001$), suggesting that the data on the density of vertebrae, the clavicle, scapula, and major tarsals presented by Suby and Guichón (2004) might be useful. I do not present them here, however, because Suby and Guichón (2004) measured an archaeological skeleton, and some of their measurements concern whole bones rather than particular scan sites.

The data in Table 4.5 are sufficient to provide significant insight to the taphonomic history of a collection and whether that collection underwent density-mediated attrition or not, but more research is needed on racial and sexual variation, as well as the aforementioned ontogenetic variation in the density of skeletal parts. In addition, we need data on bone density measured via computed tomography or a similar technique in order to control fully for the cross-section morphology and structure of each scan site. Together, detailed data on racial, sexual, ontogenetic, and cross-sectional structure will likely increase the correlation between density and survivorship. Such data may help explain some of the residual variation when a correlation coefficient between density and frequency is <1.0. We also need data for skeletal parts other than long bones, including vertebrae, crania, carpals, tarsals, phalanges, etc. Finally, even when we have much more complete data, it is important to keep in mind that modern taphonomic research must include multivariate analysis. Density is only one property with taphonomic and forensic significance. Others include bone size and shape (e.g., Darwent and

Lyman 2002) and associated soft tissue (Binford 1978). The data in Table 4.5 provide but a starting point for a thorough taphonomic analysis of human bone survivorship and its meaning.

Acknowledgments

Many thanks to P. Willey and Alison Galloway for allowing me to use their density data in new analyses and to publish it in a new form. Cynthia Irsik was more than helpful (and saved me a lot of hours) with translating an archaic and quite large data file into something which I could use.

References

Bartram, L. E., Jr. and C. W. Marean (1999) Explaining the "Klasies Pattern": Kua ethnoarchaeology, the Die Kelders Middle Stone Age archaeofauna, long bone fragmentation and carnivore ravaging. *Journal of Archaeological Science* 26:9–29.

Behrensmeyer, A. K. (1975) The taphonomy and paleoecology of Plio-Pleistocene vertebrate assemblages east of Lake Rudolf, Kenya. *Bulletin of the Museum of Comparative Zoology* 146:473–578.

Bever, J. E. (2004) Identifying necessity and sufficiency relationships in skeletal-part representation using fuzzy-set theory. *American Antiquity* 69:131–140.

Binford, L. R. (1978) *Nunamiut Ethnoarchaeology*. Academic Press, New York.

Binford, L. R. (1981) *Bones: Ancient Men and Modern Myths*. Academic Press, New York.

Binford, L. R. (1984) *Faunal Remains from Klasies River Mouth*. Academic Press, Orlando, FL.

Binford, L. R. and J. B. Bertram (1977) Bone frequencies and attritional processes. In *For Theory Building in Archaeology* ed. L. R. Binford, pp. 77–153. Academic Press, New York.

Boaz, N. J. and A. K. Behrensmeyer (1976) Hominid taphonomy: Transport of human skeletal parts in an artificial fluviatile environment. *American Journal of Physical Anthropology* 45:53–60.

Brain, C. K. (1967) Hottentot food remains and their bearing on the interpretation of fossil bone assemblages. *Scientific Papers of the Namib Desert Research Station* 32:1–7.

Brain, C. K. (1969) The contribution of the Namib Desert Hottentots to and understanding of Australopithecine bone accumulations. *Scientific Papers of the Namib Desert Research Station* 39:13–22.

Brain, C. K. (1976) Some principles in the interpretation of bone accumulations associated with man. In *Human Origins: Louis Leakey and the East African Evidence* eds. G. Ll. Isaac and E. R. McCown, pp. 97–116. W. A. Benjamin, Menlo Park, CA.

Broughton, J. M., D. Mullens, and T. Ekker (2007) Avian resource depression or intertaxonomic variation in bone density? A test with San Francisco Bay avifaunas. *Journal of Archaeological Science* 34:374–391.

Buckland, W. (1823) *Reliquiae Diluvianae, or, Observations on the Organic Remains Contained in Caves, Fissures, and Diluvial Gravel, and on Other Geological Phenomena, Attesting to the Action of an Universal Deluge*. John Murray, London, U.K.

Butler, V. L. and J. C. Chatters (1994) The role of bone density in structuring prehistoric salmon bone assemblages. *Journal of Archaeological Science* 21:413–424.

Cameron, J. R., J. G. Skofronick, and R. M. Grant (1999) *Physics of the Body*. 2nd edn. Medical Physics Publishing, Madison, WI.

Cann, C. E. (1988) Quantitative CT for determination of bone mineral density: A review. *Radiology* 166:509–522.

Carlson, K. J. and T. R. Pickering (2004) Shape-adjusted bone mineral density measurements in baboons: Other factors explain primate skeletal element representation at Swartkrans. *Journal of Archaeological Science* 31:577–583.

Chambers, A. L. (1992) *Seal Bone Mineral Density: Its Effect on Specimen Survival in Archaeological Sites*. Unpublished Bachelor's Honors thesis, Department of Anthropology, University of Missouri, Columbia, MO.

Cruz, I. and D. Elkin (2003) Structural bone density of the lesser rhea (*Pterocnemia pennata*) (Aves: Rheidae): Taphonomic and archaeological implications. *Journal of Archaeological Science* 30:37–44.

Currey, J. (1984) *The Mechanical Adaptations of Bones*. Princeton University Press, Lawrenceville, NJ.

Darwent, C. and R. L. Lyman (2002) Detecting the postburial fragmentation of carpals, tarsals, and phalanges. In *Advances in Forensic Taphonomy: Method, Theory, and Archaeological Perspectives* eds. W. D. Haglund and M. H. Sorg, pp. 355–377. CRC Press, Boca Raton, FL.

Dawkins, W. B. (1869) On the distribution of British postglacial mammals. *Quarterly Journal of the Geological Society of London* 25:192–217.

Dawkins, W. B. (1874) *Cave Hunting, Researches on the Evidence of Caves Respecting the Early Inhabitants of Europe*. Macmillan, London, U.K.

Dirrigl, F. J. (2001) Bone mineral density of wild turkey (*Meleagris gallopavo*) skeletal elements and its effect on differential survivorship. *Journal of Archaeological Science* 28:817–832.

Elkin, D. C. (1995) Volume density of South American camelid skeletal parts. *International Journal of Osteoarchaeology* 5:29–37.

Galloway, A., P. Willey, and L. Snyder (1997) Human bone mineral densities and survival of bone elements: A contemporary sample. In *Forensic Taphonomy: The Postmortem Fate of Human Remains* eds. W. D. Haglund and M. H. Sorg, pp. 295–317. CRC Press, Boca Raton, FL.

Grayson, D. K. (1984) *Quantitative Zooarchaeology: Topics in the Analysis of Archaeological Faunas*. Academic Press, Orlando, FL.

Guthrie, R. D. (1967) Differential preservation and recovery of Pleistocene large mammal remains in Alaska. *Journal of Paleontology* 41:243–246.

Gutiérrez, M., C. Kaufmann, M. González, A. Massigoge, and M. C. Álvarez (2010) Intrataxonomic variability in metapodial and femur bone density related to age in guanaco (*Lama guanicoe*): Zooarchaeological and taphonomical implications. *Journal of Archaeological Science* 37: 3226–3238.

Hill, A. P. (1980) Early postmortem damage to the remains of some contemporary East African mammals. In *Fossils in the Making: Vertebrate Taphonomy and Paleoecology* eds. A. K. Behrensmeyer and A. P. Hill, pp. 131–155. University of Chicago Press, Chicago, IL.

Ioannidou, E. (2003) Taphonomy of animal bones: Species, sex, age, and breed variability of sheep, cattle, and pig bone density. *Journal of Archaeological Science* 30:355–365.

Izeta, A. D. (2005) South American camelid bone structural density: What are we measuring? Comments on data sets, values, their interpretation and application. *Journal of Archaeological Science* 32:1159–1168.

Klein, R. G. (1989) Why does skeletal part representation differ between smaller and larger bovids at Klasies River Mouth and other archeological sites? *Journal of Archaeological Science* 16:363–381.

Korth, W. W. (1979) Taphonomy of microvertebrate fossil assemblages. *Annals of the Carnegie Museum* 48:235–285.

Kreutzer, L. A. (1992) Bison and deer bone mineral densities: Comparisons and implications for the interpretation of archaeological faunas. *Journal of Archaeological Science* 19:271–294.

Lam, Y. M., X. Chen, C. W. Marean, and C. J. Frey (1998) Bone density and long bone representation in archaeological faunas: Comparing results from CT and photon densitometry. *Journal of Archaeological Science* 25:559–570.

Lam, Y. M., X. Chen, and O. M. Pearson (1999) Intertaxonomic variability in patterns of bone density and the differential representation of bovid, cervid, and equid elements in the archaeological record. *American Antiquity* 64:343–362.

Lam, Y. M., and O. M. Pearson (2005) Bone density studies and the interpretation of the faunal record. *Evolutionary Anthropology* 14:99–108.

Lam, Y. M., O. M. Pearson, C. W. Marean, and X. Chen (2003) Bone density studies in zooarchaeology. *Journal of Archaeological Science* 30:1701–1708.

Lubbock, J. (1913) *Prehistoric Times as Illustrated by Ancient Remains and the Manners and Customs of Modern Savages* (7th edn.). Henry Holt and Company, New York.

Lyman, R. L. (1984) Bone density and differential survivorship of fossil classes. *Journal of Anthropological Archaeology* 3:259–299.

Lyman, R. L. (1993) Density-mediated attrition of bone assemblages: New insights. In *From Bones to Behavior* ed. J. Hudson, pp. 324–341. Center for Archaeological Investigations Occasional Paper No. 21, Southern Illinois University Press, Carbondale, IL.

Lyman, R. L. (1994a) Quantitative units and terminology in zooarchaeology. *American Antiquity* 59: 36–71.

Lyman, R. L. (1994b) Relative abundances of skeletal specimens and taphonomic analysis of vertebrate remains. *Palaios* 9:288–298.

Lyman, R. L. (1994c) *Vertebrate Taphonomy*. Cambridge University Press, Cambridge, U.K.

Lyman, R. L. (2008) *Quantitative Paleozoology*. Cambridge University Press, Cambridge, U.K.

Lyman, R. L., L. E. Houghton, and A. L. Chambers (1992) The effect of structural density on marmot skeletal part representation in archaeological sites. *Journal of Archaeological Science* 19:557–573.

Morlot, [K. von] A. (1861) General views on archaeology. *Smithsonian Institution Annual Report for 1860,* pp. 284–343.

Nicholson, R. A. (1992) An assessment of the value of bone density measurements to archaeoichthyological studies. *International Journal of Osteoarchaeology* 2:139–154.

Novecosky, B. J. and P. R. W. Popkin (2005) Canidae volume bone mineral density values: An application to sites in Western Canada. *Journal of Archaeological Science* 32:1677–1690.

Pavao, B. and P. W. Stahl (1999) Structural density assays of leporid skeletal elements with implications for taphonomic, actualistic and archaeological research. *Journal of Archaeological Science* 26:53–66.

Pickering, T. R. and K. J. Carlson (2002) Baboon bone mineral densities: Implications for the taphonomy of primate skeletons in South African cave sites. *Journal of Archaeological Science* 29:883–896.

Shipman, P. (1981) *Life History of a Fossil: An Introduction to Taphonomy and Paleoecology*. Harvard University Press, Cambridge, MA.

Stahl, P. W. (1999) Structural density of domesticated South American camelid skeletal elements and the archaeological investigation of prehistoric Andean ch'arki. *Journal of Archaeological Science* 26:1347–1368.

Suby, J. A. and R. A. Guichón (2004) Densidad ósea y frecuencias de hallazgos en restos humanos en el norte de Tierra del Fuego: Análisis exploratorio. *Intersecciones en Antropología* 5:95–104.

Symmons, R. (2004) Digital photodensitometry: A reliable and accessible method for measuring bone density. *Journal of Archaeological Science* 31:711–719.

Symmons, R. (2005) New density data for unfused and fused sheep bones, and a preliminary discussion on the modeling of taphonomic bias in archaeofaunal age profiles. *Journal of Archaeological Science* 32:1691–1698.

Turner, C. G., II, and J. A. Turner (1999) *Man Corn: Cannibalism and Violence in the Prehistoric American Southwest*. University of Utah Press, Salt Lake City, UT.

Voorhies, M. R. (1969) *Taphonomy and Population Dynamics of an Early Pliocene Vertebrate Fauna, Knox County, Nebraska*. University of Wyoming Contributions to Geology, Special Paper No. 1. Laramie, WY.

White, T. D. (1992) *Prehistoric Cannibalism at Mancos 5MTUMR-2346*. Princeton University Press, Princeton, NJ.

Willey, P., A. Galloway, and L. Snyder (1997) Bone mineral density and survival of elements and element portions in the bones of the Crow Creek Massacre victims. *American Journal of Physical Anthropology* 104:513–528.

Effects of Burial Environment on Osseous Remains

JAMES T. POKINES
JOAN E. BAKER

Contents

HAMLET: How long will a man lie i' the earth ere he rot?

FIRST CLOWN: I' faith, if he be not rotten before he die—as we have many pocky corpses now-a-days, that will scarce hold the laying in—he will last you some eight year or nine year: a tanner will last you nine year.

HAMLET: Why he more than another?

FIRST CLOWN: Why, sir, his hide is so tanned with his trade, that he will keep out water a great while; and your water is a sore decayer of your whoreson dead body. Here's a skull now; this skull has lain in the earth three and twenty years.

—**William Shakespeare, *Hamlet, Act V, Scene 1***

Introduction

One of the most basic questions that a forensic anthropologist working in a medical examiner's office or a similar setting must answer is whether remains are human or nonhuman. Once remains are identified as human, what can be done with these remains analytically largely devolves from the taphonomic markers of their burial or other depositional setting (surface, water, etc.) to place them into broad categories of postmortem history (Berryman et al. 1991, 1997; Duhig 2003; Hughes et al. 2012; Micozzi 1991; Schultz 2012; Schultz et al. 2003; Sledzik and Micozzi 1997; Ubelaker 1995). The taphonomic alterations left by different burial contexts (or their lack) and the duration of burial often separate remains into groups along these lines: (1) recent remains, sometimes with associated soft tissue, that are of definite forensic interest; (2) cemetery remains, whether recent or not, that likely do not represent criminal activity other than the possibility of vandalism of buried remains; (3) remains derived from historical/archaeological burials, which normally become the responsibility of state archaeological agencies (Garman 1996); (4) remains likely derived from anatomical teaching, trophy, and/or ritual contexts, which probably have not been buried; and (5) unknown remains that do not fit easily into any of these categories. The taphonomic changes brought about by burial environment or the lack thereof are therefore crucial in the categorization of human skeletal remains as being of forensic interest and their ultimate disposition.

General Effects of Burial Directly in Soil

Effects of Soil pH

General Soil Properties

The science of *pedology* is primarily the domain of agricultural and engineering concerns, but it also is a component of geological, geomorphological, archaeological, and forensic concerns. The forensic analysis of soils has numerous practical applications (Fitzpatrick 2008), and the characteristics of individual soils and components of soils examined include color, consistency, texture, structure, and inclusions.

Soils form through the complex interactions of *parent material* (the main source of mineral and organic sediments in a given location, which may derive from sources including local bedrock, alluvial deposits, aeolian deposits, volcanic ash, or glacial deposits), topography (slope and drainage), climate (including temperature and precipitation), and biological organisms (including plants, fungi, and other decomposers, and *fossorial* or burrowing animals) over time. Deep soils take centuries or millennia to reach their present forms and even then do not remain static. Soils also have complex interactions of air and groundwater within their porous structure. Disruptions in this structure are usually highly visible and are the primary clue to forensic archaeologists that a body has been buried recently in that location.

Soils have up to five main *horizons*, or types of layers, which should not be confused with the stratigraphy caused by human deposition. Not all of these horizons are present for every soil, and these main horizons usually are broken down into multiple subhorizons. The uppermost is the *O horizon*, which consists primarily of the decomposing plant matter accumulation. Surface-deposited remains are often obscured by this horizon, since continued leaf fall will cover bones slowly and continue to decompose, gradually creating soil around and on them. The *A horizon* is normally equated with the topsoil, the organic-rich horizon that often is only centimeters deep yet contains most of the nutrients taken up by plants and the majority of the biotic activity. A commonly encountered subhorizon is that portion of A horizon that has undergone plowing disturbance, normally indicated as the A_p subhorizon (or the *plow zone*). The plow zone is of practical importance in both archaeology and forensics, as the process of plowing often brings buried objects to the surface and causes their dispersal (Haglund et al. 2002). The *B horizon* is characterized by the accumulation of soluble base minerals dissolved from the A horizon and is usually lighter due to its lesser amounts of organically derived carbon. The *C horizon* consists of the less altered parent material that formed locally from the physical and chemical breakdown of the bedrock or was deposited from other locations. The *R horizon* consists of the broken-up local bedrock (or *regolith*). Bedrock itself is not a part of the soil, although it has a major effect upon the types of soils that form from it. Classification of types of soils varies by country, with one comprehensive system developed by the U.S. Department of Agriculture currently recognizing 12 soil orders (11 mineral soil orders and 1 organic soil order), which are broken down, much like biological taxonomy, into local soils on a par with individual species (Soil Survey Staff 2010). Common soil orders include Mollisols (deep soils found in plains/steppe environments), Histosols (organic soils, including those forming in peat bogs and other wetlands), Oxisols (the heavily oxidized, red soils often encountered in the tropics and subtropics), and Spodosols (often found in areas of pine forest).

Generally, soils are their most acidic in the A horizon. This is due primarily to three factors: (a) the leaching of base ions (calcium [Ca^{2+}], magnesium [Mg^{2+}], potassium [K^+], etc.) out of this horizon, where they are often accumulated in the B horizon or remain dissolved and are transported away with the creeping groundwater, (b) the concentration of decomposing organic matter and the release of organic acids (including humic and tannin), and (c) the dissolving of carbon dioxide (CO_2) produced by decomposition into water to form carbonic acid. This difference in pH is more notable where the bedrock is high in base ions, especially limestone and its principal component, calcium carbonate ($CaCO_3$). Soils forming on limestone may be acidic in their upper horizons and basic or close to neutral in their lower horizons. Soils also tend to become more acidic over time, as more soluble base ions are lost and more organic matter accumulates.

Burial Depth
Given the chemical differences in soil horizons, depth of burial may play a significant role in skeletal preservation of buried remains. While folk lore suggests that formal burials

(i.e., those in cemeteries) are "six feet under," this legend does not hold true in practice. Historical cemetery burials have been found at depths as shallow as 2–4 feet below the surface (Dockall et al. 1996b:154; Fox 1984:28–29) and as deep as 5.5 feet (Taylor et al. 1986:15, 20). In the United States, modern state and cemetery regulations differ, with actual required burial depths ranging from 1.5 to 12 feet. For example, California's Health and Safety Code, §8113.1, requires that burials are covered by 1.5 feet of soil, while Article 205 of the New York City Public Health Law, §205.25, states that "…the top of the coffin or casket shall be at least three feet below the level of the ground, but if the coffin or casket is enclosed in a concrete or metal vault, the top of the vault shall be at least two feet below the level of the ground." Generally speaking, burial depth is governed by the height of the water table (e.g., most burials are above ground in cemeteries in New Orleans, United States; Yalom 2008:140), depth of topsoil relative to bedrock, and other intrinsic geological factors. In clandestine, temporary, or other expedient burials, gravediggers are likely to excavate only to the depth necessary to ensure that remains are not (or minimally) disturbed by scavenging animals. In most cases, whether the interments are in cemeteries or clandestine, burial shaft dimensions are only slightly larger than necessary to accommodate the coffin or body, respectively, and infant or child burials typically will be smaller and shallower than adult burials (e.g., Fox 1984; Gadus et al. 2002; Taylor et al. 1986).

High water tables, such as those seen at the Texas State Cemetery (Austin, TX) and the Phillips Memorial Cemetery (Galveston, TX), can result in poor preservation through softening of the bone not only due to chemical erosion but also as the result of mechanical erosion due to contact with coffin walls, other skeletal elements, or artifact inclusions in the casket (Dockall et al. 1996a,b). Skeletal elements may be removed from their anatomical position through oscillation of the water table. In one burial at the Phillips Memorial Cemetery, foot elements were found floating in water contained between the outer box and the coffin; in another, a humerus had been pushed against the end of the coffin (Dockall et al. 1996b:211; see also Dockall et al. 1996a). These effects may be particularly evident in the small bones of the hands and feet and among the lightweight thoracic elements.

Acidic Soil Corrosion

Perhaps the most pervasive long-term destructive force acting upon bones is soil acidity (Casallas and Moore 2012; Crow 2008). In depositional environments with near-neutral or slightly basic pH, bone preservation typically is excellent. This is particularly true for deposits in limestone caverns. Due to their sediment pH typically being in the 7.5–8.0 range, the protection that they afford from other destructive taphonomic forces (including weathering and sometimes scavenging), and a long time depth allowing for repeated occupation and deep accumulation, limestone caverns have yielded the bulk of hominin fossil history into the beginning of the Holocene. Other factors interacting with the effects of soil acidity include the amount of groundwater flow. In an acidic soil water solution, the hydroxyapatite crystals, $Ca_5(PO_4)_3(OH)$, are depleted of calcium (Ca^{2+}) ions by their replacement with hydrogen (H^+) ions (derived from hydronium ions, H_3O^+) as equilibrium is reached with the soil water (White and Hannus 1983). If the water flow rate is high in this acidic environment, the effect upon skeletal remains is the constant replenishment of hydronium ions in their immediate soil solution vicinity. Any acid neutralization effect brought about by the bones' mineral content itself is quickly negated. Similarly, the concentration of phosphate (PO_4^{3-}) ions in the soil water solution reaches equilibrium with the hydroxyapatite, but these ions combine with iron (Fe) and aluminum

(Al) in highly acidic solutions and precipitate out. Any increase in water flow rate may increase the dissolution of the mineral component of the bone (constituting about 70%), even in mildly acidic conditions. Crow (2008) found experimentally that mineral apatite was highly susceptible to dissolution with decreasing pH.

The gross morphological result of these (and other related) processes is *acidic soil corrosion*, which tends to appear on all exposed surfaces of a buried element, including interior spaces where these have become in direct contact with sediments/soil solution. The decomposition of the collagen component also contributes to the general pattern of bone deterioration, and the breakdown of the collagen can form acidic compounds that further the dissolution of the mineral component (White and Hannus 1983). The surfaces left behind have lost their smooth original texture and defined features, and a scooped, irregular surface is created (Nicholson 1996). The loss is most apparent on epiphyses of long bones, where the cortical bone is thinnest and may be destroyed entirely through this process. Less dense bones with thin cortices particularly prone to this taphonomic process include the vertebrae, sternum, and innominates. Casallas and Moore (2012) found that near-complete mineral dissolution occurred among a large sample of recent burials exhumed in Columbia after 8–10 years in a soil with a pH ranging from 4.2 to 4.5. In environments with extreme soil pH, high annual temperature, and humidity, this type of osseous breakdown therefore can occur very rapidly.

Acidic soil corrosion gradually thins bone cortex such that small holes or *windowing* (Figure 5.1) may form in the weakened structure or expand from foramina. While the windowing and thinning caused by acidic soil corrosion are similar to that caused by gastric corrosion (see Chapter 9, this volume), elements that are far too large to have been swallowed by any extant terrestrial scavenger will exhibit signs of acidic soil corrosion over their entire cortical surfaces. Bone that has been partially digested and deriving from vomit or feces consists of small whole elements (carpals, small phalanges, etc.) or highly fragmented larger bone (Pokines and Kerbis Peterhans 2007). Note also that a weakened structure is left behind on bone margins affected by acidic soil corrosion, while carnivore gnawing preferentially removes weakened areas, especially at the exposed ends of long bone diaphyses.

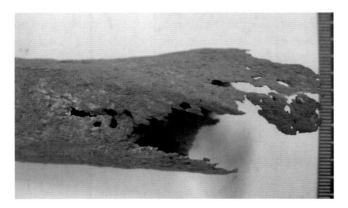

Figure 5.1 Acidic soil corrosion to distal human tibia. Note that while the windowing and thinning are similar to gastric corrosion, the element is far too large to have been swallowed and exhibits signs of corrosion over its entire cortical surface. Note also that a weakened structure is left behind, while carnivore gnawing preferentially removes weakened areas. Scale is in cm.

Bone preservation over the short term and long term is based upon a complex array of factors, including intrinsic bone properties, the actions of microbes, temperature, soil mineral composition, and soil pH (Child 1995; Hedges et al. 1995; Henderson 1987; Nielsen-Marsh and Hedges 2000; see also Chapter 1, this volume). Of these, the effects of acidic soil primarily have been studied in archaeological contexts due to the necessity for a significant burial duration to cause measurable differential preservation. Soil pH also tends to alter over the short term of decomposition due to the influx of organic and mineral nutrients in a concentrated location, before returning to original or near-original levels (Benninger et al. 2008). The long-term pH to which bone is exposed, however, is largely dictated by the prevailing soil and climate conditions prior to deposition of a body. Gordon and Buikstra (1981) presented data from multiple Late Woodland Period burial mounds in Illinois, radiocarbon dating from AD 850 to 1200. These mounds were constructed of silty loams overlooking major rivers. The remains included in the study came from 63 adult and 32 juvenile (<15 years old) skeletons and were categorized by the degree of preservation into five groups: (1) strong, complete bone, (2) fragile bone, (3) fragmented bone, (4) extremely fragmented bone, and (5) bone meal/ghost. These categories were compared with the pH from the burial fill, and a highly significant ($r = -92$, $p < .00001$, $n = 63$) inverse relationship (as pH decreases, destruction increases) was found for the adult remains. The relationship was not as significant with the juvenile remains ($r = -48$, $p < .005$, $n = 32$), likely due to the great changes in robusticity among remains of individuals over the first 15 years of life and the effect this has upon preservation independent of pH. Overall, skeletal remains fared poorly when buried in more acidic soils, to the point of near disappearance in some cases. The experimental results of Christensen and Myers (2011) using sections of cattle (*Bos taurus*) long bone confirm that bones in extreme pH solutions (very low or very high) fare extremely poorly, while those closer to neutral pH were well-preserved after 1 year of submergence.

Nicholson (1996) found that while soil pH played a large role in bone condition over the course of a 7 year experiment, it was not the only determinant of bone preservation. She noted that surface etching was common among bones buried in acidic soils (in the pH 3.5–4.5 range). Nicholson (1998) further noted that bones buried for 7 years in a compost heap were well-preserved upon excavation, but the pH in this particular depositional setting was neutral to slightly basic (7.0–7.5). A high organic content does not guarantee acidic soil conditions, and in this case, pH could have been elevated by the common inclusion of eggshells. Nicholson (1998:393) also found that the bones had undergone variable staining in blended and sometimes mottled shades of yellow/red/brown.

Effects of Soft-Tissue Decomposition upon Soil pH

The decomposition of a buried body initially causes a large influx initially of organic acids, initially increasing acidity in its immediate vicinity. This stage is followed by the influx of base ions and a general decrease therefore in the acidity of the burial fill during the next phase of decomposition (Gill-King 1997; Wilson et al. 2007). As decomposition proceeds, the mildly alkaline local environment gradually returns to more acidic conditions as nutrient cycling and dissolution reduce the amount of base ions in the burial fill. The overall effect of the burial of a whole or partial body in acidic soil is to postpone the onset of acidic soil corrosion, although the exact timing of these events is still being researched (Damann 2010).

Boot/Glove Taphonomy

Some buried objects may offer partial protection to bones. It is common for improvised burials (such as those resulting from individual homicide, genocide, or warfare) to include leather footwear. In contrast, early historical burials often do not include shoes or boots, either because they were passed down to family members due to their value or because shoes are difficult to put onto a dead body and would not be seen by mourners during a viewing anyway (see Bond et al. 2002:154; also see Fox 1984:12, 14, 40 and Rose 1985: Appendix, who found evidence of shoes in 10.1% of burials at Cedar Grove Cemetery in Texas). Leather is often preserved in acidic soils, as the acidity may provide an antiseptic effect to bacterial decomposition of the leather, and tanning hides acts to preserve them. Janaway (2008) notes the resistance of leather to decay when compared with other articles of clothing, including the frequent finds nearly 100 years later in WWI field burials in Europe where all fabric had decomposed but leather boots were still recognizable. The persistence of leather footwear (and potentially leather gloves) provides a temporary, partial barrier to other destructive taphonomic effects of burial. These include reduced direct contact with acidic soil and more restricted acidic ground-water flow, as well as lessened access by plant roots and decreased potential for disturbance by fossorial mammals. This pattern of preservation may be made more apparent by the survival of the leather items until the time of excavation, but the preferential survival of these relatively delicate hand and foot elements may indicate the former presence of leather items. The protective effect of leather boots often includes not only the foot elements but the distal portions of the tibia and fibula as well, which may be very well preserved while the midshaft and proximal portions are in far more degraded condition (Pokines 2009). These leather items also offer some protection against other non-soil-related taphonomic processes, including plowing (Haglund et al. 2002; see "Effects of Plowing on Buried Remains" section). Similar effects have also been noted with buried cranial remains contained within military helmets (pers. obs.).

Special Case of Boreal Forests

Soils associated with coniferous forests (pines, etc.) often have a highly acidic topsoil with a much more benign subsoil. These frequently are classified as Spodosols, following the USDA system (Soil Survey Staff 2010), and are found in large areas of North America and Eurasia. Skeletons from shallow burials in these contexts often become exposed to highly acidic soil only in their uppermost portions, typically the anterior skull and innominates for bodies in a supine position. Over years of exposure, this can lead to the highly localized acidic erosion of these portions of the skeleton, while the remaining portions are in a much better state of preservation. This process can lead to a "melted face" pattern of skeletal recovery (pers. obs.). Of course, any portion of the skeleton deposited near the upper portion of the burial may be affected in this manner, including hand and foot elements deposited on the upward-sloping edges of the burial feature. Since the mixed burial fill deriving from both the topsoil (highly acidic) and subsoil (less acidic) will start out with an average pH between these two extremes, the increased acidity of the upper portion of the burial fill must accrue over time through normal soil formation processes. This taphonomic pattern therefore is likely to appear only on skeletons that have been buried for multiple decades, including WWI and WWII field burials in the European Theater (pers. obs.).

Plant Root Invasion

Bones are a potential source of highly concentrated nutrients to plants, especially their nitrogen (N) and phosphate (PO_4^{3-}) content. Indeed, ground-up bone (bone meal) is a commercial organic fertilizer, applied primarily for its slow release of phosphate properties. It also reduces soil acidity through the addition of base ions, including calcium (Ca^{2+}). In the case of buried bones, the fine lattice structure of trabecular bone greatly increases the surface area for potential release of these nutrients into the environment, and this surface area initially increases as the bone gets more degraded and pores are expanded through dissolution of the mineral content and breakdown of the organic content. In addition, the porous structure of bone can trap water, further promoting the growth of plant roots through them and increasing the amount of direct contact between the two. Plant roots reaching a buried bone may grow preferentially around and into this microenvironment. Plant roots also may grow incidentally passing through foramina, including through the sacrum, vertebrae, and pelvis. Subsequent growth thickening of the root, whether directly invasive or incidental, may destroy bone from the inside (Figure 5.2). Gabet et al. (2003) summarize the bioturbation effects of plant roots and note that the potential force of growing roots is enormous and can fracture apart planes in bedrock. Radial pressures have been noted to reach up to 0.91 MPa (910,000 N/m^2 or 132 lb/in^2). Root hairs can penetrate fissures as narrow as 100 μm, and tree roots have been found 6–7 m deep within otherwise solid granite. The ability of bone to withstand this force is therefore limited, especially under tension from penetrating roots growing outward. Plant growth around a buried skeleton also may have been promoted previously in that location through the influx of nutrients from the decomposing soft tissue, further increasing the amount of root invasion into the bones. This potentially destructive process, however, may also contribute a form of postmortem interval (PMI) determination to the analysis of buried skeletal remains in the form of a minimum time since burial, since tree roots also develop annual rings that can be counted (Willey and Heilman 1987), and even smaller plant root structures may aid in determining shorter (<1 year) PMI intervals (Quatrehomme et al. 1997).

Plant roots also may destroy bone through the contact of the roots, leaving behind a pattern of surface damage in cortical bone known as *root etching*. The plant roots secrete

Figure 5.2 Secondary urn burial, undisturbed, Icla Valley, Bolivia, Tiwanaku period. Note that the plant roots growing through the tibia have nearly destroyed it from within, while the rest of the bones are in much better condition.

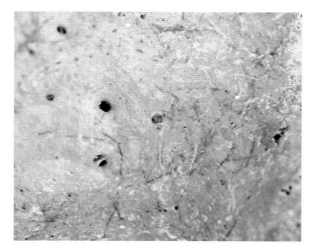

Figure 5.3 Close-up of fine root etching and staining (network of fine black lines) on bone.

multiple compounds (exudates) for a variety of purposes, which include aiding the uptake of minerals from the soil solution, deterring herbivory, acting as chemical attractants and repellents, increasing the abundance of helpful (symbiotic) bacteria, and inhibiting the growth of plant competitors (De-la-Peña et al. 2010; Walker et al. 2003). Some of these compounds include mild organic acids such as humic, citric, malic, and oxic, which may increase the available phosphorus for uptake by the plant (Bais et al. 2006; Rudrappa et al. 2008). The acidic compounds may dissolve the mineral content of the bone where the roots have grown in contact with it. Lyman (1994:376) also summarizes the conclusions of multiple researchers who have noted that the microorganisms in association with the root (fungi, etc.) or the decomposition of the root itself may produce some of the acidic compounds likely responsible for the majority of bone damage. It is probable that individual root etchings are produced from a variety of processes directly or indirectly related to the roots themselves.

The pattern of root etching is meandering and branching (Figure 5.3), with a U-shaped profile to the individual surface scores produced (Lyman 1994:376). D'Errico and Villa (1997) and Morlan (1984) note that root etching has been mistaken for incised markings on bone, including from deliberate butchery, artwork, or accidental mechanical abrasion, and that natural anatomical features including vascular grooves on the surfaces of bones also have been mistaken for all of these. D'Errico and Villa (1997:11–14) note that under high magnification, vascular channels can be seen to "tunnel" into the bone. Markings caused by sharp objects cutting into the surface of bone, regardless of the purpose or intent, should leave V-shaped profiles and parallel striations within the markings (Fisher 1995). These characteristics, which can be used to separate these types of surface marks from root etching, are summarized in Table 5.1.

Root etching also can form on the side of a bone in contact with the soil among surface-deposited remains (pers. obs.), even while the more exposed side undergoes weathering (see Chapter 11, this volume) and algae formation (Chapter 12). The root-etched lower side normally also has staining from the topsoil and may have some acidic soil corrosion (see "Acidic Soil Corrosion" section). Rootlets are often found sticking out of open structures in bones (Figure 5.4) and are an important indicator of previous (at least partial) burial or topsoil contact. This observation may indicate that the remains have been removed from

Table 5.1 Comparison of Surface Markings That May Be Mistaken for Root Etching in Forensic Contexts

Type of Surface Marking	Characteristics	Sources
Root etching	U-shaped groove profile; meandering/branching pattern; roots often still present; dark soil staining often present; follow surface contours of the bone	D'Errico and Villa (1997), Fisher (1995), Morlan (1984), Lyman (1994)
Vascular grooves	U-shaped groove profile with rounded edges; branching pattern; some "tunneling" into bone; funnel-shaped openings; follow surface contours of the bone	D'Errico and Villa (1997)
Cut marks	V-shaped groove profile; linear pattern; striations within marks; often concentrated in multiple small areas on a bone; do not follow surface contours of the bone	D'Errico and Villa (1997), Fisher (1995)
Abrasion marks	V-shaped groove profile; curving or meandering; multiple marks often created in parallel; many small, unpatterned marks	D'Errico and Villa (1997), Fisher (1995)

Figure 5.4 Severe plant root invasion of a distal nonhuman femur. Note how the roots both penetrate the cortical spaces and adhere as a mat on the surface. Scale is in cm.

a previous location when later recovered from a surface setting or if acquired from an unknown provenience. Rootlets also may leave darker staining of bones along their paths (see Figure 12.13, Chapter 12, this volume) in addition to etching or invading the surface.

Other Biological Attack

Other organisms besides plants utilize buried bone and associated soft tissue as a source of nutrients and thereby may leave behind surface damage on bone (Child 1995). Primary among these are the Kingdom Fungi, which along with bacteria are the major decomposers in most ecosystems. The microscopic effects of these organisms upon bone are covered in Chapter 2, this volume. Fungi may also leave behind macroscopic surface damage to bone, and this effect may occur in conjunction with the exudates of plant roots as noted earlier. One of the major structures of fungi is hyphae, which are the thread-like structures that give many molds their fuzzy appearance. These can invade the porous structure of bone and leave behind focal damage (Jans et al. 2002). They also may grow on the surface of bone in large masses, often initially feeding on the soft tissue still attached or the residual organic content. The overall effect is to leave behind a roughened, eaten-away surface that forms through acidic dissolution similar to acidic soil corrosion. Fungi are so ubiquitous in the upper horizons of the soil that large portions of the actual damage caused by the more general process of acidic soil corrosion may in fact be due to these species operating in conjunction with inorganic chemical reactions of dissolution of bone minerals. Fungal damage, however, may leave behind much more localized patches of surface erosion, with irregular edges (Armour-Chelu and Andrews 1996; Nicholson 1996, 1998). Andrews (1995) found areas of localized surface fungal attack (with some remaining fungal hyphae associated) on bones buried for 32 years as part of a long-term taphonomic experiment. Termites also have the potential to consume buried bones, likely due to dietary nitrogen deficiencies. These processes are covered in Chapter 9, this volume, but the presence of termite alteration to bone suggests previous burial.

Bioturbation of Skeletal Remains

Species living within the soil also may disperse bone (through the processes of *bioturbation*), which must be noted both for bone recovery and to prevent misinterpretation of this displacement as having to do with perimortem actions (Gabet et al. 2003). Armour-Chelu and Andrews (1994) examined the potential of earthworms (Oligochaeta) to displace buried microvertebrate bones and found up to 20 cm of vertical displacement within the soil column and up to 15 cm horizontal displacement over the course of 3 years. The results indicate that earthworm bioturbation has the potential to move or at least shift the orientation of smaller human elements, such as hand and foot bones.

The impact of larger fossorial taxa, such as among the Rodentia (including gophers), Lagomorpha (including rabbits and hares), Mustelidae (weasel family), and Talpidae (mole family), upon site deposits is well known to archaeologists and geomorphologists (Bocek 1992; Gabet et al. 2003; Johnson 1989; Villa 1982). These taxa, with their large tunnel systems, potentially can displace even larger human bones. In some cases, this shifting can be marked, as in the case of a primary (and otherwise intact) individual burial from the Texas State Cemetery in which the left patella was discovered in the vicinity of the right hand (Dockall et al. 1996a). Bone displacement and loss from buried remains therefore cannot be assumed to have resulted from perimortem processes (trauma, etc.) where the potential exists for these taxa to have tunneled through a burial (see Fox 1984:39). Indeed, the same types of easily tunneled soil that attract these animal species also may attract individuals undertaking clandestine burial activities, with the frequent need for speed to avoid detection. Due to later infilling and tunnel collapse, the previous presence of burrows through a human burial may not be obvious during excavation. However, in some cases, the agent of disturbance may be made clear—down to a particular taxon—through the inclusion of faunal remains in the burial itself, such as a rodent skeleton recovered from casket fill (Dockall et al. 1996a:100).

Bioturbation should not be mistaken for the natural displacement of skeletal remains as the connective soft tissues decompose and disappear. It is impossible for a body decomposing in a direct soil burial not to undergo some kind of skeletal displacement as this process occurs and remains slowly have additional space to move. Sediment compaction from the burial fill pressing down also will shift the position of some elements, as may infilling sediments from water flow. Roksandic (2002) notes that skeletal displacement will be a function of gravity and the architecture of the available empty space but is also influenced by the placement of the element(s) relative to the sequence of decomposition and subsequent disarticulation: a hand placed flat on the bottom of the grave will have its individual elements undergo little displacement, but a hand placed over the abdominal area will undergo much greater displacement and perhaps disarticulation of individual elements. These effects may be multiplied within mass graves, particularly where bodies overlay other bodies, where the bulk of soft tissue is much greater, and where the potential for movement and disarticulation (and commingling) of individual elements increases.

Soil Staining

Bones tend to take on the color of the medium into which they are deposited, due to their porous, wicking structure and initially pale coloration. Specific types of staining caused by different mineral deposits, including iron and copper oxides, are frequently encountered on buried remains (Janaway 2008) and are covered elsewhere in this volume (Chapter 12). It is, however, an important and ubiquitous taphonomic clue as to the previous burial of a bone, for example, in dark topsoil that the bone surface has become stained dark brown, whether in patches or more uniformly (see Figure 12.2, Chapter 12, this volume). It is likely that organic compounds, in particular the tannins, are primarily responsible for this color change (Barbehenn and Constabel 2011). Carbon resulting from organic breakdown is also a likely source of bone darkening. Bones buried in highly oxidized red clay soils, however, also tend to take on reddish staining from this source of pigment. Nicholson (1996) also noted areas of pink or mauve staining on osseous remains due to mold growth, which also has been noted by the authors in other contexts. This process is highly variable and requires additional research into the color changes possible from mold growth and the durability of these changes in a burial setting after the mold has died.

Few data exist on the amount of time required for bone to take on environmental staining. Nicholson (1996) noted that in a taphonomic study of various whole, fleshed, or portions of various vertebrate species buried and recovered 7 years later, very delicate recovery methods were needed, since the bones frequently had taken on the color of the surrounding sediments within that interval. These included tiny bones from rodents and fish. In order to standardize taphonomic color data gathering, Munsell® Soil Color Charts (Kollmorgen Instruments Corporation 1994) should be used. Analysis of forensic cases with known intervals between the time of burial and recovery may reveal patterns regarding the rapidity of this process and its potential use in PMI estimation, even as a gross estimate, or to match remains with their depositional context.

Adipocere Formation

Buried remains are often associated with residual *adipocere* formation, or saponified fat tissue, which is sometimes referred to as grave wax. This substance normally ranges in color from white to gray to beige, and its consistency can range from soft and paste-like to more brittle and crumbly as it ages and dries (Ubelaker and Zarenko 2011). Adipocere develops from any body fat tissue under moist, anaerobic conditions (Takatori 2001). Chemically, neutral fat triglycerides hydrolyze into fatty acids, which are then converted into insoluble hydroxy and saturated fatty acids from the actions of anaerobic bacteria, including *Clostridium perfringens* (O'Brien and Kuehner 2007). Temperature plays a role (O'Brien and Kuehner 2007), although cooler temperatures do not seem to halt the process but simply slow it down (Kahana et al. 1999). It is not unique to bodies from one kind of depositional environment and sometimes forms in coffins (Ubelaker and Zarenko 2011), soil (Fiedler et al. 2009; Forbes et al. 2005), freshwater (O'Brien and Kuehner 2007), and saltwater (Kahana et al. 1999) environments. Once formed, adipocere can persist for centuries or millennia. Fiedler et al. (2009) found that adipocere persisted for 1600 years in the case of a Late Roman period infant buried in a stone sarcophagus near the Rhine River in Mainz, Germany. The seasonal changes in groundwater level meant that the environment ranged from moist to inundated. The adipocere had formed a hard, cement-like crust that aided the preservation of the skeletal remains. Adipocere formation also may account for the traces of apparent brain tissue contained in some crania from Windover Pond, Florida, United States, a large cemetery site in a wetland that dates back ca. 7000 BP (Stojanowski et al. 2002).

When dried, adipocere can form a light-colored, flaky scale on bones (see Figure 12.4, Chapter 12, this volume). Since it is not unique to terrestrial burial environments, it cannot be used as a taphonomic indicator of such. Its presence does imply deposition of the body in a protected environment (where soft tissues could not be consumed quickly by scavengers) with restricted access to oxygen (burial or water deposition). In otherwise porous, sandy soil, adipocere still may form and persist for decades at the bottom center of mass burials and/or where remains were contained in a sealed plastic bag for over three decades (pers. obs.).

The dynamics of bodies in mass burials undergoing decomposition processes (Chapter 3, this volume) are too numerous to discuss here, although the history of investigations of these scenes is described in Chapter 10. In general, the processes of decomposition are slowed for the main mass of bodies, but the overall taphonomic processes of bodies buried in soil still hold (soil staining of bone, root etching and invasion, settling, etc.) while others are enhanced (commingling). One important observation is the *feather edge effect* (Haglund 2002), where bodies deposited at the margins of mass burials tend to decompose and skeletonize more rapidly than the bodies in the central mass of remains, where the pooling of decomposition liquid can promote adipocere formation at the bottom center of the mass (pers. obs.). Bodies at the periphery also have a greater surface area in direct contact with soil minerals, organisms, oxygen, and groundwater flow compared with bodies packed together in the center of mass, which likely leads to the more rapid skeletonization of the former. Individuals recovered from the same mass grave therefore might be in very different decomposition stages, including the degree of adipocere formation, and lacking contextual data, an analyst may assume that they came from two different burials entirely.

Effects of Plowing on Buried Remains

Plowing of agricultural fields both benefits and emperils forensic anthropological practice. Shallow burials in fields are often impacted by plowing, and the dispersal of bone across the freshly plowed (and therefore plant-denuded) surface makes the central burial location potentially much easier to locate. This mechanized destructive force, of course, also damages the very remains that are being sought, disperses them over a wide area and thereby increases the time required for and difficulty of recovery, and may cause damage that could be mistaken for perimortem trauma. Plowing also mixes the topsoil, which may destroy evidence of the burial feature and the information that it may contain in terms of the tools used to excavate it, its postdepositional history, and other data such as footprints or other impressions (Hochrein 2002). Agricultural fields also may be an attractive place for clandestine burials, despite their lack of cover, since these events frequently take place at night (see Chapter 10, this volume). The lack of tree root systems and expected deep soil allows for more rapid grave digging, and perpetrators may expect that later plowing will obscure any surface signs of digging. Plowing effects upon bone therefore are not an infre-quent taphonomic process.

The direct damage to skeletal remains caused by plowing has three main sources: the impact of the plowing, harrowing, seeding, or other multibladed heavy implement dragged through the soil; the abrasion caused by dragging through sediments; and the crush-ing caused by the wheels of the traction vehicle pulling the implement. The first type of postmortem damage can be reflected in heavy fragmentation of the bone or by visible gouges into the bone caused by both blunt and relatively sharp metal surfaces (Haglund et al. 2002). Abrasion caused by movement through the soil is similar to that caused by trampling and other accidental effects leaving surface striations (see Table 5.1; Andrews and Cook 1985; D'Errico and Villa 1997; Fisher 1995). Heavy machinery rolling over bone may cause massive crushing damage, which may get obscured by subsequent fragment dispersal.

Dispersal of remains is an equally important effect of plowing. While the increased recovery effort and loss of some remains are problem enough, the dredging up of bone from a burial context to the surface also changes its major set of taphonomic characteristics. Bone in a burial environment is exposed to the common taphonomic processes discussed in this chapter, including plant root invasion, soil staining, and acidic soil erosion. Subsequent sur-face exposure and its associated taphonomic processes, including weathering and scavenger gnawing, may overwrite those earlier taphonomic alterations and obscure the prior history of burial. Plowed remains therefore likely combine a suite of taphonomic characteristics from both buried and surface regimes. Individual fragments or portions of remains buried at the same time but from this type of context may display markedly different preservation due to these disturbances. Remains that have surfaced as a result of plowing may show a high degree of cracking, exfoliation, and sun-bleaching, while those that remained buried may be in a much better state of preservation. Context of recovery therefore is an important consideration when determining depositional history and PMI using taphonomic indica-tors, and such disparate taphonomic states in a single set of remains should not result in an automatic assessment that the remains came from multiple depositional episodes.

Odell and Cowan (1987) used an experimental setting to determine the mechanical plowing movement potential of archaeological artifacts, in this case stone tools painted for easier detection. They found in their own research (consistent with previous research on the topic) that the average recovery rate of surface objects from their large initial (n = 1000) buried sample was 5.6% over all runs. This percentage may not reflect the sur-face recovery rate for bone, given that bone when fragile will likely be highly fragmented by plowing impacts and dragging, so the population of individual bone pieces will likely increase over time for plowed osseous items. Surface detection rates for bone fragments are not only likely decreased by their blending in with soil cover but also increased in cases where surface exposure leads to their sun bleaching (see Chapter 11, this volume) and thus increased visibility to survey teams. These small bleached fragments themselves may be nondiagnostic, but their presence on the surface may lead to larger diagnostic bones. Fragmented bone may have lighter internal surfaces relative to external surface staining, so these fragments also may stand out in contrast to dark topsoil. Odell and Cowan (1987) further noted a cumulative mean horizontal movement of their artifacts of over 2 m, with the site doubling in area as measured by the perimeter created by its farthest outliers after 12 plowing runs. A greater average displacement was noted in the primary axis of plowing. Haglund et al. (2002) noted in a case study from Cyprus that 23 years of plowing in a barley field had displaced most remains from a shallow burial, leaving only some right and left foot elements *in situ*. The dispersal of these remains may have been hindered by the temporary presence of leather footwear. Human skeletal remains were scattered a maximum of 32 m east–west and 14 m north–south. The local machinery plowed to a maximum depth of approximately 25 cm.

Special Natural Burial Environments

Some natural burial environments, while rare in forensic settings, pose particular suites of taphonomic characteristics that should be recognizable due to the presence of large amounts of preserved soft tissue typically associated with the skeletal remains. The excellent soft tissue preservation therefore makes these types of burials potentially mistakable, at least initially, for more recent remains and may attract initial concern from the public or law enforcement when encountered. In addition, natural mummification may occur rapidly, so naturally mummified remains are often encountered in forensic contexts (Galloway et al. 1989).

Mummification

There are two types of mummification: those due to artificial processes, most famously from ancient Egypt, and natural (Mayer 2012; Micozzi 1991). Artificial or deliberate mummification are done typically as part of an elaborate postmortem ritual in which the remains are displayed for some time after death. Natural mummification may occur in dry environments, such as after interment in sand or other very well-drained soils in arid climates and in dry, cold environments. For example, the mummies of Xianjiang, China, are the desiccated bodies of what appears to be a family of four, naturally mummified after being buried in the stony desert of northwest China (Hadingham 1994). Similarly, naturally mummified bodies have been found in environments as diverse as the Peruvian and Argentinian highlands and Mammoth Cave in Kentucky, United States, while cemeteries in Guanajuato, Mexico, are well known for their naturally mummified remains (Iserson 1994:216). Furthermore, modern forensic case reports abound of naturally mummified remains in homes where the air is very dry or near fireplaces or heaters, or outdoors in desert environments (Galloway et al. 1989).

Ice Burials

The long-term preservative effects of frozen environments upon soft tissue are well known (Micozzi 1991, 1997) and require little elaboration here. The most famous recent example of this process is the 1991 find of the frozen remains later dubbed "Ötzi" at an altitude over 3200 m in the Italian Alps. These remains have been radiocarbon dated to ca. 3300 BC (Chalcolithic Age), with associated artifacts confirming this date (Ruff et al. 2006). Discovered melting out of a glacier, these largely intact although desiccated remains were found in such good condition that they were mistaken initially for a recent alpinist death. The excellent preservation included the internal organs and recognizable stomach contents (Gostner et al. 2011) and soft-tissue evidence of the cause of death (an arrow wound to the left shoulder) and an unrelated hand wound (Vanzetti et al. 2010). Preservation was similarly excellent for fragile associated artifacts, including leather and woven grass clothing and equipment items. It is likely that long-term preservation in such settings is greatly enhanced by actual covering by snow/ice to exclude scavengers and greater tissue loss from decomposition during thawing spells and wind abrasion. The slowly degrading sets of exposed remains from recent alpinist deaths among those attempting Mount Everest, exposed to sun and wind, are testament to the potential of these taphonomic processes. Clearly, in more benign conditions over forensic PMIs, large amounts of soft tissue preservation are expected in these environments. Recent cases of note include the separate finds of two WWII aviators who crashed on a glacier in 1942 California, United States (Stekel 2010), and who were identified by the Joint Prisoner of War/Missing in Action Accounting Command's Central Identification Laboratory, Hawaii.

Bog Burials

Bogs (wetlands characterized by the accumulation of decomposing plant remains, typically mosses of the genus *Sphagnum*) also have the potential to preserve soft tissue long term and thus cause archaeological or historical remains to be mistaken for remains of forensic interest (Brothwell et al. 1990). These remains may be encountered by accident or through commercial activities including peat harvesting. The bog burial environment is characterized by acidic water high in tannins, aerobic conditions, and large scavenger exclusion. These factors combine to allow excellent preservation of soft tissue (and organic artifacts), with skin tanning into a leather-like consistency, lesser preservation of internal organs, and demineralization of osseous elements (Brothwell et al. 1990; Micozzi 1991; Stødkilde-Jørgensen et al. 2008). Adipocere formation also is common in these environments (Evershed 1992). Deliberate burial (as opposed to simply falling into a bog and becoming buried naturally over time) apparently is a necessary ingredient for preservation, since so few animal bog bodies are known from the same European contexts that have yielded many human examples (Wilkinson et al. 2006). Ancient bog bodies also tend to be accompanied by a suite of other characteristics including frequent lack of clothing, ligatures from strangulation, and other signs of perimortem trauma (Brothwell et al. 1990). Context, including accompanying artifacts, may remove remains of this origin from further forensic consideration.

Cemetery Remains

Cemetery remains are frequently encountered from disturbed recent contexts and are turned into law enforcement for subsequent evaluation by forensic anthropologists. These cases can form a significant portion of the human remains received in a medical examiner setting (pers. obs.), perhaps increased in regions with longer settlement histories and large amounts of older cemeteries that may not have been as well-marked as more recent burials. Construction projects, natural erosion, deliberate vandalism, or purposeful theft in order to obtain human remains for religious activities (see Chapter 8, this volume) all may expose cemetery remains. Fortunately, the taphonomic characteristics typical of coffin burials are some of the best-researched in forensic anthropology (Berryman et al. 1991, 1997; Nawrocki 1995; Rogers 2005; Schultz 2012; Schultz et al. 2003; Sledzik and Micozzi 1997), likely due in part to the practical importance of and frequent need to distinguish remains of this origin from the remains of recent homicide victims.

General Effects of the Coffin Environment

Coffins do not present a constant burial environment, since coffins also proceed through a process of gradual breakdown. Their temporary nature is especially true in the case of wooden coffins. The coffin environment initially provides physical protection for a set of remains, which may have been given additional protection from decomposition by previous embalming. This physical protection may include initial prevention of direct contact with burial sediments and their destructive biota, including plant roots, bacteria, fungi, and other organisms that would utilize the remains as a source of nutrients or disturb them through fossorial activity (see Haglund 1991; Rodriguez and Bass 1985). Buried remains may decompose more slowly than those exposed on the surface not just due to physical protection from necrophagous insects and microorganisms but also because the temperature underground may be lower (Rodriguez and Bass 1985). Coffins, of course, need not be buried at all but may be placed in an above-ground mausoleum, further hindering the biological attack upon remains. In many of the United States (including Massachusetts, where one of the authors [JTP] is based), a concrete burial vault often is required by the cemetery to protect the coffin itself and to prevent subsidence of the burial fill. Vaulting was also practiced in some locations historically, where additional wooden planks were placed over the top of the coffin for protection (sometimes referred to as a "dug vault"; see Taylor et al. 1986:4). The main shaft was excavated wider than the coffin, and then a smaller hole was excavated at the base that fit the coffin more snugly. The resulting earthen shelves on either side supported planks that covered the coffin and afforded some immediate protection from the burial fill (Davidson 2012; Pye 2007; see also Fox 1984; Taylor et al. 1986). Locally obtained stone (e.g., sandstone) was used to create vaulted crypts in some nineteenth-century rural cemeteries, although in some cases, these had the unusual characteristic of covering in-ground burials (see Fox 1984:15, 53).

Beginning in the late twentieth century, vaults have been manufactured from many materials, including copper, aluminum, and fiberglass (Mitford 1998). So-called coffin liners were used throughout the nineteenth century and usually consisted of plain wooden boxes (frequently made of pine) meant to encase and protect the often ornate caskets typical of the time. Sometimes these were the original boxes used to ship the caskets, which were typically buried with the caskets out of convenience (Dockall et al. 1996b; Gadus et al. 2002; Habenstein and Lamers 2001; Holloway 1986:74). These boxes were more common after commercially manufactured coffins became widely available (i.e., after the turn of the twentieth century), and they are less common in rural communities where most coffins were built locally and where outer boxes may have been viewed as a waste (Dockall et al. 1996b:160; Gadus et al. 2002:33). Any type of additional protection to coffin burials may increase the PMI over which remains appear to have been interred recently. The gradual breakdown of a coffin allows the infiltration of sediments and the growth of plant roots into the interior (Schultz et al. 2003), both of which can now be in direct contact with remains, and the removal of a barrier to physical disturbance. The collapse of the lid, whether gradual or abrupt, places the remains under the stress of the mass of sediments crushing down and causing warping and fracturing.

Coffins also allow the breakdown of remains in an environment where evidence of this breakdown may be preserved. The repeated waterlogging and drying of bone may cause surface cracking, and acidic dissolution of the mineral component may leave the bone with a friable, chalky texture that easily disintegrates further upon handling (Berryman et al. 1991, 1997; Schultz et al. 2003; Rogers 2005). These two processes may not differ greatly from those undergone by bones buried in direct contact with soil, except bones in the latter environment are much more likely to lose the evidence of these processes as their surfaces exfoliate and the flakes adhere to the soil matrix or break down further to become indistinguishable (macroscopically) from the sediments. A bone recovered from a burial in direct contact with the soil is far more likely to exhibit a pattern of generalized erosion caused by multiple taphonomic processes due to the loss of surface layers (Fernández-Jalvo and Andrews 2003). In some cases, such as those where the burials are adjacent to a high water table (e.g., a bayou), the collapse of the casket and subsequent infill with inundated soil result in skeletal remains that have essentially melded with the wooden casket lid or bottom (e.g., Bond et al. 2002:113), making recovery difficult.

Coffin Wear

The patterned, localized destruction of some portions of a skeleton brought about by contact with a coffin floor is referred to as *coffin wear* (Rogers 2005; Schultz 2012; Schultz et al. 2003). These changes naturally take a significant passage of time to occur, making their direct observation difficult, so the exact processes are largely theoretical. Some portions of a skeleton in a coffin, once most soft tissue decomposition has occurred, naturally come into direct contact with the hard coffin floor. These logically include the posterior portions of several elements, including the occipital portion of the cranium, the vertebral spines/arches, the scapulae, the pelvis, and the limb bones (Berryman et al. 1991, 1997). Settling may be more variable for other elements, and the feet may be better protected due to the presence of leather footwear (see "Boot/Glove Taphonomy" section). The portions of the elements in contact with the floor may be attacked preferentially by the acids formed in pooling water within the coffin, leaving them in a weakened state. These portions may lose relatively flat patches of bone that sometime have a sheared appearance. Logically, the most probable portions of the skeleton to develop coffin wear are portions of bones least likely to rotate while settling and to remain with the same portions in contact with the coffin floor throughout burial. Dockall et al. (1996b:212) theorized that vibrations from a nearby train track may have contributed to coffin wear at the Phillips Memorial Cemetery in Texas through mechanical erosion.

The innominates and femora in particular may be least likely to rock from their initial relative positions due to their positions in the body and their overall morphology. The posterior surfaces of the ilia provide a broad, flat surface for stable positioning, from which it would be difficult to rotate once resting in this aspect. Figure 5.5 illustrates matching areas of coffin wear on the posterior iliac crests of paired innominates. The greatest degree of cortical erosion is concentrated where these elements would have lain flat against the coffin floor, and the missing portions of bone have a sheared appearance. Similarly, femora

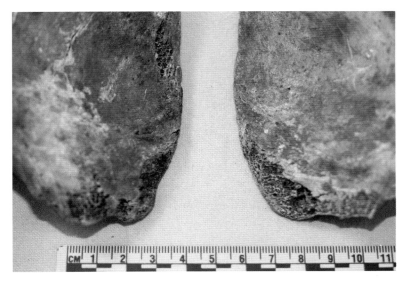

Figure 5.5 Coffin wear on posterior surfaces of iliac crests; historical context, Massachusetts. Note the flat, sheared appearance to the damaged areas.

present a stable configuration with the condyles providing two widely spaced points on the distal end and the head/neck projecting medially on the proximal end. A great deal of bone erosion or coffin contents settling/disruption must occur for the femur to be easily dislodged from this configuration once these points are resting flat on the coffin floor. Figures 5.6 through 5.9 illustrate matching areas of coffin wear on paired femora. Damage to the proximal ends (Figures 5.6 and 5.7) appears on the posterior head and trochanter areas.

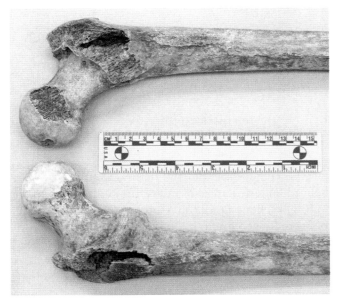

Figure 5.6 Coffin wear on posterior surfaces of proximal femora; historical context, Massachusetts. Note the matching areas of missing bone to the posterior proximal ends.

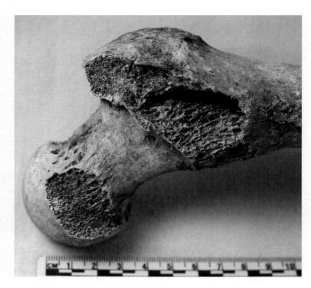

Figure 5.7 Detail of coffin wear on posterior surface of right proximal femur; historical context, Massachusetts. Note the flat, sheared appearance to the damaged areas.

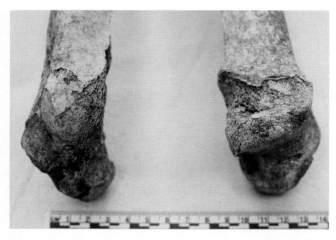

Figure 5.8 Coffin wear on posterior surfaces of distal femora; historical context, Massachusetts. Note the flat, sheared appearance to the damaged condyles.

Damage to the distal ends (Figures 5.8 and 5.9) in this example has completely removed the condyles, leaving behind flattened areas of bone. The remaining portions of these femora are in relatively good to excellent condition. Coffin wear, however, can appear on any element that comes to rest on the coffin floor, but it has more time to accrue if that element is not changing its position through further subsidence. For example, Schultz et al. (2003:145) illustrate coffin wear on the dorsal surfaces of articulated metacarpals.

Warping of skeletal remains in coffins is likely caused largely by the same factors as coffin wear (weakening of the bone with moisture/acidic attack, combined with contact with the hard coffin floor), with the increased importance of the mass of sediments pushing downward on remains in collapsed coffins (Schultz et al. 2003). Warping may be particularly

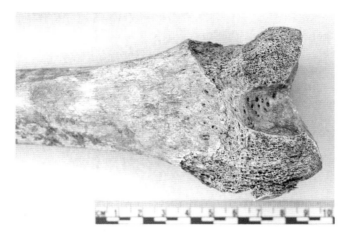

Figure 5.9 Coffin wear on posterior surfaces of a distal right femur; historical context, Massachusetts. Note the flat, sheared appearance to the damaged condyles.

prominent on the cranium, given its relatively weak structure relative to its size, combined with the small amount of soft tissue that must decompose prior to the bone coming in direct contact with the coffin floor. Cranial asymmetry caused by warping is also readily apparent, as opposed to warping of some other bones, including ribs. Cranial warping may be accompanied by signs of water ring formation and poorer preservation on the portions closest to the coffin floor, with relatively good preservation including soft tissue/hair on the portions farthest from the coffin floor. This type of taphonomic alteration, however, frequently occurs in non-coffin burials as well.

Staining

Skeletal remains from coffins often become darkly stained, including a chocolate-brown color. Schultz et al. (2003:142) note that this shade and the uniformity of staining are extremely rare in remains of forensic interest. While staining of bone typically occurs in non-coffin burials, this effect is likely intensified in coffin burials from the highly soluble organic tannins leached from the coffin wood. The same water-pooling effect that is likely instrumental in the formation of coffin wear will also concentrate around skeletal elements at the bottom of a coffin, with this organic acid leached from the coffin ceiling, walls, and floor. It is also possible that remains from non-coffin burials in sediments high in decomposing natural organic material can take on a similar coloration, since these organic compounds are produced by a wide variety of plant species. A variety of species, both hardwood and softwood, were used in wooden coffin construction, with some positive correlation between socioeconomic group and the use of more expensive hardwoods including walnut (*Juglans* spp.), mahogany (Meliaceae spp.), cherry (*Prunus* spp.), maple (*Acer* spp.), and chestnut (*Fagacea* spp.). Soft woods were most frequently used, especially pine (*Pinus* spp.) and sometimes poplar (*Populus* spp.) or willow (*Salix* spp.) (Holloway 1986; Pye 2007). Variations by region have been detected: species identified at the Texas State Cemetery also included bald cypress (*Taxodium distichum*), juniper (*Juniperus* spp.), and spruce (*Picea* spp.) (Dockall et al. 1996a), and the species identified at the Phillips Memorial Cemetery, TX, included ash (*Fraxinus* spp.) and possibly persimmon (*Diospyros virginiana*) (Dockall et al. 1996b).

All of these species potentially can leach tannins into groundwater, not just those darker in color, although in general woods that are lighter in color have fewer tannins (Barbehenn and Constabel 2011). Tannins are also highly concentrated in other parts of plants, including the leaves and nut shells, which is why tannins from natural decomposition easily can stain remains from non-coffin burials (Zelinka and Stone 2011). Schultz et al. (2003) further note that skeletal remains from above-ground crypt contexts may obtain a uniform orange-brown staining, possibly due to the combination of a lack of groundwater contact and the presence of embalming chemicals.

Signs of Previous Autopsy

Signs that remains previously had received alteration at autopsy or subsequent embalming are frequent taphonomic characteristics of modern cemetery burials (see Chapter 8, this volume). These are routinely performed where there is any question regarding the cause or manner of death of an individual, with large jurisdictions performing thousands of autopsies annually.

Signs of Previous Embalming

Embalming has a history spanning at least five millennia worldwide (Mayer 2012; Micozzi 1991) and has many ritual connotations, most arising from providing a vessel for the deceased in the afterlife or to legitimize ancestral claims by being able to produce said ancestors in a recognizable state. A variety of procedures and chemicals have been tried throughout history, with the usual goal of achieving antiseptic conditions to prevent putrefaction, at least long enough for burial rituals. Desiccation of tissues also aided in their preservation, as in deliberate attempts at mummification in ancient Egypt, Peru, and other cultures. In terms of potential forensic relevance, embalming in the United States became far more prevalent and professionalized during the Civil War, which generated large amounts of bodies, frequently during summer campaigns, and often at a great distance from their ultimate resting place. This factor coincided with a developing railway network that made rapid transportation feasible (Faust 2008). The elaborate, multistate funeral procession of Abraham Lincoln at the war's close also increased the interest in embalming as a standard practice (Faust 2008; Habenstein and Lamers 2001; Mayer 2012; Sledzik and Micozzi 1997). The goal was to have a viewable, natural-looking body that would last throughout funeral proceedings and beyond, with the illusion of incorruptibility extending into the interment period. Multiple chemical and injection methods were tried throughout the ensuing decades (Berryman et al. 1991, 1997), and some of these leave behind visible taphonomic alterations or artifacts that may allow the detection of previous embalming.

Eye caps are thin, oval devices used to hold eyelids shut on cadavers for funerary viewing purposes (Figure 5.10). While other inclusions from embalming may be easier to identify from their size and configuration, eye caps can shrivel in the ground and become highly stained (Figure 5.11). In this degraded state, they might be overlooked if they have been moved from an eye orbit. It is also possible that they may be mistaken for some other object of artificial or biological origin if not examined closely. Eye caps have been in use for several decades (Dennis Daulton, Dodge Chemical Company, pers. comm.). As listed in manufacturers' catalogs as early as 1903, eye caps were produced of wax-coated muslin.

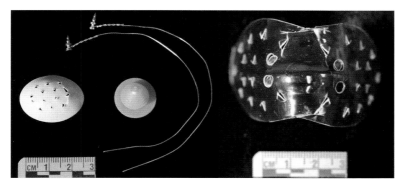

Figure 5.10 Modern (unused) embalming devices that may be recovered with recent remains. Left to right: eye cap, trocar button, needle barbs, and mouth former. (Images by Jade De la Paz.)

(a)   (b)

Figure 5.11 Eye cap, interior (a) and exterior (b) image; historical context, Massachusetts. Note the warping from burial.

At least by 1930, eye caps were being made out of aluminum and plastic/celluloid. Models today are made out of plastic (Mayer 2012).

Additional embalming artifacts, such as *trocar buttons* (Figure 5.10), have been recovered from historical burial excavations dating as early as 1940 (Dockall et al. 1996a:159), and Mayer (2012) notes the use of trocar buttons made of some material as early as the 1920s. Trocar buttons are used to seal the small incisions made during abdominal cavity embalming (Iserson 1994) and sometimes to seal gunshot wounds (Mayer 2012), although sutures can fill both of these roles. Trocar buttons resemble conical plastic screws with a flat top that appears similar to a two-hole button. The depressions are used to assist in the application of the device. One of the authors (JEB) has recovered plastic trocar buttons from burials dating to at least 1955 (Dockall et al. 1996a). A large curved needle and a rubber nipple found in separate burials at the Third New City Cemetery (TNCC) in Houston, Texas, were both hypothesized to represent embalming artifacts (Bond et al. 2002:157). Mouth formers (Figure 5.10), injector needles, sutures, and wax and cotton packing from cosmetic and restorative procedures (including to fill in the space left by donated organs) also may be found in burials (Berryman et al. 1991, 1997; Rogers 2005). Mouth formers likely came into use during the 1950s, and some early models were made of aluminum, with plastic ones also known from this early time (Dennis Daulton, Dodge Chemical Company, pers. comm.). Glue is also used frequently for cosmetic purposes (closing eyes and mouths) and to seal suture lines anywhere in the skin, and Mayer (2012) also notes the recent use of PVC pipes to replace long bones that have been removed for tissue donation. Other metal devices used to hold skeletal remains together include wires that are anchored into the maxilla and mandible (usually with a barbed point, termed *needle barbs*; Figure 5.10), then twisted together to keep the mouth closed (Mayer 2012). These, of course, would leave visible bone damage and possibly corrosion stains on these skeletal elements, even if the wires were no longer present. Small metal clamps also may be used to keep the post-autopsy sectioned calvarium attached to the remainder of the skull and prevent shifting. Schultz (2012:74) provides illustrations of these latter two metal devices recovered from field contexts. The recovery of all of these items associated with human remains should be a strong indicator of at least historical and more likely recent/modern burial origin of the associated human remains.

Berryman et al. (1991, 1997) note that the presence of patches of scalp and eyebrow hair, mold on the face, fabric impressions on skin, and cracked, desiccated skin "resembling old paint" is consistent with previous embalming and hence an original cemetery provenience. Embalming also can occasionally result in damage to skeletal remains. For example, damage to the cribriform plate may indicate use of cavity embalming of the cranium, in which a trocar is passed through the nostril or the medial corner of the eye and into the calvara, in order to replace gas and fluid with embalming chemicals (Iserson 1994:210; see also Berryman et al. 1991, 1997; Rogers 2005). Modern embalming typically also uses copious amounts of cosmetics, especially where noticeable skin changes have occurred from trauma or early decomposition (Mayer 2012), and it is possible that traces of these compounds may be found on adhering desiccated tissue.

Coffin Hardware

Assuming that no dated headstone or headstone that can be temporally seriated using stylistic motifs (Dethlefsen and Deetz 1966) is associated, the determination of the temporal and contextual origin of a set of buried remains is often aided by its other associated artifacts (Haglund 2001; Menez 2005). Forensic archaeological analysis and techniques go hand in hand with the forensic anthropological analysis of human remains in order to determine their potential origins. Thus, the professional recovery of remains is of paramount importance to their later identification. Even when the wooden portions of a coffin have completely decomposed, remnants of the metal hardware may remain behind in direct association with a buried skeleton (Bell 1990; Davidson 2010; Hacker-Norton and Trinkley 1984; Pye 2007; Springate 1998; Trinkley and Hacker-Norton 1984). Identifying the coffin hardware from the late nineteenth and early twentieth centuries is particularly important, since more recent coffin burials are likely to be better preserved and associated much more clearly with artifacts denoting their recent, yet non-forensic, context. Once a wooden coffin has decomposed, it may not be immediately apparent that the skeletal remains encountered were not buried originally in direct contact with the soil. The remnant hardware and other artifacts may present vital information that the remains come from an earlier context (Table 5.2). Even with non-coffin burials, organic materials including leather and natural fabrics can persist for decades or longer, especially in waterlogged, anaerobic deposits or arid environments (Janaway 2002). Their remnants, along with the coffin hardware discussed later, may provide useful contextual and temporal data.

Professional headstone carving became a full-time occupation by 1830 in the United States (Dethlefsen and Deetz 1966), making it much easier to date burials from this time onward. Mass-produced coffin hardware became common in the United States starting

Table 5.2   General Temporal Assignments for Certain Types of Artifacts Found in Burials

Artifact Class	Description/Status	Probable Date
Handles	Swing bail	Before 1890
	Extension bar	1911 and later
Caplifters	Absent	Before 1890
	Present	1902 and later
Coffin studs	Absent	Before 1902
	Present	1902 and later
Screws	Present	Before 1900
	Absent	1900 and later
Design motifs	Intricate	Before 1900
	Simple	1900 and later (common after 1920)
Buttons	Bone	Before 1900
	Composite/plastic	1909 and later
Snaps	Absent	Before 1900
	Present	1900 and later

Source: Dockall, H.D. et al., *Home Hereafter: An Archaeological and Bioarchaeological Analysis of an Historic African-American Cemetery (41GV125)*, Reports of Investigations No. 5. Center for Environmental Archaeology, Texas A&M University, College Station, TX, 1996b:138, Table 34.

ca. 1850, and the various styles can provide a terminus post quem for dating purposes (Hacker-Norton and Trinkley 1984; Pye 2007; Pye et al. 2004, 2007; Springate 1998). This increase in decoration was part of a trend toward the "beautification of death" (Bell 1990), which also reached the lower classes through the relatively low cost of these items made possible by their mass production. Decorative hardware has even been recovered in large amounts from paupers' cemeteries, as at the mid-nineteenth century Uxbridge Almshouse Burial Ground in southeastern Massachusetts that was in use from 1831 to 1872 (Bell 1990), thus spanning this early period of standardization. Seventeen (55%) of the graves examined there included only wooden coffin fragments constructed with cut iron nails, a few screws, and common brass hinges. Fourteen (45%), however, also contained decorative hardware fittings (see below, in this section), and two of these also included viewing windows (see below) (Bell 1990:61). Most coffins were determined to be hexagonal in overall form. Sixteen of the graves also were given uninscribed marker stones of granite quarry spalls or unmodified fieldstone (Bell 1990:61), and one had an inscribed (limestone) headstone.

Similarly, the TNCC, located in Houston's historic "Freedman's Town" and used variously as a pauper's, city (public), and hospital cemetery between 1879 and ca. 1910, yielded a large variety of coffin hardware. Despite the fact that only 79.6% of 446 possible burial features yielded identifiable human skeletal remains (mostly in very poor condition), excavations at the TNCC yielded 56 types of handles, 14 styles of caplifters, 43 kinds of thumbscrews, 27 types of escutcheons, 31 types of plaques, and 7 additional kinds of ornaments, as well as 14 styles of viewing window (Bond et al. 2002:151, Table 25; F-223–227). In summary, traces of coffin hardware can be recovered even in the extreme circumstances of minimal decorative elaboration, and more elaborate fittings are common even among burials of paupers, indigents, wards of the state, and other disenfranchised people (see also Dockall et al. 1996a).

However, dating of cemetery burials is context dependent. Hacker-Norton and Trinkley (1984) and Dockall et al. (1996b) suggest that the coffin hardware found in rural community cemeteries may not be especially useful in securing a date for burials. In the late nineteenth and early twentieth centuries in particular, conservative tastes, affordability, availability of the latest styles, and wholesale buying of large lots by local funeral vendors may have influenced the coffin and associated hardware styles in rural burials, such that rural communities may have used less expensive, outdated styles relative to their urban counterparts. This may also hold true when relative dating is applied to coffin shape. Hexagonal coffins, along with those tapered to the feet, typically date to an earlier period than rectangular caskets (Bell 1990; Dockall et al. 1996b; Rose and Santeford 1985; although see Earls et al. 1991 for early examples of rectangular caskets). However, rural communities, particularly in the southern United States, frequently preferred traditional coffin designs for nostalgic ("like what Father had"; Hacker-Norton and Trinkley 1984:44), financial, logistical, ethnic, and stylistic reasons.

Hacker-Norton and Trinkley (1984), in their study of early coffin hardware in the United States, list multiple major categories of metal coffin hardware commonly mass-produced by multiple manufacturers. These are the following:

1. *Handles* were attached around the exterior perimeter and used for carrying the coffin and therefore had to be both durable and projecting. Historically, there have been two categories of handles: bars and swing bails. Both types are affixed to the coffin with one or more lugs. Double lug short bar handles, for example, may consist of two matching metal alloy brackets (lugs) (Figure 5.12) holding an outthrust bar, which could have many configurations (including cylindrical, square, or octagonal cross sections or rope-shaped) and could be made of metal or wood. The brackets were attached to the sides of the coffin with screws or in some cases nails that were cinched on the inside. Extension bar handles also rely on bars as a carrying mechanism, but in this case, the handles typically run the length and width of the casket,

Figure 5.12 Example of a metal bracket from a handle, which held one end of a short bar for the pallbearers; historical context, Massachusetts. Remnants of screws are present.

with corner and center lugs attaching the long bars to the walls. Swing bail handles are typically metal alloy handles that swivel from their attachment points on one or two lugs (Bond et al. 2002).

Notwithstanding decorative design, the basic handle type may help determine the age of the coffin burial. Hacker-Norton and Trinkley (1984:44) noted that swing bail handles were the most popular type prior to 1880, while short bar handles were popular between 1880 and 1920. Extension bars were uncommon prior to 1912 but were sold as early as 1877 (Hacker-Norton and Trinkley 1984:44–45).

Three handles per long side was a common configuration, and exceptions include cases where there were fewer pallbearers expected, out of economic necessity, or for child coffins, and the handles for the latter were often smaller overall. At the Texas State Cemetery, the number of handles used on each casket was correlated with handle type and design, ranging in number from four to eight (notably, all were adult burials, and most of the men exhumed were wards of the state at the time of their deaths; Dockall et al. 1996a). At Houston's TNCC, archaeologists recovered one to eight swing bail handles per coffin and four to six short bar handles per casket (Bond et al. 2002:151, Table 25). The regular spacing of these items often is retained in their archaeological context.

2. *Thumbscrews* and *escutchions* (*var.* escutcheons; thumbscrew plates) were used to attach the lid to the rest of the coffin and in this function eventually replaced the nails used previously. The thumbscrews, which did not require screwdrivers for application, were threaded through holes in the escutchions and drilled into the wood. These paired items were placed at regular intervals along the lid margin. Several researchers have found a link between the use of thumbscrews and escutchions versus date of interment and particular ethnic groups, suggesting that their occurrence in a burial may be used to provide temporal and cultural context (Bell 1990; Dockall et al. 1996b; Earls et al. 1991; Fox 1984; Orser et al. 1987; Taylor et al. 1986; Trinkley and Hacker-Norton 1984). Davidson (2000:244) noted that thumbscrews date back to around 1870 and that they became the primary type of screw fastener a decade or so later.

3. *Plates* (*var.* plaques) were attached usually to the center of the coffin lid and engraved/stamped with common memorial phrases or custom-engraved with more personal messages.

4. *Caplifters* were essentially knobs attached to moveable portions of the coffin lid in order to raise them during body preparation or for later viewing. Their usage must have been in conjunction with some kind of hinge configuration (Figure 5.13), although plainer coffins may have had hinges and no caplifter. Caplifters and thumbscrews may have been used interchangeably in some cases, and they are commonly associated with base plates or escutchions (Bond et al. 2002). Early caplifters were advertised as early as 1877 and became steadily more popular with the increasing popularity of embalming (Hacker-Norton and Trinkley 1984:50).

5. *Decorative studs* were usually stamped from tin and had small tacks soldered to their undersides. These were placed on the outside of the coffin and were employed in some cases to hide nails (Figures 5.14 through 5.16). Hacker-Norton and Trinkley (1984:47) suggested that studs indicate either a coffin made prior to 1900 or a homemade coffin.

Figure 5.13 Remnant of a metal coffin hinge; historical context, Massachusetts.

Figure 5.14 Remnant of coffin wood with detail of the former extent of a star-shaped metal decorative stud preserved; historical context, Massachusetts. The remaining metal stud is to the right. The corrosion products helped preserve this piece of wood.

6. *White metal screws* (Figure 5.17) and *tacks* (Figure 5.18) were used for decoration. These could also be employed on the inside of the coffin to attach the lining fabric (Bell 1990). "White metal" refers to multiple types of lead- or tin-based alloys that were frequently silver-plated. Other typical alloys included the metals antimony, copper, nickel, and zinc. The other decorative objects noted earlier were often made of these types of alloys, with handles and hinges also sometimes made of steel or brass for their greater durability. Corrosion of the softer alloys often helped preserve other coffin features, such as fabric impressions (Figure 5.19).

Coffin construction also frequently used iron/steel nails, which can sometimes be used as temporal indicators. Wire nails were first used in the 1860s and became very popular in the early 1890s in North America; cut nails were more common prior to the 1880s (Priess 1973). However, once mass production of coffins began, finished products could be stored

Figure 5.15 Remnant of metal coffin decorative stud; historical context, Massachusetts.

Figure 5.16 Matching metal coffin studs; historical context, Massachusetts.

for long periods, while outer boxes or coffin liners, due to their simple nature, were often built at the time of or shortly before burial. Thus, cut and wire nails can occur in the same feature, particularly in cases where the coffin and the shipping container or outer box were built at different times (Bond et al. 2002:153). In contrast to nails, white metal screws were more popular at the end of the nineteenth century (Dockall et al. 1996b; Earls et al. 1991; Hacker-Norton and Trinkley 1984).

The corrosion products from the nails frequently seeped into the surrounding wood, aiding in the preservation of a small wood fragment while the remainder of the coffin

Figure 5.17 Example of a highly corroded screw surrounded by remnant portions of coffin wood; historical context, Massachusetts. The screw head is to the left. The metal oxides have helped preserve the surrounding wood.

Figure 5.18 Examples of matching metal coffin tacks; historical context, Massachusetts. These could have been used to attach fabric lining or as exterior decoration.

wood decomposed. These wood fragments or even just iron rust stains in the matrix might be all that remains of a plain wooden box coffin lacking in decorative fixtures or an outer box (coffin liner), as in either case, the lid may lack hinges and may have been simply nailed shut (e.g., Dockall et al. 1996b). An example of a coffin wood fragment held together by impregnating rust (Figure 5.20) shows the typical individual irregular shape, and collapse of the coffin during its decomposition might skew any regular pattern to their positioning.

Figure 5.19 Remnant fabric preserved by impregnating corrosion products from soft metal coffin decorative motif; historical context, Massachusetts.

Figure 5.20 Example of a highly corroded iron nail surrounded by remnant portions of coffin wood; historical context, Massachusetts. The nail head is to the left. The iron oxide has helped preserve the surrounding wood.

This type of preservation of a small "island" of wood by corrosion products of nails shows up consistently in coffin contexts from historical cemeteries in Massachusetts, but it is not seen on similar nails from contemporaneous houses that have been incorporated into site deposits after their collapse (E. Bell, Massachusetts Historical Commission, pers. comm.). This preservational difference may have to do with the immediate burial of the coffin nails in a damp, largely anoxic environment.

Additional functional (versus decorative) coffin hardware types may include metal closures, corner braces, casket rests, hinges, latches, corrugated fasteners, and box hooks (Bond et al. 2002). Closures were used to attach the sides of the coffin to the headboard, while corner braces hold the walls together. Casket rests were metal separators located on the bottom of the coffin/casket, designed to allow removal of the straps used to lower the coffin into the outer box during the burial. Hinges of various sizes and designs were used on coffin and casket lids and on viewing windows and viewing window covers. Latches were sometimes installed on viewing windows to allow the glass to slide open, allowing access to the decedent. Corrugated fasteners consist of flat corrugated strips of metal used to hold two pieces of wood together and date to the turn of the twentieth century. Box hooks, which are simple U-shaped wire loops used as handles on the outer box, have been recovered from at least one historical cemetery (Bond et al. 2002).

Other Artifacts, Alterations, and Burial Characteristics

Period clothing, even in situations where fabric is not preserved, can give important clues as to original provenience (Janaway 2002; Schultz et al. 2003). These items include buttons, which are often preserved after the fabric has decomposed or otherwise been made unidentifiable (e.g., see Fox 1984:12 for a description of a U.S. Army button found in a known Confederate sympathizer's grave). Certain types of buttons, such as those made of bone, porcelain, celluloid, Bakelite, shell, and molded plastic, were used during specific periods and can be used to date burials (Luscomb 1967; Peacock 1973). Snap fasteners typically indicate a post-1900 burial (Rose and Santeford 1985:43). Cufflinks, collar studs, bow ties, snaps, or lapel, lace, collar, or winding (shroud) pins also may be indicative of historical (i.e., non-forensic) burials (e.g., Bond et al. 2002; Dockall et al. 1996a; Rose and Santeford 1985). Clothing and/or shoes that have been cut in the back may suggest deliberate (cemetery) burial, as this was often done to ease dressing of the corpse (Berryman et al. 1991, 1997; Iserson 1994; Rogers 2005).

Other items that may be found in association with coffin-derived remains include those normally left at cemeteries as offerings (Rogers 2005; pers. obs.). These include fragmented flower vases, planters, bud holders, or small flags. Other personal votive offerings are highly variable (Elliott 1990), but some may have cultural or ethnic significance. For example, ceramics (especially bowls), eating utensils, blue beads, pierced coin jewelry, eggs, broken glass, iron pots, and milk and medicine bottles have been tied to African American and Southern U.S. folk traditions (Bond et al. 2002; Dockall et al. 1996a,b; Jordan 1982; Rose and Santeford 1985). Glass and ceramics can frequently be dated by composition, design, or manufacture, allowing burials to be dated accordingly (e.g., see Lehner 1980; Santeford 1981). Although it may be difficult to ascertain the origin or purpose of some items found in the grave shaft, they may not have been associated with the deceased person or the mourners at all, but rather with cemetery employees or cemetery surrounds. For example, a liquor bottle was discovered in a grave shaft at the Texas State Cemetery

(Dockall et al. 1996a), while fence pickets, fencing wire, and concrete "slump tests" (the last being related to road construction) were recovered from grave fill at the Phillips Memorial Cemetery (Dockall et al. 1996b).

Lining fabrics and various types of cushion fillings may be recovered in historic cemetery burials (Bell 1990; Dockall et al. 1996a; Taylor et al. 1986). For example, at the Philips Memorial Cemetery in La Marque, Texas, five of the caskets excavated included a layer of southern hard pine (*Pinus taeda*) shavings (Dockall et al. 1996b:112; see also Bell 1990; Fox 1984; Parrington and Roberts 1990). The inclusion of pine shavings in close proximity to the body may affect preservation due to increased acidity in the casket's micro-environment (see "Staining" and "Acidic Soil Corrosion" sections). Evans (1963) suggested that bodies buried in coffins with wood shavings decomposed faster than those buried in the soil because the temperature rose due to moisture in the wood shavings and subsequent fermentation of the organic material. Other organic materials, such as hay or grass, may have been used to line caskets as well (Bell 1990).

Dental attrition and style of restorations are also an important source of information in determining the burial era of a body (Rogers 2005). Dental attrition in cultures where the diet was largely derived from stone-ground grain, with constant mastication of its inherent fine grit, was much more rapid than in the modern era with highly processed foods mostly lacking this inclusion (Brothwell 1981).

Lifesaving devices (or remnants thereof) may also be found in association with coffin burials. These devices, designed to warn the living that a buried individual was still alive, became fashionable in the Victorian era, with the earliest such device patented in 1843 (Habenstein and Lamers 2001). At a time when modern medicine was in its infancy and death from communicable disease was common, the possibility of being buried alive seemed plausible (Tebb and Vollum 1905). Variants included bells or whistles that sounded above ground, speaking tubes running to the surface, electrical alarms, and flags and lamps that signaled the living. A possible accoutrement of a lifesaving device was found in an iron coffin from the Texas State Cemetery, in the form of a diamond-shaped hole in the lid of the coffin at approximately the area of the right hand (Dockall et al. 1996a). Another possible lifesaving device remnant (a circular rubber ring in the vicinity of a hole in the casket that correlated to the location of the hands) was found with a coffin from the TNCC in Houston, Texas (Bond et al. 2002:F-218). Embalming becoming common throughout this period gradually allayed this fear, and these items were largely discontinued.

In some cases, characteristics of the burial may assist in determining its origin (e.g., clandestine versus cemetery). In many Christian societies, cemetery burials are oriented with the head to the west (but see Fox 1984:43 for an example of an accidental juxtaposition of an infant in a rectangular coffin). This practice is tied to the idea that the dead will rise and face the second coming of Jesus Christ on Judgment Day (Jordan 1982:30; Yalom 2008:12). However, this rule does not always hold, as Hispanic burial grounds in the United States frequently have many burial axes; an east–west axis holds no particular meaning in Hispanic culture (Jordan 1982:70). Upside-down burials have been linked to suicides, deserters, witches, and the morally reprehensible (see Jordan 1982; Robertson 1984:155, cited in Taylor et al. 1986:42), while north–south oriented burials have been linked to criminals and suicides (Jordan 1982). In addition, folk tradition holds that husbands are buried to the south (i.e., at the right hand) of their wives, mimicking the positions of the bride and groom at the wedding altar (Jordan 1982; Fox 1984); thus, the sex of individuals, as determined via anthropological analysis, of two side-by-side burials should be considered in relation to this tradition (although see Fox 1984:40 for a historical exception to this rule). High rates of infant mortality prior to the mid-twentieth century may result in a large number of fetal and infant remains in unmarked historical cemeteries, yielding another indicator that the remains in question may not be of forensic interest. In some cases, these infant burials may be clustered in a separate section of a family or local cemetery (Fox 1984:45).

Spatial patterning of multiple graves may also be an indicator of burial origin. Modern commercial cemeteries sell plots in orderly rows, but this type of rigid organization did not always exist. Southern folk cemeteries and family cemeteries frequently may have overlapping burials, clusters of graves, or staggered rows, while early church cemeteries typically show more linear organization (Deetz 1977; Jordan 1982; Taylor et al. 1986). These types of burial characteristics may be useful in determining burial origin when human remains are encountered in an unknown context, as early colonial, folk, and small family cemeteries may have become lost over time, with headstones removed for use in local building projects or to make way for construction (prior to laws forbidding such activities; Baker et al. 2000; Fox 1984; Gadus et al. 2002; Taylor et al. 1986). In other cases, grave markers may have been made of wood, bricks, shells, or groupings of natural, unmarked stones. Wooden markers may decompose entirely or be carried away by collectors, and the bricks, shells, or stones may become scattered over time or overlooked by the casual observer as natural occurrences (Fox 1984:31, 37; 51; Gadus et al. 2002; Jordan 1982; Taylor et al. 1986; Yalom 2008:129). In still other cases, graves may have been left unmarked deliberately for socioeconomic, status, or religious reasons, as in possible slave burials at the Varnell Cemetery in Texas (Gadus et al. 2002:25; see also Yalom 2008:34, 115), early missionary burials of converted Native Americans, and early Quaker burials (i.e., predating 1850) (Yalom 2008:11).

Spatial organization may vary widely depending on the type and use dates of a given cemetery. In the 1600s and early 1700s, church cemeteries in the northeastern part of the United States were often overcrowded, with later burials intruding on earlier ones and with little regard for tracking each individual buried there. Excavations in these areas may reveal haphazard or erratic burial spacing. Family plots with individual burials became customary in the late 1700s, while the tradition of linear, organized, permanent burial plots in formally designated cemeteries did not take hold until the early 1800s (Deetz 1977). Small family cemeteries persisted in rural areas well into the late 1800s and early 1900s (Fox 1984).

On a larger scale, the larger landscape (including relative location) should also be considered when assessing the origin of buried human remains. Cemeteries are frequently found on hilltops, for example, and certain types of plants have historically been associated with cemeteries (including evergreens, irises, azaleas, and willows; Gadus et al. 2002:29; Jordan 1982; Taylor et al. 1986:14; Yalom 2008:113, 118, 135). Green spaces may persist next to public buildings and facilities for decades without any particular known reason; such suspicions can often be verified through tax and property records (Rogers 2005). Remnants of wooden, stone, or wrought iron fences may also be found on the margins of many "forgotten" cemeteries (Fox 1984; Taylor et al. 1986).

In some cases, the type of remains found, in connection with current land usage, may be helpful in ascertaining forensic significance. As Rogers (2005) pointed out, hospitals historically may have used particular locations within their cemeteries to dispose of amputated limbs, so a discovery of limbs from more than one person may be related to medical waste rather than homicide.

Coffin Viewing Windows

One particular type of coffin popular in the latter half of the nineteenth and early twentieth century featured a window for formal viewing with the coffin lid closed, allowing mourners to view the deceased individual's face. Viewing windows came in a variety of sizes and shapes (e.g., 10 styles were discovered at Houston's TNCC alone; Bond et al. 2002), and some were large enough to allow a view of a portion of the torso as well. Taylor et al. (1986:45) noted that viewing windows in infant coffins typically went the full length of the box, or nearly so. Viewing windows appeared as early as 1848 (Habenstein and Lamers 2001), were popular throughout the Victorian Era, and persisted into the early twentieth century. Springate (1998) notes that their use in the Southeastern United States ran from 1870 to 1918, and post-1878 in Ontario, Canada. These windows were commonly made of plate glass (Bell 1990) due to the stresses that would be exerted by grave fill.

Once this glass structure is breached, however, highly localized destructive taphonomic forces can be introduced to this portion of the remains (Owsley and Compton 1997). The glass allows condensation to collect on its inner surface; in fact, this phenomenon can often be viewed during the excavation process, as small amounts of air are trapped under the glass fragments. A particular taphonomic pattern of destruction of the skeletal elements under the window with relatively good preservation of the remaining elements may result. Following decomposition of the soft tissues, the trapped moisture, accompanied by the collapse and fracturing of the glass, can result in a crushing of the delicate bones of the upper body, including the sternum, ribs, vertebrae, and facial bones. This effect is compounded by the relatively thin cortex and high amount of cancellous tissue in the bones of the torso. These bones may all but disappear over decades of burial, leaving only a residue of organic material resembling bone meal (Bond et al. 2002; Dockall et al. 1996a). Fragments of plate glass will likely be found near their original position and in association with the skeletal remains, assuming sufficient excavation provenience controls are maintained.

Iron Coffins

Iron coffins present a distinct burial environment due to their durability as compared to wooden coffins and their greater ability to prevent other taphonomic agents (plant root invasion, fossorial vertebrates, acidic soil corrosion, etc.) from reaching skeletal remains. This artificial environment may be similar to the effects of burials in wet, iron-pan forming soils that have allowed excellent long-term preservation of organic materials in burial mounds due to the creation of anaerobic conditions (Breuning-Madsen et al. 2001). Owsley and Compton (1997) examined the preservation typical to cast iron coffin burials, which first came into widespread use with a mass-produced model introduced in 1848. These were replaced by sheet metal models in later years, with the cast iron models produced to around 1880. These iron models, curiously, usually contained glass viewing windows, thus at once providing a weak point in the structure that could allow the sudden introduction of multiple taphonomic forces to a localized portion of the remains despite the overall highly protective design.

Owsley and Compton (1997) note the overall excellent preservation of soft tissue and degradable artifacts (clothing and other personal items) by cast iron coffins. This is likely due to a combination of embalming and the anoxic microenvironment of the coffin, as seals were used when joining the lid to the base. The sealant used frequently was a mixture of ground lead and oil (Owsley and Compton 1997:523), which had the dual purpose of preserving the remains for viewing and preventing the venting of decomposition gases. The potential for excellent preservation makes burials of this type extremely problematic, since the remains may be mistaken for those of forensic interest. Once the coffin has been breached, often through the viewing window, the typical processes of decomposition set in. Owsley and Compton (1997:524) and Schultz et al. (2003:142) also note that the remains contained within are often stained dark/black, likely from mineral oxide leaching from the coffin. They do not note iron oxide (red rust) staining as typical.

Conclusions

No single suite of taphonomic characteristics are found on buried skeletal remains brought to or excavated by forensic anthropologists, since the circumstances of burial vary so widely in context and duration. These may include recent clandestine burials, modern coffin burials, historical or archaeological non-coffin burials, or burials where wooden coffins decomposed early. Similarly, wide differences in soil conditions and biological activity also greatly affect the ultimate state in which remains are recovered. To answer the question of the ultimate origin of a given set of remains (and with it, jurisdiction by a medical examiner's office or State archaeological agency), the accompanying burial contextual information, including artifactual evidence, is crucial and cannot be disregarded. Toward this goal, forensic archaeological field procedures and analysis of artifacts may play just as important a role as the taphonomic analysis of the skeletal remains.

Acknowledgments

The authors thank Brona Simon, Edward Bell, Jennifer Poulsen, and Jonathan Patton of the Massachusetts Historical Commission, Boston, MA, for their access to materials, bibliographic help, and photographic permission. Melissa Johnson Williams, executive director, American Society of Embalmers, and Dennis Daulton, Dodge Chemical Company, Cambridge, MA, are thanked for sharing their knowledge of the history of embalming devices. Thanks also go to Brianne Charles for her editorial assistance.

DoD Employee Statement

Dr. Baker has more than 20 years of field experience in academic, federal government, and cultural resource management areas, including field investigations and/or excavations in Vietnam, Laos, Cambodia, South Korea, France, Italy, Fiji, Jamaica, Texas, and New York. She also has worked on mass graves excavation and forensic analysis of remains in Iraq. Dr. Baker has three degrees in anthropology (B.A., M.A., and Ph.D.) from the University of Nebraska-Lincoln, Syracuse University, and Texas A&M University, respectively. Her work experience includes her current position as scientific advisor at the Defense Prisoner of War/Missing Personnel Office, as well as serving as a forensic anthropologist and laboratory manager at the Joint POW/MIA Accounting Command, Central Identification Laboratory, and as a project archaeologist and osteologist for Prewitt and Associates, Inc. and Espey-Houston and Associates. This chapter was written in the author's personal capacity and does not set forth any official positions, policies, or decisions of the Department of Defense or the U.S. Government.

References

Andrews, P. (1995) Experiments in taphonomy. *Journal of Archaeological Science* 22:147–153.

Andrews, P. and J. Cook (1985) Natural modifications to bones in a temperate setting. *Man* 20:675–691.

Armour-Chelu, M. and P. Andrews (1994) Some effects of bioturbation by earthworms (Oligochaeta) on archaeological sites. *Journal of Archaeological Science* 21:433–443.

Armour-Chelu, M. and P. Andrews (1996) Surface modification of bone from Overton Down, Wiltshire. In *The Experimental Earthwork Project 1960–1992*. Eds. M. Bell, P. J. Fowler and S. W. Hillson, pp. 178–185. Council for British Archaeology, Bootham York, U.K.

Bais, H. P., T. L. Weir, L. G. Perry, S. Gilroy, and J. M. Vivanco (2006) The role of root exudates in rhizosphere interactions with plants and other organisms. *Annual Review of Plant Biology* 57:233–266.

Baker, J. E., M. D. Freeman, and M. E. Blake (2000) *Historical Research and Archeological Investigations at the Williamson Creek Cemetery, 41TV1684, Travis County, Texas*. Technical Reports, Number 49, Prewitt and Associates, Inc., Austin, TX.

Barbehenn, R. V. and C. P. Constabel (2011) Tannins in plant-herbivore interactions. *Phytochemistry* 72:1551–1565.

Bell, E. L. (1990) The historical archaeology of mortuary behavior: Coffin hardware from Uxbridge, Massachusetts. *Historical Archaeology* 24:54–78.

Benninger, L. A., D. O. Carter, and S. L. Forbes (2008) The biochemical alteration of soil beneath a decomposing carcass. *Forensic Science International* 180:70–75.

Berryman, H. E., W. M. Bass, S. A. Symes, and O. C. Smith (1991) Recognition of cemetery remains in the forensic setting. *Journal of Forensic Sciences* 36:230–237.

Berryman, H. E., W. M. Bass, S. A. Symes, and O. C. Smith (1997) Recognition of cemetery remains in the forensic setting. In *Forensic Taphonomy: The Postmortem Fate of Human Remains*. Eds. W. D. Haglund and M. H. Sorg, pp. 165–170. CRC Press, Boca Raton, FL.

Bocek, B. (1992) The Jasper Ridge reexcavation experiment: Rates of artifact mixing by rodents. *American Antiquity* 57:261–269.

Bond, C. L., S. D. Hoyt, and E. Baxter (2002) *Archaeological Investigation Report Allen Parkway Village, 41HR886 Houston, Harris County, Texas*. Eds. E. R. Foster and L. A. Nance. PBS&J, Inc., Austin, TX.

Breuning-Madsen, H., M. K. Holst, and M. Rasmussen (2001) The chemical environment in a burial mound shortly after construction—An archaeological-pedological experiment. *Journal of Archaeological Science* 28:691–697.

Brothwell, D. R. (1981) *Digging up Bones* (3rd edn.). Cornell University Press, Ithaca, New York.

Brothwell, D. R., B. Gottlieb, and D. Liversage (1990) Radiographic and forensic aspects of the female Huldremose body. *Journal of Danish Archaeology* 9:157–178.

Casallas, D. A. and M. K. Moore (2012) High soil acidity associated with near complete mineral dissolution of recently buried human remains. *Proceedings of the American Academy of Forensic Sciences* 18:400–401.

Child, A. M. (1995) Microbial taphonomy of archaeological bone. *Studies in Conservation* 40:19–30.

Christensen, A. M. and S. W. Myers (2011) Macroscopic observations of the effects of varying fresh water pH on bone. *Journal of Forensic Sciences* 56:475–479.

Crow, P. (2008) Mineral weathering in forest soils and its relevance to the preservation of the buried archaeological resource. *Journal of Archaeological Science* 35:2262–2273.

D'Errico, F. and P. Villa (1997) Holes and grooves: The contribution of microscopy and taphonomy to the problem of art origins. *Journal of Human Evolution* 33:1–31.

Damann, F. E. (2010) *Human Decomposition Ecology at the University of Tennessee Anthropology Research Center*. Unpublished Ph.D. Dissertation, University of Tennessee, Knoxville, TN.

Davidson, J. M. (2000) The development of Freedman's Cemetery. In *Freedman's Cemetery: A Legacy of a Pioneer Black Community in Dallas, Texas* (Vol. 2). Eds. D. E. Peter, M. Prior, M. M. Green, and V. G. Clow, pp. 233–407. Report No. 21, Environmental Affairs Division, Archeology Studies Program, Texas Department of Transportation. Special Publication No. 6, Geo-Marine, Inc., Plano, TX.

Davidson, J. M. (2010) Keeping the Devil at bay: The shoe on the coffin lid and other grave charms in 19th and early 20th Century America. *International Journal of Historical Archaeology* 14:614–649.

Davidson, J. M. (2012) They laid planks 'crost the coffins: The African origin of grave vaulting in the United States. *International Journal of Historical Archaeology* 16:86–134. DOI: 10.1007/s10761-012-0170-5.

Deetz, J. (1977) In: *Small Things Forgotten: The Archeology of Early American Life*. Anchor Press/Doubleday, Garden City, New York.

De-la-Peña, C., V. D. V. Badri, Z. Lei, B. S. Watson, M. M. Branda, M. C. Silva-Filho, L. W. Sumner, and J. M. Vivanco (2010) Root secretion of defense-related proteins is development-dependent and correlated with flowering time. *The Journal of Biological Chemistry* 285:30654–30665.

Dethlefsen, E. N. and J. Deetz (1966) Death's heads, cherubs, and willow trees: Experimental archaeology in Colonial cemeteries. *American Antiquity* 31:502–510.

Dockall, H. D., D. K. Boyd, M. D. Freeman, R. L. Garza, K. E. Stork, and J. E. Baker (1996a) *Confederate Veterans at Rest: Archaeological and Bioarchaeological Investigations at the Texas State Cemetery, Travis County, Texas*. Reports of Investigations No. 107. Prewitt and Associates, Inc., Austin, TX.

Dockall, H. D., J. F. Powell, and D. G. Steele (1996b) *Home Hereafter: An Archaeological and Bioarchaeological Analysis of an Historic African-American Cemetery (41GV125)*. Reports of Investigations No. 5. Center for Environmental Archaeology, Texas A&M University, College Station, TX.

Duhig, C. (2003) Non-forensic remains: The use of forensic archaeology, anthropology, and burial taphonomy. *Science and Justice* 43:211–214.

Earls, A. C., C. R. Lintz, G. W. Gill, P. L. O'Neill, and W. N. Trierweiler (1991) *Investigations of Historic Cemeteries at O. H. Ivie Reservoir, Coleman, Concho, and Runnels Counties, Texas*. Mariah Technical Report No. 403. Mariah Associates, Inc., Austin, TX.

Elliott, J. R. (1990) Funerary artifacts in contemporary America. *Death Studies* 14:601–612.

Evans, W. E. D. (1963) *The Chemistry of Death*. Charles C Thomas, Springfield, IL.

Evershed, R. P. (1992) Chemical composition of a bog body adipocere. *Archaeometry* 34:253–265.

Faust, D. G. (2008) *This Republic of Suffering: Death and the American Civil War*. Vintage, New York.

Fernández-Jalvo, Y. and P. Andrews (2003) Experimental effects of water abrasion on bone fragments. *Journal of Taphonomy* 1:147–163.

Fiedler, S., F. Buegger, B. Klaubert, K. Zipp, R. Dohrmann, M. Witteyer, M. Zarei, and M. Graw (2009) Adipocere withstands 1600 years of fluctuating groundwater levels in soil. *Journal of Archaeological Science* 36:1328–1333.

Fisher, J. W. (1995) Bone surface modifications in zooarchaeology. *Journal of Archaeological Method and Theory* 2:7–68.

Fitzpatrick, R. W. (2008) Nature, distribution, and origin of soil materials in the forensic comparison of soils. In *Soil Analysis in Forensic Taphonomy*. Eds. M. Tibbett and D. O. Carter, pp. 1–28. CRC Press, Boca Raton, FL.

Forbes, S. L., B. H. Stuart, and B. B. Dent (2005) The effect of the method of burial on adipocere formation. *Forensic Science International* 154:44–52.

Fox, A. A. (1984) *A Study of Five Historic Cemeteries at Choke Canyon Reservoir, Live Oak and McMullen Counties, Texas*. Choke Canyon Series Vol. 9. Center for Archaeological Research, University of Texas, San Antonio, TX.

Gabet, E. J., O. J. Reichman, and E. W. Seabloom (2003) The effects of bioturbation on soil processes and sediment transport. *Annual Review of Earth and Planetary Sciences* 31:249–273.

Gadus, E. F., J. E. Baker, and A. E. Dase (2002) A mother left to mourn, archeological and historical investigations at a nineteenth-century family cemetery at the Jewett Mine. Reports of Investigations, Number 136. Prewitt and Associates, Inc., Austin, TX.

Galloway, A., W. H. Birkby, A. M. Jones, T. E. Henry, and B. O. Parks (1989) Decay rates of human remains in an arid environment. *Journal of Forensic Sciences* 34:607–616.

Garman, J. C. (1996) This church is for the living: An assessment of archaeological standards for the removal of cemeteries in Rhode Island and Massachusetts. *Northeast Historical Archaeology* 25:1–12.

Gill-King, H. (1997) Chemical and ultrastructural aspects of decomposition. In *Forensic Taphonomy: The Postmortem Fate of Human Remains*. Eds. W. D. Haglund and M. H. Sorg, pp. 93–108. CRC Press, Boca Raton, FL.

Gordon, C. G. and J. E. Buikstra (1981) Soil pH, bone preservation, and sampling bias at mortuary sites. *American Antiquity* 46:566–571.

Gostner, P., P. Pernter, G. Bonatti, A. Graefen, and A. R. Zink (2011) New radiological insights into the life and death of the Tyrolean Iceman. *Journal of Archaeological Science* 38:3425–3431.

Habenstein, R. W. and W. M. Lamers (2001) *The History of American Funeral Directing* (5th edn.). Burton and Mayer, Brookfield, WI.

Hacker-Norton, D. and M. Trinkley (1984) *Remember Man Thou Art Dust: Coffin Hardware of the Early Twentieth Century*. Chicora Foundation Research Series 2, Columbia, SC.

Hadingham, E. (1994) The mummies of Xianjiang. *Discover*, 1 April. Electronic document, http://discovermagazine.com/1994/apr/themummiesofxinj359.

Haglund, W. D. (1991) *Applications of Taphonomic Models to Forensic Investigations*. Unpublished Ph.D, Dissertation, University of Washington, Seattle, WA.

Haglund, W. D. (2001) Archaeology and forensic death investigations. *Historical Archaeology* 35:26–34.

Haglund, W. D. (2002) Recent mass graves, an introduction. In *Advances in Forensic Taphonomy: Method, Theory, and Archaeological Perspectives*. Eds. W. D. Haglund and M. H. Sorg, pp. 243–261. CRC Press, Boca Raton, FL.

Haglund, W. D., M. Connor and D. D. Scott (2002) The effect of cultivation on buried human remains. In *Advances in Forensic Taphonomy: Method, Theory, and Archaeological Perspectives*. Eds. W. D. Haglund and M. H. Sorg, pp. 133–150. CRC Press, Boca Raton, FL.

Hedges, R. E. M., A. R. Millard, and A. W. G. Pike (1995) Measurements and relationships of diagenetic alteration of bone from three archaeological sites. *Journal of Archaeological Science* 22:201–209.

Henderson, J. (1987) Factors determining the state of preservation of human remains. In *Death, Decay and Reconstruction: Approaches to Archaeology and Forensic Science*. Eds. A. Boddington, A. N. Garland, and R. C. Janaway, pp. 43–54. Manchester University Press, Manchester, U.K.

Hochrein, M. J. (2002) An autopsy of the grave: Recognizing, collecting, and preserving forensic geotaphonomic evidence. In *Advances in Forensic Taphonomy: Method, Theory, and Archaeological Perspectives*. Eds. W. D. Haglund and M. H. Sorg, pp. 45–70. CRC Press, Boca Raton, FL.

Holloway, R. G. (1986) Appendix B: Analysis of wood remains from the Morgan Chapel Cemetery, 41 BP 200. In *Archaeological Investigations at Morgan Chapel Cemetery (41 BP 200), A Historic Cemetery in Bastrop County, Texas*. Eds. A. J. Taylor, A. A. Fox, and I W. Cox, pp. 73–76. Archaeological Survey Report No. 146. Center for Archaeological Research, The University of Texas at San Antonio, TX.

Hughes, C., C. Juarez, L. Zephro, G. Fowler, and S. Chacon (2012) Past or present? Differentiating California prehistoric Native American remains from forensic cases: An empirical approach. *International Journal of Osteoarchaeology* 22:110–118.

Iserson, K. V. (1994) *Death to Dust: What Happens to Dead Bodies?* Galen Press, Tucson, AZ.

Janaway, R. C. (2002) Degradation of clothing and other dress materials associated with buried bodies of archaeological and forensic interest. In *Advances in Forensic Taphonomy: Method, Theory, and Archaeological Perspectives*. Eds. W. D. Haglund and M. H. Sorg, pp. 379–402. CRC Press, Boca Raton, FL.

Janaway, R. C. (2008) The decomposition of materials associated with buried cadavers. In *Soil Analysis in Forensic Taphonomy*. Eds. M. Tibbett and D. O. Carter, pp. 153–201. CRC Press, Boca Raton, FL.

Jans, M. M. E., H. Kars, C. M. Nielsen-Marsh, C. I. Smith, A. G. Nord, P. Arthur, and N. Earl (2002) In situ preservation of archaeological bone: A histological study within a multidisciplinary approach. *Archaeometry* 44:343–352.

Johnson, D. L. (1989) Subsurface stone lines, stone zones, artifact-manuport layers, and biomantles produced by bioturbation via pocket gophers (*Thomomys bottae*). *American Antiquity* 54:370–389.

Jordan, T. G. (1982) *Texas Graveyards: A Cultural Legacy*. University of Texas Press, Austin, TX.

Kahana, T., J. Almog, J. Levy, E. Shmeltzer, Y. Spier, and J. Hiss (1999) Marine taphonomy: Adipocere formation in a series of bodies recovered from a single shipwreck. *Journal of Forensic Sciences* 44:897–901.

Kollmorgen Instruments Corporation (1994) *Munsell® Soil Color Charts* (revised edn.). Kollmorgen Instruments Corporation, New Windsor, NY.

Lehner, L. (1980) *Complete Book of American Kitchen and Dinner Wares*. Wallace-Homestead, Des Moines, IA.

Luscomb, S. C. (1967) *The Collector's Encyclopedia of Buttons*. Bonanza Books, New York.

Lyman, R. L. (1994) *Vertebrate Taphonomy*. Cambridge University Press, Cambridge, U.K.

Mayer, R. G. (2012) *Embalming: History, Theory, and Practice* (5th edn.). McGraw-Hill, New York.

Menez, L. L. (2005) The place of the forensic archaeologist at a crime scene involving a buried body. *Forensic Science International* 152:311–315.

Micozzi, M. S. (1991) *Postmortem Change in Human and Animal Remains: A Systematic Approach*. Ed. Charles C Thomas, Springfield, IL.

Micozzi, M. S. (1997) Frozen environments and soft tissue preservation. In *Forensic Taphonomy: The Postmortem Fate of Human Remains*. Eds. W. D. Haglund and M. H. Sorg, pp. 171–180. CRC Press, Boca Raton, FL.

Mitford, J. (1998) *The American Way of Death Revisited*. Vintage Books, New York.

Morlan, R. E. (1984) Toward the definition of criteria for the recognition of artificial bone alterations. *Quaternary Research* 22:160–171.

Nawrocki, S. P. (1995) Taphonomic processes in historic cemeteries. In *Bodies of Evidence: Reconstructing History through Skeletal Analysis*. Ed. A. Grauer, pp. 49–66. Wiley-Liss, New York.

Nicholson, R. A. (1996) Bone degradation, burial medium and species representation: Debunking the myths, an experiment-based approach. *Journal of Archaeological Science* 23:513–533.

Nicholson, R. A. (1998) Bone degradation in a compost heap. *Journal of Archaeological Science* 25:393–403.

Nielsen-Marsh, C. M. and R. E. M. Hedges (2000) Patterns of diagenesis in bone I: The effects of site environments. *Journal of Archaeological Science* 27:1139–1150.

O'Brien, T. G. and A. C. Kuehner (2007) Waxing grave about adipocere: Soft tissue change in an aquatic context. *Journal of Forensic Sciences* 52:294–301.

Odell, G. H. and F. Cowan (1987) Estimating tillage effects on artifact distributions. *American Antiquity* 52:456–484.

Orser, C. E., A. M. Nekola, and J. L. Roark (1987) *Exploring the Rustic Life: Multidisciplinary Research at Millwood Plantation, a Large Piedmont Plantation in Abbeville County, South Carolina, and Elbert County, Georgia*. Mid-American Research Center, Loyola University of Chicago, Chicago, IL.

Owsley, D. W. and B. E. Compton (1997) Preservation in late 19th Century iron coffin burials. In *Forensic Taphonomy: The Postmortem Fate of Human Remains*. Ed. W. D. Haglund and M. H. Sorg, pp. 511–526. CRC Press, Boca Raton, FL.

Parrington, M. and D. G. Roberts (1990) Demographic, cultural, and bioanthropological aspects of a nineteenth-century free Black population in Philadelphia. In *A Life in Science: Papers in Honor of J. Lawrence Angel.* Ed. J. E. Buikstra, pp. 138–170. Center for American Archeology, Kampsville, IL.

Peacock, P. (1973) *Antique Buttons: Their History and How to Collect Them.* Drake Publishers, New York.

Pokines, J. T. (2009) Forensic recoveries of U.S. war dead and the effects of taphonomy and other site-altering processes. In *Hard Evidence: Case Studies in Forensic Anthropology* (2nd edn.). Ed. D. W. Steadman, pp. 141–154. Prentice Hall, Upper Saddle River, NJ.

Pokines, J. T. and J. C. Kerbis Peterhans (2007) Spotted hyena (*Crocuta crocuta*) den use and taphonomy in the Masai Mara National Reserve, Kenya. *Journal of Archaeological Science* 34:1914–1931.

Priess, P. (1973) Wire nails in North America. *Bulletin of the Association for Preservation Technology* 5:87–92.

Pye, J. W. (2007) *A Look Through the Viewing Glass: Social Status and Grave Analysis in a 19th Century Kansas Cemetery.* Unpublished M.A. Thesis, University of Arkansas, Little Rock, AR.

Pye, J. W., H. C. Smith, and D. C. Roper (2004) Excavations at the Meadowlark Cemetery, Manhattan. *Current Archaeology in Kansas* 5:77–92.

Pye, J. W., H. C. Smith, and D. C. Roper (2007) With no Stillman among them: Reburial of the Stillman Family Cemetery, Manhattan, Kansas. *Current Archaeology in Kansas* 8:77–92.

Quatrehomme, G., A. Lacoste, P. Bailet, G. Grévin, and A. Ollier (1997) Contribution of microscopic plant anatomy to postmortem bone dating. *Journal of Forensic Sciences* 42:140–143.

Robertson, J. I., Jr. (1984) *Tenting Tonight: The Soldier's Life.* Time-Life Books, Alexandria, VA.

Rodriguez, W. C. and W. M. Bass (1985) Decomposition of buried bodies and methods that may aid in their location. *Journal of Forensic Sciences* 30:836–852.

Rogers, T. L. (2005) Recognition of cemetery remains in a forensic context. *Journal of Forensic Sciences* 50:5–11.

Roksandic, M. (2002) Position of skeletal remains as a key to understanding mortuary behavior. In *Advances in Forensic Taphonomy: Method, Theory, and Archaeological Perspectives.* Eds. W. D. Haglund and M. H. Sorg, pp. 95–113. CRC Press, Boca Raton, FL.

Rose, J. C. (Ed.) (1985) *Gone to a Better Land: A Biohistory of a Rural Black Cemetery in the Post-Reconstruction South.* Arkansas Archeological Survey Research Series No. 25. Fayetteville, AR.

Rose, J. C. and L. G. Santeford (1985) Burial interpretations. In *Gone to a Better Land: A Biohistory of a Rural Black Cemetery in the Post-Reconstruction South.* Ed. J. C. Rose, pp. 130–145. Arkansas Archeological Survey Research Series No. 25. Fayetteville, AR.

Rudrappa, T., K. J. Czymmek, P. W. Paré, and H. P. Bais (2008) Root-secreted malic acid recruits beneficial soil bacteria. *Plant Physiology* 148:1547–1556.

Ruff, C. B., B. M. Holt, V. Sládek, M. Berner, W. A. Murphy, Jr., D. zur Nedden, H. Seidler, and W. Recheis (2006) Body size, body proportions, and mobility in the Tyrolean Iceman. *Journal of Human Evolution* 51:91–101.

Santeford, L. G. (1981) Medicine bottles: One man's (or woman's) cure becomes the archaeologist's tool. In *A Guide for Historical Archaeology in Illinois.* Ed. C. E. Orser, Jr., pp. 60–77. Research Paper No. 1, Mid-American Research Center, St. Louis, MO.

Schultz, J. J. (2012) Determining the forensic significance of skeletal remains. In *A Companion to Forensic Anthropology.* Ed. D. C. Dirkmaat, pp. 66–84. Wiley-Blackwell, Chichester, U.K.

Schultz, J., M. Williamson, S. P. Nawrocki, A. Falsetti, and M. Warren (2003) A taphonomic profile to aid in the recognition of human remains from historic and/or cemetery contexts. *Florida Anthropologist* 56:141–147.

Sledzik, P. and M. S. Micozzi (1997) Autopsied, embalmed, and preserved human remains: Distinguishing features in forensic and historic contexts. In *Forensic Taphonomy: The Postmortem Fate of Human Remains.* Eds. W. D. Haglund and M. H. Sorg, pp. 483–495. CRC Press, Boca Raton, FL.

Soil Survey Staff (2010) *Keys to Soil Taxonomy* (11th edn.). National Resources Conservation Service, United States Department of Agriculture, Washington, DC.

Springate, M. E. (1998) Mass-produced coffin hardware in Eastern North America: A synthesis. *Paper Presented at the Annual Conference of the Society for Historical Archaeology*, Atlanta, GA, 7–12 January. [available on-line: http://works/bepress.com/meganspringate/1]

Stekel, P. (2010) *Final Flight*. Wilderness Press, Birmingham, AL.

Stødkilde-Jørgensen, H., N. O. Jacobsen, E. Warncke, and J. Heinemeier (2008) The intestines of a more than 2000 years old peat-bog man: Microscopy, magnetic resonance imaging and 14C-dating. *Journal of Archaeological Science* 35:530–534.

Stojanowski, C. M., R. M. Seidemann, and G. H. Doran (2002) Differential skeletal preservation at Windover Pond: Causes and consequences. *American Journal of Physical Anthropology* 119:15–26.

Takatori, T. (2001) The mechanism of human adipocere formation. *Legal Medicine* 3:193–204.

Taylor, A. J., A. A. Fox, and I. W. Cox (1986) Archaeological investigations at Morgan Chapel Cemetery (41BP200), a historic cemetery in Bastrop County, Texas. Archaeological Survey Report No. 146, Center for Archaeological Research, University of Texas, San Antonio, TX.

Tebb, W. and E. P. Vollum (1905) *Premature Burial and How It May Be Prevented, with Special Reference to Trance, Catalepsy, and Other Forms of Suspended Animation* (2nd ed.). Ed. W. R. Hadwen. Swan Sonnenschein & Co., London.

Trinkley, M. and D. Hacker-Norton (1984) *Analysis of Coffin Hardware from 38CH778, Charleston County, South Carolina*. Research Series 3, Chicora Foundation, Inc., Columbia, SC.

Ubelaker, D. H. (1995) Historic cemetery analysis: Practical considerations. In *Bodies of Evidence: Reconstructing History through Skeletal Analysis*. Ed. A. Grauer, pp. 37–48. Wiley-Liss, New York.

Ubelaker, D. H. and K. M. Zarenko (2011) Adipocere: What is known after over two centuries of research. *Forensic Science International* 208:167–172.

Vanzetti, A., M. Vidale, M. Gallinaro, D. W. Frayer, and L. Bondioli (2010) The iceman as a burial. *Antiquity* 84:681–692.

Villa, P. (1982) Conjoinable pieces and site formation processes. *American Antiquity* 47:276–290.

Walker, T. S., H. P. Bais, E. Grotewold, and J. M. Vivanco (2003) Root exudation and rhizosphere biology. *Plant Physiology* 132:44–51.

White, E. M. and L. A. Hannus (1983) Chemical weathering of bone in archaeological soils. *American Antiquity* 48:316–322.

Wilkinson, D. M., H. J. O'Regan, and T. Clare (2006) Where are the non-human bog bodies? *Journal of Wetland Archaeology* 6:99–104.

Willey, P. and A. Heilman (1987) Estimating time since death using plant roots and stems. *Journal of Forensic Sciences* 32:1264–1270.

Wilson, A. S., R. C. Janaway, A. D. Holland, H. I. Dodson, E. Baran, A. M. Pollard, and D. J. Tobin (2007) Modelling the buried human body environment in upland climes using three contrasting sites. *Forensic Science International* 169:6–18.

Yalom, M. (2008) *The American Resting Place*. Houghton Mifflin, Boston, MA.

Zelinka, S. L. and D. S. Stone (2011) The effect of tannins and pH on the corrosion of steel in wood extracts. *Materials and Corrosion* 62:739–744.

Fluvial Taphonomy

THOMAS EVANS

6

Contents

It is the task of the natural scientist to search for laws which will enable him to deduce predictions. This task may be divided into two parts. On the one hand, he must try to discover such laws as will enable him to deduce single predictions ('causal' or 'deterministic' laws or 'precision statements'). On the other hand, he must try to advance hypotheses about frequencies, that is, laws asserting probabilities, in order to deduce frequency predictions.

—**Karl Popper,** *The Logic of Scientific Discovery* **(1959)**

Introduction

Human remains routinely enter fluvial systems through natural (i.e., erosion of cemeteries and archaeological sites), accidental (i.e., drowning), suicidal, and criminal (i.e., body disposal or intentional drowning) events. Regardless of the mechanisms of entry into a river, accidental or intentional, it is beneficial for human material to be recovered and subjected to a forensic or anthropological analysis. If the remains are the product of criminal activity, discovery of additional remains may be beneficial for the prosecution by increasing the potential for identification, cause, and manner of death determination (Komar and Potter 2007) and/or aiding in the location of a crime scene. Unfortunately, searching for any materials (i.e., evidence, remains, etc.) in rivers is difficult, slow, and complicated (see also Becker 2000; Dutelle 2007; McUne and Gagnon 2007; Tackett and Whitfield 1987; Teather 1994), especially due to the significant physical hazards for diving personnel (Burke and O'Rear 1998; Dutelle 2007; Falkenthal 1999; McUne and Gagnon 2007; Tackett and Whitfield 1987; Teather 1994). A greater understanding of fluvial transport and deposition of remains increases the recovery potential of evidence and remains by narrowing search areas. In addition, the forensic anthropologist can use diagnostic tools to aid in identifying potential taphonomic histories of the remains that they are asked to analyze. Such tools include an understanding of fluvial taphonomic processes and the associated taphonomic modifications due to these processes.

The purpose of this chapter is to inform the reader of our present understanding of fluvial taphonomic processes and to describe the resulting taphonomic modifications (i.e., the results of the processes). What follows covers decay in rivers, full body transport, articulated body part transport, isolated bone transport, and the analytical techniques that can be used to interpret skeletal remains recovered from a fluvial context. Each section includes a description of the taphonomic modifications that can aid investigators in diagnosing a fluvial history for remains, when this information is available.

Since there is a paucity of literature covering human fluvial taphonomy, literature from other fields (e.g., zoology and paleontology) has been incorporated; however, the reviewed literature has been restricted to observational and experimental research. Some review articles concerning fluvial taphonomic processes are not included here, but the interested reader should seek these resources directly (Haglund and Sorg 2002; Osterkamp 2011; Rodriguez 1997). In addition, no information about sediment transport theory is presented regarding isolated bone transport; a review of this literature is beyond the scope of this chapter, and the interested reader should access any of the many textbooks (Thorne et al. 1987) and reviews (Middleton and Southard 1984; Parker 2006) on the subject.

Previous Research

Historically, research concerning the transport of remains in rivers has been performed in the fields of paleontology and archaeology, and both fields face similar analytical problems to the forensic scientist: the reconstruction of the past from fragmentary or partial evidence. Since the evidence interpreted by paleontology and archaeology is nearly entirely skeletal, most research has focused on the transport and deposition of isolated bones, with few exceptions. Similarly, most literature reviews focus on isolated bones, for example, in paleontology (Behrensmeyer 1990, 1991; Rogers and Kidwell 2007; Shipman 1981), archaeology (Boaz 1982; Gifford 1981; Lyman 1994), and most recently in forensics (Evans 2006; Haglund and Sorg 2002; Nawrocki et al. 1997).

Given the interest in fluvial taphonomy in three disciplines (paleontology, archeology, and forensics), what is the state of our understanding of fluvial processes and taphonomic signatures? Surprisingly, we know very little, since most research has used small sample sizes, poor or no controls, unknown or unreported sample histories, and poorly reported experimental conditions, resulting in most data and interpretations yielding preliminary or tentative results. Presently, it is not possible to combine all studies into a coherent corpus of understanding; there are conflicting observations and conclusions, which raise doubts and concerns related to the applicability of many of the conclusions presently in the literature. There is also a considerable amount of speculation in the literature about how fluvial processes take place, most of which have no basis in published observations or experimentation. Presented here is a comprehensive and straightforward analysis of the published literature to determine what we understand and what is still opaque.

Decay in Fluvial Systems

The decay of tissues in rivers proceeds differently than decay in lakes and ponds, since the decay products are swept downstream, the biota is different in flowing water, currents physically buffet tissues (Piorkowski 1995), bodies fall apart as they impact the bed during transport (Kline et al. 1997; Piorkowski 1995), and the effects of temperature and seasonality manifest differently in rivers. Consequently, this review will not include the decay of bodies in lakes, ponds, wells, tubs, or any other standing body of water.

Decay of tissues in rivers is integral to the taphonomic history of fluvially altered remains, since decay produces the different entities that are transported and deposited in rivers. Intact bodies move and are altered differently than articulated units and isolated bones. As such, it is important to consider what units are produced during decay and how these units will be altered differently as they move in different ways downstream. Unfortunately, the disarticulation sequence of human bodies in rivers is still poorly understood, which complicates our understanding of which articulated units are transported and the approximate order in which isolated bones become available for transport.

Little information is presently available on how tissue breakdown occurs in fluvial environments or the rate at which it occurs (but see Chaloner et al. 2002; Piorkowski 1995), as well as how the processes might change depending on the season. What can be stated with confidence is that decay is slower in fluvial systems than on land (Hobischak 1997a,b; Hobischak and Anderson 2002; MacDonell and Anderson 1997), most likely due to lower temperatures (Doberentz and Madea 2010; Heaton et al. 2010; Madea 2002; Petric et al. 2004; Reh 1969; Reh et al. 1977) and lack of terrestrial vertebrates and invertebrate scavengers. Terrestrial invertebrates will colonize body parts that are exposed above the water surface, thus hastening decay (Barrios and Wolff 2011; Haglund 1993; Hobischak 1997a,b; Hobischak and Anderson 2002; Kline et al. 1997; MacDonell and Anderson 1997; Mann et al. 1990:109; Piorkowski 1995), while partial submersion in water can keep tissues wet enough for terrestrial invertebrate colonization in environments where desiccation would occur otherwise (Goff and Odom 1987:47–48). In the absence of insect consumption, soft tissue above water can become mummified, even while the rest of the body is submerged. The amount of flesh above and below water changes as bodies sink and float throughout decay (Hobischak 1997a,b; Hobischak and Anderson 2002; MacDonell and Anderson 1997).

Like terrestrial decay, the warmer the water, the faster the decay (Minshall et al. 1991). Once in water, a body is rapidly colonized by invertebrates (Brusven and Scoggan 1969; Duband et al. 2011; Kline et al. 1997; MacDonell and Anderson 1997; Piorkowski 1995; Vanin and Zancaner 2011), which facilitate tissue breakdown, including crustaceans (Duband et al. 2011; Mottonen and Nuutila 1977:1097–1098; Petric et al. 2004; Vanin and Zancaner 2011). Invertebrates can be found all over a submerged body (Chaloner et al. 2002; Duband et al. 2011; Minakawa 1997; Piorkowski 1995), although they are most often located near body orifices and locations of trauma (Brusven and Scoggan 1969; Chaloner et al. 2002; Haglund 1993; Heaton et al. 2010; Kline et al. 1997; Minakawa 1997; Piorkowski 1995; Schuldt and Hershey 1995; Vanin and Zancaner 2011) or on the sheltered underside of bodies in fast flows (Kline et al. 1997; Piorkowski 1995). Aquatic invertebrates can be used as a postmortem interval (PMI) indicator (Barrios and Wolff 2011; Wallace et al. 2007, 2008), although in some places and habitats, there is no consistent succession of invertebrates on decaying bodies (Keiper et al. 1997;

Hobischak 1997a,b; Piorkowski 1995). Unfortunately, the invertebrates present in a river change depending on the season (Hobischak 1997a,b; Hobischak and Anderson 2002) as well as the microhabitat (riffle vs. pool) (Brusven and Scoggan 1969; Chaloner et al. 2002; Hobischak 1997a,b; Hobischak and Anderson 2002; Keiper et al. 1997; MacDonell and Anderson 1997), which complicates the use of invertebrates as a PMI indicator. Mold or algae are often intimately involved in aqueous decomposition (Casamatta and Verb 2000; Chaloner et al. 2002; Haefner et al. 2004; Hobischak and Anderson 2002; Keiper et al. 1997; Kline et al. 1997; Minshall et al. 1991; Piorkowski 1995), with aquatic organisms growing faster in warmer water, thus facilitating faster decay (Minshall et al. 1991). Microbial life can also control decay in fluvial systems (Hobischak and Anderson 2002; Kline et al. 1997; Piorkowski 1995), although this mechanism of decay has rarely been reported.

Bodies from rivers tend to have a consistent sequence of decay prior to disarticulation (Doberentz and Madea 2010; Heaton et al. 2010; Hobischak 1997a,b; Hobischak and Anderson 1999, 2002; MacDonell and Anderson 1997; Madea 2002; Madea and Doberentz 2010; Perry 2005; Petric et al. 2004; Reh 1967, 1969; Reh et al. 1977; Seet 2005), beginning with the development of "washer woman's skin," skin discoloration (e.g., marbling and black discoloration), distension and bloating, skin peeling, hair loss, loss of nails, and loss of skin. Finally, progressive skeletonization and disarticulation occur, proceeding generally from distal to proximal joints (Haglund 1993), although there is variability in the observed disarticulation sequence.

Presently, there are three main fluviatile PMI indicators: invertebrate succession, algal succession, and the sequence of body decay. If local invertebrate and algal information is unavailable, then using the decomposition research of Heaton et al. (2010), Hobischak (1997a,b), Hobischak and Anderson (1999, 2002), Madea (2002), Madea and Doberentz (2010), Reh (1967, 1969), Reh et al. (1977), and Seet (2005) to estimate PMI is presently the best practice. There are a number of reviews and articles regarding the use of aquatic insects (Barrios and Wolff 2011; Haskell et al. 1989; Hawley et al. 1989; Hobischak and Anderson 2002; Keiper et al. 1997; Keiper and Casamatta 2001; Merritt and Wallace 2001) and algae (Casamatta and Verb 2000; Haefner et al. 2002, 2004; Keiper and Casamatta 2001) to determine PMI.

Full Body Transport

Little has been published concerning the transport of full bodies in fluvial environments; consequently, our understanding is extremely limited. Nearly all data on the subject come from anecdotes (Darwin 1839:141), case reports (D'Alonzo et al. 2012; Mann et al. 1990:109), or disasters (Berryman et al. 1988:844; Moore et al. 2008; Varricchio et al. 2005). Human bodies have a density near that of water (Donoghue and Minnigerode 1977). Consequently, bodies can be expected to float and sink repeatedly depending on a number of variables including state of decay and density of water (salt and sediment concentrations) (Heaton et al. 2010). Warmer water leads to faster bloating, so remains will float earlier during the PMI, consequently moving downstream sooner. The bulk density of the body determines floatation, which includes any clothing or objects attached to a body. Body floatation is common and increases the rate of transport considerably, since the body is moving slightly slower than the fluid medium. Often, transport is episodic (Strobel et al. 2009), though typically faster and more common during periods of higher water (Bickart 1984:527–528; D'Alonzo et al. 2012; Glock et al. 1980; Guatame-Garcia et al. 2008; *contra* Strobel et al. 2009). Intermittent transport is caused by a body being caught on the upstream side of woody debris, rocks, or other channel obstructions (Cederholm and Peterson 1985; Cederholm et al. 1989; 1999:9–10; Heaton et al. 2010; Hobischak and Anderson 1999; Minakawa 1997; Minakawa and Gara 2005; Piorkowski 1995; Rodriguez 1997:461; Strobel et al. 2009; Teather 1994:6–8, 10, 29–30). In addition, pools or eddies behind obstructions (woody debris or rocks) can also trap bodies and stop downstream transport (Brooks and Brooks 1984, 1997; Cederholm et al. 1989; Minakawa 1997; Minakawa and Gara 2005; Piorkowski 1995; Strobel et al. 2009). Sediment bars of any kind also can be loci of body deposition (Butler 1987:133; Glock et al. 1980; Haglund et al. 1990); however, channel obstructions and eddies/pools retain the majority of bodies (Cederholm et al. 1989; Cederholm and Peterson 1985; Minakawa 1997; Minakawa and Gara 2005; Strobel et al. 2009). Therefore, more episodic transport and lower net transport are expected in rivers with more obstructions, and faster and more continuous transport is expected in rivers with no or fewer obstructions. Bodies can be transported hundreds of miles in days or months in large river systems (Bassett and Manhein 2002; Brady 2012; D'Alonzo et al. 2012; Pampin and López-Abajo 2001); therefore, the longer a body is missing, the farther downstream it may have traveled. This is not always the case, as bodies have been found upstream of their river entry location (Bassett and Manhein 2002; Brewer 2005; Heaton et al. 2010). In larger rivers, bodies tend to stay on the same side of the river that they entered (Bassett and Manhein 2002; Brewer 2005; Dilen 1984).

It should be noted that none of the previous research concerning fluvial transport of full bodies includes a taphonomic description of the human bodies recovered. Consequently, any taphonomic interpretations of the history of a body recovered from a river should be governed by the context of recovery as well as indicators of decay taking place under water.

Articulated Unit Transport

Similar to full body transport, articulated unit transport has received little attention in the experimental or observational literature, and what has been published has entirely utilized faunal (nonhuman) remains. This is a function of the difficulty in obtaining human remains for destructive experimentation as well as difficulty in obtaining permits to run experiments in public waterways using human remains. It is useful to note that the disarticulation sequence of human body parts in rivers is nearly unknown and consequently so are the articulated parts typically transported in fluvial systems resulting from this disarticulation. In addition, the amount of soft tissue that was present on articulated parts during fluvial transport and prior to the recovery of skeletonized remains is also unknown, so no modeling or hypothesis formation can take place without further observations and experiments into fluvial decay processes.

Like full bodies, articulated elements move most often and furthest during higher flow events (Bickart 1984; Gifford 1977:166, 187; Gifford and Behrensmeyer 1977:250). It is unclear if articulated units have a greater transport potential, since articulation, in comparative studies with isolated bones, yielded both faster (Coard 1999; Coard and Dennell 1995; Trapani 1996, 1998) and slower (Coard and Dennell 1995) transport. More authors have observed an increased dispersal potential, so *in toto*, it appears that articulation generally increases transportability with some exceptions. As more skeletal elements are articulated, preferred orientations of bones become more cryptic, with bone orientations no longer reflecting flow direction (Coard 1999; Coard and Dennell 1995). Like isolated bones, articulated units often adopt long axis orientations that are either parallel or perpendicular to the flow direction (Coard and Dennell 1995). Temporary burial (complete or partial) slows net transport considerably (Trapani 1996, 1998). The shape of articulated elements contributes to transport potential (Trapani 1996, 1998), but the manner in which shape alters transport is not well understood. Dry articulated units tend to move faster than saturated parts (Coard 1999), particularly when they float. Floating can also occur from decay gases building up in tissues, causing the entire unit to float (pers. obs.). Floatation increases the transport potential of articulated units dramatically (Coard 1999). It also provides a transport mechanism that does not leave any observable trace on the soft or osseous tissues.

Little research has described the taphonomic modifications caused by the transport of articulated material. Consequently, taphonomic history interpretations of articulated remains found in rivers should be governed primarily by the context of recovery. Since articulated remains are often partially devoid of flesh, some of the taphonomic modifications isolated bones' experience from fluvial transport, may also apply to articulated remains.

Isolated Bone Transport

Introduction

Fluvial systems are immensely complicated, making the transport of any material in a river difficult to describe let alone fully understand. Presented here is a synopsis of what we understand about isolated bone transport, starting with bone floatation and saturation with water, the factors that alter bone transport rates, a discussion of what taphonomic modifications may be found on remains, some proposed analytical techniques for remains recovered from fluvial environments, and a brief discussion of sheet flow (a way in which bones enter fluvial systems).

Bone Floatation and Saturation

Bone floatation has been observed by many investigators in laboratory and field experiments as well as during aqueous decay experiments (Table 6.1). Similarly, bone floatation has been observed in bones of all sizes (rodent up to elephant) and from many taxa (amphibians, birds, and mammals) (Table 6.1). Consequently, this mode of transportation should not be ignored, since it is common and can cause rapid downstream movement without producing evidence to suggest that the process occurred. Bone floatation occurs when the bulk density of a bone (see Chapter 4, this volume) is less than the fluid medium in which it resides. These conditions can occur after dry periods with lower flow, followed by rapid river rise, potentially entraining dry skeletal material in higher flows. In addition, fresh skeletal material may float, caused by the buildup of decay gases inside the bone (Ayers 2010; pers. obs.).

Behrensmeyer (1973:31–32) measured mammal bone bulk densities, which ranged from 0.64 to 2.30 g/cm^3 (Appendix 2, pp. 174–175). Gutierrez and Kaufmann (2007) report bulk densities for juvenile guanaco (*Lama guanicoe*) bones ranged from 0.63 to 2.12 g/cm^3 (2007:156, Table 1) and 0.55 to 2.42 g/cm^3 (2007:157, Table 2) for adult bones. Kaufmann et al. (2011:341, Figures 3 and 4) depict the range of densities for wet and dry guanaco

Table 6.1 Studies of Floating Bones, Including Bones Observed, Taxa, Duration, and the Type of Aqueous Environment in Which the Bones Were Floating

Reference	Floating Bones	Taxa	Duration of Floatation	Aqueous Environment
Alley (2007:39, 40, 42)	Ribs, thoracic vertebrae, and articulated vertebrae	Pig (*Sus scrofa*)	1–2 weeks	Standing water
Ayers (2010:37, Table 3; 27, Table 5; 35, Appendix C; 82, 83, 92)	Vertebrae, phalanges, other bones	Pig (*Sus scrofa*)	1–2 days	Standing water
Behrensmeyer (1973:31)	Foot bones and vertebrae	Not reported	Hours	Standing water
Behrensmeyer (1975:485)	Foot bones and vertebrae	Not reported	Hours	Standing water
Boaz and Behrensmeyer (1976:57, Figure 2)	Cranium	Human (*Homo sapiens*)	Not reported	Flume
Coard (1999:1371)	Thoracic and lumbar vertebrae, ribs, and sacrum	Mouflon sheep (*Ovis musimon*), pig-tailed macaque (*Macaca nemestrina*), Alsatian dog (*Canis familiaris*)	7–30 m	Flume
Coard and Dennell (1995:447)	Cranium	Pig-tailed macaque (*Macaca nemestrina*)	Not reported	Flume
Dodson (1973:18)	Nearly every bone in the body	Mouse (*Mus*) and frog (*Rana*)	Few days (mouse), month (frog)	Standing water
Evans (2010:28)	Not reported	Not reported	Month and a half	River, standing water
Frison and Todd (1986:67)	Smaller elements	Indian elephant (*Elephas maximus*)	Minutes	River
Gnidovec (1978:18; 19, Figure 8; 20, Table 3; 21)	Not reported	Mammals, birds, and herpetofauna	3 hours	Standing water
Gutierrez and Kaufmann (2007:155, Figure 2; 158)	Lateral tuberosity, head, distal epiphysis of humerus, femur, caudal vertebrae, sacral vertebrae, and others	Guanaco (*Lama guanicoe*)	Several hours	Standing water
Kaufmann et al. (2011)	Many; see Tables 1–3	Guanaco (*Lama guanicoe*)	Minutes	Flume
Morden (1991a:77)	Cervical vertebra, thoracic vertebra, ribs, calcaneus, and metacarpal	Human (*Homo sapiens sapiens*)	5 days	Standing water
Trapani (1996:116, 148)	Cranium, most bird bones	Pigeon (*Columbia livia*)	Not reported	Flume
Trapani (1998:480, Table 1; 481)	Cranium	Pigeon (*Columbia livia*)	Not reported	Flume
Voorhies (1969:67, text and footnote)	Sacrum and sternum	Sheep, coyote (species not reported)	Not reported	Flume
Personal Observations	Nearly every skeletal element	Mammals, birds, frogs, salamanders, snakes, lizards	Seconds to 2.5 months	Buckets, rivers, settling columns, etc.

Table 6.2 Observations of the Time to Saturation or Time to Sinking

Reference	Time to Saturation or Sinking
Behrensmeyer (1973:31–32, Figure 2)	Hours, 70+ hours (time to saturation)
Behrensmeyer (1975:485, Figure 2; 486)	Hours, 70+ hours (time to saturation)
Coard and Dennell (1995:442)	5–7 days (time to saturation)
Dodson (1973:18)	Few days to a month (time to sinking)
Gnidovec (1978:18; 19, Figure 8; 20, Table 3; 21)	8–83 h (time to sinking)
Gutierrez and Kaufmann (2007:155, Figure 2; 158)	Hours (time to saturation)
Trapani (1996:82–83, Table 6.1; 84)	2–13 days (time to saturation)
Young (1989:12, 49)	Bones released gas for over half an hour
Personal observation	2.5 months (time to sinking)

bones, and demonstrate that both wet and dry bones can have densities below 1.0 g/cm³. Yang et al. (2011: Figures 1 and 2 and Table 1) report the dry density of Dybowski's frog (*Rana dybowskii*) femora as between ~0.55 and just slightly higher than ~1.00 g/cm³, with the density increasing slightly with age. These observations of initial bone densities suggest that many bones will at first float in water. Similarly, Young (1989:12, 49) reported densities of subfossil (partially mineralized) bone ranging from 1.40 to 3.06 g/cm³ and modern bones ranging from 1.00 to 2.10 g/cm³. His observations suggest that skeletal material on river beds can have densities close to 1.00 g/cm³ even when (partially) saturated with water, making bones easy to transport or float.

When placed in water, bones begin to hydrate, increasing their bulk density. The rate at which bones hydrate is variable, with some bones becoming saturated in a matter of hours, while others can take months (Table 6.2). Since bone density is continually changing during hydration, it is difficult to determine the transport properties of bones that have recently entered a river and are yet to undergo full saturation. During hydration, bones will move faster and more readily than when saturated, since they have a lower density and require less force to initiate and maintain transport. The analyst should be aware that bones that have been in river systems for days, weeks, and even months still may not be saturated and may be capable of partial or complete floatation, facilitating their faster and more frequent transport.

Bone floatation is undetectable, since floatation itself produces no permanent taphonomic modifications on osseous remains, so it is best to consider floatation as a possibility when interpreting any skeletal assemblage recovered from a fluvial environment.

Factors That Alter Bone Transport Rates

During fluvial transport bones move faster than other clastic material (Pavlish et al. 1998, 2002; Schick 1984, 1986, 1987), and which bones have a higher transport potential depends on a number of factors, including taxon, size (Blob 1997; Pante and Blumenschine 2009, 2010; Pavlish et al. 2002), mass (Knell 2009; Kontrovitz and Slack 1991; Morden 1991a,b), density (dry or wet) (Boaz and Behrensmeyer 1976; Coard 1999), shape (Blob 1997; Morden 1991a,b), projected surface area (Coard 1999; Kontrovitz and Slack 1991), orientation (Blob 1997; Elder 1985), age of organism (Kaufmann et al. 2011), weathering stage, and freshness (presence of grease) (Morden 1991a,b). Since many studies have disagreed on which is most important, it is unclear which, if any, factor is most important in skeletal element transport. Given the conflicting conclusions between many authors, it is prudent simply to note that all the earlier factors alter the transport of skeletal elements; however, a brief discussion of some of these factors follows.

Larger bones (length, volume, area, or diameter) tend to move slower than smaller bones (Brady 2005; Brady and Rogers 2005, 2007; *contra* Boaz and Behrensmeyer 1976), with the converse also being true; smaller bones under some conditions move farther, faster, and more readily than larger bones (Aslan and Behrensmeyer 1996; Duckworth 1904; Evans 2007; Long and Langer 1995:88; Nawrocki and Pless 1993; *contra* Andrews and Whybrow 2005). As expected, some larger bones are left behind when transport occurs to other elements (Long and Langer 1995:88; Spennemann 1992; Weigelt 1989 [1927]:36). It should be noted that there is a good deal of variation in transport potentials, so smaller bones can move less than larger bones, and vice versa (Aslan and Behrensmeyer 1996; Hanson 1980; pers. obs.). Similarly, light bones move farther, more readily, and more rapidly (Duckworth 1904; Evans 2007; Long and Langer 1995:88; Nawrocki and Pless 1993; *contra* Andrews and Whybrow 2005) than larger and heavier bones (Aslan and Behrensmeyer 1996). Denser bones tend to move slower than less dense bones as suggested by faster bone movement when bones are dry and slower movement when wet (Coard 1999; Evans 2010; Kaufmann et al. 2011; Morden 1991a). Similarly, fresh (unweathered) bones tend to move faster in a flow than degreased or weathered bones (Morden 1991a), which may be a function of bone density changes caused by degreasing.

Both shape and orientation alter bone transport, and both variables function in concert, so they are treated together here. Shape governs the transport characteristics of some bones (innominates, scapulae, vertebrae, etc.), and bone transport properties change when they break (Boaz and Behrensmeyer 1976) or are abraded. During transport or exposure to a current, skeletal material often adopts a stable orientation that yields less net transport (Frison and Todd 1986:61–69). Flat bones tend to lay flat on the river bed and not move (Boaz and Behrensmeyer 1976; Elder 1985; Evans 2007; Gifford 1977:165, 187–198; Gifford and Behrensmeyer 1977:261–263), while skeletal elements with processes or other portions that extend upward from the river bed and higher into the flow tend to have higher transport potentials (Coard and Dennell 1995). Concavo-convex elements orient convex-up most frequently (Dodson 1973; Elder 1985; Evans 2007; Gifford 1977; Gifford and Behrensmeyer 1977; Knell 2009; Trapani 1996; Voorhies 1969), and move slowly, if at all. Elongate bones tend to orient parallel or perpendicular to flow with parallel orientation most common when water depths greatly exceed the height of a bone (Boaz and Behrensmeyer 1976; Coard and Dennell 1995; Dodson 1973; Elder 1985; Morden 1991a; Pavlish et al. 2002; Voorhies 1969) and perpendicular orientation predominates with shallower flow (Voorhies 1969) or when bones orient parallel to the lee side of bedforms (Pavlish et al. 2002; Trapani 1996, 1998; Voorhies 1969). When long bones orient parallel to flow, the heaviest end tends to be downstream (Boaz and Behrensmeyer 1976; Voorhies 1969). Similarly, open diaphysis tubes (cylinders) orient parallel to flow and are filled or covered by sediment rapidly and do not move (Evans 2007; Morden 1991a).

It appears that interactions with the bed ultimately govern bone transport, since stabilization of bones in/on the bed prevents their movement temporarily or permanently (Frison and Todd 1986:61–69). Bedforms alter all aspects of bone transport, including the rate (velocity), orientation, and mode of movement (Trapani 1996, 1998). Bedform migration over bones temporarily stops their movement (Pavlish et al. 2002; Trapani 1996, 1998; Voorhies 1969), although the magnitude of this effect depends on bone length. If long bones are parallel to flow and are covered by a bedform with a shorter wavelength than the length of the bone, then those bones are never fully exposed before the next bedform migrates over them, keeping the bone permanently buried (Trapani 1996, 1998). Besides burial, scour around a bone can stabilize its location or orientation, thus reducing bone transportability (Frison and Todd 1986:61–69; Hanson 1980). Similarly, bones can trap other skeletal material by pinning them down (Pavlish et al. 2002) or creating eddies in which other bones are deposited (Brady 2005; Pavlish et al. 2002), thus stabilizing bone locations. Generally, bones move toward areas in a flow with lower flow velocities including moving upstream into the troughs of bedforms (Trapani 1996, 1998; pers. obs.).

Fluvially Derived Taphonomic Modifications

Abrasion can take many forms on a bone surface including bone smoothing, rounding, polish (sometimes shiny), scratches, gouges, frosting, pitting, denting, chipping, grooves, and notches. Rarely are long grooves and scratches produced (Shipman and Rose 1983:77–80, 1988). In addition to these individual marks, the bone surface will generally become thinner, eventually leading to small openings (*windows*) that enlarge with further abrasion (Fernández-Jalvo and Andrews 2003; Korth 1978, 1979; Nawrocki et al. 1997). Similarly, lacunae and vascular canals (any natural opening) will gradually enlarge (Bromage 1984; Nawrocki et al. 1997; Thompson et al. 2011:791, Figure 3.4). Articular surfaces rapidly thin to expose underlying cancellous bone (Fernández-Jalvo and Andrews 2003; Korth 1978, 1979; Llona and Andrews 1999), and in juvenile vertebrates, the epiphyses will detach if not fused (Fernández-Jalvo and Andrews 2003). Edges can be fractured or chipped as well (Andrews 1990).

River seeding experiments indicate that the abrasion state of skeletal material does not correlate with transport distance (Aslan and Behrensmeyer 1996:414; Van Orden and Behrensmeyer 2010). For example, lighter bones can be moved faster and further with little abrasion, while larger bones could move less and be "sandblasted" in place (Thompson et al. 2011; Van Orden and Behrensmeyer 2010). Bones have moved hundreds of meters or kilometers downstream without showing signs of abrasion (Behrensmeyer et al. 1989:116; Hanson 1980; pers. obs.), while abrasion in the form of scratches, scrapes, pitting, and gouging has been observed on bones with as little as 1 km of fluvial transport (Herrmann et al. 2004). Consequently, no correlation exists between transport distance and abrasion state, so abrasion should not be used as a transport distance estimation tool or as a PMI indicator. There is no clear picture of how much abrasion is caused by transport and with what sediment types (but see Thompson et al. 2011), although it seems that larger clasts (or higher energy) are needed to cause extensive rounding on a bone (Evans 2007). Since many bones with a known transport history show no or minimal abrasion, the presence of abrasion on bones suggests an episode of prior fluvial transport, but the opposite cannot be taken as indicative of a lack of fluvial transport.

Acid etching of bone surfaces usually occurs over nearly the entire bone surface and presents as a delocalized surface roughening (Duckworth 1904). Small pits form, expand outward, and finally connect, making irregular and rough galleries in the bone surface. Often, acid etching is accompanied by bone discoloration, probably caused by the same acids that are etching the bone. Determining when acid etching will occur is primarily a function of the ions present in the solution surrounding a bone and their concentration. For freshwater with few ions in solution, any acid in solution should start to degrade bone. Christensen and Myers (2011) observed bovine bone degradation under different pH levels and found that a pH of 7 did very little damage to the bone, while low pH levels (4 and 1) were associated with significant bone degradation. Similar results were observed for cooked salmon bones degraded in different pH solutions by Collins (2010). Harnett et al. (2011) observed the progressive dissolution of bone in HCl and H_2SO_4 and graphed mass loss over time. They noted that bone surfaces became porotic and pitted prior to complete dissolution. None of these studies are directly analogous to fluvial systems, however, since bones were allowed to react in a standing body of water, keeping the reaction products in solution with the bone and thus establishing a dynamic equilibrium over time. Fluvial systems have continuous water flow, and reaction products cannot build up around a bone, so more acid etching is expected in even mildly acidic rivers than was observed in the work of Christensen and Myers (2011), Collins (2010), or Harnett et al. (2011). Figures 6.1 and 6.2b display bones recovered from an acidic river displaying mild to advanced acid etching.

Discoloration of bones can occur from a variety of agents, most of which are poorly understood or unknown (see Chapters 11 and 12, this volume). The most common color change is to a light or medium brown (see Figure 6.2), which appears to be caused by partial or complete burial in a river bed or through submersion in discolored water (Nawrocki et al. 1997; pers. obs.). A light green staining often accompanies the growth of algae on bone surfaces (Nawrocki et al. 1997; pers. obs.), a modification that can be found on bones in nearly all rivers and which can occur in less than a year (pers. obs.). Black staining has been observed often in conjunction with adipocere formation, which is usually found in small cavities in the bone (Figure 6.3). Yellow staining appears to be the consequence of fat leaching out of the bone, discoloring its surface. Figure 6.2 displays bones recovered from two rivers, all with discoloration.

Invertebrate consumption of bone and larval casings are frequent fluvial taphonomic indicators. Larval boring appears as smooth-walled troughs, approximately U-shaped in cross section, and often meandering. At times, feeding traces can be confused with acid etching. Generally, feeding traces are much smoother, deeper, regular, and sinuous than the irregular pitting of acid etching (see Chapter 9, Figure 9.12, this volume). It should be noted that both acid etching and invertebrate feeding traces can be found on the same bone. Figure 6.4 displays bones recovered from an Alaska river with evident invertebrate casings.

Sediment impaction within cracks, hollow spaces, and foramina is common in bones recovered from sandy or coarse bed rivers (Figure 6.5). The size, composition, and variety of clasts will be a function of the river from which the remains came; however, impacted sediment on or in a bone is a good indicator of some aqueous history, freshwater or marine (see Chapter 7, this volume). If sand or gravel grains are wedged in cracks or holes in bones, it can suggest a fluvial origin, since there are few processes operating in a standing body of water (lake or pond) that can wedge sediment in to openings (Nawrocki et al. 1997). Figure 6.5 shows sand impaction in bone cracks and foramina. It is possible that shrinking and swelling of bones through wetting and drying are the mechanisms causing clastic material to be wedged tightly in cracks and holes.

Bone cracking and warping from drying can occur when skeletal material is removed from (moving or still) water. While the focus of this review is modifications to bones from fluvial taphonomic processes, it should be noted that taphonomic modifications also occur on bones when removed from fluvial systems. The most obvious change is the drying of bones either during transport or in the laboratory. Drying often causes bones to contract, which causes extensional stresses along the exterior cortical bone surfaces, particularly on long bone (humeri, radii, ulnae, femora, tibiae, or fibulae) diaphyses. The result is often

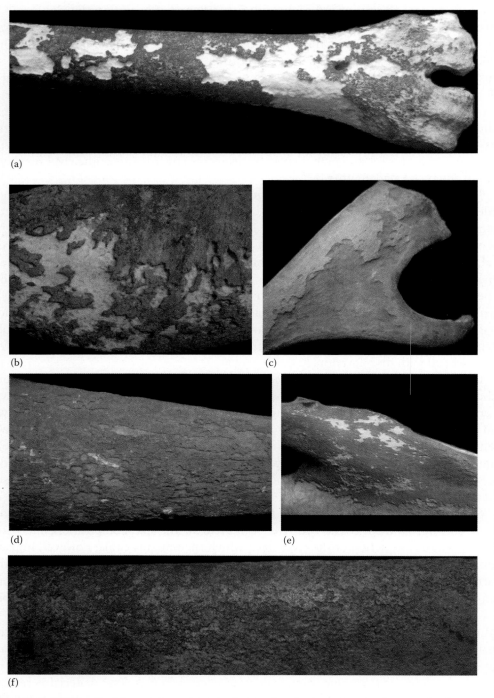

Figure 6.1 Acid-etched bones from Levelock Creek, Alaska. The creek is acidic because of acids leaching out of the surrounding tundra: (a) caribou (*Rangifer tarandus*) metatarsal showing deep cortical bone erosion, (b) caribou dentary with deep discontinuous cortical bone erosion, (c) caribou antler depicting shallow continuous cortical bone removal, (d) shallow discontinuous erosion pits on a rib, (e) surficial incipient erosion pits on cortical bone, and (f) extensively developed disconnected pitting on a diaphysis.

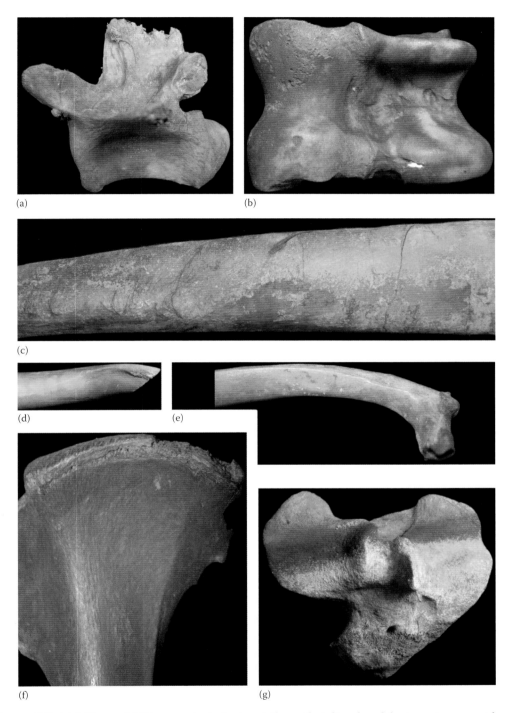

Figure 6.2 (a) Alligator (*Alligator mississippiensis*) bone that discolored during a 1-year residence in a river, (b) astragalus showing discoloration and incipient acid dissolution, (c) a rib shaft with discoloration and aquatic vegetation adhering to the bone surface, (d) sawn diaphysis with discoloration, (e) rib with deep reddish discoloration, (f) ilium with uniform brownish discoloration, and (g) proximal tibia showing bands of discoloration, likely caused by partial burial in a river.

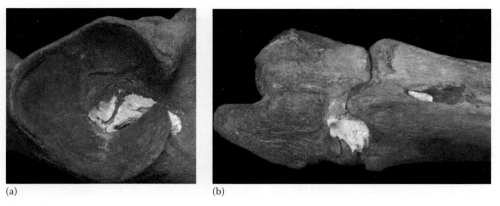

(a)   (b)

Figure 6.3 Location of adipocere formation. Adipocere, when preset, is often found in confined spaces (foramina, medullary cavity, articular fossae, etc.): (a) adipocere formation in an acetabular fossa, and (b) adipocere formation in spaces between bones as well as in a nutrient foramen.

(a)   (b)

Figure 6.4 Invertebrate casings can be of many shapes and sizes: (a) shows a calcified shell in a bone depression, and (b) shows a series of thin larval casings.

an elongate and deep crack (or cracks) extending from the exterior cortical bone into the medullary cavity often over nearly the entire length of a diaphysis (Figure 6.6). During drying of thousands of bones for experimentation, the author has observed that hundreds of long bones crack, often violently and with a sharp, loud, startling popping sound. (See also Prassack (2011) for a discussion of bone cracking during drying.) In addition to deep cracking, drying can alter the shape of skeletal material. When bones are wet, they are flexible to varying degrees. As a bone dries, it loses this flexibility and will retain the shape it was in during drying. Consequently, it is possible to bend or flex a bone while wet and dry it in a new, altered shape. This flexing is readily observable in scapulae, which can flex considerably while wet (Figure 6.7). When observing skeletal material recovered from fluvial systems, it is important to remember that any large cracking and some bending may be a function of fluvial residence and removal, rather than some other taphonomic processes.

Analytical Techniques

Six methods have been proposed to identify skeletal assemblages that have experienced fluvial transport: Voorhies Groups (Voorhies 1969), equivalent particle diameters (Behrensmeyer 1973, 1975), relative transport potentials (Hanson 1980), transport index

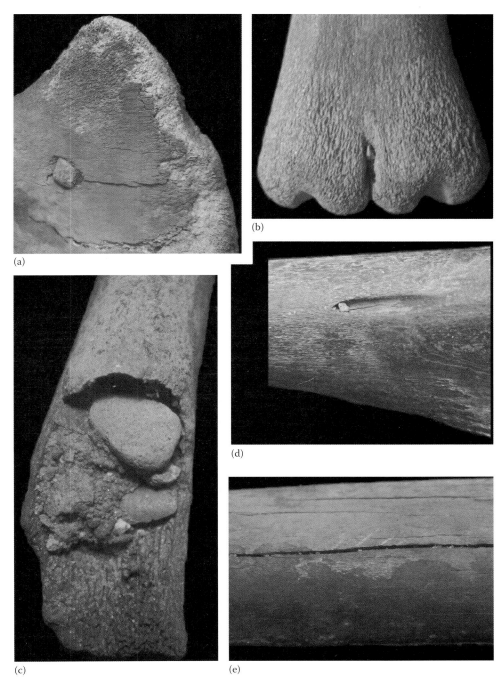

Figure 6.5 Sediment impaction in holes and cracks. Sediment is often found in small cracks or holes in bone: (a) grain of gravel pressed into an ilium while it was wet and pliable, (b) sand grain wedged in the slot between two fused metatarsals, (c) sand and gravel in a diaphysis, (d) sand grain wedged into a nutrient foramen, and (e) sand grains firmly fixed in a crack in cortical bone.

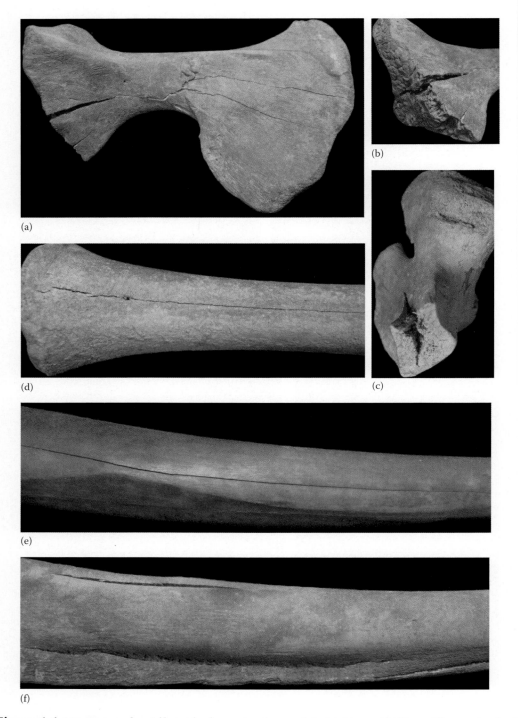

Figure 6.6 Drying cracks. All cracks formed as bones dried: (a) juvenile ilium illustrating both small and large drying cracks, (b) close up of the deepest crack in the ilium from (a), (c) sawed end of a rib demonstrating the degree of cracking and warping of cortical bone during drying, (d) crack in the anterior surface of a metacarpal shaft, (e) elongate drying crack in a tibia that extends the length of the bone and penetrates the medullary cavity, and (f) two cracks deforming the surface of a rib, causing the bone to deflect outward.

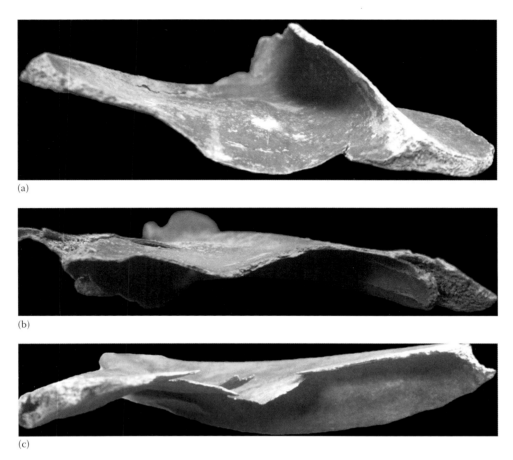

(a)

(b)

(c)

Figure 6.7 Scapulae deformation: (a) medially warped superior scapular border, (b) laterally warped superior scapular border, and (c) warped and cracked superior scapular border illustrating that bone can deform both medially and laterally simultaneously.

(Frison and Todd 1986; Trapani 1996, 1998), mobility numbers (Pavlish et al. 2002), and observing bones in preferred orientations (Lyman 1994; Voorhies 1969). Unfortunately, none of these techniques have been tested or validated, and as such, none are suitable for use in forensic casework. In addition, there are data for each method that suggest that they are not universally applicable. Consequently, this author is unaware of any analytical technique that presently can be used to identify fluvially transported skeletal remains reliably, although research is presently underway to remedy this situation. Presented in the following text is a brief overview of each method to orient the reader on this topic.

Voorhies (1969:69, Table 12) divided bones into slow-, medium-, and fast-moving groups, based upon flume experiments with coyote and sheep skeletons. Behrensmeyer (1973, 1975) continued the grouping of bones based on transport behavior and coined the term "*Voorhies Groups*," meaning grouping bones based on their relative transport rates. Since the term has never been precisely defined, some authors have generated between two and five different transport groups, depending on their method of study (settling column, flume, etc.) and the behavior of the bones that they studied. This method assumes that bones have consistent relative transport rates, and subsequent research has demonstrated that bones display many different rates of transport relative to each other (Aslan and Behrensmeyer 1996; Boaz and Behrensmeyer 1976; Dodson 1973; Kaufman et al. 2011; Korth 1978; Morden 1991a; Trapani 1996, 1998), which falsifies the underlying assumption required for the method to work.

Behrensmeyer (1973, 1975) developed an equation that roughly equates bone transport potential with the transport potential of a spherical quartz grain with the same settling velocity. The hypothesis is that by comparing the grain size on or in which bones are deposited, a transported bone assemblage can be identified. If the quartz equivalent diameters of the bones are roughly equivalent to the grain size diameters of the surrounding sediment, then the bones were likely transported and deposited with the sediment; however, if the predicted grain size and the sediment size are different, then some other transport and deposition history is likely for the skeletal material. Since being proposed, some research has suggested that this oversimplified model is incorrect (Gifford 1977; Gifford and Behrensmeyer 1977; Trapani 1996), and experiments are underway by the author to validate this method directly.

Hanson (1980:164–170) developed an equation for a dimensionless number proportional to the relative transport rate of skeletal material in a fluvial system. Since fluvial systems are complex with far too many variables to model simply, he made a few simplifying assumptions in the development of his equation. As a result, it is unclear how applicable the final equation is to the transport of bones in rivers. He then tested his equation by using it to calculate the relative transport potential of bones and compared the observed transport properties of bones in a flume to those predicted by his equation. A scatter plot (1980:171, Figure 9.5) shows a rough trend suggesting a general correlation between transport potential and his dimensionless variable, but there is significant overlap of transport behaviors across the entire figure, suggesting that the method does not work reliably enough to use in casework.

Frison and Todd (1986) proposed the Fluvial Transport Index, a dimensionless number that describes the relative dispersal potential of skeletal remains. It is a descriptive tool that can be applied to an assemblage with known transport distances downstream. This method requires further validation, and its reliance upon known transport distances makes its application to forensic situations limited, given that this information is usually unknown.

Pavlish et al. (2002) proposed "mobility numbers," which are dimensionless numbers that may be proportional to the relative transport potentials of different bones (similar to Hanson 1980). In a small-scale assessment of the method, Pavlish et al. (2002:235, Figure 2) plotted the relative distance traveled versus mobility number and found a general correlation between transport distance and mobility number, although there was a wide spread in the data. The spread in the data suggests that the tool does not have sufficient resolution to be useful in a forensic context.

It has been suggested that skeletal assemblages that have experienced fluvial transport or reorientation can be identified by measuring and plotting the orientations of bones in the assemblage. This method assumes that bones consistently adopt a known and recognizable preferred orientation relative to a flow and that full disarticulation did not occur until after final deposition (i.e., that the elements did not reach their final location as part of an articulated unit with a different combined shape and density). Field data demonstrate that the orientation of skeletal material is largely a function of bed orientation (pers. obs. and unpublished data) in addition to flow direction. Consequently, bone orientations are not a reliable indicator of interaction between bones and a fluid flow.

Sheet Flow

There are many ways in which bones can enter a river, including the action of *sheet flow* over land surfaces during rainfall events. Sheet flow is the movement of shallow sheets of water over land surfaces until the fluid and their transported objects reach gullies or other channels in which they can be entrained in channelized flow.

Generally, bones on mild slopes do not move quickly (Andrews and Whybrow 2005; Frostick and Reid 1983), although bones in small depressions parallel to slope move faster than bones on featureless surfaces (Frostick and Reid 1983). Spherical- and rod-shaped bones move downslope faster than blade- or disk-shaped bones (Frostick and Reid 1983; Pokines et al. 2011). Similarly, larger, denser bones move downslope slower than smaller, lighter bones (Andrews 1990:17; Baker 2004), and saturated bones move less than dry bones, which may float on water or water and sediment mixtures (Woodruff and Varricchio 2011). When surface flow entrains sediment and bones, there is a higher likelihood of bone breakage (Woodruff and Varricchio 2008, 2011). It has been suggested that a higher land surface slope and higher water discharge will move material downstream faster (Frostick and Reid 1983). While this seems logically sound, there are no published data to support this inference.

Recommendations for Human Remains Recovery

When searching for remains in rivers, it is recommended to look on the upstream sides of obstructions (woody debris, bridge piers, rocks, etc.) (Nawrocki and Baker 2001; Young 1989; Evans 2010; Hanson 1980; Schick 1984, 1986), in eddies behind obstructions (Schick 1984, 1986), on bars (of any kind: lateral, point, median, etc.; Behrensmeyer 1982; Nawrocki et al. 1997), and to focus the search on the same side of the river as the body/parts entered (if known). All locations with drops in flow velocity (competence) should be searched, including banks, the upstream and lateral edges of deeper pools, and the edges of large bedforms (Aslan and Behrensmeyer 1987, 1996; Evans 2010; Schick 1984, 1986). Deep pools in channels not associated with debris are less likely to capture remains. Woody debris is particularly effective at catching and retaining remains (Evans 2007), so all woody debris should be searched thoroughly. One should also search for bodies both up- and downstream in rivers with significant shipping traffic or tidal influence. If a body entered a waterway, it may be useful to contact jurisdictions downstream to determine if they have found any remains. Conversely, if remains are found, it may be useful to contact upstream jurisdictions to determine if they have missing persons. In addition, cadaver dogs can be used to facilitate searches, particularly of fleshed-out remains (Osterkamp 2011).

When searching for skeletal material in fluvial systems, the reader should be aware that it is most common to find larger bones and miss many smaller skeletal elements (Aslan and Behrensmeyer 1996; Evans 2010). Small bones can be caught in any location with a space large enough to hold them (between rocks, vegetation, or woody debris), so if searching for small bones, one should look in the spaces between material in and on the bed. It is noteworthy that skeletal material can be found in rivers, if a search is implemented, often with a potential of high recovery rates (Aslan and Behrensmeyer 1996; Schick 1984, 1986; pers. obs.). Increasing the search effort may not yield large gains in bone recovery, since smaller material may have been transported away, or buried, causing them to be increasingly difficult to locate and recover.

Conclusions

Presently, our understanding of fluvial taphonomic processes is in its infancy; thus, describing suites of taphonomic characters (*taphofacies*) expected from different river types is premature. Every river that the author has surveyed (n = 13) has yielded a different suite of taphonomic modifications on the remains found in the channel. Consequently, no one taphofacies model will suffice for "fluvial systems." What we understand about decay in river systems is largely anecdotal, and most of the research that has been performed has been on a small scale, so the variability in decay processes across different river environments is poorly understood. Similarly, transport of both full bodies and articulated parts in fluvial systems suffers from a lack of systematic, large-scale research, since most of what we know comes from isolated observations.

Comparatively, there is far more research concerning the transport and deposition of isolated (nonhuman) skeletal elements in fluvial systems. Unfortunately, the topic is far more complicated than studying the transport of standard geologic clasts (rocks, sand, etc.), since bones change shape, density, and articulation during decay and transport, and the size, sex, age, and body mass of the living organism also may affect bone transport dynamics. Shape changes occur through breakage and abrasion, while density alterations take place due to loss of grease, decay (buildup and loss of decay gases), water uptake, breakage, and abrasion. Aside from their clast properties continually changing, bones are periodically buried (partially or completely) and become fixed (armored or imbricated) in river beds. All these factors yield inconsistent or episodic transport, which is difficult to predict or even describe. As a result, the taphonomic modifications to bones and skeletal assemblages are difficult to interpret, since the process of fluvial transport is so complicated and convoluted. While highly transportable bones (small, light, less dense bones) are rapidly moved and winnowed, these are the same bones that are most easily destroyed by other taphonomic processes or buried. Consequently, correctly interpreting the taphonomic modifications to bones and skeletal assemblages in fluviatile systems is difficult at best in theory and often cryptic in practice. Often, the analyst must consider many taphonomic processes operating sequentially and/or concurrently in potentially many different microenvironments that change over time. Since fluvial processes are so variable, there is a massive variability in taphonomic modifications found on remains that have experienced fluvial environments.

References

Alley, O. A. (2007) *Aquatic Decomposition in Chlorinated and Freshwater Environments*. Unpublished M.S. Thesis, Texas State University, San Marcos, TX.

Andrews, P. (1990) *Owls, Caves and Fossils*. University of Chicago Press, Chicago, IL.

Andrews, P. and P. Whybrow (2005) Taphonomic observations on a camel skeleton in a desert environment in Abu Dhabi. *Palaeontologia Electronica* 8:1–17.

Aslan, A. and A. K. Behrensmeyer (1987) Vertebrate taphonomy in the East Fork River, Wyoming. *Geological Society of America Abstracts with Programs* 19:575.

Aslan, A. and A. K. Behrensmeyer (1996) Taphonomy and time resolution of bone assemblages in a contemporary fluvial system: The East Fork River, Wyoming. *Palaios* 11:411–421.

Ayers, L. E. (2010) *Differential Decomposition in Terrestrial, Freshwater, and Saltwater Environments; A Pilot Study*. Unpublished M.S. Thesis, Texas State University, San Marcos, TX.

Baker, A. J. (2004) *A Taphonomic Analysis of Human Cremains from the Fox Hollow Farm Serial Homicide Site*. Unpublished M.S. Thesis, University of Indianapolis, Indianapolis, IN.

Barrios, M. and M. Wolff (2011) Initial study of arthropods succession and pig carrion decomposition in two freshwater ecosystems in the Colombian Andes. *Forensic Science International* 212:164–172.

Bassett, H. E. and M. H. Manhein (2002) Fluvial transport of human remains in the lower Mississippi River. *Journal of Forensic Sciences* 47:1–6.

Becker, R. F. (2000) Mythos of underwater recovery operations. *FBI Law Enforcement Bulletin* September 2000:1–5.

Behrensmeyer, A. K. (1973) *The Taphonomy and Paleoecology of Plio-Pleistocene Vertebrate Assemblages East of Lake Rudolf, Kenya*. Unpublished Ph.D. Dissertation, Harvard University, Cambridge, MA.

Behrensmeyer, A. K. (1975) The taphonomy and paleoecology of Plio-Pleistocene vertebrate assemblages of Lake Rudolf, Kenya. *Bulletin of the Museum of Comparative Zoology* 146:473–578.

Behrensmeyer, A. K. (1982) Time resolution in fluvial vertebrate assemblages. *Paleobiology* 8:211–227.

Behrensmeyer, A. K. (1990) Bones. In *Paleobiology: A Synthesis* eds. D. E. G. Briggs and P. R. Crowther, pp. 232–235. Blackwell Scientific Publications, Oxford, U.K.

Behrensmeyer, A. K. (1991) Terrestrial vertebrate accumulations. In *Taphonomy: Releasing the Data Locked in the Fossil Record* eds. P. A. Allison and D. E. G. Briggs, pp. 291–335. Plenum, New York.

Behrensmeyer, A. K., K. D. Gordon, and G. T. Yanagi (1989) Nonhuman bone modification in Miocene fossils from Pakistan. In *Bone Modification* eds. R. Bonnichsen and M. H. Sorg, pp. 99–120. Center for the Study of the First Americans, Orono, ME.

Berryman, H. E., J. O. Potter, and S. Oliver (1988) The ill-fated passenger steamer *Sultana*: An inland maritime mass disaster of unparalleled magnitude. *Journal of Forensic Sciences* 33:842–850.

Bickart, K. J. (1984) A field experiment in avian taphonomy. *Journal of Vertebrate Paleontology* 4:525–535.

Blob, R. W. (1997) Relative hydrodynamic dispersal potentials of soft-shelled turtle elements: Implications for interpreting skeletal sorting in assemblages of non-mammalian terrestrial vertebrates. *Palaios* 12:151–164.

Boaz, D. D. (1982) *Modern Riverine Taphonomy: Its Relevance to the Interpretation of Plio-Pleistocene Hominid Paleoecology in the Omo Basin, Ethiopia*. Unpublished Ph.D. Dissertation, University of California, Berkeley, CA.

Boaz, N. T. and A. K. Behrensmeyer (1976) Hominid taphonomy: Transport of human skeletal parts in an artificial fluviatile environment. *American Journal of Physical Anthropology* 45:53–60.

Brady, M. (2005) *An Experimental and Field-Based Approach to the Taphonomy of Microvertebrate Assemblages: A Case Study in the Judith River Formation of North-Central Montana*. Unpublished Senior Thesis, Macalester College, St. Paul, MN.

Brady, T. V. (2012) The case of the frustrating floater. *Proceedings of the American Academy of Forensic Sciences* 18:273.

Brady, M. and R. Rogers (2005) An experimental and field-based approach to microvertebrate bonebed taphonomy in the Judith River Formation of north-central Montana. *Geological Society of America Abstracts with Programs* 37:24.

Brady, M. and R. Rogers (2007) Exploring the origins of microfossil bonebeds. *Journal of Vertebrate Paleontology* 27:52A.

Brewer, V. B. (2005) Observed taphonomic changes and drift trajectory of bodies recovered from the tidal Thames, London England: A 15-year retrospective study. *Proceedings of the American Academy of Forensic Sciences* 11:286.

Bromage, T. G. (1984) Interpretation of scanning electron microscopic images of abraded forming bone surfaces. *American Journal of Physical Anthropology* 64:161–178.

Brooks, S. and R. H. Brooks (1984) Effects on bone of abrasive contents in moving water. *Abstracts from the First International Conference on Bone Modification*, Carson City, NV, August 17–19, 1984:6–7.

Brooks, S. and R. H. Brooks (1997) The taphonomic effects of flood waters on bone. In *Forensic Taphonomy: The Postmortem Fate of Human Remains* eds. W. D. Haglund and M. H. Sorg, pp. 553–558. CRC Press, Boca Raton, FL.

Brusven, M. A. and A. C. Scoggan (1969) Sarcophagous habits of Trichoptera larvae on dead fish. *Entomological News* 80:103–105.

Burke, T. W. and C. E. O'Rear (1998) Forensic diving, the latest in underwater investigation. *FBI Law Enforcement Bulletin* April 1998:1–8.

Butler, V. L. (1987) Distinguishing natural from cultural salmonid deposits in the Pacific Northwest of North America. In *Natural Formation Processes and the Archaeological Record* eds. D. T. Nash and M. D. Petraglia, pp. 131–149. British Archaeological Reports, International Series 352, Oxford, U.K.

Casamatta, D. A. and R. G. Verb (2000) Algal colonization of submerged carcasses in a mid-order woodland stream. *Journal of Forensic Sciences* 45:1280–1285.

Cederholm, C. J., D. B. Houston, D. L. Cole, and W. J. Scarlett (1989) Fate of coho salmon (*Oncorhynchus kisutch*) carcasses in spawning streams. *Canadian Journal of Fisheries and Aquatic Sciences* 46:1347–1355.

Cederholm, C. J., M. D. Kunze, T. Murota, and A. Sibatani (1999) Pacific salmon carcasses: Essential contributions of nutrients and energy for aquatic and terrestrial ecosystems. *Fisheries* 24:6–15.

Cederholm, C. J. and N. P. Peterson (1985) The retention of coho salmon (*Oncorhynchus kisutch*) carcasses by organic debris in small streams. *Canadian Journal of Fisheries and Aquatic Sciences* 42:1222–1225.

Chaloner, D. T., M. S. Wipfli, and J. P. Caouette (2002) Mass loss and macroinvertebrate colonization of Pacific salmon carcasses in south-eastern Alaskan streams. *Freshwater Biology* 47:263–273.

Christensen, A. M., and S. W. Meyers (2011) Macroscopic observations of the effects of varying fresh water pH on bone. *Journal of Forensic Sciences* 56:475–479.

Coard, R. (1999) One bone, two bones, wet bones, dry bones: Transport potentials under experimental conditions. *Journal of Archaeological Science* 26:1369–1375.

Coard, R. and R. W. Dennell (1995) Taphonomy of some articulated skeletal remains; transport potential in an artificial environment. *Journal of Archaeological Science* 22:441–448.

Collins, B. R. (2010) Element survivability of *Salmo salar*. *Journal of Taphonomy* 8:291–300.

D'Alonzo, S. S., S. J. Clinkinbeard, and E. J. Bartelink (2012) Fluvial transport of human remains in the Sacramento River, California. *Proceedings of the American Academy of Forensic Sciences* 18:408–409.

Darwin, C. R. (1839) *Narrative of the Surveying Voyages of His Majesty's Ships Adventure and Beagle Between the Years 1826 and 1836: Describing Their Examination of the Southern Shores of South America, and the Beagle's Circumnavigation of the Globe.* Henry Colburn, London, U.K.

Dilen, D. R. (1984) The motion of floating and submerged objects in the Chattahoochee River, Atlanta, GA. *Journal of Forensic Sciences* 29:1027–1037.

Doberentz, E. and B. Madea (2010) Estimating the time of immersion of bodies found in water—An evaluation of a common method to estimate the minimum time interval of immersion. *Revista Espanola De Medicina Legal* 36:51–61.

Dodson, P. (1973) The significance of small bones in paleoecological interpretation. *University of Wyoming Contributions to Geology* 12:15–19.

Donoghue, E. R. and S. C. Minnigerode (1977) Human body buoyancy: A study of 98 men. *Journal of Forensic Sciences* 22:573–579.

Duband, S., F. Forest, Y. Gaillard, J.-M. Dumollard, M. Debout, and M. Peoc'h (2011) Macroscopic histological and toxicological aspects of early *Gammarus pulex* scavenging. *Forensic Science International* 209:e16–e22.

Duckworth, W. L. H. (1904) Note on the dispersive power of running water on skeletons: With particular reference to the skeletal remains of *Pithecanthropus Erectus*. In *Studies from the Anthropological Laboratory, the Anatomy School, Cambridge* ed. W. L. H. Duckworth, pp. 274–277. Cambridge University Press, Cambridge, U.K.

Dutelle, A. (2007) Underwater crime-scene response, part 1 of 2: Underwater investigative teams. *Evidence Technology Magazine* 5:24–27.

Elder, R. L. (1985) *Principles of Aquatic Taphonomy with Examples from the Fossil Record.* Unpublished Ph.D. Dissertation, University of Michigan, Ann Arbor, MI.

Evans, T. (2006) Fluvial transport of bones: Our state of knowledge and future research directions. *Proceedings of the American Academy of Forensic Sciences* 12:173.

Evans, T. (2007) Field observations of bone deposition in six rivers. *Proceedings of the American Academy of Forensic Sciences* 13:207.

Evans, T. (2010) Pilot fluvial skeletal transport experiments. *Geological Society of America Abstracts with Programs* 42:28.

Falkenthal, G. (1999) Underwater search and recovery team: A passion for diving and a desire to serve. *Law Enforcement Quarterly* 82:20–23.

Fernández-Jalvo, Y. and P. Andrews (2003) Experimental effects of water abrasion on bone fragments. *Journal of Taphonomy* 1:147–163.

Frison, G. C. and L. C. Todd (1986) *The Colby Mammoth Site: Taphonomy and Archaeology of a Clovis Kill in Northern Wyoming.* University of New Mexico Press, Albuquerque, NM.

Frostick, L. and I. Reid (1983) Taphonomic significance of sub-aerial transport of vertebrate fossils on steep semi-arid slopes. *Lethaia* 16:157–164.

Gifford, D. P. (1977) *Observations of Modern Human Settlements as an Aid to Archaeological Interpretation.* Unpublished Ph.D. Dissertation, University of California, Berkeley, CA.

Gifford, D. P. (1981) Taphonomy and paleoecology: A critical review of archaeology's sister disciplines. *Advances in Archaeological Method and Theory* 4:365–438.

Gifford, D. P. and A. K. Behrensmeyer (1977) Observed formation and burial of a recent human occupation site in Kenya. *Quaternary Research* 8:245–266.

Glock, J. W., G. Hartman, and L. Conquest (1980) *Skagit River Chum Salmon Carcass Drift Study.* City Light Department, City of Seattle, WA.

Gnidovec, D. M. (1978) *Taphonomy of the Powder Wash Vertebrate Quarry, Green River Formation (Eocene), Uintah County, Utah.* Unpublished M.S. Thesis, Fort Hays State University, Hays, KS.

Goff, M. L. and C. B. Odom (1987) Forensic entomology in the Hawaiian islands: Three case studies. *American Journal of Forensic Medicine and Pathology* 8:45–50.

Guatame-Garcia, A. C., L. A. Camacho, and T. Simmons (2008) Computer simulation for drift trajectories of objects in the Magdalena River, Colombia. *Proceedings of the American Academy of Forensic Sciences* 14:319–320.

Gutierrez, M. A. and C. A. Kaufmann (2007) Criteria for the identification of formation processes in guanaco (*Lama guanicoe*) bone assemblages in fluvial-lacustrine environments. *Journal of Taphonomy* 5:151–176.

Haefner, J. N., J. R. Wallace, and R. W. Merritt (2002) A new technique to estimate a postmortem submersion interval (PMSI) using algal growth rates. *Proceedings of the American Academy of Forensic Sciences* 8:184–185.

Haefner, J. N., J. R. Wallace, and R. W. Merritt (2004) Pig decomposition in lotic aquatic systems: The potential use of algal growth in establishing a postmortem submersion interval (PMSI). *Journal of Forensic Sciences* 49:330–336.

Haglund, W. D. (1993) Disappearance of soft tissue and disarticulation of human remains from aqueous environments. *Journal of Forensic Sciences* 38:806–815.

Haglund, W. D., D. G. Reichert, and D. T. Reay (1990) Recovery of decomposed and skeletal human remains in the "Green River Murder" investigation: Implications for medical examiner/coroner and police. *American Journal of Forensic Medicine and Pathology* 11:35–43.

Haglund, W. D. and M. H. Sorg (2002) Human remains in water environments. In *Advances in Forensic Taphonomy: Method, Theory, and Archaeological Perspectives* eds. W. D. Haglund and M. H. Sorg, pp. 201–218. CRC Press, Boca Raton, FL.

Hanson, C. B. (1980) Fluvial taphonomic processes: Models and experiments. In *Fossils in the Making* eds. A. K. Behrensmeyer and A. P. Hill, pp. 156–181. University of Chicago Press, Chicago, IL.

Harnett, K. M., L. C. Fulginiti, and F. D. Modica (2011) The effects of corrosive substances on human bone, teeth, hair, nails and soft tissue. *Journal of Forensic Sciences* 56:954–959.

Haskell, N. H., D. G. McShaffrey, D. A. Hawley, R. E. Williams, and J. E. Pless (1989) Use of aquatic insects in determining submersion interval. *Journal of Forensic Sciences* 34:622–632.

Hawley, D. A., N. H. Haskell, D. G. McShaffrey, R. E. Williams, and J. E. Pless (1989) Identification of a red "fiber": Chironomid larvae. *Journal of Forensic Sciences* 34:617–621.

Heaton, V. G., A. Lagden, C. Moffatt, and T. Simmons (2010) Predicting the postmortem submersion interval for human remains recovered from U.K. waterways. *Journal of Forensic Sciences* 55:302–307.

Herrmann, N. P., B. Bassett, and L. M. Jantz (2004) High velocity fluvial transport: A case study from Tennessee. *Proceedings of the American Academy of Forensic Sciences* 10:282.

Hobischak, N. R. (1997a) *Freshwater invertebrate succession and decompositional studies on carrion in British Columbia.* Unpublished M.S. Thesis, Simon Fraser University, Burnaby, BC.

Hobischak, N. R. (1997b) Freshwater invertebrate succession and decompositional studies on carrion in British Columbia. Canadian Police Research Centre, Technical Report TR-10-98, Ottawa, Ontario, Canada.

Hobischak, N. R. and G. S. Anderson (1999) Freshwater-related death investigations in British Columbia in 1995–1996. A review of coroners cases. *Canadian Society of Forensic Sciences Journal* 32:97–106.

Hobischak, N. R. and G. S. Anderson (2002) Time of submergence using aquatic invertebrate succession and decompositional changes. *Journal of Forensic Sciences* 47:142–151.

Kaufmann, C., M. A. Gutierrez, M. C. Alvarez, M. E. Gonzalez, and A. Massigoge (2011) Fluvial dispersal potential of guanaco bones (*Lama guanicoe*) under controlled experimental conditions: The influence of age classes to the hydrodynamic behavior. *Journal of Archaeological Science* 38:334–344.

Keiper, J. B. and D. A. Casamatta (2001) Benthic organisms as forensic indicators. *Journal of the North American Benthological Society* 20:311–324.

Keiper, J. B., E. G. Chapman, and B. A. Foote (1997) Midge larvae (Diptera: *Chironomidae*) as indicators of postmortem submersion interval of carcasses in a woodland stream: A preliminary report. *Journal of Forensic Sciences* 42:1074–1079.

Kline, T. C., J. J. Goering, and R. J. Piorkowski (1997) The effect of salmon carcasses on Alaskan freshwaters. In *Freshwaters of Alaska: Ecological Syntheses* eds. A. M. Milner and M. W. Oswood, pp. 179–204. Springer-Verlag, New York.

Knell, M. (2009) Experiments in actualistic taphonomy using modern freshwater turtle remains for interpreting fossil turtle localities in fluvial depositional environments. *Journal of Vertebrate Paleontology* 29:128A.

Komar, D. A. and W. E. Potter (2007) Percentage of body recovered and its effect on identification rates and cause and manner of death determination. *Journal of Forensic Sciences* 52:528–531.

Kontrovitz, M. and J. M. Slack (1991) Transport of human teeth: An experimental study. *Geological Society of America Abstracts with Programs* 23:253.

Korth, W. W. (1978) *Taphonomy of Microvertebrate Fossil Assemblages.* Unpublished M.S. Thesis, University of Nebraska, Lincoln, NE.

Korth, W. W. (1979) Taphonomy of microvertebrate fossil assemblages. *Annals of the Carnegie Museum* 48:235–285.

Llona, A. C. P. and P. J. Andrews (1999) Amphibian taphonomy and its application to the fossil record of Dolina (Middle Pleistocene, Atapuerca, Spain). *Palaeogeography, Palaeoclimatology, Palaeoecology* 149:411–429.

Long, D. J. and M. R. Langer (1995) Nassariid gastropods as destructive agents in preservation and fossilization of marine fishes. *Cellular and Molecular Life Sciences* 51:85–89.

Lyman, L. (1994) *Vertebrate Taphonomy.* Cambridge University Press, Cambridge, U.K.

MacDonell, N. and G. Anderson (1997) Aquatic forensics determination of time since submergence using aquatic invertebrates. Canadian Police Research Centre, Technical Report TR-09-97, Ottawa, Ontario, Canada.

Madea, B. (2002) Estimation of duration of immersion. *Nordisk Rettsmedisin* 8:4–10.

Madea, B. and E. Doberentz (2010) Comment on: Heaton V., Lagden A., Moffatt C. Simmons T., Predicting the postmortem submersion interval for human remains recovered from U.K. waterways. *Journal of Forensic Sciences* 55:1666–1667.

Mann, R. W., W. M. Bass, and L. Meadows (1990) Time since death and decomposition of the human body: Variables and observations in case and experimental field studies. *Journal of Forensic Sciences* 35:103–111.

McUne, E. L. and J. E. Gagnon (2007) Underwater body recovery procedures in adverse conditions. *Proceedings of the American Academy of Forensic Sciences* 13:206.

Merritt, R. W. and J. R. Wallace (2001) The role of aquatic insects in forensic investigations. In *Forensic Entomology: The Utility of Arthropods in Legal Investigations* eds. J. H. Byrd and J. L. Castner, pp. 177–222. CRC Press, Boca Raton, FL.

Middleton, G. V. and J. B. Southard (1984) *Mechanics of Sediment Movement: Lecture Notes for Short Course No. 3* (2nd edn.). Society of Economic Paleontologists and Mineralogists, Tulsa, OK.

Minakawa, N. (1997) *The Dynamics of Aquatic Insect Communities Associated with Salmon Spawning.* Unpublished Ph.D. Dissertation, University of Washington, Seattle, WA.

Minakawa, N. and R. I. Gara (2005) Spatial and temporal distribution of coho salmon carcasses in a stream in the Pacific Northwest, USA. *Hydrobiologia* 539:163–166.

Minshall, G. W., E. Hitchcock, and J. R. Barnes (1991) Decomposition of rainbow trout (*Oncorhynchus mykiss*) carcasses in a forest stream ecosystem inhabited by non-anadromous fish populations. *Canadian Journal of Fisheries and Aquatic Sciences* 48:191–195.

Moore, J., D. Varricchio, and F. Jackson (2008) Identifying taphonomic pathways in modern bone assemblages using ordination analysis. *Journal of Vertebrate Paleontology* 28:118A.

Morden, J. L. (1991a) *Hominid Taphonomy: Density, Fluvial Transport, and Carnivore Consumption of Human Remains with Application to Three Plio/Pleistocene Hominid Sites.* Unpublished Ph.D. Dissertation, Rutgers, Piscataway, NJ.

Morden, J. L. (1991b) Models of fluvial transport of human bones, with application to modern fossil hominid sites. *Journal of Vertebrate Paleontology* 11:47–48.

Mottonen, M. and M. Nuutila (1977) Postmortem injury caused by domestic animals, crustaceans, and fish. In *Forensic Medicine, A Study in Trauma and Environmental Hazards, Volume II Physical Trauma* eds. C. G. Tedeschi, W. G. Eckert, and L. G. Tedeschi, pp. 1096–1098. W. B. Saunders, Philadelphia, PA.

Nawrocki, S. P. and A. Baker (2001) Fluvial transport of human remains at the Fox Hollow serial homicide site. *Proceedings of the American Academy of Forensic Sciences* 7:246–247.

Nawrocki, S. P. and J. E. Pless (1993) Transport of human remains in fluvial environments: A review. *Proceedings of the American Academy of Forensic Science* 1993:146.

Nawrocki, S. P., J. E. Pless, D. A. Hawley, and S. A. Wagner (1997) Fluvial transport of human crania. In *Forensic Taphonomy: The Postmortem Fate of Human Remains* eds. W. D. Haglund and M. H. Sorg, pp. 529–552. CRC Press, Boca Raton, FL.

Osterkamp, T. (2011) K9 water searches: Scent and scent transport considerations. *Journal of Forensic Sciences* 56:907–912.

Pampin, J. B. and B. A. López-Abajo Rodríguez (2001) Surprising drifting of bodies along the coast of Portugal and Spain. *Legal Medicine* 3:177–182.

Pante, M. C. and R. J. Blumenschine (2009) Fluvial transport of hominin- and carnivore-modified long bone fragments. *Program of the Seventy-Eighth Annual Meeting of the American Association of Physical Anthropologists,* Chicago, IL, pp. 286–287.

Pante, M. C. and R. J. Blumenschine (2010) Fluvial transport of bovid long bones fragmented by the feeding activities of hominins and carnivores. *Journal of Archaeological Science* 37:846–854.

Parker, G. (2006) Gary Parker's Morphodynamics Web Page. Electronic document, http://vtchl.uiuc.edu/people/parkerg/ (accessed December 1, 2011).

Pavlish, L. A., M. R. Kleindienst, and P. J. Sheppard (1998) Flume experiments with stone and bone. *Program and Abstracts of the 31st International Symposium on Archaeometry, Budapest,* 27 April–1 May 1998, p. 118.

Pavlish, L. A., M. R. Kleindienst, and P. J. Sheppard (2002) Flume experiments with stone and bone. In *Archaeometry 98* eds. E. Jerem and K. T. Biro, pp. 231–237. British Archaeological Reports, International Series S1043, Oxford, U.K.

Perry, P. A. (2005) Human decomposition in the Detroit River. *Proceedings of the American Academy of Forensic Sciences* 11:285–286.

Petric, M. S., N. R. Hobischak, and G. S. Anderson (2004) Examination of factors surrounding human decomposition in freshwater: A review of body recoveries and coroner cases in British Columbia. *Canadian Society of Forensic Science Journal* 37:9–17.

Piorkowski, R. J. (1995) *Ecological effects of Spawning Salmon on Several Southcentral Alaskan Streams.* Unpublished Ph.D. Dissertation, University of Washington, Seattle, WA.

Pokines, J. T., A. Nowell, M. S. Bisson, C. E. Cordova, and C. J. H. Ames (2011) The functioning of a natural faunal trap in a semi-arid environment: Preliminary investigations of WZM-1, a limestone sinkhole site near Wadi Zarqa Ma'in, Hashemite Kingdom of Jordan. *Journal of Taphonomy* 9:89–115.

Prassack, K. A. (2011) The effect of weathering on bird bone survivorship in modern and fossil saline-alkaline lake environments. *Paleobiology* 37:633–654.

Reh, H. (1967) Anhaltspunkte fur die Bestimmung der Wasserzeit. *Deutsche Zeitschrift fur die Gesamte Gerichtliche Medizin* 59:235–245.

Reh, H. (1969) *Diagnostik des Ertrinkungstodes und Bestimmung der Wasserzeit.* Michael Triltsch Verlag, Dusseldorf, Germany.

Reh, H., K. Haaroff, and C. D. Vogt (1977) Die Schatzung der Todeszeit bei Wasserleichen. *Zeitschrift fur Rechtsmedizin* 79:261–266.

Rodriguez, W. C. (1997) Decomposition of buried and submerged bodies. In *Forensic Taphonomy: The Postmortem Fate of Human Remains* eds. W. D. Haglund and M. H. Sorg, pp. 459–467. CRC Press, Boca Raton, FL.

Rogers, R. R. and S. M. Kidwell (2007) A conceptual framework for the genesis and analysis of vertebrate skeletal concentrations. In *Bonebeds, Genesis, Analysis and Paleobiological Significance* eds. R. R. Rogers, D. A. Eberth, and A. R. Fiorillo, pp. 1–63. University of Chicago Press, Chicago, IL.

Schick, K. D. (1984) *Processes of Palaeolithic Site Formation: An Experimental Study.* Unpublished Ph.D. Dissertation, University of California, Berkeley, CA.

Schick, K. D. (1986) *Stone Age Sites in the Making: Experiments in the Formation and Transformation of Archaeological Occurrences.* British Archaeological Reports, International Series 319, Oxford, U.K.

Schick, K. D. (1987) Experimentally derived criteria for assessing hydrologic disturbance of archaeological sites. In *Natural Formation Processes and the Archaeological Record* eds. D. T. Nash and M. D. Petraglia, pp. 86–107. British Archaeological Reports, International Series 352, Oxford, U.K.

Schuldt, J. A. and A. E. Hershey (1995) Effect of salmon carcass decomposition on Lake Superior tributary streams. *Journal of the North American Benthological Society* 14:259–268.

Seet, B. L. (2005) *Estimating the Postmortem Interval in Freshwater Environments.* Unpublished M.S. Thesis, University of Tennessee, Knoxville, TN.

Shipman, P. (1981) *Life History of a Fossil.* Harvard University Press, Cambridge, MA.

Shipman, P. and J. J. Rose (1983) Early hominid hunting, butchering, and carcass processing behaviors: Approaches to the fossil record. *Journal of Anthropological Archaeology* 2:57–98.

Shipman, P. and J. J. Rose (1988) Bone tools: An experimental approach. In *Scanning Electron Microscopy in Archaeology* ed. S. L. Olsen, pp. 303–335. British Archaeological Reports, International Series 452, Oxford, U.K.

Spennemann, D. H. R. (1992) Differential representation of human skeletal remains in eroded and redeposited coastal deposits: A case study from the Marshall Islands. *International Journal of Anthropology* 7:1–8.

Strobel, B., D. R. Shiveley, and. B. B. Roper (2009) Salmon carcass movements in forest streams. *North American Journal of Fisheries Management* 29:702–714.

Tackett, E. C. and K. Whitfield (1987) *Underwater Crime Scene Investigation: Organizing, Training, and Equipping the Dive Team on a Budget.* Sub-Sea Services, Woodland, WA.

Teather, R. G. (1994) *Encyclopedia of Underwater Investigations.* Best Publishing, Flagstaff, AZ.

Thompson, C. E. L., S. Ball, T. J. U. Thompson, and R. Gowland (2011) The abrasion of modern and archaeological bones by mobile sediments: The importance of transport modes. *Journal of Archaeological Science* 38:784–793.

Thorne, C. R., J. C. Bathurst, and R. D. Hey (1987) *Sediment Transport in Gravel-Bed Rivers.* Wiley, New York.

Trapani, J. (1996) *Hydrodynamic Sorting of Avian Skeletal Remains.* Unpublished Senior Honors Thesis, State University of New York, Binghamton, New York.

Trapani, J. (1998) Hydrodynamic sorting of avian skeletal remains. *Journal of Archaeological Science* 25:477–487.

Vanin, S., and S. Zancaner (2011) Post-mortal lesions in freshwater environment. *Forensic Science International* 212:e18–e20. DOI: 10.1016/j.forsciint.2011.05.028.

Van Orden, E. and A. K. Behrensmeyer (2010) Bone abrasion and transport distance: Taphonomic experiments in the East Fork River, Wyoming. *Journal of Vertebrate Paleontology* 30:181A.

Varricchio, D., F. Jackson, B. Scherzer, and J. Shelton (2005) Don't have a cow, man! It's only actualistic taphonomy on the Yellowstone River of Montana. *Journal of Vertebrate Paleontology* 25:126A.

Voorhies, M. R. (1969) Taphonomy and population dynamics of an early Pliocene fauna, Knox County, Nebraska. *University of Wyoming Contributions to Geology, Special Papers* 1:1–69.

Wallace, J. R., R. W. Merritt, R. K. Kimbaraskas, M. E. Benbow, and M. McIntosh (2007) Caddisfly cases assist homicide case: Determining a postmortem submersion interval (PMSI) using aquatic insects. *Proceedings of the American Academy of Forensic Sciences* 13:291–292.

Wallace, J. R., R. W. Merritt, R. Kimbirauskas, M. E. Benbow, and M. McIntosh (2008) Caddisflies assist with homicide case: Determining a postmortem submersion interval using aquatic insects. *Journal of Forensic Sciences* 53:219–221.

Weigelt, J. (1989 [1927]) *Recent Vertebrate Carcasses and Their Paleobiological Implications.* Reprint edition, translated by J. Schaefer. University of Chicago Press, Chicago, IL.

Woodruff, D. and D. Varricchio (2008) Modeling an *Oryctodromeus cubicularis* (Dinosauria) burrow. *Journal of Vertebrate Paleontology* 28:162A.

Woodruff, D. and D. Varricchio (2011) Experimental modeling of a possible *Oryctodromeus Cubicularis* (Dinosauria) burrow. *Palaios* 26:140–151.

Yang S. H., X. M. Huang, R. Xia, Y. C. Xu, and T. D. Dahmer (2011) Use of femur bone density to segregate wild from farmed Dybowski's frog (*Rana dybowskii*). *Forensic Science International* 207:61–65.

Young, T. S. (1989) *A Taphonomic and Paleoecological Study of the Late Pleistocene Vertebrate Deposit from the St. Marks River, Wakulla County, Florida.* Unpublished M.S. Thesis, University of Georgia, Athens, GA.

Marine Environmental Alterations to Bone

NICHOLAS D. HIGGS
JAMES T. POKINES

Contents

Well, this is not a boat accident! And it wasn't any propeller, and it wasn't any coral reef, and it wasn't Jack the Ripper! It was a shark.

—**Oceanographer Matt Hooper,** *Jaws*

143

Introduction

Coastal areas are a frequent setting for forensic investigations, given the frequency of deaths at sea from homicide, suicide, and accidents (Boyle et al. 1997; Copeland 1987; Ebbesmeyer and Haglund 1994, 2002), burials at sea (London et al. 1997), the use of the ocean for deliberate remains disposal after terrestrial homicide (Ebbesmeyer and Haglund 2002), and the potential for transport of remains from river systems into the ocean (Bassett and Manheim 2002; Brooks and Brooks 1997; Dilen 1984; Haglund and Sorg 2002; Nawrocki et al. 1997). Coastal margins present an impenetrable barrier to the further transport of bodies or isolated skeletal elements moved by currents or wave action, with tidal fluctuations allowing objects to be deposited above the water line (Berkeley 2009; Liebig et al. 2003; Liebig et al. 2007; Pyenson 2010; Vullo 2009). Coastal margins also attract large numbers of people into a setting where any remains (skeletonized or fleshed) washing ashore are usually deposited in an exposed area devoid of plant cover. The overall effect is the concentration of many casual observers into a narrow area where exposed remains are typically easier to spot than in other terrestrial settings (forests, grasslands, etc.). The discovery of remains with soft tissue also may be aided by the attraction of avian and terrestrial scavengers feeding in groups. Bodies floating in harbors or other waterways high in marine traffic also increase their chances of discovery, as do suicides or accidental falls from bridges spanning these areas (Ebbesmeyer and Haglund 1994, 2002). This intersection of human activity with the other factors noted increases the frequency of discovery and recovery of human remains from these settings, and the attraction of humans to marine areas with their inherent lethal dangers increases the relative amount of remains in these environments.

This chapter focuses upon the taphonomic alterations typical of skeletal remains recovered from marine environments and how these differ from alterations caused in freshwater or terrestrial environments. Knowledge of these taphonomic alterations is crucial toward understanding the depositional context of the remains as well as distinguishing natural alterations to bone from human sources, including perimortem trauma. Aquatic habitats also offer increased opportunities for biological organisms to colonize remains over terrestrial habitats, creating some taphonomic alterations that are highly distinctive in this regard. Since transport, decomposition, and scavenging of soft tissue affect the taphonomic alterations to bones, these factors also are examined.

Decomposition and Scavenging in Marine Environments

A general pattern has been found across a range of environments that remains decompose more slowly in water than in terrestrial environments (Anderson 2008; Anderson and Bell 2010; Anderson and Hobischak 2002; Sorg et al. 1997; Weigelt 1989 [1927]). This reduced rate of soft tissue loss is a function of multiple factors. Perhaps the most important among these is the reduced ability (floating bodies) or complete exclusion (sunken bodies) of fly (dipteran) maggot masses to colonize a body (Westling 2012). When unscavenged by larger taxa in terrestrial environments, maggot feeding is responsible for the bulk of tissue consumption in a decomposing vertebrate, provided that the temperature and other environmental requirements (including a lack of desiccation of the carcass soft tissue) are met. Additional invertebrate feeding also removes the soft tissue, including beetles of the family Dermestidae, which tend to become more dominant at a set of vertebrate remains after the fly mass has reduced and the remaining soft tissue has become desiccated. Decomposition in water is also inhibited by the generally reduced temperatures, which slow bacterial growth. Additionally, aerobic bacterial growth is inhibited by the anoxic conditions sometimes reached. Scavengers may be partially excluded in cases where bodies are lost in shipwrecks or air crashes and are sealed inside, although a multitude of marine organisms may still reach bodies under these conditions, especially arthropods (Foecke et al. 2010; Raymer 1996). Rapid siltation of portions of wrecks also may exclude macroscavengers, thus leaving behind relatively intact and articulated sets of skeletal remains even hundreds of years later, or highly commingled and incomplete remains where these conditions are not met (Bell and Elkerton 2008; Bell et al. 2009; Stirland 2005). Notable shipwrecks in this regard include the discovery in 2002 of two largely intact skeletons of crewmembers of the USS *Monitor*, which sank in a storm in 1862. These skeletons were in excellent condition and in articulation and were found under the turret of the ship (Fox 2003). In contrast, despite multiple expeditions with crewed and remote submersibles and its deep, cold water resting place, no human remains from the RMS *Titanic* have been discovered to date. Some possible intact remnants of clothing with apparently no remains contained within have been located (National Oceanic and Atmospheric Administration 2012).

As an illustration of the great differences in soft tissue preservation that may occur in deep marine environments, Dumser and Türkay (2008) report the preservational state of remains from two separate air crashes, one west of Namibia in the Atlantic Ocean and the other south of Sicily in the Mediterranean Sea. In both cases, human remains were recovered from a depth of 540–580 m, with a postmortem submergence interval (PMSI) of 3 months for the Namibia air crash and 34 days for the Sicilian air crash. The former site yielded a set of completely skeletonized remains, still loosely associated via their surrounding clothing, while the latter yielded a complete set of remains, still clothed, and with skeletonization only of the skull. While the Namibian remains had a PMSI triple that of the Sicilian remains, Dumser and Türkay (2008) attribute the great difference in soft tissue preservation (and the lack of skeletal disarticulation afforded by it) to the presence of large biomasses of amphipods (tiny arthropods) of the family Lysianassidae or related taxa in the Namibian waters. The Mediterranean waters are depauperate of these highly necrophagous taxa, which in many ways may fill the role of primary soft tissue reduction in marine environments that dipteran maggots play in terrestrial ecosystems. Dumser and Türkay (2008) also note that the small amounts of soft tissue consumption of the Sicilian remains likely can be attributed to larger arthropods, order Decapoda (including crabs, lobsters, etc.).

The rate at which small marine vertebrate and invertebrate scavengers can reduce a mammal carcass has been measured by Jones et al. (1998). They observed the rates of carcass consumption of three small cetacean (dolphin and porpoise species *Lagenorhynchus acutus*, *Phocoena phocoena*, and *Delphinus delphis*) full or partial carcasses placed on the abyssal plain at depths of 4000–4800 m in the northeast Atlantic Ocean. These species are comparable in mass to adult humans. Scavenging loss of tissue was measured over intervals of 36, 152, and 276 h. Even at this great depth, scavenging ensued and proceeded rapidly. The carcasses were monitored remotely, which showed that the carcasses were scavenged rapidly by multiple species of fish and invertebrates. Removal of soft tissue proceeded at rates ranging from 0.05 to 0.4 kg/h. The half-carcass used for the 276 h interval was nearly skeletonized, with only connective tissue still remaining. The main vertebrate scavengers were grenadier fish (*Coryphaenoides armatus*). Primary invertebrate scavengers again were amphipods (at least seven species present), and species of decapod and mollusk (gastropods) were also noted. A turnover of species was also noted over time, similar to terrestrial colonization of carcasses by arthropods. The introduction of large vertebrate carcasses into deep marine environments means the rapid influx of nutrients into an otherwise largely barren environment (Allison et al. 1991) past where sunlight penetrates sufficiently to allow photosynthesis (the euphotic zone), and multiple species have evolved to exploit these nutrients (Tunnicliffe et al. 2010).

Bloating and Water Pressure

The multiple atmospheres of pressure exerted by deep water can prevent a decomposing set of remains from ever rising to the surface from the expansion of decomposition gases, even very large taxa such as whales (Allison et al. 1991). Each 10 m of water exerts one additional atmosphere of pressure, so remains sunk into deep water have little chance of rising to the surface once decay gases are generated internally. The temperatures at great depths are also usually low enough to slow bacterial activity, further delaying decay and the generation of gases. Eventually, an advanced state of decomposition will allow the decay gases to vent, eliminating any further chance of the remains rising to the surface (Allison et al. 1991). The duration that a body decomposing in a marine environment may float is therefore variable and also influenced by prior trauma. Raymer (1996) notes in his personal account of U.S. Navy salvage operations aboard the sunken USS *Arizona* months after the attack that several bodies were still floating within the flooded compartments, largely held together by their clothing. A bloated body, floating to the surface remains approximately 80% under water (Dilen 1984), limiting its exposure even when at the surface to colonization by non-marine organisms.

Given individual variation, amounts of trauma and postmortem scavenging (which would allow some decomposition gases to vent), and ocean temperature (varying the amount of bacterial activity), there is no absolute minimum depth beyond which a human body decomposing on the bottom will fail ever to rise to the surface from decompositional bloating. Certainly, for most areas of the open ocean where depths exceed 3 km (the abyssal plain), the amount of water pressure makes it impossible for a sunken body ever to rise to the surface unaided. Most bodies in coastal areas, however, are likely floating only in hundreds of meters of water or less. Data also are limited by the lack of experimentation on human bodies. Anderson and Hobischak (2002) decomposed a total of twelve 20–25 kg pigs off the coast of British Columbia, Canada. These pigs were tethered to the bottom at two locations, at depths of 7.6 and 15.5 m, with tidal variances in the 1.5–3.0 m range. Only head trauma was accrued when the pigs were euthanized. The pigs could not be observed on a continual basis due to the location, but it appears that at least some of the pigs never floated from among the samples at both depths. Anderson (2008) was able to monitor a 26 kg pig carcass (euthanized by electrocution) remotely in 94 m of ocean water in this same marine area. The temperature at this depth was from 9.5°C to 9.8°C, and the water was poorly oxygenated. This carcass also was tethered to the bottom and did not refloat during the entire length of the experiment (23 days). It is unknown if a human at this depth would refloat, but pressure at this depth added over nine atmospheres above surface pressure.

Adipocere Formation

Multiple studies in both freshwater and saltwater environments have noted the formation of adipocere, and otherwise skeletonized remains from these environments may still be associated with this decomposition product adhering. Adipocere forms from the fat tissues of decomposing bodies and is a white to gray to beige soap-like product that may remain friable or become more dried and brittle, but resists additional decomposition and may persist for centuries or longer (see Chapter 5, this volume). As the adipose tissue breaks down, the triglycerides turn into fatty acids aided by the lipases present in the host body, which are subsequently hydrolyzed and hydrogenated. It is known to form through bacterial action under anaerobic conditions. In particular, the presence of the anaerobic bacteria *Clostridium perfringens* and the optimal temperature range of this species (21°C–45°C) facilitate adipocere formation (O'Brien and Kuehner 2007). Adipocere forms under a broad range of environments in both terrestrial and aquatic environments, including freshwater, saltwater, wetlands/bogs, soil burials, coffin burials, and surface deposits (see Ubelaker and Zarenko [2011] for a recent summary of adipocere research). Its formation is also enhanced by a lack of scavenging, that is, if more fatty tissue remains for breakdown instead of being consumed by macroscavengers (large vertebrates) and microscavengers (amphipods, dipteran larvae, etc.), then the available supply of fatty tissue for conversion is much greater. With the majority of its remaining soft tissue converted to adipocere or consisting of less digestible connective tissue, individual carcasses often become far less attractive to subsequent scavengers, and the adipocere may persist even in an exposed setting. Adipocere may continue to adhere to bones, even when recovered disarticulated and largely unprotected from a marine environment (JTP, pers. obs.) and may be the only remnants of soft tissue on the exterior.

Adipocere formation has been detected in a variety of marine contexts, even where this optimal temperature range is not met (as is usually the case in ocean water, especially at depth). Anaerobic conditions and a frequent lack of scavenging normally prevail in these environments. Adipocere therefore may still form, but slowly. Kahana et al. (1999) examined the remains of 13 crewmembers recovered over the course of 433 days, trapped in the sunken ship *Mineral Dampier* at an approximate depth of 65 m in the East China Sea. These cadavers were recovered over the course of multiple dives to the wreck, after periods of 25, 38, 68, 109, and 433 days, from the same mostly sealed interior environment. Adipocere was detected on the subcutaneous tissue of the cadavers at 38 days from the time of their deaths. The seawater at that depth was 10°C–12°C, far below the optimal range for *Clostridium perfringens*. By 68 days, adipocere formation was extensive, and by 109 days, total saponification had occurred, with the formation of a friable crust and complete skeletonization. Other researchers have indicated the presence of adipocere, including Lewis et al. (2004) on the remains recovered from the fishing trawler *Ehime Maru* off the coast of Oahu, USA. Eight sets of largely intact remains were recovered from inside the ship, which initially sank at 610 m and was moved to shallower water (35 m) for the interior recovery. The remains therefore spent the majority of time in a cold water environment, as the water temperature at the initial wreck site was 5°C–6°C, where the ship remained for 8 months, and 25°C at the final site, where recovery began immediately after moving and proceeded for 3 weeks. Six of seven sets of mostly intact remains, with varying degrees of soft tissue preservation, exhibited adipocere formation.

Marine Transport

The relatively slow decomposition rate in marine environments combined with the action of currents on floating remains can lead to the long-distance transport of bodies, even without attached flotation devices. Regarding the latter occurrence, it is noteworthy that remains were recovered scattered over an area hundreds of square miles around where the RMS *Titanic* sank on April 15, 1912. Some bodies were found as late as June that year, with 337 recovered total from the deceased (Maritime Museum of the Atlantic 2012). By June, the life jackets (constructed primarily of natural materials) were starting to give way and release their remains into the water. Modern life jackets are composed of durable artificial materials that likely would resist falling apart for longer than human remains could persist while decomposing (in temperate or warm waters). Dispersal of bodies with flotation devices attached therefore could take place over hundreds of miles of ocean. Ebbesmeyer and Haglund (2002) describe the 1875 sinking of the paddlewheel steamship *Pacific* at the mouth of the Juan de Fuca Strait (dividing Washington state, USA, and British Columbia, Canada), where 250–300 people aboard drowned. Likely most of the individuals were wearing some kind of life preserver. Bodies were recovered ashore and at sea over the course of a month afterward, with drifts as far as 100 miles back into the strait. Only about 6% of the bodies were ever recovered, despite the narrowness of the waterway, amount of ship traffic, and amount of shoreline searching that took place.

Natural Flotation

Bodies without flotation devices attached follow different trajectories, depending upon the presence of air in the lungs, gases in the intestinal tract, and later the presence of decomposition gases building up internally. The specific gravity (density relative to freshwater) of a human body with these potential gas pockets filled is greater than freshwater (1.000, by definition) or typical seawater (1.026). As a body begins to sink, the increasing pressure of the water (one additional atmosphere per 10 m of depth) on the remaining gas pockets will cause them to contract, further decreasing the body's buoyancy (Donoghue and Minnigerode 1977). The main determinant of whether a body sinks or floats initially is the amount of air remaining in the lungs. Even at residual lung capacity (the amount of air remaining after maximum exhalation), 69% of bodies float in seawater, following the sample of 98 (living, healthy) adult males examined by Donoghue and Minnigerode (1977). In freshwater, with its lower density due to the lower amounts of dissolved minerals, the amount that floated under these conditions plummets to 7%. Variations among individuals are caused by multiple factors, including relative lung volume and amount of adipose tissue. The residual lung capacity is roughly equivalent to the amount of air in a recently deceased person entering the water, provided that water has not filled the lungs and decreased overall buoyancy. Only minor amounts of additional mass are needed to sink a body, so drowning victims are more likely on average to sink initially. Weighting down by dense objects typically attached to persons in or around water, including tools, fishing gear and nets, heavy footwear, or deliberate weighting for divers to achieve neutral or negative buoyancy, also may interrupt this delicate balance and cause a body to sink.

The distances traveled by floating bodies can be enormous, depending upon the prevailing currents and lack of landfall to halt progress, and travel can be rapid. Giertsen and

Morild (1989) report the long-distance floating of two separate bodies in the North Sea from Denmark to Norway, with a distance of approximately 500 km. Both bodies were the results of falls from fishing vessels, with one floating for 4–6 months and the other floating for 4–6 weeks. Ebbesmeyer and Haglund (1994) found that a body traveled over 32 km to the location ashore that it was recovered in a maximum of 56.5 h in the Puget Sound (Washington state, USA) after a voluntary plunge from a high bridge. Following the collapse of a bridge in Portugal, Blanco Pampín et al. (2001) report that bodies were swept downriver and then transported distances of over 220 km along the Portuguese and Spanish coast, in as little as 3 days in some cases. In this instance, bodies recovered within 5 days of the accident showed little signs of decomposition, while those recovered after 20 days showed advanced decomposition.

Dispersal of Body Parts

The decomposition and float patterns of bodies in water lead to the gradual dispersal of individual portions of a body, as these are successively lost (Dodson 1973; Haglund 1993; Stojanowski 2002; Voorhies 1969). As Haglund and Sorg (2002) note, the typical alignment of a floating human body is very different from that of most other animals. Human arms and legs are very long and large relative to trunk size, and these along with the head tend to dangle inferiorly freely as the body drifts, posterior side up. Due to the relative density of the head, arms, and legs vs. the less dense trunk (which has some gas spaces filled or the body would not be floating at all without artificial help), this position is relatively stable. Advanced bloating of the abdomen may change this relationship and cause a human body to float anterior side up (Haglund and Sorg 2002). Other animals, such as pigs (*Sus scrofa*), have limbs that are shorter and smaller relative to their trunks, so their floating position is likely to be much more variable, especially after advanced decomposition begins. This difference in overall body plan makes pigs, the usual human analog for taphonomic experiments, particularly unsuited to study the effects of human body movement in water, which is in part why multiple experimenters (Dilen 1984; D'Alonzo et al. 2012) opt to use dummies to mimic natural human drift characteristics. This typical human drift position also allows the extremities to be dragged across shallow bottom surfaces or to become snagged on objects to a greater degree than for many other drifting species, for example, seals with their shorter limbs and streamlined bodies.

As decomposition proceeds in water environments, the extremities tend to be lost first (Haglund 1993; Haglund and Sorg 2002). This includes the mandible, which can swing freely in this environment. Haglund (1993) plotted the loss of body parts from 11 sets human remains from previous investigations in the Seattle and New York City areas and including multiple water settings (still and flowing freshwater and saltwater). He noted that the loss of skeletal parts followed a general sequence: bones of the hands and wrists, being more exposed, were typically lost first. These were followed by the bones of the feet and ankles and then the mandible and cranium. Element loss continued to the lower legs and forearms, followed by the upper arms. This sequence, of course, can be modified by the prior occurrence of perimortem trauma (including boat propeller or marine animal attack), later scavenging, changes in body float position, or elements becoming trapped in clothing. Soft tissue loss occurred most rapidly in areas where it thinly overlays bone, including the skull, hands, and anterior tibia. As bones drop off of a floating body in open ocean, it is very unlikely that these isolated elements will be recovered.

Direct Marine Alterations to Bone

Many data about the taphonomic alterations to bones from marine settings must be derived post hoc, due to the difficulties involved in direct observations of marine feeding behavior even under controlled experimental conditions (Anderson 2008; Anderson and Hobischak 2002). These difficulties include the specialized equipment and training necessary, such as boats, SCUBA, or underwater monitoring equipment; the physical difficulties of operating in an energetic or deep marine environment; the corrosive salt-water environment; the limited visibility; the necessity in many jurisdictions to acquire permits before depositing decomposing remains in the ocean; and the presence of many macroscavengers that may terminate experiments prior to the observation of slower taphonomic processes.

Sediment and Substrate Abrasion

Marine environments, especially coastal margins, present perhaps the most energetic environment for sedimentary abrasion and rounding of bone. Freshwater fluvial systems have not been found to abrade bone significantly under experimental conditions (Chapter 6, this volume). This difference likely includes the differences in substrate, with shorelines being dominated by sand-sized particles of mineral or biological (coral, shell, etc.) origin. Freshwater fluvial systems often are dominated by silt and clay deposits with rounded, rocky beds. Isolated bones in fluvial systems often undergo transport until they are captured by some obstacle and may remain in one place for extended periods. The constant wave action of coastal marine environments tumbles any mobile objects in them through an abrasive substrate, often punctuated with sharp, rocky areas. The overall effect abrades bone to give it a characteristic rounding of edges (Figure 7.1). Irmis and Elliot (2006) attempted to recreate the effects of the repeated sediment abrasion on bone in an experimental setting, using modern shark (*Odontaspis* sp.) and eagle ray (*Myliobatis* sp.) teeth, fine siliceous

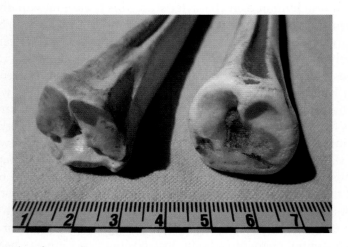

Figure 7.1 Example of rounding in a marine coastal environment: the white-tailed deer (*Odocoileus virginianus*) metatarsal on the left is intact, and the one on the right was recovered from a marine coastal environment. Note the rounding of the original precise margins and projections and the bleaching. Scale is in cm.

sand, and saltwater in a reciprocal shaker to simulate wave action. Agitation proceeded in 100 h cycles for a total of 1000 h, at 180 cycles per minute. While this degree of abrasion may seem excessive, 1000 h represent only less than 42 days in total. Bones recovered from marine coastal margins may have been agitated in the natural environment for much longer, although they likely go through periods of temporary burial in the sand alternating with periods of constant wave action, proceeding constantly (though at a slower rate than 180 cycles/min). Bones in a natural setting are also likely exposed to coarser sand. Irmis and Elliot (2006) noted progressive rounding of the crown and root margins and cracking across the crowns. They also noted that sometimes the mass of individual teeth increased, despite the slow erosion through abrasion, due to embedding of sand particles in the cracks formed. Many portions of mammal bone (especially thin cortical areas of the epiphyses) are less dense and thick than the teeth used in their experiment and so may be far more susceptible to abrasion, with rounding giving way to sudden exposure of cancellous bone and further degradation.

Further rounding experiments by Fernández-Jalvo and Andrews (2003) examined a variety of large mammal bone types (fresh, lightly weathered/dry, highly weathered, and fossilized) in multiple abrasive (very coarse sand, coarse sand, fine sand and silt, and silt and clay) settings. Only previously unabraded bone fragments were used. The bones were agitated in a series of rock tumblers under a constant speed of 15 cm/s, yielding a notional movement of the bones relative to the sediment of 540 m/h. Experimental periods ran for 72, 192, and 360 h. Overall, coarser sediments produced greater degrees of rounding on fresh and lightly weathered/dry bone, but this relationship was reversed on highly weathered and fossilized bone. Fresh bones introduced into a marine coastal environment, with their typically coarse sediments, can undergo high amounts of polishing from natural wave agitation. It is also noteworthy that sediment abrasion polishing of bone surfaces can remove earlier signs of weathering, indicating that highly reworked bones recovered from marine coastal environments may no longer have traces of prior deposition on land. Deep cracks from previous advanced weathering in a terrestrial environment, however, may be retained even after substantial abrasion (Fernández-Jalvo and Andrews 2003:159).

Bones also may get dragged by wave action over jagged rocky outcrops and other sharp objects, which can leave traces of abrasion behind, provided that further polishing does not remove these traces. This type of surface scoring can be oriented in any direction, although multiple scores often will be created in parallel as the bone is dragged across an object with multiple projections. This type of surface scoring is analogous to that caused by tramping of bone in terrestrial settings, where the bone is pushed against surface rocks or against those adjacent to it in the soil.

Sediment Embedding

Osseous remains recovered from coastal settings frequently have embedded sand particles in their exposed medullary cavities, trabecular bone, foramina, and surface cracks (Irmis and Elliot 2006). During initial recovery, transport, processing, storage, and analysis, it is important to retain this evidence of the specimen's origin, since sand particles adhere less strongly to bone than do terrestrial sediments heavy in clay and organic content. This simple but effective source of contextual evidence therefore can be lost readily or is frequently not recorded in forensic taphonomic examinations.

Concretion

Concretion is the deposition of a cement-like substance around ferrous objects in saltwater (Green 2004:262), which can encompass any adjacent object, including bone. This form of taphonomic alteration is more relevant to underwater archaeological excavations than to forensic recoveries due to the time needed for this process to accrue. The presence of concretion on bone therefore may be a useful indicator that bone is of historical/archaeological age than recent.

Bleaching and Staining

Bones recovered from marine environments typically become bleached white (Figure 7.1) from chemical reactions with the saltwater. Very little is understood about the timing of this change, likely due to the difficulties of recovering experimentally placed bones at known intervals from saltwater settings without significant recovery loss and the amount of time necessary likely exceeding that of available research programs.

Marine bleaching can be distinguished from the bleaching caused by sunlight in the subaerial weathering of bone (see Chapter 11, this volume) by its overall pattern, which typically affects all areas of a bone simultaneously and is unsurprising given the saltwater environment affecting all exposed bone surfaces. Subaerial weathering often advances to greater degrees on the portion of a bone most exposed to sunlight, while the downward-facing aspect of the bone lags multiple weathering stages behind. Bleaching caused by subaerial weathering is also accompanied by cracking and exfoliation of the bone surface, which is not typically the case for marine-bleached bone. Bones washed ashore after having undergone marine bleaching are often in an exposed position and can start to proceed through the subaerial weathering stages that are typical to terrestrial surface deposits. Thus, many received bones from coastal margins have both types of bleaching. Salt crystal formation from drying bone (see later) also may mimic the more common cracking caused by subaerial weathering. Some marine settings also cause the mineral staining of bone (see Chapter 12, this volume).

Salt Crystal Formation

Bones submerged in saltwater for extended periods absorb salt ions (primarily Na^+ and Cl^-) into their porous structure. This porosity is increased by the breakdown of the organic collagen component and the partial dissolution of the mineral portion, expanding extant pores and channels. When the bone is dried, the salt can recrystallize, with the crystal expansion causing cracking and surface flaking of the bone (see Figure 12.14, Chapter 12, this volume). Skeletal remains that have been submerged long term in the ocean must be flushed with freshwater in order to reduce the salt content. Following the guidelines put forth by Hamilton (1997, 1999/2001, 2010), the recommended conservator process is to keep the bone in 100% saltwater until ready for processing. It is then placed into successive dilutions of saltwater to freshwater: 75% saltwater/25% freshwater; 50% saltwater/50% freshwater; 25% saltwater/75% freshwater; and then 100% freshwater. The bone is then passed through successive rinses of freshwater or through running freshwater until the soluble salt level reaches that of the local freshwater. Distilled water then replaces the freshwater until the soluble salts are removed or reach minimal levels, as determined by an electrical conductivity meter. The bone can then be slowly air-dried at this time.

Human skeletal remains washed up ashore and recovered some time later are likely to have dried out and begun salt crystallization. This process can be highly damaging to the bone (Prassack 2011) and is already unavoidable under these circumstances.

Adhering Marine Taxa

Multiple marine taxa adhere themselves to hard substrates, either for support (sessile life forms) or to feed upon organisms already colonizing that substrate, such as limpets (a common gastropod) feeding upon algae. The buildup of these colonizing organisms on artificial surfaces, such as ships hulls and propellers, is termed *biofouling* (Bixler and Bhushan 2012). This term may also be extended to natural inorganic particulate buildup. When these taxa adhere themselves to bone, either the attaching organisms themselves or traces of their attachment method may be preserved on the surface and indicate its deposition in a saltwater (or at least an aquatic) environment. Many of these taxa disperse via a tiny larval stage, so that the adult forms may grow and develop seemingly spontaneously. These species are very common in the intertidal and shallow marine zones and are frequently encountered or in many cases harvested commercially.

Algae and Kelp

Algae are a diverse and disparate group of marine organisms that range in size from microscopic protists to large seaweeds and kelp. They are found throughout the world in almost every environment. Only the marine macroalgae or "seaweeds" will be considered here, although microalgae may play a role in the bioerosion of skeletal matter in the marine environment. The classification and evolutionary relationships of algae are a matter of current research, but it has become increasingly clear that the algae are not a taxonomically coherent group of organisms and belong to at least four different kingdoms. The seaweeds have been traditionally divided into three groups: the green algae (Chlorophyceae), the brown algae (Phaeophyceae), and the red algae (Rhodophyceae). This classification is useful for the nonexpert and forms the basis for an excellent color guide to the common macroalgae of the world's oceans by Braune and Guiry (2011). Almost all species of brown algae and most species of red algae occur in the marine realm, but a significant proportion of green algae also occur in brackish and freshwater environments.

Algae will colonize almost any hard substrate, including shells and bone as long as they are reasonably stable (Zimmerman and Wallace 2008). Most produce their own food through photosynthesis, so they are restricted to the euphotic zone, which will vary in depth depending on the turbidity of the local seas. Growth rates can vary and are affected by seasonality, as well as a host of other factors such as wave exposure, nutrient availability, and temperature.

The simplest forms of macroalgae are made up of thin filaments that can be branching or unbranching, which can form dense mats that proliferate rapidly to cover their substrate. Larger forms of algae have a more complex three-dimensional structure, termed the thallus. This can be divided into various regions such as leafy fronds or lamina. In some forms such as kelp, there is a stem-like structure called the stipe, which is attached to the substrate by a holdfast. Holdfasts may be simple disk shapes or have ramulose appendages called haptera that embed the thallus to the substrate. The holdfasts attach to their substrate using a glycoprotein or acid-polysaccharide/protein complex that is strong enough to create a distinct holdfast scar if the algae are ripped away by waves (Bromley and Heinberg 2006).

Additionally, the algae may leave etching traces on the bone surface. It may be possible to use holdfast diameter to gain an approximation of PMSI, but the relationship between age and holdfast diameter is strongly influenced by wave exposure. The diversity of algal colonization has also been used to estimate PMSI in brackish water (Zimmerman and Wallace 2008), and similar PMSI estimation has been attempted using bacterial colonization in marine water (Dickson and Poulter 2010). Interestingly, algal growth also may be responsible for transporting skeletal elements when the buoyancy of attached algae overcomes the mass of the bone (e.g., Gilbert 1984).

In contrast to the more ornate forms taken on by seaweeds, several families of red algae form calcified crusts on their substrate. These are known as the crustose coralline algae (CCA) and are some of the most common algal forms found throughout the oceans (Steneck 1986). Coralline algae vary from flat simple crusts to complex three dimensionally branching structures known as rhodoliths. The calcareous structures produced by CCA do record growth increments, but their slow growth rates mean that they are probably of more use to archaeological studies. In general, the flat thin forms grow faster than thicker forms. Branching forms typically grow at 0.3–10 mm per year (Steneck 1986).

Bryozoa

Bryozoa (literally: moss animals) are colonial filter-feeding animals found in both freshwater and marine environments. Colonies are made up of minute (~0.5 mm) individual zooids, housed in a protective covering that may be organic or mineralized (e.g., calcium carbonate), which may survive long after the animal has died. These zooid colonies can grow into extensive arborescent or foliose forms, but more commonly, they form mats that spread over the surface of a firm substrate. Sorg et al. (1997) suggested that bryozoans might be useful in a forensic context, since the size of the mat colony may be used to indicate a minimum PMSI; however, their variable growth rates mean that this can only ever be an approximation at best. There is no record of bryozoans being used in a forensic context, but their presence on human bones from shipwrecks suggests that there may be some forensic utility warranting further investigation (Steptoe and Wood 2002).

Barnacles

Barnacles (infraclass: Cirripedia) are members of the Arthropoda Subphylum Crustacea, which includes crabs, shrimp, and lobster. These taxa have a long history of biological study, including early research by Charles Darwin (Love 2002). When in a larval stage, they drift in marine waters until reaching a stable surface on which to grow and remain sessile for their adult lives. They are found in deep water but most abundantly in shallow water and the intertidal zone and only in marine and brackish environments, so their growth on an object indicates its at least temporary deposition in an oceanic setting. They normally grow on rocks but are also commonly found on other biological organisms, including whales, mollusk shells, turtle shells, and upon each other (Figure 7.2). They also grow on artificial objects, including ships' hulls, wooden pilings, driftwood, rope, anchor cables, breakwaters, or any solid object tossed into the ocean. Their removal is a constant requirement of maritime maintenance (Bixler and Bhushan 2012; Dickinson et al. 2009). Acorn barnacles (order Sessilia) are attached directly to substrates and have a rounded shape (Figure 7.3), while stalked or gooseneck barnacles (order Pedunculata) attach by means of a flexible stalk. Their bodies are protected by calcified plates, and these hard parts commonly are preserved after the barnacle dies and the soft tissue decomposes or desiccates

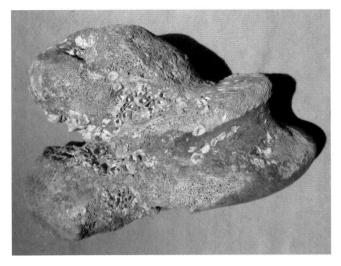

Figure 7.2 Example of acorn barnacle growth on bone recovered from a marine environment. Note the round patches left behind after barnacles have detached, the clustering of barnacles in depressions, and the erosion of exposed cortical bone.

Figure 7.3 Example of acorn barnacle growth on bone recovered from a marine environment. Note the round patches left behind after barnacles have detached. Scale is in cm.

(Figure 7.4). Due to their design and direct attachment to substrates, acorn barnacles are more likely to remain adhered to a bone or other objects after it has been deposited on land.

Acorn barnacles attach themselves by their dorsal surface to a hard substrate, and most species capture plankton and other microscopic food by fanning their appendages. Their adhesive is also a natural protein polymer that holds them tightly even to moving objects (marine mammals and ships' hulls) and rocks subjected to heavy wave action (Dickinson et al. 2009; Stewart et al. 2011). Since barnacles are sessile organisms, indicators of their growth may provide a useful means of determining a minimum value for PMSI. Barnacle growth is recorded in their calcareous plates as incremental growth bands

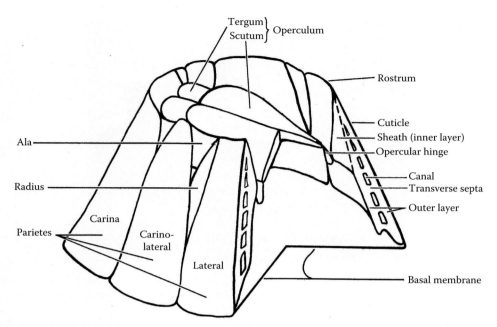

Figure 7.4 Anatomy of an acorn barnacle's skeleton. (Slightly modified with kind permission from Springer Science + Business Media: *Skeletal Growth of Aquatic Organisms*, eds. Rhoades, D.C. and Lutz, R.A., Barnacle shell growth in relation to environmental factors, 1980, 469, Bourget, E.)

(Bourget and Crisp 1975). Several types of skeletal increments have been recorded in barnacle hard parts: (a) growth bands seen in radial thin sections of the parietes (wall plates), (b) ridges on the external surfaces of the parietes, (c) prominent ridges on the operculum (plates surrounding the aperture), and (d) circular increments of the base plate (Clare et al. 1994; Crisp and Bourget 1985). These increments are influenced by numerous cyclical factors, both internal and external, ranging in their temporal scale from tidal to annual (Crisp and Bourget 1985).

Growth bands seen in radial sections of barnacle wall plates appear to represent cycles of feeding (rapid growth) and stress (reduced growth) that are dominated by the tidal regime of their surroundings. Consequently, barnacles from the intertidal zone, which are subject to tidal cycles of submergence and exposure, show the most defined bands, while those that are continuously submerged (i.e., grow underwater) show less-defined banding. Laboratory experiments have shown that the number of bands corresponds directly to tidal cycles of submergence and emergence, even when the period is artificially manipulated (Bourget and Crisp 1975). Barnacles grown under uniform conditions in the laboratory, continuously submerged, produce two growth bands per day, presumably because of endogenous rhythms (Bourget 1980). Seasonal variations in the thickness of the growth bands have been recorded where thin bands represent periods of reduced growth in the winter and so may provide a means of aging specimens that are several years old.

Growth ridges on the surface of the plates have received less attention than cross-sectional growth banding, but studies to date show that the two types of growth increment are asynchronous and probably have different underlying causes (Bourget and Crisp 1975). The major ridges (also called hirsute ridges by some authors) on the parietes and opercular plates (a and b, provided earlier) can be considered together, since they seem to increase synchronously (Clare et al. 1994). These ridges are the result of the animal's molting cycle but are not always laid down on every molt and would seem to be of little use in aging individuals. Nevertheless, the number of external ridges on the opercula of *Balanus amphitrite* showed a linear relationship with the age of the barnacle over the first 25 days of measurement (Clare et al. 1994). In this instance, each ridge represented 1.3–1.8 days of growth, but the authors note that in another species, *B. improvisus*, each ridge took 1.8–2.3 days to form, so caution must be exercised when considering this method of aging. In regions of extreme seasonality, "winter rings" may be observed on the outer surface of parietes as distinct overhangs or notches, where growth has severely reduced during the winter (Bourget 1980). These seasonal growth rings offer a means to age animals in the longer term and have been used to age animals on several occasions (Bourget 1980; Crisp 1954).

The fourth type of growth increment, growth rings found on the basal plate, has received almost no attention, but is likely to the most useful to forensic investigators because of its durability on the attachment surface. In the absence of data on the periodicity of growth ring formation on the base plate, the total size of the base plate can be considered as an indicator of time since colonization and possibly used to determine a minimum PMSI. The diameter of the base plate increases linearly during the early phases of growth but decreases after maturity. By dividing the total diameter of the base plate by the maximum recorded growth rate, it is possible to obtain a very conservative estimate of PMSI. This method should be used only as a last resort, since growth varies markedly depending on a host of factors. For example, recorded growth rates the basal diameter of *Balanus balanoides* vary between 33 and 169 µm per day, as do growth rates for a variety of other species (Crisp and Bourget 1985:212–214). Growth rates should be considered on a species-by-species basis, since large species grow more slowly, as do those growing at high tide levels.

Barnacle growth increments have rarely been utilized in forensic cases, but are not without precedent. The use of barnacles to estimate the time of immersion for a cadaver recovered from the sea was reported well over a century ago, showing that "in certain cases, zoology can aid forensic science" (Mégnin 1894:110). Two more recent cases where the basal diameter of barnacles was used to provide a minimum estimate of time since death were reported by Sorg et al. (1997) and Skinner et al. (1988). The analysis of growth increments or ridges on barnacle plates was attempted by Dennison et al. (2004) to estimate a minimum time since death, although little methodological information was provided.

Mollusks

Members of Phylum Mollusca, Class Bivalvia (i.e., bivalves), include those mollusk species having two shells joined by a hinge, such as mussels, clams, oysters, and scallops. Many of these species are sessile and attach themselves permanently to hard substrates in marine (and freshwater) environments. From there, they filter-feed from the environment. Dispersal is achieved through larval drift, until the larvae attach themselves and begin to grow. Attachment of mussels (including the commonly consumed marine mussels of the family Mytilidae) to their substrate is achieved with byssal threads known commonly the "beard" strands. This natural adhesive is formed from secreted cross-linked proteins (Hight and Wilker 2007; Waite 2002). The byssal threads are silklike and very strong, having to hold mussels firmly attached in the energetic intertidal zone. Byssal threads may still be attached to a bone or other object after the mussel has been detached. Other bivalves, including some clams and freshwater mussels, also attach themselves to substrates using byssal threads, so the presence of these can be used only as an indicator of bone deposition in an aquatic, not necessarily marine, environment.

Members of Phylum Mollusca, Class Gastropoda, include some mollusk species having just a single, spiral shell (snails) or no shell (slugs). Common marine snails include Littorinidae, the winkles and periwinkles. Limpets (Patellogastropoda) are a ubiquitous taxon of marine snails having a conical, instead of spiral, shell. Both of these groups are commonly found in the intertidal zone, attached to rocks and other hard surfaces. These species are not sessile and move about on these surfaces when feeding (Figures 7.5 and 7.6). When needed, including when exposed to the air during low tide, these species adhere tightly to the surface and are difficult to pry loose. Attachment is aided by the secretion of an adhesive mucus (Smith 2002). Their resting spots may also leave an identifiable patch on the substrate. When removed from the ocean attached to a bone or other object, the mollusk will eventually dehydrate and die and may remain attached. Their presence therefore may indicate marine deposition, although their attachment will not be as permanent as other taxa discussed here.

Figure 7.5 Example of mollusk encrustation on bone recovered from a marine environment. As the mollusks desiccate and die, they can remain attached or flake off, as in the case of the large mollusk detached above from the oval area on the bone. Scale is in cm.

Figure 7.6 Close-up of mollusk encrustation on bone recovered from a marine environment. As the mollusks desiccate and die, they can remain attached or flake off, leaving behind oval marks on the bone (center).

Coral

Corals (Phylum Cnidaria, Class Anthozoa, which also includes anemones) are an abundant, diverse group of sessile marine life forms found throughout the world. Their fertilized eggs drift until reaching a hard substrate, where they attach and begin to grow into their adult polyp form. Some of these (the stony corals or order Scleractinia) form coral reefs through the gradual deposition of calcium carbonate ($CaCO_3$) to house these colonial organisms and act as an exoskeleton. Many of these hard coral species are also symbiotic with forms of algae and therefore are found only in the euphotic zone. Hard corals and reef formation are most common in shallow tropical waters. Substrates for coral formation include rock, dead coral, artificial objects, and potentially bone.

The rates at which coral species can begin to deposit calcium carbonate in an identifiable manner is variable and affected by environmental conditions (Bessat and Buigues 2001; Lough and Cooper 2011; Rasher et al. 2012). Deposition of calcium carbonate has been measured (linearly) in terms of a few millimeters per year. The annual banding of coral (Lough and Cooper 2011) also has potential as a dating source to provide a minimum age of deposition, although this has not been applied to forensics.

Marine Bioerosion

The term *bioerosion* is defined as the removal of bone by living organisms, as a result of tunneling into the bone for shelter or nutrition or through marking the surface in conjunction with feeding on attached soft tissues or other adhering organisms. The study of bone bioerosion in marine contexts has been limited to date, and most of the available information has been gleaned from studies of marine mammal remains and paleontological evidence of bone bioerosion. Nevertheless, a wide variety of marine organisms are known to bioerode bone, and this behavior is recorded well back into the fossil record (Belaústegui et al. 2012 and references therein). Recent human remains deposited into the ocean therefore are subjected to alteration by taxa that have evolved for millions of years to exploit these large packages of nutrients in an otherwise nutrient-poor environment (Britton and Morton 1994; Jones et al. 1998).

Human anatomy differs in several respects from that of marine vertebrates in multiple relevant aspects, so some types of taphonomic alteration that are recorded on other specimens are far less likely to occur on human bones. The size of humans is at the lower end of the scale when compared to extant marine mammals, the largest of which (whales) include the largest vertebrate species ever to evolve on the planet. In addition, the structure of human bones differs from sea mammals. Whale bone has a very high lipid content that serves as an abundant, long-lasting nutrient supply to the organisms colonizing a whale carcass on the ocean floor (Allison et al. 1991; Higgs et al. 2011a). Manatee (*Trichechus* spp.) long bones and ribs have a very high density due to increased mineralization and a reduction of interior spaces (pachyostosis), likely an adaptation to help maintain neutral buoyancy (Clifton et al. 2008). Other differences include reduction or absence of rear appendages of some sea mammals, making their skeletons not easily analogous to humans even where there is a general body size overlap. Deep layers of subcutaneous fat also may alter patterns of decomposition between humans and sea mammals, making skeletonization follow different paths (Higgs et al. 2011a).

Differences in taphonomic alterations between humans and marine vertebrates may also relate to the normal depth range inhabited by the taxon causing the alteration. While human remains may reach that depth as a result of shipwreck or air crash, they are unlikely to be recovered from it as they are from shallower coastal contexts. Newer technology and methods, however, are allowing the recovery of human remains from depths over 500 m (Dumser and Türkay 2008; Lewis et al. 2004). In a more extreme case, several sets of remains were recovered 2 years later from the June 2009 crash of Air France Flight 447 in the South Atlantic off the coast of Brazil. All 228 aboard were killed, and the causes of the crash are still under investigation (BEA 2011). The depth of this Airbus A330–203 wreckage ranged up to 4000 m (the abyssal plain), and the recovery of bodies and key pieces of wreckage were through the use of remote submersibles (BEA 2011; Clifford 2011; Purcell et al. 2011). Deep-water dwelling taxa that alter human remains therefore will become more important to forensic analyses as recoveries of this type from ships and aircraft become common.

Belaústegui et al. (2012) in their review of vertebrate remains in marine settings list microbioerosion (i.e., microboring) and five categories of macrobioerosion: (1) invertebrate grazing traces, (2) osteophagous crab traces, (3) worm borings, (4) bivalve borings, and (5) vertebrate predator/scavenger traces. Additionally, Higgs et al. (2012) highlighted evidence of sponge borings in bone as another source of bioerosion. The categories that have the highest relevance to forensic, as opposed to paleontological or marine biological, analyses are discussed in the following text.

Microboring

Marine microboring into bone is caused by microscopic organisms, including fungi, bacteria, and cyanobacteria (Arnaud et al. 1978; Ascenzi and Silvestrini 1984; Davis 1997; Yoshino et al. 1991). These taphonomic alterations (focal destruction) are also evident in bones from terrestrial settings and are discussed in more detail in Chapter 2 of this volume. Evidence from the few available studies indicates that there is a contrast in microboring morphology between terrestrial and marine environments. Wedl-type tunneling is the most common type of focal destruction observed in bone from marine environments (Bell and Elkerton 2008; Trueman and Martill 2002; Yoshino et al. 1991), whereas bacterial focal destruction is more common in terrestrial settings. It is generally thought that Wedl tunneling is caused by cyanobacteria (Bell and Elkerton 2008; Davis 1997) or fungi (Trueman and Martill 2002). The onset of bioerosion may be rapid: Davis (1997) reports that experimentally deployed bones were bioeroded within 4 days off the coast of Florida, USA.

Microorganisms play key roles in bone bioerosion by enabling and encouraging larger animals to graze the bones. Firstly, the nutritive value of the microorganisms attracts larger animals to graze the surface layers. The bone mineral–collagen matrix is a highly refractile, indigestible food source, but the microbial bioeroders are able to unlock collagen nutrients and make them available to larger animals in the food chain. Secondly, the degree to which the microorganisms penetrate the bone severely compromises its structural integrity, allowing grazers easily to erode the bone.

Invertebrate Grazing Traces

A wide variety of invertebrates are known to graze hard substrates for the microorganisms and algae growing in or on them, including several chitons and gastropod mollusks, sea urchins, and crabs. Representatives from all of these groups have been identified grazing on bones in the marine environment and leave telltale evidence of grazing activity on the bone's surface. Mollusks have a chitinous feeding appendage called the radula that is studded with rows of minute teeth, often hardened by the incorporation of metal compounds.

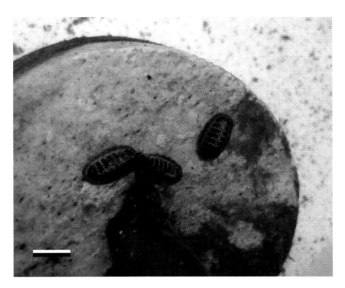

Figure 7.7 Chitons (class Polyplacophora) grazing a sample of whale bone. Note the dark algal growth on the bone's surface (lower right), which has been grazed off the rest of the bone. The surface also shows slight pitting from the grazing action of the chitons. Scale is 1 cm.

They use the radula to scrape away or rasp algae that are embedded in the bone, thereby removing layers of bone as they do so (Figure 7.7). Radular grazing traces (known as *radulichnus*) consist of parallel striations having a surface relief of 20–100 μm (Bromley 1994). They occur in multiple blocks of parallel striations and may cover a large surface area. Several families of deep-water gastropods are known to specialize on bone and have been found with guts full of bone debris (e.g., Haszprunar 1988; Marshall 1987; Warén 2011). Large deep-sea snails of the genus *Rubyspira* were found feeding on whale bones at a depth of 2890 m in the Monterey Canyon off California, USA, but have not been found on other skeletons shallower than 1500 m in the canyon (Johnson et al. 2010). Bones deposited in shallow waters also may become rapidly colonized by grazing mollusks, but little is known about the rates at which bones are degraded in different marine environments.

Sea urchins have a five-toothed jaw apparatus that they use to scrape the surface of bones, producing a star-shaped pattern of grooves in the surface. In the paleontological literature, these traces have been given the name *gnathichnus pentax* and are highly distinctive. They indicate marine deposition but offer little information on minimum submergence interval and occur in both deep and shallow settings. Figure 7.8 shows experimentally deployed whale bones being grazed by pencil urchins in deep waters off of Scotland.

Osteophagous Crab Traces
Grazing crabs have been documented only on bones from deep-water environments to date. Squat lobsters are frequently observed on whale skeletons on the deep-seabed (Smith and Baco 2003; Lundsten et al. 2010) and have been shown to be grazing the bone directly (Hoyoux et al. 2012). Tanner crabs have been observed to destroy and consume bones containing *Osedax* worms, probably preying on the worms themselves (see Braby et al. 2007 and their supplemental video footage). Nevertheless, this can lead to rapid destruction of bones that have already been weakened by the boring activities of other invertebrates. This type of bioerosion does not create distinctive traces but leads to a general erosion of friable parts of the bone.

Figure 7.8 Cidarid sea urchins grazing on whale bones on the deep seabed.

Worm Borings

Annelids are some of the most prolific borers of hard substrates in the marine realm, particularly polychaetes worms of the Spionidae and the Cirratulidae families. Their borings have been well studied because of their economic significance as blight on oyster shells (Blake and Evans 1973), as well as their paleontological and ecological significance. The borings may take a variety of forms but are typically U-shaped with two openings at the surface. Almost all worm borings are thought primarily to be protective domiciles, since very few hard substrates can provide nourishment. The shell-boring spionid polychaetes are known to orient their excavations with feeding currents or those created by the host, affording some nutritional benefits to the organism. Despite the ubiquity of polychaete borings in calcareous substrates, only one highly specialized genus of these worms has been recorded boring into bone.

Osedax (literally "bone devourers") worms subsist entirely on the skeletal remains of vertebrates on the seabed (Figure 7.9). Initially described from whale skeletons, they also have been documented living on experimentally implanted pig, cow, and fish bones (Jones et al. 2008; Rouse et al. 2011). There are over 20 known species of *Osedax* worms, mostly inhabiting deep waters below 100 m depth (Fujikura et al. 2006; Glover et al. 2005, 2008; Rouse et al. 2004; Vrijenhoek et al. 2009); however, a few specimens have been found living on bones at 30 m during winter at high latitudes (Dahlgren et al. 2006). These worms have been recorded in deep waters of most of the world's oceans, and some species have been found on both sides of the Pacific. They can colonize bones within 2 months and occur in high densities, up to 30/cm^2 (Braby et al. 2007; Goffredi et al. 2004). The worms remain in the same place once they begin to bore into the bone and do so using specialized root tissue that releases a combination of acids and proteolytic enzymes, capable of dissolving the bone's collagen/mineral matrix (Higgs et al. 2011b).

Unlike other worm borings, those of *Osedax* are not U-shaped, and only small round openings of the borings can be seen from the surface of the bone. Inside the bone, the

Figure 7.9 Close-up of *Osedax* worms living on whale bone.

Figure 7.10 A whale bone after colonization by *Osedax* worms. Inset to the right shows a close-up of the pitted texture of the bone's surface where numerous borings have merged and the surface layer of bone has eroded. Bore holes can be seen in intact bone at the top of the inset. Scale is 10 cm.

borings expand into bulbous chambers that may merge to create large subsurface cavities (Higgs et al. 2010, 2011b). Sometimes the thin surface layer of bone may collapse, leaving behind round pits or extensive areas of eroded bone (Figure 7.10; see also Higgs et al. 2012). Recorded rates of penetration into the bone vary widely depending on the species, but the only data available suggest that it occurs on the order of 4–10 mm per year. In some cases, whole bones may be destroyed in 3–10 years (Higgs et al. 2012; Lundsten et al. 2010). There are not enough data available to estimate PMSI using *Osedax* borings, but the presence of live specimens may allow a rough approximation to be made based on the recorded growth rates from individual species (e.g., Rouse et al. 2008, 2009). Species of *Osedax* show depth stratification in well-studied regions (Lundsten et al. 2010), so the identification of a particular species may be able to provide information on the depth at which remains were deposited.

Mollusk Borings
At least nine families of bivalve mollusks (phylum Mollusca, class Bivalvia) are known to bore into hard substrates, using both chemical and mechanical boring techniques

(reviewed by Savazzi 1999). Pholadid bivalves (piddocks) are particularly versatile and have been found in various types of rock, shells, wood, coal, lead, concrete, and plastic. Especially pertinent is the report that they have been found boring into "recent and fossil bone" (Savazzi 1999:210). This is further supported by evidence of bivalve borings in fossil bone. In most cases, it has not been possible to tell if the borings occurred in bones before or after they had become fossils (e.g., Boreske et al. 1972, Tapanila et al. 2004); however, evidence presented by Belaústegui et al. (2012) seems to show that bivalve borings do occur in pre-fossilized bone.

Typically, boring bivalves create flask-shaped (clavate) borings that have a narrow neck leading from a surficial opening that smoothly tapers into a rounded interior chamber (known as *gastrochaenolites* in the paleontological literature). From the exterior, bivalve borings appear as holes in the bone's surface and can vary in outline from round to an hourglass shape to two adjoining holes, depending on the degree to which the two tubes leading from the chamber of the boring are merged (Kelly and Bromley 1984). Some species produce a calcareous lining to their borings, which may be useful in determining the identity of bivalve that created the boring if the organism has since perished. If the bivalve shells are present, growth bands may be used to estimate PMSI based on growth rates (e.g., Evans 1968).

Sponge Borings

Rock boring demosponges (mainly in the family Clionaidae) are common bioeroders and can cause significant damage to calcareous hard substrates and skeletal material. They are found throughout tropical and temperate seas in both shallow and deep environments, but they tend to be most prolific down to ~70 m depth. Despite their ubiquity in marine environments, sponges rarely have been documented on submerged bones. A single record comes from human skeletal remains found in a 200 year old shipwreck at 33 m depth off of Australia (Steptoe and Wood 2002).

Sponge boring is carried out at a cellular level where sponge tissue comes into contact with the surface of its host substrate (Pomponi 1980). Cellular projections chemically penetrate the substrate and then join up to encapsulate a small fragment or chip. Once surrounded, the fragment is detached and mechanically ejected through the exhalent papillae. Interestingly, this process shows many similarities to the mechanism by which osteoclasts in human bodies resorb bone during the process of remodeling (Pomponi 1980). As the sponges grow into the substrate, they create a network of inter-linked subsurface chambers, which are connected to the surface via a series of canals where the sponge's siphons stick out. Rates of excavation by sponges can vary depending on the density and composition of the substrate and on the supply of food available (Calcinai et al. 2007).

From the bone's surface, sponge borings appear as small round holes, similar to those produced by *Osedax* worms, but several features distinguish the two. Firstly, because the exhalent and inhalant siphons of the sponge are of contrasting sizes, there are usually many small holes, accompanied by a few relatively large holes. Secondly, the holes created by sponges occur in a much more regular pattern across the bone's surface rather than the haphazard pattern of *Osedax* borings. The surface layer of sponge borings also may collapse, leaving a large pit of eroded bone, at which point the trace is very similar to *Osedax* borings. Sponge borings described by Steptoe and Wood (2002) were similarly eroded. In this case, only the remnants of actual sponge tissue allowed identification of the organism responsible for the damage.

Effects of Large Vertebrate Predators and Scavengers

Apart from the massive soft tissue damage that large marine predators and scavengers can cause to a human body, they also may leave traces upon bone in the form of digestive corrosion and tooth marks. An examination of terrestrial scavenger effects upon bone is presented in Chapter 9, this volume. These effects have been little researched among marine environments due to the obvious difficulties of retrieving altered bone under these extreme field circumstances. Even post hoc analyses are limited by the numbers of known cases of shark or other marine species attacks upon humans. Ihama et al. (2009) also note the lack of autopsy data, due to the rarity of attacks, the frequent lack of recovery of known victims, and states of advanced decomposition making the assessment of trauma patterns difficult. These attacks are relatively rare despite their reputation to the contrary (Bendersky 2002), although attacks or at least the reporting thereof seem to be increasing in recent years due to increased human population and water activity (West 2011). Lentz et al. (2010) examined a sample of 96 documented shark attacks dating since 1921 for which complete medical records were available and found that only 8.3% were fatal. Bites were found to be often very minor, ranging up to large amounts of soft tissue loss leading to death, frequently through exsanguination and shock.

The most aggressive species toward humans worldwide are great white sharks (*Carcharodon carcharias*), tiger sharks (*Galeocerdo cuvier*), and bull sharks (*Carcharhinus leucas*), with several other species known to attack humans in more isolated occurrences (Bury et al. 2012; Byard et al. 2006; Clua and Séret 2010; Ihama et al. 2009; International Shark Attack File 2012; Martin et al. 2009; Nakaya 1993; Rathbun and Rathbun 1997; Ritter and Levine 2005; Rtshiladze et al. 2011; West 2011). These three species grow to a relatively large size, making their feeding behavior inherently more damaging and less survivable. Great white sharks are among the largest predators known, and their maximum bite force of approximately 4000 lb may be the highest of any extant species (Wroe et al. 2008). Shark teeth among all predatory species, however, are relatively fragile and grow in multiple lines (series) attached to the mandibles by flexible tissues. As teeth are lost, new teeth rotate forward to take their place in the same row (Figure 7.11). Feeding does not involve mastication so much as shredding by shaking the head laterally to rip through soft tissue with

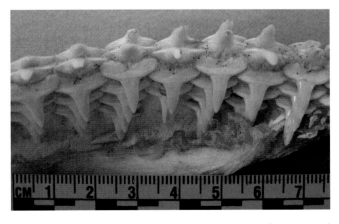

Figure 7.11 Mandible of blacktip reef shark (*Carcharhinus melanopterus*) showing multiple lines (series) of replacement teeth emerging in rows posterior to the front series. The teeth in this species lack serrations.

these sharp, often serrated teeth. The teeth tips penetrate the soft tissue, then the lateral movement of the head slices the distally and mesially facing margins of the teeth through it, shredding it and allowing detachment (Whitenack and Motta 2010). Sometimes, this behavior is directed at assessing an object as a potential food source, so soft tissue is greatly damaged, while little is actually consumed (Byard et al. 2000; Ritter and Levine 2005). Shark attacks often terminate after this initial trauma. When consumption is pursued, chunks of soft tissue or whole smaller species or juveniles are swallowed, and whole teeth or fragments thereof are sometimes left in wounds (Ihama et al. 2009; İşcan and McCabe 1995; Lentz et al. 2010). Subsequent decomposition or movement in ocean water may cause many of these left-behind teeth to be lost prior to recovery.

This pattern of feeding behavior is why shark bites tend to be so jagged through remaining soft tissue, with often a crescent-shaped area of removed flesh (Ihama et al. 2009). Smaller sharks of any species would find it difficult to crush through large mammal bones (including humans), since their feeding structures are not morphologically suited for this purpose. Traumatic lesions therefore are often confined to the soft tissue, and any alteration of bones can be minor even when accompanied by large amounts of soft tissue damage (Byard et al. 2000). Severing of body parts usually occurs at joints, with very little crushing or breakage of bone detected, except damage to ribs (Ihama et al. 2009). Bites from predation are often directed at human legs and abdominal areas, as these areas are often lowest in the water among swimming humans as the shark approaches from below (Ihama et al. 2009; Ritter and Levine 2005). Ihama et al. (2009:219) note that the characteristics of shark bites into soft tissue include incision without abrasion, wounds with serrated edges, a triangular or rectangular flap of skin left behind at the wound site, and a regular arrangement of marks that correspond to the spacing of shark teeth. Large portions of a human can be swallowed whole, as in the case examined by İşcan and McCabe (1995) from the coastal waters of Florida, where a tiger shark swallowed a likely intact leg and at least the intact femoral portion of the other leg.

Some species of shark frequently prey upon marine mammals (LeBoeuf et al. 1982; Lucas and Stobo 2000), and instances of attacks upon humans may be in part due to humans being mistaken for this prey, especially where humans in dark-colored wet suits (surfers and divers) present a form even more like the other prey species. These include pinnipeds (walruses, fur seals, true seals, and sea lions), which are frequent shark prey, especially juvenile pinnipeds. Great white sharks are a frequent pinniped predator, as indicated by the analysis of their stomach contents (LeBoeuf et al. 1982). As among humans, many shark attacks are survived, as indicated by the frequency of bite marks on living pinnipeds.

Shark tooth morphology and size varies by taxon (and individual) and can be identified even to species level in some cases from teeth alone. Overall shapes range from broadly triangular, to more sloped (tip angled, with one margin indented), to dagger-like, and these morphological types correspond to broad classes of feeding behavior (Whitenack and Motta 2010). In addition, some species' tooth margins are serrated in characteristic patterns (Nambiar et al. 1996), while others present a sharp, unserrated edge. Examples from common species with different tooth morphologies are depicted in Figures 7.12 and 7.13. Great white shark and bull shark teeth are triangular and broad, with serrated edges. The crown of tiger shark teeth has an indentation and multiple small cusps, with overall serrated edges. Mako shark (*Isurus* spp.) teeth are dagger-shaped and non-serrated. Hammerhead shark (*Sphyrna* spp.) teeth are intermediate in morphology between those of tiger sharks and mako sharks, with a serrated edge. Minor variations in morphology and size are also

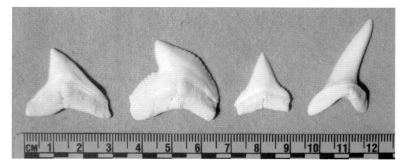

Figure 7.12 Examples of teeth of (left to right) common species of shark known to attack and/or consume humans: bull (*Carcharhinus leucas*), tiger (*Galeocerdo cuvier*), great white (*Carcharodon carcharias*), and mako (*Isurus* sp.) shark. Note that size variations displayed here are largely due to the body size attained by the individual sharks and are not interspecific indicators.

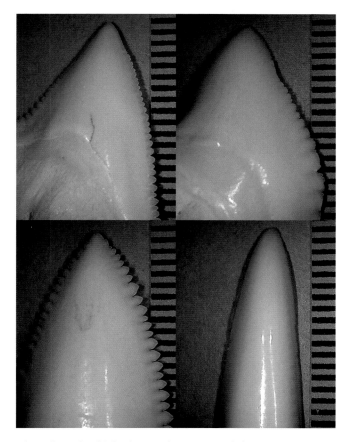

Figure 7.13 Examples of teeth of (clockwise from upper left) common species of shark known to attack and/or consume humans: bull (*Carcharhinus leucas*), tiger (*Galeocerdo cuvier*), mako (*Isurus* sp.), and great white (*Carcharodon carcharias*) shark. Note the variations in serration pattern that potentially could leave marks on bone, including the lack of serrations of mako teeth. Scales are in mm.

encountered based upon location of the tooth in the shark's mouth, based upon maxillary or mandibular and mesial to distal location (Nambiar et al. 1996; Ritter and Levine 2005). As indicated earlier, shark teeth or fragments thereof can be left behind in soft tissue, making it possible to identify the consuming species directly and not just by inference from the bite mark morphology or from witness statements.

In some cases, direct alterations to human bones from shark feeding do occur (Allaire et al. 2009, 2012). Ihama et al. (2009) examined 12 cases of shark attack and/or scavenging from the waters off Okinawa, Japan, and noted that 7 of these cases retained tooth marks on bones. The large species involved with these cases were most likely tiger sharks and bull sharks. Multiple researchers have noted the presence of distinctive shark tooth markings or patterned damage in objects associated with victims. These objects include surf boards, clothing, wetsuits (Ihama et al. 2009), and other diving equipment (Byard et al. 2006).

The damage to bones most frequently consists of parallel striations (linear marks not penetrating the cortical layer) or furrows (linear marks penetrating the cortical layer) (see Chapter 9, this volume, for a discussion of terminology of predator tooth marks). These are caused by multiple teeth margins simultaneously scraping across the surface of the bone (Byard et al. 2000, 2002; Ihama et al. 2009; İşcan and McCabe 1995). Allaire and Manhein (2009) and Allaire et al. (2012) go into more detail in describing the types of dental markings left by shark feeding on a body recovered from the Gulf of Mexico. They noted the following types of bone trauma: (1) punctures without associated fractures, caused by teeth entering the bone in a straight-on tooth impact; (2) punctures with associated fractures, caused by teeth entering weaker portions of bone (ribs, etc.) in a straight-on impact and creating compression fractures; (3) striations with bone shaving, where the margin of the tooth scraped a protuberance of the bone then slid off (Figure 7.14); (4) overlapping striations, caused by multiple passes with the teeth in the same location as the shark's head shakes from side to side; and (5) incised bone gouges (i.e., furrowing; Figure 7.15).

Figure 7.14 Tooth striation on a human clavicle likely fed upon by bull shark (*Carcharhinus leucas*) in the Gulf of Mexico. (Image from Allaire, M.T., Manhein, M.H., and Burgess, G.H.: Shark-inflicted trauma: A case study of unidentified remains recovered from the Gulf of Mexico. *J. Forensic Sci.* 2012. 57. 1675–1678. Copyright Wiley-VCH Verlag GmbH & Co. KGaA. Reprinted with permission.)

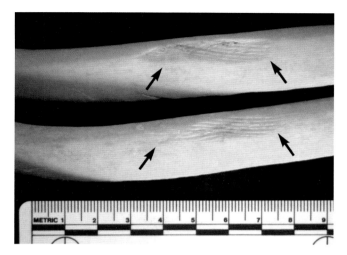

Figure 7.15 Human ribs likely fed upon by bull shark (*Carcharhinus leucas*) in the Gulf of Mexico (Allaire et al. 2012). Note the gouged surfaces with parallel striations (arrows), which could be used to eliminate some species of shark as potential scavengers (see Figures 7.12 and 7.13). Scale is in cm. (Image from Allaire, M.T., Manhein, M.H., and Burgess, G.H.: Shark-inflicted trauma: A case study of unidentified remains recovered from the Gulf of Mexico. *J. Forensic Sci.* 2012. 57. 1675–1678. Copyright Wiley-VCH Verlag GmbH & Co. KGaA. Reprinted with permission.)

The striations in this case indicated that a species with serrated tooth margins was responsible for some of the damage, with the size and patterning indicating that a bull shark was likely involved, with other areas of damage possibly caused by much smaller requiem sharks (*Carcharhinus* spp.).

Traces of shark teeth scraping across bones of marine mammals also are known paleontologically (Bianucci et al. 2010; Ehret et al. 2009; Kallal et al. 2012), which is unsurprising given the ancient fossil history of sharks and the diversity of potential prey items. Due to their cartilage skeletons, most direct traces of shark fossil history are confined to their ossified teeth.

The pattern of serrations incised into bone by shark teeth may be identifiable to taxa of various levels. Nambiar et al. (1996) examined whole jaw sets of great white shark from three individuals (two adult and one juvenile). They found that the serration patterns varied from tooth to tooth within the same individual, including peaks that were bifid and trifid, with neither consistent overall pattern in serration size nor arrangement. Individual serration peaks also tended to get fractured away, further altering the potential pattern of individual tooth marks during the life of the shark. They also noted the variations of tooth size and form within each specimen, with the largest teeth mesial, and that some areas of the mandibular teeth of the juvenile had no serrations or very small ones. Nambiar et al. (1991) did note a general correlation between bite and tooth mark size and the overall body length of the great white shark causing the trauma, which is potentially useful in determining which species or individual caused the trauma in a particular forensic case.

It is unknown the degree to which sharks may scavenge human remains, and available data indicate that shark digestion is a slow process when they do. Rathbun and Rathbun (1997) note the (serendipitous) find of partial human remains (left knee portion; see Figure 7.16) in the stomach of a tiger shark, which is one of the few shark species

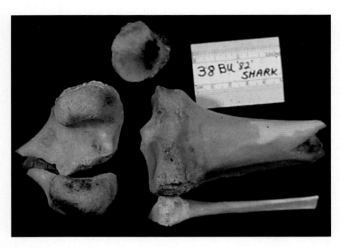

Figure 7.16 Human remains (knee portion), after removal of adhering soft tissue, recovered from a tiger shark (*Galeocerdo cuvier*) stomach off the coast of North Carolina, USA. Lower scale is in cm. (Image courtesy of T. Rathbun, personal collection.)

known to scavenge frequently, including human remains. They were able to trace the possible origin of the remains back to a jetliner crash in the general (coastal North Atlantic) vicinity earlier in the same month. The trauma separating the femur in this case may have occurred as a result of the air crash (or other unknown trauma), although the tibia did have clear scoring from shark teeth (T. Rathbun, pers. comm.). İşcan and McCabe (1995) note that the portions of human legs recovered from a tiger shark off the coast of Florida that they examined may have been scavenged. An infamous homicide case (Castles 1995) from 1935 in Sydney, Australia, included human remains that likely were scavenged by a tiger shark. A human left arm, complete with identifiable tattoo and manila rope around the wrist, was regurgitated by a 4-m tiger shark recently brought for display to an aquarium. This tiger shark, the first live one on display in the world, was found to have consumed *another*, smaller shark that may have consumed the human arm first. This likely crudely dismembered arm probably had been disposed of in the nearby ocean in an attempt to hide evidence of a homicide and so must have been scavenged. (Other evidence pointed to the victim being murdered and dismembered on land.) Identifiable remains therefore persisted in this case for a minimum of 8 days in the tiger shark's stomach and as long as 17 days (from the date the victim was last seen alive). The state of preservation was such that the victim's fingerprints could be obtained and were used for positive identification, along with the tattoo. Ihama et al. (2009) and Makino et al. (2004) note cases of probable suicide victims who were later recovered with traces of shark feeding trauma, and Ihama et al. (2009) further note one case of a floating corpse that was witnessed to receive subsequent shark scavenging. Byard et al. (2002) notes a case of accidental drowning that also bore these traces. Scavenging therefore occurred in at least some of these cases after death had occurred. A variety of shark species are suspected in these cases, including cookie-cutter shark (*Isistius* sp.) (Makino et al. 2004) and what must have been larger species.

Some species of sharks have been found to practice gastric eversion, or the pushing of their stomachs inside-out and partially outside of their mouths (Brunnschweiler et al. 2005, 2011). This behavior fills the same role as peristaltic vomiting in mammals, and it may be common though as yet undocumented. The purpose may be the ejection of indigestible stomach contents, including bone or debris swallowed accidentally, and thus in practice, it is analogous to the vomiting of pellets as practiced by numerous species of avian raptors, including owls and many hawk, eagle, falcon, and other diurnal species. Ejection of indigestible stomach contents among taxa is therefore frequently encountered where prey is swallowed whole or with minimal mastication and among scavenging species (including, among terrestrial scavengers, hyenas) where marginal nutrition sources may be consumed in large amounts. The lack of mastication may be compensated for in part through very high shark stomach acidity, which has been measured as low as a pH of 0.4 (Papastamatiou et al. 2007). Shark gastric eversion is little understood in terms of frequency, timing within the digestion process, or variations by species. In terms of forensics, it makes recovery of partial human remains less likely, given that after digestion of most soft tissues, the remaining portions will be less likely to be recovered: many cases of shark consumption of humans are discovered only after the shark has been killed and its stomach contents examined. It also means that isolated human remains bearing shark tooth marks may have been consumed previously, as a result of predation or scavenging, and may have been transported a great distance from the initial location of feeding. This increase in distance between discovery and initial feeding greatly increases the potential pool of deceased individuals and decreases the likelihood of their identification.

Conclusions

Multiple environmental (mechanical, sedimentary, and chemical) and biological (adhesion, boring, and feeding) processes occurring commonly in marine environments alter osseous remains in ways that frequently are characteristic of this environment. The ultimate postmortem origin of osseous remains therefore often can be traced by these taphonomic alterations to marine settings, specifically high-energy and high-biodiversity/biomass shallow coastal areas. This portion of the oceans (the littoral/euphotic zone) is frequented the most by humans and has the highest instance of the introduction and recovery of human remains over the open ocean (pelagic) or deep-water (benthic) zones. These same taphonomic processes also have the potential to allow estimation of the PMSI but require additional research in most cases to refine the successful application of these techniques.

Acknowledgments

The authors thank Ted Rathbun for his access to previous data on shark taphonomy and images and Maria T. Allaire for her permission to reprint images. Adrian Glover and Ben Wigham kindly provided the image of sea urchins. Parts of this chapter are based on original research supported by the Natural Environment Research Council Facility for Scientific Diving (NFSD/2010/04), U.K. The authors thank Brianne Charles for her editorial assistance.

References

Allaire, M. T. and M. H. Manhein (2009) Shark-inflicted trauma on human skeletal remains. *Proceedings of the American Academy of Forensic Sciences* 15:317–318.

Allaire, M. T., M. H. Manhein, and G. H. Burgess (2012) Shark-inflicted trauma: A case study of unidentified remains recovered from the Gulf of Mexico. *Journal of Forensic Sciences* 57:1675–1678.

Allison, P. A., C. R. Smith, H. Kukert, J. W. Deming, and B. A. Bennett (1991) Deep-water taphonomy of vertebrate carcasses: A whale skeleton in the bathyal Santa Catalina Basin. *Paleobiology* 17:78–89.

Anderson, G. (2008) Determination of elapsed time since death in homicide victims disposed of in the Ocean. Canadian Police Research Centre, Technical Report TR-10-2008, Ottawa, Ontario, Canada.

Anderson, G. and L. S. Bell (2010) Deep coastal marine taphonomy: Interim results from an ongoing experimental investigation of decomposition in the Saanich Inlet, British Columbia. *Proceedings of the American Academy of Forensic Sciences* 16:381–382.

Anderson, G. and N. Hobischak (2002) Determination of time of death for humans discovered in saltwater using aquatic organism succession and decomposition rates. Canadian Police Research Centre, Technical Report TR-09-2002, Ottawa, Ontario, Canada.

Arnaud, G., S. Arnaud, A. Ascenzi, E. Bonucci, and G. Graziani (1978) On the problem of the preservation of human bone in sea-water. *Journal of Human Evolution* 7:409–420.

Ascenzi, A. and G. Silvestrini (1984) Bone-boring marine micro-organisms: An experimental investigation. *Journal of Human Evolution* 13:531–536.

Bassett, H. E. and M. H. Manhein (2002) Fluvial transport of human remains in the lower Mississippi River. *Journal of Forensic Sciences* 47:719–724.

BEA (2011) *Interim Report no.3 on the Accident on 1st June 2009 to the Airbus A330–203 Registered F-GZCP Operated by Air France Flight AF 447 Rio de Janeiro—Paris.* Bureau d'Enquêtes et d'Analyses pour la Sécurité de l'Aviation Civile, Ministère de l'Écologie, du Développement Durable, des Transports et du Logement, Paris, France.

Belaústegui, Z., J. M. de Gibert, R. Domènech, F. Muñiz, and J. Martinell (2012) Clavate borings in a Miocene cetacean skeleton from Tarragona (NE Spain) and the fossil record of marine bone bioerosion. *Palaeogeography, Palaeoclimatology, Palaeoecology* 323–325:68–74.

Bell, L. S. and A. Elkerton (2008) Human skeletal material recovered from the medieval warship *Mary Rose*. *International Journal of Osteoarchaeology* 18:523–535.

Bell, L. S., J. A. Lee Thorp, and A. Elkerton (2009) The sinking of the *Mary Rose* warship: A medieval mystery solved? *Journal of Archaeological Science* 36:166–173.

Bendersky, G. (2002) The original "Jaws" attack. *Perspectives in Biology and Medicine* 45:426–432.

Berkeley, A. (2009) Understanding the role of taphonomy and post-depositional processes on the intertidal stratigraphic record. *Palaios* 24:271–272.

Bessat, F. and D. Buigues (2001) Two centuries of variation in coral growth in a massive *Porites* colony from Moorea (French Polynesia): A response of ocean-atmosphere variability from south central Pacific. *Palaeogeography, Palaeoclimatology, Palaeoecology* 175:381–392.

Bianucci, G., B. Sorce, T. Storai, and W. Landini (2010) Killing in the Pliocene: Shark attack on a dolphin from Italy. *Palaeontology* 53:457–470.

Bixler, G. S. and B. Bhushan (2012) Biofouling: Lessons from nature. *Philosophical Transactions of the Royal Society A* 370:2381–2417. DOI: 10.1098/rsta.2011.0502.

Blake, J. A. and J. W. Evans (1973) *Polydora* and related genera as borers in mollusk shells and other calcareous substrates. *Veliger* 15:235–249.

Blanco Pampín, J. and B. A. López-Abajo Rodríguez (2001) Surprising drifting of bodies along the coast of Portugal and Spain. *Legal Medicine* 3:177–182.

Boreske, J., L. Goldberg, and B. Cameron (1972) A reworked cetacean with clam borings: Miocene of North Carolina. *Journal of Paleontology* 46:130–139.

Bourget, E. (1980) Barnacle shell growth in relation to environmental factors. In *Skeletal Growth of Aquatic Organisms*, eds. D. C. Rhoades and R. A. Lutz, pp. 469–491, Plenum, New York.

Bourget, E. and D. J. Crisp (1975) An analysis of the growth bands and ridges of barnacle shell plates. *Journal of the Marine Biological Association of the UK* 55:439–461.

Boyle, S., A. Galloway, and R. T. Mason (1997) Human aquatic taphonomy in the Monterey Bay area. In *Forensic Taphonomy: The Postmortem Fate of Human Remains*, eds. W. D. Haglund and M. H. Sorg, pp. 605–614. CRC Press, Boca Raton, FL.

Braby, C. E., G. W. Rouse, S. B. Johnson, W. J. Jones, and R. C. Vrijenhoek (2007) Bathymetric and temporal variation among *Osedax* boneworms and associated megafauna on whale-falls in Monterey Bay, California. *Deep-Sea Research Part I* 54:1773–1791.

Braune, W. and M. D. Guiry (2011) *Seaweeds: A Colour Guide to Common Benthic Green, Brown and Red Algae of the World's Oceans*. Koeltz Scientific Books, Konigstein, Germany.

Britton, J. C. and B. Morton (1994) Marine carrion and scavengers. In *Oceanography and Marine Biology: An Annual Review* (Vol. 32), eds. H. Barnes, A. D. Ansell, R. N. Gibson, and M. Barnes, pp. 369–434. University College, London Press, London, U.K.

Bromley, R. G. (1994) The palaeoecology of bioerosion. In *The Palaeobiology of Trace Fossils*, ed. S. K. Donovan, pp. 134–154. John Wiley & Sons, Chichester, U.K.

Bromley, R. G. and C. Heinberg (2006) Attachment strategies of organisms on hard substrates: A palaeontological view. *Palaeogeography, Palaeoclimatology, Palaeoecology* 232:429–453.

Brooks, S. and R. H. Brooks (1997) The taphonomic effects of flood waters on bone. In *Forensic Taphonomy: The Postmortem Fate of Human Remains*, eds. W. D. Haglund and M. H. Sorg, pp. 553–558. CRC Press, Boca Raton, FL.

Brunnschweiler, J. M., P. L. R. Andrews, E. J. Southall, M. Pickering, and D. W. Sims (2005) Rapid voluntary stomach eversion in a free-living shark. *Journal of the Marine Biological Association of the U.K.* 85:1141–1144.

Brunnschweiler, J. M., F. Nielsen, and P. Mottac (2011) in situ observation of stomach eversion in a line-caught Shortfin Mako (*Isurus oxyrinchus*). *Fisheries Research* 109:212–216.

Bury, D., N. Langlois, and R. W. Byard (2012) Animal-related fatalities-Part I: Characteristic autopsy findings and variable causes of death associated with blunt and sharp trauma. *Journal of Forensic Sciences* 57:370–374.

Byard, R. W., J. D. Gilbert, and K. Brown (2000) Pathologic features of fatal shark attacks. *The American Journal of Forensic Medicine and Pathology* 21:225–229.

Byard, R. W., R. A. James, and J. D. Gilbert (2002) Diagnostic problems associated with cadaveric trauma from animal activity. *The American Journal of Forensic Medicine and Pathology* 23:238–244.

Byard, R. W., R. A. James, and K. J. Heath (2006) Recovery of human remains after shark attack. *The American Journal of Forensic Medicine and Pathology* 27:256–259.

Calcinai, B., F. Azzini, G. Bavestrello, L. Gaggero, and C. Cerrano (2007) Excavating rates and boring pattern of *Cliona albimarginata* (Porifera: Clionaidae) in different substrata. In *Porifera Research: Biodiversity, Innovation and Sustainability—2007* (Vol. 28), ed. M. Reis Custódio, pp. 203–210. Série Livros, Museu Nacional, Universidade Federal do Rio de Janeiro, Rio de Janeiro, Brazil.

Castles, A. C. (1995) *The Shark Arm Murders: The Thrilling True Story of a Tiger Shark and a Tattooed Arm*. Wakefield Press, Kent Town, South Australia, Australia.

Clare, A. S., S. C. Ward, D. Rittschof, and K. M. Wilbur (1994) Growth increments of the barnacle *Balanus amphitrite amphitrite* Darwin (Cirripedia). *Journal of Crustacean Biology* 14:27–35.

Clifford, C. (2011) Bodies from Air France crash arrive in France. Electronic document: http://articles.cnn.com/2011-06-16/world/france.bodies.arrive_1_bodies-dental-records-victims-relatives?_s = PM:WORLD (accessed November 30, 2012).

Clifton, K. B., J. Yan, J. J. Mecholsky, Jr., and R. L. Reep (2008) Material properties of manatee rib bone. *Journal of Zoology* 274:150–159.

Clua, E. and B. Séret (2010) Unprovoked fatal shark attack in Lifou Island (Loyalty Islands, New Caledonia, South Pacific) by a great white shark, *Carcharodon carcharias*. *American Journal of Forensic Medicine and Pathology* 31:281–286.

Copeland, A. R. (1987) Suicide by drowning. *American Journal of Forensic Medicine and Pathology* 8:18–22.

Crisp, D. J. (1954) The breeding of *Balanus porcatus* (Da Costa) in the Irish Sea. *Journal of the Marine Biological Association of the UK* 33:473–496.

Crisp, D. J. and E. Bourget (1985) Growth in barnacles. *Advances in Marine Biology* 22:199–244.

D'Alonzo, S. S., S. J. Clinkinbeard, and E. J. Bartelink (2012) Fluvial transport of human remains in the Sacramento River, California. *Proceedings of the American Academy of Forensic Sciences* 18:408–409.

Dahlgren, T. G., H. Wiklund, B. Källstrom, T. Lundälv, C. R. Smith, and A. G. Glover (2006) A shallow-water whale-fall experiment in the north Atlantic. *Cahiers de Biologie Marine* 47:385–389.

Davis, P. G. (1997) The bioerosion of bird bones. *International Journal of Osteoarchaeology* 7:388–401.

Dennison, K. J., J. A. Kieser, J. S. Buckeridge, and P. J. Bishop (2004) Post mortem cohabitation-shell growth as a measure of elapsed time: A case report. *Forensic Science International* 139:249–254.

Dickinson, G. H., I. E. Vega, K. J. Wahl, B. Orihuela, V. Beyley, E. N. Rodriguez, R. K. Everett, J. Bonaventura, and D. Rittschof (2009) Barnacle cement: A polymerization model based on evolutionary concepts. *The Journal of Experimental Biology* 212:3499–3510.

Dickson, G. C. and R. T. M. Poulter (2010) Microbial marine deposition: Marine bacteria as an indicator of postmortem submersion interval. *Proceedings of the American Academy of Forensic Sciences* 16:361–362.

Dilen, D. R. (1984) The motion of floating and submerged objects in the Chattahoochee River, Atlanta, GA. *Journal of Forensic Sciences* 29:1027–1037.

Dodson, P. (1973) The significance of small bones in paleoecological interpretation. *Contributions to Geology, University of Wyoming* 12:15–19.

Donoghue, E. R. and G. C. Minnigerode (1977) Human body buoyancy: A study of 98 men. *Journal of Forensic Sciences* 22:573–579.

Dumser, T. K. and M. Türkay (2008) Postmortem changes of human bodies on the bathyal sea floor—Two cases of aircraft accidents above the open sea. *Journal of Forensic Sciences* 53:1049–1052.

Ebbesmeyer, C. C. and W. D. Haglund (1994) Drift trajectories of a floating human body simulated in a hydraulic model of Puget Sound. *Journal of Forensic Sciences* 39:231–240.

Ebbesmeyer, C. C. and W. D. Haglund (2002) Floating remains on Pacific Northwest waters. In *Advances in Forensic Taphonomy: Method, Theory, and Archaeological Perspectives*, eds. W. D. Haglund and M. H. Sorg, pp. 219–240. CRC Press, Boca Raton, FL.

Ehret, D. J., B. J. MacFadden, and R. Salas-Gismondi (2009) Caught in the act: Trophic interactions between a 4-million-year-old white shark (*Carcharodon*) and mysticete whale from Peru. *Palaios* 24:329–333.

Evans, J. W. (1968) Growth rate of the rock-boring clam *Penitella penita* (Conrad 1837) in relation to hardness of rock and other factors. *Palaeogeography, Palaeoclimatology, Palaeoecology* 4:271:278.

Fernández-Jalvo, Y. and P. Andrews (2003) Experimental effects of water abrasion on bone fragments. *Journal of Taphonomy* 1:147–163.

Foecke, T., L. Maa, M. A. Russell, D. L. Conlin, and L. E. Murphy (2010) Investigating archaeological site formation processes on the battleship *USS Arizona* using finite element analysis. *Journal of Archaeological Science* 37:1090–1101.

Fox, M. (2003) Turret excavation reveals insights into ship's sinking. *Cheesebox* 13:8–11.

Fujikura, K., Y. Fujiwara, and M. Kawato (2006) A new species of *Osedax* (Annelida: Siboglinidae) associated with whale carcasses off Kyushu, Japan. *Zoological Science* 23:733–740.

Giertsen, J. C. and I. Morild (1989) Seafaring bodies. *American Journal of Forensic Medicine and Pathology* 10:25–27.

Gilbert, R. (1984) The movement of gravel by the alga *Fucus vesiculosus* (L.) on an arctic intertidal flat. *Journal of Sedimentary Petrology* 54:463–468.

Glover, A. G., B. Källstrom, C. R. Smith, and T. G. Dahlgren (2005) World-wide whale worms? A new species of *Osedax* from the shallow north Atlantic. *Proceedings of the Royal Society B* 272: 2587–2592.

Glover, A. G., K. M. Kemp, C. R. Smith, and T. G. Dahlgren (2008) On the role of bone-eating worms in the degradation of marine vertebrate remains. *Proceedings of the Royal Society B* 275:1959–1961.

Goffredi, S. K., C. Paull, K. Fulton-Bennett, L. Hurtado, and R. Vrijenhoek (2004) Unusual benthic fauna associated with a whale fall in Monterey Canyon, California. *Deep-Sea Research Part I* 51:1295–1306.

Green, J. (2004) *Maritime Archaeology: A Technical Handbook*, 2nd edn. Elsevier, San Diego, CA.

Haglund, W. D. (1993) Disappearance of soft tissue and the disarticulation of human remains from aqueous environments. *Journal of Forensic Sciences* 38:806–815.

Haglund, W. D. and M. H. Sorg (2002) Human remains in water environments. In *Advances in Forensic Taphonomy: Method, Theory, and Archaeological Perspectives*, eds. W. D. Haglund and M. H. Sorg, pp. 201–218. CRC Press, Boca Raton, FL.

Hamilton, D. L. (1997) *Basic Methods of Conserving Underwater Archaeological Material Culture*. Legacy Resource Management Program, U.S. Department of Defense, Washington, DC.

Hamilton, D. L. (1999/2001) Conservation of cultural materials from underwater sites. *Archives and Museum Informatics* 13:291–323.

Hamilton, D. L. (2010) *Methods of Conserving Underwater Archaeological Material Culture* (rev. 2). Nautical Archaeology Program, Texas A&M University, College Station, TX. [Available on-line: http://nautarch.tamu.edu/class/ANTH605.]

Haszprunar, G. (1988) Anatomy and relationships of the bone-feeding limpets, *Cocculinella minutissima* (Smith) and *Osteopelta mirabilis* (Marshall) (Archaeogastropoda). *Journal of Molluscan Studies* 54:1–20.

Higgs, N. D., A. G. Glover, T. G. Dahlgren, and C. T. S. Little (2010) Using computed-tomography to document borings by *Osedax mucofloris* in whale bone. *Cahiers de Biologie Marine* 51:401–405.

Higgs, N. D., A. G. Glover, T. G. Dahlgren, and C. T. S. Little (2011b) Bone-boring worms: Characterizing the morphology, rate, and method of bioerosion by *Osedax mucofloris* (Annelida, Siboglinidae). *Biological Bulletin, Marine Biological Laboratory, Woods Hole* 221:307–316.

Higgs, N. D., C. T. S. Little, and A. G. Glover (2011a) Bones as biofuel: A review of whale bone composition with implications for deep-sea biology and palaeoanthropology. *Proceedings of the Royal Society B* 278:9–17.

Higgs, N. D., C. T. S. Little, A. G. Glover, T. G. Dahlgren, C. R. Smith, and S. Dominici (2012) Evidence of *Osedax* worm borings in Pliocene (~3 Ma) whale bone from the Mediterranean. *Historical Biology* 24:269–277.

Hight, L. M. and J. J. Wilker (2007) Synergistic effects of metals and oxidants in the curing of marine mussel adhesive. *Journal of Material Science* 42:8934–8942.

Hoyoux, C., M. Zbinden, S. Samadi, F. Gaill, and P. Compère (2012) Diet and gut microorganisms of *Munidopsis* squat lobsters associated with natural woods and mesh-enclosed substrates in the deep South Pacific. *Marine Biology Research* 28:28–47.

Ihama, Y., K. Ninomiya, M. Noguchi, C. Fuke, and T. Miyazaki (2009) Characteristic features of injuries due to shark attacks: A review of 12 cases. *Legal Medicine* 11:219–225.

International Shark Attack File (2012) Electronic document: http://www.flmnh.ufl.edu/fish/Sharks/Statistics/statistics.htm. Ichthyology at the Florida Museum of Natural History (accessed November 30, 2012).

Irmis, R. B. and D. K. Elliot (2006) Taphonomy of a Middle Pennsylvanian marine vertebrate assemblage and an actualistic model for marine abrasion of teeth. *Palaios* 21:466–479.

İşcan, M. Y. and B. Q. McCabe (1995) Analysis of human remains recovered from a shark. *Forensic Science International* 72:15–23.

Johnson, S. B., A. Warén, R. W. Lee, Y. Kano, A. Kaim, A. Davis, E. E. Strong, and R. C. Vrijenhoek (2010) *Rubyspira*, new genus and two new species of bone-eating deep-sea snails with ancient habits. *Biological Bulletin* 219:166–167.

Jones, E. G., M. A. Collins, P. M. Bagley, D. Addison, and I. G. Priede (1998) The fate of cetacean carcasses in the deep sea: Observations on consumption rates and succession of scavenging species in the abyssal north-east Atlantic Ocean. *Proceedings of the Royal Society of London, B* 265:1119–1127.

Jones, W. J., S. B. Johnson, G. W. Rouse, and R. C. Vrijenhoek (2008) Marine worms (genus *Osedax*) colonize cow bones. *Proceedings of the Royal Society of London B* 275:387–391.

Kahana, T., J. Almog, J. Levy, E. Shmeltzer, Y. Spier, and J. Hiss (1999) Marine taphonomy: Adipocere formation in a series of bodies recovered from a single shipwreck. *Journal of Forensic Sciences* 44:897–901.

Kallal, R. J., S. J. Godfrey, and D. J. Ortner (2012) Bone reactions on a Pliocene cetacean rib indicate short-term survival of predation event. *International Journal of Osteoarchaeology* 22:253–260.

Kelly, S. and R. Bromley (1984) Ichnological nomenclature of clavate borings. *Palaeontology* 27:793–807.

LeBoeuf, B. J., M. Riedman, and R. S. Keyes (1982) White shark predation on pinnipeds in California coastal waters. *Fishery Bulletin* 80:891–895.

Lentz, A. K., G. H. Burgess, K. Perrin, J. A. Brown, D. W. Mozingo, and L. Lottenberg (2010) Mortality and management of 96 shark attacks and development of a shark bite severity scoring system. *The American Surgeon* 76:101–106.

Lewis, J. A., Jr., C. Y. Shiroma, K. Von Guenthner, and K. N. Dunn (2004) Recovery and identification of the victims of the *Ehime Maru*/USS *Greeneville* collision at sea. *Journal of Forensic Sciences* 49:539–542.

Liebig, P. M., K. W. Flessa, and T.-S. A. Taylor (2007) Taphonomic variation despite catastrophic mortality: Analysis of a mass stranding of false killer whales (*Pseudorca crassidens*), Gulf of California, Mexico. *Palaios* 22:384–391.

Liebig, P. M., T.-S. A. Taylor, and K. W. Flessa (2003) Bones on the beach: Marine mammal taphonomy of the Colorado Delta, Mexico. *Palaios* 18:168–175.

London, M. R., F. J. Krolikowski, and J. H. Davis (1997) Burials at sea. In *Forensic Taphonomy: The Postmortem Fate of Human Remains*, eds. W. D. Haglund and M. H. Sorg, pp. 615–622. CRC Press, Boca Raton, FL.

Lough, J. M. and T. F. Cooper (2011) New insights from coral growth band studies in an era of rapid environmental change. *Earth-Science Reviews* 108:170–184.

Love, A. C. (2002) Darwin and *Cirripedia* prior to 1846: Exploring the origins of the barnacle research. *Journal of the History of Biology* 35:251–289.

Lucas, Z. and W. T. Stobo (2000) Shark-inflicted mortality on a population of harbor seals (*Phoca vitulina*) at Sable Island, Nova Scotia. *Journal of Zoology, London* 252:405–414.

Lundsten, L., K. L. Schlining, K. Frasier, S. B. Johnson, L. Kuhnz, J. B. J. Harvey, G. Clague, and R. C. Vrijenhoek (2010) Time-series analysis of six whale-fall communities in Monterey Canyon, California, USA. *Deep-Sea Research I* 57:1573–1584.

Makino, Y., K. Tachihara, S. Ageda, T. Arao, C. Fuke, and T. Miyazaki (2004) Peculiar circular and C-shaped injuries on a body from the sea. *American Journal of Forensic Medicine and Pathology* 25:169–171.

Maritime Museum of the Atlantic (2012) *Titanic*'s Halifax connection. Electronic document, http://museum.gov.ns.ca/mmanew/en/home/whattoseedo/Titanic/default.aspx (accessed November 30, 2012).

Martin, R. A., D. K. Rossmo, and N. Hammerschlag (2009) Hunting patterns and geographic profiling of white shark predation. *Journal of Zoology* 279:111–118.

Marshall, B. A. (1987) Osteopeltidae (Mollusca: Gastropoda): A new family of limpets associated with whale bone in the deep sea. *Journal of Molluscan Studies* 53:121–127.

Mégnin, J. P. (1894) *La Faune des Cadavres Application de l'Entomologie à la Médecine Légale.* G. Masson, Paris, France.

Nakaya, K. (1993) A fatal attack by a white shark in Japan and a review of shark attacks in Japanese waters. *Japanese Journal of Ichthyology* 40:35–42.

Nambiar, P., T. E. Bridges, and K. A. Brown (1991) Allometric relationships of the dentition of the great white shark, *Carcharodon carcharias*, in forensic investigations of shark attacks. *Journal of Forensic Odonto-Stomatology* 9:1–16.

Nambiar, P., K. A. Brown, and T. E. Bridges (1996) Forensic implications of the variation in morphology of marginal serrations on the teeth of the great white shark. *Journal of Forensic Odonto-Stomatology* 14:3–9.

Nawrocki, S. P., J. E. Pless, D. A. Hawley, and S. A. Wagner (1997) Fluvial transport of human crania. In *Forensic Taphonomy: The Postmortem Fate of Human Remains*, eds. W. D. Haglund and M. H. Sorg, pp. 529–552. CRC Press, Boca Raton, FL.

National Oceanic and Atmospheric Administration (2012) National Marine Sanctuaries. The 2010 Scientific Expedition to *Titanic*. Electronic document: http://sanctuaries.noaa.gov/maritime/titanic/2010_expedition.html (accessed November 30, 2012).

O'Brien, T. G. and A. C. Kuehner (2007) Waxing grave about adipocere: Soft tissue change in an aquatic context. *Journal of Forensic Sciences* 52:294–301.

Papastamatiou, Y. P., S. J. Purkis, and K. N. Holland (2007) The response of gastric pH and motility to fasting and feeding in free swimming blacktip reef sharks, *Carcharhinus melanopterus*. *Journal of Experimental Marine Biology and Ecology* 345:129–140.

Pomponi, S. A. (1980) Cytological mechanisms of calcium carbonate excavation by boring sponges. *International Review of Cytology* 65:301–319.

Prassack, K. A. (2011) The effect of weathering on bird bone survivorship in modern and fossil saline-alkaline lake environments. *Paleobiology* 37:633–654.

Purcell, M., S. Pascaud, D. Gallo, M. Rothenbeck, M. Dennett, G. Packard, and A. Sherrell (2011) Use of REMUS 6000 AUVs in the search for the Air France Flight 447. *Proceedings of the IEEE Oceans 2011 Conference*, Hilo, HI, September 19–22, 2011.

Pyenson, N. D. (2010) Carcasses on the coastline: Measuring the ecological fidelity of the cetacean stranding record in the eastern North Pacific Ocean. *Paleobiology* 36:453–480.

Rasher, D. B., S. Engel, V. Bonito, G. J. Fraser, J. P. Montoya, and M. E. Hay (2012) Effects of herbivory, nutrients, and reef protection on algal proliferation and coral growth on a tropical reef. *Oecologia* 169:187–198.

Rathbun, T. A. and B. C. Rathbun (1997) Human remains recovered from a shark's stomach in South Carolina. In *Forensic Taphonomy: The Postmortem Fate of Human Remains*, eds. W. D. Haglund and M. H. Sorg, pp. 449–456. CRC Press, Boca Raton, FL.

Raymer, E. C. (1996) *Descent into Darkness; Pearl Harbor, 1941: The True Story of a Navy Diver.* Presidio Press, Novato, CA.

Ritter, E. K. and M. L. Levine (2005) Bite motivation of sharks reflected by the wound structure on humans. *American Journal of Forensic Medicine and Pathology* 26:136–140.

Rouse, G. W., S. K. Goffredi, S. B. Johnson, and R. C. Vrijenhoek (2011) Not whale-fall specialists, Osedax worms also consume fishbones. *Biology Letters* 7:736–739.

Rouse, G. W., S. K. Goffredi, and R. C. Vrijenhoek (2004) *Osedax*: Bone-eating marine worms with dwarf males. *Science* 305:668–671.

Rouse, G. W., N. G. Wilson, S. K. Goffredi, S. B. Johnson, T. Smart, C. Widmer, C. M. Young, and R. C. Vrijenhoek (2009) Spawning and development in *Osedax* boneworms (Siboglinidae, Annelida). *Marine Biology* 156:395–405.

Rouse, G. W., K. Worsaae, S. B. Johnson, W. J. Jones, and R. C. Vrijenhoek (2008) Acquisition of dwarf male 'harems' by recently settled females of *Osedax roseus* n. sp. (Siboglinidae; Annelida). *Biological Bulletin* 214:67–82.

Rtshiladze, M. A., S. P. Andersen, D. Q. A. Nguyen, A. Grabs, and K. Ho (2011) The 2009 Sydney shark attacks: Case series and literature review. *ANZ Journal of Surgery* 81:345–351.

Savazzi, E. (1999) Boring, nestling and tube-dwelling bivalves. In *Functional Morphology of the Invertebrate Skeleton*, ed. E. Savazzi, pp. 205–237. John Wiley & Sons, Chichester, U.K.

Skinner, M. F., J. Duffy, and D. B. Symes (1988) Repeat identification of skeletonized human remains: A case study. *Journal of the Canadian Society of Forensic Science* 21:138–141.

Smith, A. M. (2002) The structure and function of adhesive gels from invertebrates. *Integrative and Comparative Biology* 42:1164–1171.

Smith, C. R. and A. Baco (2003) Ecology of whale falls at the deep-sea floor. *Oceanography and Marine Biology: An Annual Review* 41:311–354.

Sorg, M. H., J. H. Dearborn, E. I. Monahan, H. F. Ryan, K. G. Sweeney, and E. David (1997) Forensic taphonomy in marine contexts. In *Forensic Taphonomy: The Postmortem Fate of Human Remains*, ed. W. D. Haglund and M. H. Sorg, pp. 567–604. CRC Press, Boca Raton, FL.

Steneck, R. S. (1986) The ecology of coralline algal crusts: Convergent patterns and adaptive strategies. *Annual Review of Ecology and Systematics* 17:273–303.

Steptoe, D. P. and Wood W. B. (2002) The human remains from HMS *Pandora*. *Internet Archaeology* 11 (electronic journal).

Stewart, R. J., T. C. Ransom, and V. Hlady (2011) Natural underwater adhesives. *Polymer Physics* 49:757–771.

Stirland, A. J. (2005) *The Men of the Mary Rose: Raising the Dead* (rev. ed.). Sutton Publishing, Phoenix Mill, U.K.

Stojanowski, C. M. (2002) Hydrodynamic sorting in a coastal marine skeletal assemblage. *International Journal of Osteoarchaeology* 12:259–278.

Tapanila, L., E. M. Roberts, M. L. Bouaré, F. Sissoko, and M. A. O'Leary (2004) Bivalve borings in phosphatic coprolites and bone, Cretaceous–Paleogene, northeastern Mali. *Palaios* 19:565–573.

Trueman, C. and D. M. Martill (2002) The long-term survival of bone: The role of bioerosion. *Archaeometry* 44:371–382.

Tunnicliffe, V., G. Anderson, K. Nikolich, and R. K. Dewey (2010) Cadavers in support of forensic and hypoxia research. In *Proceedings from the AGU Ocean Sciences Meeting*, pp. 22–26, Portland, OR, February 2010.

Ubelaker, D. H. and K. M. Zarenko (2011) Adipocere: What is known after over two centuries of research. *Forensic Science International* 208:167–172.

Voorhies, M. R. (1969) Taphonomy and population dynamics of an Early Pliocene vertebrate fauna, Knox County, Nebraska. *University of Wyoming, Contributions to Geology*, Laramie, WY, Special Paper No. 1.

Vrijenhoek, R. C., S. Johnson, and G. W. Rouse (2009) A remarkable diversity of bone-eating worms (*Osedax*; Siboglinidae; Annelida). *BMC Biology* 7:74.

Vullo, R. (2009) Taphonomy of vertebrate microfossil assemblages in coastal environments: In search of a modern analogous model. *Palaios* 24:723–725.

Waite, J. H. (2002) Adhesion à la moule. *Integrative and Comparative Biology* 42:1172–1180.

Warén, A. (2011) Molluscs on biogenic substrates. In *The Natural History of Santo*, eds. P. Bouchet, H. Le Guyader, and O. Pascal, pp. 438–448. MNHN, Paris, France; IRD, Marseille, France; PNI, Paris, France.

Weigelt, J. (1989 [1927]) *Recent Vertebrate Carcasses and Their Paleobiological Implications*. Reprint edition, translated by J. Schaefer. University of Chicago Press, Chicago, IL.

West, J. G. (2011) Changing patterns of shark attacks in Australian waters. *Marine and Freshwater Research* 62:744–754.

Westling, L. (2012) *Underwater Decomposition: An Examination of Factors Surrounding Freshwater Decomposition in Eastern Massachusetts*. Unpublished M.S. Thesis, Boston University, Boston, MA.

Whitenack, L. B. and P. J. Motta (2010) Performance of shark teeth during puncture and draw: Implications for the mechanics of cutting. *Biological Journal of the Linnean Society* 100:271–286.

Wroe, S., D. R. Huber, M. Lowry, C. McHenry, K. Moreno, P. Clausen, T. L. Ferrara, E. Cunningham, M. N. Dean, and A. P. Summers (2008) Three-dimensional computer analysis of white shark jaw mechanics: How hard can a great white bite? *Journal of Zoology, London* 276:336–342.

Yoshino, M., T. Kimijima, S. Miyasaka, H. Sato, and S. Seta (1991) Microscopical study on estimation of time since death in skeletal remains. *Forensic Science International* 49:143–158.

Zimmerman, K. A. and J. R. Wallace (2008) The potential to determine a postmortem submersion interval based on algal/diatom diversity on decomposing mammalian carcasses in brackish ponds in Delaware. *Journal of Forensic Sciences* 53:935–941.

Contemporary Cultural Alterations to Bone

8

JOSEPHINE M. PAOLELLO
ALEXANDRA R. KLALES

Contents

> The ancient teachers of this science... promised impossibilities and performed nothing. The modern masters promise very little; they know that metals cannot be transmuted and that the elixir of life is a chimera but these philosophers, whose hands seem only made to dabble in dirt, and their eyes to pore over the microscope or crucible, have indeed performed miracles... They ascend into the heavens; they have discovered how the blood circulates, and the nature of the air we breathe. They have acquired new and almost unlimited powers; they can command the thunders of heaven, mimic the earthquake, and even mock the invisible world with its own shadows.
>
> —**Mary Wollstonecraft Shelley,** *Frankenstein; or the Modern Prometheus*

Introduction

The following is an analysis of the most prevalent taphonomic features observed on human osseous remains commonly derived from contemporary contexts in the United States: anatomical collection, personal display, and ritual sources. These remains have in common their manipulation and alteration in recent contexts and their ubiquitous appearance as cases requiring examination in Medical Examiner and other forensic laboratory settings. They also tend to overlap in multiple taphonomic characteristics due to frequent common origins as remains pillaged from cemetery contexts or culled from teaching collections and subsequent use or display.

A review of the cultural practices affecting human osseous remains throughout history and prehistory would be the work of several volumes. Since the Lower Paleolithic period, osseous tissues (bones, teeth/ivory, and antler) have been a frequently used material of great utility in tool manufacture (Backwell and d'Errico 2003; Bonnichsen and Sorg 1989; Brain 1981; Lesnik 2011; Morlan 1984) due to their relative ease of shaping combined with their durability and flexibility (MacGregor 1985). They also have been a frequent cross-cultural venue for artistic expression, both as a relatively innocuous raw material and as a cultural signifier themselves when their original morphology is deliberately retained, especially with human remains. Skull motifs in particular (whether signifying rebellion, intimidation, death, or sciences involving osteology, for example) are commonly seen on clothing, personal items, and tattoos, and retain a general acceptance in contemporary U.S. society. The display of actual human skulls, however, is less accepted by the general public and is more confined to specific subcultural segments. Such human remains tend to be an anatomical or personal display specimen or a ritual object used in contemporary religions/cults. *Anatomical remains* are processed bones used in medical, teaching, or research facilities, and these often find their way into the hands of the general public or are discarded in contexts requiring their later forensic examination. These have many taphonomic characteristics in common with *personal display* bones, many of which originally derived from anatomical teaching specimens. Human remains used in ritual or ceremonial practices may derive from anatomical remains, cemetery contexts, or other more direct sources and be modified for religious purposes, such as in some Afro-Caribbean cultures (Wetli and Martinez 1981). The taphonomic characteristics of remains from these sources will be examined in the following text.

Anatomical Specimens

History of Anatomical Specimens

Despite cultural stigma, human remains have been used for dissection and medical/anatomical education as early as the third century B.C. by the Greeks (Walker 2008). Widespread documented use of human cadavers for medical purposes in Western cultures, however, did not occur until the Renaissance Period (fourteenth to seventeenth centuries A.D.). During this time, religious stigmatization decreased, and the value of human remains for scientific research and medical education began to be realized (Walker 2008). Blakely and Harrington (1997:165) note that the "clash between beliefs about death—both medical and religious—and the needs of the medical profession reached a zenith in the eighteenth and nineteenth centuries." By the eighteenth century, the utilization and demand for human cadavers increased significantly. In Europe, medical students were required to learn human anatomy and to have hands-on practice with cadavers. Similarly, in order to become a licensed doctor in the United States, an individual was required to have practical experience in anatomical dissection; however, both dissection and the possession of cadavers were largely illegal at that time, thereby creating what Iserson (2001:414) calls a "Catch-22."

At that time, many countries lacked legal venues for human body acquisition to meet the increased demands of medical schools (Iserson 2001). Laws were created to satisfy the shortage, yet religious stigmas and ethnocentric belief systems influenced the acquisition and sources of human cadavers during this period. In 1752, the English Parliament enacted the Murder Act, whereby the bodies of convicted murderers were prohibited from being buried, and public dissection following execution was mandated (Halperin 2007). Throughout both Europe and North America, adult anatomical specimens began to be legally procured from people who died as a result of duels, executed criminals, prison inmates who died naturally, and the unclaimed corpses of the poor, while the remains of children came from orphans, stillbirths, or unbaptized infants, usually of the poor. However, the supply of legal remains proved insufficient, and medical schools soon began the opportunistic procurement of cadavers from relatives of those teaching, body snatching or grave robbing, and in extreme cases from people murdered for the use of their bodies (Halperin 2007; Roach 2003).

In the United States, the majority of remains for anatomical dissection were acquired from disenfranchised groups that could neither object nor prevent their dead from being stolen, namely, the poor, the mentally and physically disabled, criminals, immigrants, and African Americans (Blakely and Harrington 1997; Halperin 2007; Stubblefield 2011). Laws were enacted to make grave robbing and illegal acquisition of human remains a crime in both the United States, beginning with New York in 1789, and in Europe (Blake 1955). The Warburton Act (or Anatomy Act) of 1832, passed by the United Kingdom Parliament, required individuals who practiced anatomy to have a license and to report the source of their cadavers. State governments in the United States began to enact similar laws concerning the legal acquisition of cadavers beginning in 1831 with Massachusetts (Blake 1955). However, the U.S. anatomy laws were passed only on a state-by-state basis; therefore, there was no national uniformity (Humphrey 1973; Iserson 2001).

During this period, skeletons used for teaching specimens were frequently "leftovers" from anatomical dissections. In the modern era (from the mid-1960s to present), most remains used for anatomical dissections are acquired from individuals who have willed or actively donated their remains to science. In most of these instances, virtually all of the tissue is either cremated or returned for burial depending on the individual's or family's wishes following dissection. Because of this, skeletal material used for teaching in the modern era usually is purchased after the tissue has been removed and processed and is not acquired from dissections. Typically, India is considered to be the primary modern source of anatomical material (Stubblefield 2011). During the twentieth century, major sources of anatomical specimens in the United States were those purchased and acquired from India and Bangladesh prior to the 1980s' ban on the export of human material from those countries (Carney 2007; Hefner et al. 2008). Today, human skeletal remains can be purchased by several U.S. biological supply companies that source material from India, which has since lifted the ban on the export of human remains, and also from other parts of Asia including China (Cauble 2010; Quigley 2001). Additionally, anatomically prepared human remains can be purchased from private sellers on Internet sites, as it is legal to own and sell human skeletal remains in most states. In the case of most, if not all, of these sources of human anatomical remains, the provenience and demographic information is lacking.

Collectors of human remains, including medical professionals and laypersons, often display the skeletal material as curiosities, typically skulls having visible medical anomalies such as pathological conditions, trauma, and other interesting cases (Walker 2008). Human skeletal remains also were often preserved for extended display as anatomical art for public viewing (Hansen 1996). Many of these collections were preserved and appropriated to either museums or educational facilities. Disposal of unwanted anatomical specimens prior to the 1970s was an "informal process" that often resulted in interment at a waste site (Stubblefield 2011). In other instances, disposal of anatomical display skulls rested on the relatives of the deceased previous owners who inadvertently found these items among the deceased's belongings. Since disposal often involves haphazard discard leading to later discovery, contact with law enforcement and the involvement of forensic anthropologists often follow.

Comparative Analysis of Anatomical and Personal Display Skeletal Remains

Skulls from this context fall into two categories based on the intended use of the remains: (1) those prepared for teaching purposes in medicine and biological anthropology and (2) those prepared for personal display as a "curiosity," art, or prop. The former category sometimes includes remains that have been previously altered during autopsy. Information for this analysis comes from the personal observations of the authors and more specifically from cases submitted for forensic anthropological analysis either by private citizens or by police agencies to the Department of Applied Forensic Sciences at Mercyhurst University, Erie, PA. The taphonomic features present on four cases consisting of five individuals were compared from primary analyses to determine the taphonomic characteristics of anatomical and display remains (Figure 8.1).

Commingling

Commingling is expected in cases of anatomical remains, as many skeletons would be processed in batches and then later reassembled. Therefore, a minimum number of individuals (MNI) greater than one provides supporting evidence that skeletal remains may be anatomical in origin. The preparation processes also may result in having ill-fitting teeth in alveolar sockets, a mandible that does not properly articulate to the cranium (including malocclusion between the maxillary and mandibular teeth), or mismatched ribs (Carney 2007). Careful attention should be given to the determination of the minimum number of elements and the MNI in these cases. Human remains have been found in association

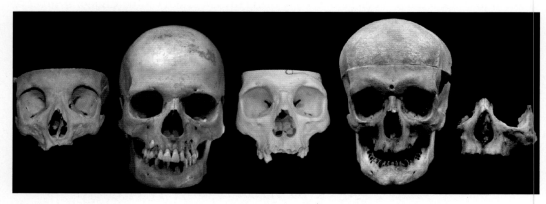

Figure 8.1 Sample of anatomical specimens analyzed. From left to right: MC-2, MC-3, MC-4, MC-5a, and MC-5b. (Images by A. Klales, courtesy of D. Dirkmaat at Mercyhurst University, Erie, PA.)

with nonhuman bones (Saul and Saul 1987) when comparative faunal collections were discarded with human material.

Taphonomic Characteristics

There are a number of common taphonomic features observed on remains that have been prepared for teaching and display purposes. The observed taphonomic features have been categorized according to three proposed occurrences relating to (1) the original preparation, (2) features from display and use for anatomical education, or (3) features related to subsequent curation and storage of the remains. These categories are generalizations and are not observed in all cases.

Taphonomic Characteristics Related to Preparation   *Bleaching/whitening:* There are a number of methods used in modern times to *macerate* (remove soft tissue from) human osseous remains, and a number of these techniques are employed in combination or sequentially and may leave recognizable alterations on skeletal material. Common methods of tissue removal include boiling or prolonged warm water submersion, often with the use of common laundry detergents, hydrogen peroxide (Na_2O_2), or bleach (sodium hypochlorite, NaClO) (Fenton et al. 2003; Snyder et al. 1975; Stephens 1979). Boiling is often accompanied by manual scrubbing to remove adhering soft tissue, which may leave behind characteristic micro-abrasions or other tool marks. Other methods of defleshing include consumption of dried tissue by dermestid beetles (*Dermestes maculatus*) and consumption of moist tissue by blowfly maggots (Calliphoridae) during outdoor decomposition, which may leave evidence of environmental exposure. Varnish is also frequently applied following initial preparation of the skeletal material in order to prevent flaking and damage to the bone (Snyder et al. 1975).

Sectioning cuts: Remains prepared for anatomical specimens often exhibit sectioning cuts in order to make interior portions of bones (typically the endocranium and tooth crypts) available for visual inspection. In addition, the most common autopsy cut of the skull is circumferential calvarium sectioning for the removal of the calotte and brain (Figure 8.2). This particular cut typically is oriented transversely across the frontal bone just superior to the orbits and passes through the temporal bones along the squama and through the occipital planum, occasionally involving the parietals (McFarlin and Wineski 1997). Cuts along the sagittal plane of the skull also are commonly found in medically prepared specimens to exhibit the internal structures of the endocranium. Additional

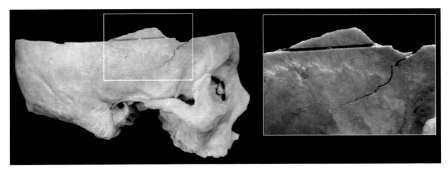

Figure 8.2 Bone splintering resulting from an autopsy cut for the removal of the calotte. (Images by A. Klales, courtesy of D. Dirkmaat at Mercyhurst University, Erie, PA.)

sectioning includes longitudinal cuts specifically through the petrous portion and external auditory meatus of the temporal bones, along the mastoid processes, through the occipital bone to create an "occipital wedge," and along the frontal and zygomatics to expose the orbits and sinuses (McFarlin and Wineski 1997:138; Stubblefield 2011). McFarlin and Wineski (1997:108) found that many "dissection approaches, instrumentation, and techniques have not changed substantially over the past 150 years." Postcranially, the body and manubrium of the sternum may be cut completely or exhibit tool marks from the Y-shaped incision made to open the chest cavity. As such, anatomical preparation cuts are the most distinct taphonomic feature of anatomically prepared remains and can be used to distinguish easily these from forensically significant human remains.

The presence of these cuts also includes temporal information for determination of the postmortem interval, since mechanical devices for sectioning crania have only been employed on a large scale in modern times. The most ubiquitous of these devices is the Stryker saw, known for its deep, narrow, and vertical bone cuts, which has been available commercially only since 1948 (Breneman 1993:116). Various powered devices were patented prior to the Stryker saw and may have been employed in this role on a more limited scale. One of the earliest patents was in 1890 by Milton J. Roberts for a powered surgical saw ("Electro Osteotome", U.S. Patent No. 436,804, Sept. 23, 1890). Prior to the commercialization of powered devices, dissections and amputations typically were conducted using either a hand saw, a hand-crank powered blade, or a gigli saw (Mr. Steve Carusillo, VP, R&D Technology, Stryker Instruments, pers. comm.).

Reconstruction material: Plaster and other reconstructive materials are sometimes applied to any damaged, fragile, or loose areas of the skeletal elements. In particular, reconstructive material has been used along the alveoli to prevent tooth loss and the cranial sutures to prevent disarticulation. In some cases, glue is also used to affix the sectioned calotte to the cranium.

Taphonomic Characteristics Related to Display and Use   *Articulation-related:* Skeletal remains (specifically skulls) prepared for teaching purposes typically have drill holes and associated metal hardware from the assembly and reconstruction of the bones into anatomical order. Anatomical specimens are prepared with holes to affix all portions of a sectioned cranium, to connect the mandible, and to articulate the postcrania for mounting and display of the remains. Holes are often located on the mandible to affix it to the rest of the cranium, and the corresponding hardware holes are most frequently found on the temporal bone but may also be located on the frontal bone, especially when springs are used (Figure 8.3). These holes are generally small (approximately 2–3 mm in diameter). For display, holes are most common near the anatomical landmark bregma or along the sagittal suture for hanging skeletons. Sometimes, preparation holes or hardware also can be found in the posterior portion of the cranium near opisthocranion for mounting the skeleton on a wall or display plaque. Those holes drilled for hanging and mounting are larger (usually >5 mm in diameter) in comparison to those made for assembling the individual skeletal elements. Preparation holes tend to be circular with clean edges. The hardware includes springs, metal rods and wiring, hooks, clasps, nails, and screws, and sometimes makeshift hardware is devised for the same tasks by nonprofessionals.

Springs are attached to nails or hooks in the mandible (either through the ramus, coronoid process, or condyles) and to the cranial vault (either on the parietals, temporal, or frontal) to attach the two so that the jaw can still be opened and closed. In these

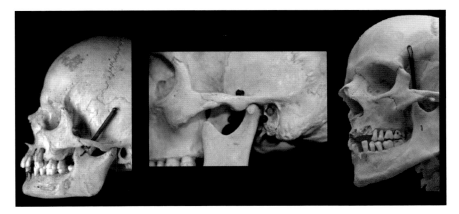

Figure 8.3 Variation in articulation holes and hardware associated with affixing the mandible to the cranium. From left to right: attachment of mandible to the squamous portion of the temporal, attachment to the zygomatic process of the temporal, and attachment to the frontal bone. (Images by A. Klales, courtesy of D. Dirkmaat at Mercyhurst University, Erie, PA.)

cases, damage to the teeth is common from the springs being released too quickly, causing chipping and flaking of the enamel. Hooks, clasps, or levers are frequently used to attach the calotte to the rest of the skull and can be located on the parietals and temporal bones. Thin metal rods inserted into the diploë of the flat cranial bones can be used in conjunction with the aforementioned hardware or separately to attach the calotte (Figure 8.4).

Anatomical markings and writing: Anatomical markings on skeletal remains are a common addition to the preparation of modern commercial anatomical specimens. These markings include the labeling of anatomical features including muscle attachment points, arteries, veins, and nerves. Writing often includes names or serial numbers from the company distributing and selling the remains. Older specimens sometimes have the location

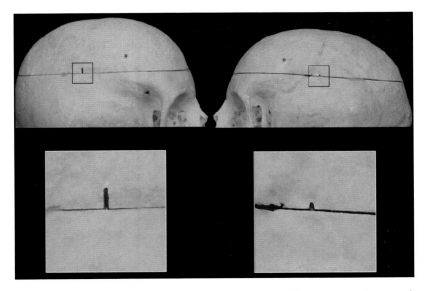

Figure 8.4 Example of metal rods used to affix the calotte to the cranium. (Images by A. Klales, courtesy of D. Dirkmaat at Mercyhurst University, Erie, PA.)

of preparation or individual who prepared the remains. Paint specks or marks resembling paint are also commonly present on anatomical remains from curation, molding materials, and accidental exposure. Unintentional marks or incidental writing can also be found on anatomical and teaching specimens, especially around locations involving craniometric landmarks and measurements, the instructions for which in many cases advocate the use of a temporary pencil mark to indicate a midpoint (Buikstra and Ubelaker 1994), which may be forgotten and left behind.

Taphonomic Characteristics Related to Curation   *Handling alteration:* Remains prepared for anatomical or display purposes frequently exhibit postmortem alteration, including breakage from repeated handling, especially along the fragile portions of the skull (the eye orbits, interior nasal bones, styloid processes, alveolar bone, and zygomatic processes). Damage also may be present around the areas of articulation as a result of abrupt or repeated contact between the moveable parts. As indicated earlier, broken teeth are common, as the springs joining the mandible to the cranium often cause the mandibular teeth to close forcibly against the maxillary teeth. Furthermore, fully articulated skeletons are difficult to handle, and transport and damage can occur when limbs are not stabilized and are free to swing. Such remains, by their very nature, exist to be manipulated by multiple persons often initially unfamiliar with their fragility. The same bones often are used in academic settings for decades, slowly acquiring destructive modification over that span.

Glue and tape: Glue and other adhesives, such as rubber cement or from adhesive tape, are used frequently in anatomically prepared human remains to reconstruct broken or loose elements throughout normal use. Remnants of adhesives also can be found on anatomically prepared specimens after features have been labeled for exemplars during instruction and from test preparation (or to cover serial numbers known to the test-takers). Dust, debris, and dirt adhere more readily to these residual adhesive areas, giving them a darkened appearance (Figure 8.5). In other cases, the tape or adhesive removes previous

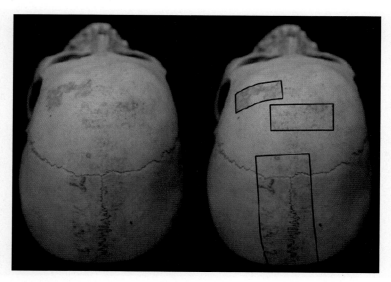

Figure 8.5 Left: remnants of adhesive tape creating differential staining on the cranium of MC-3. Right: edges of tape outlined in black. (Images by A. Klales, courtesy of D. Dirkmaat at Mercyhurst University, Erie, PA.)

buildup of dust and debris and creates a lightened area of bone. Frequently, the precise out-line of the adhesive material is preserved, and areas tend to be symmetrical, rectangular in shape, and have distinctly outlined corners or edges.

Dust: A fairly thick coating of dust is referred to as *attic dust* because of long-term accumulation from storage and frequently will be found on internal structures due to exposure from the cuts made during preparation. The pattern of dust accumulation found on the remains can indicate how the skull was displayed or stored and how regularly it was handled. Endocranial dust accumulation suggests that the skull was stored without the calotte in place and protecting the internal structures. Ectocranial dust accumulation is often found along the top of the skull, along the inferior portion of the eye orbits, at the base of the zygomatic arches on the temporal bones, and inside the nasal aperture. Specimens handled less frequently during prolonged periods of curation can be expected to have more dust buildup present.

Patina and polish: *Patina* is an accrued darkened film as a result of long-term expo-sure to dust and handling, the composition of which includes oils and other substances from human skin (see Chapter 12, this volume, Figure 12.5f for an example). This may be accompanied by a glossy *polish* or burnish, as a result of repeated handling. The presence or degree of the patina or gloss largely depends on how often the remains were handled. Skulls displayed as art or curiosities generally are not handled as often as teaching speci-mens. Differential staining may also result from the processing method or from the rem-nants of the aforementioned adhesives. Care should be taken not to confuse the darkened appearance from differential staining or patina with soil staining from burials.

Shelf wear: This taphonomic alteration is caused by unintentional, accrued postmor-tem forces affecting the base of the cranium, including the occipital condyles, mastoid processes, and inferior mandibular margin, specifically characterized by erosion and flak-ing of the outer cortical bone from repeatedly setting the skull down on hard surfaces (Figure 8.6). Repeated rubbing and wear on a surface creates a dense, smooth, shiny, whit-ened appearance similar to ivory.

Taphonomic Characteristics of Anatomical Remains   The primary analysis of anthro-pological cases involving anatomical and display remains has revealed a suite of taphonomic

(a)

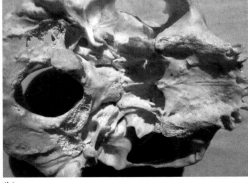
(b)

Figure 8.6 Examples of shelf wear. The inferior mandible (a) and cranium (b) show damage typical to surfaces from repeated handling, in this case, from years of use in teaching in a medical school.

characteristics common on such remains. While not all of the taphonomic signatures presented here were found in every case, each case did exhibit multiple indicators that the remains were for anatomical, teaching, or display purposes. Generally, remains prepared for anatomical specimens are clean and free of all soft tissue from processing and almost always belonged to adult individuals. Compared to subadults, adult remains are more easily acquired, and areas of anatomical interest are better exhibited and easier to locate since the features are larger. All but one individual were males, which corresponds with previous published literature that, historically, males were preferred over females for dissection and for skeletal remains (Blakely and Harrington 1997).

All of the cases exhibit evidence of handling damage from repeated use. Damage was usually restricted to the fragile areas of the skull. All of the cases, except for one, had paint, writing, or a combination of both present. Over half of the cases also had sectioning cuts, glue or tape, patina, and shelf wear. Half of the cases had bleaching or evidence of whitening, articulation-related holes or hardware, and dust. Only one case showed evidence of tissue removal in the form of soap remnants, and one case had differential staining throughout. Although there were no instances of anatomical markings present on the cases, these are common inclusions on commercial anatomical products that may be encountered on cases of haphazard disposal. Similarly, none of the cases have reconstructive materials present, although it should be considered when assessing anatomical remains. The combination of several of these traits is indicative of a taphonomic pattern that can be used to identify anatomical specimens from forensically significant modern cases.

Contemporary Ritual Remains

In the United States, multiple instances of human remains encountered from a ritual context have been attributed to practices of Santería and Palo Mayombe (Gill et al. 2009; Wetli and Martinez 1981), with the former being perhaps the largest sect of the extensive underground religions (Brandon 1993). These findings are most frequent in cities with large Afro-Caribbean populations, especially around New York City, Miami, Los Angeles, Chicago, Boston, and Washington, D.C., among other cities (Brandon 1993). While human osseous remains from other less numerous or less formal modern ritual practices may no doubt be encountered in forensic settings, these two ritual systems often cause specific taphonomic characteristics that may indicate the origin of some collections of skeletal remains.

History of Santería

The beliefs of Santería stem from the African slave trade in colonial Cuba and the combination of Christianity, influenced largely by Spanish Catholicism, with the African Yoruba religion, primarily of Nigeria, into what is referred to as a syncretic faith. The early, or formative, period of Santería in Cuba developed from about 1760 through 1870, after which time Cuban slavery slowly became abolished, and a period of transformation brought the religion into the predominant form (Brandon 1993). Following the Cuban Revolution and resultant diaspora, Santería began to take root in New York in 1959 (Brandon 1993).

Santería also has been referred to as *Regla de Ocha* ("Rule of Ocha"; variably spelled *Ochaö*) and *Lucumí* ("friendship"; variably spelled *Lukumi*), an ethnic term that was used in Cuba to describe the Yoruba slaves and their culture (Brandon 1993; De La Torre 2004).

Hybrids of the syncretic religion developed as the Yoruba slaves were transferred to different Caribbean regions, such as Voodoo (variably *Vodou* or *Voudun*) in Haiti and New Orleans as expressed through French Catholicism (De La Torre 2004).

According to the principles of Santería, the deities are secondary gods known as the *orishas*, of which there is no exact number, but the pantheon may include around 20–25 in Latin America and range from 400 to more than 1000 in Africa (De La Torre 2004; González-Wippler 1989). In order to mask the practice from the slave owners, the *orishas* were associated with Catholic saints and celebrated on the respective Saint's Days, hence the term "Santería," literally meaning "the way of the saints." The association of the *orishas* with saints continues to be practiced, even though Santería is becoming less of an underground religion.

Specific *orishas* are associated with certain colors and sacred objects and offerings, to include preferred animal sacrifices. Initiates of Santería receive beaded necklaces (*collares* or *elekes*) in the respective color sequences for five major *orishas*, followed by those of additional *orishas* if their protection is deemed necessary (González-Wippler 1989). The finding of such necklaces in association with ritual remains or altars has been reported in investigations by Gill et al. (2009) and Wetli and Martinez (1981).

Several *orishas* are invoked during a single ritual by the *santeros*, or priests. One of the most influential *orishas* is *Elegguá*, for the Yoruba word meaning "messenger of the gods." *Elegguá* is the patron saint of pathways and crossroads, and he is believed to be the intermediary between humans and *Olodumare*, the one God of Santería. As such, *Elegguá* is always the first *orisha* invoked during a ritual so that he will pass on the requests of the practitioners, and a portion of every sacrifice is offered to him. He is referred to as the trickster, because, in part, of the stories that he would often hide behind doors of houses to eavesdrop for information. The colors of *Elegguá* are red and black, and his necklace consists of three red beads alternating with three black beads. His associated objects, offerings, and animal sacrifices are not limited to: roosters, goats, deer, opossum, coconuts, rum, toasted corn, cigars, whistles, guns, and children's toys. This particular *orisha* is represented as a clay or cement head with a face made out of cowrie shells, and the object may often be found behind a door, a finding that is further verified in a case by Wetli and Martinez (1981).

When a *santero* dies, a group of *santeros* gather and consult the *orishas* through cowrie shells to determine how to discard the previous owner's paraphernalia, with options of burying the objects with the person, giving them to an heir, or giving them back to nature by tossing them into a river or ocean. This action may account for cases involving bags of bones with other items found along riverbanks, such as reported by Gill et al. (2009).

Palo Mayombe

Another popular spiritual hybrid developed from the slave trade as African beliefs originating from the Kongo culture of central Africa were syncretized with Christianity to form Palo. The practice of Palo uses magic associated with *brujería*, or witchcraft, and it is said to be "the dark side of Santería" (De La Torre 2004:27), although they are separate belief systems. In addition, practitioners of Palo can progress later as initiates of Santería, while the reverse is not allowed (De La Torre 2004; Murrell 2009). Also, leaders of Palo may often choose to incorporate myths and symbols of Santería into their own practice, depending on individual interpretations (Murrell 2009).

Figure 8.7 The practice of Palo Mayombe uses ceremonial cauldrons such as these, containing the remains of RMEO-1 and sacrificial objects. (Image courtesy of G. Hart, State of New Jersey Regional Medical Examiner's Office, New Jersey.)

Palo is a Spanish term for "branch" or "wooden stick" and derives its name from the incorporation of wood branches and herbs in its spells. The branches or sticks are part of the foundation used to fill the ceremonial cauldrons, known as *prendas* or by the African name *ngangas* (Figure 8.7). Alternatively, the *ngangas* may take the form of a sack. Other elements of the foundation typically include graveyard soil, stones, insects, animal carcasses, and human bones, ideally of a skull with some of the brain still present (De La Torre 2004). A variety of other items will be added for the spells such as coins, candles, scraps of a person's clothes, and cigar butts, and foodstuffs like rum, lime, and wine besides the many herbs and spices. Further, quicksilver (mercury) is often added to give the spirit speed, and the remains of a dog will help the spirit in its search (González-Wippler 1989). The presence of mercury among ritual cases is stressed by Gill et al. (2009), and dog remains were noted in ritual cases during their research.

Palo Mayombe is one of the major sects of Palo. The influence of Christianity on Palo Mayombe is reflected through the division of the good "baptized" versus the bad "unbaptized" branches of the practice. The "baptized" add holy water to their *ngangas* and only work with good spirits of the dead. This Mayombero Christiano sect of Palo Mayombe uses "white magic," and it can be distinguished from evil magic because the altar will always have a crucifix associated with it (Wetli and Martinez 1983). The "unbaptized" work with evil spirits, as in those from criminals or the insane, who would be more likely to fulfill their malevolent requests (De La Torre 2004; González-Wippler 1989). The spirits are obtained through a bone of the deceased, and in return for the favors, blood and animal sacrifices are offered. Notably, a railroad spike is a symbolic item of the "unbaptized" *paleros* (i.e., Palo practitioners).

Of the several steps required in the initiation ritual to become a *palero*, the final ordination may be of forensic interest. A human tibia wrapped in black cloth is received as a scepter used to invoke the spirits of the *nganga*. In choosing spirits of the dead for the *nganga*, human remains from a cemetery are usually acquired from recent corpses whose identity is known to the *palero*, in hopes that the brain is present and to be sure that their requests will be followed. Fingers, toes, and ribs are often taken along with the head and tibia. There is no set preference as to the racial affiliation of the deceased individual, but it is said that remains from a white person are favored in beliefs that their brains are "easier to influence than that of a [B]lack man and that it will follow instructions better" (González-Wippler 1989:244). When a *palero* dies, his *nganga* is either passed on to another or else it is dismantled and buried in the woods, preferably near the base of an anthill, and the earth is topped with rum and chicken's blood (González-Wippler 1989). This is done to constrain the associated evil spirits (González-Wippler 1973:30; Wetli and Martinez 1983:633).

These Afro-Caribbean religions lack a central organization or formal dogma; therefore, the beliefs and practices will vary in different regions and even among neighboring house-temples. Variations in the religions also developed from the combination of assorted African tribes that were united because of the slave trade in the Caribbean. When human remains are involved in the rituals, the practice is more likely related to Palo. The beliefs of Palo focus largely on veneration of the dead, namely, by invoking their spirits (known as *nkitas* among other synonymous terms). Worship, however, does include some counterparts of the *orishas*.

Comparative Analysis of Ritual Remains

Generalizations from the religious beliefs of Santería and Palo Mayombe support the interpretation of taphonomic features observed on reported case studies of ritual remains from nine reported investigations with a total of 15 skulls/crania, along with other human and nonhuman remains. Wetli and Martinez (1981) describe five ritualistic cases involving a total of seven skulls and other human and faunal remains from the Dade County Medical Examiner's Office in Miami, FL, designated here as DCME-1–5. Gill et al. (2009) describe two cases consisting of three skulls from the New York City Office of Chief Medical Examiner (OCME) and Department of Forensic Medicine, designated here as OCME-1a, 1b, and 2. Ms. Gina Hart of the State of New Jersey Regional Medical Examiner's Office (RMEO) in Newark contributed anthropology reports describing two cases with a total of five human skulls, designated here as RMEO-1a, 1b, 1c, 2a, and 2b, along with many other human and nonhuman faunal remains.

Commingling

It is apparent that ritual cases will involve the remains of multiple individuals disbursed over several cauldrons or vessels. In RMEO-1, all three skulls were without their calvaria, and three nonmatching calvaria were present. In addition, postcranial remains found in a white sack at the residence were matched to RMEO-1c, and postcranial elements from another individual were reassociated from throughout the case. Of interest, both of these individuals were able to be identified by pair-matching, articulation, and taphonomic similarities (e.g., coloration) of elements compared to remains recovered from disturbed cemetery crypts with deaths dating to 1930 and 1935.

Human remains also tend to be commingled with nonhuman remains, as animal offerings and sacrifices are a fundamental aspect of Santería and Palo Mayombe rituals.

Nonhuman remains associated with the cases include reports of chicken heads and bodies, a duck head, and several other avian species, a turtle carapace/plastron, goat skulls, dog heads, deer antlers, and cow horns, along with a number of unidentified nonhuman bones.

Biological Profiles

As stated earlier, human remains used for ritual purposes are not limited to a specific biological profile. Two black males (DCME-1 and -2a) and one white female (DCME-4) were reported by Wetli and Martinez (1981), and Gill et al. (2009) report probable male and probable female remains of indeterminate ancestry among OCME-1. The skulls involved in the RMEO cases were determined to be of three white males (RMEO-1a, 1c, and 2b) and two females and one white (RMEO-2a) and one either white or Hispanic (RMEO-1b). All of the crania were determined to be from adults or older adults, although a subadult calvarium also was present among RMEO-1.

Antemortem tooth loss was reported in cases of older adults; RMEO-1a, 1c, and 2a are edentulous crania, and two maxillary dentures were included in RMEO-1. Antemortem lesions noted on RMEO-1b suggested a disease such as tuberculosis. There were no reports of perimortem trauma observed among the cases.

Taphonomic Characteristics

Remains acquired for ritual practice may derive from anatomical specimens and thus exhibit some taphonomic characteristics as described earlier. The practitioner using DCME-1 had supplied a receipt of purchase for the item from a botánicas store. One cranium from DCME-3 had a broken spring and screw attached to the mandible with a corresponding screw in the maxilla (Wetli and Martinez 1981), suggesting its origin as an anatomical specimen. The observed taphonomic features on the other remains have been categorized as relating to either previous interment or as a result of cultural practices.

Taphonomic Characteristics Related to Previous Interment   Gill et al. (2009) report that the remains from OCME-1 and 2 are consistent with having a historical origin from a long-term burial, which is a similar finding for the RMEO cases. Taphonomic characteristics consistent with a previous burial will lack many features of environmental exposure, such as sun bleaching and scavenging, with the major exceptions of adherent soil and soil staining (see Chapter 5, this volume).

Adherent soil: Dried soil and dark staining were reported in a majority of the sample. The presence of soil was abundant around the orbits, nasal aperture, and other openings. In some cases, adherent soil may also be attributed to cultural modification, as soil is an integral part of the cauldron foundation, or it may occur postdepositionally with discarded remains. It is most likely that a thick coating of soil and dark staining on the remains are related to previous interment.

Autopsied or embalmed: The preservation of autopsied and embalmed remains is highly variable and, thus, not a reliable indicator of postmortem interval (see Chapter 5, this volume). Embalming hinders and alters the typical decomposition process (Mann et al. 1990), often leaving remnant desiccated tissue. Berryman et al. (1991) note that evidence of embalming includes adhering head and facial hair; fungal growth particularly on the hands and face from cosmetic make-up and elsewhere from the dark, moist environment; flaking of the skin from continual shrinkage; flaking and erosion of cortical bone from changes between wet/dry episodes and "pressure point" contact with the coffin

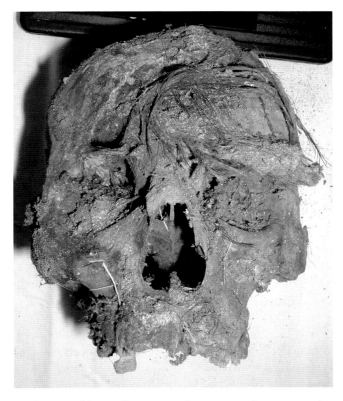

Figure 8.8 Soil and clumps of hair adhering to the RMEO-2b cranium. (Image courtesy of G. Hart, State of New Jersey Regional Medical Examiner's Office, New Jersey.)

surface (i.e., coffin wear; see Chapter 5, this volume); differential decomposition; and brain preservation. Many of these traits were described in these cases. The presence of desiccated tissue was noted on RMEO-1a and 1c, and on several postcranial elements associated with the case, especially articulating finger bones and vertebrae. Further, clumps of hair were adhering to RMEO-2b (Figure 8.8). Cortical exfoliation or flaking were reported on three cases (OCME-1 and 2 and RMEO-2), possibly as a result of coffin wear. Also a mummified brain present in the cranial cavity was reported in one case (DCME-4). Fungal growth was not reported; however, a dark greenish coloration was observed on remains from RMEO-1, which may be related to embalming. As noted earlier, the three crania from RMEO-1 are without their calvaria, but three other calvaria are present, and all but one of these (RMEO-1b) are consistent with the smooth-cut sectioning done by a Stryker saw during autopsy.

Taphonomic Characteristics Related to Cultural Practices   *Associated and residual artifacts:* Indications of ritual remains are obvious when found in the context of altars or cauldrons. Prolonged contact with other ceremonial offerings may leave residual traces on the remains that may still be present when they are taken out of that context or discarded. After taking a radiograph of OCME-2, Gill et al. (2009) discovered a glass jar containing mercury within the mud-filled cranial vault. The cranial cavity of RMEO-2a was full of plastic, paper, and miscellaneous objects visible through the foramen magnum.

Wetli and Martinez (1981) note the presence of dried grass on three crania (DCME-3a, 3b, and 5), which is probably the result of additives to the cauldrons, such as from herbs and spices. Green leaves, likely of an herbal nature, were present within the cauldrons and crania of RMEO-1, while particles of dried grass were apparent on the RMEO-2b cranium. In these cases, postdepositional adherence of dried grass seems less probable, since the DCME remains were encountered within bags or wrapped in cloth. The presence of these botanical remains as a result of previous interment, however, cannot be excluded. Direct contact with copper and corroded metal items can result in a green oxide staining (DCME-3) or rust-colored stain (DCME-2), respectively (see Chapter 12, this volume). Feathers were abundant over most of the items from RMEO-1 and reported for DCME-2. Glitter was also noted throughout RMEO-1. Finally, blood residue can be expected, as it is a sacred offering of Santería and Palo Mayombe, and it may transfer from association with recently sacrificed animal remains. Only in DCME-1 and DCME-4 was the presence of blood on the remains noted. The presence of blood may be underreported, or less obvious, when dried on remains with thick adhering soil or when combined with other taphonomic staining sources.

Odor: A foul odor was noted on the remains of RMEO-1 due to contact with a mixture of items within the cauldrons including herbs and spices, rotting fruit, decomposing animal carcasses, and likely from incense and candles.

Graffiti: Certain symbols and emblems are associated with the spells of Palo Mayombe. One popular emblem is of the Earth and four cardinal points to signify the crossing of ways, where the evil spell is sent to the victim (González-Wippler 1989:242). The representation is comprised of circles, arrows, and crosses, which may be made out of chalk, paint, blood, or other media. These symbols are present on the cranial vaults of OCME-1 and within a cauldron of RMEO-1, while other similar symbols are present on the blades of machetes associated with both cases.

Postmortem cutmarks: For unknown reasons, postmortem cutmarks or saw marks to the ends of long bones are common among ritual cases and includes several elements of RMEO-1 and 2 and DCME-2 and 4. Likewise, rough and inexpert saw marks are attributed to the sectioning of the calvarium of both DCME-5 and RMEO-1b (Figure 8.9).

Taphonomic Characteristics of Ritual Remains

These findings indicate that the taphonomic characteristics relate to the original source of the remains and also to their later alterations through ritual use. Ritual remains associated with Santería or Palo Mayombe tend to originate from burials or are acquired as anatomical specimens. The recognition of burial remains may include thickly adherent soil and desiccated tissue and hair remnant from the embalming process. The most common artifacts resulting from ritual use include adherent grass and herbs, blood residue, feathers, and drawn symbols. Additionally, artifacts may be lodged within cranial vaults. Remains also may acquire a foul odor from the assorted collection of items within the cauldrons, especially from decomposing animal carcasses and rotting fruit. The identification of ritual remains is much more apparent when the bones are found in the context of cauldrons and altars. The artifacts have specific meanings in the rituals of Santería and spells of Palo Mayombe. When remains have been discarded, residual artifacts and other associated sacred objects, like beaded necklaces, support the assessment of ritual remains. Following these ritual beliefs, if a priest dies, the ritual paraphernalia may be discarded in cemeteries or along riverbanks.

Figure 8.9 Saw marks atypical of autopsy cuts are present in the cranium of RMEO-1b. Included with the case was a dog (*Canis familiaris*) skull. (Image courtesy of G. Hart, State of New Jersey Regional Medical Examiner's Office, New Jersey.)

Conclusions

When human remains are found among a person's belongings, or out of context, analysis of the taphonomic characteristics is important in determining forensic significance and functional categorization of the remains, as discussed here for cases of anatomical and ritual remains in the United States. Forensic anthropologists are frequently called upon to determine whether unidentified human remains are forensically significant and, in turn, their role is to be able to recognize the potentially unique suite of taphonomic modifications found in each of these types of cases in order to accurately classify the remains. A review of past literature concerning the taphonomic signatures of these case types often focuses solely on individual case reports. The most inclusive descriptions of such non-forensically significant remains can be found in Komar and Buikstra (2008). This research has (1) comparatively analyzed the frequencies of observed and/or reported taphonomic traits to identify and interpret the corresponding taphonomic characteristics of such cases and (2) included figures, where relevant, to illustrate the taphonomic modifications frequently encountered.

Once a case is determined to lack forensic significance, aspects of an anthropological analysis may be underreported or omitted, thus possibly skewing some of the results presented here for cases that could not be directly analyzed by the authors. It is important to note, however, that while remains classified as anatomical or ritual are not always considered to be forensically significant because no cause and manner of death will be determined, these types of remains may still be of legal interest depending on how the material was procured (Komar and Buikstra 2008). Variations from the taphonomic characteristics reported here are stressed, as the limits of human alterations to bone are conceivably endless. There are a number of instances where human remains are repurposed for reasons not relating to anatomical display and education, or for religious and ritual uses; however, the discussion of the myriad of alterations to human skeletal material is beyond the scope of this chapter.

Acknowledgments

The authors thank Dr. Dennis Dirkmaat, Mr. Luis Cabo-Pérez, and Dr. Stephen Ousley of Mercyhurst University; Mr. Christopher Rainwater of the New York Office of Chief Medical Examiner; and Ms. Gina Hart of the New Jersey Regional Medical Examiner's Office.

References

Backwell, L. and F. d'Errico (2003) Additional evidence on the early hominid bone tools from Swartkrans with reference to spatial distribution of lithic and organic artefacts. *South African Journal of Science* 99:259–267.

Berryman, H. E., W. M. Bass, S. A. Symes, and O. C. Smith (1991) Recognition of cemetery remains in the forensic setting. *Journal of Forensic Sciences* 36:230–237.

Blake, J. B. (1955) The development of American anatomy acts. *Journal of Medical Education* 30:431–439.

Blakely, R. L. and J. M. Harrington (1997) Grave consequences: The opportunistic procurement of cadavers at the Medical College of Georgia. In *Bones in the Basement: Postmortem Racism in Nineteenth-Century Medical Training* Eds. R. L. Blakely and J. M. Harrington, pp. 162–183. Smithsonian Institution Press, Washington, DC.

Bonnichsen, R. and M. H. Sorg (Eds.) (1989) *Bone Modification.* Center for the Study of the First Americans, University of Maine, Orono, ME.

Brain, C. K. (1981) *The Hunters or the Hunted? An Introduction to African Cave Taphonomy.* University of Chicago Press, Chicago, IL.

Brandon, G. (1993) *Santeria from Africa to the New World: The Dead Sell Memories.* Indiana University Press, Bloomington, IN.

Breneman, J. C. (1993) *The Stryker Story: Homer's Iliad.* Paul Schubert and Associates, Kalamazoo, MI.

Buikstra, J. E. and D. H. Ubelaker (1994) *Standards for Data Collection from Human Skeletal Remains.* Arkansas Archeological Survey Research Report No. 44, Fayetteville, AR.

Carney, S. (2007) Into the heart of India's underground bone trade. Electronic document, http://www.npr.org (accessed July 7, 2011).

Cauble, R. (2010) About bones. Electronic document, http://www.boneroom.com (accessed July 7, 2011).

De La Torre, M. A. (2004) *Santería: The Beliefs and Rituals of a Growing Religion in America* Ed. W. B. Eerdmans. Grand Rapids, MI.

Fenton, T. W., W. H. Birkby, and J. Cornelison (2003) A fast and safe non-bleaching method for forensic skeletal preparation. *Journal of Forensic Sciences* 48:274–276.

Gill, J. R., C. W. Rainwater, and B. J. Adams (2009) Santeria and Palo Mayombe: Skulls, mercury, and artifacts. *Journal of Forensic Sciences* 54:1458–1462.

González-Wippler, M. (1973) *African Magic in Latin America: Santería.* Julian Press, New York.

González-Wippler, M. (1989) *Santería: The Religion.* Harmony Books, New York.

Halperin, E. C. (2007) The poor, the Black, and the marginalized as the source of cadavers in the United States anatomical education. *Clinical Anatomy* 20:489–495.

Hansen, J. V. (1996) Resurrecting death: Anatomical art in the cabinet of Dr. Frederik Ruysch. *The Art Bulletin* 78:663–679.

Hefner, J. T., N. Uhl, and N. V. Passalacqua (2008) Beyond taphonomy: Craniometric variation among anatomical specimens. *Proceedings of the American Academy of Forensic Sciences* 14:317–318.

Humphrey, D. C. (1973) Dissection and discrimination: The social origins of cadavers in America, 1760–1915. *Bulletin of the New York Academy of Medicine* 49:819–827.

Iserson, K. V. (2001) *Death to Dust: What Happens to Dead Bodies?,* 2nd edn. Galen Press, Tucson, AZ.

Komar, D. A. and J. E. Buikstra (2008) *Forensic Anthropology: Contemporary Theory and Practice.* Oxford University Press, New York.

Lesnik, J. J. (2011) Bone tool texture analysis and the role of termites in the diet of South African hominids. *PaleoAnthropology* 2011:268–281. DOI: 10.4207/PA.2011.ART57.

MacGregor, A. (1985) *Bone, Antler, Ivory & Horn: The Technology of Skeletal Materials since the Roman Period.* Barnes and Noble, London, U.K.

Mann, R. W., W. M. Bass, and L. Meadows (1990) Time since death and decomposition of the human body: Variables and observations in case and experimental field studies. *Journal of Forensic Sciences* 35:103–111.

McFarlin, S. C. and L. E. Wineski (1997) The cutting edge: Experimental anatomy and the reconstruction of the Nineteenth-Century dissection techniques. In *Bones in the Basement: Postmortem Racism in Nineteenth-Century Medical Training* Eds. R. L. Blakely and J. M. Harrington, pp. 107–161. Smithsonian Institution Press, Washington, DC.

Morlan, R. E. (1984) Toward the definition of criteria for the recognition of artificial bone alterations. *Quaternary Research* 22:160–171.

Murrell, N. S. (2009) *Afro-Caribbean Religions: An Introduction to Their Historical, Cultural, and Sacred Traditions.* Temple University Press, Philadelphia, PA.

Quigley, C. (2001) *Skulls and Skeletons: Human Bone Collections and Accumulations.* McFarland and Company, Jefferson, NC.

Roach, M. (2003) *Stiff: The Curious Lives of Human Cadavers.* W. W. Norton and Co., New York.

Saul, F. P. and J. M. Saul (1987) An osteobiographical analysis of an early dissecting "room" population. *Anatomical Record* 218:1–120A.

Snyder, R. G., A. Burdi, and G. Gaul (1975) A rapid technique for preparation of human fetal and adult skeletal material. *Journal of Forensic Sciences* 20:576–580.

Stephens, B. G. (1979) A simple method for preparing human skeletal material for forensic examination. *Journal of Forensic Sciences* 24:660–662.

Stubblefield, P. R. (2011) The anatomical diaspora: Evidence of early American anatomical traditions in North Dakota. *Journal of Forensic Sciences* 56:1–4.

Walker, P. L. (2008) Bioarchaeological ethics: A historical perspective on the value of human remains. In *Biological Anthropology of the Human Skeleton,* 2nd edn. Eds. M. A. Katzenberg and S. R. Saunders, pp. 3–40. Wiley-Liss, Hoboken, NJ.

Wetli, C. V. and R. Martinez (1981) Forensic sciences aspects of Santeria, a religious cult of African origin. *Journal of Forensic Sciences* 26:506–514.

Wetli, C. V. and R. Martinez (1983) Brujeria: Manifestations of Palo Mayombe in South Florida. *Journal of the Florida Medical Association* 70:629–634, 634a.

Faunal Dispersal, Reconcentration, and Gnawing Damage to Bone in Terrestrial Environments

9

JAMES T. POKINES

Contents

> Sing, O goddess, the anger of Achilles son of Peleus, that brought countless ills upon the Achaeans. Many a brave soul did it send hurrying down to Hades, and many a hero did it yield a prey to dogs and vultures, for so were the counsels of Jove fulfilled from the day on which the son of Atreus, king of men, and great Achilles, first fell out with one another.
>
> —Homer, *Iliad*, translation by Samuel Butler

Introduction

Humans and their relatives in the family Hominidae have a long history of being eaten by species that have evolved to do precisely that (Brain 1980, 1981; Corbett 1944; Domínguez-Rodrigo 1999; Hart 2002; Hart and Sussman 2008; Kerbis Peterhans 1990; Kerbis Peterhans and Gnoske 2001; Kruuk 2002; Patterson 1996; Payne 1983; Treves and Naughton-Treves 1999; Wroe et al. 2005). This sometimes unpleasant trophic relationship also applies to our extant relatives among the Hominoidea (Boesch 1991; Fay et al. 1995; Galdikas 1978; Kerbis Peterhans et al. 1993) and other large primates (Hart 2002; Pickering and Carlson 2004; Simons 1966). This relationship extends to remains examined in forensic anthropology, since a large number of these hunting/scavenging species still coexist with humans, despite the generally severe decreases in population sizes and restrictions and fragmentations of territories of the former over the past several 1000 years. A hominid body, whether it was one of our distant ancestors felled by a leopard in East Africa or a recent murder victim dumped into the New England woods, represents an enormous temporary boost in consumable resources for the local ecosystem into which it was introduced. Thousands of vertebrate and invertebrate species have evolved for millennia to exploit those and similar resources as efficiently and fully as possible, or their own survival would not be as secure. In short, a deceased human is nothing new to the many populations of decomposers and consumers that would exploit it. These interactions follow similar patterns with other large mammal carcasses, despite variations in anatomy and body mass.

The interaction with a human cadaver goes beyond consumption of soft tissue: other resources are present, and other interactions occur besides direct consumption. The bones themselves are a valuable resource, especially the large fat reserves contained within the marrow cavities of the long bones of adult mammals and their mineral content. Bones are also transported away from the initial location of body deposition and sometimes reconcentrated in other locations. Bone gnawing therefore is just one component of feeding behavior and must be examined within the larger process of remains utilization. One must also note that it is rare for a set of remains in an outdoor setting to have been scavenged by only one species, so bone alteration and movement are likely amalgams of the behavior of multiple agents. Careful analysis may allow the distinction of these separate taphonomic processes, including in some cases the order in which they occurred.

This chapter covers the typical processes of bone gnawing, dispersal, and, in some cases, reconcentration in terrestrial environments. The taxa discussed in the following text include those most potentially relevant to forensic settings: carnivores, rodents, pigs and other ungulates, and termites. The specific taphonomic actions of birds are covered in Chapter 16, this volume.

Reasons for Bone Gnawing, Other Damage, and Dispersal

Bones are gnawed upon for multiple reasons by many common terrestrial taxa. These include, most importantly, the following.

A byproduct of predation: The act of capturing and killing prey by a large predator can start the bone damaging process. Often, the more fragile bones are damaged as the predator lands upon the prey or its teeth or claws are employed in order to kill it. This process is much more damaging in the case of prey smaller than adult humans, such as a canid snatching and crushing the skeleton of a bird or rodent at the moment of capture. In larger prey, the skeleton is often avoided as much as possible at the moment of capture due to the increased difficulty of biting through bony portions. Often, attacks are directed toward the throat or to kill by disembowelment (Kruuk 1972, 2002).

Dismemberment of prey: The dismemberment of prey during feeding often begins the process of skeletal disarticulation. Bone breakage will likely occur during this process, as limbs are detached for transport away from the place of initial carcass/cadaver deposition, and more fragile elements (particularly among the thoracic area) are broken in order to access their associated soft tissue. The mass of the consuming animal also may break bone, especially in the thoracic cage of the consumed (Berryman 2002).

Associated exterior soft tissue: Damage to skeletons also occurs as the soft tissue is consumed from it, from incidental tooth action of the consuming species (Pobiner 2007). More extensive damage and dismemberment normally follow after this initial phase, where the easier-to-consume soft tissue is attacked first (Blumenschine 1986, 1988). Smaller species, especially rats (*Rattus* spp.) and other omnivorous rodents, also will consume bone as they gnaw through associated soft tissue or to access interior soft tissue.

Marrow and grease content of bones: Bones are a valuable source of fat (Brink 1997; Lupo 1998; Madrigal and Holt 2002; Morin 2007), which can be a scarce resource among wild animals, especially during the winter months in the temperate and more northern zones and drier months in the subtropical and tropical zones. Marrow fat reserves are often the last to be depleted during times of nutritional stress (Bear 1971; Lochmiller et al. 1985). Humans raised in modern industrial societies are used to consuming farm-raised species specifically bred and fed to encourage an overall fat content not normally encountered among their wild counterparts. A larger component of stored fat among terrestrial wild game therefore is contained within the long bone cavities as opposed to dispersed among the muscle tissue or stored subcutaneously. As a consequence of this anatomical pattern, many species of carnivores have evolved to exploit this resource. These include, to some degree, most large carnivores encountered in North America and Eurasia (including canids, ursids, mustelids, and felids) and especially hyaenids encountered in Africa and Eurasia, which have evolved as the most damaging extant bone gnawers (Becker and Reed 1993; Kerbis Peterhans 1990; Kruuk 1972; Pokines and Kerbis Peterhans 2007).

Nutrients from the mineral content of the bones: Bone gnawing supplies minerals (Ca^{2+} and PO_4^{3-} but also Na^- and K^-) to multiple species, including rodents. Old World porcupines (*Hystrix* spp.), in particular, have been determined experimentally to consume a portion of the bones upon which they gnaw (Duthie and Skinner 1986), specifically in pursuit of dietary sodium (Roze 2009). Other rodents known to gnaw upon and possibly consume dry bone include pocket gophers (*Geomys* spp.) (Smith 1948) and squirrels (*Sciurus* spp.) (Carlson 1940; Coventry 1940). Multiple ungulate species also are known to practice *osteophagia* (bone consumption) in response to local environmental mineral (likely phosphorus) nutritional deficiencies. These geographically dispersed taxa include sheep (*Ovis aries*) (Brothwell 1976), deer (Cervidae) (Bowyer 1983; Cáceres et al. 2011; Kierdorf 1993, 1994; Sutcliffe 1973, 1977), and giraffe (*Giraffa camelopardalis*) (Wyatt 1971).

Rodent incisor sharpening: Many rodent species will also gnaw upon a variety of available hard substances, including (dry) bone, wood, and in some cases metal (Minetz 2010) and carbonate rocks (Gobetz and Hattin 2002). The presumed reason for this behavior is sharpening and wearing of their continuously growing incisors, although in the case of carbonate rocks, the gnawing also may be in response to dietary deficiency (Gobetz and Hattin 2002). Rodent incisor honing also occurs naturally through edge-to-edge incisor contact and also occurs in rodent species that are not known to collect and gnaw bones. Given the >2200 described species of rodents throughout the world (Wilson and Reeder 2005), research into those that gnaw bone and how they gnaw has barely been touched upon. Perhaps this is so because of the great overlap in the size of rodent incisors among species worldwide and the dental formula common to all rodents of two upper and two lower incisors.

Boredom, especially among domestic or zoo animals: Many studies of zoo, captive, and domesticated animals gnawing upon bones note their greater tendency to damage bone, likely due to the greater amount of time devoted to a single bone combined with a lack of other diversion (Domínguez-Solera and Domínguez-Rodrigo 2009; Haynes 1983; Marean et al. 1992; Pobiner 2007; Willey and Snyder 1989). Domestic dogs often are given commercially prepared large leg bone portions (typically cattle bones) to gnaw upon, despite all the easily obtained nutrients already having been removed through cleaning of interior and exterior soft tissues. These bones may receive much more attention than wild-caught or scavenged bones would, again due to their singularity and the increased leisure time among domestic animals. They are also sometimes deliberate objects of play and can receive additional damage in this manner. Highly advanced rounding/polish (Figure 9.1) can develop under these circumstances.

Mechanics of Terrestrial Carnivore Bone Gnawing

The mechanics of terrestrial carnivore bone gnawing differ greatly, for example, from gnawing and consumption by sharks. While having jaws that can crush down with a large amount of force (Wroe et al. 2005), sharks primarily dismember their prey by shaking their heads laterally, producing a shredding effect with their multiple rows of sharp, serrated, yet relatively fragile teeth (see Chapter 7, this volume). Bones normally are not crushed as a result of this action, which can produce a great deal of dismemberment regardless. Since fish are typical shark prey, their relatively small and fragile bones present much less of

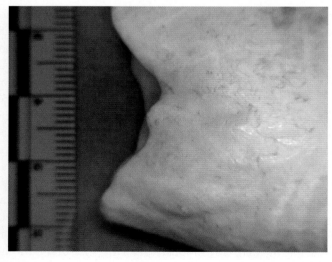

Figure 9.1 Large mammal long bone rounded and polished through repeated gnawing by a large dog (*Canis familiaris*). Scale is in cm.

an obstacle to dismemberment and consumption. In contrast, large terrestrial mammals, including humans, have stored in their long bones a valuable fat reservoir, and multiple carnivore species have evolved to gnaw upon these bones to get at this resource, or crush smaller bones that are associated with more desirable tissue.

Leverage and Bone Crushing

It is useful to visualize the main mastication function of a carnivore's maxilla and mandible as a (class 3) lever system, with the temporomandibular joint (TMJ) as the fulcrum and the force supplied by the mastication muscles mostly between the fulcrum and the chewed object (Figure 9.2). The least amount of bite force is applied at the incisors, since these are farthest away from the TMJ fulcrum. Halving the distance to the fulcrum roughly doubles the amount of force that can be applied. Since this force increases the farther back an object can be fit into the mouth, the behavior is often observed among carnivores of turning their heads sideways to gnaw upon a bone with their rear teeth (premolars and molars) when the bone is too large to fit effectively into the mouth. The teeth adapted to do the principle amount of shearing (similar to two scissor blades meeting) in a carnivore are the *carnassial* teeth (Searfoss 1995). The teeth evolved to fill this role differ among carnivore taxa. Large intact bones generally cannot be fit deeper into a carnivore's mouth than at the carnassial teeth or molars immediately posterior to them, which also therefore is the site of the maximum amount of bite force that can be applied. Larger bones, which normally are stronger overall (e.g., long bone shafts or mandible bodies), therefore cannot be put into the mouth as deeply as smaller weaker bones (e.g., ribs, partial vertebrae, or sternum), which conversely do not require as much crushing force. Larger and more durable bones, especially long bones, therefore are typically attacked incrementally by bone gnawers, which must wear down a bone by slow fragmentation. The fragments created are often consumed.

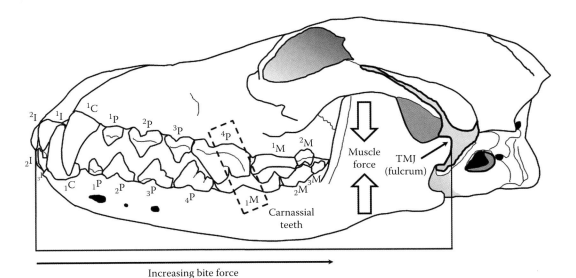

Figure 9.2 Mechanics of mandibular leverage, using a coyote (*Canis latrans*) skull, left side. Bite force increases closer to the fulcrum of the TMJ; force (primarily by the masseter and temporalis muscles) is supplied between the TMJ and the posterior-most teeth, and most shearing action occurs at the carnassials (^{4}P and $_1$M in the case of this species). Note that the least amount of bite force can be generated at the anterior teeth (first incisors not visible).

Table 9.1   Maximum Bite Force (lbs-force) Measured for
Multiple Taxa

Taxon	Maximum Bite Force (lbs-force)
Great white shark (*Carcharodon carcharias*)	≥4000[a]
Alligator (*Alligator mississippiensis*)	2960[b]
Spotted hyena (*Crocuta crocuta*)	1000[c]
Lion (*Felis leo*)	940[d]
Wolf (*Canis lupus*)	400[d]
Dusky shark (*Carcharhinus obscurus*)	330[d]
Domestic dogs (*Canis familiaris*)	3–313[e]
Human	55–280[f]

[a] Wroe, S. et al., *J. Zool.* (London), 276, 336, 2008; estimated.
[b] Erickson, G. M. et al., *J. Zool.* (London), 262, 21, 2004.
[c] Binder, W. J. and B. Van Valkenburgh, *J. Zool.* (London), 252, 273, 2000.
[d] Erickson, G. M. et al., *Nature*, 382, 706, 1996.
[e] Lindner, D. L. et al., *J.Vet. Dent.*, 12, 49, 1995.
[f] Hidaka, O. et al., *J. Dent. Res.*, 78, 1336, 1999.

Maximum bite force (Table 9.1) varies greatly among taxa, although few have been measured to date. The difficulties in gathering data on the maximum bite force of wild species have been reported frequently (Binder and Van Valkenburgh 2000; Erickson et al. 1996, 2004; Hidaka et al. 1999; Lindner et al. 1995; Wroe et al. 2008). The greatest bite force for an extant predator species is of the great white shark (*Carcharodon carcharias*), although this force is applied over multiple shearing teeth instead of concentrated on chisel-shaped teeth anchored in bony jaws, as is the case with spotted hyena (*Crocuta crocuta*). Lions (*Felis leo*) have been recorded as generating similar amounts of bite force, but this species lacks the specialized bone-crushing teeth of hyenas. Humans and various breeds of domesticated dog (*Canis familiaris*) have generated a wide range of bite force data, likely dependent upon the characteristics of the tested individuals including age and size. Note that the ability of dogs, a species that is perhaps the most common gnawer on bones of forensic interest, to gnaw and crush bone therefore varies greatly.

Long Bone Gnawing Sequences

This battle of attrition waged by the bone gnawer vs. a long bone normally means attacking by way of the epiphyses, where the cortical bone is much thinner than that along the diaphysis (Figure 9.3). The usual gnawing proceeds as gradual crushing followed by large amounts of consumption of these dislodged fragments (which contain bone grease). As gnawing proceeds, the marrow cavity is gradually exposed, although the contents cannot yet be removed. As the gnawing moves toward the diaphysis, the cortical bone continues to get thicker. As a result, more effort must be expended to detach each bone fragment. Each freshly exposed break surface is therefore subjected to more dental abrasion as the bone is gnawed, often forming a rounded edge on the newly exposed surface (Fisher 1995). Gnawing often continues until the marrow cavity is exposed sufficiently for a portion of its contents to be accessed and may continue until all of the marrow is consumed. Abandonment may occur sooner. The final result, if the long bone is attacked long enough from both ends, is the formation of a bone *cylinder* (a change from a tube with closed ends to a tube with open ends).

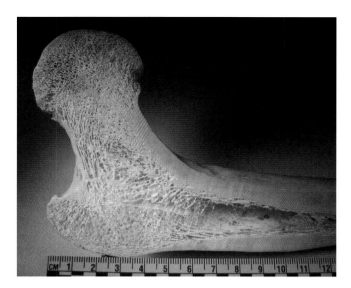

Figure 9.3 Human proximal femur sawn lengthwise to show the range in cortical thickness at the extremities, from less than one millimeter at the epiphyses (left) to close to one cm along the diaphysis (right) in this individual.

The weaker (i.e., less dense; see Chapter 4, this volume) epiphyses of large mammal long bones are often attacked preferentially to the stronger (more dense) ones on the same bones. An example of this general gnawing pattern comes from a cave den sample from Masai Mara National Reserve, Kenya (Kerbis Peterhans 1990; Pokines and Kerbis Peterhans 2007). In this case, gnawing data are presented on ungulate (hooved animals, including a range of sizes from cape buffalo *Syncerus caffer* to small antelopes such as Thomson's gazelle *Gazella thomsoni*) long bones. This size range includes humans. These bones were transported from kill sites to a den for further gnawing by spotted hyenas. The results of gnawing on long bones are presented in Table 9.2. A clear pattern emerges of a preferential gnawing on weaker portions of long bones, even by the terrestrial scavenger species most adapted to effective bone gnawing. Among the humeri ($n = 110$), which have among all large terrestrial mammals species a relatively weak proximal portion and strong, dense distal portion, the proximal portion tended to be destroyed preferentially. Only one proximal humerus had not been destroyed by gnawing, although multiple complete humeri were present and had not yet undergone significant gnawing. In addition, 13 adult humeri in this sample were so gnawed on both the proximal and distal ends that only the shaft portion remained (i.e., a bone cylinder). The radii ($n = 105$) tended to have a weaker distal relative to proximal portion. The distal portion was destroyed preferentially, although as with the humeri sometimes both ends were gnawed away, leaving a bone cylinder. The femora ($n = 79$), with relatively weak proximal and distal extremities, tended to be gnawed on both ends: few proximal or distal portions survived among bones that had undergone gnawing. The tibiae ($n = 102$) exhibited a pattern similar to the humeri. Their weaker proximal ends were destroyed preferentially to their stronger, denser distal ends, which survived preferentially.

This pattern is also followed in a more typical example. In an experiment, three large dogs (ranging from 26 to 45 kg) were fed mostly defleshed, commercially available large juvenile pig long bones in multiple settings. In one test series, a fresh pig humerus was

Table 9.2   Long Bone Survivorship: Spotted Hyena Gnawing on Combined Large Ungulate Sample

Humerus (n = 110)			Radius (n = 105)		
Portion	Total	%	Portion	Total	%
Complete	16	14.5	Complete	32	30.5
Cylinder	13	11.8	Cylinder	20	19.0
Diaphysis (unfused)	16	14.5	Diaphysis (unfused)	2	1.9
Distal	14	12.7	Distal	1	1.0
Distal half	27	24.5	Distal half	1	1.0
Distal + shaft	18	16.4	Distal + shaft	3	2.9
Proximal	1	0.9	Distal epiphysis	2	1.9
Shaft fragment	5	4.5	Proximal	13	12.4
			Proximal half	21	20.0
			Shaft fragment	10	9.5

Femur (n = 79)			Tibia (n = 102)		
Portion	Total	%	Portion	Total	%
Complete	10	12.7	Complete	16	15.7
Complete minus head	3	3.8	Cylinder	7	6.9
Cylinder	20	25.3	Diaphysis (unfused)	1	1.0
Diaphysis (unfused)	13	16.5	Distal	15	14.7
Distal	3	3.8	Distal half	21	20.6
Distal half	6	7.6	Distal + shaft	17	16.7
Distal + shaft	5	6.3	Distal epiphysis	8	7.8
Distal epiphysis	2	2.5	Proximal	4	3.9
Proximal	1	1.3	Proximal half	2	2.0
Proximal half	2	2.5	Proximal + shaft	1	1.0
Proximal epiphysis	2	2.5	Proximal epiphysis	2	2.0
Shaft fragment	12	15.2	Shaft fragment	8	7.8

Source: Pokines, J.T. and J.C. Kerbis Peterhans, *J. Archaeol. Sci.*, 34, 1914, 2007.

given to each of the three dogs for timed feeding bouts of 6, 12, 18, and 24 min. All feeding was by individual dogs acting on individual elements. The three dogs were observed for the entire feeding periods, and no discarded fragments were noted. In the other series of tests, the same dogs were given pig humeri and femora and allowed to gnaw upon them for up to 24 h, at which point they were taken away if the dogs had not already abandoned them. Feeding in the latter series therefore could have involved more than one dog in succession, as the dogs were not monitored during the entire span. All bones were then macerated for examination. Figure 9.4 shows one series of 6-, 12-, 18-, and 24-min feeding bouts from one of these dogs. The majority of damage proceeded in a linear progression, with increasing amounts of destruction of the proximal end over time. A very similar damage sequence was produced by one of the other dogs, while the third (and oldest) dog showed variable amounts of interest. It is noteworthy that despite the edible meat attached to the bones, in each case, the dog was more attracted to gnawing the bone (likely to obtain the fat, large quantities of which were lacking from their usual diet) than consuming the attached tissue, which was largely ignored.

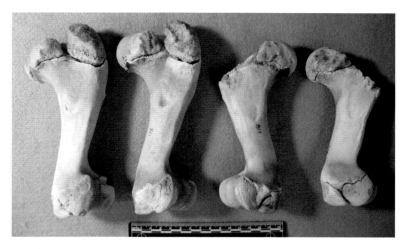

Figure 9.4 Subadult pig humeri gnawed on by a large (26 kg) domestic dog (*Canis familiaris*). Left to right: 6 min of gnawing, 12, 18, and 24 min. The proximal end in each case has been gnawed preferentially to the distal end. Note that detached epiphyses have been glued to their original locations after cleaning. Scale is in cm.

When given more time, in each case, these dogs reduced the pig humeri and femora to a cylinder by destroying both ends and exposing the marrow, little or none of which was left upon retrieval. Figure 9.5 shows a typical sample of these bones. In the most extreme case (Figure 9.6), little of the shaft cylinder remained. This element, with a little more gnawing, could have been reduced to nothing but fragments and possibly consumed entirely.

Multiple studies comparing the results of a range of carnivores and large mammal prey (Becker and Reed 1993; Behrensmeyer 1991; Brain 1981; Carson et al. 2000; Domínguez-Rodrigo 1999; Faith and Behrensmeyer 2006; Haglund 1997a; Harding and Wolf 2006; Haynes 1980a,b; Hill 1980, 1989; Hill and Behrensmeyer 1984; Pobiner 2007; Pokines and Kerbis Peterhans 2007), including those which specifically address large carnivore

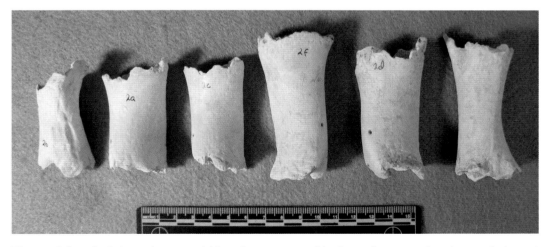

Figure 9.5 Subadult pig (*Sus scrofa*) long bones gnawed by large domestic dogs (26–45 kg) until abandonment, less than 24 h later. Note that in each case, the elements (humeri and femora) were reduced to a cylinder. Scale is in cm.

Figure 9.6 Subadult pig (*Sus scrofa*) humerus reduced to a residual cylinder by large domestic dog gnawing, less than 24 h later. Scale is in cm.

consumption of humans or other large primates (Galdikas 1978; Haglund 1997a; Haglund et al. 1988, 1989; Hart and Sussman 2008; Horwitz and Smith 1988; Kerbis Peterhans et al. 1993; Kerbis Peterhans and Gnoske 2001; Merbs 1997; Milner and Smith 1989; Morton and Lord 2006; Pickering and Carlson 2004), indicate that once consumption has begun, the weaker elements have a much poorer chance of survival and are often consumed entirely. In general, stronger elements equate with long bone diaphyses and mandibular bodies, with the other elements of the human body more easily consumed/fragmented due to their less dense construction (especially the cranium, sternum, vertebrae, ribs, scapulae, and innominates) and/or smaller size (hand and foot elements), making it possible to swallow them whole or after minor fragmentation.

Direct Marks on Bone

As mentioned earlier, the repeated wear of gnawing teeth (or tongue) against the exposed margin of a bone may form *edge polish* (Figure 9.7). This tends to occur where more robust sections of cortical bone have been exposed by flake removal, since repeated gnawing on a weaker bone or portion thereof tends to remove a new flake and expose a clean, unpolished surface.

Other direct markers of carnivore gnawing damage are often divided among four main categories of *tooth marks* left behind on bone, which have been defined through general usage in the taphonomic and zooarchaeological literature (Binford 1981; Lyman 1994:205–214; Pobiner 2007; Pokines and Kerbis Peterhans 2007) as given below.

Tooth pits (Figure 9.7) are circular to irregular-shaped depressions in the cortical bone, which do not penetrate to the bone interior (i.e., either cancellous bone or the marrow cavity, brain case, or other interior space). These are defined as having a maximum length no more than three times their maximum width.

Tooth punctures (Figure 9.8) are deeper depressions that do penetrate into the interior. Since full penetration of the cortical bone is involved, the margins of a tooth puncture tend to be more broken/crushed in form than tooth pits (Pobiner 2007:167). Tooth punctures may preserve the shape of the tooth that caused them, which potentially may be used to identify which species or species size class did the gnawing. Paired/multiple tooth punctures may also help in identification, as in the case of suspected leopard

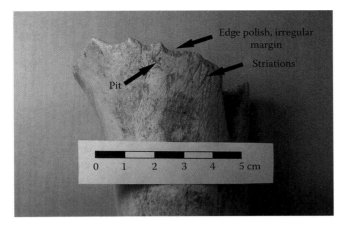

Figure 9.7 Heavily gnawed nonhuman long bone. The epiphysis has been completely removed to access the marrow cavity. Note the scores and pits present, and the edge polish formed by repeated tooth contact, but the exposed margin itself is irregular. (Image courtesy of Dr. R. Lee Lyman.)

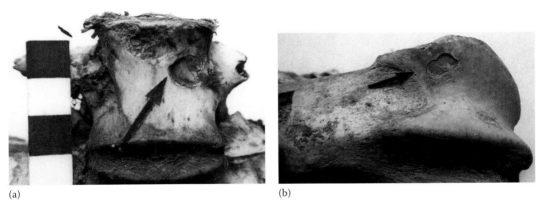

(a)   (b)

Figure 9.8 Puncture marks caused on nonhuman bone by spotted hyenas: (a) lumbar vertebra and (b) distal femur. (Reprinted from *J. Archaeol. Sci.*, 34, Pokines, J.T. and J.C. Kerbis Peterhans, Spotted hyena (*Crocuta crocuta*) den use and taphonomy in the Masai Mara National Reserve, Kenya, 1914–1931, Copyright (2007), with permission from Elsevier.) The chisel-like shape of the crushing teeth does not match other families of predator found in East Africa.

(*Panthera pardus*) carrying of an *Australopithecus* cranium from the South African early hominin site of Swartkrans (Brain 1981). In this example, the distance between paired canine punctures matches that typically found in leopards. The term *tooth punctures* more generally may be applied to holes made into accompanying artifacts, such as clothing associated with remains.

Tooth scores (or *striations*) (Figure 9.7) are the same penetrative form as tooth pits, only these are three times or more longer in maximum diameter than width. Scores may occur at most places on the bone, not preferentially on a gnawed extremity, as they often mark where the bone was gripped for transport or repositioning by a carnivore. Scores located randomly along a long bone diaphysis therefore are sometimes termed *gripping marks* and are usually formed by bone manipulation for gnawing or to secure it for transport. These marks may also be comprised wholly or partially of tooth pits, although due to

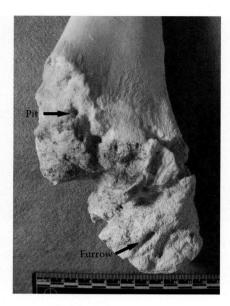

Figure 9.9 Adult cattle (*Bos taurus*) distal femur gnawed on by a zoo lion (*Felis leo*) as a dietary supplement. Note the multiple deep furrows and punctures in the cancellous bone, too large to have been made by small mammal gnawing. Scale is in cm.

their usual location along a diaphysis, they rarely include a puncture or furrow component. Tooth scores are also sometimes formed in a parallel manner by multiple teeth dragging simultaneously.

Tooth furrows (Figure 9.9) are in the same penetrative form as tooth punctures, only these are three times or more longer in maximum diameter than width. Tooth furrows can also be left in cancellous bone exposed by previous gnawing, forming a secondary stage of damage usually by canines having been dragged through it. These secondary furrows are often destroyed by continued gnawing, as all of the cancellous bone of a long bone epiphysis restricts access to the marrow cavity.

Pits and punctures tend to be formed by direct pressure of the tooth approximately perpendicular to the bone surface, while scores and furrows tend to be formed by the dragging of the tooth across the surface (Pobiner 2007:167–168). The latter may be V- or U-shaped in cross section, varying by the shape and angle of the tooth. Gnawing damage also may be so extensive in one area that individual marks can no longer be differentiated, or that portion of bone has already been completely removed. Such areas are simply grouped under the general term *gnawing damage*, although individual tooth marks frequently are preserved at or past the margins of this damaged or missing area.

Gastric Corrosion

The bone fragments produced by gnawing (and intact, small elements such as carpals and phalanges) are often consumed by the carnivore, either for digestion or later regurgitation along with less digestible body portions (hair, hooves, etc.). *Gastric corrosion* often appears on these flakes of bone (or small bones consumed whole, such as carpals) and is characterized by a sculpted appearance (Table 9.3; Figures 9.10 and 9.11a and b) on cortical surfaces, thinning or sharpening (*feathering*) of exposed margins as their thickness is eaten away (Esteban-Nadal et al. 2010; Payne and Munson 1985; Schmitt and Juell 1994),

Table 9.3   Characteristics of Gastric Corrosion on Bone

- Derived from carnivore/omnivore feces, regurgitation, or stomach contents
- Affects fragments or small whole elements
- Thinning of edges
- Windowing of bone common
- Sculpted appearance to cortical surfaces
- Hair/fur often imbedded in hollow spaces
- May be accompanied by indigestible remains (hair, fur, feathers, clothing, etc.)

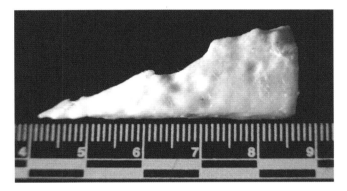

Figure 9.10 Gastrically corroded (previously machine-butchered; note right-angle cut on bottom and right sides) nonhuman long bone fragment, derived from domestic dog vomit. Note the scooping of the surface. Scale is in cm.

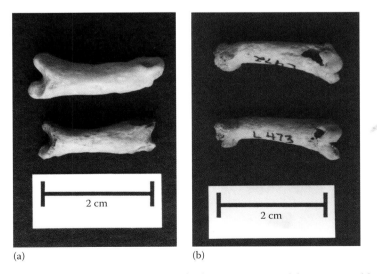

(a)   (b)

Figure 9.11 Gastrically corroded nonhuman phalanges, retrieved from striped hyena (*Hyaena hyaena*) feces, Israel. (From Kerbis Peterhans, J.C., 1990, *The Roles of Porcupines, Leopards, and Hyenas in Ungulate Carcass Dispersal: Implications for Paleoanthropology*. Unpublished PhD Dissertation, Department of Anthropology, University of Chicago, Chicago, IL.) Note the (a) sculpted appearance to the surfaces and (b) the windowing.

and *gastric windowing* (Figure 9.11a and b), where the digestive acid has eaten small holes through the bone. These flakes, found in regurgitation piles or feces, often have their pore spaces packed with hair or fur. (*Corrosion* as used here refers specifically to acidic damage to bone. The term *erosion* is applied to more general loss of bone, the sources of which may include acidic damage, plant action, abrasion, and excavation damage.)

Gastric corrosion may mimic the effects of acidic soil corrosion (see Chapter 5, this volume), since the chemical processes are largely the same. Gastric corrosion, by definition, can attack only fragments or whole bones small enough to be consumed by a carnivore (Esteban-Nadal et al. 2010; Payne and Munson 1985; Schmitt and Juell 1994). While acidic soil certainly will cause damage to small pieces of bone as well, it also very visibly attacks bones far too large to have been swallowed (see Chapter 5, this volume). The more fragile elements, particularly the epiphyses, are damaged preferentially, and large reductions in the diameter of long bones can be caused by the gradual eating away by acidic attack. Differing frequencies in skeletal part recovery are also a key discriminating factor, since gastric corrosion must be accompanied by a large amount of bone gnawing and breakage. Payne and Munson (1985) note that domestic dog digestion of bone fragments recovered from their feces removed all clear traces of previous gnawing on those fragments; Schmitt and Juell (1994) note similar findings for bone fragments recovered from coyote feces. Fragments with gastric corrosion, since they are dietary in origin, also likely contain a mixture of species including smaller vertebrate taxa whose bones are more likely to be swallowed whole and therefore survive the digestive process in an identifiable state (Schmitt and Juell 1994; Stiner 1994).

Body Part Consumption Sequences

With a notable exception (see below in this section), the carcasses of most large mammals deposited into terrestrial environments tend to be consumed in a patterned body portion sequence (Table 9.4), and this pattern is followed by a variety of large mammal predators or scavengers throughout the world (Blumenschine 1986, 1988; Domínguez-Rodrigo 1999; Haynes 1980b; Kruuk 1972; Pobiner 2007). The degree of similarity in this regard is striking and therefore likely a product of accessible nutrients relative to expended effort (Blumenschine 1986), although the effects of ease of detachment of some portions of a body for transport elsewhere must be considered. In general, the highest yield/least effort portions of the body are consumed first, followed in the order of decreasing yield/greater effort. Other variables that affect consumption are intraspecies competition (number of individuals feeding), the need to provision juveniles awaiting feeding at a den, interspecies competition, the size of the carcass being eaten, the developmental age of the deceased, and the relative availability of food resources in that environment. Consumption sequence patterning therefore will affect both the skeletal elements most likely to be consumed and the order in which they tend to become detached from a skeleton and made available for transportation away from the scene of initial deposition.

The abdominal area normally gets fed upon first in order to gain access to the internal organs. This venue of attack requires the least amount of effort relative to the nutritional gain, since little bone is in the way besides the relatively thin and weak ribs and sternum, and these can be largely bypassed at this stage. Viscera are often already partially consumed before death has even occurred, since some carnivores such as spotted hyenas (*Crocuta crocuta*) kill their prey by evisceration (Kruuk 1972). In the case of smaller carnivores or

Table 9.4 Carnivore Consumption Sequences

	Haynes (1980b)	Haglund (1997a)	Blumenschine (1986)
Consuming taxa	Large canids (*Canis lupus*)	Large canids (*C. latrans* and *C. familiaris*)	Spotted hyena, lion, and vultures (*Crocuta crocuta*, *Panthera leo*, and mult. species)
Consumed taxa	White-tailed deer (*Odocoileus virginianus*)	Humans	Large game, size classes I–V (small antelopes to elephants)
MNI of consumed taxa	$n = 94$	$n = 53$	$n = 260$
Source	Kill/scavenged sites	Scavenged sites	Kill/scavenged sites
Location	Minnesota, USA	Pacific NW, USA	Tanzania
Environment	Boreal forest	Boreal forest	Savanna
Consumption Sequence: (Start → Finish)	• Paunch penetrated; organs and blood • Upper hindquarters • Ribs and vertebrae • Upper forelegs, shoulder • Throat/face • Disarticulation of limbs	• Throat/face • Thoracic elements/ internal organs • Legs consumed/ detached • Disarticulation of remaining portions • Disarticulation/ gnawing of elements	• [Internal organs][a] • Hindquarters flesh • Forequarters flesh and thoracic cage • Head flesh • Hindlimb marrow • Forelimb marrow • Head contents

[a] Internal organs were not a specific part of this study, which concerned the skeletal effects of scavenging.

other small scavengers being the first ones to happen upon a fresh carcass, this area allows access to the heart, liver, lungs, and other soft organs without the need for bone to be destroyed. Early feeding therefore largely leaves bone undamaged and undispersed.

Feeding (Blumenschine 1986) normally proceeds to the upper hindquarters/rump area, as this is the largest mass of muscle tissue available, and the associated skeletal elements are contained well within. Feeding on this area can often cause disarticulation of one or both hind legs. Feeding then proceeds to the upper forequarters as the next largest muscle mass available. Little bone is damaged in this stage, as the pursued nutrients are largely external, but disarticulation of the forelimbs begins. Disarticulation of the forelimb from the thorax is expedited by the lack of interlocking skeletal articulation, including the absence of a clavicle in ungulate species. Feeding into the thoracic cage causes large amounts of damage to the ribs, vertebrae, and sternebrae, as these easily destroyed elements are often consumed with their associated soft tissue or at least snapped off through direct gnawing action or through the mass of the consuming species pressing down upon them. The external soft tissue of the head and throat area (including the tongue) is pursued next. While little-protected, it represents a lower-yield portion of the carcass. This feeding naturally may cause disarticulation of the skull from the rest of the carcass and the mandible from the cranium. With the majority of easily accessible external soft tissue consumed at this point, attention normally turns to the skeletal elements themselves and the nutrients that they contain in the form of stored fat within the marrow cavity and cancellous spaces. Hindlimb long bones (femur and tibia) normally are attacked first, followed by the forelimb long bones (humerus and radius/ulna). The rear limb long bones contain on average larger marrow yields compared with the forelimb long bones of the same species (Brink 1997; Lupo 1998; Madrigal and Holt 2002; Morin 2007), hence their higher nutrient value to consuming species. Head contents tend to be pursued last. While the braincase contents include a high proportion of valuable fatty tissue (Stiner 1994), these tend to be well protected in adult animals, including humans. The cranial size and shape, with its gradual curve, are harder for a carnivore to grip and gnaw through. It is also in many cases too large to transport, depending upon the relative size of the consumed to the consuming species (Pokines and Kerbis Peterhans 2007). Other skeletal elements generally are more transportable, in partial articulation or not, and dispersal begins as soon as each body area begins to be consumed. The later stages of consumption (marrow extraction) therefore often take place away from the initial kill site, where more time can be expended upon this harder to extract but valuable caloric source.

Variations in this sequence do occur, as noted by Haynes (1980b) in his study of wolves (*Canis lupus*) consuming white-tailed deer (*Odocoileus virginianus*) in Minnesota, USA (Table 9.4). His research noted that upper hindquarters tend to be consumed prior to thoracic portions, *contra* the research of Blumenschine (1986) on the Tanzanian savanna. Since Haynes (1980b) reports a single carnivore and prey relationship, it is possible that the relative size of the consuming species and particular nutrient yield pattern of the prey increase the desirability of the thoracic region in this case, or that more fragmentation of the thoracic region occurs during accessing or consumption of the internal organs. Haynes (1982) studied wolf winter consumption sequences on two larger species, moose (*Alces alces*) and bison (*Bison bison*), in Canada and the United States and found that their carcasses were consumed in much the same pattern (1982:271): internal organs/ rump, including early rib damage; shoulder area; pelvic area; vertebral damage; greater damage to upper long bones and scapulae; soft portions of the head; followed by greater consumption/damage to bones throughout the body.

Haglund et al. (1989) and Haglund (1997a) (Table 9.4) report a more forensically important variation regarding human consumption and dispersal sequences by large canids (*Canis latrans* and *C. familiaris*) in the Pacific Northwest. They found that consumption normally began with the throat and facial area of humans, then proceeded in almost the same pattern typical of other large mammals: abdominal/internal organs and thoracic region, legs, then the remaining portions. This pattern variation may be explicable by human bodies usually being covered by clothing, which tends to be of the heavier variety in their study area in most seasons. The facial and throat area of a human body therefore might present on average the most easy point at which to begin consumption by a large canid, with consumption generally following from there to the areas of the body with a higher nutrient payoff relative to effort expended. Clothing also likely hinders dismemberment and may alter the transportability of disarticulated human skeletal elements. This apparent difference in consumption pattern between humans and other large mammals theoretically would be more pronounced in winter, where human bodies typically would average greater and thicker clothing coverage in a variety of scenarios involving outdoor deposition.

Bone Dispersal

Large and small carnivores also disperse bone away from the point of initial body deposition (Haynes 1982, 1983; Hill 1979; Moraitis and Spiliopoulou 2010). In forensic terms, whether a bone was entirely consumed or transported so far away from an initial crime scene that it could not be located, the material result is that the bone is not available for analysis and can shed light only on the disarticulation/dispersal status of the remains. *Primary dispersal* is defined here as bone movement away from their point of initial deposition, without any prior movement of the entire, intact mass of remains as a unit. Dispersal in any environment can range from zero (remains still intact on the surface or buried) through severe, with few if any traces of the remains at their place of initial deposition. Some dispersal is likely under most circumstances from incidental agencies of bone dispersal, such as downslope wash, feeding displacement, and accidental trampling by wildlife. Even buried remains may undergo minor dispersal if partially dug into by scavengers or through the efforts of fossorial (burrowing) fauna displacing bone after the soft tissue has decomposed. More advanced dispersal is likely the result of dispersal agents including mammalian scavengers, porcupines, and flowing water channels. Larger teams employing integrated searching techniques are necessary to recover remains in these situations, especially where more time has passed and vegetation (living and dead) has built up over and obscured isolated elements/fragments. As dispersal increases, more intensive survey techniques will be required, including line searches with members advancing at ground level and the use of cadaver dogs (see Chapter 17, this volume). Heavier dispersal likely corresponds with a greater postmortem interval (PMI) and/or amounts of large carnivore involvement, and the recovered remains are likely in a poorer preservational state. Heavy amounts of dispersal also likely involve more species, including the common scenario of scavenging and dispersal by large mammals, followed months or years later by movement of these surviving elements by large rodents gnawing on the now-dry bones. The taphonomic alterations left upon the bones likely increases as the PMI and amount of dispersal both increase. Some species such as hyenas habitually transport individual pieces of remains for feeding elsewhere such as a home den, normally causing severe dispersal of remains. Severe dispersal also can occur where mass flooding events spread remains downstream.

Secondary dispersal is defined here as occurring when remains have been moved, largely intact, from the point where initial deposition/death occurred to another location. From this secondary deposition point, secondary dispersal will then proceed. The movement of largely intact remains may be caused by (accidental or deliberate) deposition into water (Chapters 6 and 7, this volume), transportation of murder victims (Chapter 10, this volume), or caching or other transport behavior by large predators (see "Caching" section).

There are multiple reasons for bone dispersal by carnivores. Dispersal begins as a direct result of feeding behavior: as a body is consumed, bones get disarticulated, then moved at least a short distance as limbs are detached from the axial skeleton, ribs are broken and removed, and the cranium is removed over the course of hours or days. It is also the typical behavior across a range of carnivores, large and small and including domesticated dogs (Hudson 1993; Kent 1981), wolves (Mech 1970; Willey and Snyder 1989), and bears (Carson et al. 2000), to remove portions of a carcass to feed on them in different location. Haynes (1980b) noted that single wolves typically removed carcass portions for gnawing away from the point of deposition yet usually within 30 m of it.

This reduces interspecies and intraspecies competition for food, by taking a small portion some distance from the main source. Feeding often continues within the sight of the main source, with repeated forays to secure more food, which is then removed to a safe distance. Bones can in this manner be scattered tens or hundreds of meters from their site of initial deposition. Bones with or without meat attached are also deliberately transported by many species in order to feed their young at a denning site and also to feed nursing females (Harrison and Gilbert 1985; Kuyt 1972; Mech 1970; McLoughlin et al. 2002; Peterson 1977). This type of dispersal also leads to the later reconcentration of remains in other locations (see later). Carnivore defecation also may occur repeatedly in the same locations in order to mark home territories (Kruuk 1972; Pickering 2001; Schmitt and Juell 1994). These many processes make dispersal as much a characteristic of carnivore interaction with bone as gnawing damage and mean that bones may be transported several kilometers, making their recovery less likely.

The size of body portions ranging from partial, single skeletal elements up to major portions of a carcass that may be transported varies with the size of the consuming animal transporting that food item. Haynes (1982) observed wolves running through several hundred meters of deep (60 cm) snow carrying disarticulated lower limbs of bison (*Bison bison*). Research in Kenya indicates that transport of larger species' intact crania by spotted hyena (*Crocuta crocuta*) is usually restricted to the smaller ungulates in their diet or to the juveniles of such large species as Cape buffalo (*Syncerus caffer*) (Pokines and Kerbis Peterhans 2007). Transport of body portions this large by typical scavengers indicates that long-distance transport of partially articulated human remains is possible for many species. In addition, Horwitz and Smith (1988) detected movement of human remains, including crania, by striped hyenas (*Hyena hyena*) in Israel to a den site over 35 km from their likely source.

Bone Aggregation (Reconcentration)

Multiple species also aggregate (usually heavily commingled) bone in locations away from their point of initial deposition, typically at a *denning* or other home site. The primary reasons are to continue feeding in a more protected location within one's home range, where it is less easy for interspecies competitors to steal food. The home den also often offers other amenities, such as shade, shelter, a location near a water source, and presumed continued access to other food sources. The provisioning of young, as discussed earlier, also occurs among many species, where carcass portions are brought to juveniles too young to participate directly in hunting activities or to nursing females. In North America, this primarily includes wolves, which hunt/scavenge within a home territory, and the pups of the alpha male and female are raised collectively and left in a home den during the spring and early summer (Fuller 1989; Kuyt 1972; Mech 1970; Peterson 1977). Food, in between the time when pups are weaned but before they are old enough to hunt with the pack, is transported to the den, where the adults also may feed on it. Food may also be delivered to pups in the form of regurgitation (Harrison and Gilbert 1985; Mech 1970), which may contain bone fragments or whole small elements.

In the Old World, all three extant hyena species are avid bone collectors (Hill 1989; Horwitz and Smith 1988; Kerbis Peterhans 1990; Kerbis Peterhans and Horwitz 1992; Pokines and Kerbis Peterhans 2007), the fossil bone concentrations of which must be distinguished from accumulations by hominins (Behrensmeyer 1991; Blumenschine 1988;

Brain 1980, 1981; Crader 1983; Domínguez-Rodrigo 1999; Tappen 1995). As indicated earlier, feeding in a favored tree or cave by leopards may concentrate bones, and these concentrations may have paleoecological implications (Brain 1981; Cavallo and Blumenschine 1989; Kerbis Peterhans 1990).

Den Characteristics

Most bone aggregation occurs at denning sites, which are also important archaeologically and paleontologically, as these depositional settings greatly increase the chances for the long-term preservation of osseous assemblages. Den sites, both modern and ancient, also increase greatly the chances for remains to be discovered, as they increase the forensic, archaeological, or paleontological visibility of that concentration.

Large animal dens throughout most world regions rarely have just one occupying species, as they tend to get reused by multiple species (Barthelmess 2006; Behrensmeyer 1991; Brain 1980; Harrison and Gilbert 1985; Kerbis Peterhans 1990; Pokines and Kerbis Peterhans 2007). This is true of more temporary dens, such as burrows or borrowed human structures (culverts, under buildings, etc.), or more permanent features (caves; see Figure 9.12). The former category tends to persist for decades, while the latter persists for millennia or longer—long enough temporal spans to accumulate large, commingled bone assemblages drawn from the surrounding area via multiple sources. The mixture of species that may occupy a single den in succession in large portions of North America include porcupines, canids (domestic dogs, wolves, and coyotes), lynxes (*Felis canadensis*), bobcats (*Felis rufus*), mountain lions (*Puma concolor*), and bears. These dens are used for adult and juvenile shelter and therefore also tend to build up large concentrations of feces, urine, hair, and arthropods that are attracted to these environments. Dens also may be used for hibernation (especially among bears), and deaths that occur during this period (weaker or unhealthy individuals) may build up large amounts of skeletal remains from these species. Dens also provide a protective environment for bone, which tends to preserve them for much longer than had they been exposed on the surface and subjected to weathering (see Chapter 11, this volume).

Figure 9.12 Example of dense animal bone reconcentration in a den, in this case by striped hyenas (*Hyaena hyaena*) and porcupines (*Hystrix* sp.) alternately using a cave in Hell's Gate National Park, Kenya.

Wolf dens in North America are not known to build up large amounts of osseous remains, since most wolf dens are earthen burrows, which are used only for a portion of a birthing season then abandoned (Fuller 1989; Kuyt 1972; Mech 1970; Peterson 1977; Thiel et al. 1998; and G. Haynes, pers. comm.). Some reuse of dens over multiple seasons does occur, and these locations have the greater potential to accumulate osseous remains in and around them from feces, regurgitation, and the remnants of feeding. As such, these locations are of forensic interest. Habitation of these sites by wolves is normally during the spring. Coyote denning, while less studied than that of wolves, is lesser in its potential to accumulate osseous remains (Harrison and Gilbert 1985) due to the higher proportion of vegetable foods and human garbage in coyote diet (Gehrt et al. 2009; Schmitt and Juell 1994).

Other species reconcentrate bone for other reasons. Multiple species of porcupines found throughout the world are avid bone collectors, transporting usually dry, weathered bone back to a home den for continued gnawing (Alexander 1956; Barthelmess 2006; Becker and Reed 1993; Kerbis Peterhans 1990; Pokines and Kerbis Peterhans 2007; Woods 1973). Packrats also transport bones, along with many other assorted items, back to their nests and may incidentally pick up bones of interest to homicide investigators (Betancourt et al. 1990).

Caching

Multiple species *cache* prey for later, more paced consumption by moving usually an entire body/carcass and hiding it by shallow burial under loose sediments and plant debris or storing in a less accessible place, including trees, rock features, or under water. Subsequent competition is reduced or excluded, and multiple bouts of feeding may occur on the same carcass over multiple days. This behavior extends the time of access by the predator to the prey carcass, since no single large terrestrial predator can consume an entire large mammal approaching its own body mass in one feeding bout. Decomposition is also slowed through the partial exclusion of colonizing arthropods (Bischoff-Mattson and Mattson 2009).

Brown bears (Elgmork 1982) and mountain lions (Murad 1997; Pierce et al. 1998) in North America are the most forensically relevant caching taxa, as are leopards (*Panthera pardus*) in Africa and southern Asia. Other species of bear (black bears and polar bears) are not known to cache prey as frequently (Elgmork 1982:607). Leopards typically store kills in trees, usually for more immediate consumption and to prevent food from being stolen by larger/social predators (Brain 1981; Cavallo and Blumenschine 1989; Kerbis Peterhans 1990; Pobiner 2007). Caching behavior in this case may cause osseous aggregation, since leopards often return repeatedly to favorite feeding trees. Leopards also are known to store prey in caves (Simons 1966). Caching by bears and mountain lions is unlikely to cause osseous aggregation, since they only rarely return prey repeatedly to the same caching location (Elgmork 1982). Their storage of prey does cause immediate dispersal from its initial point of deposition (the kill site) and does serve to limit later dispersal by competing scavengers.

Caching behavior likely is more prevalent among these solitary predators, because pack predators can consume single prey items much more rapidly. Some exceptions have been noted among pack predators, such as spotted hyenas caching prey (Kruuk 1972), although these exceptions tend to occur when these species are hunting alone. Food transport among pack carnivores, due to interspecies competition, is more likely to take the form of moving portions of a carcass for feeding elsewhere. Some of these portions can be hidden, as among canids. This includes stereotypical bone-burying behavior of domestic dogs, as well as similar behavior among their wild relatives, including African wild dog (*Lycaon pictus*) (Malcolm 1980).

Distances of carcass transport for caching purposes vary by individual, predator species, size of prey, and environmental conditions. Prevalence of cover is also a likely factor, as ground-dwelling predators living in more open (e.g., savanna) environments have less opportunity to hide carcasses effectively. Mountain lions, bears, and leopards typically cache whole carcasses after predation. The latter species is more observable in this behavior, since it usually terminates with the carcass dragged up a tree for feeding, and the need for cover to prevent its loss to scavengers is therefore greatly reduced. Little direct observational data exist on this behavior, as both a singular kill episode and cached carcass must be linked. The location of initial predation/carcass deposition may contain only small traces of the predation incident, including blood, hair, environmental disturbance (foliage displacement, tracks, etc.), and, in the case of human prey, also artifactual evidence. Leopards can drag small antelopes approaching their own body mass up a feeding tree (Brain 1981). It is unknown how much transport was required to reach the trees, but distances on the order of hundreds of meters are plausible given the dispersal of game and suitable feeding trees in that semi-arid savanna environment.

Caching therefore can greatly increase the initial dispersal category of remains, given that they are normally removed from their kill site some distance. Secondary dispersal likely occurs from the point of caching/feeding, unless the remains are abandoned or lost for some reason.

Carnivore Gnawing Characteristics

A suite of common characteristics defines the damage caused by most large carnivores to large mammalian prey skeletons, including humans (Table 9.5). In North America and Eurasia, these large species are most commonly ursids (brown/grizzly bear [*Ursus arctos*], black bear [*U. americanus*], and polar bear [*U. maritimus*]), large felids (mountain lion/cougar/puma [*Felis concolor*] and leopard [*Panthera pardus*]), large canids (wolves

Table 9.5   Characteristics of Large Carnivore Interaction with Carcasses/Bodies

- Fresh bone
- Massive removal of soft tissue
- Destruction of long bone epiphyses
- Destruction of more delicate elements (ribs, vertebrae, sternum, etc.) or portions thereof
- Edge polish to exposed margins (rounding; irregular margins)
- Tooth pitting and scoring near exposed margins
- Scoring in other locations (diaphyses) from gripping and manipulating with teeth
- Furrowing of exposed cancellous bone
- May include tooth punctures, though these tend to get erased as more gnawing occurs
- Dispersal of bone 10 s of meters to kilometers
- May reconcentrate bone in a den or other favored feeding spot
- Damage to surrounding soft tissue may retain visible tooth marks
- Differentiation between gnawing taxa aided greatly by tracks, feces, and presence of distinctive tooth punctures
- Some species live in close proximity with humans (domesticates and those frequenting garbage, including coyotes, bears, etc.)

[*Canis lupus*], coyotes [*C. latrans*], large breeds of domestic dog [*C. familiaris*]), and hyae-nids (which only include striped hyena [*Hyaena hyaena*] in this range). Sub-Saharan Africa in particular has many species of large and small carnivore, and data derived from these species will be drawn upon in this discussion. There is also a great amount of overlap with the behavior of small carnivores, the most common ones in North America and Eurasia including small canids (most commonly red fox [*Vulpes vulpes*], small domestic dog breeds, and black-backed jackal [*Canis mesomelas*]), small felids (including domestic cats [*Felis catus*] and lynx [*Felis canadensis*]), most members of the Mustelidae (weasels, minks, martens, etc.), and a single member of Procyonidae (raccoon [*Procyon lotor*], which have also been introduced to Europe), and their separate suite of characteristics is differentiated where possible. There is, of course, a preference among all of these species for remains with soft tissue still attached, which is generally consumed first without great damage to bone in the early stages of carcass availability. Bone breakage upon initial prey consumption often consists of bones in the way of soft tissue access, usually the bones of the thoracic cage (sternum, ribs, and vertebrae). Fragile bones of the hands and face may also be attacked and/or transported away, especially from human remains where access to the rest of the body may be restricted due to the presence of clothing. Bone dispersal in the initial phase of consumption is also usually restricted to easily removed elements.

The commonalities of large carnivore skeletal destruction (Table 9.5) consist of a pref-erence for fresh bone, with nutrients in the form of soft tissue still attached and fat/grease contained within. Dry and/or weathered bone devoid of attached soft tissue is generally avoided by carnivores, as it lacks these nutrients. As discussed earlier, gnawing damage tends to be extensive and occurs rapidly. This damage includes the destruction of weaker elements (Hudson 1993), swallowing small elements whole, and destruction of long bone epiphyses through incremental gnawing to access the marrow spaces. The amount of edge polish to exposed long bone margins is very high, accompanied by tooth pitting and scoring near margins and on diaphyses, with the latter usually caused by gripping/manipulation. Tooth punctures and furrows also may be present, but these tend to be caused in softer bone (long bone epiphyses and the axial skeleton) and consequently are often destroyed by later gnawing if the carnivores expend ample time on the remains. Dispersal of bones due to carnivore activity is extremely high and can extend from the immediate area of the carcass/body to kilometers away; initial sites of remains deposition can lack any surviv-ing bone whatsoever as carnivores continue to damage and disperse a skeleton (Haynes 1980b, 1982; Kruuk 1972) and transport the remains elsewhere (Carson et al. 2000; Kerbis Peterhans 1990; Kerbis Peterhans and Horwitz 1992; Kerbis Peterhans and Gnoske 2001; Pokines and Kerbis Peterhans 2007).

Four clear rules emerge from cross-comparison of large carnivore consumption of prey:

1. When prey is abundant, carcass utilization (i.e., the proportion of tissue of an indi-vidual prey item that is consumed, including the degree to which bones are gnawed) generally decreases. What wolves leave behind at a kill, for example, is much greater when prey is abundant or more easily hunted. An example is feeding upon moose (*Alces alces*) in deep snow conditions where hard pack has formed, and the moose break through while the wolves do not (Mech 1970; Peterson 1977). If the next prey item can be killed by the wolf pack, they tend to abandon the previous prey item more quickly, use less of it (i.e., leave more bones behind), or return to it less often.

2. Juvenile prey, including humans, are far more quickly and completely destroyed relative to adult remains of that same prey species (Morton and Lord 2006; Pokines and Kerbis Peterhans 2007). Even taxa that are not noted bone gnawers (such as the felids and ursids) can leave very little trace behind of juvenile prey.
3. Seasonality affects carcass utilization in temperate and more northerly climates. Large carnivores consistently show lesser interest in frozen carrion that they have found vs. fresh prey that they have killed in winter. This means that heavy utilization of frozen remains is often delayed until the spring thaw, although winters relatively poor in game will mean an increase in frozen carcass utilization. It also may not be possible to access all of a frozen carcass (Haynes 1982).
4. As the number of large carnivores feeding increases, carcass utilization increases (Haynes 1980b), including the amount of bone damage (Haynes 1982; Pobiner 2007:113). This scenario is especially relevant to pack animals (as is typical among canids).

When combined, these rules indicate that except under specialized conditions, drawing conclusions about PMI using only the degree to which a set of remains has been consumed by large carnivores can be very tenuous (Haglund et al. 1989). What is clear is that consumption of remains can be very rapid, occurring over the course of hours or just a few days in order to render the remains of large prey (including humans) down to very few traces still at the point of initial deposition.

Distinguishing among Carnivore Bone Gnawers, Large and Small

Numerous studies have attempted to discriminate among the damage caused by large carnivore families (canids, ursids, and felids) typically encountered in North America and other avid bone gnawers (hyaenids) (Andrés et al. 2012; Carson et al. 2000; Delany-Rivera et al. 2009; Domínguez-Rodrigo and Piqueras 2003; Faith and Behrensmeyer 2006; Fisher 1995; Haglund et al. 1988; Haynes 1983; Miller 1969; Murmann et al. 2006; Payne 1983; Pobiner 2007, 2008; Pobiner and Blumenschine 2003; Pokines and Kerbis Peterhans 2007; Richardson 1980). This problem has several inherent difficulties, which include the following: (1) the general dental size overlap among these taxa, (2) the conical shape of canines, allowing them to leave tooth punctures of very different diameters, even when caused by the same individual bone gnawer, (3) the other multiple congruencies in dental morphology among these taxa, especially as their teeth undergo age-related attrition, (4) the effects of repeat damage, where new gnawing damage overlaps with, obscures, or destroys previous gnawing damage, (5) the infinite attack angles available to a bone gnawer when gnawing a bone, (6) the inherent problem that the portions of a gnawed bone most likely to preserve a tooth puncture potentially identifiable to the creating taxon are the least durable and therefore the least likely to survive continued gnawing and other postmortem destructive forces, (7) the possibility that more than one scavenging species gnawed on a bone, and (8) the bone dispersal that typically accompanies large carnivore bone gnawing. As Haynes (1983) notes, bones only lightly gnawed upon by a lion will be indistinguishable from bones only lightly gnawed upon by a bear. In addition, the use of other information such as field signs left behind by the scavengers (Einarsen 1952) including their droppings (Gilmour and Skinner 2012; Murad 1997) or the exclusion of other scavengers in an indoor setting (Steadman and Worne 2007) can aid greatly in differentiating among the species that may have interacted with a set of remains.

In terms of pure destructive force to bone, hyaenids represent the worst-case scenario of skeletal damage and dispersal in terrestrial environments (Kruuk 1972; Kerbis Peterhans and Horwitz 1992; Pobiner 2007; Pokines and Kerbis Peterhans 2007). Fortunately for forensic practitioners in the New World and Europe, these species' extant range is only in Africa and spanning southern Asia. Spotted hyenas (*Crocuta crocuta*) are the most destructive of these, having evolved both as an efficient social hunter and as a scavenger in Africa (Kruuk 1972). Other species, such as wolves, can achieve the overall effects of hyena ravaging to a carcass by taking more time to reach the same results. Since many hours or days are a common interval between death and discovery of remains, large scavenging carnivores often have ample time during the early PMI to gnaw upon remains until they have lost interest and abandoned them. If this takes more time because they are less efficient bone gnawers, then the gnawing efficiency of the taxon involved is unlikely to be discernable through forensic analysis of the overall state of gnawing damage and dispersal.

Figure 9.13 illustrates the great degree of overlap between large and small carnivore behavior, in this case unfused freshly butchered pig humeri gnawed on by a large (26 kg) and small (9 kg) domestic dog. In the case of the former, gnawing occurred for 24 min, and for the latter gnawing occurred for approximately 2 h. The gnawing by the small dog progressed much further, destroying more of the proximal end and involving the distal

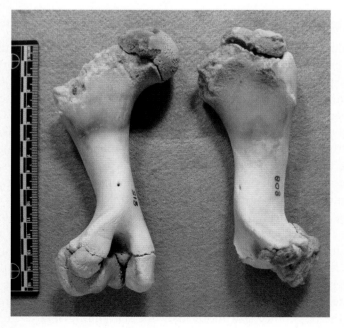

Figure 9.13 Juvenile pig humeri gnawed on by domestic dogs. Left: gnawed for 24 min by a large (26 kg) dog, damaged on the proximally only; right: gnawed for approximately 2 h by a small (9 kg) dog, damaged proximally and distally. Smaller dogs can cause amounts and types of damage similar to that of large dogs if given longer periods to gnaw, and the differences in gnawing duration will be largely undetectable during common forensic PMIs (days or weeks). Note that detached epiphyses have been glued to their original locations after cleaning. Scale is in cm.

end. Each individual left behind furrowing in the cancellous bone, edge polish of the cortical bone, and multiple pits and striations, but the large dog left behind no clear marks so large that they could not have been created by the dentition of the smaller dog. While data are limited, other small carnivores can damage large vertebrate skeletons to significant degrees (pers. obs.). Even domestic cats (*Felis catus*) have been demonstrated to leave minor damage on the weaker areas of large vertebrate bones (Moran and O'Connor 1992), although the large vertebrate remains in their experiment were both unfused and cooked, leaving them weaker than uncooked adult bones.

Overall Skeletal Damage and Locations

Table 9.6 compares the amount of skeletal damage caused to large vertebrates from multiple studies of large carnivores worldwide to different classes of large mammalian prey, including humans in some cases. The weaker elements or portions thereof with thinner cortical bone (including vertebrae, sterna, ribs, and pelves) underwent greater amounts of destruction, regardless of which large carnivore taxon was doing the gnawing. Smaller durable bones such as carpals may still be damaged or lost by being consumed whole and deposited elsewhere. There is enough overlap among all of these predators that determination of which taxon has scavenged a partial set of remains is extremely difficult when simply relying upon the degree of scavenging. For example, while hyenas tend to destroy and transport away more of a given large vertebrate skeleton than other large terrestrial scavengers, the same skeleton may reach a similar (and indistinguishable) degree of damage when scavenged by other taxa for a longer duration or by more individuals. Canids tend to be the next most destructive to skeletons, likely due in part to the commonness of pack instead of individual behavior. Steadman and Worne (2007) note that canid scavenging of human remains in a confined indoor setting over an interval of multiple weeks can leave very few identifiable osseous remains behind. In this case, the two dogs had exhausted their other food options and had to consume their former owner to survive a long period unattended. Ursids and felids tend to damage vertebrate skeletons to lesser degrees among the taxa presented in Table 9.6, with suids the least damaging.

Carson et al. (2000) suggest that overall human skeletal representation left at a scene of initial deposition may help to separate the scavenging action of black bears vs. large canids in their study area in New Mexico, USA. The largest difference that they noted in skeletal recovery from multiple cases ($n = 7$) of likely black bear scavenged remains is a reduced recovery of vertebral elements and sterna when compared with the canid scavenging pattern on human remains found by Haglund et al. (1989) in the Pacific Northwest. Overall elemental damage was comparable, with preferential attack of the long bone epiphyses to reach the marrow cavities and general attack upon the softer elements (scapulae, innominates, etc.). Note that this difference, if real, also holds true if the vertebral and sternal elements were transported away from the immediate scene for later consumption elsewhere or consumed on the spot. The effects of the more marginal environment in the bear study area (desert uplands) are unknown, in that greater carcass utilization may hold where scavengeable remains are more scarce. In contrast, Willey and Snyder (1989) found a very high degree of vertebral consumption/destruction of the carcasses of white-tailed deer (*Odocoileus virginianus*) fed to five captive wolves, which had greater time to consume each carcass fully.

Table 9.6 Comparison of Large Carnivore Interaction with Large Vertebrate Remains

	Domínguez-Rodrigo (1999)	Pobiner (2007)	Pobiner (2007)	Phillips (1993)
Taxa—consumer	Felidae Lion (*Panthera leo*)	Felidae Lion (*Panthera leo*)	Felidae Lion (*Panthera leo*)	Felidae Cheetah (*Acinonyx jubatus*)
Taxa—consumed	Large ungulates	Large ungulates	Small ungulates	Small antelopes and other bovids (30–50 kg)
MNI consumed taxa	*n* = 28	*n* = 7	*n* = 9	*n* = 24
Location	Kenya	Kenya	Kenya	Namibia
Source	Kill sites	Kill sites	Kill sites	Kill sites
Environment	Savanna	Savanna (game preserve)	Savanna (game preserve)	Savanna
Typical gnawing damage				
Crania	Little modification	Modification to face, base, vault	Heavy modification to face, base, vault	Little modification
Mandibles	Little modification	Little modification	Heavy modification	Little modification
Vertebrae	Processes damaged	Processes damaged; sometimes consumed	Processes damaged; sometimes consumed	Processes damaged
Ribs	Distal ends broken	Generally heavy damage	Generally heavy damage	Up to half consumed
Sterna	(No data)	(No data)	(No data)	(No data)
Innominates	Tooth marks on margins	Moderate damage to margins	Heavy damage to margins	(No data)
Clavicles	N/A	N/A	N/A	N/A
Scapulae	Tooth marks	Moderate damage to margins	Heavy damage to margins	(No data)
Long bones	Minor damage on extremities from defleshing	Little to moderate damage to epiphyses	Generally heavy damage to epiphyses	Abandoned at feeding sites
Metapodials	Rare tooth marks	Rare damage	Rare damage to epiphyses	(No data)
Carpals/tarsals/phalanges	Not consumed	Rare damage	Rare damage	Untouched
Aggregation of bone	Individual kills dragged to shade for feeding	None	None	None

	Simons (1966)	Horwitz and Smith (1988)	Pokines and Kerbis Peterhans (2007)	Carson et al. (2000)
Taxa—consumer	Felidae Leopard (*Panthera pardus*)	Hyaenidae Striped hyena (*Hyaena hyaena*)	Hyaenidae Spotted hyena (*Crocuta crocuta*)	Ursidae Black bear[a] (*Ursus americanus*)
Taxa—consumed	Baboon (*Papio* sp.)	Human	Large ungulates	Humans
MNI consumed taxa	n = 22	n = 10	n = 151	n = 7
Location	Kenya	Israel	Kenya	New Mexico, USA
Source	Kill site/cave den	Cave dens	Cave den	Scavenged sites
Environment	Savanna	Desert	Savanna	High desert
Typical gnawing damage				
Crania	Frequent tooth marks; damage to facial area	Reduced to calvaria	Most reduced to tooth rows	Generally intact; some minor damage
Mandibles	Tooth rows recovered	Tooth rows recovered	Tooth rows recovered	Unmodified
Vertebrae	Few recovered; some damage	None recovered	Frags. only remain	Many destroyed; spinous processes damaged
Ribs	None recovered	None recovered	Frags. only remain	Heavy damage
Sterna	None recovered	None recovered	All destroyed	All destroyed
Innominates	Margins removed	None recovered	Highly fragmented	Gnawing to margins, tooth marks
Clavicles	None recovered	None recovered	N/A	Frequently modified or unrecovered
Scapulae	Margins gnawed	None recovered	Glenoid and frags. remain	Frequently modified or unrecovered
Long bones	Most epiphyses gnawed off	Shafts only recovered	Weakest epiphyses consumed, many reduced to cylinders	Weakest epiphyses consumed
Metapodials	Few recovered	None recovered	Weakest epiphyses consumed, many reduced to cylinders	Few recovered
Carpals/tarsals/phalanges	Few recovered	None recovered	Often consumed	Few recovered
Aggregation of bone	Significant at feeding sites	Maximal among extant taxa	Maximal among extant taxa	Limited

(continued)

Table 9.6 (continued) Comparison of Large Carnivore Interaction with Large Vertebrate Remains

	(Haynes 1980b, 1982)	Haynes (1980a)	Haglund (1997)	Domínguez-Solera & Domínguez-Rodrigo (2009)
Taxa—consumer	Canidae Wolf (Canis lupus)	Canidae Wolf (Canis lupus)	Canidae Coyote and dog (Canis latrans, C. familiaris)	Suidae Pigs (Sus scrofa)
Taxa—consumed	White-tailed deer (Odocoileus virginianus), bison (Bison bison), moose (Alces alces)	White-tailed deer (Odocoileus virginianus)	Humans	Partially disarticulated lamb (Ovis aries), cattle (Bos taurus), and pigs
MNI consumed taxa	N/A; general observations	n = 94	n = 53	N/A
Location	Canada and Minnesota, USA	Minnesota, USA	Pacific NW, USA	Spain
Source	Kill/scavenged sites	Fall/winter kill/scavenged sites	Scavenged sites	Captive and wild feeding
Environment	Boreal forest/wetlands	Mixed forest	Boreal forest	Farm and forest
Typical gnawing damage				
Crania	Juvenile crania often destroyed; damage to weaker areas	Often removed; variable damage from only to weaker areas to only tooth rows remaining	Damage to weaker areas (face, etc.)	(Not tested)
Mandibles	Light damage	Often removed; variable damage	Variable damage	(Not tested)

Vertebrae	Frequent damage to processes; often removed/destroyed	Frequent damage to processes; often removed/destroyed	Frequent damage to processes; often removed/destroyed	Most consumed completely
Ribs	(No data)	Often removed; heavy damage	Frequent damage; often removed/destroyed	(Not tested)
Sterna	(No data)	Usually completely splintered/consumed	Often removed/destroyed	(Not tested)
Innominates	Gnawing to margins	Gnawing to margins; often only acetabulum remains	Gnawing to margins/removed	Most consumed completely
Clavicles	N/A	N/A	Often removed/destroyed	N/A
Scapulae	Gnawing to margins	Often removed; gnawing to margins	Gnawing to margins	Margins gnawed
Long bones	Weakest epiphyses consumed; gradual reduction to cylinders noted	Weakest epiphyses consumed to greater damage noted	Weakest epiphyses consumed; gradual reduction to cylinders noted	Tooth marks including incisal furrowing on epiphyses
Metapodials	Proximal damage common	Lower legs often all remaining at kill site	Frequently missing	Some swallowed whole
Carpals/tarsals/phalanges	(No data)	Lower legs often all remaining at kill site	Frequently missing	(Not tested)
Aggregation of bone	Not noted	Not noted	Not noted	None

a Some canid involvement could not be ruled out

Dental Arcade Bite Pattern and Size

An impression of all or a portion of the gnawing species' dental arcade may narrow down which taxon has scavenged remains. Repeated gnawing of the same area obscures clear bite mark impressions, and most bone areas are generally too dense to leave a clean impression of multiple teeth crushing inward all at once. Exceptions include ribs, innominates, and scapulae. Bite force is also at the minimum, since the impressing teeth most often are in the anterior apex of the dental arcade and farthest from the fulcrum point at the TMJ (Figure 9.3). For this reason, clear bite mark patterns are more likely to be found in soft tissue (Lyver 2000) or associated articles of clothing. In addition, since the canines are much longer and larger than the incisors in all of these species, these teeth are far more likely among the anterior teeth to leave an impression behind in bone.

The great overlap in carnivore species' dental arcade size also makes this determination difficult. (The number of anterior teeth in each case is the same: three incisors and the canine in each quadrant.) If a larger portion of the dental arcade than just the canines leaves an impression, the overall pattern is more distinctive. Murmann et al. (2006) measured intercanine distances and made impressions of the common North American (Nearctic) scavengers (Table 9.7). They noted clear differences by carnivore family (Ursidae, Canidae, Felidae, and Mustelidae) in anterior arcade shape. Felids were distinctive in their flat, long row of incisors, with an intermediate amount of curvature for ursids and mustelids and the greatest amount of anterior curvature among canids. Their study also included juveniles and had large samples for each species, drawing upon a number of available subspecies. Murmann et al. (2006) found large amounts of overlap in intercanine width among and between Carnivore families, although the larger species can be separated from the smaller using their data.

Table 9.7   Intercanine Width of Common North American Carnivores

Taxon	*n*	Maxillary (cm)	Mandibular (cm)
Felidae			
Domestic cat (*Felis catus*)	25	0.7–2.2	0.4–1.8
Bobcat (*Lynx rufus*)	39	1.1–3.1	0.5–2.4
Lynx (*Lynx canadensis*)	34	1.3–3.0	0.5–2.5
Mountain lion (*Puma concolor*)	39	2.1–4.5	1.0–4.0
Canidae			
Gray fox (*Urocyon cinereoargenteus*)	52	0.9–2.2	0.4–2.0
Red fox (*Vulpes vulpes*)	54	1.1–2.7	0.4–2.5
Domestic dog (*Canis familiaris*)	35	1.3–4.8	0.6–4.9
Coyote (*Canis latrans*)	54	1.5–3.6	0.7–3.9
Gray wolf (*Canis lupus*)	53	2.3–5.1	1.1–4.5
Mustelidae			
Wolverine (*Gulo gulo*)	31	1.8–4.3	0.7–3.2
Ursidae			
Black bear (*Ursus americanus*)	35	2.0–6.4	1.1–5.2
Brown (Grizzly) bear (*Ursus arctos*)	35	3.4–9.6	1.5–9.1

Source: Murmann D.C. et al., *J. Forensic Sci.,* 51, 846, 2006.

Tooth Mark Morphology and Size

Tooth mark morphology and size may indicate a single carnivore or class of carnivores, especially when the known types of carnivores in an area are restricted to fewer viable options. Pobiner (2007) studied multiple species of African carnivore (lions, spotted hyenas, leopards, cheetahs, and jackals [*Canis mesomelas*]) and their interaction with many sizes of large nonhuman mammal in both a game park and an animal rehabilitation facility. This research included noting the type of tooth mark and maximal dimensions. She found that while all of these carnivores left tooth marks that are relatively small in size, only the largest two species (lions and spotted hyenas) left large tooth marks. Andrés et al. (2012) similarly noted a great deal of overlap of the measured lengths of tooth pits left on long bone ends by the range of gnawing species that they studied, including large and small carnivores and humans. They found that statistically significant separation could be achieved only for the very largest gnawers (spotted hyenas and lions) vs. the other species. Other distinctions among smaller gnawing taxa may be possible using additional dimensions measured for tooth pits. Differences in markings were also more distinctive when the gnawed-upon species was adult/larger, and the bones were not so easily destroyed by gnawing Andrés et al. (2012). Large scavengers therefore may leave behind individual tooth marks that are too large to have been created by small scavengers, despite the great deal of overlap normally encountered.

Pig Gnawing Characteristics

Domestic and feral pigs (*Sus* spp.) are avid omnivorous scavengers, which will include animal protein in their diet when available, including human and other large primate tissues (Berryman 2002; Galdikas 1978; Greenfield 1988; Wilcox and Van Vuren 2009). Their interactions with large mammal carcasses are similar in some respects with large carnivores, although their teeth are neither adapted to bone crushing nor particularly effective at soft tissue shearing (Hillson 1986). Contra what has apparently reached popular myth status, pigs cannot consume an entire human skeleton and leave little trace. Their ubiquitous presence throughout the world in urban, rural, and wilderness settings, however, increases their taphonomic significance (Greenfield 1988). This species, along with domestic/feral dogs, are in many ecosystems throughout the world the largest terrestrial scavengers, such as in Australia, Papua New Guinea, the Hawaiian Islands, other geographically isolated locations, and physically enclosed local ecosystems (i.e., pig farms).

Berryman (2002) describes a case of probable pig scavenging of a human in Tennessee. The largely articulated body had undergone some skeletal scavenging and displayed postmortem damage predominantly upon the more delicate portions: the facial area, vertebral column, innominates, and ribs. Additional anterior tooth scoring was noted on a femur, tibia, and both medial clavicles. Much of the thoracic cavity breakage was attributable to the opening of this area to feed upon viscera and therefore may have been caused more by scavenger mass pressing down than by direct mastication behavior. The overall pattern shows a confinement to the softer portions of the body in contrast to the type of feeding and bone damage caused by large carnivores. These results parallel the partially controlled pig-feeding experiments of Greenfield (1988), where domestic pigs were found to destroy

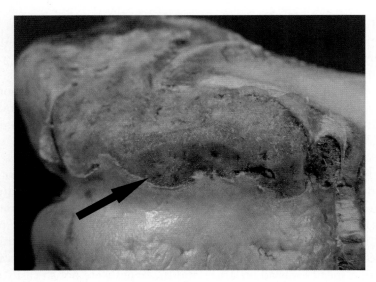

Figure 9.14 Damage to long bone epiphysis caused by pig gnawing; note the removal of the thin cortical bone (arrow) over the cancellous bone. (Image courtesy of Dr. Manuel Domínguez-Rodrigo.)

smaller, weaker isolated large mammal elements (vertebrae and sacrum) and leave some gnawing damage on long bone epiphyses (Figure 9.14). Berryman (2002) notes that parallel scoring caused by the lower incisors may be indicative of pig scavenging. Other damage and some missing elements indicate that other scavenger involvement with these remains was possible, but the proximity of domesticated pigs indicates that most damage likely was caused by them. This individual was dead for a maximum of 10 days, which indicates a much lower overall rate of scavenging, osseous damage, and dispersal by the pigs relative to large carnivores.

Experimental feeding experiments among *Sus* taxa (Domínguez-Solera and Domínguez-Rodrigo 2009) generally indicate an ability among pigs to consume/destroy weaker elements (scapulae, vertebrae, and innominates) and modify the epiphyses of long bones (femora and tibiae). Whether this represents habitual consumption patterns in the wild when confronted with largely intact carcasses is unknown, as many of the experimental runs involved defleshed and disarticulated elements from pigs, lambs, and cattle. Minor experiments using wild pigs showed a similar pattern of bone destruction: weaker elements modified or consumed, and long bone epiphyses gnawed upon with fragmentation of shafts prevalent among smaller elements. Some whole small bones (tarsals) likely were consumed in their entirety. Dispersal was minor, and interest in individual elements by penned animals generally ceased after 1.5 h.

Damage possibly indicative of pig involvement with remains was discovered in the form of broad furrows formed by pig incisors (Domínguez-Solera and Domínguez-Rodrigo 2009:356). This modification is significant in that pigs use their broad, flat incisors for gnawing, whereas the cheek teeth are normally used by most terrestrial carnivores including felids, hyaenids, canids, and ursids. An example of this type of furrowing and scoring is shown in Figure 9.15. Pigs also show a preference for remains of smaller large mammals, those <50 kg mass, which includes much of the human size range. Bones from larger species including cattle are less heavily modified.

Figure 9.15 Damage to nonhuman long bone epiphysis caused by pig gnawing, showing blunt, parallel scoring made by the incisors. (Image courtesy of Dr. Manuel Domínguez-Rodrigo.)

Ungulate Osteophagia Characteristics

Despite numerous references to osteophagia among a variety of ungulate species, this phenomenon has undergone little systematic study, and knowledge of it derives primarily from chance observational reports (Bowyer 1983; Brothwell 1976; Kierdorf 1993, 1994; Sutcliffe 1973, 1977; Wyatt 1971). The reason for bone consumption is likely a response to dietary mineral deficiencies based upon environment, so not all members of an animal population will practice bone consumption. Due to the broad occlusal molar surfaces of ungulates that evolved for a herbivorous or omnivorous diet, damage to the bone should consist of a battered, ground appearance with heavy tooth pitting. Beginning and intermediate stages of alteration consist of broad, rounded grooves consistent with the broad cusps of herbivores that gradually wear away the bone (Cáceres et al. 2011:2769). Heavy wear leads to a characteristic Y-fork shape left on the ends of long bones (Figure 9.16).

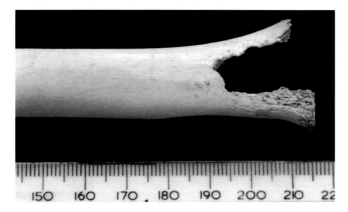

Figure 9.16 Damage to a sheep (*Ovis aries*) metapodial caused by osteophagia by a sheep, Wales. Note the characteristic Y-fork shape to the end. (Image courtesy of Dr. Peter Andrews.)

Given

Given the number of potential osteophagic taxa involved throughout the world, a high degree of variation is expected, and this specific taphonomic feature may be difficult to identify especially in its early stages.

Porcupine and Other Large Rodent Gnawing Characteristics

Among large rodents, porcupines (most commonly North American porcupine *Erethizon dorsatum* and *Hystrix* spp. in Africa and southern Eurasia) are the most avid bone gnawers (Kerbis Peterhans 1990; Roze 2009) (Table 9.8). *Hystrix* is also an avid bone collector, concentrating large amounts in den sites. This extreme behavior regarding bones has not been detected in the repertoire of other large rodents, although relatively little study has been done in this area. Porcupines have broad upper and lower incisors and therefore leave broader, flatter (and deeper) gnaw marks upon bone than smaller rodents. Their distinctive furrows (Figure 9.17) are concentrated on the margins of elements, and repeated gnawing often obliterates distinct furrows, leaving behind

Table 9.8 Characteristics of Large Rodent (e.g., Porcupine) Interaction with Bone

- Dryer, weathered bones are preferred
- Transport of larger elements to a den is typical of some species
- Tend to sample all bone sources in home area regardless of taxon
- Damage caused (parallel striations) is similar to that caused by smaller rodents, but more damage than is typical of the latter
- Incisor sharpening and nutrient ingestion of the dry bone
- Not known to scavenge fresher bones/carcasses to consume soft tissue
- Repeated gnawing often obliterates distinct furrows, leaves behind a more even margin
- Porcupines normally avoid human contact and are excluded from many scenes of potential forensic interest

Figure 9.17 Large rodent gnawing (North American porcupine, *Erethizon dorsatum*) upon dry, weathered large mammal bone. Note the irregular sculpting of the upper margin and the sets of more regular, shallower, and older convergent striations below. Scale is in cm.

a more even margin. They leave similar marks behind on wood, especially on objects where perspiring human hands have touched repeatedly (tool handles, door frames, etc.) and left behind salts (Roze 2009). They do not normally seek out fresher remains, as they are otherwise herbivores, although Roze (2009) does report an isolated instance of *Erethizon dorsatum* feeding upon the bones from the remains of a fresh white-tailed deer (*Odocoileus virginianus*). The majority of this gnawing behavior is dietary in nature, in order to compensate for sodium intake in otherwise low-sodium environments (Duthie and Skinner 1986; Roze 2009).

Denning behavior differs between these two ubiquitous genera. Concentration of bones within dens has not been reported for *E. dorsatum* (Betancourt et al. 1986; Roze 2009). In the northeastern United States, for example, dens of *E. dorsatum* are normally occupied only in winter for the thermal benefits (Roze 2009). Food is not transported to dens, and the vegetal remains that may build up there are almost entirely derived from fecal matter (Betancourt et al. 1986). It is, of course, possible that bones already transported to a den that is used by other species may be gnawed upon later in that location by *E. dorsatum* (Dixon 1984). *Hystrix*, in contrast, are avid bone transporters (Alexander 1956; Kerbis Peterhans 1990). They tend to sample all bones (above a certain size, avoiding smaller mammal bones) indiscriminately within their home ranges.

Porcupines as indicated earlier show a marked preference for dry/weathered bone as opposed to fresh, greasy bone. Data from the mixed spotted hyena/*Hystrix*-accumulated sample in Masai Mara Cave, Kenya (Pokines and Kerbis Peterhans 2007), show a clear trend for the weathered bones to have been gnawed by porcupines while the unweathered, fresh bones were collected and gnawed by the hyenas. (Deposition into a cave or similar protected setting curtails continued weathering.) Of the 31 identified skeletal elements with porcupine gnawing in this sample, 15 (48.4%) had reached weathering stages 1–4 (i.e., at least mostly degreased), compared with 7.3% of the total sample, a statistically significant difference (chi square = 70.56, p $\leq$ 0.001, d.f. = 1). Brain (1981) noted similar results among osseous remains collected from another recent porcupine den in South Africa (Nossob): only 15 of 1620 osseous elements (0.9%) retained residual grease. This weathering state corresponds with stage 0, with the remaining 99.1% falling into Stage 1 or higher. Of course, any given skeletal element encountered during a forensic investigation could first have undergone gnawing by a carnivore then abandonment, followed by drying out and weathering, then gnawing and possibly transport by a porcupine. This sequence of events may be determinable by the weathered state of the residual carnivore gnawing marks, with fresher traces of porcupine gnawing.

Small Rodent Gnawing Characteristics

Small rodents present two separate suites of characteristics when interacting with skeletal remains. The better known of the two is gnawing upon dry bone (see later). This behavior is exhibited by many species of rodent and likely by many that have not yet been studied in this regard, since over 2200 species of rodent have been described (over 40% of all mammal species). Omnivorous rodents (in forensic terms, most importantly black rats *Rattus rattus* and Norway rats *Rattus norvegicus*) also will consume fresh remains and gnaw into fresh bone while doing so (Haglund 1992, 1997b; Klippel and Synstelien 2007; Patel 1994; Tsokos et al. 1999). Given their cosmopolitan world distribution, avid feeding activity, sometimes local abundance, commensalism, the potential exclusion of scavenging vertebrate competitors from many indoor death scenes, and the frequency in which increasing human social isolation leads to deaths going unreported or unnoticed for months or years, the forensic importance of these taxa is greatly increased.

Fresh Remains

The characteristics of small rodent gnawing upon fresh remains are presented in Table 9.9, in contrast with their gnawing patterns upon dry bone, and the commonalities in these two behaviors. These two modes of behavior also likely have areas of overlap, such as gnawing upon remains in the early PMI that are largely defleshed and retain their greasy texture. One set of remains in isolation also may pass from perimortem/recent postmortem involvement by rodents and slowly into later postmortem involvement, as the remains decompose and receive continued rodent feeding attention (see the following text). In addition, one species of omnivorous rodent (spiny mouse *Acomys cahirinus*) found in Egypt and neighboring areas is known to nest in archaeological sites and causes recent gnawing damage on the dried external soft tissue and marrow of mummies (Osborn and Helmy 1980:299). Commonalities in these two modes of behavior include a general inability or disinclination to disperse remains from their point of origin, the main exception

Table 9.9 Characteristics of Small Rodent Gnawing on Fresh Remains and Dry/Weathered Bones

Fresh Bones/Bodies/Carcasses	Dry/Weathered Bones
• Primary purpose: consumption of nutrients	• Primary purposes: incisor sharpening and consumption of nutrients
• Consume soft tissue and continue into delicate bone areas (epiphyses, nasal margins, etc.)	• Often will gnaw wood or other hard objects in the same manner
• Adjacent soft tissue not typically penetrated, unlike carnivores	• Leave behind short, parallel striations
• Leave behind pedestaled areas of bone when gnawing into epiphyses	• Often prefer sharp margins of dense bone
	• Striations single row (mandibular incisors engaged while maxillary incisors hold the bone in place) or convergent row (both sets of incisors converge at a point)
• Uniform pitch to gnaw margins	• May be a caused by a variety of small rodent taxa (rats, squirrels, voles, gerbils, etc.)
• Fresh bone consumption therefore more likely from an omnivorous small rodent taxon (rats instead of squirrels)	
• See Haglund (1997b)	

Characteristics Common to Both

- Tend not to disperse large elements away from initial area of deposition
- (Exceptions: packrats [*Neotoma* spp.] will transport and concentrate small elements or fragments; burrowing by many species will displace buried bones)
- Marks on bones lack associated pits, punctures, and striations characteristic of carnivore gnawing
- Uniform pitch and parallel damage to bone margins (carnivore margins irregular, rounded)
- Other: presence of rodent droppings or live rodents themselves (less likely to be frightened away immediately by human presence)
- Other: exclusion—some scenes allow only rodent access to a body, such as house interiors

being packrats (*Neotoma* spp.), which are found mostly in the western United States and northern Mexico but also extend into the eastern United States and Canada (Betancourt et al. 1990). Burrowing behavior by a multitude of rodent species, however, can accidentally disturb buried remains in most world locations and cause significant bone displacement. Rodent gnaw marks, in contrast to those of carnivores, consist of fine parallel grooves confined to smaller surfaces that they can fit into their relatively small mouths. Their gnawing also lacks the associated pits and other damage away from the main areas of damage concentrated on bone margins, unlike carnivore damage, which normally encompasses more of a given bone. Rodent involvement may also be indicated by their ubiquitous droppings or fur at a scene and by the exclusion of access by other possible scavengers (closed buildings, etc.).

Small rodent gnawing on fresh remains includes the recently deceased, so a great deal of soft tissue damage may occur (Haglund 1997b; Patel 1994) and without any bone involvement (Tsokos et al. 1999), especially when competing scavengers are excluded from a death scene. Soft tissue damage is normally confined to exposed areas, so faces and hands often receive the most attention. Gnawing of soft tissue often continues into the osseous tissues, especially thin margins of bone (such as the nasal region) or into softer bone (the epiphyses). In the latter case, *pedestaling* often occurs, where an epiphysis is gnawed into, leaving areas of untouched bone adjacent to the damaged location. (Note that small carnivores such as small breeds of dog may also cause pedestaling, although they tend to leave much more ragged margins and cause other kinds of tooth damage elsewhere on the same bone.) Fine parallel striations are still found on the margins of cortical bone gnawed by small rodents (Figure 9.18).

Figure 9.18 Close-up of *Rattus* sp. gnawing upon fresh, still-greasy animal vertebrae. Note the faint, parallel, convergent striations on the left element margins and the deep gouging into the soft cancellous bone on the right.

Dry/Weathered Bone

Rodent damage to dry/weathered bone often has the ultimate cause of incisor sharpening instead of nutrient ingestion, although multiple species of small rodent consume dry bone for the mineral nutrient content (Carlson 1940; Coventry 1940). Small rodents will also leave similar gnaw marks on wood and other hard materials. Since the species are small, they often attack preferentially the thinner, exposed margins of bones, such as long bones where the epiphyses have already been removed by other processes (carnivore action, weathering, etc.). The striations left behind can be of two types: *singular*, where only the maxillary or mandibular paired incisors have been dragged across the surface while the other holds the bone steady, and *convergent*, where the maxillary and mandibular incisors are used simultaneously to drag against the bone while converging on each other (Figures 9.19 and 9.20). The distinctive, parallel markings are difficult to confuse with other kinds of taphonomic observations. The width of the markings varies according to rodent incisor size, although there is a great deal of overlap among taxa, and individual species determination is likely not possible.

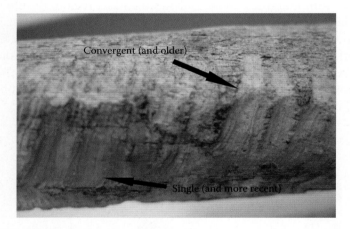

Figure 9.19 Small rodent (likely *Mus musculus* or *Rattus* sp.) gnawing upon dry, weathered human bone. Note that the gnawing can proceed either singly (one row of teeth dragged; fresher damage) or convergently (upper and lower teeth dragged, converging on a margin).

Figure 9.20 Small rodent (likely *Mus musculus* or *Rattus* sp.) gnawing upon human bone. Note the preferential attacking of thinner, already exposed margins and that the bone had undergone previous weathering.

Termite Gnawing Characteristics

Termites (Insecta Order: Isoptera; multiple families, approximately 3000 described species; see Bignell et al. 2010) are known to tunnel through bone. The reasons for this are unclear, since the termites derive their sustenance by the breaking down of plant cellulose through a symbiotic relationship with protozoans (primarily *Trichonympha* spp.) inhabiting their digestive tract. Their tunneling therefore normally proceeds through wood and other plant materials, which can supply this resource. They may, however, derive nitrogen and phosphorus nutrients from bone (Watson and Abbey 1986) and sometimes may be attracted to fresher remains (Backwell et al. 2012; Thorne and Kimsey 1983). It is also possible that the bones, when encountered, are simply in the way of subterranean tunneling (Derry 1911), as termites also tunnel through soil. These well-known pests are more prevalent in the subtropical and tropical zones, although their range extends into the temperate zone, including much of North America and Eurasia. Their potential to affect bones of forensic interest therefore is significant, and they have been posited as a source of damage to archaeological (Backwell et al. 2012; Huchet et al. 2011) and fossil bones as well (Kaiser 2000; Watson and Abbey 1986).

The suite of characteristics of termite tunneling through bone (Table 9.10) includes most visibly the "Swiss cheese" effect that they leave behind, which resembles the tunnels that they leave through wood. Investigators have noted that the bones or surrounding soil may still contain live termites (Danielson 2005, 2006). Termite gnawing may be mistaken for generalized acid soil corrosion. Indeed, the two may often be found on the same element, since termite gnawing is more likely to occur on buried remains, and there is some correspondence between the range of termites and acidic tropical soils. Acidic soil corrosion (see Chapter 5, this volume) thins out the entire portion of the element in contact with the soil, but typically produces windowing only at the thinnest margins. Termite tunneling takes place throughout a bone, regardless of thickness, and will also leave in some places adjacent bone completely undamaged. Extensive termite attack may so damage a bone (through decreasing its structural integrity and increasing its surface area) that it makes it more susceptible to other destructive forces (acidic erosion, trampling, and recovery), which may mask the earlier termite involvement. It is likely that other arthropod taxa have a similar potential to destroy bone through direct gnawing, but this topic requires additional investigation.

Termite damage to wood and bone can be characterized into three basic types: (1) *surface deflation*, where whole layers have been stripped away; (2) *channeling*, where narrow tunnels have left their traces along the surface or through the interior; and (3) *entrance/exit holes*, where these tunnels terminate (Danielson 2005, 2006). Figure 9.21a and b illustrate these damage traces to a human innominate on a macroscopic scale. Figure 9.22 shows

Table 9.10 Macroscopic Characteristics of Termite Interaction with Bone

- Occurs more often on dryer, defleshed bone
- Formation of surface deflation, channeling, and entry/exit holes; some surface defects may be star-shaped (Backwell et al. 2012)
- Overall "Swiss cheese" effect of interconnected tunnels and holes through the bone
- Bone normally from a buried context and therefore may also have soil staining, plant root damage, plant roots infiltrating, etc. (see Chapter 5, this volume)

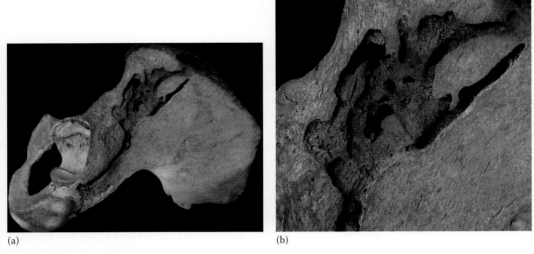

(a)   (b)

Figures 9.21 (a) Termite damage to a human innominate. (From Huchet, J.-B., D. Deverly, B. Gutierrez, and C. Chaucat: Taphonomic evidence of a human skeleton gnawed on by termites in a Moche-civilisation grave at Huaca de la Luna, Peru. *Int. J. Osteoarchaeol.* 2011. 21. 92–102. Copyright John Wiley & Sons. Reproduced with permission.) (b) Close-up of same. Note sheeting, galleries, tunneling, and overall "Swiss cheese" effect.

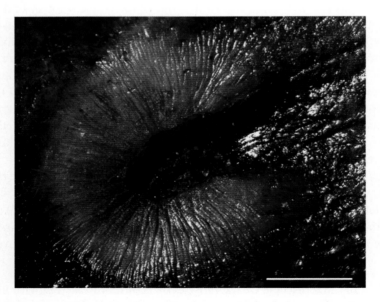

Figure 9.22 Experimentally derived termite damage to fresh bone after 1 year of burial in a termite mound; note the stellate pattern of radiating striations around the central cavity (Reprinted from *Palaeogeography, Palaeoclimatology, Palaeoecology*, 337–338, Backwell, L.R., E.M. Roberts, F. d'Errico, and J.-B. Huchet (2012) Criteria for identifying bone modification by termites in the fossil record, 72–87, Copyright (2012), with permission from Elsevier.) Scale bar is 1 mm.

experimentally derived termite damage to bone on a microscopic scale. Termite gnawing can form stellate-shaped lesions in bone with striations radiating out from a central hole. Other variations in microscopic traces of termite gnawing occur and have been noted in archaeological specimens (Backwell et al. 2012).

Surface deflation, in theory, could be confused with large-scale surface corrosion in an acidic soil environment. Acidic soil corrosion normally affects all buried portions of an element to some degree, although some cortical areas may be more deeply removed than others. Termite surface deflation affects some areas of bone cortex deeply, yet completely bypasses others and leaves intact cortical surface in isolated areas. Similarly, entrance/exit holes could be confused with windowing in bone caused by acidic soil corrosion or gastric acid. The latter types of holes generally are small, irregular, and pierce only the thinnest portions of bone. The acidic holes also do not have distinct channels leading to them. The exception to this pattern is where a nutrient foramen has been enlarged by acidic action, thus leaving the appearance of a tunnel leading into an interior cavity. The singular, isolated occurrence of these taphonomically enlarged foramina and their location in typical anatomical positions and angles separates them from termite damage.

Conclusions and Recommendations

Gnawing by terrestrial carnivores is one of the most damaging taphonomic processes that may happen to a bone, since many of these taxa have evolved behavioral, masticatory, and digestive mechanisms specifically to exploit bones as a nutritional resource. (The commonness of this type of taphonomic alteration is indicated by the necessity for forensic research facilities decomposing large vertebrate remains to have these areas fenced in order to limit wholesale loss of remains, their dispersal, and their gnawing damage.) Normal scavenging feeding behavior includes a heavy component of bone dispersal away from the point of initial carcass/body deposition, further confounding efforts to analyze skeletal remains forensically. Similarly, gnawing attacks by rodents and other species further degrade bones in ways that may make them unidentifiable or unrecoverable. Through careful field recovery and analysis, the suites of characteristic (and potentially unique signatures) of these gnawing taxa possibly can be detected, even where these overlap on a set of remains. A number of recommendations to deal with this pervasive taphonomic force are as follows:

1. Know what bone-altering taxa live in your area as a list of potential suspects. These should be obtainable from regional mammal guides or researchers in other academic and museum departments. When in doubt, please note that many wildlife species are in fact reestablishing themselves in portions of their former North American ranges, including wolves (Thiel et al. 1998), coyotes, moose (*Alces alces*), mountain lions, and smaller species, due to environmental protection, the loss of smaller agricultural operations, and deliberate reintroductions. Please also note that some of these species, especially coyotes, have more urban ranges than normally assumed (Gehrt et al. 2009) and can be a factor in outdoor crime scene scavenging within city limits.

2. Obtain examples of gnawed bone from sources where the gnawing species is known. Long bones gnawed by domestic dogs should be easy to obtain and are valuable comparative material.
3. Determine the pH of soils at investigation scenes in order to control for the possible effect that this variable has had upon osseous remains degradation and to separate its potential effects from the others described in this chapter.
4. Taphonomic research of this nature lends itself well to thesis projects and is an underexplored area of investigation within forensic anthropology and among related fields.

Acknowledgments

Portions of this research were supported by the Field Museum, Division of Mammals and Division of Birds, Chicago, and The Bill Curtis Foundation. Some images were generously supplied by Dr. Manuel Domínguez-Rodrigo, Dr. Peter Andrews, Dr. Lucinda Backwell, Dr. Jean-Bernard Huchet, and Dr. Julian Kerbis Peterhans. Bibliographic assistance was supplied by Dr. Matthew Connior. Thanks also go to Dr. R. Lee Lyman, Ms. Allysha Winburn, Mr. Sean Tallman, and Ms. Josie Paolello for their reviews of this research and to Ms. Brianne Charles for her editorial assistance.

References

Alexander, A. J. (1956) Bone carrying by a porcupine. *South African Journal of Science* 52:257–258.

Andrés, M., A. O. Gidna, J. Yravedra, and M. Domínguez-Rodrigo (2012) A study of dimensional differences of tooth marks (pits and scores) on bones modified by small and large carnivores. *Archaeological and Anthropological Sciences.* DOI: 10.1007/s12520–012-0093-4.

Backwell, L. R., A. H. Parkinson, E. M. Roberts, F. d'Errico, and J.-B. Huchet (2012) Criteria for identifying bone modification by termites in the fossil record. *Palaeogeography, Palaeoclimatology, Palaeoecology* 337–338:72–87.

Barthelmess, E. L. (2006) Hystrix africaeaustralis. *Mammalian Species* 788:1–7.

Bear, G. D. (1971) Seasonal trends in fat levels in pronghorns, *Antilocapra americana*, in Colorado. *Journal of Mammalogy* 53:583–589.

Becker, B. and C. A. Reed (1993) Studies of the bone detritus of the striped hyena (*Hyaena hyaena*) at a site in Egyptian Nubia, and the interaction of the bone breakage by striped hyenas. In *Skeletons in her Cupboard* Eds. A. Clason, S. Payne, and H.-P. Uerpmann, pp. 157–182. Oxbow Monograph 34, Oxford, U.K.

Behrensmeyer, A. K. (1991) Terrestrial vertebrate accumulations. In *Taphonomy: Releasing the Data Locked in the Fossil Record* Eds. P. A. Allison and D. E. G. Briggs, pp. 291–335. Springer, Dordrecht, the Netherlands.

Berryman, H. E. (2002) Disarticulation pattern and tooth mark artifacts associated with pig scavenging of human remains: A case study. In *Advances in Forensic Taphonomy: Method, Theory, and Archaeological Perspectives* Eds. W. D. Haglund and M. H. Sorg, pp. 487–495. CRC Press, Boca Raton, FL.

Betancourt, J. L., T. R. Van Devender, and P. S. Martin (Eds.) (1990) *Packrat Middens: The Last 40,000 Years of Biotic Change.* University of Arizona Press, Tucson, AZ.

Betancourt, J., T. Van Devender, and M. Rose (1986) Comparison of plant macrofossils in woodrat (*Neotoma* sp.) and porcupine (*Erethizon dorsatum*) middens from the western United States. *Journal of Mammalogy* 67:266–273.

Bignell, D. E, Y. Roison, and N. Lo (Eds.) (2010) *Biology of Termites: A Modern Synthesis* (2nd edn.). Springer, Dordrecht, the Netherlands.

Binder, W. J. and B. Van Valkenburgh (2000) Development of bite strength and feeding behaviour in juvenile spotted hyenas (*Crocuta crocuta*). *Journal of Zoology* (London) 252:273–283.

Binford, L. R. (1981) *Bones: Ancient Men and Modern Myths*. Academic Press, New York.

Bischoff-Mattson, Z. and D. Mattson (2009) Effects of simulated mountain lion caching on decomposition of ungulate carcasses. *Western North American Naturalist* 69:343–350.

Blumenschine, R. J. (1986) Carcass consumption sequences and the archaeological distinction of scavenging and hunting. *Journal of Human Evolution* 15:639–659.

Blumenschine, R. J. (1988) An experimental model of the timing of hominid and carnivore influence on archaeological bone assemblages. *Journal of Archaeological Science* 15:483–502.

Boesch, C. (1991) The effects of leopard predation on grouping patterns in forest chimpanzee. *Behaviour* 117:220–242.

Bowyer, R. T. (1983) Osteophagia and antler breakage among Roosevelt elk. *California Fish and Game* 69:84–88.

Brain, C. K. (1980) Some criteria for the recognition of bone-collecting agencies in African caves. In *Fossils in the Making: Vertebrate Taphonomy and Paleoecology* Eds. A. K. Behrensmeyer and A. P. Hill, pp. 107–130. University of Chicago Press, Chicago, IL.

Brain, C. K. (1981) *The Hunters or the Hunted? An Introduction to African Cave Taphonomy*. University of Chicago Press, Chicago, IL.

Brink, J. W. (1997) Fat content in leg bones of *Bison bison*, and applications to archaeology. *Journal of Archaeological Science* 24:259–274.

Brothwell, D. R. (1976) Further evidence of bone chewing by ungulates: The sheep of North Ronaldsay, Orkney. *Journal of Archaeological Science* 3:179–182.

Cáceres, I., M. Esteban-Nadal, M. Bennàsar, and Y. Fernández-Jalvo (2011) Was it the deer or the fox? *Journal of Archaeological Science* 38:2767–2774.

Carlson, A. J. (1940) Eating of bone by the pregnant and lactating gray squirrel. *Science* 91:573.

Carson, E. A., V. H. Stefan, and J. F. Powell (2000) Skeletal manifestations of bear scavenging. *Journal of Forensic Sciences* 45:515–526.

Cavallo, J. A. and R. J. Blumenschine (1989) Tree-stored leopard kills: Expanding the hominid scavenging niche. *Journal of Human Evolution* 18:393–399.

Corbett, J. (1944) *Man-Eaters of Kumaon*. Oxford University Press, Delhi, India.

Coventry, A. F. (1940) The eating of bone by squirrels. *Science* 92:128.

Crader, D. C. (1983) Recent single-carcass bone scatters and the problem of "butchery" sites in the archaeological record. In *Animals and Archaeology: 1. Hunters and their Prey* Eds. J. Clutton-Brock and C. Grigson, pp. 107–141. BAR International Series 163, Oxford, U.K.

Danielson, D. (2005) Bioarchaeological implications concerning the effects of termites (Isoptera) on human osseous remains. *Poster presented at the 70th Annual Meeting of the Society for American Archaeology*, Salt Lake City, UT, 31st March 2005.

Danielson, D. (2006) Bioarchaeological implications concerning the effects of termites (Isoptera) on human osseous remains recovered in Papua New Guinea and the Socialist Republic of Vietnam. *Poster presented at the 71st Annual Meeting of the Society for American Archaeology*, San Juan, Puerto Rico, 28th April 2006.

Delany-Rivera, C., T. W. Plummer, J. A. Hodgson, F. Forrest, F. Hertel, and J. S. Oliver (2009) Pits and pitfalls: Taxonomic variability and patterning in tooth mark dimensions. *Journal of Archaeological Science* 36:2597–2608.

Derry, D. E. (1911) Damage done to skulls and bones by termites. *Nature* 86:245–246.

Dixon, E. J. (1984) Context and environment in taphonomic analysis: Examples from Alaska's Porcupine River caves. *Quaternary Research* 22:201–215.

Domínguez-Rodrigo, M. (1999) Flesh availability and bone modifications in carcasses consumed by lions: Palaeoecological relevance in hominid foraging patterns. *Palaeogeography, Palaeoclimatology, Palaeoecology* 149:373–388.

Domínguez-Solera, S. D. and M. Domínguez-Rodrigo (2009) A taphonomic study of bone modification and of tooth-mark patterns on long limb bone portions by suids. *International Journal of Osteoarchaeology* 19:345–363.

Domínguez-Rodrigo, M. and A. Piqueras (2003) The use of tooth pits to identify carnivore taxa in tooth-marked archaeofaunas and their relevance to reconstruct hominid carcass processing behaviors. *Journal of Archaeological Science* 30:1385–1391.

Duthie, A. G. and J. D. Skinner (1986) Osteophagia in the Cape porcupine *Hystrix africaeaustralis*. *South African Journal of Zoology* 21:316–318.

Einarsen, A. S. (1956) Determination of some predator species by field signs. *Oregon State Monographs Studies in Zoology* 10:1–34.

Elgmork, K. (1982) Caching behavior of brown bears (*Ursus arctos*). *Journal of Mammalogy* 63:607–612.

Erickson, G. M., A. K. Lappin, T. Parker, and K. A. Vliet (2004) Comparison of bite performance between long-term captive and wild American alligators (*Alligator mississippiensis*). *Journal of Zoology* (London) 262:21–28.

Erickson, G. M., S. D. Van Kirk, J. Su, M. E. Levenston, W. E. Caler, and D. R. Carter (1996) Bite-force estimation for *Tyrannosaurus rex* from tooth-marked bones. *Nature* 382:706–708.

Esteban-Nadal, M, I. Cáceres, and P. Fosse (2010) Characterization of a current coprogenic sample originated by *Canis lupus* as a tool for identifying a taphonomic agent. *Journal of Archaeological Science* 37:2959–2970.

Faith, J. T. and A. K. Behrensmeyer (2006) Changing patterns of carnivore modification in a landscape bone assemblage, Amboseli Park, Kenya. *Journal of Archaeological Science* 33:1718–1733.

Fay, J. M., R. Carroll, J. C. Kerbis Peterhans, and D. Harris (1995) Leopard attack on and consumption of gorillas in the Central African Republic. *Journal of Human Evolution* 29:93–99.

Fisher, J. W. (1995) Bone surface modifications in zoo archaeology. *Journal of Archaeological Method and Theory* 2:7–68.

Fuller, T. K. (1989) Denning behavior of wolves in north-central Minnesota. *American Midland Naturalist* 121:181–184.

Galdikas, B. M. F. (1978) Orangutan death and scavenging by pigs. *Science* 200:68–70.

Gehrt, S. D., C. Anchor, and L. A. Whitehome (2009) Range and landscape use of coyotes in a metropolitan landscape: Conflict or coexistence? *Journal of Mammalogy* 90:1045–1057.

Gilmour, R. and M. Skinner (2012) Forensic scatology: Preliminary experimental study of the preparation and potential for identification of captive carnivore scat. *Journal of Forensic Sciences* 57:160–165.

Gobetz, K. E. and D. E. Hattin (2002) Rodent-gnawed carbonate rocks from Indiana. *Proceedings of the Indiana Academy of Science* 1:1–8.

Greenfield, H. J. (1988) Bone consumption by pigs in a contemporary Serbian village: Implications for the interpretation of prehistoric faunal assemblages. *Journal of Field Archaeology* 15:473–479.

Haglund, W. D. (1992) Contribution of rodents to postmortem artifacts of bone and soft tissue. *Journal of Forensic Sciences* 37:1459–1465.

Haglund, W. D. (1997a) Dogs and coyotes: Postmortem involvement with human remains. In *Forensic Taphonomy: The Postmortem Fate of Human Remains* Eds. W. D. Haglund and M. H. Sorg, pp. 367–381. CRC Press, Boca Raton, FL.

Haglund, W. D. (1997b) Rodents and human remains. In *Forensic Taphonomy: The Postmortem Fate of Human Remains* Eds. W. D. Haglund and M. H. Sorg, pp. 405–414. CRC Press, Boca Raton, FL.

Haglund, W. D., D. T. Reay, and D. R. Swindler (1988) Tooth mark artifacts and survival of bones in animal scavenged human skeletons. *Journal of Forensic Sciences* 33:985–997.

Haglund, W. D., D. T. Reay, and D. R. Swindler (1989) Canid scavenging/disarticulation sequence of human remains in the Pacific Northwest. *Journal of Forensic Sciences* 34:587–606.

Harding, B. E. and B. C. Wolf (2006) Alligator attacks in southwest Florida. *Journal of Forensic Sciences* 51:674–677.

Harrison, D. J. and J. R. Gilbert (1985) Denning ecology and movements of coyotes in Maine during pup rearing. *Journal of Mammalogy* 66:712–719.

Hart, D. L. (2002) *Primates as Prey: Ecological, Morphological, and Behavioral Relationships between Primate Species and Their Predators*. Unpublished PhD Dissertation. Washington University, St. Louis, MO.

Hart, D. L. and R. W. Sussman (2008) *Man the Hunted: Primates, Predators, and Human Evolution* (rev. edn.). Westview Press, Cambridge, MA.

Haynes, G. (1980a) Evidence of carnivore gnawing on Pleistocene and Recent mammalian bones. *Paleobiology* 6:341–351.

Haynes, G. (1980b) Prey bones and predators: Potential ecologic information from analysis of bone sites. *Ossa* 7:75–97.

Haynes, G. (1982) Utilization and skeletal disturbances of North American prey carcasses. *Arctic* 35:266–281.

Haynes, G. (1983) A guide to differentiating mammalian carnivore taxa responsible for gnaw damage to herbivore limb bones. *Paleobiology* 9:164–172.

Hidaka, O., M. Iwasaki, M. Saito, and T. Morimoto (1999) Influence of clenching intensity on bite force balance, occlusal contact area, and average bite pressure. *Journal of Dental Research* 78:1336–1344.

Hill, A. (1979) Disarticulation and scattering of mammal skeletons. *Paleobiology* 5:261–274.

Hill, A. (1980) Early postmortem damage to the remains of some contemporary East African mammals. In *Fossils in the Making: Vertebrate Taphonomy and Paleoecology* Eds. A. K. Behrensmeyer and A. P. Hill, pp. 131–152. University of Chicago Press, Chicago, IL.

Hill, A. (1989) Bone modification by modern spotted hyenas. In *Bone Modification* Eds. R. Bonnichsen and M. H. Sorg, pp. 169–178. Center for the Study of the First Americans, Orono, ME.

Hill, A. and A. K. Behrensmeyer (1984) Disarticulation patterns of some modern East African mammals. *Paleobiology* 10:366–376.

Hillson, S. (1986) *Teeth*. Cambridge University Press, Cambridge, U.K.

Horwitz, L. and P. Smith (1988) The effects of striped hyaena activity on human remains. *Journal of Archaeological Science* 15:471–481.

Huchet, J.-B., D. Deverly, B. Gutierrez, and C. Chaucat (2011) Taphonomic evidence of a human skeleton gnawed on by termites in a Moche-civilisation grave at Huaca de la Luna, Peru. *International Journal of Osteoarchaeology* 21:92–102.

Hudson, J. (1993) The impacts of domestic dogs on bone in forager camps; Or, the dog-gone bones. In *From Bones to Behavior: Ethnoarchaeological and Experimental Contributions to the Interpretation of Faunal Remains* Eds. J. Hudson, pp. 301–323. Center for Archaeological Investigations, Occasional Paper No. 21, Southern Illinois University, Carbondale, IL.

Kaiser, T. M. (2000) Proposed fossil insect modification to fossil mammalian bone from Plio-Pleistocene hominid-bearing deposits of Laetoli (Northern Tanzania). *Annals of the Entomological Society of America* 93:693–700.

Kent, S. (1981) The dog: An archaeologist's best friend or worst enemy—the spatial distribution of faunal remains. *Journal of Field Archaeology* 8:367–372.

Kerbis Peterhans, J. C. (1990) *The Roles of Porcupines, Leopards, and Hyenas in Ungulate Carcass Dispersal: Implications for Paleoanthropology*. Unpublished PhD Dissertation, Department of Anthropology, University of Chicago, Chicago, IL.

Kerbis Peterhans, J. C. and T. Gnoske (2001) The science of 'man-eating' among lions *Panthera leo* with a reconstruction of the natural history of the Man-Eaters of Tsavo. *Journal of East African Natural History* 90:1–40.

Kerbis Peterhans, J. C. and L. Horwitz (1992) A preliminary report on a bone assemblage from a striped hyaena den (*Hyaena hyaena*) in the Negev. *Israel Journal of Zoology* 37:225–245.

Kerbis Peterhans, J., R. W. Wrangham, M. L. Carter, and M. D. Hauser (1993) A contribution to tropical rainforest taphonomy: Retrieval and documentation of chimpanzee remains from Kibale Forest, Uganda. *Journal of Human Evolution* 25:485–514.

Kierdorf, U. (1993) Fork formation and other signs of osteophagia on a long bone swallowed by a red deer stag (*Cervus elaphus*). *International Journal of Osteoarchaeology* 3:37–40.

Kierdorf, U. (1994) A further example of long-bone damage due to chewing by deer. *International Journal of Osteoarchaeology* 4:209–213.

Klippel, W. E. and J. A. Synstelien (2007) Rodents as taphonomic agents: Bone gnawing by brown rats and gray squirrels. *Journal of Forensic Sciences* 53:765–773.

Kruuk, H. (1972) *The Spotted Hyaena*. University of Chicago Press, Chicago, IL.

Kruuk, H. (2002) *Hunter and Hunted: Relationships Between Carnivores and People*. Cambridge University Press, Cambridge, U.K.

Kuyt, E. (1972) Food habits of wolves on barren-ground caribou range. *Canadian Wildlife Service, Report Series* 21:1–36.

Lindner, D. L., S. M. Marretta, G. J. Pijanowski, A. L. Johnson, and C. W. Smith (1995) Measurement of bite force in dogs: A pilot study. *Journal of Veterinary Dentistry* 12:49–52.

Lochmiller, R. L., E. C. Hellgren, W. E. Grant, and L. W. Varner (1985) Bone marrow fat and kidney fat indices of condition in collared peccaries. *Journal of Mammalogy* 66:790–795.

Lupo, K. D. (1998) Experimentally derived extraction rates for marrow: Implications for body part exploitation strategies of Plio-Pleistocene hominid scavengers. *Journal of Archaeological Science* 25:657–675.

Lyman, R. L. (1994) *Vertebrate Taphonomy*. Cambridge University Press, Cambridge, U.K.

Lyver, P. O'B. (2000) Identifying mammalian predators from bite marks: A tool for focusing wildlife protection. *Mammal Review* 30:31–44.

Madrigal, T. C. and J. Z. Holt (2002) White-tailed deer meat and marrow return rates and their application to Eastern Woodlands archaeology. *American Antiquity* 67:745–759.

Malcolm, J. R. (1980) Food caching by African wild dog (*Lycaon pictus*). *Journal of Mammalogy* 61:743–744.

Marean, C. W., L. M. Spencer, R. J. Blumenschine, and R. J. Capaldo (1992) Captive hyena bone choice and destruction, the Schlepp effect, and Olduvai archaeofaunas. *Journal of Archaeological Science* 19:101–121.

McLoughlin, P. D., H. D. Cluff, and F. Messier (2002) Denning ecology of barren-ground grizzly bears in the central arctic. *Journal of Mammalogy* 83:188–198.

Mech, L. D. (1970) *The Wolf: The Ecology and Behavior of an Endangered Species*. Natural History Press, Garden City, New York.

Merbs, C. F. (1997) Eskimo skeleton taphonomy with identification of possible polar bear victims. In *Forensic Taphonomy: The Postmortem Fate of Human Remains* Eds. W. D. Haglund and M. H. Sorg, pp. 249–262. CRC Press, Boca Raton, FL.

Miller, G. J. (1969) A study of cuts, grooves, and other marks on recent and fossil bones. 1. Animal tooth marks. *Tebiwa* 12:9–19.

Milner, G. R. and V. G. Smith (1989) Carnivore alteration of human bone from a Late Prehistoric site in Illinois. *American Journal of Physical Anthropology* 79:43–49.

Minetz, J. A. (2010) Rodent gnawing, wildfire, and cultural modification: Using forensic techniques to interpret historic artifacts from the Spencer Site. *Paper presented at the 62nd Annual Meeting of the American Academy of Forensic Sciences*, 24th February 2010, Seattle, WA.

Moraitis, K. and C. Spiliopoulou (2010) Forensic implications of carnivore scavenging on human remains recovered from outdoor locations in Greece. *Journal of Forensic and Legal Medicine* 17:298–303.

Moran, N. C. and T. P. O'Connor (1992) Bones that cats gnawed upon: A case study in bone modification. *Circaea* 9:27–30, 31–34.

Morin, E. (2007) Fat composition and Nunamiut decision-making: A new look at the marrow and bone grease indices. *Journal of Archaeological Science* 34:69–82.

Morton, R. J. and W. D. Lord (2006) Taphonomy of child-sized remains: A study of scattering and scavenging in Virginia, USA. *Journal of Forensic Sciences* 51:475–479.

Murad, T. A. (1997) The utilization of faunal evidence in the recovery of human remains. In *Forensic Taphonomy: The Postmortem Fate of Human Remains* Eds. W. D. Haglund and M. H. Sorg, pp. 395–404. CRC Press, Boca Raton, FL.

Murmann, D. C., P. C. Brumit, B. A. Schrader, and D. R. Senn (2006) A comparison of animal jaws and bite mark patterns. *Journal of Forensic Sciences* 51:846–860.

Osborn, D. J. and I. Helmy (1980) *The Contemporary Land Mammals of Egypt (Including Sinai).* Fieldiana: Zoology, New Series, No. 5, Chicago, IL.

Patel, F. (1994) Artefact in forensic medicine: Postmortem rodent activity. *Journal of Forensic Sciences* 39:257–260.

Patterson, J. H. (1996) *The Man-Eating Lions of Tsavo.* Field Museum, Chicago, IL.

Payne, S. B. (1983) Bones from cave sites: Who ate what? In *Animals and Archaeology: 1. Hunters and Their Prey* Eds. J. Clutton-Brock and C. Grigson, pp. 149–162. BAR International Series 163, Oxford, U.K.

Payne, S. B. and P. J. Munson (1985) Ruby and how many squirrels? The destruction of bones by dogs. In *Paleobiological Investigations: Research Design, Methods, and Data Analysis* Eds. N. R. J. Feller, D. D. Gilbertson, and N. G. A. Ralph, pp. 31–40. BAR International Series 266, Oxford, U.K.

Peterson, R. O. (1977) *Wolf Ecology and Prey Relationships on Isle Royale.* U.S. National Park Service Scientific Monograph Series No. 11, Washington, DC.

Phillips, J. A. (1993) Bone consumption by cheetahs at undisturbed kills: Evidence for a lack of focal-palatine erosion. *Journal of Mammalogy* 74:487–492.

Pickering, T. R. (2001) Carnivore voiding: A taphonomic process with the potential for the decomposition of forensic evidence. *Journal of Forensic Sciences* 46:406–411.

Pickering, T. R. and K. J. Carlson (2004) Baboon taphonomy and its relevance to the investigation of large felid involvement in human forensic cases. *Forensic Science International* 144:37–44.

Pierce, B. M., V. C. Bleich, C.-L. B. Chetkiewcza, and D. Wehausen (1998) Timing of feeding bouts of mountain lions. *Journal of Mammalogy* 79:222–226.

Pobiner, B. L. (2007) *Hominin-Carnivore Interactions: Evidence from Modern Carnivore Bone Modification and Early Pleistocene Archaeofaunas (Koobi Fora, Kenya; Olduvai Gorge, Tanzania).* Unpublished PhD Dissertation, Department of Anthropology, Rutgers University, Newark, NJ.

Pobiner, B. L. (2008) Paleoecological information from predator tooth marks. *Journal of Taphonomy* 6:373–397.

Pobiner, B. L. and R. J. Blumenschine (2003) A taphonomic perspective on the Oldowan hominid encroachment on the carnivoran paleoguild. *Journal of Taphonomy* 1:115–141.

Pokines, J. T. and J. C. Kerbis Peterhans (2007) Spotted hyena (*Crocuta crocuta*) den use and taphonomy in the Masai Mara National Reserve, Kenya. *Journal of Archaeological Science* 34:1914–1931.

Richardson, P. R. K. (1980) Carnivore damage to bones and its archeological implications. *Palaeontologia Africana* 23:109–125.

Roze, U. (2009) *The North American Porcupine* (2nd edn.). Cornell University Press, Ithaca, New York.

Schmitt, D. N. and K. E. Juell (1994) Toward the identification of coyote scatological faunal accumulations in archaeological contexts. *Journal of Archaeological Science* 21:249–262.

Searfoss, G. (1995) *Skulls and Bones: A Guide to the Skeletal Structures and Behavior of North American Mammals.* Stackpole Books, Mechanicsburg, PA.

Simons, J. W. (1966) The presence of leopard and a study of the food debris in the leopard lairs of the Mount Suswa Caves, Kenya. *Bulletin, Cave Exploration Group of East Africa* 1:51–69.

Smith, C. F. (1948) A burrow of the pocket gopher (*Geomys bursarius*) in eastern Kansas. *Transactions of the Kansas Academy of Science* 51:313–315.

Steadman, D. W. and H. Worne (2007) Canine scavenging of human remains in an indoor setting. *Forensic Science International* 173:78–82.

Stiner, M. C. (1994) *Honor Among Thieves: A Zooarchaeological Study of Neandertal Ecology.* Princeton University Press, Princeton, NJ.

Sutcliffe, A. J. (1973) Similarity of bones and antlers gnawed by deer to human artefacts. *Nature* 246:428–430.

Sutcliffe, A. J. (1977) Further notes on bones and antlers chewed by deer and other ungulates. *Deer* 4:73–82.

Tappen, M. (1995) Savanna ecology and natural bone deposition: Implications for early hominid site formation, hunting, and scavenging. *Current Anthropology* 36:223–260.

Thiel, R. P., S. Merrill, and L. D. Mech (1998) Tolerance by denning wolves, *Canis lupus*, to human disturbance. *Canadian Field-Naturalist* 122:340–342.

Thorne, B. L. and R. B. Kimsey (1983) Attraction of Neotropical *Nasutitermes* termites to carrion. *Biotropica* 15:295–296.

Treves, A. and L. Naughton-Treves (1999) Risk and opportunity for humans coexisting with large carnivores. *Journal of Human Evolution* 36:275–282.

Tsokos, M., J. Matschke, A. Gehl, E. Koops, and K. Puschel (1999) Skin and soft tissue artifacts due to postmortem damage caused by rodents. *Forensic Science International* 104:47–57.

Watson, J. A. L. and H. M. Abbey (1986) The effects of termites (Isoptera) on Bone: Some archeological implications. *Sociobiology* 11:245–254.

Wilcox, J. T. and D. H. Van Vuren (2009) Wild pigs as predators in oak woodlands of California. *Journal of Mammalogy* 90:114–118.

Willey, P. and L. M. Snyder (1989) Canid modification of human remains: Implications for time-since-death estimations. *Journal of Forensic Sciences* 34:894–901.

Wilson, D. E. and D. M. Reeder (Eds.) (2005) *Mammal Species of the World* (3rd edn.). The Johns Hopkins University, Baltimore, MD.

Woods, C. A. (1973) Erethizon dorsatum. *Mammalian Species* 29:1–6.

Wroe, S., D. R. Huber, M. Lowry, C. McHenry, K. Moreno, P. Clausen, T. L. Ferrara, E. Cunningham, M. N. Dean, and A. P. Summers (2008) Three-dimensional computer analysis of white shark jaw mechanics: How hard can a great white bite? *Journal of Zoology* (London) 276:336–342.

Wroe, S., C. McHenry and J. Thomason (2005) Bite club: Comparative bite force in big biting mammals and the prediction of predatory behavior in fossil taxa. *Proceedings of the Royal Society B: Biological Sciences* 272(1563):619–625.

Wyatt, J. R. (1971) Osteophagia in Masai giraffe. *African Journal of Ecology* 9:157.

Deposition and Dispersal of Human Remains as a Result of Criminal Acts

Homo sapiens sapiens as a Taphonomic Agent

10

DEREK CONGRAM

Contents

> The mopping-up operations practiced by the Black Squads have an evocative name: el paseo ["the stroll"]. They are carried out to such a characteristic pattern that one can talk of a method.
> —**Couffon, in Gibson (1973:73)**

Introduction

Scavenging behavior of human remains by wild and domestic animals has been widely researched (see Chapter 9, this volume). Likewise, the natural decomposition processes of human remains have received much scientific attention in the form of forensic case reports (e.g., Bucheli et al. 2009; Prieto et al. 2004; Ross and Cunningham 2011) and through such research institutions as the University of Tennessee's Anthropology Research Facility (e.g., Mann et al. 1990; Vass 2011; see also Chapter 3, this volume). Despite these advances, the variable that arguably accounts for the most destructive effects upon human remains and that which most frustrates human remains recovery and identification is that of deliberate dispersal and disposal behavior by *Homo sapiens sapiens*. Considering this, there is remarkably little forensic anthropological study of *H. sapiens sapiens* as a taphonomic agent. This situation is surprising, given early definitions of anthropology as a scientific study of "man as an animal" (*Oxford English Dictionary* 2011).

This chapter examines how people dispose of and disperse the remains of other people in different criminal contexts and the geographic or geometric taphonomic signature of such behavior. In essence, this chapter examines ecological behavior of humans relative to a sociopolitical niche that is quite unique to humans (e.g., killing conspecifics is, generally, very actively discouraged and severely punished when it occurs during peacetime, whereas it is actively encouraged during armed conflict). This chapter presents recent research conducted by the author (Congram 2010) on the locations of unmarked mass burials of civilians who were victims of summary execution by the rearguard of the Spanish Civil War (1936–1939). Different contexts and categories of body disposal are discussed, and the characteristics of body disposal sites are examined relative to different cultural and geographic variables such as populated areas and degree of ground cover. This chapter adopts a geographic approach by employing spatial analysis to examine trends in disposal behavior and will reference observations from other modern criminal investigative contexts including individual and serial murder in several countries.

The aim of this chapter is to understand better this intraspecies predatory behavior, as a means of improving methods of body search and recovery, and ultimately the identification of both the offender and the victim. In an effort to move beyond anecdote and the linking of seeming cross-context coincidences, this chapter will demonstrate that predatory behavior by *H. sapiens sapiens* is often constrained by multiple measurable factors and results in predictable, limited disposal and dispersal patterns.

Study of *H. sapiens sapiens* as a Taphonomic Agent

In a forensic context, Haglund et al. (2001) warn against interpreting human behavior and processes, instructing that forensic anthropologists should document only facts and give defensible expert opinion (2001:67). What constitutes fact and defensible expert opinion, however, is debatable and dependent upon the onus of proof of a legal jurisdiction or the forum in which forensic anthropological evidence is presented. I argue that not only are forensic anthropologists potentially qualified to make certain interpretations about human behavior based on contextual, artifactual, spatial, relational, and taphonomic variables, but also that they should. Anthropological training and experience as the study of people generally enables one to do so with sufficient skill, depending on the context and circumstances of the case and question at hand. Competently analyzing and commenting on human behavior and processes may answer critical questions related to forensic death investigation, body identification, and if applicable offender location or identification.

There are sensible reasons why anthropologists generally do not incorporate the social and behavioral study of people into their forensic practice. One reason is that forensic anthropologists are physical anthropologists; their focus on the skeleton is largely biological, not sociocultural. When one, however, considers the forensic anthropologist as a bioarchaeologist (Skinner et al. 2003), the study of sociocultural behavior and its impact on the skeleton is much more apropos.

A serious consideration for the lack of sociocultural research by forensic anthropologists is the pressure for experts to employ tested methods and quantifiable results, particularly in light of recent judgments (e.g., Daubert v. *Merrell Dow Pharmaceuticals*). Some forensic anthropological methods conform to evidentiary standards of the admissibility of scientific evidence; for example, calculating stature from long bones is generally straightforward, and point estimates are accompanied by a prediction interval. This seems to be what Haglund et al. (2001) were driving at when they warned against interpreting human behavior and advocated only the reporting of facts: avoid speculation about things of which you are uncertain and cannot be certain. Conclusions about human behavior are grounded in social sciences, whereas conventional forensic anthropology is mostly about biological science. Nevertheless, as forensic anthropologists have been employed in different contexts, or have found themselves being asked different questions by investigative agencies, they are beginning to incorporate conventional anthropological practice that studies social behavior into the forensic realm. One example of this is the examination of material culture by anthropologists as a line of both physical and cultural evidence (e.g., Baraybar 2008; Komar and Lathrop 2008; Maeyama and Fernández-Congram 2008; Skinner et al. 2009).

Patterns of Body Disposal during Armed Conflict

In the past 30 years, forensic anthropologists have increasingly been involved in large-scale investigations of genocide, crimes against humanity, and war crimes that have required them to locate and excavate clandestine mass graves (Steadman and Haglund 2005). These types of graves can include mass burials of battle casualties (e.g., Skinner 2007; Wessling and Loe 2011), executed prisoners of war (POWs), including combatants (e.g., Kamenetsky 1989), mass killings of civilians (e.g., Browning 1998; Flavel and Barker 2009), or a combination of these in a single burial, at a single burial site with multiple graves, and/or across a broader temporal and geographic area (e.g., Congram and Sterenberg 2009:441, 442; Skinner et al. 2002). Despite this increasing involvement, the work has been very task-oriented, and there has been disappointingly little published anthropological analysis of data derived from these types of investigations. One reason for the lack of available literature and research is due to the evidence related to mass graves being used in ongoing trials of people responsible for the killings, such as the recently arrested (May 2011) former Bosnian Serb military general Ratko Mladić at the International Criminal Tribunal for the former Yugoslavia (ICTY). Until criminal trials have concluded—and they may take several years each, particularly if the detention of an accused is not immediate as in the case of Mladić—prosecutors are wont to make evidence (i.e., data) available for scientific scrutiny.

WWII Mass Grave Investigations

The lack of information and analysis is also true for those victims buried in mass graves from the WWII era, despite the atrocious numbers of victims and the relatively long time passed since both the events and the subsequent Nuremberg trials of political and military leaders. The most obvious reason for this lack is that millions of victims of the Nazi extermination policy were not buried at all but cremated at internment camps (Ball 1999:41). However, internment camp exterminations were preceded by systematic mass shootings and burial by the Nazis, particularly in Eastern Europe and Russia. Some information is available for cursory analysis, although mostly via witness testimony and documentary evidence (e.g., Browning 1998; Desbois 2008; Rhodes 2002), not from systematic grave excavations. Another reason for a lack of grave excavations in Europe may relate to continuing political sensitivity about the crimes. In Estonia, for example, the killing of Gypsies was so pervasive that almost no group members survived to call for social or legal justice, and although the Germans orchestrated and implemented the killings, many Estonians of the time considered the Gypsies an annoyance and had wished for their elimination (although not necessarily their extermination) (Weiss-Wendt 2003).

Accounts of WWII-era grave excavations do exist, but many lack detail, are anecdotal, are limited to single burials, or the identification of victims and/or offenders are uncertain (e.g., Gojanović and Sutlović 2007; Mark 2010 on Romania; Palo et al. 2007; Raszeja and Chróścielewski 1994; Susa 2007 on Hungary). Despite an entire text being dedicated to the "archaeology of twentieth century conflict" and much attention given to WWII (Schofield et al. 2002), there is no mention of grave excavations from the war. Immediately following World War II, Mant (1987) led the opening of several mass burials for the purpose of collecting evidence for the Nuremberg trials, but observations made by Mant related mostly to taphonomic factors related to human decomposition, which was the topic of his medical degree thesis.

Eastern European concentration camps and Natzweiler in France were destroyed as Nazis fled Allied advances, in an attempt to hide evidence of the camps' existence (Beech 2002:201; Rees 2005:194). Forests were planted over the destroyed sites at Belzec, Treblinka, and Sobibor (Rhodes 2002:265). This is an important observation for those investigating missing persons: the sociopolitical sensitivity of killings may lead offenders to destroy, or disguise—so far as is possible—traces of the killings and body disposal sites.

Other reasons for a dearth of grave excavations include a lack of political desire to confront the past (e.g., Beech 2002:206; Walston 1997), Jewish religious prohibitions related to the "disturbance" of the dead (Wolentarska-Ochman 2006), lack or unreliability of witnesses, financial constraints (Maver n.d.), and fear of reviving interethnic rivalry (Bax 1997). Access to archives and documents, particularly those in the custody of the former USSR, was severely restricted until recently, although Desbois (2008) reports that postwar Soviet commissions created 16 million pages of documentation of Nazi crimes and often opened victim mass burials to verify the testimonies of the killings (p. 173, footnote 4 of Chapter 5). A copy of these archives exists in the U.S. Holocaust Memorial Museum. Lack of access to information in the custody of the Russians is also a factor in the case of the Spanish Civil War, where archives from toward the end of the war were confiscated by the Soviets, who heavily supported the Republicans and prevented documents from public review until recently (Petrou 2005). On the other side of the conflict in Spain, the postwar dictatorship ensured that the Nationalist narrative of the war dominated, extolling a single offender (the Republicans), grossly exaggerating the number of Nationalist victims, and seriously understating their own culpability and the scale of Nationalist killings (Badcock 2005:69; Espinosa 2006:95–97; Graham 2005:133; Richards 2007). To maintain this narrative, access to Nationalist archives from the war and postwar repression that were not destroyed has been severely restricted (Espinosa 2006:5, 6, 318; Reig Tapia 1979; Ruíz 2009).

Despite all of the earlier explanations for a lack of comparable and analyzable data, there are a couple of unusual and fascinating examples of mass grave excavations and exhumations led by the Nazi Germans during WWII. Probably the earliest controlled excavation of mass burials for medico-legal (and political) purposes was conducted by representatives of the Nazi Third Reich in 1942 and 1943 in German-occupied Poland and Ukraine. The excavations were at times conducted with international medico-legal experts and representatives of the Red Cross as witnesses with the purpose of documenting mass executions committed by the Soviets only a few years prior (Kamenetsky 1989), and these are discussed in greater detail in the following text.

In 1990 and 1991, mass graves were excavated as part of an investigation of Nazi crimes (Wright et al. 2005). These investigations were conducted by a joint Australian and Soviet team, employing Australian archaeologist Richard Wright to excavate WWII mass burials of Jewish victims at Serniki and Ustinovka, Ukraine. Evidence indicated that the victims had been murdered by the Nazis 1 year *before* the Nazi-led exhumations and their accusations of Soviet mass murder described earlier.

Site Selection Decision Factors

Patterns of victim body disposal likely exist in the context of armed conflict for three reasons: resources are generally limited, especially personnel and equipment; geographic constraining factors—particularly when the number of victims is in the thousands; and sociopolitical factors that influence whether killings and victims will be hidden or, less commonly, made public as an example to others. The extent to which body disposal patterns are consistent within and between contexts, however, is unknown. A systematic study comparing these events has not previously been published, but a cursory analysis of publications and personal experience suggests that logistics and the sensitivity of the killings (based in part on victim identity and the sociopolitical context) are the two primary factors that determine where and how killers dispose of victim bodies. The presence of labor to dig graves, locations to which the typically large groups of victims can be transported, and the availability of preexisting features for burial are all logistical considerations that appear to factor strongly in killer decisions about where and how to dispose of victim bodies. The logistics of mass body disposal also include the necessity of detaining victim groups; preparing or locating suitable body disposal sites; moving victims to detention, execution, and disposal sites; and arranging personnel to gather, guard, transport, and then kill. All of these things generally must occur within a limited geographic area that has constraints including but not limited to transportation infrastructure, topography (e.g., mountainous areas), geology (e.g., exposed bedrock preventing burial), bodies of water, and secure territory under the control of those conducting the killings. Kalyvas (2006) notes that "war entails more constraints and less consent... [and] the stakes are incomparably higher for everyone involved" (2006:38), and so killer options with respect to body disposal are generally quite limited unless a significant proportion of the power of a state is available and applied toward the task (e.g., Nazi Germany). In other cases where states have committed their resources toward large-scale noncombatant murder and body disposal, the worst crimes appear to have occurred while war was either pending or just ending, thus enabling the mobilization of resources for noncombat activity (e.g., the Soviet Union in 1937 and 1938 or Iraq under the Baath Party and their purge of the Kurdish population following the Iran–Iraq war).

Given the horrendous scale of the killings and the typically limited resources of the killers during active armed conflict, logistics play a major role in how and where victims are disposed. Rhodes (2002:xi–xii) comments on the role of the Nazi *Einsatzgruppen*—Nazi paramilitary death squads—who were tasked with eliminating Jews and other "enemies" in the rearguard in Eastern Europe and Russia: "their assignment was to murder Jews, not indirectly by herding them into gas chambers but directly, by *shooting them into antitank ditches, natural ravines or pits freshly dug by Russian prisoners of war...* the *Einsatzgruppen* massacres preceded the invention of the death camps and significantly influenced their development" [emphasis added].

An example of sociopolitical sensitivity during WWII is given by Browning (1998), who cites an order by Nazi Colonel Max Montua regarding executions of Jews in Poland: "The shootings are to take place away from cities, villages, and thoroughfares. The graves are to be leveled in such a way no pilgrimage site can arise. I forbid photographing and the permitting of spectators at the executions. Executions and grave sites are not to be made known." In many instances, selecting burial sites at or just outside of prisons or military installations served the dual purposes of ensuring against investigation of the killings as well as making victim transport to burial sites logistically simple, as these places are where the victims were often detained and killed. There are many instances of victims being buried at military facilities in various conflicts, including the Orchard site in Vinnytsia described later, in Iraq (Human Rights Watch 2004), Bosnia (Berman 2003), Kosovo (Jennings 2009), Guatemala (AP 2003), and Serbia (ICMP 2004), to name only a few.

Body Disposal Methods

A disturbingly common question that forensic anthropologists tend to hear is "So, what is the best way to get rid of a body?" In fact, we do not know. It stands to reason that the "best," to follow the line of thought of the questioner, is that which goes undiscovered. As such, the best method evades detection. The most common method, however, appears to be burial. Nevertheless, other body disposal methods are employed besides burial.

Surface Deposition and the Use of Preexisting Features   In some instances, the twin parameters of discretion and logistics work against each other. The desire to kill in an area of heavy cover (e.g., forest) can preclude one's ability to bury at the same location because of an abundance of tree roots and inaccessibility of the location to heavy machinery to dig large graves. It is unknown if this was the reason that victims were not buried, for example, in the initial killings in July 1942 by Nazi paramilitary (German Reserve Police Battalion 101) in occupied Poland at Józefów. Burial of subsequent mass killing victims by the same unit, however, suggests that this is so, as with the September 1942 mass killing of Jews from Serokomla at an open quarry and waste dump in Poland (see Table 10.1).

One of the clearer examples of the importance of logistics is the massacre of almost 34,000 Jewish men, women, and children by a few hundred members of *Einsatzgruppe* C in September 1941. When the Germans defeated the Soviets at Kiev, they took the Jewish population to a ravine called Babi Yar on the western edge of Kiev, where they were shot. The task of so few soldiers killing and burying so many was so great that a use of a pre-existing feature as a grave was necessary. With a summer of experience in mass killing behind them, the *Einsatzgruppen* "had become expert at picking killing sites; Babi Yar

Table 10.1 WWII Mass Burial Characteristics

Site	Site Type	No. of Graves	Victims	Offender	Victims	Circumstances of Death	Killed at Burial Loc.?	Distance from Populated Area	Site Disguised Post-Killing?	Grave Features	Additional Observations
Vinnytsia 1, Ukraine	Orchard, NKVD shooting range	34	5644 (53 females)	Soviets, NKVD	Civilians; Mostly Ukrainians, also	Mostly execution at back of neck/head by small caliber pistol, 1938–1939	No	1.8 km	Yes (fenced, guarded)	~2–3.8 m in depth; often a layer of clothing and clothing over bodies	Bodies examined in situ 1943; winter clothing suggests killings in winter; site 1: bodies laid out neatly unlike sites 2 and 3; hands, elbows, or upper arms of men bound behind back with twine
Vinnytsia 2, Ukraine	Former Orthodox cemetery	40 (+2 empty)	2405 (85 females)		Russians, Jews, Gypsies, Poles		No	600 m		possessions over bodies; lime over bodies	
Vinnytsia 3, Ukraine	Park, outside NKVD prison	13 found, poss. more graves	≥2583 (31 females)				No	North of Vinnytsia 2			
Katyn, Russia	Forest by NKVD "rest house"	8	4599	Soviets, NKVD	Polish troops, officers, and civilians (POWs)	February–May 1940, mostly executed at back of neck/head by 7.65 mm caliber pistol at NKVD prison in Smolensk and abattoir; 3.5%–4.7% had blunt force skull trauma	Some	Smolensk to Katyn Forest ca. 15 km; 6.5 km from Gnezdovo train stn.; 1.2 km from main road	Pine, fir, or birch trees planted over graves (reports differ)	1.8–3.4 m deep; bodies stacked neatly in 12 layers; graves prepared in advance	Investigated by Nazis in 1943, vic. hands generally tied behind backs, blunt force and stab trauma to some; sand over bodies helped to mummify; killers given vodka

(continued)

Table 10.1 (continued) WWII Mass Burial Characteristics

Site	Site Type	No. of Graves	Victims	Offender	Victims	Circumstances of Death	Killed at Burial Loc.?	Distance from Populated Area	Site Disguised Post-Killing?	Grave Features	Additional Observations
Ulla, Belarus	Field	≥26	800–1000, exhumations suspended before complete	Nazis	Mostly Polish, ~200 Jews, a few Lithuanians, mostly middle–upper class	June 27, 1941; prisoners were being marched when Soviet base came under German air attack. Prisoners were told to take cover in a field and then shot	Yes	Within 1 km of small town of Ulla, near Nikolayev			Buried by inhabitants of Nikolayev under order of the NKVD
Serniki, Ukraine		1	553 Jews: 407 female; 98 male; 48 undetermined according to cranial features	Nazis	Jewish civilians	September 1942; 74% gunshot to head; 1.8% depressed skull trauma; 24% undetermined cause of death; many appear shot by 9 mm handguns; apparently two groups killed differently, buried together	Yes	3 km		Grave prepared in advance	Bodies examined in situ and not removed from grave; some bodies clothed, others not and clothing found in overburden
Ustinovka, Ukraine		1	19 children, 100–150 adults	Nazis	Jewish civilians	1942	Yes			Two layers of bodies: children; 20 cm soil; adults	Ramped grave
Bialystok, Poland	Forested area outside the city		>3000	German Reserve Police Batts.	Local Jewish civilians		Yes				

Józefów, Poland	Forest	0	1500	German Reserve Police Batt. 101	Local Jewish civilians	July 13, 1942	Yes	Several km from the city	Victims left on surface	Batt. physician instructed shooters on how to shoot to kill: aiming with bayonet at back of neck; bodies left lying on surface in forest, not buried
Łomazy, Poland	Forest	1	1700	Hiwis, Trawnikis[a] German Reserve Police Batt. 101, 2nd Co.	Local Jewish civilians	August 17, 1942		1 km from city	Local Jews were forced to dig the grave, ramped grave	Victims were forced to undress; shooters were drunk
Serokomla, Poland	Gravel pits and waste dump	0	200–300	German Reserve Police Batt. 101, 1st and 3rd Co.		September 1942	0	<1 km from city	Victims not buried	
Miedzyrec, Poland	Cemetery		Local Jewish civilians; ~150 mostly women and children			October 3, 1942: victims did not fit on a deportation train. Were shot in groups of 20, men first, then women and children				Shooters were given vodka prior to shootings

could have swallowed the entire population of Kiev" (Rhodes 2002:173). At the end of each day of killings, workers shoveled sand down the ravine walls to cover the bodies. After 3 full days of killings, the walls of the ravine were dynamited, burying the victims (Rhodes 2002:178).

This pattern of using preexisting features as execution and burial sites is very common—in WWII (e.g., Desbois 2008:209), the Spanish Civil War (e.g., Herrero Balsa and Hernández García 1982; Silva and Macías 2003), the Balkan wars of the 1990s (Human Rights Watch 1997; Manning 2000; Simmons 2002; Wright 2010), Colombia (El Tiempo 2007; Gómez-López and Patiño Umaña 2007), and others—and typically indicates not only that a massacre was intended, but that it was planned in advance (Browning 1998; Rhodes 2002).

Not in all instances where preexisting features were used were the victims subsequently buried. There are many examples of bodies simply being thrown in wells, including in Kosovo (e.g., Hirz 1999; Lecomte and Vorhauer 1999; OSCE 1999) and Guatemala (e.g., Flavel and Barker 2009). A further category that lies somewhere between "surface deposit" and "burial" includes the disposal of bodies into rivers, as during the Spanish Civil War (Herrero Balsa and Hernández García 1982; Zavala 2006) and in Columbia (El Tiempo 2007), and out of airplanes over the ocean as during Argentina's "Dirty War" (Tremlett 2005).

Understanding these methods of body disposal is rather complicated. The action of throwing a murdered victim into a body of water generally requires little effort. The possibility of victim's body discovery, however, can be great, as at certain postmortem stages, bodies can float and wash ashore (see Chapter 6, this volume). Body disposal in wells almost guarantees discovery in the cases where wells are common public places. In the case of victims thrown out of airplanes off the coast of Argentina, however, the disposal method over water appears to have been very deliberate, with weights attached to victims' feet to prevent their floating to the surface, and victims thrown out at great heights (Tremlett 2005), perhaps to cause more damage to the body and prevent identification.

Mass Burial in Graves   Surprisingly good evidence of mass killings and burials in Poland, Ukraine, and Belarus is available from a series of Nazi-led exhumations in June–September, 1943. The Germans, blaming the Soviets for the deaths, widely distributed details about the events as part of a propaganda campaign designed to mobilize public opinion in favor of the Nazis and against the Soviets, the territory having been under the control of both groups at various times before and throughout the war. Dozens of mass graves were excavated, and the victims were examined by German scientists. These excavations were monitored by members of an international investigations commission from 13 European countries. In Ulla, Belarus, it is interesting to note that exhumations were stopped prematurely when the Nazis discovered that the victims were Poles and not Latvians (as they had previously suspected). The Nazis had been trying to gain political and military support from the Latvians against the Russians (Kamenetsky 1989:33–34). Kamenetsky claims that these three sites in Eastern Europe are the best-documented of Soviet secret police force (NKVD) executions and mass graves. Despite the age of the documentation (in and around 1943) and the overtly political motivation of the exhumations, they represent among the best publicly available data on mass grave excavations to date.

Graves at Vinnytsia, Ukraine, are reported to have been between 2 and 3.8 m deep (Kamenetsky 1989:97–98). There was often a layer of clothing and sometimes other personal artifacts found above the level of the bodies, suggesting that some of the victims had been stripped—perhaps to rob them of valuables—before being killed. In total, 9432 bodies were exhumed from 86–87 mass graves (numbers differ according to various reports), with all the victims civilians so far as could be determined from clothing. The German government report reproduced by Kamenetsky (1989:91–141) also makes observations about the use of lime and other taphonomic aspects of the victims and graves, including the formation of adipocere, which was used to estimate a minimum postmortem interval (PMI). The author noted the important fact that victims exhumed from graves at Vinnytsia were shot at close range in the back of the head and neck and had their hands bound behind their backs, with rope tied by knots the same as those found at Katyn, Poland (1989:34). Some victims (3.5%–4.7% ranging across three sites) had crushing skull trauma, probably from being hit with rifle butts (1989:116–117). The German Forensic Medical Report notes, however, that the method of binding differed somewhat in certain cases from Katyn, where victims had been tied at the elbows. The vast majority of the victims exhumed in these cases were male, all but one of whom were bound. Women were not tied.

Allen (2010) (see also FitzGibbon 1971, 1975; Raszeja and Chróścielewski 1994) relates that over 4000 bodies were exhumed from graves at Katyn. Seven mass graves found in March 1943 held the bodies of Polish Army officers and other civilians (men and women), 2730 of whom were identified via documentation found with the individual bodies (FitzGibbon 1971:146). The largest grave was L-shaped and measured 26 m long and 8 m at its widest point. In it were 12 layers of approximately 2800 bodies, neatly stacked and with heads and feet alternating. The vast majority were executed by a gunshot to the back of the neck at the base of the skull, using 7.65 mm pistol ammunition. The graves were between 1.8 and 3.4 m deep (Allen 2010:110–112). Evidence of broken jaws and stab wounds, presumably suffered prior to being shot, were also noted. FitzGibbon (1971:140) goes on to quote the police report: "From the position of the bodies it may be assumed that the majority were murdered outside the graves. The bodies were in a complete tangle, except in graves Nos. 1, 2 and 4, where some of them lay side by side or on the top of each other... Very many of the dead had their hands tied behind their back." According to the reports discussed by Kamenetsky (1989), a general lack of shell casings at the sites led the investigators to the conclusion, supported by local witness testimony, that the executions had occurred at prisons. Documents showed that the Ukrainian victims were killed in a garage that had a special sewer to drain away the blood. Executions at one location and mass burial at another are therefore consistent with the testimony given about the killings at Katyn. This and other features of the burials demonstrate a common modus operandi by Soviet forces, which unsurprisingly suggests a coordinated effort.

Of primary relevance to this research is the location of these mass burials, as well as the fact that the burial site was often not the site of the killings. Kamenetsky (1989) reports that the Soviets wanted to give the survivor population the impression that the prisoners had actually been sent to corrective labor camps. The killings were apparently conducted with much secrecy, although that thousands could be executed in such a short time to the complete ignorance of the local populace is somewhat dubious. In Vinnytsia, there were three burial sites, each with multiple mass graves. One site was in an orchard approximately 2 km from the city center, which at the time of the killings was being used as a shooting range by the NKVD. A second site was at the edge of a former (then in disuse) Orthodox Cemetery about 600 m from the city center. A third site bordered an NKVD prison, slightly further than the second site from the city center.

The work conducted in 1990 and 1991 by the Australians and Soviets was subject to publication limitations for judicial reasons, but different accounts about the two Ukrainian sites investigated do exist from which we know the following.

At Ustinovka, there were two layers to the mass grave. The uppermost layer held 19 children, beneath which was about 20 cm of fill, then 100–150 adults (Quantum 2000; Wright 1995). The stratigraphic sequence of bodies indicates that adults were killed first, then the children. That soil was placed on top of the bodies of the adults suggests that the children were not present when the adults were killed. This layering of bodies—representing the shooting of individual groups of victims, which were covered by soil prior to the delivery and execution of a subsequent group of victims—is a method that also was sometimes employed by the Nazis in Poland (Browning 1998).

The grave had a ramp, which according to a witness was used by victims to walk into the grave before being shot. Browning (1998) reports the same feature in some graves created by the Nazis in Poland. The position of the bodies contrasted at the two different ends of the Serniki grave: at the end farthest from the ramp, victims were found lying parallel to one another, face down and in rows where they had been shot in the backs of their heads (Wright 1995; Wright et al. 2005:144). A smaller number of bodies were lying in the grave in a much more disorganized fashion at the base of the ramp, consistent with a witness statement that most victims had been lying down when shot, while others who arrived in a later group were beaten with clubs and thrown into the grave (Wright 2010). Bevan (1994:58–59) reports 410 of 553 (74%) victims with gunshot trauma to the head, 10 (1.8%) with depressed skull fractures, and 133 (24%) with undetermined cause of death. It is important to note that full exhumations and autopsies were not performed on these bodies; only skulls were examined and in situ. Bevan also mentions that many appeared to have been shot with German 9 mm (hand gun) ammunition. The two different body deposition types in the grave and the prevalence of cranial trauma at the base of the ramp indicate a diachronic change in the killings. This change is consistent with reports by Browning (1998) of Nazi killings in Poland showing increasing killer impatience and sadism, fuelled in part by alcohol, as killings progressed. A further change in victim treatment was observed by Wright (1995) at the grave at Ustinovka, where only some victims were wearing remaining pieces of clothing (parts having degraded over time), but clothing presumably from other, undressed victims had been found throughout the overburden, suggesting that it had been picked through and thrown in during the backfilling of the grave. Changes in victim treatment and killing at a single site complicate the search for commonalities among mass grave patterns but at the same time indicate patterns in human behavior when similar series of events are observed elsewhere. At both Ustinovka and Serniki, it was determined that the Nazis were responsible for the killings (Wright 1995). Bevan (1994:59) also notes that based on examinations of the skulls at Serniki, 407 of the bodies were estimated to be female, 98 male, and 48 undetermined. Possible explanations for this unusual demographic is that males were deported to work as slave labor for the Nazi war effort, or that males were killed separately, both of which often occurred during Nazi occupation (see Browning 1998).

Burning of Bodies   Burning of victim bodies is not uncommon in domestic and armed conflict contexts. Nevertheless, it is a costly method, since destruction of bodies is not easily accomplished by fire (see Chapter 14, this volume; Warren and Maples 1997). Burning of bodies was a more elaborate means of disposal at the beginning of the Spanish Civil War (Reig Tapia 2006:529). This method was notoriously employed on the victims of the Badajoz massacre, where, in 1936, thousands of prisoners were machine-gunned in the city bullring. The killing and burning of bodies at a local cemetery were reported and photographed by several foreign journalists, creating international alarm over the mass executions (Espinosa 2006; Pons Prades 2006). Influential countries including the United Kingdom, United States, and France were officially neutral during the Spanish Civil War, and to a degree, they limited or prohibited supplies from outside Spain reaching either party in the conflict. Recognizing that what was planned as a military coup was turning into a civil war and that resources such as fuel were in short supply, the Nationalists were keen to avoid negative publicity from massacres that might move other countries to support the Republicans. After Badajoz, the Nationalists seem to have turned to a different program of detention and smaller-scale but still systematic killings followed by victim burial as the primary body disposal method.* Other sources record the burning of victim bodies early in the war in Bosnia (Berman 2003:278) and in Serbia of Kosovo Albanians (ICMP 2004).

Burning bodies as a means of disposal was not the first choice by the Nazis during WWII. Rees (2005:101–102) recounts prisoner testimony about how, prior to the completion of the crematorium at Auschwitz, bodies were buried by prisoners, although covered only with a shallow layer of lime and soil. When the bodies began decomposing in the summer heat of 1942, they became exposed. Members of the *Schutzstaffel* (SS), the elite Nazi paramilitary group under Himmler, ordered prisoners to exhume the bodies and then assist with burning them, fueled by wood and gasoline. In 1943 when it became apparent that the Nazis were losing the war on the Eastern front, they prepared to retreat. SS personnel were ordered to exhume bodies from mass graves and burn them (Auerbach 1979:38–40; Browning 1998:141). *Einsatzgruppe* leader Paul Blobel was tasked with the following:

> [R]emoving the traces of executions carried out by the Einsatzgruppen in the East... [and he] spent a grisly summer at Chelmno investigating fuels and systems for destroying masses of corpses. The bodies of the victims murdered in the gas chambers at Chelmno had been buried in mass graves. Blobel ordered them exhumed and used them in his experiments... he alternated bodies with railroad ties; then they were doused with gasoline or other flammable liquids (Browning 1998:259).

In June–August of 1943, Blobel oversaw mass burial exhumations and the burning of bodies. At one grave near Kiev, it took about 2 days to destroy the bodies in the grave. The same process was undertaken in Lithuania at Ninth Fort under SS direction: bodies were dragged from the grave and laid out in layers on the ground, alternating with layers of wood, with all drenched in gasoline (Browning 1998:260).

It seems that burning is attractive to organized killers initially, perhaps as a panic-response to early massacres where the desire is to eliminate traces of victims' remains and

---

* The author thanks Professor of Archaeology Jordi Estevez from the Universitat Autònoma de Barcelona for first suggesting this change in killing behavior by the Nationalist forces.

impede their identification. The time and resource costs, as well as the obviousness of such acts during the actual combustion, however, are quickly realized, and mass perpetrators tend to abandon body burning as a consistent body disposal method except when deemed urgent.

Postburial Treatment of Victim Remains

The final example of the earlier section illustrates how mass burial was the first choice of victim disposal for the Nazis, and only when they were losing territory and desperate to eliminate evidence of their crimes did they resort to the burning of bodies. This activity of postburial exhumation and alternative disposal of victim remains is not unique to the Nazis in latter stages of WWII.

Fischer (2005) describes the political controversy that surrounded the NKVD murders and mass burials at Katyn. During and following the war, the Soviets insisted that the victims were from Nazi massacres. According to aerial photoreconnaissance imagery, the NKVD bulldozed the area and removed some bodies from the graves sometime between 1941 and 1944.

The best-documented evidence of postburial treatment of remains in the context of armed conflict comes from grave excavations in Bosnia from 1996 to 2001. Much of this evidence has been presented at trial at the ICTY. In July 1995, up to 8000 men and boys from the enclave of Srebrenica, in western Bosnia, were taken prisoner by Bosnian Serb military forces. Over the next few days, they were systematically executed and buried in multiple mass graves throughout the local area. In October 1995, when the United Nations began to investigate the whereabouts of the missing, the killers coordinated a series of grave "exhumations," removing bodies from the primary burial sites and relocating the remains to more clandestine locations. Over the next 6 years, archaeologists and anthropologists assisted the Office of the Prosecutor of ICTY locate and excavate primary and secondary graves containing the remains of those missing from the Srebrenica massacre and others (Manning 2000; Skinner and Jessee 2005; Tuller 2012; Wright 2010).

Manning (ICTY 2003) also notes that an empty pit at the Zeleni Jadar site, near Srebrenica, probably indicates that a tertiary grave exists elsewhere, as other burials at that location were demonstrated to be secondary sites. According to Manning, the empty pit was a robbed secondary burial. The archaeological and other investigative evidence (shell casings, blindfolds, ligatures, soil, pollen, glass from a bottling factory, and other artifacts) successfully linked execution sites with primary and secondary burial sites. In total, over 50 burial sites have been linked to the Srebrenica massacre (Reddick 2006:149). Thus, killer logistical behavior is extremely well-established in this series of cases: from the point of victim detention, to execution, primary burial, criminal exhumation, secondary burial, and finally exhumation as part of a medico-legal investigation. The Zeleni Jadar site is significant because its geographical characteristics differ significantly from the primary sites. The primary sites are along major roads and tend to be in more open areas (e.g., fields). The locations of secondary sites reflect the deliberate effort to hide the bodies better from investigators: off tertiary roads, farther from populated areas, and more often in forested areas.

Political sensitivity to international investigations inspired a more complicated body disposal method in Bosnia. The availability of resources (transportation, fuel, and personnel under a chain of command) of the Bosnian Serb armed forces enabled them to employ this method. In some respects, the removal of bodies from Kosovo to Serbia in 1999 can be seen as an extension of this pattern. Once NATO began bombing Kosovo and Serbia and it was clear that the Serbs would be abandoning Kosovo, they removed bodies out of the territory altogether for secondary and subsequently tertiary burial. The scale of individual killing events appears to have been much smaller in Kosovo than Bosnia, but this may be a reflection of a more rural population in Kosovo as well as an example of "lessons learned in Bosnia" by Serbian military and paramilitary who were responsible for the majority of the killings in Kosovo. By keeping killing events frequent but with fewer individuals per event, the large mass graves containing hundreds of victims that were found in Bosnia would not be found in Kosovo. The change of tactics in the Balkans seems quite similar to the evolution of the killings in the Spanish Civil War Nationalist rearguard (discussed in the following text).

Skinner et al. (2002) note that postburial disturbance may not necessarily be the result of perpetrators trying to hide evidence. There are some instances in which bodies are traded by opposing militaries or unilaterally handed over during and following conflict, those that are exhumed for preliminary forensic analysis, and also those that are exhumed by family members. Skinner et al. (2002:297–306) observed examples of all of these in the former Yugoslavia and emphasized that distinguishing one type of postburial disturbance from another can be very difficult, particularly when exhumations fail to employ standard archaeological methods.

Holland et al. (2002) also discuss causes of alterations of human remains and related burials from armed conflict in Southeast Asia. Although there has been question on the motive for osseous alterations and whether or not it was criminal in intent, the most common explanation is simply careless or naive discovery and curation. In other instances, bone trading is responsible, which of course is a criminal act in most countries. In this latter instance, however, the intention for the modification is not to hide criminal acts, but economic gain through illegal activity unrelated to the circumstances of death of the individuals' remains (such as dividing remains into smaller pieces potentially to increase the profits from their sale).

"Noncriminal" postburial disturbance has also been seen in Iraq, where, following the disruption or fall of Iraqi government authority in 1991 (Gulf War) and 2003 (Operation Iraqi Freedom), families and community members of victims went out to search for graves (Bouckaert 2003; Hess 2004; Recknagel 2003). Given the political sensitivity of such acts, they may have been done very quickly and relatively discretely. Like criminal postburial transfer of bodies, however, the family-organized exhumations in Iraq seldom involved the use of archaeologists and anthropologists. As such, traces of the original burials and human remains probably exist. Personal experience of the author in various countries has shown that inexpert grave excavations and exhumations typically leave significant traces of burials in the form of remaining in situ human remains, traces of decomposition fluids, burial artifacts, or undamaged portions of the burial feature.

Body Disposal as Part of Systematic Repression   It is unclear if coordinated killings and body disposal in times of less organized and more indirect conflicts result in patterns that resemble those that occur in full-scale war. This is unfortunately the situation despite decades of forensic archaeological work in Latin America, where conflict generally has been characterized by government or government-sponsored (e.g., paramilitary) forces combating less organized and less formal enemies over prolonged periods of time. Unconventional armed groups may not have uniforms, and membership may be loosely defined or organized. In fact, this is likely one reason why civilians are so often victimized in such contexts, as it is difficult for formal government armed forces to define who is an enemy and who, therefore, is considered a legitimate target. Although such killings as at My Lai in Vietnam (BBC 1998) and the massacre at El Mozote (Doretti and Snow 2003) in El Salvador might be cited as an illustration of this confusion, these incidents more accurately demonstrate how offenders in the blatant and knowing killing of civilians use such "confusion" as a way of attempting to justify or explain the killing of civilians. Nevertheless, in prolonged periods of armed repression, killers are constrained by similar logistic, geographic, and sociopolitical factors that greatly influence how and where victim bodies are disposed. These constraints should result in similar modes and patterns of body disposal as in formal armed conflict.

Killings and Body Disposal during the Spanish Civil War

The study presented here sets a precedent by examining burial sites on a macroscale and as a series and not as isolated features. The patterns evident in Spain may also be reflected in other contexts: different types of armed conflict (e.g., civil war or interstate war) in other countries and under quite different sociopolitical circumstances.

The war in Spain started in 1936 as a military coup, soon turned into a full-scale civil war, and quickly evolved into a systematic repression by the Nationalists who supported the coup. Even with Nationalist victory under General Francisco Franco in 1939, the conflict continued with the fighting of guerrillas and the detention and killing of other unarmed, perceived ideological enemies. Like in much of Latin America during different recent conflicts, organized, state-sponsored killings and body disposal continued in Spain for years, even decades, after the formal, large-scale conflict had ended.

As in other contexts and as alluded to earlier, a variety of body disposal site types were used in the Nationalist rearguard of the Spanish Civil War, including preexisting features such as wells. The use of cemeteries as killing and burial sites was quite common, particularly at the beginning of the war or when the territory was freshly captured by Nationalist forces (see the following text). However, the use of "cemetery" in the context of Spanish Civil War killings is contentious. Many people in Spain and in the documentation from the time of the killings employ the term (*cementerio* in Spanish). In a strict sense, a modern cemetery is a formally recognized and legal burial place. In times of large numbers of deaths, alternative areas may be used to dispose of bodies, and they become—officially or unofficially—cemeteries. Remote areas of formal cemeteries or even plots of land adjacent to cemeteries or on the property of public or religious grounds may be used as mass burial sites (e.g., Congram et al. n.d.). In the situation of illegal killings and burial, the label of "cemetery" may also be used to "protect" burials, which is to say prohibit investigation, because of the special status of cemeteries and the general taboo of removing remains from them. In such instances, archaeological expertise is often necessary in distinguishing legal from illegal deaths and burials (Figure 10.1).

Two types of rearguard killings predominated in Spain and resulted in clandestine victim burial: *paseos* and *sacas*. Zavala (2006) traces the use of *paseo* to the American mafia of the 1920s and 1930s and their euphemistic use of the term "stroll" or "walk" (e.g., "Let's take him for a walk"). *Sacas* ("to take out, to remove") appear in official documents showing that prisoners were released, but upon exiting the front gates, trucks with paramilitaries or civil guards would be waiting to drive the prisoners to their place of extra-judicial execution (Rilova Pérez 2001). Zavala (2006:95) distinguishes between these two types of

Figure 10.1 Modern mass burial cross-cutting legal cemetery burial. The partially excavated mass burial runs left to right and intersects an older legal burial (center of photo) that conforms with cultural norms related to the depth, size, and orientation. The trowel points north.

killings by calling *sacas* "industrialized" versions of *paseos*, meaning that they demonstrated greater coordination by the authorities and produced larger numbers of deaths per killing event. *Paseos* and *sacas* committed by the Nationalists in Spain were strategic, preemptive killings of perceived ideological enemies (Herreros and Criado 2009).

Research on killings during the Spanish Civil War shows an evolution of body disposal methods that appears to be a response to sociopolitical sensitivity about the deaths, based in part on symmetry of control in an area. In the first weeks of the attempted coup, executions were more commonly done in public places. As a failed coup turned into civil war, and parties fought to garner support from both the public and international partners (or at least stave off intervention that would hurt their cause), killings became more clandestine (Castro 2006:220; Congram 2010; Vilaplana 1977:87, 170).

Kalyvas (2003, 2006) analyzed the dynamics and mechanisms of violence in civil war, specifically under what circumstances civilians are targeted and killed by authorities. Congram (2010) built upon this to examine the dynamics of victim disposal once they have been killed. A key observation of Kalyvas is that where a group in a civil war is contending for control, the degree of selective violence that it employs is directly related to the level of control that they possess in an area and the persuasion they can employ on potential informants who provide the vying authorities with targets for their violence. The pattern observed by Kalyvas is parabolic when one plots the degree of control along the x-axis (with one contending group at one end of the scale and another group at the opposite end of the scale) against the use of selective violence along the y-axis: when one group's political control is great, the need for and the use of selective violence against the civilian population are low; when control is threatened, violence increases; and when two sides seem to be vying equally for control, the general population avoids taking sides, and contending authority groups avoid violence against the general population for fear of turning people against them. Following this logic, how bodies are disposed of will depend in part on the degree of control the killers have over the territory in which the killing takes place and the sensitivity of these killings.

The evolution of killings by Nationalist forces in Spain seems to have gone through three general phases:

1. An initial, more anarchic, though deliberate stage of large-scale killings by military forces as they moved into new territory. The most notorious examples of these are large-scale killings at cemeteries in Andalusia (Gibson 1973; Jackson 1965:299–300; Zavala 2006:272) and the machine-gunning of prisoners in Badajoz described earlier (Espinosa 2007:371). These killings generally occurred immediately following the conquest of populous territory and were committed by the advancing troops, partly as a means of protecting the military from having to return to combat continuing resistance in the previously conquered territory (Armengou and Belis 2004:37–38; Jackson 1965:536).

2. Over the first 4 months following the attempted coup, the predominant form of killing (far exceeding battle casualties; Bahamonde 2005:139; Bennassar 2005:102; Castro 2006:250; Jackson 1965:533) was targeted, more covert executions of civilians by the Nationalist rearguard, mostly by *Falange* paramilitary. The killings during this phase are characterized by *paseos* and *sacas*, whereby people were detained at their homes or taken from prisons at night, driven out of urban areas, and shot at roadside locations. Castro (2006:220) reports that these were the predominant forms of killing, and in little over 2 months, 26 *sacas* produced at least 400 deaths of prisoners from the Burgos Central Prison alone. Castro calculates that *paseos* and *sacas* accounted for at least 75%–80% of all deaths in Burgos (where the coup was largely successful) in the first 3 months following the coup (2006:221).

3. A consolidation and formalization of political and military authority under the *Generalissimo* Francisco Franco took place in the late autumn and winter of 1936. Following this, courts martial were imposed, and killings were preceded by mass incarceration, group "show trials" lasting only minutes, mass sentencing, and formal, "legal," or legitimized executions (Espinosa 2007:402; Rodrígo 2008). This last phase would become the dominant mode of killing from 1937 and beyond the end of the civil war and has been referred to as the "institutionalized repression" (Prada Rodríguez 2006:202–295). This repression is said to have been instigated by foreign allies of the Nationalists (presumably the Nazi Germans and Italians; Vilaplana 1977:87, 170), probably due to sensitivity of negative press related to the less formal mass killings (e.g., Martín Barrio et al. 1988:373). Given the legitimized nature of the killings at this stage, they would more often take place publicly or at least not in the clandestine form of *paseos* and *sacas* of the second stage of the repression (e.g., Torres 2002:247).

The second phase of the repression is of interest and relevance to this study. The killings from both the first and third phases were more likely to result in cemetery burials (e.g., Botella López, pers. comm. on Andalusia; Rilova Perez 2001 on Burgos).

The aim of the study upon which this section of the chapter is based (Congram 2010) was to identify patterns of killer behavior. This information could then be used to facilitate the search for further graves of victims of rearguard killings. The sample for the study included data from 44 excavated burial sites of victims of Nationalist rearguard killings, mostly from the last half of 1936 (the first 6 months of the war).

Table 10.2   Independent Variables as Recommended for Consideration during Stages of Investigation

Variable	Used for Predictive Model (Stage 1)	Used as an Investigative Guide Based on Statistical Analysis (Stage 2)	No Significance Detected
Victim		X	
Distance traveled		X	
Land use/cover		X	
Road side (L/R)			X
Road type	X		
Distance to last town[a]	X	X	
Distance to next town[a]	X	X	
Towns crossed		X	
Distance from road to grave	X	X	
Population density relative to sites		X	

[a] Distances between the grave and the populated areas on either side of it were taken as a single variable in the predictive models: included as a population layer and the measurement of the *single* nearest populated area was modeled. These two variables should also be considered in the second investigative stage independently based on the results of the descriptive statistics.

Frequency statistics were calculated on several variables relative to burial locations, and other variables were used to create suitability maps, which highlighted areas of greater and lesser suitability for burial based on landscape characteristics. These maps were based on three predictive models using either inductive or deductive approaches. Table 10.2 illustrates which variables were examined, according to this study, and in which way.

Among other things, the results of the study demonstrated that killers traveled to foreign and lower-density municipalities before shooting their victims. This trend is particularly useful to investigators, as it indicates that witness and archival information related to killings is more likely to be found in municipalities that surround that of the victim origin. Generally, unless burials were conducted in cemeteries, there appeared to be a buffer around populated areas, showing that killers preferred to travel a certain distance beyond towns before killing. Even for cemetery killings, the cemeteries chosen were often located a short distance outside of towns.

Prior to being able to employ the results of this study's work, one should identify the incident type that resulted in a disappeared person or persons to ensure that it is consistent with the killing incident studied (*paseos*). One also must ensure that there is little or no possibility that the victims were interred in or around a previously existing cemetery local to the detention site. This should be done by examining cemetery and local government and church registries (including both religious and civil burial sites). Surprisingly, work by historians has shown that despite the criminality of the killings, many victim burials were registered in one form or another (Espinosa 2009). Of equal, if not greater importance, investigators should conduct directed questioning of locals, who have sometimes proven to be valuable sources of information even 75 years after the majority of the killings (Gomez and Junquera 2008).

If cemeteries and preexisting features appear not to have been used as body disposal sites, the following guidelines can be used to search for the victim grave in a two-stage investigative process. The predictive model that performed most accurately to create a suitability surface is used in "Stage 1" of the guidelines and is based on area road types, distances from roads, and distances from populated areas relative to the victim origin (i.e., the point of detention by the killers).

"Stage 2" is based upon the results of other variables analyzed using univariate and bivariate tests of statistical significance and descriptive statistics. The second stage considers information that could not be modeled and involves creating two prioritized probability areas, labeled "a" and "b" according to higher and lower probability respectively (within the high suitability area). Probability area "a" includes 67% of the cases from the study sample according to the values of the independent variables. Probability area "b" includes 95% of the cases according to the values of the independent variables. As the independent variables used for this second investigative stage demonstrated strong positive skewness, the cases considered for each of the probability areas were taken around the median. Independent variables considered here include "distance traveled," "towns crossed," "distance to last town," "distance to next town," "land-use/cover," and "population density." Sites discovered to date show that these can be expected to be within 200 m of a road, although most will be within 100 m.

Stage 1: Examine the suitability map and identify the high suitability area within 50 km of the origin site.

Stage 2 will take place entirely within this high suitability area.

Higher probability area "a"

1. Distances within 14.5 km of the origin
2. Along roadways between the origin and the next two towns in all directions
3. Areas between 350 m and 3.12 km of all towns passed in the direction of travel (assuming no other towns are crossed)
4. Areas between 4 km and 250 m of all towns being approached in the direction of travel (assuming no other towns are crossed)
5. Property that was farmed at the time of victim disappearance (orchards, vineyards, and fields)
6. Municipalities with a lower population density than the origin

Lower probability area "b"

1. Distances within 36.15 km of the origin
2. Along roadways between the next two to six towns in all directions
3. Areas between 250 m and 9 km of the last town passed in the direction of travel (assuming no other towns are crossed)
4. Areas between 12.3 km and 350 m of all towns being approached in the direction of travel (assuming no other towns are crossed)
5. Areas of all but heavy cover (i.e., forested) at the time of victim disappearance
6. Municipalities with population density equal to or less than the origin

These investigative guidelines obviously are meant only for the discovery of primary disposal sites. There are instances of both "criminal" and "noncriminal" body removal from primary sites during and following the Spanish Civil War.* There is limited oral evidence of clandestine grave exhumations by victim family members during and soon after the war (Molina, pers. comm.). Following Franco's death, and during a transition to democratic governance in Spain, limited exhumations of victims of Nationalist killings were conducted by families of the victims without legal mandates or support (Baviano 1980; Ferrándiz 2009:83–85; Herrero Balsa and Hernández García 1982; Silva and Macías 2003).

Postburial exhumations and body transfers also occurred at the behest of the Franco government during the 1950s. Having carved a massive memorial—the "Valley of the Fallen"—out of a mountain, using prison labor, the government set about exhuming those who were killed or died fighting for the Nationalist cause. The inflated number of victims propagated by the Nationalists during the war came to light and resulted in much empty space at the memorial. The government's solution was to exhume victims of Nationalist execution and bury them at the Valley of the Fallen as well. Many of the families of the victims of Nationalist killings were unaware of the original clandestine burial sites and so were equally ignorant that the bodies had subsequently been relocated to the monument honoring their killers. Only through recent investigations have family members come to realize that the victims do not lie in anonymous mass graves near their place of disappearance, but at the war monument, Franco had built for those who died fighting for the Nationalists (Barcala 2010). In May 2011, the Spanish government announced that identification of those interred at the Valley of the Fallen would be impossible (Barcala 2011). This reconcentration of remains has precedent in prehistoric and historic contexts (e.g., Olson 1966), as well as in the animal kingdom (see Chapter 9, this volume), although the motivation for the behavior obviously can differ greatly both on an inter- and on an intraspecies level.

Criminological Study of Peace-Time Serial and Individual Murder

Early examples of criminological studies, as exemplified by the Chicago School (Becker 1999), adopted an ethnographic fieldwork approach to studying urban crime and relating human behavior to ecological factors. More recent criminological work, particularly those in environmental criminology and offender profiling, has analyzed geographic patterns of offender movement in cases of individual murders and serial murders in a "peace-time" context. The focus of these studies is on the mindset and behavior of murderers and how this is manifested geographically, as in offender residence relative to offense locations. Such lines of inquiry are of obvious relevance to forensic anthropologists and the study of *H. sapiens sapiens* as a taphonomic agent. Although the conventional forensic anthropologist is more likely to be concerned with the geographic information that comes from these studies (e.g., knowing where and how murderers tend to dispose of their victims), the study of killer thought processes and activity is within the realm of broader anthropological study as discussed at the beginning of this chapter.

---

* For the sake of this work, "criminal" removal of bodies is considered that which is not sanctioned or known by victim families and communities, and "noncriminal" is that organized or conducted by victim families and communities. It is acknowledged that either or both may be technical violations of criminal law or entirely legal, but moral rather than legalistic reasoning is used here to define these terms.

Much of the criminological study on body disposal involves the use of several principal concepts including the distance decay effect (Rengert et al. 1999; Rossmo 2000), which relates to Tobler's first law of geography (Sui 2009). Tobler's law states that things that are nearer in space are more similar, or have stronger relationships, than things that are more distant (also referred to as spatial autocorrelation). Rossmo (2000) presents a thorough overview of criminological work on geographic analysis of offender behavior, which culminates in geographic profiling, which Rossmo (2000:211) refers to as "a strategic information management system designed to support serial violent crime investigations."

There is significant variation in victim disposal patterns among murderers, and some of this variation is dependent upon the nature of the crime (e.g., sexual or emotional), offender (e.g., individual or serial murderer), and the victim (e.g., child or adult). Disagreement also exists among researchers about the validity of various categories of murderers (e.g., "organized" versus "disorganized," Canter et al. 2004; Ressler et al. 1986). Distinguishing patterns according to the many groups and criteria is akin to trying to isolate the relative influence of individual factors in human decomposition: the complex interplay of many variables makes the extraction of meaningful information about a single variable extremely difficult.

Kraemer et al. (2004) studied 157 serial homicide offenders with 608 victims and compared a subsample of serial homicide offenses with a control group of single homicide offenses. They observed that serial homicide offenders kill for apparent sexual motivation more often than for any other reason, while single homicide offenders kill most often out of anger. Perhaps the impulsivity of single homicides versus the planned serial homicides helps explain the observation made by the authors that for single homicide offences, different elements of the crime (the initial contact site, the murder site, and the body disposal site) tend to be at the same location, whereas these elements tend to be distinct sites for serial homicides. The authors further note that "The only significant difference in method of body disposal was the increased likelihood that serial homicide offenders dump the body in a remote location" (2004:335–336).

Reinforcing the parallels between human and nonhuman animal behavior asserted in this chapter, Kraemer et al. (2004:327–328) conclude of single and serial murderers:

> Borrowing from ecological biology models, we observe that animals kill for two reasons: competition and predation (Lord et al. 2002). Most homicide offenses are between two males who know each other, and can be understood as eliminating competition of peers (Daly and Wilson 1988). Serial homicide offenders, however, although also predominantly male, more frequently target women and children who are strangers. Killing such victims may be a form of predation, to acquire a desired resource such as sex.

Although several studies demonstrate some differences between serial and single homicide offender motivation and behavior, including travel patterns for victim disposal, there are many similarities when victims are not left in the home of the offender or victim.

Serial Murder

Serial murder is very uncommon, despite its ubiquity in fiction. Killers show trends in victim body disposal behavior, but some studies also show that killers adapt their behavior over time as they kill. Adaptation to circumstances and the complexity of human decision

Table 10.3 Attempt to Hide Victim Body by Serial Killers

Characteristic	% (Number)
Displayed	7.3 (13)
Dumped	10.7 (19)
Other, not hidden	34.3 (61)
Casually hidden	10.1 (18)
Well hidden	25.3 (45)
Other	12.4 (22)

Source: Rossmo, D.K., Geographic profiling: Target patterns of serial murderers, Unpublished PhD thesis, Simon Fraser University, Burnaby, British Columbia, Canada, 317, 1995.

processes and behavior (including those killers who suffer a degree or particular form of psychopathy) frustrate investigative efforts to classify and model patterns. Nevertheless, certain information can be derived from these studies that assist with crime resolution, including victim discovery and identification.

In developing geographic profiling, Rossmo studied patterns of serial murderers, which included data on victim body disposal sites ($n = 104$). The body disposal site area was "residential" (as defined by city maps and/or as reported in various crime documents, Rossmo, pers. comm.) in almost half of the sites analyzed (45.2%, with almost 17% actually at the offender residence). The next highest category of disposal site type was, ironically, the opposite: "wilderness or uninhabited" (21.2%). The dominance of these two very different location types illustrates the great variability of locations selected by serial murderers. Slightly over 20% were categorized as "river, lake, or marsh." Almost three quarters of disposal sites were outdoor, public places (Rossmo 2000:175). Table 10.3, taken from Rossmo (1995:317), shows the variation demonstrated in attempts to hide (or not) victim bodies. As with body disposal location type, there is little consistency in attempts to hide victim bodies.

The mean distance of body dump sites from victim–offender encounter sites is 11.9 km. Remarkably, this result is very consistent with the distances between detention and body disposal sites from the study of burials from the Spanish Civil War rearguard (mean distance between victim–offender encounter and burial location of 13.11 km, 67% of burials within 14.5 km). However, the standard deviation of this distance measure in Rossmo's data is high (25.9 km). It should be noted here that the distribution of these data—in studies by Rossmo and others—is seldom normally distributed, so both the mean and the standard deviation can be misleading. Rossmo notes that "optimal body disposal sites are often situated in uninhabited regions located some distance from urban areas" (2000:176), although this seems to stand in contradiction to the high frequency of residential area disposal sites selected (as well as some disposal sites being in the home of the offender) in his study.

A further observation made by Rossmo is that serial killers tend to mimic the hunting behavior of certain nonhuman predators by repeatedly visiting the same sites, which includes revisiting body dump sites. Although Rossmo suggests that this behavior is motivated at least in part by offender fantasies (2000:179), it is also reasonable to believe that once killers have found a "good" body disposal site, they continue to use it. Site reuse has been seen in the context of armed conflict, as evidenced by the agglomeration of secondary mass burials of Bosnian Muslim victims in the area of Zeleni Jadar as discussed earlier or the continued mass killings and burials in the forest north of Granada or throughout Burgos province during the Spanish Civil War (Gibson 1973; Jimenez, pers. comm.). Just as nonhuman animal behavior demonstrates the repeated use of geographic and ecological space, so too is *H. sapiens sapiens* a creature of habit.

Godwin and Canter (1997) studied the relative distances between offender homes, the "point of fatal encounter" between offender and victim, and the body dump sites of victims of 54 male U.S. serial murderers, each convicted of at least 10 murders. The authors concluded that the data demonstrated a consistent effort to dump bodies beyond the point of first encounter, which is to say farther away from the offender's residence than the point of encounter. They also noted that serial murderers appear to spread the location of dump sites (i.e., subsequent disposals in the opposite direction as the previous disposal), possibly as a means of reducing the risk of detection. The mean distance between offender residence and body dump site was 22.9 km, with a standard deviation of 8 km. The mean distance from the point of first offender–victim encounter to the body dump site was 20.5 km with a very small standard deviation of 2 km. It is surprising that these results are quite different from those of Rossmo, particularly because the datasets certainly included many of the same offenders and sites, although some of this can be attributed to different sample criteria (Rossmo [2000] analyzed murderers with at least five victims; Godwin and Canter [1997] studied those with at least 10 victims) as well as distinct analytical methods. Interestingly, Godwin and Canter (1997) document a fairly consistent and significant decrease in distance between offender residence and body dump site with each consecutive killing. It is possible that confidence of the offenders in avoiding detection results in their committing less effort to dispose of victims as time goes on.

Snook et al. (2005) analyzed 53 serial killers in Germany. Unfortunately, these authors also used slightly different criteria from both Rossmo (2000) and Godwin and Canter (1997) for selecting cases for analysis. Also somewhat problematic for comparison with other studies is the failure by Snook et al. to distinguish among the victim–offender encounter site, the murder site, and the body disposal site. The only two locations examined were the offender base (typically his residence) and the body disposal site. Despite these differences, the overall results are informative and broadly comparable. Snook et al. (2005) report a median distance between offender residence and body disposal site of 6.5 km. In this instance, the reporting of the median distance rather than the mean is most useful, as the distribution of distances is negatively skewed with a very long tail (i.e., a small proportion of very remote outliers of murderers who traveled very far to dispose of bodies). They conclude by saying that "German serial murderers generally dispose of their victims' bodies in close proximity to the murderer's homes… [and the distance] follows a decay pattern" (2005:161), in accordance with Tobler's Law. Table 10.4 shows the percentage of cases relative to distances from offender residences as observed by Snook et al. (2005) for German serial murderers. The authors of the study do not attempt to explain the relatively short distances when compared with North American serial killer spatial behavior. One possible explanation is the greater population density in Germany, which gives killers few reasonably close unpopulated disposal sites. The possibility of a higher prevalence of urban or semiurban parks within a larger high population density

Table 10.4   Distances between Offender Residences and Victim Body Disposal Sites

Distance from Offender Residence (km)	Cumulative % Victim Body Disposal Sites
<1	6.5
<2	17
<3	28
<4	34
<5	45
<10	63
<20	78
<30	84

Source: Snook, B. et al., *J. Invest. Psychol. Offender Profil.*, 2, 147, 2005.

area in Germany as opposed to North America may make the parks the most reasonable choice for body disposal, and their relative ubiquity close to murderer residences would account for the shorter distances observed in Germany. Higher population density could also explain the long tail and very long distances traveled by only a few of those studied by Snook et al. (2005), as killers unwilling to dispose of bodies in an urban or semiurban environment would have to travel great distances to go beyond urbanized areas. A final possible explanation relates to the sample size of the populations analyzed. In a study of U.S. and U.K. serial murderers, Lundrigan and Canter (2001a) demonstrated that the distance between an offender's residence and body disposal sites generally increases with subsequent victims. This is the opposite of what was shown in Godwin and Canter's (1997) study discussed earlier, which calls their explanation (increasing killer confidence to avoid detection) into question. The study by Snook et al. (2005) included killers with a minimum of three victims and an average of five (247 victims of 53 murderers). Lundrigan and Canter's study included those convicted of killing a (comparable) minimum of two victims, but the average was seven for both groups (898 victims of 126 American murderers and 207 victims of 29 British murderers). It could be that the greater number of average victims per killer in the United States and United Kingdom explains some of the difference in distances. Nevertheless, distances from Lundrigan and Canter's study showed a median offender home to body disposal site distance of 15 km (mean of 40 km) for U.S. serial murderers and a median distance of 9 km (mean of 18 km) for U.K. serial murderers, which could also be interpreted as supporting the hypothesis posited here on the influence of population density on distances traveled to dispose of victims. Lundrigan and Canter attribute the difference in distances in their study to topography and ease of travel, and this remains a further possible explanation. Although they do not explain what they mean by "ease of travel," this could be based in whole or part on relative measures of traffic congestion, which would reflect back on the influence of population density.

Other conclusions drawn by Lundrigan and Canter (2001a) include the observation that "the locations at which serial killers dispose of their victims' bodies reflect the inherent logic of the choices that underlie their predatory activities." The authors demonstrate that although a murder and its motivation may be irrational, the location choice of victim disposal site is often rational and one that avoids immediate detection and apprehension

Table 10.5 Distances between Serial Murderer Residences and Body Disposal Sites

Distance of Offender Residence to Disposal Site (km)	Cumulative % of Cases
<5	25
<15	50
<40	75

Source: Lundrigan, S. and Canter, D., *Behav. Sci. Law*, 19, 595, 2001a.

of the offender. Table 10.5 shows the proportions of distances between U.S. and U.K. serial murderer residences and body disposal sites.

Lundrigan and Canter (2001b:423) also analyzed serial murderers using the approach of environmental psychology, through which they surmised that although the murders committed may not be considered rational, "environmental psychology hypotheses predict that their choice of disposal site location may be guided by a recognizable rationality… evident through their spatial patterns of disposal locations." The authors found that the offender residence was central, spatially, to their choice of disposal sites. They also found that previous disposal site locations influenced subsequent location choices, although this influence was stronger for those whose geographic range was smaller. This could be interpreted as the short-range murderer being more concerned with avoiding detection and association of one murder to the next.

Salfati and Bateman (2005) examined serial murders and crime scene characteristics in an attempt to identify behavioral consistency, which could in turn be used to discern multiple crimes/crime scenes from potentially multiple offenders. Although many of the crime-scene behaviors observed are not relevant to the present research, the authors do note that in 65% of the cases that they studied, the victim body recovery site was indoors. They also observed that in 44.9% of cases, the killer appeared to be unconcerned with disposal of body, whereas in 34.8% of cases, the victim body was hidden or placed to prevent discovery. These results are similar to those of Rossmo (2000), who found that victim bodies were either casually or well hidden in just over 35% of cases (Table 10.3). As with other studies, this should not be surprising, as the cases examined and the criteria used by both Rossmo (2000) and Salfati and Bateman (2005) are the same (i.e., an offender arrested for a minimum of three murders over time).

As part of a forensic search for victims, information about the nature of the crime—be it individual, serial, or mass murder—might affect how a search is conducted. Studies analyzing individual murderer behavior patterns and some comparing individual and serial murderer patterns are therefore critical to understanding the taphonomic signature of *H. sapiens sapiens* predatory behavior.

Individual Murder

Häkkänen et al. (2007) examined murder victim body disposal sites in Finland (*n* = 46). The authors found that 73% of bodies were disposed of in wooded areas and 27% in water, leaving one to wonder if there were only two categories for disposal site location. Unfortunately, the authors restricted their study to victim disposal in rural areas of Finland. Nevertheless, the authors do report the distances among offender residences, homicide sites, and body

Table 10.6   Distances between Victim–Offender
Encounter Sites and Victim Body Disposal Sites
for Rural Homicides in Finland

Distance from Encounter Site to Body Dump (km)	Cumulative % Victim Body Disposal Sites
<5	33.3
<15	50.0
<25	63.4
<50	83.3

Source: Häkkänen, H. et al., *J. Invest. Psychol. Offender Profil.*, 4, 181, 2007.

disposal sites. The statistics on these distances can be loosely compared with those studies already mentioned measuring similar distances when disposal sites at victim or offender residences have been removed from calculations. Table 10.6 shows the proportion of distances traveled between homicide sites and victim body disposal sites for the cases examined by Häkkänen and colleagues. These are relatively farther than distances in other studies, and this is almost certainly attributable in part to the sample criterion of rural victim disposal site.

In 20% of cases, there was an attempt to burn the victim's body. Slightly over one quarter of victims were deposited within 200 m of a road, almost one half (43.9%) within 500 m, and 29.2% over 1 km from the nearest road. Although most other studies on victim disposal behavior do not report distances from road (for an exception, see the discussion of Manhein et al. 2006 (following text)), this is a measure that is of obvious use for investigators of missing persons. The measure of distance from the nearest road of burials from the Spanish Civil War was made only indirectly, due to lack of reported detail of sites (e.g., datum used for recording global positioning system (GPS) coordinates). Nevertheless, personal experience of the author in this context, discussions with colleagues, and reference to photographs from the excavation reports demonstrate that burials of civilian victims executed in the rearguard were seldom more than 100 m from the nearest road, but it is reasonable to believe that those closer to roads are more likely to be discovered.

An interesting observation by Häkkänen et al. (2007) is that three of the five female victims were transported a relatively long distance for disposal (>50 km). This difference of treatment of female victims was posited in the study of Spanish Civil War killings, but a small sample size (victim groups that included at least one female in the Spanish study numbered three) meant that statistical significance of other variables related to female victims could not be reliably tested. A further important observation by Häkkänen et al. (2007) was that psychopathy in the offender showed no significant correlation with distance patterns, reinforcing the assertion that murderer behavior with respect to victim body disposal generally demonstrates rational thinking.

Nethery (2002) studied abduction and murder victims of both serial and individual murderers in Canada and Washington State, United States. She observed that the majority of victims were killed in isolated and secluded areas, which most often served as the body disposal site, principally wooded areas. Child victims (less than 12 years old) also were sometimes disposed of on farmland or in bodies of water. Nethery notes that in most cases, body disposal was planned by the offender prior to the murder. Taking the victims to the disposal site while alive and killing them there facilitate body disposal. This was the modus operandi for the rearguard killings of the Spanish Civil War and during WWII, where truckloads of victims were often taken to prepared graves, where they would be shot and buried.

According to Nethery's research, in cities or towns with a population of less than 50,000, 50% of child victims were disposed of in locations over 25 km away from the victim's home (and the abduction point was within 3 km of the victim's home in all cases). In areas with a population greater than 50,000, only 16% of victim bodies were disposed of more than 25 km away from the victim's home. Further, in the largest city in the study—Toronto, with a population of 2.5 million—offenders traveled the shortest distances to dispose of victims' remains. Mean distances from the murder scene to the body disposal sites were 4 km for larger cities and 15 km for smaller cities. These data support the conclusion that offenders travel shorter distances in more urban areas, as seen in the studies of serial killers in Germany and the United Kingdom. This is especially apparent considering that most victims' bodies in Canada are disposed of in isolated or secluded areas, meaning that these areas exist within very short distances of urban or residential areas where victims and offenders meet. Population density figures between 1970 and 2010 show Germany ranging around 219 people/km^2; the United Kingdom between 229 and 255; Canada at a constant 3; and the United States at 32 for 2010 (previous data not reported) (United Nations 2011). To assess the possible influence of population density more accurately, however, one must consider the more local density in the areas of the murders. In the case of Canada, the overall population density figure is misleading, as a vast majority of the population is concentrated near the southern border with the United States, and this is where most serial murder occurs.

Also in Nethery's study, for young adult victims (13–17 years old) in Canada, 16 of 17 were disposed of less than 10.9 km from the murder site. Among adults (at least 18 years old), four of five were disposed of less than 5.9 km from the murder site. Though informative, confidence in this distribution is very limited due to small sample sizes.

Morton and Lord (2002) summarized two studies focused on child abduction and homicide (Boudreaux et al. 1999; Hanfland et al. 1997). Overall, a clear majority of victims from both studies were disposed of less than 8 km from the victim's residence. Overall, body disposal distances appear to be relatively short for children, which is probably related to the nature of the crimes and relationships between offenders and victims, many offenders being related to or acquainted with their victim. Morton and Lord concluded by stating that, generally, the younger the victim, the closer to the home their body will be found.

Van Patten and Delhauer (2007) studied 197 sexual killings in Los Angeles County, USA. As with other serial murder studies, Van Patten and Delhauer's sample is skewed by a small proportion of murderers who traveled very long distances (e.g., the distance from one offender's home residence to the body dump site was 3411 miles, or 5457 km). Such cases should be treated differently so as to get a more realistic measure of general spatial behavior. For this and similar reasons, some researchers refer to an offender's "base," which may include a residence or another location at which they spend a significant amount of time (e.g., workplace) and from which they travel to commit murders. In the instance of outliers, it is probable that murderers have a local base that is unrecorded, leaving researchers to include an unusually distant residence instead. Specifically because of this bias inherent in the data, Van Patten and Delhauer—like other researchers discussed here—rely more on median distances rather than the arithmetic mean. In a large

**Table 10.7   Distances between Victim–Offender
Encounter Sites and Body Disposal Sites for Sexual
Homicides in Los Angeles County**

Distance from Encounter Site to Body Dump (km)	% Victim Body Disposal Sites
0–4.22	50.0
0–8	62.7
8–16	20.4

Source: Van Patten, I.T. and Delhauer, P.Q., *J. Forens. Sci.*, 52, 1129, 2007.

proportion of cases (41%), the offender disposed of the victim body at the victim's residence. This is an important consideration for investigators of missing persons, particularly when offender sexual motivation is suspected. Nevertheless, removing these cases where no travel has occurred, the median distance from offender residence to encounter site was 2.67 km, and the median distance from offender residence to body disposal site was 3.9 km. The mean distance of encounter site to the body disposal site was 11 km, and the median distance was 4.2 km. Table 10.7 shows distances between victim–offender encounter site and victim body disposal site.

Forensic Anthropological Study of the Taphonomic Signature of *H. sapiens sapiens*

Listi et al. (2007) explored the use of GPS as a technique for mapping surface-scattered human remains, but concluded that the inaccuracy of recorded locations of elements relative to one another makes traditional archaeological mapping techniques preferable. Manhein et al. (2006) used geographic information systems (GIS) and spatial analysis in Louisiana to examine possible patterns of where and when human remains are dumped as well as to determine if PMI correlates with distance of remains scatter and direction of scatter. The authors used the terms "spatial forensic taphonomy" and "geo-forensic taphonomy" to refer to the use of GIS and spatial analysis to answer taphonomic questions in forensic contexts. Unsurprisingly, the authors found that a significant number of body dump sites were within 400 meters of a road and away from structures. Remains are also more likely to be found in wooded rather than open environments.

Apart from several limitations acknowledged by Manhein et al. (2006), there are several others that should be considered for those building upon what is a promising line of research methods. As this volume demonstrates, PMI estimation is very complex, and precise intervals—particularly for skeletonized remains—should be critically examined. The data used in these analyses, as in all other similar studies, are biased toward the types of places in which remains are found (i.e., those that are less effectively hidden or placed in less remote locations and so more likely to be discovered). This explanation may account for the majority of dump sites appearing to be close to roads. The complete range of body disposal behavior is indeterminable in most cases, where the number of victims is unknown. In situations outside of armed conflict, a missing person is not necessarily a murder victim: they might have migrated elsewhere, died through another cause in a remote location, committed suicide, or be intentionally avoiding contact with others (Skinner and Lazenby 1983).

Although these explanations are also possible for disappearances in the context of armed conflict, one can safely presume that they constitute a much smaller proportion of the missing and that the majority have been killed and their bodies hidden.

Discussion

Only recently have cultural anthropologists actively started to study violent human behavior in a modern context (e.g., Leyton 2005). In *Annihilating Difference: The Anthropology of Genocide,* Laban Hinton (2002) observes that "Although anthropologists have long been at the forefront of advocating for the rights of indigenous people and have conducted rich analyses of violence, conflict, and warfare in substate and prestate societies, they have only recently (since the 1980s) begun to focus their attention intensively on political violence in complex state societies." Forensic anthropologists, despite for decades being actively engaged in death-scene investigations, grave search, and excavation and skeletal analysis, have seldom explored beyond the realm of basic archaeological search and recovery techniques and osteological observations related to biological profile and trauma. This situation exists despite the four-field anthropology emphasis taught in most of North American universities, where forensic anthropology has been focused—both in research and practice. Only very recently have forensic anthropologists ventured into broader aspects of anthropological work such as material culture analysis and spatial analysis.

The nature of killings and body disposal, in both peace-time and armed conflict contexts, may evolve over time due to different circumstances. Serial killers may become more brazen, careless, or adept with each subsequent kill. The Nazi Germans and the Nationalists during the Spanish Civil War demonstrated a learning process with respect to body disposal. Not only is it difficult to destroy a human body, it can be costly in terms of resources, as when one uses fuel to try to burn them, which is otherwise needed in large quantities to support the mechanized forces engaged in the main war effort.

Concerning the clandestinity of body disposal sites, the motivation to hide a body is driven largely by sociopolitical factors. Cases of domestic and serial homicides seem to show a concerted effort to hide the body or at least to disassociate the offender from the victim, which is natural given the almost certain consequences for the offender who is caught and convicted (minimally, incarceration). In the context of wide-scale killings of noncombatants during armed conflict, there is a range of behavior that reflects sociopolitical circumstances and mandates. In the Spanish Civil War, in areas of secure control and at the beginning of the war—when the war was still very much perceived as being a coup d'état—killings were often at or around established cemeteries, and attempts were made to burn bodies en masse. When publicity of Nationalist mass killings threatened to move international support toward the Republicans, Nationalist military orders were issued to dispose of bodies more discretely.

In Bosnia–Herzegovina, initial killings and mass body disposals (typically burials) were done only somewhat clandestinely, taking into consideration that United Nations and other foreign body agents were operating throughout the territory. Later, remarkable efforts were conducted to remove bodies from their primary burial place and rebury them in more clandestine secondary or even tertiary locations. Subsequently, in Kosovo, bodies were sometimes transported out of the territory and buried on military bases or other more secure locations in Serbia (Tuller et al. 2008). Thus, when one seeks the bodies of victims, one must take into account the objectives and constraints of the killers given the sociopolitical context at the time of and subsequent to the killings.

An important conclusion reached by several authors who have studied individual and serial murderers is that their spatial decisions and movement related to their crimes and victim body disposal are not unlike that of other serial criminals (e.g., burglars and rapists). This observation lends weight to the feasibility of modeling the spatial behavior of those who are often popularly conceived of and portrayed by the media as unpredictable, incomprehensible psychopaths (e.g., Leyton 2005:327–330; Owen 2006). Research on body disposal patterns of homicide and serial homicide victims demonstrates that serial killers in different countries employ an "inherent logic" and are guided by rationality in their spatial choices. Studies of serial killers in several countries support the idea that behavior patterns are based on factors that transcend cultural and political boundaries.

In the study of the Spanish Civil War killings, it was posited that the near or actual impunity of killers led to their traveling only short distances (albeit at night) and killing victims along mostly primary roads. Data from studies on serial homicide and sexual homicide demonstrate that there is remarkably little difference (with some exceptions) in the distances traveled between victim–offender encounter site and body disposal site. The coincidence of geometry across these seemingly very different types of killings suggests that the root of body disposal location is simply logical universal human behavior. The overall evidence related to the taphonomic signature of *H. sapiens sapiens* suggests that the behavior of victim disposal in various contexts is logical and patterned. This conclusion should provoke further study in what is certainly within the professional realm of anthropologists.

References

Allen, P. (2010) *Katyn: Stalin's Massacre and the Triumph of Truth*. Northern Illinois University Press, DeKalb, IL.

AP (2003) Mass grave unearthed in Guatemala. *The Guardian*, Monday 1st September. Electronic document, http://www.guardian.co.uk/world/2003/sep/01/1, accessed June 28, 2011.

Armengou, M. and R. Belis (2004) *Las Fosas del Silencio*. Random House, Barcelona, Spain.

Auerbach, R. (1979) In the fields of Treblinka. In *The Death Camp Treblinka* ed. A. Donat, pp. 19–74. Holocaust Library, New York.

Badcock, J. (2005) Saved by the war. *Index on Censorship* 2:68–71.

Bahamonde, A. (2005) *Un Año con Queipo de Llano*. Espuela de Plata, Sevilla, Spain.

Ball, H. (1999) *Prosecuting War Crimes and Genocide: The Twentieth-Century Experience*. University of Kansas, Lawrence, KA.

Baraybar, J. P. (2008) When DNA is not available, can we still identify people? Recommendations for best practice. *Journal of Forensic Sciences* 53:533–540.

Barcala, D. (2010) Mi padre está en la caja 198, en la cripta derecha. *Público*, 13th October. Electronic document, http://www.publico.es/espana/341266/mi-padre-esta-en-la-caja-198-en-la-cripta-derecha, accessed July 3, 2011.

Barcala, D. (2011) El Gobierno concluye que los cuerpos del Valle de los Caídos no son identificables. *Público*, 4th May. Electronic document, http://www.publico.es/especiales/memoriapublica/374360/el-gobierno-concluye-que-los-cuerpos-del-valle-de-los-caidos-no-son-identificables, accessed May 5, 2011.

Baviano, J. M. (1980) El juicio contra el alcalde de Torremegía el recuerdo de los fusilamientos de 1936. *El País*, 22nd June. Electronic document, www.elpais.com/articulo/espana/badajoz/jucio/alcalde/torremegia/recuerdo/fusilamientos/1936/elpepiesp/19800622elpepinac_3/tes/, accessed June 3, 2009.

Bax, M. (1997) Mass graves, stagnating identification, and violence: A case study in the local sources of the war in Bosnia Hercegovina. *Anthropological Quarterly* 70:11–19.

BBC (1998) Murder in the name of war—My Lai, Monday 20th July. Electronic document, http://news.bbc.co.uk/2/hi/asia-pacific/64344.stm, accessed June 30, 2011.

Becker, H. S. (1999) The Chicago School, So-called. *Qualitative Sociology* 22(1):3–12.

Beech, J. G. (2002) The differing development paths of Second World War concentration camps and the possibility of an application of a principle of equifinality. In *Matériel Culture; The Archaeology of Twentieth-Century Conflict* eds. J. Schofield, W. G. Johnson, and C. M. Beck, pp. 199–207. Routledge, London, U.K.

Bennassar, B. (2005) *El Infierno Fuimos Nosotros*. Taurus, Madrid, Spain.

Berman, D. M. (2003) Calling the wandering souls: A journey through the heartland of ethnic cleansing. *War, Literature and the Arts* 15:267–282.

Bevan, D. (1994) *A Case to Answer: The Story of Australia's First European War Crimes Prosecution*. Wakefield Printing, Kent Town, South Australia, Australia.

Bouckaert, P. (2003) The mass graves of al-Mahawil: The truth uncovered. Human Rights Watch report, 15(5) (E), May 2003. Electronic document, http://hrw.org/reports/2003/iraq0503/, accessed October 18, 2011.

Boudreaux, M. C., W. D. Lord, and R. L. Dutra (1999) Child abduction: Age-based analyses of offender, victim, and offense characteristics in 550 cases of alleged child disappearance. *Journal of Forensic Sciences* 44:539–553.

Browning, C. (1998) *Ordinary Men; Reserve Police Battalion 101 and the Final Solution in Poland*. Harper Perennial, New York.

Bucheli, S. R., J. A. Byetheway, and S. M. Pustilnik (2009) Insect successional pattern of a corpse in cooler months of subtropical southeastern Texas. *Journal of Forensic Sciences* 54:452–455.

Canter, D. V., L. J. Alison, E. Alison, and N. Wentink (2004) The organized/disorganized typology of serial murder: Myth or model? *Psychology, Public Policy and Law* 10:293–320.

Castro, L. (2006) *Capital de la Cruzad: Burgos durante la Guerra Civil*. Crítica, Barcelona, Spain.

Congram, D. (2010) *Spatial Analysis and Predictive Modelling of Clandestine Graves from Rearguard Repression of the Spanish Civil War*. Unpublished doctoral thesis, Simon Fraser University, Burnaby, British Columbia, Canada.

Congram, D., A. Flavel, and K. Maeyama (n.d.) Ignorance is not bliss: Evidence of human rights violations from Civil War Spain. In *Human Rights and Forensic Science* eds. E. O'Brien and N. Hayes. TMC Asser Press, The Hague, the Netherlands.

Congram, D. and J. Sterenberg (2009) Grave problems in Iraq. In *Handbook of Forensic Archaeology and Anthropology* eds. S. Blau and D. H. Ubelaker, pp. 441–453. Left Coast Press, Walnut Creek, CA.

Couffon, C. (1962) *A Grenade, sur les Pas de Garcia Lorca*. Seghers, Paris, France.

Daly, M. and M. Wilson (1988) *Homicide*. Aldine de Gruyter, New York.

Daubert v. *Merrell Dow Pharmaceuticals, Inc.*, 509 U.S. 579 (1993).

Desbois, P. (2008) *The Holocaust by Bullets*, Palgrave MacMillan, New York.

Doretti, M. and C. C. Snow (2003) Forensic anthropology and human rights: The Argentine experience. In *Hard Evidence: Case Studies in Forensic Anthropology* ed. D. W. Steadman, pp. 290–310. Prentice Hall, Upper Saddle River, NJ.

El Tiempo (2007) Por siete ríos corrió la sangre derramada, Las Fosas de los Paras. *El Tiempo* Tuesday 24th April, pp. 1–9.

Espinosa, F. (2006) *Contra el Olvido: Historia y Memoria de la Guerra Civil*. Crítica, Barcelona, Spain.

Espinosa, F. (2007) *La Columna de la Muerte*. Crítica, Barcelona, Spain.

Espinosa, F. (2009) Informe sobre la represión franquista. In *La Gran Represióni* ed. M. Nuñez Díaz-Balart, pp. 433–469. Flor del Viento, Barcelona, Spain.

Ferrándiz, F. (2009) Fosas comunes, paisajes del terror. *Revista de Dialectología y Tradiciones Populares* LXIV(1):61–94.

Fischer, B. B. (2005) The Katyn controversy; Stalin's killing field. Studies in Intelligence Winter 1999–2000. Available online at https://www.cia.gov/library/center-for-the-study-of-intelligence/csi-publications/csi-studies/studies/winter99–00/art6.html, accessed December 20, 2011.

FitzGibbon, L. (1971) *Katyn*. Tom Stacey, London, U.K.

FitzGibbon, L. (1975) *Unpitied and Unknown; Katyn... Bologoye... Dergachi*. Bachman & Turner, London, U.K.

Flavel, A. and C. Barker (2009) Forensic anthropology and archaeology in Guatemala. In *Handbook of Forensic Archaeology and Anthropology* eds. S. Blau and D. H. Ubelaker, pp. 426–440. Left Coast Press, Walnut Creek, CA.

Gibson, I. (1973) *The Death of Lorca*. W. H. Allen, London, U.K.

Godwin, M. and D. Canter (1997) Encounter and death: The spatial behavior of US serial killers. *Policing: An International Journal of Police Strategy and Management* 20:24–38.

Gojanović, M. D. and D. Sutlović (2007) Skeletal remains from World War II mass grave: From discovery to identification. *Croatian Medical Journal* 48:520–527.

Gómez, L. and N. Junquera (2008) Dónde acabaron? *El País, Domingo*, September 14.

Gómez-López, A. M. and A. Patiño Umaña (2007) Who is missing? Problems in the application of archaeology and anthropology in Colombia's conflict. In *Forensic Archaeology and Human Rights Violations* ed. R. Ferllini, pp. 170–204. Charles C. Thomas, Springfield, IL.

Graham, H. (2005) *The Spanish Civil War*. Oxford University Press, Oxford, U.K.

Haglund, W. D., M. Connor, and D. D. Scott (2001) The archaeology of contemporary mass graves. *Historical Archaeology* 35:57–69.

Häkkänen, H., K. Hurme, and M. Liukkonen (2007) Distance patterns and disposal sites in rural area homicides committed in Finland. *Journal of Investigative Psychology and Offender Profiling* 4:181–197.

Hanfland, K. A., R. D. Keppel, and J. G. Weis (1997) *Case Management for Missing Children Homicide Investigation*. Attorney General of Washington and U.S. Department of Justice Office of Juvenile Justice and Delinquency Prevention, Olympia, WA.

Herrero Balsa, G. and A. Hernández García (1982) *La represión en Soria Durante la Guerra Civil*. Herrero Balsa and Hernández García, Soria, Spain.

Herreros, F. and H. Criado (2009) Pre-emptive or arbitrary: Two forms of lethal violence in a civil war. *Journal of Conflict Resolution* 53:419.

Hess, P. (2004) Evidence to be unearthed from mass graves. *The Washington Times*, 7 January. Electronic document, http://www.washingtontimes.com/news/2004/jan/6/20040106-093959-2372r/, accessed October 18, 2011.

Hirz, R. (1999) *Republic of Austria, Federal Ministry of the Interior, Kosovo Crime Scene Team, Crimes Scene: XXI*. International Criminal Tribunal for the former Yugoslavia, Translation 03010876.

Holland, T. D., B. E. Anderson, and R. W. Mann (2002) Human variables in the postmortem alteration of human bone: Examples from U.S. war casualties. In *Advances in Forensic Taphonomy: Method, Theory, and Archaeological Perspectives* eds. W. D. Haglund and M. H. Sorg, pp. 263–274. CRC Press, Boca Raton, FL.

Human Rights Watch (1997) Bosnia and Hercegovina: The unindicted; Reaping the rewards of ethnic cleansing. Electronic document, http://www.hrw.org/reports/1997/bosnia/Bosnia-06.htm#P731_154719, accessed October 14, 2011.

Human Rights Watch (2004) Iraq: State of the Evidence. *Human Rights Watch Report* 16(7):1–41.

ICMP (2004) Summary report on the forensic monitoring activities relating to the excavation and recovery of human remains from several related features located at Batajnica, Serbia and Montenegro, August to December 2002.

ICTY (2003) *International Criminal Tribunal for the Prosecution of Persons Responsible for Serious Violations of International Law Committed in the Territory of the Former Yugoslavia since 1991,* Witness Statement, document X0169239.

Jackson, G. (1965) *The Spanish Republic and the Civil War.* Princeton University Press, Princeton, NJ.

Jennings, S. (2009) Kosovo victims relatives testify about mass graves. Institute for War and Peace Research. Electronic document, http://iwpr.net/report-news/kosovo-victims%E2%80%99-relatives-testify-about-mass-graves, accessed June 28, 2011.

Kalyvas, S. N. (2003) The ontology of political violence: Action and identity in civil wars. *Perspectives on Politics* 1:475–494.

Kalyvas, S. (2006) *The Logic of Violence in Civil War.* Yale University Press, New Haven, CT.

Kamenetsky, I. (ed.) (1989) *The Tragedy of Vinnytsia.* Ukrainian Historical Association, Toronto, Ontario, Canada.

Komar, D. A. and S. Lathrop (2008) The use of material culture to establish the ethnic identity of victims in genocide investigations: A validation study from the American Southwest. *Journal of Forensic Sciences* 53:1035–1039.

Kraemer, G. W., W. D. Lord, and K. Heilbrun (2004) Comparing single and serial homicide offenses. *Behavioral Sciences & the Law* 22:325–343.

Laban Hinton, D. (2002) The dark side of modernity. In *Annihilating Difference: The Anthropology of Genocide* ed. A. L. Hinton, pp. 1–39. University of California Press, Berkeley, CA.

Lecomte, D. and W. Vorhauer (1999) *French Forensic Mission Kosovo—Summer 1999; Site Report, Cirez Site 2nd and 3rd July 1999.* International Criminal Tribunal for the former Yugoslavia, court document 03035631 (K017-6651–K017-6756).

Leyton, E. (2005) *Hunting Humans.* McClelland and Stewart, Toronto, Ontario, Canada.

Listi, G. A., M. H. Manhein, and M. Leitner (2007) Use of the global positioning system in the field recovery of scattered human remains, *Journal of Forensic Sciences* 52:11–15.

Lord, W. D., M. C. Boudreaux, J. P. Jarvis, J. Waldvogel, and H. Weeks (2002) Comparative patterns in life course victimization: Competition, social rivalry, and predatory tactics in child homicide in the United States. *Homicide Studies* 6:325–347.

Lundrigan, S. and D. Canter (2001a) Spatial patterns of serial murder: An analysis of disposal site location choice. *Behavioral Sciences & the Law* 19:595–610.

Lundrigan, S. and D. Canter (2001b) A multivariate analysis of serial murderers disposal site location choice. *Journal of Environmental Psychology* 21:423–432.

Maeyama, K. and A. Fernández-Congram (2008) Cultural objects analysis and the recovery of evidence. Paper presented at the *Society of Historical Archaeology 41st Annual Conference*, January 12, 2008, Albuquerque, NM.

Manhein, M. H., G. A. Listi, and M. Leitner (2006) The application of geographic information systems and spatial analysis to assess dumped and subsequently scattered human remains. *Journal of Forensic Sciences* 51:469–474.

Mann, R. W., W. M. Bass, and L. Meadows (1990) Time since death and decomposition of the human body: Variables and observations in case and experimental field studies. *Journal of Forensic Sciences* 35:103–111.

Manning, D. (2000) *Srebrenica Investigation; Summary of Forensic Evidence—Execution Points and Mass Graves.* United Nations International Criminal Tribunal for the former Yugoslavia.

Mant, A. K. (1987) Knowledge acquired from post-war exhumations. In *Death, Decay and Reconstruction: Approaches to Archaeology and Forensic Science* eds. A. Boddington, A. N. Garland and R. C. Janaway. Manchester University Press, Manchester, U.K.

Mark, J. (2010) What remains? Anti-communism, forensic archaeology, and the retelling of the national past in Lithuania and Romania. *Past & Present* 206:276–300.

Martín Barrio, A., M. de los Angeles Sampedro Talabán, and M. J. Velasco Marcos (1988) Dos formas de violencia durante la guerra civil. La represión en Salamanca y la Resistencia armada en Zamora. In *Historia y Memoria de la Guerra Civil* (vol. 2) ed. J. Aróstegui, pp. 367–438. Junta de Castilla y León, Valladolid, Spain.

Maver, D. (n.d.) Historical overview: The ethnic wars phenomena towards the end of the second millennium and some problems of investigation of war crimes. Electronic document, http://www.fpvv.uni-mb.si/conf2004/papers/maver.pdf, accessed November 16, 2006.

Morton, R. J. and W. D. Lord (2002) Detection and recovery of abducted and murdered children: Behavioral and taphonomic influences. In *Advances in Forensic Taphonomy: Method, Theory and Archaeological Perspectives* eds. W. D. Haglund and M. H. Sorg, pp. 151–171. CRC Press, Boca Raton, FL.

Nethery, K. (2002) Non-familial abductions that end in homicide: An analysis of the distance patterns and disposal sites. Unpublished Master of Arts thesis, Simon Fraser University, Burnaby, British Columbia, Canada.

Olson, A. P. (1966) A mass secondary burial from Northern Arizona. *American Antiquity* 31:822–876.

OSCE (1999) Violation of the right to life. In *Kosovo/Kosova; As Seen, as Told*. Organization for Security and Co-operation in Europe, Office for Democratic Institutions and Human Rights. Electronic document, http://www.osce.org/odihr/17773?download = true, accessed October 14, 2011.

Owen, D. (2006) Hubris and nemesis in heads of government. *Journal of the Royal Society of Medicine* 99:548–551.

Oxford English Dictionary (2011) Online edition. Available at http://www.oed.com/, accessed November 30, 2011.

Palo, J. U., M. Hedman, N. Söderholm, and A. Sajantila (2007) Repatriation and identification of Finnish World War II Soldiers. *Croatian Medical Journal* 48:528–535.

Petrou, M. (2005) Sex, spies and Bethune's secret. *Maclean's* 118(43):46–52.

Pons Prades, E. (2006) *Las Escuadras de la Muerte*. Flor del Viento Ediciones, Barcelona, Spain.

Prada Rodríguez, J. (2006) *De la agitación Republicana a la represión Franquista. Ourense 1934–1939*. Ariel, Madrid, Spain.

Prieto, J. L., C. Magaña, and D. Ubelaker (2004) Interpretation of postmortem change in cadavers in Spain. *Journal of Forensic Sciences* 49:1–6.

Quantum (2000) Unearthing evil. Electronic document, http://www.abc.net.au/quantum/stories/s124137.htm, accessed November 16, 2006. Australian Broadcasting Corporation.

Raszeja, S. and E. Chróścielewski (1994) Medicolegal reconstruction of the Katyn forest massacre. *Forensic Science International* 68:1–6.

Recknagel, C. (2003) Iraqis open Saddam Hussein's mass graves, demand justice (Part 1). *Radio Free Europe*, July 7. Electronic document, http://www.rferl.org/content/article/1103735.html, accessed October 18, 2011.

Reddick, A. (2006) *The Use of Spatial Techniques in the Location and Excavation of Contemporary Mass Graves*. Unpublished Master of Philosophy thesis, Institute of Archaeology and Antiquity, University of Birmingham, Birmingham, U.K.

Rees, L. (2005) *Auschwitz: The Nazis and the 'Final Solution'*. BBC Books, London, U.K.

Reig Tapia, A. (1979) En torno al estudio de la represión franquista. *Tiempo de Historia* 58:4–23.

Reig Tapia, A. (2006) Represión y esfuerzo humanitarios. In *La Guerra Civil Española* ed. E. Malefakis, pp. 521–552. Taurus, Madrid, Spain.

Rengert, G. F., A. R. Piquero, and P. R. Jones (1999) Distance decay reexamined. *Criminology* 37:427–446.

Ressler, R. K., A. W. Burgess, J. E. Douglas, C. R. Hartman, and R. B. D'Agostino (1986) Sexual killers and their victims: Identifying patterns through crime scene analysis. *Journal of Interpersonal Violence* 1:288–308.

Rhodes, R. (2002) *Masters of Death: The SS-Einsatzgruppen and the Invention of the Holocaust*. Random House, New York.

Richards, M. (2007) Los límites de la cuantificación: Represión franquista y la metodología histórica. *Hispania Nova* 7. Electronic document, http://hispanianova.rediris.es/7/dossier/07d015.pdf, accessed June 28, 2010.

Rilova Pérez, I. (2001) *Guerra Civil y Violencia Política en Burgos (1936–1943)*. Editorial Dorsales, Burgos, Spain.

Rodrigo, J. (2008) *Hasta la Raíz*. Editorial Alianza, Madrid, Spain.

Ross, A. H. and S. L. Cunningham (2011) Time-since-death and bone weathering in a tropical environment. *Forensic Science International* 204:126–133.

Rossmo, D. K. (1995) *Geographic Profiling: Target Patterns of Serial Murderers*. Unpublished PhD thesis, Simon Fraser University, Burnaby, British Columbia, Canada.

Rossmo, D. K. (2000) *Geographic Profiling*. CRC Press, Boca Raton, FL.

Ruíz, J. (2009) Seventy years on: Historians and repression during and after the Spanish Civil War. *Journal of Contemporary History* 44:449–472.

Salfati, C. G. and A. L. Bateman (2005) Serial homicide: An investigation of behavioural consistency. *Journal of Investigative Psychology and Offender Profiling* 2:121–144.

Schofield, J., W. G. Johnson, and C. M. Beck (2002) *Matériel Culture: The Archaeology of Twentieth-Century Conflict*. Routledge, London, U.K.

Silva, E. and S. Macías (2003) *Las Fosas de Franco*. Temas de Hoy, Madrid, Spain.

Simmons, T. (2002) Taphonomy of a karstic cave execution site at Hrgar, Bosnia-Herzegovina. In *Advances in Forensic Taphonomy: Method, Theory, and Archaeological Perspectives* eds. W. D. Haglund and M. H. Sorg, pp. 263–275. CRC Press, Boca Raton, FL.

Skinner, M. (2007) Hapless in Afghanistan: Forensic archaeology in a political maelstrom. In *Forensic Archaeology and Human Rights Violations* eds. R. Ferllini, pp. 233–265. Charles C. Thomas, Springfield, IL.

Skinner, M., D. Alempijevic, and M. Djuric-Srejic (2003) Guidelines for international forensic bio-archaeology monitors of mass grave exhumations. *Forensic Science International* 134:81–92.

Skinner, M., A. Fernández, and D. Congram (2009) Material culture analysis in forensic cases: A call for formal recognition by forensic anthropologists. *Proceedings of the American Academy of Forensic Sciences* 15:336–337.

Skinner, M. and E. Jessee (2005) A typology of mass grave and mass grave-related sites. *Forensic Science International* 152:55–59.

Skinner, M. and R. Lazenby (1983) *Found! Human Remains: A Field Manual for the Recovery of the Recent Human Skeleton*. Archaeology Press, Simon Fraser University, Burnaby, British Columbia, Canada.

Skinner, M. F., H. P. York, and M. A. Connor (2002) Postburial disturbance of graves in Bosnia-Herzegovina. In *Advances in Forensic Taphonomy: Method, Theory, and Archaeological Perspectives* eds. W. D. Haglund and M. H. Sorg, pp. 293–307. CRC Press, Boca Raton, FL.

Snook, B., R. M. Cullen, A. Mokros, and S. Harbort (2005) Serial murderers' spatial decisions: Factors that influence crime location choice. *Journal of Investigative Psychology and Offender Profiling* 2:147–164.

Steadman, D. W. and W. D. Haglund (2005) The scope of anthropological contributions to human rights investigations. *Journal of Forensic Sciences* 50:1–8.

Sui, D. Z. (2009) Tobler's first law of geography: A big idea for a small world? *Annals of the Association of American Geographers* 94:269–277.

Susa, E. (2007) Forensic anthropology in Hungary. In *Forensic Anthropology: Case Studies from Europe* eds. M. Brickley and R. Ferllini, pp. 203–215. Charles C. Thomas, Springfield, IL.

Torres, R. (2002) *Desaparecidos de la Guerra de España (1936 - ?)*. La Esfera de los Libros, Madrid, Spain.

Tremlett, G. (2005) Argentinean jailed for throwing prisoners from plane. *The Guardian,* April 20. Electronic document, http://www.guardian.co.uk/world/2005/apr/20/argentina.gilestremlett, accessed June 27, 2011.

Tuller, H. (2012) Mass graves and human rights: Latest developments, methods and lessons learned. In *A Companion to Forensic Anthropology* eds. D. C. Dirkmaat. Wiley-Blackwell, Hoboken, NJ.

Tuller, H., U. Hofmeister, and S. Daley (2008) Spatial analysis and mass grave mapping data to assist in the reassociation of disarticulated and commingled remains. In *Recovery, Analysis, and Identification of Commingled Remains* eds. B. Adams and J. Byrd, pp. 7–30. Humana Press, Totowa, NJ.

United Nations (2011) *UN Data.* Electronic document, http://data.un.org/Data.aspx?q=population+density&d=PopDiv&f=variableID%3a14, accessed October 3, 2011.

Van Patten, I. T. and P. Q. Delhauer (2007) Sexual homicide: A spatial analysis of 25 years of deaths in Los Angeles. *Journal of Forensic Sciences* 52:1129–1141.

Vass, A. A. (2011) The elusive universal post-mortem interval formula. *Forensic Science International* 201:34–40.

Vilaplana, R. (1977) *Doy Fe*, 3rd edn. Epidauro, Barcelona, Spain.

Walston, J. (1997) History and memory of the Italian concentration camps. *The Historical Journal* 40:169–183.

Warren, M. W. and W. R. Maples (1997) The anthropometry of contemporary commercial cremation. *Journal of Forensic Sciences* 42:417–423.

Weiss-Wendt, A. (2003) Extermination of the Gypsies in Estonia during World War II: Popular images and official policies. *Holocaust and Genocide Studies* 17:31–61.

Wessling, R. and L. Loe (2011) The Fromelles project—The recovery and identification of British and Australian WWI soldiers from mass graves in Northern France. *Proceedings of the American Academy of Forensic Sciences, Annual Meeting,* Chicago, IL, p. 369.

Wolentarska-Ochman, E. (2006) Collective remembrance in Jedwabne: Unsettled memory of World War II in postcommunist Poland. *History & Memory* 18:152–178.

Wright, R. (1995) Investigating war crimes: The archaeological evidence. *The Sydney Papers* 7:39–44.

Wright, R. (2010) Where are the bodies? In the ground. *Public Historian* 32:96–107.

Wright, R., I. Hanson, and J. Sterenberg (2005) The archaeology of mass graves. In *Forensic Archaeology: Advances in Theory and Practice* eds. J. Hunter and M. Cox, pp. 137–158. Routledge, London, U.K.

Zavala, J. M. (2006) *Los Horrores de la Guerra Civil.* DeBosillo, Madrid, Spain.

Subaerial Weathering

11

CHRISTINE A. JUNOD
JAMES T. POKINES

Contents

> KING HENRY V: And those that leave their valiant bones in France,
> Dying like men, though buried in your dunghills,
> They shall be fam'd; for there the Sun shall greet them,
> And draw their honours reeking up to heaven.
> **—William Shakespeare, *Henry V, Act IV, Scene 3***

Introduction

Subaerial bone weathering can be described in lay terms as grossly similar to what happens to exterior house paint: it bleaches, loses moisture, cracks, and flakes due to exposure to solar radiation, temperature fluctuations, precipitation, and sometimes from chemical processes and is spalled off in thin fragments (Figure 11.1). While the chemical (Nielsen-Marsh et al. 2000) and physical processes undergone by weathering bones are very different than paint, the end result is a bone that is fragmenting apart to become part of the lithosphere, completing its taphonomic pathway. The relevance of osseous weathering to forensic analyses is

Figure 11.1 Detail of a weathered nonhuman long bone surface. Note the delamination. Scale is in cm.

twofold. First, it is necessary to distinguish this type of taphonomic alteration from other sources, including other processes that bleach and/or crack bone, in order to understand the context from where the bone came. This includes taphonomic alterations that might link a bone to a certain depositional setting, such as weathered remains from a surface deposit, which later get moved to a new location. Similarly, the movement of a bone from its original position while remaining in the same general location is often discernible from its weathering pattern. Second, and of most importance in forensic anthropology, is the information that osseous weathering can give regarding the postmortem interval (PMI). Estimation of the PMI in the middle range between where decomposition and entomological studies leave off (typically less than 1 year) and radiocarbon dating (prior to AD 1950) begins. Forensic anthropologists have few viable options within this interval (Beary 2005) and often must rely upon artifactual evidence accompanying remains (clothing or other personal objects), broad taphonomic patterns indicating a lack of forensic relevance (see Chapter 5, this volume), or related analyses such as the development of annual rings in trees in direct association with remains (Willey and Heilman 1987). Weathering analysis also has the potential for misuse where temporal standards developed in different environments are applied uncritically to estimate the PMI (Lyman 1994; Lyman and Fox 1989, 1997).

The effects of differing environment (including temperate deciduous forest, semiarid equatorial savanna, or tundra) and microhabitat within that environment (i.e., patches of forest, brush, wetland, or grass cover within a temperate deciduous forest) upon the rates of osseous weathering have been little researched in any world region (Andrews and Cook 1985; Cutler et al. 1999; Hill 1976; Janjua and Rogers 2008; Miller 2009; Misner et al. 2009; Pokines 2009; Purdy and Clark 1987; Ross and Cunningham 2011; Tappen 1969, 1976, 1994; Ubelaker and Sperber 1988; Western and Behrensmeyer 2009; White and Hannus 1983). This gap in our knowledge is likely due to the time needed to gather observations of weathering changes over a meaningful time span (Behrensmeyer 1978; Behrensmeyer and Miller 2012; Toots 1965; Western and Behrensmeyer 2009), or the need to have bones of known depositional age with which to commence a study (Miller 2009). In addition, a large sample size in a natural setting, where the same skeletal elements can be identified and their individual changes recorded year after year, must be utilized. Due to potential seasonality effects, one must also know the timing of deposition within a given year. Only long-term research projects spanning decades can answer these questions, combined where possible with naturalistic observations of bones deposited at known times in the past (Miller 2009).

Subaerial weathering also makes bones in some cases more susceptible to other kinds of taphonomic alteration. Most importantly, many species of rodent preferentially gnaw on dry, weathered bone. These include many species of porcupines, large rodents with wide ranges throughout the world that can damage bones greatly in order to wear their incisors and obtain mineral salts from bone (Brain 1980, 1981; Kerbis Peterhans 1990; Roze 2009; see Chapter 9, this volume). The breakdown of the bone surface also makes it susceptible to subsequent rounding and wear when introduced into an abrasive fluvial environment (Fernández-Jalvo and Andrews 2003), making the loss of the surface layers more rapid. The loss of surface features from both of these processes limits the biological information that can be derived from a bone, including element, species, development, and evidence of perimortem trauma. Dry, weathered bone also is altered differently when burned than is fresh, green bone (Buikstra and Goldstein 1973; Buikstra and Ubelaker 1994), providing important clues regarding the timing of postmortem thermal alteration. Micozzi (1991) notes that the end process of weathering may delete the less robust bones from a surface assemblage first, changing the relative proportions of skeletal elements surviving for analysis. Drying and loss of organic component accompanying the weathering process also make bones of less interest to large scavengers, decreasing the likelihood for further gnawing and dispersal by these taxa (Faith and Behrensmeyer 2006). Surface deposition also makes bones far more likely to undergo multiple other taphonomic processes, including algal and other biological interactions (see "Other Effects of Surface Exposure" section). Subaerial weathering is one part of an interlocking pattern of taphonomic changes that skeletal remains may undergo.

Processes of Weathering

Bone Properties

The exact mechanisms of bone weathering are poorly understood experimentally, but the gross physical processes involve the loss of organic content, loss of moisture, bleaching of the surface layers, and cracking (Beary 2005; Behrensmeyer 1978; Behrensmeyer and Miller 2012; Brain 1967; Cutler et al. 1999; Miller 1975). In materials science, *fatigue* is the localized, cumulative structural damage caused by repeated loading and unloading of an object that leads to cracking, fracture, and failure. Schütz (1996) provides a detailed history of the study of fatigue, emphasizing the German contribution made during the mid-1900s, and these same principles from engineering may be applied to organic supportive tissues. Living bone is subjected to constant stresses and may fail cumulatively under these conditions (forming a stress fracture) or more rapidly under more extreme loading (Cox and Yang 2007; Doblaré et al. 2004; Galloway 1999; Tomar 2009), but living bone can repair damage and reshape itself in response to repeated stress (Wolff's law). Dead bone no longer has the capacity for self-repair, and cumulative fatigue through multiple environmental stresses leads to crack propagation and its gradual flaking apart in more advanced stages.

Since the collagen fibers in living/fresh bone limit crack propagation through the mineral (largely hydroxyapatite) matrix, any collagen loss or breakdown also will reduce a bone's ability to withstand cracking. Using SEM imaging, Thurner et al. (2007) noted that bone fails by the delamination and separation of mineralized collagen fibrils, which results in the whitening of the bone. The collagen component is also largely responsible for the ability of bone to withstand tensile forces (Doblaré et al. 2004), so any taphonomic process that expands bone is more likely to cause cracking when the collagen component is degraded. Similarly, partial dissolution of the mineral component also will weaken bone and increase the ease with which other taphonomic processes can cause cracking and flaking. This process is paralleled in living persons with osteoporosis, whose bones break far more easily (and often just from muscle contraction without any corresponding blunt force trauma) as the mineral component decreases (Doblaré et al. 2004; McGee et al. 2007).

Patterns of Physical Degradation to Osseous Remains

Miller (1975) and Behrensmeyer (1978) first laid out stages of osseous weathering for large mammals (i.e., those above 5 kg average adult body mass, classified as megafauna), describing six *weathering stages* (WS 0 through WS 5) based on the progressive pattern of linear cracking and flaking of the cortical surface, followed by formation of a rough fibrous texture, and eventual loss of bone structure. [These stages with accompanying photographs are reproduced in their entirety in Buikstra and Ubelaker (1994).] These proceed as outlined in Table 11.1. When determining which weathering stage should be assigned, Behrensmeyer (1978) indicated that the most advanced stage covering an area larger than 1 cm^2 should be recorded, avoiding areas of physical damage, and all observers must agree concerning the stage before it is recorded. This progressive pattern of cracking and flaking is the basis for determining weathering stages and is broadly indicative of the period of surface exposure (Behrensmeyer 1978). While the rate of weathering is highly dependent upon climate and microenvironment, the stages of weathering seem to follow the same pathway as the pattern described earlier, regardless of environmental conditions (Behrensmeyer and Miller 2012; Buikstra and Ubelaker 1994; Madgwick and Mulville 2012; Miller 2009; Tappen 1994).

Weathering is characterized by both cracking, where splits penetrate inward, and delamination, where splits occur circumferentially and layers of bone peel away from the remainder, slowly reducing its overall size and integrity. More general flaking can occur where irregular fragments spall off. Bone cracking due to weathering normally runs parallel to the orientation of the osteons, following the *split-line orientation* of a bone (Buckland-Wright 1977; Tappen 1969, 1976; Tappen and Peske 1970). In practical terms, cracking tends to proceed parallel to the long axes of the ribs, long bones, metapodials, and other bones with a long, narrow structure (Hill 1976) (Figure 11.2). On other irregularly shaped elements such as vertebrae (Figure 11.3), the direction of cracking follows the less-linear overall osteon orientation, which must orient in more than one direction to follow multiple directions of stress. Weathering cracks of these elements therefore tend to be more irregular.

The microscopic structure of bone is also key to understanding how it weathers and how variations in the major structural type of bone may affect how weathering proceeds. Plexiform (or fibrolamellar) bone is found in very young humans, but is a common microscopic structural type in large nonhuman mammals due to their rapid growth requirements

Table 11.1 Summary of Weathering Stages as Defined by Behrensmeyer (1978)

WS	Bone Condition	Soft Tissue
0	Bone surface shows no sign of cracking or flaking due to weathering	Usually bone is still greasy, marrow cavities contain tissue, skin and muscle/ligament may cover part or all of the bone surface
1	Bone shows cracking, normally parallel to the fiber structure (e.g., longitudinal in long bones). Articular surfaces may show mosaic cracking of covering tissue as well as in the bone itself	Fat, skin, and other tissue may or may not be present
2	Outermost concentric thin layers of bone show flaking, usually associated with cracks, in that the bone edges along the cracks tend to separate and flake first. Long thin flakes, with one or more sides still attached to the bone, are common in the initial part of Stage 2. Deeper and more extensive flaking follows, until most of the outermost bone is gone. Crack edges are usually angular in cross section	Remnants of ligaments, cartilage, and skin may be present
3	Bone surface is characterized by patches of rough, homogenously weathered compact bone, resulting in a fibrous texture. In these patches, all the external, concentrically layered bone has been removed. Gradually the patches extend to cover the entire bone surface. Weathering does not penetrate deeper than 1.0–1.5 mm at this stage, and bone fibers are still firmly attached to each other. Crack edges usually are rounded in cross section	Tissue rarely present at this stage (or beyond)
4	The bone surface is coarsely fibrous and rough in texture; large and small splinters occur and may be loose enough to fall away from the bone when it is moved. Weathering penetrates into inner cavities. Cracks are open and have splintered or rounded edges	
5	Bone is falling apart in situ, with large splinters lying around what remains of the whole, which is fragile and easily broken by moving. Original bone shape may be difficult to determine. Cancellous bone usually exposed, when present, and may outlast all traces of the former more compact, outer parts of the bones	

Source: Behrensmeyer, A.K., *Palaeobiology*, 4, 150, 1978. Reprinted with permission from the Paleontological Society, Inc./BioOne.

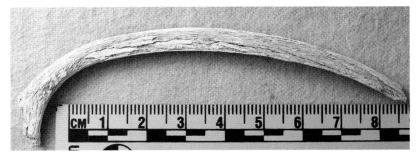

Figure 11.2 Weathered caprine rib, WS 3. Note how the cracks orient parallel to the shaft of the rib, with patches of delamination exposing a rough, fibrous texture and some deeper cracking.

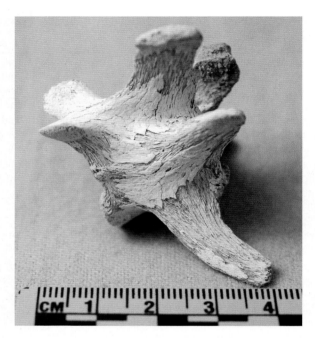

Figure 11.3 Weathered (WS 3) caprine vertebra. Note how the cracks orient parallel to the major structures of the bone and note the patches of delamination exposing the rough, fibrous texture.

(Hillier and Bell 2007; Morris 2007; Weiner and Wagner 1998) and short lifespans in the wild or under most domesticated systems of butchery timing, where subadults are normally culled. These include many of the species of quadrupeds (primarily Bovidae) whose remains were analyzed by Behrensmeyer (1978) in her original systemization of weathering stages. Plexiform bone has a regular, "brick like" structure and is laid down in radial bands, which in bovids are approximately 200 μm thick (Currey 2002:18). The microscopic plexiform structure consists of layers of parallel-fiber woven bone, which is laid down rapidly, with lamellar bone more slowly filling in the cavities in the woven structure. This structure may get transformed gradually into lamellar bone as the animal ages, including primary and secondary osteon formation (Stover et al. 1992). In the lamellar bone of adult humans, the osteonal structure does not fit the regular osteonal banding of plexiform bone, and indeed the constant remodeling of secondary osteons rewrites/replaces the primary osteonal structure (Mulhern and Ubelaker 2001). No osteonal banding is present, so spalling of lamellar bone surfaces due to weathering (apart from the surface layer) is likely to be much more irregular than that in plexiform bone, although the cracking of the surface of lamellar bone tends to parallel the underlying osteonal structure (Buckland-Wright 1977; Tappen 1969, 1976; Tappen and Peske 1970). Models of bone weathering derived from nonhuman mammal species therefore may not be precisely applicable to adult human remains, but a great deal of long-term research using human bones in controlled settings in direct comparison with nonhuman bones is required to answer this question.

Examples of the slow breakdown of bone by weathering are shown in Figures 11.2 through 11.9, which also illustrate the effects that the presence of plexiform bone, with its regular layered structure, has upon surface flaking/spalling. Note that while the surface of the bone is highly cracked and beginning to spall (Figure 11.4), the interior cortical

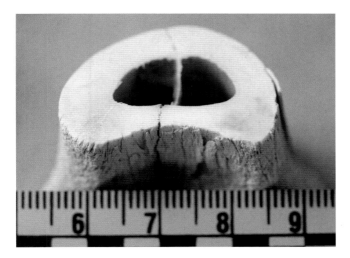

Figure 11.4 Sectioned metacarpal shaft of cattle (*Bos taurus*), showing intact inner cortex of plexiform bone, surface cracking, and a large patch of delamination (right side of photograph). Most of the visible exterior surface corresponds with WS 2. Scale is in cm.

Figure 11.5 Sectioned metacarpal shaft (plexiform bone) of cattle (*Bos taurus*), showing the variability of weathering states, ranging from unweathered (WS 0; top of photograph), to mildly weathered (WS 1; center of photograph), to weathered and delaminating (WS 2; bottom of photograph). Note also the unweathered bone exposed underneath the surface-delaminated area on the right.

structure is undamaged and highly intact. Subsequent removal of the outer weathered surface of this bone (such as through sand abrasion in a marine coastal environment) would leave little trace that the bone had been weathered previously (Fernández-Jalvo and Andrews 2003). Bone also frequently displays areas of different weathering stages over different surfaces, such as the metacarpal illustrated in Figure 11.5, which ranges from WS 0 (unweathered) to WS 2. This bone was located, as is typical, with the unweathered surface in contact with the ground, and the WS 2 surface the uppermost and therefore the more exposed to environmental effects. Transitional areas of WS 1 bone are in between. Examples of WS 3 bone are depicted in Figure 11.2 (rib) and Figure 11.3 (vertebra), with rougher, fibrous patches of bone revealed under the spalling surface layers. More advanced weathering (WS 4) is depicted in Figures 11.6 through 11.8, in this example a juvenile cattle

Figure 11.6 Sectioned distal right humerus (plexiform bone) of cattle (*Bos taurus*), showing unweathered interior cortex structure underlying the highly weathered (WS 4) exterior.

Figure 11.7 Sectioned distal right humerus of cattle (*Bos taurus*), showing unweathered interior cortex structure underlying the highly weathered (WS 4) exterior. Note the penetrating cracks reaching the marrow cavity and the delamination of the outer layers. The spalling of the osteonal layers of the plexiform bone is highly regular.

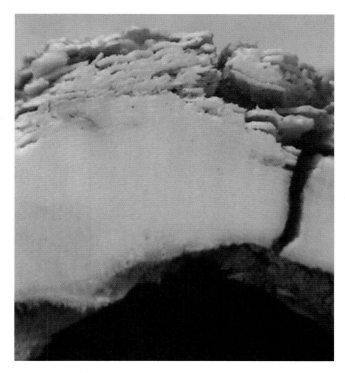

Figure 11.8 Close up of sectioned distal right humerus (plexiform bone) of cattle (*Bos taurus*), showing unweathered interior cortex structure underlying the highly weathered (WS 4) exterior. Note the penetrating crack reaching the marrow cavity and the regular spalling of the outer layers, with intact osteonal layers (each around 200 μm thick) visible.

(*Bos taurus*) humerus whose main microscopic structure is plexiform bone. Deeper cracks have penetrated all the way to the marrow cavity, with areas of bone weathering carrying deeper into the cortex along these cracks. The surface is heavily spalled, with clear delamination following the underlying concentric osteonal bands (Figure 11.8). The majority of the cortex, however, still appears undamaged. The final stage of weathering (WS 5) is reached where the bone is falling apart into fragments (Figure 11.9), and most data about the element, size, type, development, species, and other taphonomic alterations are lost.

Effects of Solar Radiation on Bleaching

Bleaching is one component of the overall suite of weathering changes and begins to show up early in the weathering process (see Chapter 12, this volume, for illustrations of sun bleaching and specific comparisons of this source of bone bleaching with other sources, including chemical). Beary (2005) examined the direct effects of solar (specifically, UV) radiation on the surface color of osseous remains under controlled experimental conditions. As he noted, the surface color of bone has gone largely unexplored in taphonomic research, with bone starting off its usual light beige color (i.e., "ivory" colored or similar descriptor) and becoming progressively bleached by solar radiation. Any quantification of this change was confined to comparison with *Munsell*® Soil Color Charts (Kollmorgen Instruments Corporation 1994). This procedure naturally includes all the variable effects of color

Figure 11.9 The final stage of weathering (WS 5): a bone disintegrating into fragments. The element can no longer be identified.

determination, including differences in light source and interobserver and intraobserver errors. In order to increase accuracy and replicability, Beary (2005) used a digital spectrophotometer to determine the degree of bleaching accrued on a sample of 60 white-tailed deer (*Odocoileus virginianus*) rib segments, half exposed to controlled dosages of generated UV light and half exposed to natural sunlight. Color changes were measured daily for over 1 month. He found highly significant relationships between the duration of UV insolation and the degree of color change (progressive bleaching). The results for the outdoor-exposed rib segments were more variable, as the effects of humidity also had a significant impact, including the degree to which wet bone reflects incident light to the spectrophotometer. The research indicated that bleaching begins immediately (even if it is not detectable by the human eye) upon exposure, although a terminal color was not reached in either portion of the study. The eventual goal is the determination of PMI based upon the accumulated amount of UV light exposure for that location.

Effects of Moisture

The loss of moisture from a bone through surface exposure follows multiple pathways. These include the desiccation or decomposition of protective adhering soft tissue, the presence of which generally halts or greatly slows the weathering process. Continued exposure causes the bone to lose its internal water, although this can get replenished from precipitation cycles. More gradual is the decline in grease content as this decomposes, gets consumed, or slowly leaches to the surface and is lost to dissolution and consumption. Weathering in general appears to be slower where bones are kept moist and protected by vegetation and other forms of cover (Behrensmeyer 1978; Miller 2009), although moisture has long been recognized as an important factor in the breakdown of the organic component of bone (Hare 1974). Tappen (1994) and Pokines (2009) found weathering crack formation to be slower in a tropical rain forest environment than in open savannas and therefore likely partly related to moisture and/or drying cycles of the bones. These environments also presented much more uniform annual temperature with a complete lack of seasonal or daily freezing.

Moisture in the bone, of course, is necessary for the damaging effects of freeze–thaw cycles to take effect (see "Effects of Freezing and Thawing" section). As bone is repeatedly wet and dried, crack formation may be enhanced by the shrinking and swelling of the material, although these effects have been little studied in the context of weathering. Waterlogged bone that dries rapidly may crack suddenly and extensively (see Chapter 6, this volume).

Effects of Heating and Cooling

Heating and cooling through the daily (or more rapid) cycles of direct sunlight upon a bone cause expansion and contraction. Pal and Saha (1989) found that in the range of −20°C to 20°C, the coefficient of thermal expansion in a human tibia ranges from 23 to 32×10^{-6}/°C (i.e., the bone will undergo a linear fractional change in size in the range of 0.000023–0.000032/°C within this range). From 30°C to 60°C (i.e., the interval one would expect bones and other objects lying in direct sunlight in warm environments to attain), they found that the linear fractional change was larger: 37.1×10^{-6}/°C. The normal in vivo temperature of human bone is 37°C. Depending upon the depositional environment, temperature swings of tens of °C per day would be expected for bone lying on the surface between when direct sunlight strikes during day and night or other exclusion of sunlight.

The role that thermal expansion and contraction play in the weathering of bedrock has been examined (Hall 1999). As the cycles of thermal expansion and contraction accrue, material fatigue accumulates, which may cause microfracturing (thermal stress fatigue) or sudden failure (thermal shock) (Hall 1999:48). This model applies to bone, where expansion/contraction damage may accrue slowly over many diurnal cycles and sudden changes in temperature may induce localized failure of the bone structure (Conard et al. 2008), especially in parallel to the heterogeneous structures of osteons including cement lines, resorption spaces, and central canals (Skedros et al. 2005). Bone, however, is more homogenous in composition overall than many types of rock, since the latter may have a highly heterogeneous crystalline structure (such as granite), be composed of heterogeneous sedimentary materials, have metamorphic recrystallization, or have veins of different minerals interrupting the main structure. Differing rates of thermal expansion/contraction in these adjacent mineral crystals in rocks therefore may cause fracturing along their boundaries, while bone is much more homogenous in its composition. Expansion and contraction may explain, however, why the much more highly mineralized (and therefore more brittle) teeth (Currey 2002) with their different structural organization (Weiner and Wagner 1998) often have fractured to a higher degree than their associated cranium or mandible. This different cracking and fragmentation pattern is the reason why teeth are normally excluded from designations of weathering stage for a set of remains.

Effects of Freezing and Thawing

Beyond the linear expansion and contraction of bone with changes in temperature, freezing of water within the cracks already formed within a bone or in other internal spaces has a high potential destructive force. Around 12% of fresh cortical bone volume consists of pore spaces (Nielsen-Marsh et al. 2000), so even the denser portions of a bone can absorb water. Water reaches its maximum density at 4°C, and it undergoes ~9% volume expansion dropping from 4°C to 0°C as it freezes and the H_2O molecules form a hexagonal crystal structure—hence, the property of ice floating. Since water exerts up to

30,000 lb-force/in^2 (207 MPa) as it expands while freezing (Matsuoka and Merton 2008), this force has the greatest potential in the natural environment to spread existing cracks in bone wider and deeper and propagate them longitudinally. The maximum tensile strength of rock (and bone) is far exceeded by this force, especially force directed transversely to bone (Pietruszczak et al. 2007; Turner et al. 2001; Weiner and Wagner 1998). Subsequent thawing then allows the water to penetrate more deeply into these newly expanded cracks before refreezing perhaps during the same diurnal cycle (Matsuoka and Merton 2008). Multiple trips through this cycle may be the dominant destructive force in temperate zone physical weathering of bone, although this process needs further controlled experimentation. These processes are well understood in the geological sciences regarding the mechanical breakdown of rocks (Hall and Thorn 2011; Matsuoka and Merton 2008; Yavuz 2011). The rapidity of this cycling and its occurrence multiple times per day in Spring and Fall in the temperate zone (Matsuoka 1996) may work to destroy bone faster than during summer and winter with their fewer changes in temperature moving above or below the freezing point. Snow cover or ambient temperatures remaining below freezing for long periods would act to inhibit the rate of weathering (Miller 2009). Habitats that cycle through freezing/thawing most frequently (i.e., the temperate zone) may weather bone more rapidly than habitats with more constant temperature above (subtropical and tropical) or below (boreal forest and tundra) this middle range. Locations along bodies of water, with their greater humidity, are also likely to increase the incidence and severity of frost damage (Matsuoka and Merton 2008).

Theoretically, any taphonomic process increasing the pre-cracking or amount of pore space in bone would increase its susceptibility to freezing/thawing damage. These processes might include focal destruction by invading fungi (see Chapter 2, this volume) or plant rootlets (see Chapter 5, this volume), indicating that habitats with high amounts of biological activity may predispose bone to a greater degree of this potential source of weathering damage, provided that they also have seasonal cold phases (including temperate environments).

Effects of Mineral Crystallization

The formation of crystals within bone can also cause cracking, as these minerals expand and force apart the existing bone structure, much as freezing water forms expanding crystals (Trueman et al. 2004). Other effects of mineral crystallization also may cause expansion, including differential thermal expansion of the porous substance versus the impregnating minerals, osmotic swelling of clays, hydration pressure, and enhanced wet/dry cycling (Doehne 2002; Prassack 2011). Minerals that commonly crystallize near the surface of bedrock include halite (NaCl), nitratite (NaNO$_3$), gypsum (CaSO$_4$·2H$_2$O), calcite (CaCO$_3$), and dolomite (CaMg(CO$_3$)$_2$), depending upon the local groundwater solution and other factors (Matsuoka 1995).

This phenomenon has been noted directly affecting bone. Behrensmeyer (1978), Cutler et al. (1999), and Trueman et al. (2004) note the frequent presence of alkaline soils in Amboseli Park, Kenya, where they observed long-term large mammal bone weathering. In some cases, weathering was more advanced on the bone surfaces in contact with the ground than on the opposite surface exposed to more direct solar radiation. They attribute this reverse pattern to the formation of crystals on the undersides of bone that forced apart cracks and increased the overall degree of fragmentation. This phenomenon is known to damage archaeological monuments and artifacts and is indeed one of the primary forces acting against their long-term preservation (Doehne 2002; Johnson 1998; Rodriguez-Navarro and Doehne 1999). Matsuoka (1995) describes how salt crystal formation can fracture bedrock in a similar manner, even in cold Antarctic desert conditions. Crystallization therefore may affect bone weathering in environments where other sources of weathering damage are less prevalent.

Key to this taphonomic (diagenetic) process is the infiltration of groundwater with soluble/exchangeable minerals from the soil (Pate and Hutton 1988; Pate et al. 1989; Sillen 1989). As this solution reaches the surface of bone and other porous materials, the water evaporates, leaving behind the minerals to crystallize (Rodriguez-Navarro and Doehne 1999). This process affects archaeological monuments even in arid environments, such as the well-known tombs carved directly into sandstone at Petra, Jordan, by the Nabataean culture and dating back to the sixth century B.C. The effect is concentrated at the surface layers where the minerals crystallize, with flaking exposing deeper portions of the rock that then become the new surface layer and are exposed to attack. This repeated spalling of the surface layer gradually erodes away the structure of the stone building or monument and is the focus of much conservation effort. Other factors in their weathering include the dissolution of more-soluble minerals, weakening the overall structure (Walderhaug 1998), similar to the breakdown of the organic component through digestion by microbes and chemical breakdown (Nielsen-Marsh et al. 2000; Smith et al. 2005; Turner-Walker 2008), weakening its overall resistance to weathering.

In a study of bones from the Amboseli Basin, Kenya, Trueman et al. (2004) thin-sectioned multiple weathered bones from known large mammal species to detect the microscopic effects of weathering. They found within pore spaces formed by natural bone structures or from postmortem alteration that several mineral types had recrystallized from uptake from the groundwater, including calcite, barite, dahlite, crandallite, trona, and possibly sepiolite, with calcite the most common. The formation of these crystals alters the physical structure of the bones, making their composition less homogenous and more prone to thermal stress, as discussed earlier. The diagenetic effect of recrystallization of bone minerals themselves also may contribute to this cause of weathering. Dissolved bone minerals in the soil water solution can recrystallize the intact hydroxyapatite, also altering the microscopic structure of the bone (Hedges et al. 1995; Nielsen-Marsh et al. 2000; Trueman et al. 2004). The differential thermal expansion and contraction of both types of crystals could aid in the formation of microcracks within the bone, speeding the rate of weathering in locations with a high surface evaporation rate. The recrystallization of the hydroxyapatite also weakens the bone and makes it more susceptible to breakage from mechanical forces, and this effect is similar to that caused by recrystallization due to calcination of burned bone (Stiner et al. 1995).

Other Effects of Surface Exposure

Other taphonomic changes often accompany weathering in surface environments. Most common among these is algae growth on bone surfaces, which commonly is found on lightly weathered bones (see Figure 12.12A, Chapter 12, this volume). The environmental conditions needed for the algae to grow (nutrients, moisture, and sunlight) also favor bone weathering. Algae, of course, can develop on submerged bone in shallow (fresh or salt) water (Haefner et al. 2004), so its presence is only an indicator of sunlight and wet conditions to some degree and not uniquely surface deposition. In general, algae forms on the more exposed portion of the bone, just as these portions also tend to have the most advanced weathering. Very dry conditions, however, can lead to the death of the algae, especially on these more exposed (and more likely to desiccate) bone portions. Skeletal elements within the same surface scatter often have differing degrees of algal growth, from none visible to extensive, based upon minor differences in microhabitat (amounts of sunlight, moisture, etc.), in the same way that these elements display different degrees of weathering, inter- and intraelement.

Lichens and moss are also common growths on bone and other solid objects lying exposed on the ground surface. Mosses (Division Bryophyta) are simple plants that are limited in size due to their lack of a vascular system and derive energy through photosynthesis. They also therefore must have a moist (mesic) environment to survive. Their growth on bone can leave behind surface staining (see Chapter 12, this volume). Lichens (Figure 11.10) are symbiotic life forms consisting of a fungus (most commonly within Division Ascomycota) and a photosynthetic algae or cyanobacteria. They can grow on a wide variety of substrates (living and nonliving) and in a range of environments, including dry (xeric) conditions. Their derivation of energy through photosynthesis also means that their presence is indicative of sunlit terrestrial environments. Lichens growth rates have even been applied as a type of dating on archaeological sites, although these are normally confined to dating rock structures or geological formations (Benedict 2009). The generally slow growth rates of lichens means that they are unlikely to cover extensive portions of a bone, since the bone will be exposed on the surface and subject to other destructive forces throughout that interval. The degree to which lichens might erode bone surfaces is little known, although they

Figure 11.10 Example of lichens growth on bone exposed for over 40 years in Idaho, USA. Scale is in cm. (Image courtesy of Adeline Lustig.)

do contribute to the surface weathering of rocks (Banfield et al. 1999). Fungi are known to cause microscopic focal destruction of bone (see Chapter 2, this volume).

Weathering and the Postmortem Interval

Applications to Forensic Anthropology

The use of weathering data in forensic anthropology, apart from contextual information, is primarily to estimate the PMI of a skeletal assemblage in situations where other types of data no longer apply. These include decomposition stage, the timing of which in a known temperature environment may allow estimation of the PMI (Megyesi et al. 2005), arthropod succession, or other more immediate changes in a recently deceased individual such as cooling or degree of *rigor mortis* (Geberth 2006). Past the skeletonization stage, further breakdown of the skeleton itself often is the only available method of PMI estimation derived from the remains themselves, as opposed to using artifactual evidence found with the remains. Bone weathering therefore fills the gap between early (largely soft tissue) methods and ^{14}C determinations of bone age.

Weathering data also may give, along with soil staining, algae growth, and water ring formation, a clear indication that a bone from a surface assemblage has been moved recently if the most bleached, weathered surface (in most temperate settings) is no longer the most exposed surface of the bone. This information may be relevant in the documentation of recent site disturbance, including the corroboration of witness testimony regarding their discovery of a surface skeletal deposit. Weathering alterations also must be distinguished from other forms of taphonomic alteration (see "Confusion with Other Taphonomic Effects" section).

Effects of Macrohabitat

The rate of weathering (Table 11.2) varies across regions, based on broad differences in temperature regimes, precipitation, and vegetation, and these parameters are major factors when estimating PMI from weathering stage (Ubelaker 1997). Previous research has demonstrated that skeletal remains deposited in cooler, temperate climate areas can experience a longer duration of survival (Andrews and Armour-Chelu 1998; Andrews and Cook 1985; Fiorillo 1995; Miller 2009) than skeletal remains deposited in a semiarid savanna climate (Behrensmeyer 1978; Coe 1978; Isaac 1967; Tappen 1992, 1994; Western and Behrensmeyer 2009). Furthermore, rainforest environments are known to slow the rate of weathering and extend the period of bone survival due to constant moisture, lack of freeze/thaw cycles, and dense protective vegetation (Kerbis Peterhans et al. 1993; Pokines 2009; Tappen 1994, 1995). These patterns generally indicate that the rate of weathering is slower in colder environments and locations where bones are protected from direct sunlight and that warmer climates with a high UV index and/or high daily fluctuating temperatures tend to accelerate the rate of weathering. However, this remains variable as other previous research has indicated contradictory results (Andrews and Whybrow 2005).

Miller (2009), in a large landscape study of natural osseous deposition in Yellowstone National Park (USA), noted that individual surface-exposed elements could survive to a recognizable state (WS 4) for over 200 years as determined by ^{14}C dating. Snow covering the bones for at least half of each year likely is a dominant factor in their long-term preservation.

Table 11.2   Rates of Osseous Subaerial Weathering in Different Environments

Location/Environment and Sample	Weathering Rate Observations	Source(s)
Savanna		
Amboseli Park, Kenya Semiarid savanna with a mean annual temperature of 26°C–34°C and a mean annual rainfall of 350 mm. The area is a flat-lying basin with minimal vegetation coverage and soils tend to be alkaline. The remains are of multiple large species	WS 0: 0–1 years WS 1: 0–3 years WS 2: 2–6 years WS 3: 4–15+years WS 4: 6–15+years WS 5: 6–15+years	Behrensmeyer (1978)
Tsavo (East) National Park, Kenya Semiarid grassland with a mean annual temperature of 28°C. Mean annual rainfall is 538 mm but is highly variable. Remains were of two subadult and one adult African elephant (*Loxodonta africana*) carcasses that died at known times	Cortical flaking occurred within 4 years of exposure, with an estimated bone survival interval of at least 20 years	Coe (1978)
Parc National des Virunga, Zaire Medium and tall grass savanna with a mean annual rainfall of 900 mm. Dry seasons are shorter and less severe than other East African savannas. Soils generally have a neutral pH. Remains were from a single cape buffalo (*Syncerus caffer*) skeleton found recently dead, still greasy, with some connective tissue, and without previous cracks	WS 1 was reached 2 years after death, and WS 2 was reached 4 years after death. The weathering rate is comparable to Amboseli Park, Kenya (Behrensmeyer 1978), but the duration of the study is not sufficient for the later stages	Tappen (1992, 1994, 1995)
Olorgesailie, Kenya Mixed acacia brushland within a savanna environment. The bones of subadult *Capra hircus* and some *Bos taurus* were protected under wire mesh and wood frame	Some elements reached approximately WS 4 within 7 years (based upon descriptions)	Isaac (1967)
Tropical Rainforest		
Ituri Rain Forest, Zaire Dense vegetation with a high annual rainfall average of 1900 mm and notable wet and dry seasons. Mean annual temperature is 31°C, and soils are generally acidic, with a pH of 4.0–4.25. Remains were of eight *Loxodonta africana* skeletons that were killed and eaten by inhabitants of the Ituri	Bone weathering is significantly delayed and sometimes absent due to dense vegetation and the wet environment. PMI is known for only some of the bones. WS 0 was seen up to 16 years after death at one site, and the most advanced weathering stage observed (WS 3) was noted after 15+years at another site	Tappen (1994)

Papua New Guinea Tropical rain forest with generally acidic topsoil and less acidic subsoil. Dense forest canopy and/or aircraft wreckage provided partial protection. Remains were from an aircrew of 10 individuals from a WWII airplane crash, the remains of which were largely at the surface or thinly buried over that interval by accumulating decaying leaf litter	No weathering (WS 0) occurred after 58 years, although not all remains were exposed for this full time	Pokines (2009)
Temperate Grassland		
UK Pasture with surrounding woodlands. Remains were of a single *Bos taurus* carcass deposited at the base of a slope and sheltered by vegetation and topography	No weathering (WS 0) occurred after 8 years, with some natural scree slope burial of elements	Andrews and Cook (1985)
Nebraska, USA Grassland with a mean annual temperature of 9°C and mean annual precipitation of 403 mm. Remains were of one subadult and two adult *Bos taurus* carcasses that had died at known times	WS 1 was reached by 3 years, WS 2 was reached by 5 years, and WS 4 was reached by 13 years	Potmesil (2005)
Nebraska, USA Grassland/prairie, open and unshaded. Bones were of adult *Bos taurus* and juvenile *Sus scrofa* selected from domestic carcasses that had died of natural causes at known times	WS 0: 0.2 years WS 1: 1–3 years WS 2: 3–5 years WS 3: 5–8 years WS 4: 7–8 years WS 5: 7–8 years	Fiorillo (1989)
Boreal/Mixed Forest		
Yellowstone National Park, USA Primarily boreal forest with a mean annual temperature of 4.6°C and mean annual precipitation of 387 mm. Snow pack is deeper than one foot for at least half the year, and vegetation densities are higher compared to Amboseli Park, Kenya. Annual freeze–thaw cycles total >50. Remains were of local large fauna	WS 0: 0–1 years WS 1: 0.3–6.5 years WS 2: 2–10 years WS 3: 3–20+years WS 4: 6.5–200+years WS 5: 35–200+years	Miller (2009)
Southern Ontario, Canada Mixed deciduous and coniferous forest with average monthly temperatures ranging from −6°C to 23°C and total monthly precipitation ranging between 20 and 120 mm. Soil pH is neutral. Defleshed *Sus scrofa* femora and metatarsals obtained from a butcher and a farm were set in wooden-framed wire cages that did not have a floor	Longitudinal cracking (WS 1) first appeared after 6 months. No cortical bone flaking (WS 2) was observed after 9.5 months	Janjua and Rogers (2008)

(continued)

Table 11.2   (continued) Rates of Osseous Subaerial Weathering in Different Environments

Location/Environment and Sample	Weathering Rate Observations	Source(s)
Colorado, USA Subalpine, open grassland with annual temperatures that range from −40°C to 32°C and mean annual precipitation of 325 mm. The remains consisted primarily of medium to large ungulates, rodents, and lagomorphs, as well as some bird and fish specimens	PMI is unknown. The majority of bones were recorded as WS 0, possibly a result of the predominantly low temperatures	Fiorillo (1995)
Qikirtaq Island, Canada Semiarid arctic herbaceous tundra with a mean annual temperature of −7°C and a mean annual precipitation of 310 mm, with 53% falling as snow. Surrounding soils are generally acidic. Remains were of local, medium-to-large marine and terrestrial fauna	AMS ^{14}C dating indicated an age range of 1900–2500 years BP. Bones were excavated from three main archaeological levels, and bone preservation was excellent, with the majority of bones recorded as WS 1 and WS 2	Todisco and Monchot (2008)
Desert		
Abu Dhabi, United Arab Emirates Wadi bed in a desert environment that lacks vegetation and experiences large daily temperature fluctuations and high solar radiation. Remains were from a single *Camelus dromedarius*	Weathering rates appeared to be slower, with WS 1 reached only by a few elements after 2 years (initial contact point). After 8 years, no elements had reached WS 2; WS 2 was reached on some elements by 10 years, and WS 3 was reached on some elements by 15 years. Bones that had become buried showed little or no weathering after 15 years	Andrews and Whybrow (2005)
Wadi Enoqiyya, Azraq Basin, Jordan Eastern basalt/sand desert grazed by Bedouin herds, adjacent to a wadi bed. Annual temperatures have an average low of 10°C, average maximum of 24.5°C, and average daily of 17.5°C, and annual precipitation is <100 mm. Remains were a single small adult *Bos taurus* carcass that died in the early summer, the bulk of which became mummified but with some elements dispersed	All exposed bones reached WS 1 in less than 6 weeks. By 1 year later, multiple exposed elements had reached WS 2. By 3 years later, most exposed elements had reached WS 2. Elements/portions thereof protected by desiccated soft tissue remained unweathered (WS 0)	Pokines (new data)

Andrews and Cook (1985) studied bone modifications of a single cattle carcass in a temperate environment in the United Kingdom and determined that the skeletal elements did not portray any signs of weathering (WS 0) after an 8 year period. These elements were largely protected by the local vegetation and terrain. Similarly, in central Wales, Andrews and Armour-Chelu (1998) studied a surface assemblage from natural deaths of sheep and found that the majority of skeletal elements showed no signs of weathering, and none of the bones had reached the most advanced stage of weathering (WS 5). The time of exposure was unknown, but continuous observations indicated that weathering rates tend to be much slower when compared to equatorial Africa (Behrensmeyer 1978). Fiorillo (1995) also noted a prolonged survival rate of ungulate remains studied in a subalpine, open grassland climate of southwest Colorado. Colder temperatures led to depressed microbial activity, a destructive process associated with warmer, moist environments (Bell et al. 1996).

In contrast to cooler, temperate climates, Behrensmeyer (1978) found skeletal elements to reach WS 1 or 2 within a year and WS 5 within 15 years of death in the Amboseli Basin, southern Kenya. Coe (1978) studied elephant (*Loxodonta africana*) remains in Tsavo (East) National Park, Kenya, and noted that most skeletal remains showed flaking of the outer surface (WS 2) within 4 years of exposure, estimating that bone survival intervals are at least 20 years. Isaac (1967) studied taphonomic changes of subadult goat (*Capra hircus*) and some additional cattle (*Bos taurus*) remains in southern Kenya and noted that advanced stages of weathering occurred after 7 years. While this research predates the stage system of Behrensmeyer (1978), from the descriptions given (crumbled, cracked, friable, and fragile), it is clear that the majority of bones had reached at least WS 3 or more likely WS 4. Similarly, Tappen (1992, 1994) found that bone weathering in the savanna environment at Parc National des Virunga, Zaire, is comparable to the morphological changes and rates noted by Behrensmeyer (1978). However, in the same study, Tappen (1994) determined that bone weathering is significantly delayed and sometimes absent in the Ituri Rain Forest, Zaire. This can be attributed to the preservation of moisture content due to vegetation coverage and the wet environment and the protection from solar radiation. Kerbis Peterhans et al. (1993) also suggested that much less subaerial weathering occurs in rainforest environments than in savanna contexts based on observations made in Kibale Forest, Uganda. All chimpanzee (*Pan troglodytes*) skeletal elements that were located were reported to be in WS 0. The minimal degradation that was noted on this sample was attributed to mammalian carnivore and scavenger activity.

In contrast to the earlier findings, the findings reported by Andrews and Whybrow (2005) on the monitoring of a camel (*Camelus dromedarius*) skeleton for 15 years in a desert environment near Abu Dhabi, United Arab Emirates, indicated a much slower rate of weathering. Total exposure time was thought to be closer to 17 years, since the skeleton was disarticulated and the presence of soft tissue was minimal at the time of initial discovery, estimated at 2 years after the death of the camel. This arid environment lacks shading vegetation and experiences large daily temperature fluctuations. Under these environmental conditions, the potential for bone survival was expected to be low, but weathering was noted to be substantially slower when compared to weathering rates in tropical environments of similar latitudes. After 8 years of exposure, most bones had barely reached WS 1; after 10 years, most bones were between WS 1 and WS 2; and after 15 years, only four bones of the 15 that could be recorded at that time had reached WS 3. This pattern was observed for bones that were exposed on the surface for the entirety of the study, and bones that had become deeply buried showed little or no weathering after 15 years. This rate of weathering is in sharp contrast to the findings (ongoing research of the junior author) at a location in the eastern basalt desert north of Azraq, Jordan. A small adult cattle carcass with an approximate time of death reported by its Bedouin owners was plotted for dispersal and assessed for rates of weathering for multiple years. This carcass is adjacent to a wadi, lying on a flat, sand surface with intermittent boulders and low scrub vegetation. Dispersal is primarily through domestic dogs, trampling by sheep/goat herds, and seasonal water transport of the few elements that made it into the wadi. While the presence of mummi-fied soft tissue has protected a large portion of the central mass of skeletal remains (WS 0), all exposed bones reached WS 1 in less than 6 weeks. By 1 year after first analysis, multiple exposed elements had reached WS 2. By 3 years after deposition, most exposed elements had reached WS 2. This desert environment, too, is noted for its temperature fluctuations, which reach extremes of subzero to 45°C. Unlike the camel remains examined by Andrews and Whybrow (2005), no evidence exists that the cattle elements spent any time buried except for the few in the wadi. Andrews and Whybrow (2005) note that their remains were at or near the bottom of the wadi, so the potential for temporary burial was much higher and that some of the dispersed remains started off with desiccated skin attached.

Effects of Microhabitat

Given the prevalence for one portion of a bone to have reached a more advanced weather-ing stage than other portions of the same bone, despite the only differences in these por-tions being the underlying structure of the bone itself and the slight rotation toward more direct solar radiation while occupying an otherwise identical environment, it is clear that even minor variations in microhabitat can have a profound effect upon osseous weathering.

Tappen (1994) and Pokines (2009) noted very low rates of weathering in dense forest conditions where the remains were surface exposed but otherwise consistently protected from direct sunlight exposure. In the case of the latter study, no osseous weathering nor gnawing was detected on 10 sets of human remains that had been exposed on the surface in a rainforest environment in Papua New Guinea as the result of a WWII bomber crash, which was excavated 58 years later. The protective nature of partial wreckage, dense for-est canopy, and the slow buildup of decaying leaf litter prevented any of the remains from reaching even WS 1, and the lack of significant large terrestrial scavengers in this environ-ment limited the dispersal of remains. Most bone alteration in this environment was due to contact with acidic topsoil and infiltration and surface etching by plant roots.

Caves also may provide constant protection from direct sunlight exposure and con-tribute to bone preservation over a long period. Brain (1980) studied bovid bone accu-mulations in caves in various parts of Southern Africa. Most bones that were located in a porcupine lair displayed signs of weathering, suggesting that the bones had weathered from surface exposure prior to being collected by porcupines. Porcupines tend to show a preference for bleached, defatted bone. He noted that unless bones are defatted before col-lection in a cave, the bones will continue to exude grease indefinitely due to the protection from sun exposure. Pokines et al. (2011) studied taphonomic changes of megafauna and microfauna remains located within a large, open sinkhole in a semiarid environment near Wadi Zarqa Ma'in, Jordan. Very few elements had undergone significant weathering. The rate of weathering was slowed due to the lack of direct sunlight and whole carcass deposi-tion, resulting in limited scavenging, slower decomposition rates, and mummification of the soft tissue.

Conversely, skeletal remains that are deposited in open grassland and receive minimal shade will progress through weathering stages at an accelerated rate. Fiorillo (1989), in an analysis of partial ungulate skeletons deposited in an open field in Nebraska, noted that the remains appeared to correspond to the same pattern and rate of weathering as observed by Behrensmeyer (1978) in southern Kenya. Similarly, Potmesil (2005) studied taphonomic changes to cattle bone in an open grassland in Nebraska and noted that the bones deteriorated at a constant rate, with each site representing a different weathering stage. The bones were exposed for approximately 13 years, 5 years, and 3 years and reached WS 4, WS 2, and WS 1, respectively. Ubelaker and Sperber (1988) noted that weathering can be highly localized on a skeletal element where sun exposure strikes only that part of the element in an otherwise protected artificial environment. High temperatures resulting from direct sun exposure accelerate the rate of collagen loss, leading to a change in bone matrix organization and ultimately resulting in a mineral "ghost" (Collins et al. 2002).

Microenvironment also may affect how quickly skeletal remains become partially or completely buried after deposition, influencing the exposure time and ultimately hindering weathering processes (Andrews 1995; Behrensmeyer 1978, 1983; Miller 2009; Ross and Cunningham 2011; Serjeantson 1991; Shipman 1981; Tappen and Peske 1970; Todisco and Monchot 2008). Well-preserved buried bones may indicate rapid burial, whereas highly weathered buried bones imply a longer exposure length prior to burial (Todisco and Monchot 2008). Miller (2009) determined the proportion of buried bones to surface-deposited bones for four different microenvironments in Yellowstone National Park, USA. The bone assemblages located in grasslands displayed the slowest rates of burial, followed by river margins, forests, and lake margins. These differences are likely due in most part to the degree to which decaying leaf litter builds up in these habitats. In turn, the burial environment will affect skeletal preservation based on soil pH and water fluctuations. For example, waterlogged soils are more likely to preserve organic materials than well-drained soils, and highly acidic environments will increase the rate of degradation (Crow 2008; Gordon and Buikstra 1981). Hill (1980) noted that buffalo skeletal remains buried in a mud wallow in southwest Uganda were found in near-perfect condition after 52 months since death. Furthermore, Conard et al. (2008) studied a faunal accumulation in the Geelbek Dunes of South Africa, which is continuously effected by cycles of open-air exposure and burial. This cycle subjects the elements to daily heating and cooling and wetting and drying, leading to the more rapid destruction of cortical bone and the survival of more porous bone. Although the extent of weathering is related to the time of exposure, weathering progresses at different rates in various microenvironments, thus making it more difficult to determine a standard rate at which weathering stages occur (Shipman 1981:115). General patterns among various macroenvironments have been recognized in relation to the rate of weathering (Table 11.2), with colder environments and less solar radiation acting to slow the rate of weathering and warmer, arid environments with high solar radiation accelerating the rate of weathering. However, contradicting results exist, and microenvironments can also significantly alter this rate, indicating that more research is still needed.

Confusion with Other Taphonomic Effects

Weathering can be mistaken for the gross effects of taphonomic forces that cause whitening of bone, including calcination from prolonged intense thermal exposure or boiling (Chapter 14, this volume) and bleaching from submersion in saltwater (Chapter 7, this volume). Macroscopic examination of weathered bone should reveal clear differences between these other common alterations. The analyst is cautioned that weathering is often found in conjunction with other taphonomic alterations. For example, marine alteration could be followed by deposition on a shoreline followed by subaerial weathering.

Distinguishing Weathering from Calcination

Calcination of bone as a result of extreme thermal alteration (see Chapter 14, this volume) can mimic superficially the effects of advanced weathering. Both processes turn bone various shades of white/gray, and both processes crack bone. Upon close visual inspection, the two taphonomic effects can be distinguished. The orientation of weathering cracks on articular surfaces may follow a pattern similar to that observed on dry lake beds, where the drying clay forms multisided shapes. The orientation of cracks elsewhere, however, typically follows the long axis of the bone along the main orientation of the osteons (Tappen 1969, 1976; Tappen and Peske 1970). Weathering cracking is accompanied by cortical exfoliation at lower stages and deeper flaking at more advanced stages. The appearance of these flakes is far more ragged than the fragments formed by thermal alteration/calcination. In addition, the surfaces of calcined bone present a much smoother appearance around these cracks than the surfaces of weathered bone. Crack orientation also follows multiple paths and often is perpendicular to the long axis of a bone. Calcination also often affects only a portion of a bone or bone fragment, with zones of carbonization deeper or adjacent. Unburned bone also may be adjacent to these areas of carbonization. Weathering does not cause bone to turn black, and inner portions of a bone where sun bleaching has not penetrated may retain the original (beige) color (see Chapter 12, this volume). Finally, calcination also can be accompanied by bone warping and fine bone ash, neither of which are caused nor mimicked by weathering.

Distinguishing Weathering from Saltwater Immersion

Bone in marine environments undergoes bleaching that may mimic the appearance of sun bleaching (Ubelaker 1997). Similarly, bones removed from marine environments may later crack as a part of the drying process that may include the formation of salt crystals forcing the bone apart. The overall patterns of taphonomic alteration, however, are distinguishable upon close examination. Except in rare cases, saltwater bleaching affects all surfaces of a bone relatively equally (see Chapter 7, this volume). This is because the ions in the liquid medium can penetrate all surfaces from all angles. In contrast, the changes that a weathered bone undergoes, including sun bleaching, is rarely uniform, and the portion of the bone facing the ground surface often can lag as much as two weathering stages behind the most exposed upper surface. Marine-altered bones also tend to become rounded from the abrasion of sand particles, selectively removing more exposed portions of the element (Fisher 1995; Isaac 1967). Weathering itself produces no such rounding effect, although later abrasion of a previously weathered bone might (Andrews and Armour-Chelu 1998). Marine-altered bones, of course, are often discovered after their deposition in beach contexts where they subsequently may weather, thus combining characteristics of both. Previous rounding may be detected on subsequently weathered bone, and weathering will likely be more advanced on the uppermost exposed surfaces. Salt cracking, however, may proceed equally in all directions.

Conclusions

Osseous weathering is a progressive process that follows a pattern of linear cracking and flaking of the cortical surface, followed by formation of a rough fibrous texture and eventual loss of bone structure (Behrensmeyer 1978). The analysis of bone weathering is particularly important to the field of forensic anthropology, with the potential to contribute to PMI estimations for cases involving advanced stages of decomposition (i.e., skeletonization followed by skeletal breakdown). The rate of weathering is highly variable among different climates (i.e., temperate deciduous forest, semiarid equatorial savanna, or tundra) and various microenvironments within that climatic zone (i.e., patches of forest, brush, wetland, or grass cover within a temperate deciduous forest), and all environmental aspects must be considered when assessing PMI. This variation has been little researched and demonstrates the need for further investigation of bone weathering across different regions. It is also clear that weathering of nonhuman (largely plexiform) bone may differ significantly in patterning and timing from adult human (largely lamellar) bone, and future forensic research must focus on the latter.

Acknowledgments

The authors thank Don Siwek for his sectioning of bone and other research assistance and Martha Tappen, Mark Beary, MariaTeresa Tersigni-Tarrant, and Brianne Charles for their valuable comments. Adeline Lustig kindly provided an image.

References

Andrews, P. (1995) Experiments in taphonomy. *Journal of Archaeological Science* 22:147–153.

Andrews, P. and M. Armour-Chelu (1998) Taphonomic observations on a surface bone assemblage in a temperate environment. *Bulletin de la Société Géologique de France* 169:433–442.

Andrews, P. and J. Cook (1985) Natural modifications to bones in a temperate setting. *Man* 20:675–691.

Andrews, P. and P. Whybrow (2005) Taphonomic observations on a camel skeleton in a desert environment in Abu Dhabi. *Palaeontologica Electronica* 8:23A:1–17.

Banfield, J. F., W. W. Barker, S. A. Welch, and A. Taunton (1999) Biological impact on mineral dissolution: Application of the lichen model to understanding mineral weathering in the rhizosphere. *Proceedings of the National Academy of Sciences of the United States of America* 96:3404–3411.

Beary, M. O. (2005) *Estimation of Bone Exposure Duration Through the Use of Spectrophotometric Analysis of Surface Bleaching and Its Application in Forensic Taphonomy.* Unpublished M.S. Thesis, Mercyhurst College, Erie, PA.

Behrensmeyer, A. K. (1978) Taphonomic and ecologic information from bone weathering. *Palaeobiology* 4:150–162.

Behrensmeyer, A. K. (1983) Patterns of natural bone distribution on recent land surfaces: Implications for archaeological site formation. In *Animals and Archaeology: 1. Hunters and Their Prey,* eds. J. Clutton-Brock and C. Grigson, pp. 93–106. BAR Int Series 163, Oxford, London, U.K.

Behrensmeyer, A. K. and J. H. Miller (2012) Building links between ecology and paleontology using taphonomic studies of recent vertebrate communities. In *Paleontology in Ecology and Conservation,* ed. J. Louys, pp. 69–91. Springer-Verlag, Berlin, Germany.

Bell, L. S., M. F. Skinner, and S. J. Jones (1996) The speed of post mortem change to the human skeleton and its taphonomic significance. *Forensic Science International* 82:129–140.

Benedict, J. B. (2009) A review of lichenometric dating and its applications to archaeology. *American Antiquity* 74:143–172.

Brain, C. K. (1967) Bone weathering and the problem of bone pseudo-tools. *South African Journal of Science* 63:97–99.

Brain, C. K. (1980) Some criteria for the recognition of bone-collecting agencies in African caves. In *Fossils in the Making*, eds. A. K. Behrensmeyer and A. P. Hill, pp. 107–130. University of Chicago Press, Chicago, IL.

Brain, C. K. (1981) *The Hunters or the Hunted? An Introduction to African Cave Taphonomy*. University of Chicago Press, Chicago, IL.

Buckland-Wright, J. C. (1977) Microradiographic and histological examination of the split-line formation in bone. *Journal of Anatomy* 124:193–203.

Buikstra, J. E. and L. Goldstein (1973) *The Perrins Ledge Crematory*. Illinois State Museum, Report of Investigations No. 28, Springfield, IL.

Buikstra, J. E. and D. H. Ubelaker (eds.) (1994) *Standards for Data Collection from Human Skeletal Remains*. Arkansas Archeological Survey Research Series No. 44, Fayetteville, AR.

Coe, M. (1978) The decomposition of elephant carcasses in the Tsavo (East) National Park, Kenya. *Journal of Arid Environments* 1:71–86.

Collins, M. J., C. M. Nielsen-Marsh, J. Hiller, C. I. Smith, J. P. Roberts, T. J. Wess, T. J. Csapo, A. R. Millard, R. V. Priyodich, and G. Turner-Walker (2002) The survival of the organic matter of bone: A review. *Archaeometry* 44:383–394.

Conard, N. J., S. J. Walker, and A. W. Kandel (2008) How heating and cooling and wetting and drying can destroy dense faunal elements and lead to differential preservation. *Palaeogeography, Palaeoclimatology, Palaeoecology* 266:459–469.

Cox, B. N. and Q. Yang (2007) Cohesive zone models of localization and fracture in bone. *Engineering Fracture Mechanics* 74:1079–1092.

Crow, P. (2008) Mineral weathering in forest soils and its relevance to the preservation of the buried archaeological resource. *Journal of Archaeological Science* 35:2262–2273.

Currey, J. D. (2002) *Bones: Structure and Mechanics* (2nd edn.). Princeton University Press, Princeton, NJ.

Cutler, A. H., A. K. Behrensmeyer, and R. E. Chapman (1999) Environmental information in a recent bone assemblage: Roles of taphonomic processes and ecological change. *Palaeogeography, Palaeoclimatology, Palaeoecology* 149:359–372.

Doblaré, M., J. M. García, and M. J. Gómez (2004) Modelling bone tissue fracture and healing: A review. *Engineering Fracture Mechanics* 71:1809–1840.

Doehne, E. (2002) Salt weathering: A selective review. *Geological Society Special Publication: Natural Stone, Weathering Phenomena, Conservation Strategies and Case Studies* 205:51–64.

Faith, J. T. and A. K. Behrensmeyer (2006) Changing patterns of carnivore modification in a landscape bone assemblage, Amboseli Park, Kenya. *Journal of Archaeological Science* 33:1718–1733.

Fernández-Jalvo, Y. and P. Andrews (2003) Experimental effects of water abrasion on bone fragments. *Journal of Taphonomy* 1:147–163.

Fiorillo, A. R. (1989) An experimental study of trampling: Implications for the fossil record. In *Bone Modification* eds. R. Bonnichsen and M. Sorg, pp. 61–72. Center for the Study of the First Americans, Orono, ME.

Fiorillo, A. R. (1995) Possible influence of low temperature on bone weathering in Curecanti National Recreation Area, southwest Colorado. *Current Research in the Pleistocene* 12:69–71.

Fisher, J. W. (1995) Bone surface modifications in zooarchaeology. *Journal of Archaeological Method and Theory* 2:7–68.

Galloway, A. (ed.) (1999) *Broken Bones: Anthropological Analysis of Blunt Force Trauma*. Charles C Thomas, Springfield, IL.

Geberth, V. J. (2006) *Practical Homicide Investigation* (4th edn.). CRC Press, Boca Raton, FL.

Gordon, C. G. and J. E. Buikstra (1981) Soil pH, bone preservation, and sampling bias at mortuary sites. *American Antiquity* 46:566–571.

Haefner, J. N., J. R. Wallace, and R. W. Merritt (2004) Pig decomposition in lotic aquatic systems: The potential use of algal growth in establishing a postmortem submersion interval (PMSI). *Journal of Forensic Sciences* 49:1–7.

Hall, K. (1999) The role of thermal stress fatigue in the breakdown of rock in cold regions. *Geomorphology* 31:47–63.

Hall, K. and C. Thorn (2011) The historical legacy of spatial scales in freeze-thaw weathering: Misrepresentation and resulting misdirection. *Geomorphology* 130:83–90.

Hare, E. P. (1974) Amino acid dating of bone—The influence of water. *Carnegie Institute of Washington Yearbook* 73:576–581.

Hedges, R. E. M., A. R. Millard and A. W. G. Pike (1995) Measurements and relationships of diagenetic alteration of bone from three archaeological sites. *Journal of Archaeological Science* 22:201–211.

Hill, A. (1976) On carnivore and weathering damage to bone. *Current Anthropology* 17:335–336.

Hill, A. (1980) Early postmortem damage to the remains of some contemporary East African mammals. In *Fossils in the Making: Vertebrate Taphonomy and Paleoecology*, eds. A. K. Behrensmeyer and A. P. Hill, pp. 131–152. University of Chicago Press, Chicago, IL.

Hillier, M. L. and L. S. Bell (2007) Differentiating human bone from animal bone: A review of histological methods. *Journal of Forensic Sciences* 52:249–263.

Isaac, G. L. (1967) Towards the interpretation of occupation debris: Some experiments and observations. *The Kroeber Anthropological Society Papers* 37:31–57.

Janjua, M. A. and T. L. Rogers (2008) Bone weathering patterns of metatarsal v. femur and the postmortem interval in Southern Ontario. *Forensic Science International* 178:16–23.

Johnson, J. S. (1998) Soluble salts and deterioration of archeological materials. *Conserve O Gram National Park Service US* 6/5(August):1–4.

Kerbis Peterhans, J. C. (1990) *The Roles of Porcupines, Leopards, and Hyenas in Ungulate Carcass Dispersal: Implications for Paleoanthropology*. Unpublished PhD Dissertation, Department of Anthropology, University of Chicago, Chicago, IL.

Kerbis Peterhans, J., R. W. Wrangham, M. L. Carter, and M. D. Hauser (1993) A contribution to tropical rainforest taphonomy: Retrieval and documentation of chimpanzee remains from Kibale Forest, Uganda. *Journal of Human Evolution* 25:485–514.

Kollmorgen Instruments Corporation (1994) *Munsell® Soil Color Charts* (rev. edn.). Kollmorgen Instruments Corporation, New Windsor, NY.

Lyman, R. L. (1994) *Vertebrate Taphonomy*. Cambridge University Press, Cambridge, U.K.

Lyman, R. L. and G. L. Fox (1989) A critical evaluation of bone weathering data as an indication of bone assemblage formation. *Journal of Archaeological Science* 16:293–317.

Lyman, R. L. and G. L. Fox (1997) A critical evaluation of bone weathering as an indication of bone assemblage formation. In *Forensic Taphonomy: The Postmortem Fate of Human Remains*, eds. W. D. Haglund and M. H. Sorg, pp. 223–247. CRC Press, Boca Raton, FL.

Madgwick, R. and J. Mulville (2012) Investigating variation in the prevalence of weathering in faunal assemblages in the UK: A multivariate statistical approach. *International Journal of Osteoarchaeology* 22:509–522.

Matsuoka, N. (1995) Rock weathering and landform development in the Sør Rondane Mountains, Antarctica. *Geomorphology* 12:323–339.

Matsuoka, N. (1996) Soil moisture variability in relation to diurnal frost heaving on Japanese high mountain slopes. *Permafrost and Periglacial Processes* 7:139–151.

Matsuoka, N. and J. Merton (2008) Frost weathering: Recent advances and future directions. *Permafrost and Periglacial Processes* 19:195–210.

McGee, M. E., K. W. Magic, D. L. Miller, A. J. Maki, and S. W. Donahue (2007) Black bear femoral porosity decreases and mechanical properties increase with age despite annual periods of disuse (hibernation). *Engineering Fracture Mechanics* 74:1942–1952.

Megyesi, M. S., S. P. Nawrocki, and N. H. Haskell (2005) Using accumulated degree-days to estimate the postmortem interval from decomposed human remains. *Journal of Forensic Sciences* 52:618–626.

Micozzi, M. S. (1991) *Postmortem Change in Human and Animal Remains.* Charles C Thomas, Springfield, IL.

Miller, G. J. (1975) A study of cuts, grooves, and other marks on recent and fossil bones. 2. Weathering cracks, fractures, splinters, and other similar natural phenomena. In *Lithic Technology: Making and Using Stone Tools,* ed. E. H. Swanson, Jr., pp. 211–226. Aldine, Chicago, IL.

Miller, J. H. (2009) *The Large-Mammal Death Assemblage of Yellowstone National Park: Historical Ecology, Conservation Biology, Paleoecology.* Unpublished PhD Dissertation, University of Chicago, Chicago, IL.

Misner, L. M., A. C. Halvorson, J. L. Dreier, D. H. Ubelaker, and D. R. Foran (2009) The correlation between skeletal weathering and DNA quality and quantity. *Journal of Forensic Sciences* 54:822–828.

Morris, Z. H. (2007) *Quantitative and Spatial Analysis of the Microscopic Bone Structures of Deer* (Odocoileus virginianus), *Dog* (Canis familiaris), *and Pig* (Sus scrofa domesticus). Unpublished M.A. Thesis, Louisiana State University, Shreveport, LA.

Mulhern, D. M. and D. H. Ubelaker (2001) Differences in osteon banding between human and non-human bone. *Journal of Forensic Sciences* 46:220–222.

Nielsen-Marsh, C. M., A. M. Gernaey, G. Turner-Walker, R. E. M. Hedges, A. W. G. Pike, and M. J. C. Collins (2000) The chemical degradation of bone. In *Human Osteology in Archaeology and Forensic Science* eds. M. Cox and S. Mays, pp. 439–454. Greenwich Medical Media, London, U.K.

Pal, S. and S. Saha (1989) Coefficient of thermal expansion of bone. In *Biomechanics,* eds. K. B. Sahay and R. K. Saxena, pp. 52–60. John Wiley & Sons, New York.

Pate, F. D. and J. T. Hutton (1988) The use of soil chemistry data to address post-mortem diagenesis in bone mineral. *Journal of Archaeological Science* 15:729–739.

Pate, F. D., J. T. Hutton, and K. Norrish (1989) Ionic exchange between soil solution and bone: Toward a predictive model. *Applied Geochemistry* 4:303–316.

Pietruszczak, S., K. Gdela, C. E. Webber, and D. Inglis (2007) On the assessment of brittle-elastic cortical bone fracture in the distal radius. *Engineering Fracture Mechanics* 74:1917–1927.

Pokines, J. T. (2009) Forensic recoveries of U.S. war dead and the effects of taphonomy and other site-altering processes. In *Hard Evidence: Case Studies in Forensic Anthropology,* 2nd edn., ed. D. W. Steadman, pp. 141–154. Prentice Hall, Upper Saddle River, NJ.

Pokines, J. T., A. Nowell, M. S. Bisson, C. E. Cordova, and C. J. H. Ames (2011) The functioning of a natural faunal trap in a semi-arid environment: Preliminary investigations of WZM-1, a limestone sinkhole site near Wadi Zarqa Ma'in, Hashemite Kingdom of Jordan. *Journal of Taphonomy* 9:89–115.

Potmesil, M. (2005) Bone dispersion, weathering, and scavenging of cattle bones. *Nebraska Anthropologist, Paper 6.* [Available online: http://digitalcommons.unl.edu/nebanthro/6.]

Prassack, K. A. (2011) The effect of weathering on bird bone survivorship in modern and fossil saline-alkaline lake environments. *Paleobiology* 37:633–654.

Purdy, B. A. and D. E. Clark (1987) Weathering of inorganic materials: Dating and other applications. *Advances in Archaeological Method and Theory* 11:211–253.

Rodriguez-Navarro, C. and E. Doehne (1999) Salt weathering: Influence of evaporation rate, supersaturation and crystallization pattern. *Earth Surface Processes and Landforms* 24:191–209.

Ross, A. H. and S. L. Cunningham (2011) Time-since-death and bone weathering in a tropical environment. *Forensic Science International* 204:126–133.

Roze, U. (2009) *The North American Porcupine* (2nd edn.). Cornell University Press, Ithaca, NY.

Schütz, W. (1996) A history of fatigue. *Engineering Fracture Mechanics* 54:263–300.

Serjeantson, D. (1991) Rid grasse of bones: A taphonomical study of bones from midden deposits at the Neolithic and Bronze Age site at Runnymede, Surrey, England. *International Journal of Osteoarchaeology* 1:73–89.

Shipman, P. (1981) *Life History of a Fossil.* Harvard University Press, Cambridge, MA.

Sillen, A. (1989) Diagenesis of the inorganic phase of the cortical bone. In *The Chemistry of Prehistoric Bone*, ed. T. D. Price, pp. 211–229. Cambridge University Press, Cambridge, U.K.

Skedros, J. G., J. L. Holmes, E. G. Vajda, and R. L. Bloebaum (2005) Cement lines of secondary osteons in human bone are not mineral-deficient: New data in a historical perspective. *The Anatomical Record Part A* 286A:781–803.

Smith, C. I, O. E. Craig, R. V. Prigodich, C. M. Nielsen-Marsh, M. M. E. Jans, C. Vermeer, and M. J. Collins (2005) Diagenesis and survival of osteocalcin in archaeological bone. *Journal of Archaeological Science* 32:105–113.

Stiner, M. C., S. L. Kuhn, and O. Bar-Yosef (1995) Differential burning, recrystallization, and fragmentation of archaeological bone. *Journal of Archaeological Science* 22:223–237.

Stover, S. M., R. P. Pool, B. Martin, and J. P. Morgan (1992) Histological features of the dorsal cortex of the third metacarpal bone mid-diaphysis during postnatal growth in thoroughbred horses. *Journal of Anatomy* 181:455–469.

Tappen, M. (1992) *Taphonomy of a Central African Savanna: Natural Bone Deposition in Parc National des Virunga, Zaire*. Unpublished Ph.D. Dissertation, Harvard University, Cambridge, MA.

Tappen, M. (1994) Bone weathering in the tropical rain forest. *Journal of Archaeological Science* 21:667–673.

Tappen, M. (1995) Savanna ecology and natural bone deposition: Implications for early hominid site formation, hunting, and scavenging. *Current Anthropology* 36:223–260.

Tappen, N. C. (1969) The relationship of weathering cracks to split-line orientation in bone. *American Journal of Physical Anthropology* 31:191–197.

Tappen, N. C. (1976) Advanced weathering cracks as an improvement on split-line preparations for analysis of structural orientation in compact bone. *American Journal of Physical Anthropology* 44:373–377.

Tappen, N. C. and R. Peske (1970) Weathering cracks and split-line patterns in archaeological bone. *American Antiquity* 35:383–386.

Thurner, P. J., B. Erickson, R. Jungmann, Z. Schriock, J. C. Weaver, G. E. Fantner, G. Schitter, D. E. Morse, and P. K. Hansma (2007) High-speed photography of compressed human trabecular bone correlates whitening to microscopic damage. *Engineering Fracture Mechanics* 74:1928–1941.

Todisco, D. and H. Monchot (2008) Bone weathering in a peri-glacial environment: The Tayara Site (KbFk-7), Qikirtaq Island, Nunavik (Canada). *Arctic* 61:87–101.

Tomar, V. (2009) Insights into the effects of tensile and compressive loadings on microstructure dependent fracture of trabecular bone. *Engineering Fracture Mechanics* 76:884–897.

Toots, H. (1965) Sequence of disarticulation in mammalian skeletons. *Contributions to Geology* 4:37–39.

Trueman, C. N. G., A. K. Behrensmeyer, N. Tuross, and S. Weiner (2004) Mineralogical and compositional changes in bones exposed on soil surfaces in Amboseli National Park, Kenya: Diagenetic mechanisms and the role of sediment pore fluids. *Journal of Archaeological Science* 31:721–739.

Turner, C. H., T. Wang, and D. B. Burr (2001) Shear strength and fatigue properties of human cortical bone determined from pure shear tests. *Calcified Tissue International* 69:373–378.

Turner-Walker, G. (2008) The chemical and microbial degradation of bones and teeth. In *Advances in Human Palaeopathology*, eds. R. Pinhasi and S. Mays, pp. 3–29. John Wiley & Sons, Chichester, U.K.

Ubelaker, D. H. (1997) Taphonomic applications in forensic anthropology. In *Forensic Taphonomy: The Postmortem Fate of Human Remains*, eds. W. D. Haglund and M. H. Sorg, pp. 77–90. CRC Press, Boca Raton, FL.

Ubelaker, D. H. and N. D. Sperber (1988) Alterations in human bones and teeth as a result of restricted sun exposure and contact with corrosive agents. *Journal of Forensic Sciences* 33:540–548.

Walderhaug, O. (1998) Chemical weathering at rock art sites in western Norway: Which mechanisms are active and how can they be retarded? *Journal of Archaeological Science* 25:789–800.

Weiner, S. and H. D. Wagner (1998) The material bone: Structure-mechanical function relations. *Annual Review of Materials Science* 28:271–298.

Western, D. and A. K. Behrensmeyer (2009) Bone assemblages track animal community structure over 40 years in an African savanna ecosystem. *Science* 324:1061–1064.

White, E. M. and L. A. Hannus (1983) Chemical weathering of bone in archaeological soils. *American Antiquity* 48:316–322.

Willey, P. and A. Heilman (1987) Estimating time since death using plant roots and stems. *Journal of Forensic Sciences* 32:1264–1270.

Yavuz, H. (2011) Effect of freeze-thaw and thermal shock weathering on the physical and mechanical properties of an andesite stone. *Bulletin of Engineering Geology and the Environment* 70:187–192.

Taphonomic Bone Staining and Color Changes in Forensic Contexts

12

TOSHA L. DUPRAS
JOHN J. SCHULTZ

Contents

I know for sure that I have an instinct for color, and that it will come to me more and more, that painting is in the very marrow of my bones.
—Vincent van Gogh, letter to Theo van Gogh, 3 September 1882

Introduction

A component of forensic skeletal analysis is to identify various postmortem modifications and to reconstruct the depositional history of the remains. Describing any color changes associated with bones is important to this process, as it may provide clues when reconstructing the post-depositional environment of skeletal remains. The purpose of this chapter is to discuss the common types of taphonomic bone stains and color changes and discuss the causative agents for those stains. The aim of this chapter is not to provide an exhaustive list of every example of stain that has been discussed in the literature but rather to highlight examples of bone staining such as organic, metal, and soil, which are more commonly encountered by the forensic anthropologist.

To understand how bone changes color, it is important to be familiar with the normal color of unstained bone when describing staining found on bones. Normal fresh bone devoid of flesh has been described as having a yellowish-white to yellowish-brown color (Figure 12.1a through c) due to the retention of lipids and other fluids (Byers 2008; Schafer 2001). Interestingly, fresh skulls with a bright yellow color have been associated with individuals who suffered from diabetes (Gruspier 1999). While Schafer (2001) did not find an increased yellow coloration in a small sample of fresh diabetic skulls compared to a sample of nondiabetic skulls, he did find a correlation of increased yellow hue with increased age at death.

A suggested method to document bone color is by the use of a Munsell® Color chart (e.g., Cain 2005) which identifies color based on three dimensions: value, hue and chroma. The color of bone will change during the decomposition process and when the bone is completely dry. In a controlled study designed to analyze the early postmortem interval (PMI) up to 8 weeks, Huculak and Rogers (2009) concluded that color changes occurring on various skeletal elements that were either on the ground surface or buried were the result of soil, sun, hemolysis, decomposition, and fungi. During decomposition, bones can display areas of dark reddish brown coloration due to hemolysis, or the breakdown of red blood cells (Figure 12.1a), and a dark reddish gray coloration due to decomposition staining (Huculak and Rogers 2009). When bones become dry during the postmortem period, the yellowish hue may change to an ivory or off-white color (Figure 12.1b) (Byers 2008). There are, however, many taphonomic and environmental conditions which can cause a myriad of color changes to bone. In fact, bones recovered from outdoor environments often display differential patterns of staining that represent multiple taphonomic processes (Figures 12.2a and b). At the same time, it is important to recognize that different taphonomic processes can cause similar color changes to bone. For example, a variety of taphonomic processes can result in a white coloration to bone such as adipocere remnants, burning, sun bleaching, adhered concretions, and commercial preparation of skeletal remains for teaching (discussed below).

Chemical Staining and Natural Bleaching

Sun Bleaching

In some cases bones may appear to be a variant of the color white, from gray to brilliant white. Ultraviolet radiation from sunlight will cause natural bleaching of exposed bones (see Chapter 11, this volume). Solar UV radiation can be responsible for the degradation and/or decomposition of many organic compounds, and it does so by breaking chemical bonds during photolytic and photo-oxidative reactions (Zayat et al. 2007). In bone, UV radiation assists in breaking down the organic components that contribute to the color of bone such as blood, lipids, and proteins. Eventually, after substantial exposure to UV radiation and other environmental conditions, all that may remain is the mineral portion of bone, hydroxyapatite, which is naturally white in color.

The color of bleached bones will depend on the length of exposure, and it is observed that the longer the exposure, the more bleached the bones can become. After significant exposure bones may appear a brilliant white color (Beary 2005; Haglund et al. 2002; Ubelaker 1997). Several authors note changes in bone color due to sun bleaching

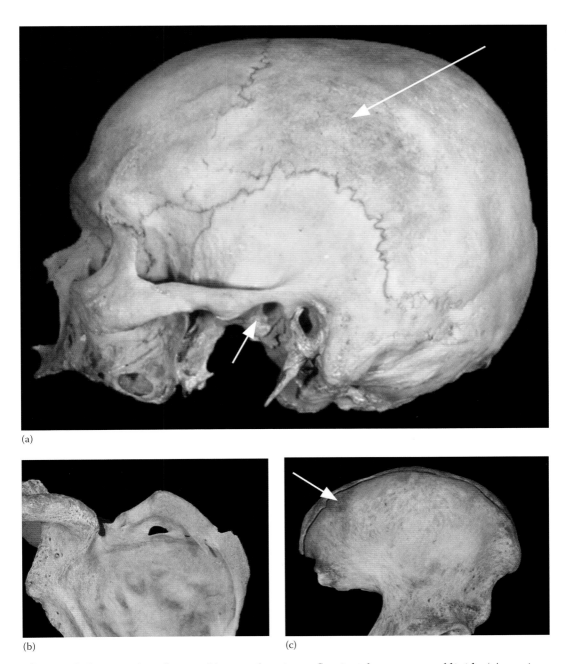

(a)

(b)   (c)

Figure 12.1 Examples of natural bone coloration reflecting the presence of lipids: (a) cranium showing examples of hemolysis (top arrow) and adipocere (bottom arrow); (b) scapula with tissue and lipid retention; and (c) ilium with darker coloration representing concentrated areas of lipid retention (arrow).

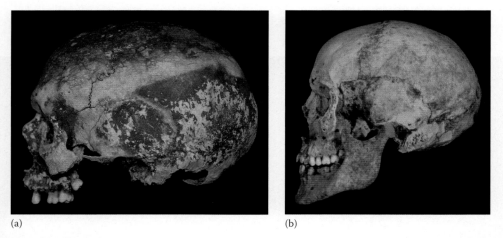

(a)   (b)

Figure 12.2 Differential staining: (a) sun-bleached cranium exhibiting a darker soil stain on the superior aspect due to contact with an organic soil horizon, algae staining on the face and sides of the cranial vault; and (b) sun-bleached skull with minimal algae staining on the vault and face and prominent soil staining of the mandible and dentition.

(e.g., Calce and Rogers 2007; Galloway et al. 1989; Huculak and Rogers 2009; Quatrehomme and İşcan 1997; Schultz 2012). Figure 12.3a through c shows the effects of sun bleaching on bones from different contexts. Figure 12.3a shows a left femur from an archaeological context in Egypt in which the bone had been exposed on the surface for over a year. In addition to bleaching, bones may show substantial surface cracking and exfoliation due to exposure to additional environmental conditions such as cold, heat, moisture, and wind (Figure 12.3a) (see Chapter 11, this volume). Bones may also be differentially bleached dependent on their position relative to the ground surface. For example, Figure 12.3b shows a skull from a forensic context in which the left side of mandible remained in contact with the soil, while the cranium was resting on the surface with the left side exposed to the sun. Figure 12.3c shows a differentially stained sacrum from an archaeological context. In this case the sacrum remained partially buried with only the superior aspect exposed to the sun.

It is important to note that bones may also appear white due to other circumstances. For example, exposure to intense heat or fire may also change bones to a variant of the color white (calcined). Much like UV radiation, intense heat can destroy organic materials in and associated with bone, therefore leaving only the inorganic component (see Chapter 14, this volume). Figure 12.3d shows a vertebra exposed to fire and the associated white color which could be easily mistaken for sun bleaching. Bone also may have a white appearance due to the presence of adipocere, the remnants of the process of lipid hydrolysis during decomposition (Aufderheide 2011; Ubelaker and Zarenko 2011; see also Chapter 5, this volume). While bleaching and fire change the entire constitution of the bone, adipocere is normally adhered only to the internal and external surfaces of the bone, and has a waxy, greasy texture that turns friable when dried. Figure 12.4 shows examples of adipocere associated with bones from forensic contexts. Figure 12.4a shows adipocere on the proximal end of a right ulna, while Figure 12.4b shows adipocere on the internal surface of the medullary cavity of a femoral diaphysis. Adipocere also can be noted on the inferior surface and external auditory meatus of the cranium in Figure 12.1a.

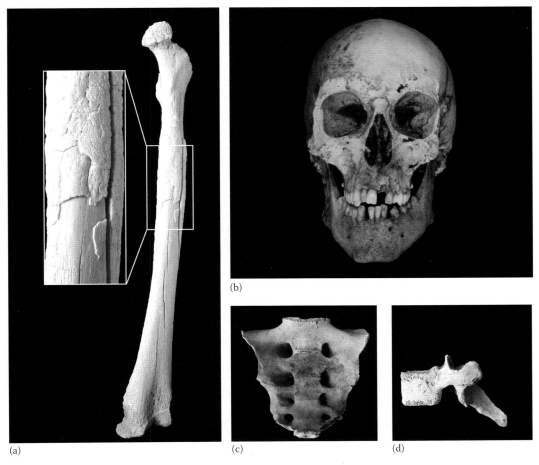

(b)

(a)   (c)   (d)

Figure 12.3 White coloration due to sun bleaching and fire exposure: (a) archaeological left femur displaying sun bleaching with surface cracking and exfoliation; (b) skull with sun bleaching on face and cranial vault; (c) archaeological sacrum showing sun bleaching of superior aspect; and (d) calcined thoracic vertebra.

Other Chemical Staining

During the process of preparing skeletal remains from forensic contexts for examination, or for commercial preparation (e.g., teaching specimens), chemical agents may be used for the purposes of degreasing and/or whitening bones (Figure 12.5). Dependent on the amount of soft tissue and lipids remaining, different chemicals may be used to treat skeletal remains. As more organic components are removed, the bone will become increasingly white; however, it is very difficult to remove all the organic material associated with or in bone without altering the chemical composition, surface, or shape of the bone (see Figure 12.5a). In the preparation of skeletal materials for forensic examination, once an acceptable level of soft tissue and lipids are removed with the use of a degreasing agent, preparation will cease (Mairs et al. 2004). This is imperative for the preservation of evidence and molecular structures such as DNA (Fenton et al. 2003; Steadman et al. 2006). A mixture of detergent, sodium carbonate, hot water, boiling

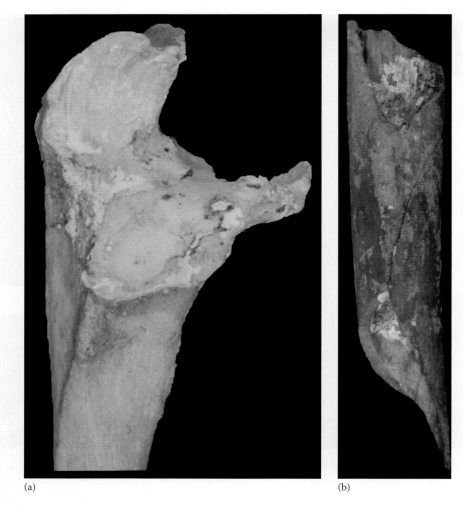

(a)   (b)

Figure 12.4 Adipocere: (a) proximal right ulna with minimal adipocere development (white areas); and (b) femoral shaft exhibiting adipocere in the medullary cavity.

water, and microwaving has been found to be one of the most efficient methods of maceration that also yielded the most total DNA (Lee et al. 2010; Steadman et al. 2006). Methods such as this will degrade the proteins of soft tissues and lipids, and caution must be taken so that over-processing does not affect the structural integrity of the bone (Figure 12.5a). After this process the bone may still have a yellowish hue due to the retention of some lipids.

If the skeletal remains are commercially prepared for sale as teaching materials, the next step after lipid removal will be to treat the bones with a bleaching agent such as sodium hypochlorite (NaClO) or hydrogen peroxide (H_2O_2) (Rennick et al. 2005). A bleaching agent is a chemical which can whiten or decolorize any substances which contains *chromophores*—groups of atoms which absorb visible light, and reflect or transmit the light that is not absorbed, as color. Bleaching agents destroy chromophores through oxidation or reduction, resulting in the removal of color (Joiner 2006). Unfortunately, many bleaching agents also attack and destroy the organic and mineral component of

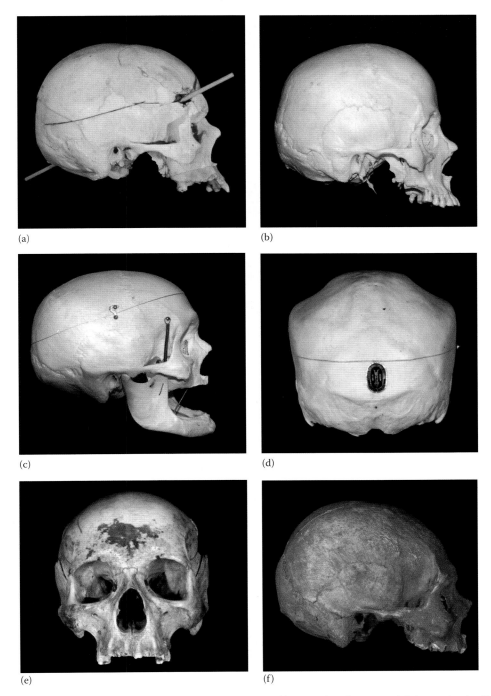

Figure 12.5 Chemically treated crania showing differential coloration: (a) forensic skull displaying white coloration due to over-processing; (b) commercially prepared teaching cranium from China, bleached off-white; (c) commercially prepared teaching skull most likely from India, bleached white; (d) commercially prepared teaching cranium most likely from India, bleached white; (e) slightly dirty commercially prepared teaching cranium bleached white with adhered packing material; and (f) commercially prepared teaching cranium that is dirty from handling.

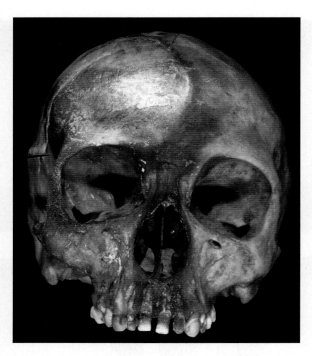

Figure 12.6 Cranium from forensic context showing chemical staining produced by hydro-chloric acid that was used in an attempt to dissolve identifying features.

bone, so this step is not advised for treating materials from forensic contexts (Rennick et al. 2005; Steadman et al. 2006). After this process skeletal materials are usually a bright white color (Figure 12.5c,d).

A number of authors have discussed how assailants have used corrosive chemicals in an attempt to dispose of or mutilate a body (e.g., Maples and Browning 1994; Ubelaker and Sperber 1988). At present there are very few publications that reference the clandestine use of corrosive chemicals on human remains, and research in this area only briefly mentions associated color changes (e.g., Cope and Dupras 2009; Hartnett et al. 2011). Areas of dark brown staining have been noted on remains which have been exposed to hydrochloric acid (HCl) (Figure 12.6), while suspected exposure to sodium hydroxide (NaOH) is thought to whiten bone (Christensen and Meyers 2011; Cope and Dupras 2009).

Staining—Skeletal Teaching Materials

Most material in skeletal teaching collections, particularly those in North America, were likely procured from India or China. Due to variation in commercial preparation techniques, the color of this material may vary (Schultz 2012). Figure 12.5 shows several examples of skeletal material legally purchased from clearing houses for the purposes of teaching. Figure 12.5b shows a cranium that originated in China, and it is common that the color of these materials vary from white to yellowish-white. Figure 12.5d,e show the materials that were prepared in India, and these materials are usually a bright white color, although they may show dark staining on the alveolar region due to the chewing of betel nut (Schultz 2012). Figure 12.5e is also interesting in that the cranium has paper (appearing as dark areas) adhered to the frontal and right zygomatic due to the long term storage of this particular specimen. It is also important to note that after significant handling in the classroom setting, teaching material that was once bright white may become very dirty, forming a *patina* of residual skin oils and dust or other particle and showing as a dark brown or gray color with variable glossiness (Figure 12.5f). These color changes likely will be accompanied by other, physical alterations to remains professionally prepared for teaching, including sectioning and mounting (see Chapter 8, this volume).

Soil Staining

It is very common to observe staining on bones from outdoor contexts resulting from burial of the remains, or bone surfaces that are in contact with the soil surface (e.g., Figures 12.2a,b and 12.3b,c). The coloration of the staining is related to the soil composition which can include various minerals and organic matter. Color is the most obvious characteristic of soil that we first notice, which is the result of either clean soil particles or the coatings of the soil particles (Schaetzl and Anderson 2005). For example, white soil coloration can be due to sodium salts, carbonates, and silt-sized or smaller quartz grains without pigmenting coatings. Dark soils with a black or brown coloration are the result of organic matter (humus) as well as magnetite (Fe_3O_4). Black or bluish-black colorations are the result of reduced manganese (Mn^{2+}). Bright red and brown colorations are associates with well-drained soils and oxidizing conditions (iron-bearing).

In forensic contexts, soil staining on bone may be represented by various colors. The organic horizons of a mineral soil profile begin at the ground surface and are formed from the residues of decaying plant and animal remains (Brady and Weil 2002). A black or darker brown coloration on bones in contact with the ground surface is associated with the darkly colored organic matter that comprises the organic horizons (see Chapter 5, this volume). It should be noted that teeth also may be stained differentially by soil contact. It is common for the anterior (single-rooted) teeth to be soil-stained, since they may be in contact with or become buried under the ground surface after detaching from the alveolus during decomposition (Figure 12.7).

It is common for buried skeletal remains from forensic contexts to exhibit brownish colorations. At the same time, buried skeletal remains from historical contexts have been described as displaying a uniform medium to rich chocolate brown coloration resulting from either tannins in the soil solution (soil water and dissolved load) or iron oxides in the soil (Schultz et al. 2003; see also Chapter 5, this volume). The interaction of bone within an environment is dominated by water, which transports ions, molecules, and particles in and out of bone (Millard 1996). Further, the chemical interaction between buried objects and the burial medium is mainly the result of the chemical nature of the soil solution (Pollard 1996), as the chemistry, pH, and Eh of the soil solution will control the diagenetic change to bone (Millard 1996). Therefore, in the burial environment bone staining will occur due to contact with the soil and through the interaction with the soil solution. While darker-colored minerals and organic matter present in the soil solution will result in darker staining such as dark brown, buried bone exhibiting a lighter-colored staining such as tan (e.g., Figure 12.8) may be buried in a lighter colored mineral soil low in organic matter and comprised of smaller quartz grains without

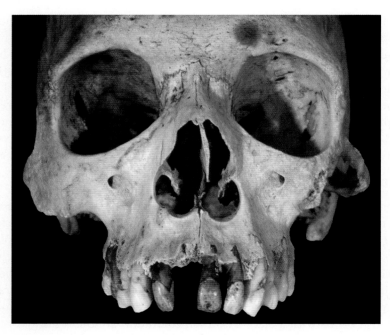

Figure 12.7 Sun-bleached cranium showing differential staining of teeth. After decomposition the incisors detached from the alveolus and were stained by contact with the soil.

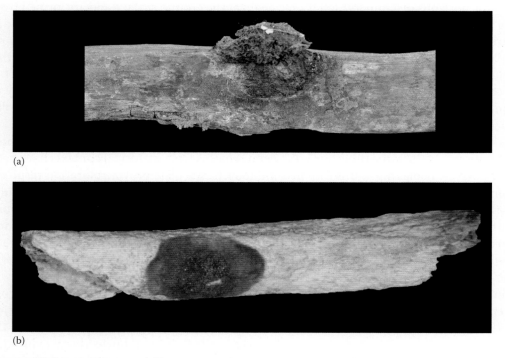

(a)

(b)

Figure 12.8 Iron staining: (a) large mass of iron corrosion products adhered to femoral diaphysis; and (b) prominent orange area of iron staining with adhered rust on long bone diaphysis. The light brown color is most likely due to exposure to sandy soil matrix.

pigmentation coatings. Soil staining on bones that have been in contact with the ground surface is also important in determining if skeletal remains had been moved prior to discovery by investigators. For example, if the soil-stained surface is facing up and not in contact with the ground surface, this would be a clear indication that the remains had been disturbed.

Manganese, present in many minerals, is one of the most abundant metals in soil (Emsley 2001). Depending on its state, manganese can form compounds with different colors, and these compounds may stain bone different colors. For example, manganese dioxide (MnO_2) will stain bone a black color (Cukrowska et al. 2005; Shahack-Gross et al. 1997), manganese (II) carbonate ($MnCO_3$) can stain bones a pink to red or brown color (Anthony et al. 2010), and permanganate ions ($KMnO_4$) may stain bone a purple color (House 2008).

Metal Staining from Artifacts

According to Goffer (2007), corrosion is a natural destructive environmental process resulting in decay or waste of most metals and alloys. This natural tendency of metal and alloy corrosion, with the exception of noble metals such as gold and platinum, results by combining them with an oxidizing substance (e.g., oxygen, fluoride, etc.). This corrosion process is a reversal of the metallurgical process back to the natural chemically combined form found in the crust of the earth. For example, rust found on the surface of exposed iron and steel has the same chemical composition as natural iron ore (Goffer 2007). Corrosion of metal in contact with bone results in metal staining and possibly adhered corrosion products to the bone. In a forensic context, common metals that stain bone are iron (Schultz 2012; Schultz et al. 2003) and copper (Buikstra and Ubelaker 1994; Schultz 2012; Schultz et al. 2003), with mercury staining less commonly reported (Ubelaker 1996).

According to Janaway (2008), corrosion of metal in a burial environment is influenced by a number of variables that include the PMI, the chemical nature of the burial environment, and the composition and structure of the metal artifact. If the burial environment contains high levels of moisture, metals will corrode much faster, and corrosion products such as oxides, carbonates, and sulphates are produced when metals react with environmental chemicals such as oxygen, carbon dioxide, and salts (Cronyn 1990). In forensic contexts, the burial environment will obviously contain moisture related to the decomposition process, as well as percolating rainwater and possible proximity to shallow water tables. Further, Edwards (1996) and Banwart (1996) assert that the combination of pH and redox (an increase in oxidation or the loss of electrons) are chemical variables of the burial environment that will influence metal corrosion. For example, metal will not corrode in a burial environment with low redox (decrease in oxidation or a gain in electrons) values, while metals with high redox values will be more susceptible to corrosion (Janaway 2008). At the same time, while an alkaline (higher pH) burial environment will tend to stabilize the corrosion matrix in most metals, acidic (lower pH) conditions will corrode metals (Janaway 2008).

Janaway (2008) further emphasizes how the chemical nature of the buried object will influence corrosion, by dividing metals into three groups based on their susceptibility to corrosion. The first group of metals is classified as corrosion-resistant and common examples include gold or surgical steel used for body piercings and titanium alloys used for implants. The second group of metals is susceptible to an initial rapid corrosion phase, followed by the creation of a layer of stable corrosion products (e.g., copper). In addition, these metals can have an extensive metallic core preserved hundreds of years after burial. The third group of metals corrodes rapidly and does not form a layer of protective corrosion products. Iron would be an example of a rapidly corroding metal that can be characterized as completely lost over an extended PMI, or it can remain as a large mass of corrosion that may cover a reduced metallic core (Figure 12.8a).

Iron

Rust, a brown, crumbly corrosion product composed of hydrated iron oxide, is formed when iron and its alloys are exposed to a moist, oxygenated environment (Cronyn 1990; Goffer 2007). As corrosion proceeds into the metal, a thick overlying concretion of corrosion products can be formed over the iron artifact (Figure 12.8a) (Cronyn 1990). Eventually, the metal can be completely corroded and only represented by a void within the overlying concretion. According to Cronyn (1990), in moist and oxygenated environments, the oxidized iron can produce an area of corrosion products that can be considerably larger than the dissolved metal. Hence, staining of bone can occur (Figure 12.8b) when the item is in direct contact with the corroding iron object or in proximity to the corrosion products in the soil. Iron staining of bone also may be used to recognize out-of-context cemetery remains, as iron artifacts associated with the coffin such as nails (see Chapter 5, this volume) can stain bone an orange color, and adhered corrosion products also may be present (Schultz 2012; Schultz et al. 2003).

Corrosion of iron results in a layer/crust of corrosion products that can display a variety of colors (Cronyn 1990). Iron excavated from damp, aerated sites is commonly recovered as a mass with a red/brown coloration composed of iron oxides and carbonates. The corrosion products consist of iron (III) oxyhydroxides (FeO·OH), with the main component in the form of red/brown/yellow goethite (αFeO·OH), including orange lepidocrocite (γFeO·OH). A black coloration to the corrosion products of iron can occur from a number of different compounds. When iron objects are subjected to a wet, anaerobic burial environment because of iron (II) sulphide (FeS) formed by sulphate-reducing bacteria, a black layer can be formed. Also, a black coloration due to the formation of black oxide magnetite (Fe_3O_4) can form at marine sites with low oxygen. Interestingly, Cronyn (1990) further mentions that green-colored rust is also possible as a mixture of iron (II) and iron (III) hydrated oxides. While it is observed occasionally on marine cast and wrought iron, it also has been observed on wrought iron from land sites. Considering that the green coloration from copper and copper alloys found on bone is most often a stain and not an adhered green corrosion product, this rare example more than likely does not have to be considered when interpreting green staining as copper-derived.

Lastly, a bright blue to blue-black coloration is much rarer and can be displayed on bone resulting from deposits of vivianite (iron phosphate). In the form of iron (II) phosphate ($Fe_3(PO_4)_2 \cdot 8H_2O$), vivianite exhibits a whitish-gray coloration in its unoxidized condition when first excavated, but when exposed to air the mineral changes color to a brilliant blue (Cronyn 1990; Guthrie 1990). When referring to paleontological bones, this mineral staining occurs on buried organic remains that are high in phosphates and low in iron and that are buried in damp soils rich in iron and low in phosphates (Guthrie 1990). With the combination of a phosphate and iron source, there must be a reducing and acidic environment for vivianite to form (Courty et al. 1989). Examples of a reducing environ-ment include acid groundwater, deep water, waterlogged soil, and anaerobic conditions (Courty et al. 1989; Johanson 1976; Mann et al. 1998; Martill 1991; Thali et al. 2011). While vivianite staining traditionally has been reported in the paleontological literature (Guthrie 1990; Martill 1991), this staining also has been sampled on skeletal remains from U.S. servicemen listed as missing in action from the Vietnam War, which indicates that this staining can be produced on bone during much shorter PMIs than previously believed (Holland et al. 1997; Mann et al. 1998). According to Mann et al. (1998) based on experi-ence and summarizing the literature, the iron source for the formation of vivianite on bone can also come from a nearby piece of iron in addition to the soil, a common occurrence on battlefield and air crash sites.

Copper and Copper Alloys

Copper and copper alloy staining is fairly recognizable on bone as a green to green-bluish coloration (Buikstra and Ubelaker 1994; Schultz 2012; Schultz et al. 2003). Copper stain-ing has been reported in the literature dealing with taphonomic clues to recognize out-of-context cemetery remains as artifacts comprised of copper, including coffin hardware or jewelry, can corrode and stain bone a greenish coloration (Figure 12.9) (Schultz 2012; Schultz et al. 2003). In forensic contexts copper staining may be present on bone as a result of the copper alloy-based clothing artifacts such as buttons and zippers and also from the copper jacket of a bullet (Figure 12.10).

The two most common alloys of copper are bronze and brass. Brass, which is stron-ger and harder than copper, is primarily a mixture of copper and zinc, while bronze, which is harder and has a higher tensile strength than copper, is primarily a mixture of copper and tin (Goffer 2007). While copper and copper alloys are generally resis-tant to corrosion under normal atmospheric conditions, these metals will tarnish by contact with pollutants such as hydrogen sulfide and/or carbon dioxide (Goffer 2007). Eventually, corrosion will produce a green surface layer referred to as a patina with the metallic core remaining unchanged. Compounds such as copper carbonates, oxides, and chlorides comprise the copper patina, while the patina for bronze and brass also includes oxides of tin and lead (Goffer 2007). Slow, controlled corrosion to the sur-face of copper and copper alloys is due to moisture, carbon dioxide, oxygen, air pollut-ants, and sea water (Cronyn 1990; Goffer 2007). Conversely, buried copper objects may become severely corroded as they react with soil pollutants and components of the soil (Goffer 2007).

According to Cronyn (1990), there also can be color variation of the corrosion prod-ucts resulting from the environment and type of copper alloy. For example, the common green coloration observed on bone is the result of emerald/dark-green malachite, basic copper (II) carbonate ($CuCO_3 \cdot Cu(OH)_2$). The hue of the green can be darkened by the addition of sulphides of copper and lead, or lightened by the addition of lead carbonate and other compounds. A blue color can also develop from another basic copper (II) carbonate, azurite ($2CuCO_3 \cdot Cu(OH)_2$), while yellow-green patinas can form on copper alloys exposed to the atmosphere from basic copper (II) sulphate, brochantite ($CuCO_4 \cdot 3Cu(OH)_2$). Further, corrosion of copper artifacts can also produce a crust of corrosion products that usually contain the same minerals as the patinas (Cronyn 1990).

On occasion, the presence of copper also will aid in the preservation of organic materials (McIntosh 1999). For example, if cotton clothing is present, the copper may act

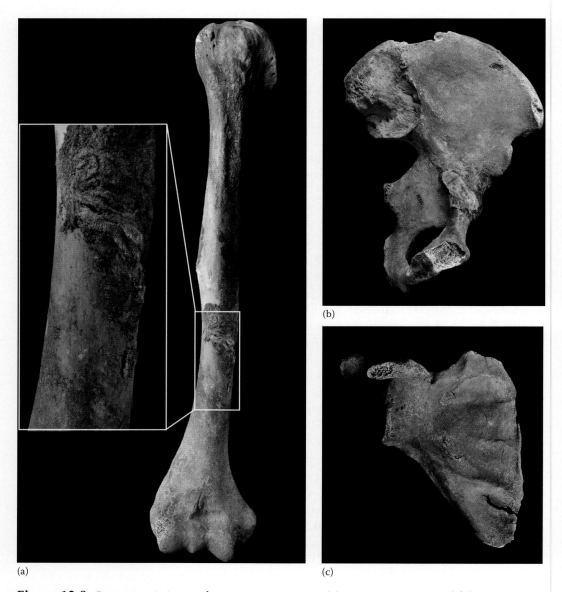

Figure 12.9 Copper staining on historic-era remains: (a) copper staining and fabric preservation on the diaphysis of a right humerus; (b) copper staining and fabric preservation on the superior pubic ramus and ilium of a left innominate; and (c) copper staining along the anterior axial border of a right scapula.

as a preserving agent, and it is not uncommon to see small pieces of cloth adhered to areas that are stained green. For example, both the historic-era humerus and innominate in Figure 12.9a and b show preservation of cotton material adhered to the stained areas.

Mercury

Mercury staining from dental amalgam restorations is one of the less commonly reported chemical stains. A dental amalgam is classified as a solid emulsion metal mixture comprised

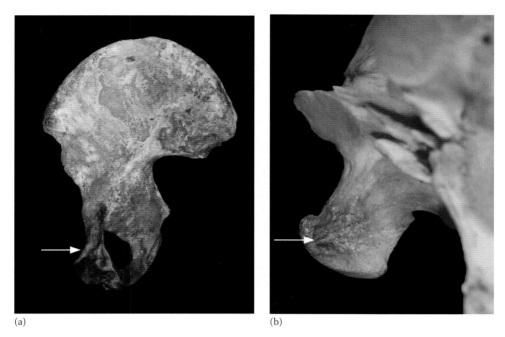

(a)   (b)

Figure 12.10 Copper staining on remains from forensic contexts: (a) prominent staining of the superior pubic area (arrow) most likely from clothing fasteners; decomposition staining is notable on the iliac blade; and (b) faint staining on the spinous process of a thoracic vertebra from a copper bullet jacket (arrow).

of approximately 50% metallic mercury (Hg^0) by mass (Richardson et al. 2011). While the formulations will vary in the Hg content from 43% to 50.5% by mass, the powder mixture typically will contain a variety of metals such as silver (40%–70%), copper (12%–30%), tin (12%–30%), indium (0%–4%), zinc (0%–1%), and palladium (0.5%) (Berry et al. 1994). Although it is now accepted that there is a continual release and therefore exposure of Hg^0 in living persons with amalgam fillings (USFDA 2009), it is not common to see mercury staining of the dental anatomy.

Mercury stains on osseous material have been the result of postmortem deterioration of the amalgam fillings. In the only case study describing the causative agent of mercury stains to the dental anatomy, Ubelaker (1996) described a metallic black stain to the oral cavity of an exhumed cemetery skeleton with a significant number of dental amalgam restorations. Staining was present on the anterior dentition of both the maxillary and mandibular teeth, as well as the mandible. In addition, it was reported that the dental amalgam restorations were deteriorated. While the causative agent for the deterioration of the amalgam fillings and resultant staining of the osseous surfaces was not known, Ubelaker (1996) suggested that the staining may been produced from the presence of sulfuric acid (H_2SO_4) in the burial environment. For example, sulfur dioxide (SO_2) could have been released from decomposition, producing sulfuric acid in the humid environment of the vault. The interaction of the sulfuric acid, or possibly some other compound, released the mercury from the amalgam restorations, producing the staining. Figure 12.11a through c shows an example of the deterioration of

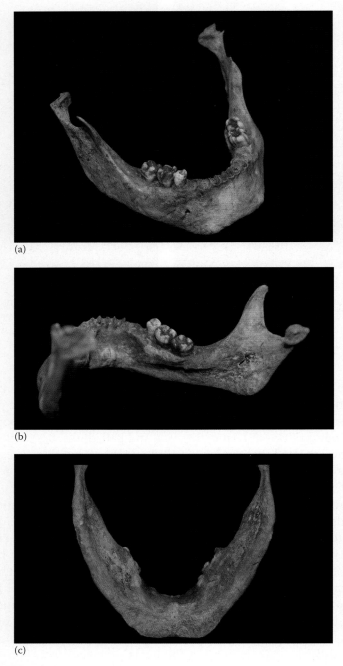

Figure 12.11 Mandible with amalgam mercury staining: (a) anterior view showing staining on buccal side of enamel; (b) posterior view showing staining on the lingual surfaces of enamel and alveolus; and (c) inferior view showing bone staining.

amalgam fillings of the mandible in a forensic case. In this example, there is a grayish stain on the enamel of the teeth with amalgam fillings and the concomitant bone surfaces. In particular, there is a prominent stain on the lingual surface of the mandible. It is important to note that this stain was only located on the mandible and may be the result of a unique compound in the postmortem environment reacting with the amalgam fillings.

Organic Staining

Bones from outdoor contexts typically will interact with plant and tree materials, resulting in organic stains on the bone. According to Bass (1997), bones in shady areas may exhibit moss or green algae growth (see Chapter 11, this volume) during the first year of exposure. Green staining from moss and algae is the result of pigments such as chlorophyll (greens), xanthrophylls (yellows), and carotenoids (oranges and reds) (Davies 2004) invading and binding tightly with the bone surface. Other examples of organic staining present on bones can be due to the interaction of bone with roots or the decomposition of pine needles (see Chapter 5, this volume).

Algae

While algae growth on human remains in aquatic environments has been associated with the determination of the postmortem submersion interval (PMSI) (Casamatta and Verb 2000; Haefner et al. 2004; Zimmerman and Wallace 2008; see also Chapter 7, this volume), green staining from algae is also commonly found on terrestrial bones in moist shaded areas (Bass 1997; Janjua and Rogers 2008; Ubelaker, 1997). Algae are nonvascular plants without true roots, stems or leaves that typically possess chlorophyll and are photosynthetic (Hall 2012). Forensically, algae also may be important botanical evidence. For example, algae can be important when linking a suspect to a specific aquatic scene, as well as placing a suspect at a scene during a specific time of year (Hall 2012; Hardy and Wallace 2012; Siver et al. 1994). Algae typically are associated with different types of aquatic ecosystems and also can grow in wet terrestrial environments (Hall 2012; Hardy and Wallace 2012). While it is common to find green algae growth on submerged remains, it is also common to observe green organic staining from algae growing on bone in terrestrial environments (Figure 12.12a), and this would indicate that the bones had been in a moist, shady environment.

Mosses

Mosses are nonvascular and flowerless plants of the class Musci that can grow on bone and also produce green staining (Bass 1997). Mosses grow in moist and shady areas (Coyle 2004), and are usually the first plants to colonize newly exposed bare rocks, ground, and other abiotic surfaces (Hallingbäck and Hodgetts 2000). While mosses may appear to have stems, roots, and leaves, they are a small green organism lacking these structures (Hall 2012). Although they have no true roots, they contain root-like structures that allow them to cling to various surfaces (Hallingbäck and Hodgetts 2000). Also, while they are usually small organisms, mosses can grow as large mats across the ground and are on average only a few centimeters in height from their surface of attachment (Coyle 2004).

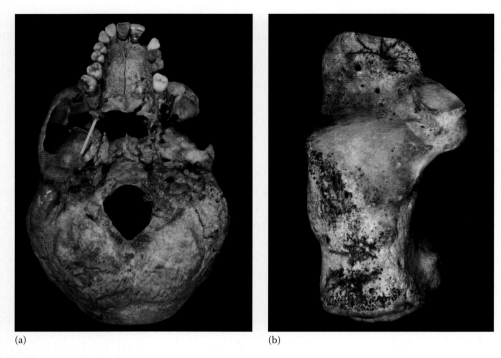

(a)   (b)

Figure 12.12 Organic staining: (a) inferior cranium showing algae staining; and (b) sun-bleached left calcaneus with moss and soil staining. Note that the moss growth corresponds with the exposed (sun-bleached) areas.

Forensically, mosses also can be useful in establishing a portion of the PMI (Cardoso et al. 2010; Hall 2012). Green organic staining also may occur from mosses adhered to and growing on bone (Figure 12.12b).

Root and Decomposing Plant Material Staining and Etching

Root etching is a common taphonomic modification that is recognized on the bone surface as a dendritic pattern of shallow grooves or tracts (Behrensmeyer 1978; Buikstra and Ubelaker 1994; Schultz 2012; Schultz et al. 2003; White and Folkens 1991; see also Chapter 5, this volume). According to Behrensmeyer (1978:154), the pattern results from "dissolution by acids associated with the growth and decay of roots or fungus in direct contact with the bones surfaces." Discoloration of the tracts may also occur through acid decalcification of the bone (Buikstra and Ubelaker 1994). Root etching is more commonly observed on archaeological material, and it is not common to observe this taphonomic modification on forensic remains due to shorter PMIs (Schultz 2012; Schultz et al. 2003). It is possible, however, to observe dendritic patterns of darker staining from plant roots on the bone surface of forensic remains (Figure 12.13a).

Another example of organic staining found on bones can be the result of decomposing plant materials, including leaves and pine needles (see Chapter 5, this volume, for discussion of tannins as they relate to coffin burials). In addition to discoloration, pine needles will also etch the bone, and this taphonomic change can be observed as an unorganized pattern of linear staining with shallow etching (Dupras et al. 2011).

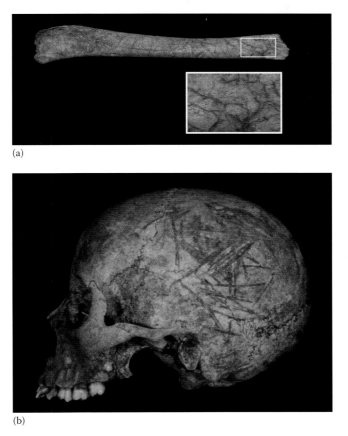

(a)

(b)

Figure 12.13 Organic staining: (a) juvenile deer (*Odocoileus virginianus*) tibia showing dendritic pattern of root staining; and (b) sun-bleached cranium with minimal algae staining and pine needle etching with accompanying tan-colored staining.

The staining can be present as a tannish coloration (Figure 12.13b). More than likely, the bone is etched because the decomposing pine needles are acidic and react with the base ions of the bone surface.

Mineral Precipitates and Other Encrustations

On some occasions bone surfaces may be altered by either mineral precipitates or other mineral encrustations and thus alter the bone's color. For example, in both marine and mineral-laden burial environments, sodium chloride (NaCl or "salt") may be dissolved in solution. This solution may penetrate the bone, and as the water evaporates the salt will begin to crystalize (see Chapter 7, this volume). The crystals may expand and cause damage to the bone, or form crystals on the bone surface (Figure 12.14a). Other minerals such as vivianite (see previous discussion on iron) may form encrustations on the surface. In the marine environment bones may also show color and surface alteration due to barnacles. Although not a mineral, but an animal, barnacles may grow on bone thereby altering the

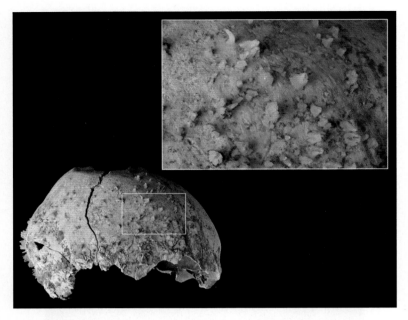

Figure 12.14 Cranium showing salt precipitates with close-up (inset).

bone surface, and also affecting the color of the bone (see Chapter 7, this volume, for discussion of barnacles in marine environments).

Bones in marine or burial environments with groundwater also may have stains and encrustations associated with calcium carbonate ($CaCO_3$). Calcium carbonate commonly manifests as segregations in soil, and occurs in a variety of forms, sizes and consistencies (Fitzpatrick 2008). In precipitate form calcium carbonate may permeate the bone and exchange for minerals in the hydroxyapatite, or it may form layers on the bone surface where it will appear as a white or off-white encrustation (Figure 12.15a through c). This type of mineral concretion forms frequently where water pools and evaporates, and the traces of it may form a distinct ring indicating the orientation of the bone while this process occurred. Later movement of this element may be detectable by the lack of horizontal alignment of the calcium carbonate ring.

Conclusions

In forensic cases involving the analysis of human skeletal remains, it may become vital to reconstruct and interpret associated taphonomic events. Taphonomic criteria can be useful in determining information such as forensic context (Schultz 2012), body movement, identification of associated artifacts, and possible perimortem events. Bone staining and color changes may provide vital clues about the burial or depositional environment and about associated burial artifacts. Determining the cause of bone staining may be very helpful with the interpretation of taphonomic events, but it is imperative to recognize that different causative agents can create similar coloration or staining on bone. For example, bones with a white color may have been sun bleached, burnt, have mineral or adipocere adhesions, or have been chemically altered. Green staining may be related to algae or moss growth, or

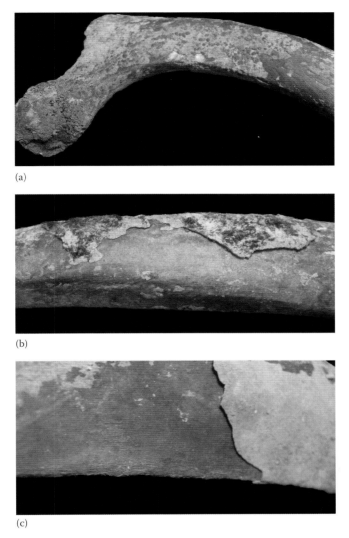

(a)

(b)

(c)

Figure 12.15 Calcium carbonate concretions from a fresh water environment: (a) cow (*Bos taurus*) rib showing calcium carbonate concretions with algae growth; (b) layer of calcium carbonate with algae growth; and (c) close-up showing layer of calcium carbonate on bone surface. Scale bar is 1 cm. (Images courtesy of Tom Evans.)

oxidation of copper artifacts. Bones with brown coloration may have been in contact with soils, water, or may be dirty from handling. It is also possible, as shown in Figure 12.2, that bones may also display multiple color changes related to different taphonomic events. See Table 12.1 for summary of taphonomic processes and associated color changes.

Much like differential diagnosis in paleopathology, all bone surfaces should be examined and documented for any noticeable staining or color changes. Once colors are documented it is then possible to go to the literature to identify possible causes through the process of elimination. Additional clues from the depositional context and/or associated artifacts also may be very useful to assist in interpretation. For example, a bright white skull with hardware such as springs to hold the mandible in place, and screws and hooks

Table 12.1   Taphonomic Processes and Associated Bone Color Changes

Taphonomic Process	Possible Associated Color
Chemical Staining and Natural Bleaching	
Sun bleaching	Bright white to gray
Commercial preparation	Yellow to bright white
Industrial chemicals	Brown, white (dependent on chemical)
Soil Staining	
Humic acids	Dark brown, black
Manganese dioxide	Black
Manganese carbonate	Pink, red, brown
Permanganate	Purple
Metal Staining	
Iron	Orange, red, brown, black
Vivianite	Bright blue to blue-black
Copper and copper alloys	Green to bluish-green
Mercury	Gray/silver to black
Organic Staining	
Algae	Green
Mosses	Green
Roots and decomposing plant materials	Light brown to black
Mineral Precipitates	
Salts	White (opaque crystals)
Calcium carbonates	White to off-white

to keep the calotte secured to the cranium, would indicate teaching or anatomical material (Schultz 2012; see also Chapter 9, this volume), and the bright white coloration would be due to deliberate chemical alteration from preparation. The anatomical location of the staining also may help to determine the causative agent. For example, gray staining on the alveolus and enamel most likely caused by the mercury in amalgam fillings, and it would be very unlikely to find this kind of staining on other parts of the skeleton. Forensic anthropologists should be aware of the most common types of bone staining and color alteration as part of their investigation and interpretation of taphonomic events.

Acknowledgments

We would like to extend our thanks to Dr. Rimantas Jankauskus (Vilnius University) for permission to photograph bone samples with iron staining. We also extend thanks to Dr. Lana Williams for her assistance with some of the photography and to Tom Evans for allowing us to use the images for Figure 12.15.

References

Anthony, J. W., R. A. Bideaux, K. W. Bladh, and M. C. Nichols (2010) *Handbook of Mineralogy*. Mineralogical Society of America, Chantilly, VA.

Aufderheide, A. C. (2011) Soft tissue taphonomy: A paleopathology perspective. *International Journal of Paleopathology* 1:75–80.

Banwart, S. A. (1996) Groundwater geochemistry in the burial environment. In *Preserving Archaeological Remains* in situ, eds. M. Corfield, P. Hinton, T. Nixon, and M. Pollard, pp. 66–72. Museum of London Archaeology Service, London, U.K.

Bass, W. M. (1997) Outdoor decomposition rates in Tennessee. In *Forensic Taphonomy: The Postmortem Fate of Human Remains*, eds. W. D. Haglund and M. H. Sorg, pp. 181–186. CRC Press, Boca Raton, FL.

Beary, M. O. (2005) *Taphonomic Effects of UV Light on Bone Surface: An Experimental Approach*. Unpublished M.A. Thesis, Mercyhurst College, Erie, PA.

Behrensmeyer, A. K. (1978) Taphonomic and ecologic information from bone weathering. *Paleobiology* 4:150–162.

Berry, T. G., J. Nicholson, and K. Troendle (1994) Almost two centuries with amalgam: Where are we today? *Journal of the American Dental Association* 125:392–399.

Brady, N. C. and R. R. Weil (2002) *The Nature and Properties of Soils* (13th edn.). Prentice Hall, Upper Saddle River, NJ.

Buikstra, J. E. and D. H. Ubelaker (1994) *Standards for Data Collection from Human Skeletal Remains*. Arkansas Archeological Survey Research Series No. 44. Arkansas Archeological Survey, Fayetteville, AR.

Byers, S. N. (2008) *Introduction to Forensic Anthropology* (3rd edn.). Pearson Education, Boston, MA.

Cain, C. R. (2005) Using burned animal bone to look at Middle Stone Age occupation and behavior. *Journal of Archaeological Science* 32:873–884.

Calce, S. E. and T. L. Rogers (2007) Taphonomic changes to blunt force trauma: A preliminary study. *Journal of Forensic Sciences* 52:519–527.

Cardoso, H. F. V., A. Santos, C. Garcia, M. Pinto, C. Sérgo, and T. Magalhaes (2010) Establishing a minimum postmortem interval of human remains in an advanced state of skeletonization using the growth rate of bryophytes and plant roots. *International Journal of Legal Medicine* 124:451–456.

Casamatta, D. and R. Verb (2000) Algal colonization of submerged carcasses in a mid-order woodland stream. *Journal of Forensic Sciences* 45:1280–1285.

Christensen, A. M. and S. W. Meyers (2011) Macroscopic observations of the effects of varying fresh water pH on bone. *Journal of Forensic Sciences* 56:475–479.

Cope, D. J. and T. L. Dupras (2009) The effects of household corrosive chemicals on human dentition. *Journal of Forensic Science* 54:1238–1246.

Courty, M. A., R. Goldberg, and R. Macphail (1989) *Soils and Micromorphology in Archaeology*. Cambridge University Press, Cambridge, MA.

Coyle, H. M. (2004) Plant diversity. In *Forensic Botany: Principles and Applications to Criminal Casework,* ed. H. M. Coyle, pp. 81–96. CRC Press, Boca Raton, FL.

Cronyn, J. M. (1990) *The Elements of Archaeological Conservation*. Routledge, London, U.K.

Cukrowska, E. M., T. S. McCarthy, S. Pole, L. Blackwell, and C. Steininger (2005) The chemical removal of manganese dioxide coatings from fossil bones from the cradle of humankind, South Africa. *South African Journal of Science* 101:101–103.

Davies, K (2004) An introduction to plant pigments in biology and commerce. In *Plant Pigments and Their Manipulation,* ed. K. Davies, pp. 1–22. Annual Plant Reviews, Vol. 14. Blackwell Publishing, Oxford, U.K.

Dupras, T. L., J. J. Schultz, S. M. Wheeler, and L. J. Williams (2011) *Forensic Recovery of Human Remains: Archaeological Approaches* (2nd edn.). CRC Press, Boca Raton, FL.

Edwards, R. (1996) The effect of changes in groundwater geochemistry on the survival of buried metal artefacts. In *Preserving Archaeological Remains* in situ, eds. M. Corfield, P. Hinton, T. Nixon, and M. Pollard, pp. 86–92. Museum of London Archaeology Service, London, U.K.

Emsley, J. (2001) *Nature's Building Blocks: An A-Z Guide to the Elements*. Oxford University Press, Oxford, London, U.K.

Fenton, T. W., W. H. Birkby, and J. Cornelison (2003) A fast and safe non-bleaching method for forensic skeletal preparation. *Journal of Forensic Science* 48:274–276.

Fitzpatrick, R. W. (2008) Nature, distribution and origin of soil materials in the forensic comparison of soils. In *Soil Analysis in Forensic Taphonomy: Chemical and Biological Effects of Buried Human Remains*, eds. M. Tibbett and D. O. Carter, pp. 1–28. CRC Press, Boca Raton, FL.

Galloway, A., W. H. Birkby, A. M. Jones, T. E. Henry, and B. O. Parks (1989) Decay rates of human remains in an arid environment. *Journal of Forensic Sciences* 34:607–616.

Goffer, Z. (2007) *Archaeological Chemistry*. John Wiley and Sons, Hoboken, NJ.

Gruspier, K. L. (1999) Pathological changes in human skeletal remains: Before, during or after? In *Forensic Osteological Analysis: A Book of Case Studies*, ed. S. I. Fairgrieve, pp. 199–225. Charles C Thomas, Springfield, IL.

Guthrie, R. D. (1990) *Frozen Fauna of the Mammoth Steppe: The Story of Blue Babe*. University of Chicago Press, Chicago, IL.

Haefner, J. N., J. R. Wallace, and R. W. Merritt (2004) Pig decomposition in lotic aquatic systems: The potential use of algal growth in establishing a postmortem submersion interval (PMSI). *Journal of Forensic Sciences* 49:330–336.

Haglund, W. D., M. Connor, and D. D. Scott (2002) The effect of cultivation on buried human remains. In *Advances in Forensic Taphonomy: Method, Theory, and Archaeological Perspectives*, eds. W. D. Haglund and M. H. Sorg, pp. 133–150. CRC Press, Boca Raton, FL.

Hall, D. W. (2012) Plants as evidence. In *Forensic Botany: A Practical Guide*, eds. D. W. Hall and J. H. Byrd, pp. 12–44. John Wiley and Sons, Oxford, U.K.

Hallingbäck, T. and N. Hodgetts (2000) *Mosses, Liverworts, and Hornworts: Status Survey and Conservation Action Plan for Bryophytes*. IUCN/SSC Bryophyte Specialist Group, Cambridge, U.K.

Hardy, C. R., and J. R. Wallace (2012) Algae in forensic investigations. In *Forensic Botany: A Practical Guide*, eds. D. W. Hall and J. H. Byrd, pp. 145–173. John Wiley and Sons, Oxford, U.K.

Hartnett, K. M., L. C. Fulginiti, and F. Di Modica (2011) The effects of corrosive substances on human bone, teeth, hair, nails, and soft tissue. *Journal of Forensic Sciences* 56:954–959.

Holland, T. D., B. E. Anderson, and R. W. Mann (1997) Human variables in postmortem alteration of human bone: Examples from U.S. war casualties. In *Forensic Taphonomy: The Postmortem Fate of Human Remains*, eds. W. D. Haglund and M. H. Sorg, pp. 263–274. CRC Press, Boca Raton, FL.

House, J. E. (2008) *Inorganic Chemistry*. Academic Press, Burlington, MA.

Huculak, M. A. and T. L. Rogers (2009) Reconstructing the sequence of events surrounding body disposition based on color staining of bone. *Journal of Forensic Sciences* 54:979–984.

Janaway, J. C. (2008) The decomposition of materials associated with buried cadavers. In *Soil Analysis in Forensic Taphonomy: Chemical and Biological Effects of Buried Human Remains*, eds. M. Tibbett and D. O. Carter, pp. 153–201. CRC Press, Boca Raton, FL.

Janjua, M. A. and T. L. Rogers (2008) Bone weathering patterns of metatarsal v. femur and the postmortem interval in southern Ontario. *Forensic Science International* 178:16–23.

Johanson, G. (1976) Iron from cannon balls in teeth and jaws. *Ossa* 3–4:183–187.

Joiner, A. (2006) The bleaching of teeth: A review of the literature. *Journal of Dentistry* 34:412–419.

Lee, E. J., J. G. Leudtke, J. L. Allison, C. E. Arber, D. A. Merriwether, and D. W. Steadman (2010) The effects of different maceration techniques on nuclear DNA amplification using human bone. *Journal of Forensic Sciences* 55:1032–1038.

Mairs, S., B. Swift, and G. N. Rutty (2004) Detergent: An alternative approach to traditional bone cleaning methods for forensic practice. *American Journal of Forensic Medicine and Pathology* 25:276–284.

Mann, R. W., M. E. Feather, C. S. Tumosa, T. D. Holland, and K. N. Schneider (1998) A blue encrustation found on skeletal remains of Americans missing in action in Vietnam. *Forensic Science International* 97:79–86.

Maples, W. R. and M. Browning (1994) *Dead Men Do Tell Tales: The Strange and Fascinating Cases of a Forensic Anthropologist*. Doubleday, New York.

Martill, D. M. (1991) Bones as stones: The contribution of vertebrate remains to the lithologic record. In *The Processes of Fossilization*, ed. S. K. Donovan. pp. 270–292. Columbia University Press, New York.

McIntosh, J. (1999) *The Practical Archaeologist: How We Know What We Know About the Past*, 2nd edn. Checkmark Books, New York.

Millard, A. (1996) Bone in the burial environment. In *Preserving Archaeological Remains* in situ, ed. M. Corfield, P. Hinton, T. Nixon, and M. Pollard, pp. 93–102. Museum of London Archaeology Service, London, U.K.

Pollard, M.A. 1996. The chemical nature of the burial environment. In *Preserving Archaeological Remains* in situ, eds. M. Corfield, P. Hinton, T. Nixon, and M. Pollard, pp. 60–65. Museum of London Archaeology Service, London, U.K.

Quatrehomme, G. and M. Y. İşcan (1997) Postmortem skeletal lesions. *Forensic Science International* 89:155–165.

Rennick, S. L., T. W. Fenton, and D. R. Foran (2005) The effects of skeletal preparation techniques on DNA from human and non-human bone. *Journal of Forensic Sciences* 50:1016–1019.

Richardson, G. M., R. Wilson, D. Allard, C. Purtill, S. Douma, and J. Graviere (2011) Mercury exposure and risks from dental amalgam in the US population, post-2000. *Science of the Total Environment* 409:4257–4268.

Schaetzl, R. and A. Anderson (2005) *Soils: Genesis and Geomorphology*. Cambridge University Press, New York.

Schafer, A. T. (2001) The colour of the human skull. *Forensic Science International* 117:53–56.

Schultz, J. J., M. A. Williamson, S. P. Nawrocki, A. B. Falsetti, and M. W. Warren (2003) A taphonomic profile to aid in the recognition of human remains from historic and/or cemetery contexts. *Florida Anthropologist* 56:141–147.

Schultz, J. J. (2012) Determining the forensic significance of skeletal remains. In *A Companion to Forensic Anthropology*, eds. D. Dirkmaat, pp. 66–84. Wiley-Blackwell, Oxford, U.K.

Shahack-Gross, R., O. Bar-Yosef, and S. Weiner (1997) Black-coloured bones in Hayonim Cave, Israel: Differentiating between burning and oxide staining. *Journal of Archaeological Science* 24:439–446.

Siver, P. A., W. D. Lord, and D. J. McCarthy (1994) Forensic limnology: The use of freshwater algal community to link suspects to an aquatic crime scene in southern New England. *Journal of Forensic Sciences* 39:847–853.

Steadman, D. W., L. L. DiAntonio, J. J. Wilson, K. E. Seridan, and S. P. Tammariello (2006) The effects of chemical and heat maceration techniques on the recovery of nuclear and mitochondrial DNA from bone. *Journal of Forensic Sciences* 51:11–17.

Thali, M. J., B. Lux, S. Losch, F. W. Rosing, J. Hurlimann, P. Feer, R. Dirnhofer, U. Konigsdofer, and U. Zollinger (2011) "Brienzi"—The blue Vivianite man of Switzerland: Time since death estimation of an adipocere body. *Forensic Science International* 211:34–40.

Ubelaker, D. H. (1996) The remains of Dr. Carl Austin Weiss: Anthropological analysis. *Journal of Forensic Sciences* 41:60–79.

Ubelaker, D. H. (1997) Taphonomic applications in forensic anthropology. In *Forensic Taphonomy: The Postmortem Fate of Human Remains*, eds. W. D. Haglund and M. H. Sorg, pp. 77–89. CRC Press, Boca Raton, FL.

Ubelaker, D. H. and N. D. Sperber (1988) Alterations in human bones and teeth as a result of restricted sun exposure in contact with corrosive agents. *Journal of Forensic Sciences* 33:540–548.

Ubelaker, D. H. and K. M. Zarenko (2011) Adipocere: What is known after over two centuries of research. *Forensic Science International* 208:167–172.

U.S. Food and Drug Agency (USFDA) (2009) *White Paper: FDA Update/Review of Potential Adverse Health Risks Associated with Exposure to Mercury in Dental Amalgam*. USFDA, National Center for Toxicological Research, Washington, DC.

White, T. and P. Folkens (1991) *Human Osteology*. Academic Press, San Francisco, CA.

Zayat, M., P. Garcia-Parejo, and D. Levy (2007) Preventing UV-light damage of light sensitive materials using a highly protective UV-absorbing coating. *Chemical Society Reviews* 36:1270–1281.

Zimmerman, K. A. and J. R. Wallace (2008) The potential to determine a postmortem submersion interval based on algal/diatom diversity on decomposing mammalian carcasses in brackish ponds in Delaware. *Journal of Forensic Sciences* 53:935–941.

Taphonomy and the Timing of Bone Fractures in Trauma Analysis

13

STEVEN A. SYMES
ERICKA N. L'ABBÉ
KYRA E. STULL
MARCELLE LACROIX
JAMES T. POKINES

Contents

In skeletal trauma analysis the mistake of inferring too much from too little is one of the greatest problems in an anthropologist's routine analysis of bone injuries. In the absence of soft tissue or a lack of knowledge regarding the context in which the remains were discovered, the anthropologist needs to be conservative in trauma interpretations. As in a court of law, the interpretation of either the cause and or manner of death from one or multiple skeletal elements has tremendous implications for the accused, not to mention the career of the anthropologist.

—Symes et al., in Dirkmaat (2012:382–383)

Introduction

Determining the cause of bone fractures is not only a difficult assessment but also has larger implications and repercussions, particularly when a forensic anthropologist is tasked with differentiating human-induced injuries relevant to the cause and manner of death from either geological or biological alterations (Nawrocki 2009). The latter is often classified as *pseudotrauma*, and is defined as an alteration to wet/fresh skeletal remains that appears to be human-induced but in fact has natural origins. *Wet* or *fresh* bone is defined as retaining moisture and organic contents (including water and lipid), whereas, *dry* bone lacks an organic component (primarily collagen) and experiences degradation. These processes are a consequence of an increase in the postmortem interval (PMI). The exact time of change from wet to dry bone is not straightforward and varies greatly with depositional context (e.g., Dirkmaat and Adovasio 1997; Hill 1980; Nawrocki 2009).

Archaeologists routinely discuss fracture characteristics of wet and dry bone as a means to differentiate human-induced butchery practices from other taphonomic influences (Biddick and Tomenchuk 1975; Hill 1980; Johnson 1985; Morlan 1984). Physical anthropologists are also interested in deciphering culturally induced modifications to bone from other terrestrial (see Chapter 9, this volume) and marine (Chapter 7) animal alterations, water abrasion (Chapters 6 and 7), and plant action (Chapters 5 and 12). Furthermore, unintentional human alterations such as plowing and cemetery burial (Chapter 5) and excavation itself (Chapter 17) may also alter bones in ways that could be erroneously mistaken for fatal injuries. Thus, accurate assessment of the timing of a traumatic injury is paramount when establishing the sequence of events at a crime scene and in determining whether a crime was committed.

In the anthropological literature, the timing of an injury—perimortem or postmortem—is often used simultaneously to explain the death event (Galloway 1999; Komar and Buikstra 2008; Sauer 1998). However, the anthropologist describes all injuries occurring to wet/fresh bone as perimortem, despite the fact that somatic death already occurred. The latter is the purview of a forensic pathologist whose definition of the perimortem interval is purely based on somatic death, not bone degradation (Cunha and Pinherio 2009).

Instead of focusing on the death event, forensic anthropologists need to provide a description of the bone fracture which is associated with the bone's condition (wet or dry) at the time of injury and within the context of the scene recovery. For example, bone trauma that immediately follows death, such as dismemberment or burning, occurs while the bones are fresh; thus, the bone responds as fresh bone does to injury. While damage to dry bone may be easily recognizable (such as rodent gnawing or obvious color differentiation between outer and inner cortical layers), the circumstances surrounding a bone fracture are more difficult to infer without information on scene context. Thus, any direct association between the timing of a bone injury and the cause/manner of death should not be made without knowledge of the scene or the recovery process (Dirkmaat and Adovasio 1997; Dirkmaat et al. 2008; Nawrocki 2009).

Variability is the rule, not the exception, in both taphonomic and bone trauma analysis. Similar to the biological profile used to estimate age, sex, ancestry, and stature, a taphonomic profile is compiled as a means to interpret the circumstances surrounding death (Nawrocki 2009; Nawrocki et al. 1997). According to Nawrocki (2009:288), a taphonomic profile is "a set of hypotheses regarding the perimortem and postmortem history of the remains, drawn from a detailed description of the condition of the bones, soft tissues and the immediate recovery site." In order to create this profile, three main influences are addressed: cultural/assailant behavior, biotaphonomy, and geotaphonomy (Nawrocki 2009; Nawrocki et al. 1997). Cultural behavior (Chapter 10) refers to the assailant's altering the environment such as digging a hole, dragging the body, or throwing the body into a ravine. The assailant's actions are likewise dependent on his or her skill/strength in disposing of human remains and in the intrinsic characteristics of the victim such as mass and body position. Biotaphonomy addresses both intrinsic (e.g., decomposition) and extrinsic modifications (e.g., carnivore activity) to a victim. The influences from the geological environment on the assailant, the victim, and the location of the body are referred to as geotaphonomy (Nawrocki 2009). When all of these relationships are examined in situ, the death event can be more objectively (and ultimately, scientifically) interpreted with an anthropologist obtaining a clearer picture as to the cause of death and any possibly traumatic injuries associated with death.

The aim of this chapter is to describe basic biomechanics and fracture characteristics of wet and dry bone. With the use of a case study, the authors emphasize the complexities of deciphering wet and dry bone fractures and associate the correspondence of these interpretations to a sequence of events. Even a complete skeleton may not be informative enough to assist a forensic pathologist in the interpretation of cause or manner of death; more in-depth interpretations may be achieved with the knowledge gained from scene context. Furthermore, the authors stress the need for anthropologists to recognize the biomechanical processes associated with each bony response for accurate fracture pattern interpretations and trauma analyses.

Bone Biomechanics: Basic Terminology

Bone biomechanics, in general, and wet and dry bone, specifically, can be explained with the use of Young's Modulus of Elasticity and stress–strain curves for any material (Figure 13.1) (Currey 2002; Frankel and Nordin 2001; Özkaya and Nordin 1999). Young's Modulus of Elasticity is used to test the strength, or stiffness, of a material with a known stress (tensile, compressive, or shear) and rate of loading. The strength of any material is the amount of energy that material can absorb prior to deformation. *Stress* is calculated as force divided by surface area and is often expressed in N/m^2 or $lbf/in.^2$ (Low and Reed 1996). *Strain* is the elastic deformation of a material under a known stress and rate of load (Harkess and Ramsay 1996; Tencer 2006). A stress–strain curve measures the point of resistance to the point of failure and is calculated by the change in length (mm) divided by the original length (mm) (Currey 2002; Low and Reed 1996).

Young's Modulus of Elasticity and stress–strain curves illustrate two distinctly different concepts. Young's Modulus, or Modulus of Elasticity, is the strength (stiffness) of a material. The stress–strain curve goes on to describe plastic strain and the eventual failure of a material. As expected, only materials that contain elastic properties can deform; in less elastic materials, such as glass and dry bone, failure occurs quickly after surpassing the ultimate strength threshold.

In Figure 13.1, Young's Modulus of Elasticity and stress–strain curves for different materials, different loads, and different bone conditions are illustrated. The area under the curve demonstrates the ductility of a material and essentially refers to the ability to deform, or undergo a greater strain prior to failure (Currey 2002). A stress–strain curve is presented and is not associated with any particular type of material in insert a of Figure 13.1. Various stress–strain curves for bone are located beneath this image. When stress and strain are in proportion, the material maintains a normal shape and is within the strength levels for Young's Modulus of Elasticity (a). When stress and strain produces a straight line (elastic deformation, i.e., Young's Modulus), elastic deformation occurs and is recoverable. If stress exceeds strain (stress–strain curve), and the material reaches the *yield point*, even if stress is removed, the material is unable to return to its normal shape and has been subjected to forces above the material's elastic limits (Currey 2002; Low and Reed 1996; Reilly and

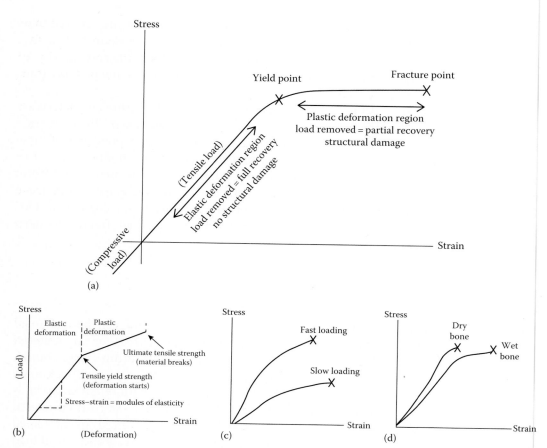

Figure 13.1 Four examples of Young's Modulus and stress–strain curves. (a) A general stress–strain curved created for illustration and descriptive purposes (not associated with any particular type of material). (From Symes, S.A. et al., Interpreting traumatic injury from bone in medicolegal investigations, in *A Companion to Forensic Anthropology*, ed. D.C. Dirkmaat, Wiley-Blackwell, London, U.K., 2012, p. 347.) The small "X" on the left represents the yield point and transition from the elastic phase to the plastic phase. The larger "X" on the right represents the fracture point. (b) Bone stress vs. strain. (From Galloway, A. ed., *Broken Bones: Anthropological Analysis of Blunt Force Trauma*, Charles C Thomas, Springfield, IL, 1999, p. 38.) (c) Fast vs. slow-loaded bone. (From Özkaya, N. and Nordin, M., *Fundamentals of Biomechanics: Equilibrium, Motion, and Deformation*, 2nd edn., Springer, New York, 1999, p. 208.) (d) Wet vs. dry bone. (From Özkaya, N. and Nordin, M., *Fundamentals of Biomechanics: Equilibrium, Motion, and Deformation*, 2nd edn., Springer, New York, 1999, p. 210.)

Burnstein 1974). When stress is removed and the material remains deformed, it has entered the plastic phase of deformation (b). In this phase, the material is compromised, even if it is only detectable at the microscopic level, and any additional stress may cause the material to fail completely. Anthropologists need to remember that all strain modes—tension, compression, and shear—act simultaneously to produce a bone fracture. Fracture morphology is attributed to a complex interaction of tension, compression, and shear forces that can be loaded in a quasi-static (slow) or dynamic (rapid) manner (Symes et al. 2012; Thornton and Cashman 1986).

Biomechanics and Bone Structure

Bone, comprised of organic and inorganic material, serves to support the body, to protect internal organs, to anchor muscles, and to assist in movement (Currey 2002; Low and Reed 1996; Pierson and Lieberman 2004; Tencer 2006). At the microscopic level, bone tissue contains organic collagen fibers imbedded within inorganic crystals of calcium hydroxy-apatite, a combination that provides strength, density, and elasticity. Living bone contains 65%–70% organic and 25%–30% inorganic materials (Pierson and Lieberman 2004).

When considered as a material, bone is nonhomogeneous, anisotropic, viscoelastic, and brittle (Currey 2002; Özkaya and Nordin 1999; Reilly and Burnstein 1974; Tencer 2006). Nonhomogeneous refers to gross types and shapes of bone (e.g., skull vs. femur), the location and surface of a bone (e.g., proximal vs. midshaft), the structure of bone (e.g., cortical vs. trabecular or spongy), and the microstructure of bone (e.g., apatite [biphasic]) (Currey 2002; Özkaya and Nordin 1999; Tencer 2006). Since bone is nonhomogeneous, the material also presents with an anisotropic response to a mechanical load. Anisotropic implies that the mechanical properties of a long bone respond with different strengths when loaded in different directions (Currey 2002; Frankel and Nordin 2001; Özkaya and Nordin 1999). The structural foundation and remodeling abilities in a long bone follows a longitudinal pattern (primary and secondary osteons); these structures enhance long bone strength in axial loads—similar to rebar inserted into concrete—but offer less resistance to failure in angled or perpendicular impacts (Currey 2002; Frankel and Nordin 2001; Özkaya and Nordin 1999). Therefore, the differential resistance of long bones to directional stress is an important variable to consider in any bone trauma analysis.

Each skeletal element is designed to perform a certain mechanical function in the body, which also contributes to its specific anisotropic response. For example, the femur supports the body's weight, while the radius is responsible for lifting, hanging, and carrying objects. When the two bones are biomechanically tested for tensile and compressive strength along a longitudinal plane, the femur presents with weaker tensile strength and greater compressive strength than the radius (Reilly and Burnstein 1974). Therefore, the strength and corresponding strain of a bone in response to an applied force (tensile, compressive, and shear) are also directly dependent on the function of that bone within the skeletal structure (Currey 2002; Reilly and Burnstein 1974). Simply defined, *anisotropy* refers to the varying response a bone has to external stress due to the intrinsic qualities and function of each bone within the skeletal structure. For this reason, the type of bone, the location of a traumatic injury, and the direction of force have important implications for interpreting the mechanism of injury.

Viscoelastic refers to the bony response to the length of time and the rate of speed at which an external load is placed (Currey 2002; Özkaya and Nordin 1999). In order to understand the mechanism of fracture and fracture morphology, an important determinant to consider is speed (Hansen et al. 2008; Symes et al. 2012; Zioupos et al. 2008). With moving objects, kinetic energy is equal to one half the mass of the object multiplied by the velocity of the object squared ($1/2 \, mv^2$). A fracture occurs when a bone can no longer absorb energy from either a slow-loaded force, such as a car bumper to the tibia (mph), or a fast-loaded force (fps), such as a bullet.

When a slow-loaded force is applied to bone and then removed before failure, bone can respond by bending and then return to its original shape. If the slow-loaded force continues, the bone may not recover and it will plastically deform (presents with ductility) and eventually fail (see aforementioned stress–strain curves). With a rapid-loaded force, bone immediately absorbs a greater amount of energy, is unable to mechanically bend due to the rapid stress (does not experience ductility), becomes resistant, and shatters (e.g., Berryman and Symes 1998; Hansen et al. 2008; Smith et al. 1987; Symes et al. 1996, 2012; Thornton and Cashman 1986; Zioupos et al. 2008).

External forces are usually classified into magnitude, duration, and rate. When focusing on speed (mph and fps), the ductile vs. brittle response of bone is revealed and manifested within fracture production. Fractures associated with slow-loaded forces are often linear (less fractures) and exhibit visible tension and compression, whereas fractures associated with rapid-loaded forces are comminuted and exhibit failure due to high-energy absorption (more fractures). For a complete explanation of slow and fast-loaded bone trauma classifications, see Berryman and Symes (1998), Smith et al. (1987), and Symes et al. (2012).

Microstructure of bone is also an important determinant in fracture production and morphology. Skeletal elements of white-tailed deer (*Odocoileus virginianus*), pig (*Sus scrofa*), and cattle (*Bos taurus*) have been used to simulate fracture morphology and fracture patterns to different forces, weapons, and environmental conditions (Calce and Rogers 2007; de Gruchy and Rogers 2002; Janjua and Rogers 2008; Wieberg and Wescott 2008). However, the nonhomogeneous and anisotropic features of bone preclude analogizing fracture morphology and mechanism of fracture of nonhuman bone to human material (Hansen et al. 2008; Keller et al. 1990). Skeletal systems evolved to serve the mechanical needs of each species, particularly with regard to compressive strength and strain, so the biomechanical response to an external force is considered species- or at least genus-specific.

Furthermore, many domestic animals utilized in bone trauma research are subadults at the age of slaughter, which further confounds the issue. Since the distribution and structural foundation of primary and secondary osteons differ considerably between subadults and adults (Pierson and Lieberman 2004), differences in strength and strain modes (tension, compression, and shear) will also exist, affecting the mechanism of fracture and overall fracture morphology.

Biomechanics of Wet and Dry Bone

In research on the tensile strength of dry and wet human long bones, Reilly and Burnstein (1974:38) observed less tensile strength and higher tensile strain in wet bone when compared to dry bone (see Figure 13.1, insert b). Simply, wet bone is stiff and elastic, while dry bone is stiff and brittle. The reason is due to the loss of viscoelastic properties in dry bone, which will not necessarily affect a bone's strength, or Young's Modulus of Elasticity, but will lessen a bone's ability to undergo strain (Özkaya and Nordin 1999; Reilly and Burstein 1974). Without viscoelasticity, the fracture mechanism of dry bone differs as it is not able to withstand as much strain as wet bone and immediately fractures soon after the ultimate strength threshold is reached. Like wet bone, dry bone also fails in tension, shear, and compression, but the bone's responses to these stresses are almost simultaneous.

Many of the earlier examples only explain strength differences of wet and dry bone in one stress mode—tension. In order to distinguish wet and dry bone fractures, information on both tensile and compressive strength/strain is necessary. Under pure tensile stress, both wet and dry bone split apart and osteons are torn from Haversian systems (Pechníková et al. 2011); in macroscopic cross section, the surface area of the bone appears mottled. Since dry bone merely fractures quicker than wet bone under tensile stress, no distinctly obvious fracture differences should be observed between the two conditions.

Compressive (bending) stress is perhaps more easily observable than tensile stress in fracture morphology on wet and dry bone. Due to the elasticity in wet bone, the bone can resist compressive strain almost two times longer than either tensile or shear strains (Frankel and Nordin 2001; Harkess and Ramsay 1996; Hildebrand and Goslow 2001; Özkaya and Nordin 1999). For this reason, under a slow-loaded force, bone fails first under a tensile strain mode prior to that of a compressive strain mode. However, the degree of bending and the subsequent appearance of fracture morphology differ between wet and dry bone, as the latter is less ductile.

Fracture Characteristics for Distinguishing Wet and Dry Bone

Multiple features have been used to differentiate fracture patterns on wet and dry bones, namely: color; fracture outline, angle, surface; and termination of radiating fractures (Karr and Outram 2012b; LaCroix 2013; Morlan 1984; Shattuck 2010; Wheatley 2008; Wieberg and Wescott 2008).

Color

Differences in color on the external and internal surfaces of cortical bone are reliable in distinguishing the timing of a fracture (Dirkmaat and Adovasio 1997; Ubelaker and Adams 1995). Taphonomic processes, such as soil and decompositional staining, sun bleaching, and root etching, influence the external surface differently, or at a different rate, than the internal surface of bone (Berryman et al. 1991; Nawrocki 2009; see also Chapters 5, 11, and 12, this volume). Therefore, any fracture subsequent to deposition will present with a color differentiation between the old and newly exposed bone surfaces.

However, the opposite is not true. A homogeneous distribution of color on the external and internal cortical bone surfaces does not always imply a perimortem injury; further information about the deposition of the material such as a primary or secondary burial, is needed (Johnson 1985; Morlan 1984; Ubelaker and Adams 1995). Bones can be altered prior to deposition, during interment, or during excavation (Morlan 1984). For example, a bone is broken prior to a deliberate or accidental reinterment. During reinterment, the external and cross-sectional cortical surface of the broken bone acquires a homogeneous color. Without recovery context or observation of additional fracture morphology characteristics, an absence of color differences may not be useful to the anthropologist in evaluating perimortem vs. postmortem timing of a fracture.

Fracture Morphology: Outlines, Angles, and Surfaces

In an attempt to quantify fracture morphology, anthropologists have categorized wet and dry long bone fractures into three types: outline, angle, and surface. Outline refers to the general appearance of the fracture lines; angle refers to the slope between the external and internal cross-sectional surfaces; and surface refers to the roughness or smoothness of the cross-sectional edges of the fracture (Johnson 1985). Descriptions of fracture outlines are critical to fracture classifications (spiral, transverse, oblique, and butterfly). Anthropologists use fracture classifications such as these to describe discontinuities in fresh/wet bone, but dry bone is described as brittle with fractures lines that run along (longitudinal cracking) or perpendicular (transverse) to the grain of the bone. Wet bone is described as having curved or V-shaped fracture lines (Figures 13.2 and 13.3) (Galloway 1999; Shattuck 2010; Villa and Mahieu 1992).

Johnson (1985) and Einhorn (2005) noted angled/obtuse surfaces on wet bone and right-angled/perpendicular surfaces on dry bone, whereas Morlan (1984) found acute/obtuse angles on both wet and dry bone and perpendicular angles on fossilized bone. Furthering the debate, Bonnichsen (1979) also noted perpendicular angles on wet bone. While no consistency in fracture angles has been observed between wet and dry bone, researchers

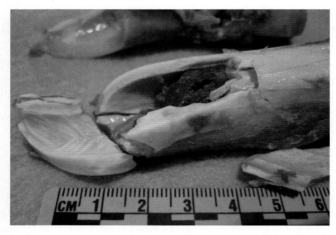

Figure 13.2 Perimortem breakage to fresh white-tailed deer (*Odocoileus virginianus*) bone. (From LaCroix, M., 2013, *A Study of the Impact of Weathering Upon the Minimal Force Required to Fracture Bone*, Unpublished M.S. thesis, Boston University, Boston, MA.)

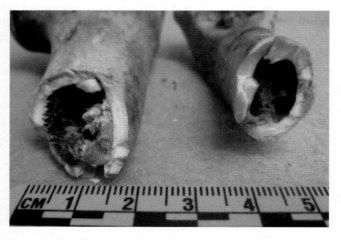

Figure 13.3 Postmortem breakage to dry white-tailed deer (*Odocoileus virginianus*) bone after 28 weeks of subaerial exposure. (From LaCroix, M., 2013, *A Study of the Impact of Weathering Upon the Minimal Force Required to Fracture Bone*, Unpublished M.S. thesis, Boston University, Boston, MA.)

generally note a trend in angled surfaces associated with wet bone and perpendicular surfaces associated with dry bone (LaCroix 2013).

Fracture surface refers to the cross-sectional topography and is considered smooth on wet bone and jagged and/or stepped on dry bone (Figures 13.2 and 13.3) (Bonnichsen 1979; Morlan 1984; Villa and Mahieu 1992; Wieberg and Wescott 2008). Researchers noted that crack formation due to weathering (longitudinal cracking) in dry cortical bone prompts the formation of stepped fractures. As the fracture extends from the point of impact, the cracked cortical surface is interrupted and redirects the fracture's propagation (Honeycutt 2012; Shattuck 2010).

Fracture Termination

The termination location of radiating fractures has also been considered a key to distinguishing wet or dry bone. Most researchers have observed radiating fractures terminating prior to or at the epiphyses in wet but not in dry bone (Karr and Outram 2012a; Morlan 1984). The composition of cancellous bone, which is found in the epiphyses and metaphyses, is approximately 500% more ductile than diaphyseal bone and is designed to absorb shock more effectively in a longitudinal direction (Currey 2002; Simon et al. 1972). Diaphyses are found to fragment more than epiphyses in both wet and dry bone samples (Karr and Outram 2012b).

One of the authors (ML) performed a study on weathering and the biomechanical responses of wet and dry bone over a 9-month period in an open microhabitat situated in a coastal environment in southeastern Massachusetts, USA (LaCroix 2013). The breakage patterns and the minimal force required to fracture bone were specifically analyzed. Results revealed trends similar to other experimental studies (Table 13.1); an increase in PMI and a loss of bone moisture were directly associated with morphological variation in the fracture outline, angle, and surface (LaCroix 2013; Wheatley 2008; Wieberg and Wescott 2008). With an increase in PMI, smooth fracture surfaces, obtuse or acute angles, and curved/V-shaped outlines slowly changed to jagged surfaces, more right angles, and fewer curved fractures (LaCroix 2013; Wheatley 2008; Wieberg and Wescott 2008). Most studies note a significant decrease in bone moisture after 2 months, followed with a plateau phase, and a subsequently slower rate of drying (Wieberg and Wescott 2008). Similarly, Shattuck (2010) observed dry transverse fractures after 42 days PMI, jagged fractures after 70 days PMI, and other dry bone characteristics after 5 months PMI.

Biomechanics and Fracture Characteristics

Differences in fracture morphology of wet and dry bone are directly attributed to the biomechanical response of the fleshed/fresh bone verse dry skeletal material to a load (stress). Forces applied to wet and dry bone may be identical, but bending features are expected to differ. Essentially, ductile wet bone progresses through tension, shear, and compression, demonstrating a resistance to bending, where fractures and microfractures appear and adjust, particularly to crushing and shearing. The adjustments in bending bone transitions create sharp edges and notches that represent failure, adjustment to force, and finally complete failure. Dry bone is brittle, and while diagnosis of tension and compression are possible, they are not dynamic in the plastic phase and essentially show complete failure at the

Table 13.1 Summary of Breakage Experiment of White-Tailed Deer (*Odocoileus virginianus*) Long Bones (n = 31) over 0–28 Weeks of Surface Exposure

Element	Mass (g)	Weeks Exposed	Force (lbs)	Fracture Type	No. of Fragments	Fracture Lines	Fracture Angle	Shape of Broken Ends	Fracture Surface Texture	Weathering Stage[a]
Humerus	197.8	0	2000+	Comminuted	11	Present	Sharp	Curved	Smooth	0
Humerus	230.3	0	1205	Comminuted	8	Present	Sharp	Curved	Smooth	0
Humerus	206.5	0	1140	Comminuted	20	Present	Sharp	Curved	Smooth	0
Femur	229.7	6	1382	Butterfly	7	Present	Mixed	Curved	Smooth	0
Tibia	228.8	6	1826	Segmental	11	Present	Sharp	Curved	Smooth	0
Tibia	199.3	6	342	Oblique	9	Present	Sharp	Curved	Smooth	0
Femur	217.3	6	1570	Segmental	13	Present	Sharp	Curved	Smooth	0
Femur	229.5	6	1382	Segmental	7	Absent	Mixed	Curved	Smooth	0
Tibia	210.5	6	1800	Comminuted	15	Present	Mixed	Curved	Smooth	0
Tibia	225.6	10	902	Oblique	0	Present	Sharp	Curved	Smooth	0
Femur	219.2	10	744	Oblique	3	Present	Sharp	Curved	Smooth	0
Femur	214.7	10	2000+	Comminuted	12	Present	Mixed	Curved	Smooth	0
Tibia	201.9	10	681	Transverse	0	Present	Mixed	Jagged	Smooth	0
Tibia	182.4	15	2000+	Segmental	10	Present	Mixed	Jagged	Smooth	0
Femur	198.2	15	355	Comminuted	2	Present	Mixed	Curved	Smooth	0
Tibia	239.4	15	2000+	Segmental	9	Absent	Sharp	Jagged	Smooth	0
Femur	192.3	15	233	Oblique	2	Present	Mixed	Jagged	Smooth	0
Tibia	206.1	15	529	Oblique	0	Absent	Sharp	Curved	Smooth	0
Tibia	218.6	20	770	Butterfly	3	Present	Mixed	Curved	Smooth	0
Tibia	174.6	20	639	Segmental	4	Present	Mixed	Jagged	Smooth	0
Humerus	173.5	20	2000+	Comminuted	20	Present	Mixed	Jagged	Rough	0
Humerus	136.1	24	889	Butterfly	3	Present	Sharp	Curved	Rough	0
Humerus	152.7	24	888	Transverse	2	Present	Mixed	Transverse	Rough	0
Humerus	133.2	24	843	Transverse	2	Present	Sharp	Curved	Smooth	0
Humerus	125.3	24	892	Segmental	3	Present	Right	Curved	Rough	1
Humerus	165.4	24	782	Oblique	5	Present	Mixed	Jagged	Rough	0
Tibia	180.3	28	2000+	Comminuted	13	Absent	Mixed	Jagged	Smooth	0
Femur	192.5	28	448	Butterfly	5	Absent	Mixed	Curved	Smooth	0
Humerus	180.5	28	346	Butterfly	1	Present	Right	Curved	Smooth	0
Humerus	249.5	28	1191	Segmental	2	Present	Mixed	Curved	Smooth	1
Humerus	178.5	28	399	Oblique	1	Present	Mixed	Curved	Smooth	0

a Following Behrensmeyer, A. K., *Palaeobiology*, 4, 150, 1978.

yield point, as opposed to being able to resist strain in predictable manners. Dry bone fails easier in shear with few microfractures or readjustments when maximum stress is reached. According to Johnson (1985), dry bone fractures "exhibit horizontal tension failure" such that the bone is transversely split on the longitudinal axis and produces right angles in cross section (e.g., fracture surfaces).

Bone deformation is "dependent upon many factors including the magnitude, direction, and duration of the applied force, the material properties of the object, the geometry of the object, and the environmental factors such as heat and humidity" (Özkaya and Nordin 1999:127). The greatest predictor for fracture morphology in wet bone is speed of load, whereas in dry bone it is the lack of elasticity of the material. However, the elastic component of a bone cannot be easily evaluated from its gross morphology. For example, an elastic response has been noted on a seemingly dry bone (Ubelaker and Adams 1995). Karr and Outram (2012b) addressed the speed of moisture loss in varying climates and noted that bone degraded and dried much faster in hot, dry climates than in wet, cold climates. Like any decomposition process, bone degradation is highly variable and is not easily predicted (LaCroix 2013; Sauer 1998). The bone structure and the compositional properties do not change at an exact time; rather, they are gradual processes dependent on the environment, geology, and human intervention.

Most wet and dry experimental studies have been conducted on long bones. Human long bones are tubular with relatively thick cortical bone and less spongy bone in the shaft. When a stress is applied to a long bone, the tubular shaft maintains its shape until the point that stress exceeds strain and the bone bends plastically. As a bone bends, compressive and tensile strains act on opposite sides of the bone (Figure 13.4) (Tencer 2006). Since bone

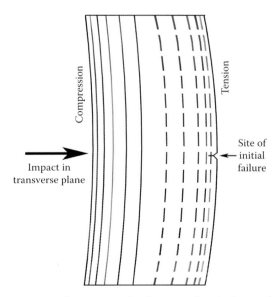

Figure 13.4 When a transverse force is applied perpendicularly to the shaft of a long bone, compression occurs on the side of the impact, while tension is occurring on the opposite side. (For simplification purposes, a solid cylinder is shown to depict areas of stress.) The lines drawn within the cylinder represent the paths followed by units of force as they pass through the object. The solid lines represent compression lines, while the dashed lines represent tension lines. Since bone is stronger at resisting compressive forces, it will fail first in tension. (Illustration courtesy of Erin N. Chapman.)

usually resists compressive strain longer than tensile strain, the bone fails first transversely in tension, and the fracture assumes a steeper oblique orientation as the failure approaches pure compression (Berryman et al. 1991; Symes et al. 2012). The cross-sectional morphology of these fractures is reminiscent of a butterfly and is colloquially described as a *butterfly fracture* with the triangular piece being referred to as a butterfly fragment (Lee et al. 2004). In butterfly fractures, the body represents tension and the wings indicate compression and these can be used to ascertain the direction in which the bone bent (Symes et al. 2012, 2013). As always, the true direction of bending is indicated by examining pure tension and maximum compression.

The characteristic microscopic features of a butterfly fracture include a bone tear, a breakaway spur or notch, possibly minor fracture lines for strain adjustment, and an area of shear between tension and compression. Bone tears can be noted on the tension side where the fractured bone surface appears mottled and billowy. Breakaway spurs and notches are jagged in appearance with at least one bone fragment exhibiting a "dog-eared" notch, where the bone likely fails in a complete fracture (Symes et al. 2012:355). The bending, strain, and eventually failure of a butterfly fracture is analogous to the fracture outline, angle, and surface characteristics of wet bone. Classifying the various features of a butterfly fracture, however, will not provide more information as to the timing of that fracture. In order to do this, biomechanical features, such as tension, compression, and shear must be used to describe the appearance of trauma injuries, and to relate these to either wet or dry bone.

Trabecular bone is more compliant than cortical bone to a compressive load, a quality that is responsible for the distribution and dissipation of energy in this material and, consequentially, fracture patterns. Simon et al. (1972) noted variation in mechanical properties between trabecular and cortical bone and attributed these differences to stiffness of the material. Epiphyses demonstrate a higher degree of compressive strength and strain than the diaphyses. Thus, they are more resistant to failure under a compressive force (Karr and Outram 2012a). This resistance to failure has been observed through the location of termination of fractures (Morlan 1984). The explanation for the ability of cancellous bone to absorb shock can either be attributed to the viscous flow of interstitial fluid or limited trabecular fractures (Simon et al. 1972 and references within; also Swanson et al. 1966).

The compliance of trabecular bone is most likely responsible for the termination or diversion of fractures. These actions also emphasize different mechanical properties in a single bone. Similar to other fracture characteristics, as bone degrades the compliance is lost, resulting in a higher frequency of fractures running through the epiphyses in dry bone than wet bone. As Karr and Outram (2012a) noted, however, the frequency of epiphyseal fractures is still lower than the frequency of diaphyseal fractures of bones with similar moisture content.

Discrepancies among studies investigating fracture patterns of dry and wet bone may be due in part to the classification system anthropologists have adopted from the medical or biomechanical literature (Symes et al. 2013). Bone trauma classification terminology such as transverse, oblique, spiral, incomplete butterfly (tension wedges), transverse fractures (initiation), failure angle shifts of 45°, breakaway spurs, and further untested, but frequently cited, terminology like concentric hoop, circumferential hoop, ballistic butterfly, wastage, and hinge (Byers 2010; Fenton et al. 2012; Galloway 1999; Klepinger 2006) are not useful or accurate when describing an injury and ultimately interpreting a total body fracture pattern. Bone is a dynamic structure, which offers tremendous variety in gross shape, size, and microstructure and therefore trauma is not as easily classifiable as other aspects of a skeletal report such as ancestry, sex, or stature. With this in mind, anthropologists are encouraged to adopt a biomechanical and not classificatory approach to describing injuries in skeletal remains.

Case Study: Using a Taphonomic Profile and Bone Trauma Analysis to Interpret the Circumstances of Death

In the spring of 2010, two men in Pennsylvania, USA, searching for scrap metal in the bottom of a steep, wooded ravine surprisingly came upon a pair of laced-up leather work boots in the leaf litter (Figure 13.5). More shocking was the fact that protruding from these weathered boots was a pair of human leg bones (Figure 13.6) that led to a skeleton, lying face up on a bed of humus. Leaf litter concealed most of the relatively complete and dry skeleton that was haphazardly covered with remnants of tattered clothing.

For the forensic scientist field recovery, context documentation, evidence removal, and laboratory analysis are not entities unto themselves but form an integral part of any death investigation (Dirkmaat et al. 2008; Nawrocki 2009). An accurate field recovery is the first step in a comprehensive death scene and body (skeletal) analysis and aids in interpreting the circumstances of death. For this case, Pennsylvania death investigators requested that the Mercyhurst Forensic Anthropology Recovery Team at Mercyhurst University scientifically document and recover the remains and perform a laboratory analysis.

Along the bottom of the narrow ravine and in the immediate vicinity of the body, the recovery team observed large and small boulders and copious amounts of trash. Miscellaneous trash and rocks defined the topography of this impromptu dumping site. The team began a systematic archaeological recovery, clearing years of vegetation and fallen leaves and flagging all skeletal elements and associated evidence, after which the

Figure 13.5 Area of scene and recovery process for case study, with mapping grid in place.

Figure 13.6 Initial finds of human remains and artifacts including boots, still in situ, case study.

group of trained (graduate) students established an east–west baseline through the main longitudinal axis of the site (Figure 13.7). They took measurements of artifacts and bones in association with the baseline and produced a hand-drawn map (Figure 13.8). Following the mapping process, they systematically numbered and removed skeletal elements from the surface and subsoil and placed these bones in individually numbered bags that corresponded to their map; they also screened loose soil and leaf litter for previously undetected skeletal material or artifacts.

While the crime scene was extremely complicated (cluttered) and difficult to interpret at first glance, an accurate map clarified the situation (Figure 13.8). Site maps form invaluable tools for investigations that invariably mature long after the initial scene disturbance. This case was no exception: an encroaching boulder appeared to intrude next to the body; in fact, the map suggests that the boulder may even be on top of the body and that other large rocks in the area may also be associated with the boulder. Since rocks are essentially

Figure 13.7 Field recovery team under supervision of Dr. Dennis C. Dirkmaat, Mercyhurst University (upper right corner).

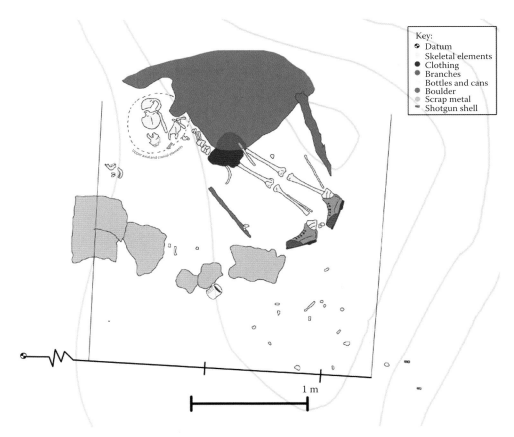

Key:
● Datum
  Skeletal elements
● Clothing
● Branches
  Bottles and cans
● Boulder
● Scrap metal
● Shotgun shell

Upper axial and cranial elements

1 m

Figure 13.8 Diagram of recovery scene based on a systematic flagging and recovery process, case study.

on both sides of the body, can we assume that the boulder has influenced the skeleton? The map also illustrates the poor condition of the skull and upper body.

Other influences include rodent gnawing as observed on the skeleton and in this depositional setting activity from large carnivores was also probable. All bones had a red-brown tint with the exception of some lighter-colored remains, due to both subaerial weathering/bleaching as well as old and recent rodent gnawing (Figure 13.9). Numerous expended shotgun shells from more than one gauge of shotgun were also found in close association to the body (Figure 13.8). Weathering on all artifacts associated with the body was obvious and added to information as to the PMI but also further enhanced the complexity of the recovery scene. Based on the available taphonomic evidence at the scene, the senior author (SAS) along with Dennis C. Dirkmaat of Mercyhurst University suggested a PMI greater than 5 years but within a rough upper limit of 10 years. Initial field estimates of PMI are always tentative, a fact about which all investigators should be routinely reminded.

As the scene was systematically dismantled, the recovery team removed skeletal remains associated with a single person, but all the bones were not recovered. After years of decomposition, deposition, and intrusion, and regardless of various archaeological methods to prevent loss, missing skeletal elements are not to be considered unusual. Despite the presence of laced-up boots, many of the right foot bones were missing. Upon closer examination of the boot (Figure 13.10), the anthropologists suggested that rodents likely nested

Figure 13.9 Right humerus with weathering and old and recent rodent modification, case study.

Figure 13.10 Close-up of the victim's right boot, indicating rodent activity that disrupted bones of the right foot.

in the boot and displaced the skeletal remains. Other notable missing elements included the right parietal, right zygomatic, and right maxilla.

At the end of the day, the investigating officers provided the recovery team with more information. An 18-year-old White male had disappeared from a nearby residence, approximately 10 years prior to discovery of the skeleton. The recovery crew suddenly had a

Figure 13.11 Mandibular remains, case study. Note the red-brown tint with lighter areas due to weathering and exposure. In situ fractures appear to have occurred to dry and weathered bone as seen with color differentiation, transverse fracture outlines, and minimal compressive strains.

suspected identity to assign to the discolored and dry bones examined in the ravine. Initial examination of the skeleton revealed that the bones belonged to a large, adolescent male, so a high probability existed that the investigation was on the right track. Unfortunately, the most important question—why a deceased 18-year-old male was lying in a ditch in the woods—had yet to be answered.

At the scene, anthropologists observed the broken bones of the cranium and associated cranial fragments in close proximity to the boulder; additionally, some bones appeared to have fractured while in a postmortem state. The left humerus and mandible (Figure 13.11) had relatively old in situ crushed fractures associated with dry/degraded and weathered bone as evidenced with transverse fracture outlines and minimal evidence of compressive strains. Color change in this case was not relevant in that the dry fractures occurred long ago, and all color was the same except where the bone was exposed to the sun. Could the boulder have rolled onto the body and fractured the bones after death, or could the "expected violence" to a missing 18-year old male be the rock, itself, which could have trapped the victim and caused his death? An accurate interpretation of the circumstances surrounding the victim's death was dependent on identifying the boulder/body sequence.

The bones found near the partial skull contributed to the perimortem findings and were even identified in the field (Figure 13.12). Fracture characteristics observed on these skeletal elements did not resemble dry bone fractures like those of the mandible or left humerus but appeared bent as a consequence of wet (dynamic) bone bending in resistance to a blunt impact. The right parietal fragment, shown in Figure 13.13, exhibited a depressed impact with plastic deformation, radiating and concentric fractures.

Radiating fractures travel away from the point of impact in adult bone, following the path of least resistance. Concentric fractures, circumferential to the point of impact, are the result of bone caving in due to blunt force (see also a reconstructed example Figure 13.14). Concentric fractures are generally secondary to radiating fractures (Berryman and Symes 1998; Smith et al. 1987; Symes et al. 2012) and are beveled inward. The external and internal aspects of the right parietal fragment of the victim are shown in Figure 13.13. The internal view of the bone is reversed so that the orientation is identical for each view. The

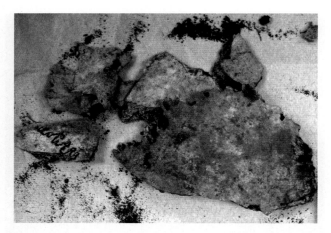

Figure 13.12 Cranial fragments associated with the right parietal. Their fracture characteristics are dissimilar to dry bone fractures. Radiating and concentric fractures are visible, and the concentric fractures have beveling.

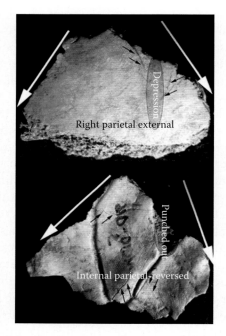

Figure 13.13 External and internal aspects of a parietal fragment, case study. The internal view has been reversed so the orientation is identical for each. Unfortunately, this fragment cannot be positioned exactly in the skull due to missing fragments of bone from the surrounding areas. While many fragments in the cranium suggest perimortem trauma, this is a classic indicator and essentially presents one of the "pie" pieces.

large white arrows denote both external and internal radiating fractures. Since radiating fractures travel away from impact sites in adults, the point of impact for this fragment is approximately where the tails of each white arrow converge (i.e., the top of each image). The small black arrows indicate minor, incomplete tension fractures surrounding an impact depression on the external surface (top image) with a resulting punched-out area on the

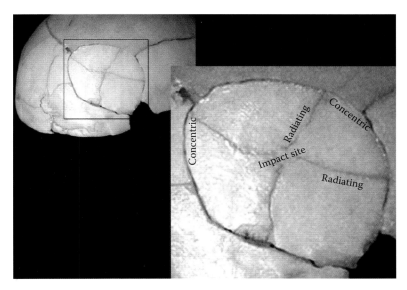

Figure 13.14 Exemplar of fresh blunt fractures (unrelated to the case study described in this chapter), illustrating wet bone failure with expressions of impact site and radiating and concentric fractures.

internal surface (lower image). Finally, a beveled fracture surface is present (top image) and is magnified in Figure 13.15. The arrows pointing downward indicate initial failure in tension on the external surface as the bone bent inward. The angled arrows indicate areas of secondary failure in compression.

A depressed impact with radiating and concentric fractures likely occurred as a consequence of wet (dynamic) bone bending inward as a response to blunt force trauma. While this fragment cannot be positioned exactly in the skull due to missing bone, this fragment and others in the cranium suggest perimortem trauma. While not shown, radiating

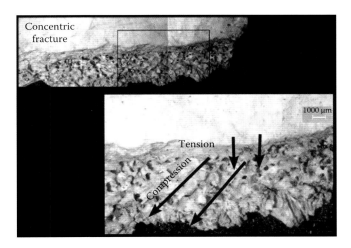

Figure 13.15 Close-up of the bevel of the parietal fragment shown in Figure 13.13, case study. The arrows pointing down indicate pure tension that occurred initially to the external surface, as the bone bends inward at the point of impact. The angled arrows are indicative of areas of secondary compression failure on the bone.

Figure 13.16 Residual rodent modification on the skull. The area may have been a perimortem fracture site, but now the area is obscured as the result of postmortem influence.

fractures also extended from the right external auditory meatus to the cribriform plate of the ethmoid and exemplify severe cranial trauma in fresh bone.

With both perimortem and postmortem trauma diagnosed on the skull, the rodent-gnawed bones found under the boulder were essential for interpreting the order of events and for demonstrating the necessity of understanding the full suite of taphonomic processes (Figure 13.16). Herbivorous rodents tend to gnaw on dry bones devoid of soft tissue, which is generally months or years after death (Klippel and Synstelien 2007; see also Chapter 9, this volume). For rodents to reach specific skull and arm bones, the elements had to be dry and exposed. Therefore, the boulder had fallen into the current position months or more likely years after the body had been deposited and decomposed.

Without a thorough analysis and knowledge of the scene and bone trauma, one may be quick to assume that all defects were due to the boulder. However, the fracture patterns suggested that the boulder fell on top of the remains following their deposition and decomposition. The location of the rodent-gnawed bones corroborates this scenario. Without a forensic anthropologist on scene, the context of the rodent-gnawed bones would have been lost and furthermore, the ability to interpret the order of events fully would have been impossible. The case study illustrates the complexities of a forensic anthropological analysis that involves dry and wet bone fractures as well as taphonomic modifications. In the current example, it was crucial to decipher the differences between wet and dry bone fractures as well as to interpret the order of events. Ensuing investigations led to matching the bones to the missing 18-year-old. The eventual questioning of a likely suspect produced an initial confession describing an accidental hunting death due to a shotgun wound. Prior knowledge of blunt force as opposed to a gunshot wound to the head eventually enabled investigators to get a full confession from the suspect, describing a lethal beating.

Conclusions

How do forensic archaeologists and anthropologists interpret the circumstances surrounding death, and can they supply information as to the cause and manner of death? How does one decide whether a body had been dumped or whether a person died on the scene? What are the repercussions for supplying an incorrect analysis to law enforcement or a court of law? These questions form an intellectual foundation for research in both taphonomy and bone trauma analysis. In a criminal trial, the role of the forensic anthropologist has always remained unclear. Unlike forensic pathologists and coroners who are paid to make decisions on the cause and manner of death, a forensic anthropologist is not pressured to do so. Therefore, in a court, comments and evidence from a forensic anthropologist are purely voluntary. As such, the implications of their statements are less often reviewed, discussed, or debated in the literature, yet all testimony—mandatory or voluntary—has implications for both the accused and for the outcome of a court case, particularly in a homicide. Despite continual pontifications among forensic anthropologists on the *Daubert* ruling and the associated rules for expert testimony, less attention is given to the implications of this testimony, either for the anthropologist or for the trial. Any skeletal analysis may adhere to a series of guidelines and may be acceptable in court; however, the interpretation of the outcome of the analysis, particularly with regard to bone trauma analysis, is far more important.

This chapter describes the biomechanical properties and fracture morphology of wet and dry bone. A connection to the theoretical foundation (biomechanical principles) is necessary in order to make meaningful, or valid, observations in trauma analysis (Houle et al. 2011). As scientists, we need to ensure that "inferences about [our variables] reflect the underlying reality that we intend to represent" (Houle et al. 2011:4). In other words, our work has to be valid, and in trauma analysis, biomechanics are the basis of bone failure analysis. The fracture morphology of fresh or dry long bones under a slow-loaded or rapid-loaded force is based on the biomechanical properties of the impactor and the material (nonhomogeneous, viscoelastic, anisotropic, and brittle).

Despite the literature on fracture classification, anthropologists need an awareness of bone reaction to force. Fracture patterns or angles of the failure are important to describe and for ease of recognition; however, the features of strain modes appear to be the best indicators for fracture interpretation. Anthropologists need to grasp the biomechanical concepts that are reflective in the fracture characteristics and acknowledge the properties in anthropological reports and in testimony. In other words, anthropologists need to return to the basic interpretation of long bone fractures (Symes et al. 2012, 2013).

The theoretical issue surrounding wet and dry bone fractures can be split into two categories, description and interpretation.

Description

Overall, the literature regarding fracture characteristics is sparse, and few studies have tested samples with a PMI greater than 5 months. Although general trends can be seen in the results, so can inconsistencies with diagnostic features for dry bone observed in wet bone samples and vice versa. Varying results are most likely the consequence of differing environments and microenvironments that ultimately affect the moisture in the skeletal sample. As noted earlier, the moisture content is the main variable that directly influences a bone's response to force. Moisture loss is a gradual and variable process such that a discrete time period may be impossible to provide. Furthermore, a descriptive approach is recommended until research that evaluates the probability of a PMI based on the observed fracture characteristics is completed. Above all, knowledge of taphonomic influences that affected the remains is necessary in order to develop an accurate interpretation of any skeletal trauma (Dirkmaat and Adovasio 1997; Dirkmaat et al. 2008).

Interpretation

Anthropologists attempt to categorize a continuous variable of unspecified duration into two arbitrary divisions: perimortem and postmortem. Division of a gradual and ambiguous process such as decomposition into two events is discordant with the available material (decomposed or skeletonized remains) (Shattuck 2010; Wheatley 2008; Wieberg and Wescott 2008). Similarly, it is ineffective when attempting to describe a fracture. Forensic pathologists use the terminology to signify a temporal period rather than the physical condition of bone. Anthropologists need to refer to the bony response as indicative of either wet or dry bone, as one observes the state that the bone is in when it is exposed to forces that caused a fracture (Symes et al. 2012).

In summary, the interpretation of traumatic injury on bone is a critical component of forensic anthropological case reports. Unlike biological profiles that focus on victim identification, a trauma report is based on the use of soft or hard tissue injuries to provide an opinion on the type of trauma inflicted and perhaps the mechanism from which these injuries occurred. In a court of law, the interpretation of either the cause and/or manner of death from skeletal elements has tremendous implications. In any reconstruction of traumatic injury to bone, descriptions of "wet" and "dry" need to be used to clarify bone condition. Further interpretations as to the timing of the injury, perimortem or postmortem, can be ascertained only when the context in which the remains were found is known, and even then interpretation has been shown to be difficult (Dirkmaat and Adovasio 1997; Dirkmaat et al. 2008).

Acknowledgments

The authors thank Dennis C. Dirkmaat for use of the images and recovery scene information for the case study and to Erin N. Chapman for her illustration help. Thanks also go to Brianne Charles and Alieske Anholts for their editorial assistance.

References

Behrensmeyer, A. K. (1978) Taphonomic and ecologic information from bone weathering. *Palaeobiology* 4:150–162.
Berryman, H. E. and S. A. Symes (1998) Recognizing gunshot and blunt cranial trauma through fracture interpretation. In *Forensic Osteology: Advances in the Identification of Human Remains* (2nd edn.) ed. K. J. Reichs, pp. 333–352. Charles C Thomas, Springfield, IL.
Berryman, H. E., S. A. Symes, O. C. Smith, and S. J. Moore (1991) Bone fracture II: Gross examination of fractures. *Proceedings of the 43rd Annual Meeting of the American Academy of Forensic Sciences.* pp. 150, Anaheim, CA.
Biddick, K. A. and J. Tomenchuk (1975) Quantifying continuous lesions and fractures on long bones. *Journal of Field Archaeology* 2:239–249.
Bonnichsen, R. (1979) *Pleistocene Bone Technology in the Beringian Refugium*. Archaeological Survey of Canada. Paper 89:1–280.
Byers, S. N. (2010) *Introduction to Forensic Anthropology* (4th edn.). Pearson Custom Anthropology, Upper Saddle River, NJ.
Calce, S. E. and T. L. Rogers (2007) Taphonomic changes to blunt force trauma: A preliminary study. *Journal of Forensic Sciences* 52:519–527.

Cunha, E. and J. E. Pinherio (2009) Antemortem trauma. In *Handbook of Forensic Anthropology and Archaeology* eds. S. Blau and D. H. Ubelaker, pp. 246–262. Left Coast Press, Walnut Creek, CA.

Currey, J. D. (2002) *Bones: Structure and Mechanics* (2nd edn.). Princeton University Press, Princeton, NJ.

de Gruchy, S. and T. L. Rogers (2002) Identifying chop marks on cremated bone: A preliminary study. *Journal of Forensic Sciences* 47:933–936.

Dirkmaat, D. C. and J. M. Adovasio (1997) The role of archaeology in the recovery and interpretation of human remains from an outdoor forensic setting. In *Forensic Taphonomy: The Postmortem Fate of Human Remains* eds. W. D. Haglund and M. H. Sorg, pp. 39–64. CRC Press, Boca Raton, FL.

Dirkmaat, D. C., L. L. Cabo, S. D. Ousley, and S. A. Symes (2008) New perspectives in forensic anthropology. *Yearbook of Physical Anthropology* 51:33–52.

Einhorn, T. A. (2005) The science of fracture healing. *Journal of Orthopedic Trauma* 19:S4–S6.

Fenton, T. W., A. E. Kendell, T. S. Deland, and R. C. Haut (2012) Determination of impact direction based on fracture patterns in human long bones. *Proceedings of the American Academy of Forensic Sciences* 18:398.

Frankel, V. H. and M. Nordin (2001) Biomechanics of bone. In *Basic Biomechanics of the Musculoskeletal System* (3rd edn.) eds. V. H. Frankel and M. Nordin, pp. 26–59. Lippincott Williams and Wilkins, Philadelphia, PA.

Galloway, A. (ed.) (1999) *Broken Bones: Anthropological Analysis of Blunt Force Trauma*, pp. 35–62. Charles C Thomas, Springfield, IL.

Hansen, U., P. Zioupos, R. Simpson, J. D. Currey, and D. Hynd (2008) The effect of strain rate on the mechanical property of human cortical bone. *Journal of Biomechanical Engineering* 130(011011):1–8.

Harkess, J. W. and W. C. Ramsey (1996) Principles of fractures and dislocations. In *Rockwood and Green's Fractures in Adults* (4th edn.) eds. C. A. Rockwood, D. P. Green, R. W. Bucholz, and J. D. Heckman, pp. 3–21. Lippincott-Raven, Philadelphia, PA.

Hildebrand, M. and G. Goslow, Jr. (2001) *Analysis of Vertebrate Structure* (5th edn.). John Wiley & Sons, New York.

Hill, A. P. (1980) Early postmortem damage to the remains of some contemporary East African mammals. In *Fossils in the Making: Vertebrate Taphonomy and Paleoecology* eds. A. K. Behrensmeyer and A. P. Hill, pp. 131–155. University of Chicago Press, Chicago, IL.

Honeycutt, K. K. (2012) *Fracture Patterns and Taphonomic Processes in a Mass Grave Environment: A Quantitative Analysis*. Unpublished M.A. Thesis, North Carolina State University, Raleigh, NC.

Houle, D., C. Pélabon, G. P. Wagner, and T. F. Hansen (2011) Measurement and meaning in biology. *Quarterly Review of Biology* 86:3–32.

Janjua, M. A. and T. L. Rogers (2008) Bone weathering patterns of metatarsal verses femur and the postmortem interval in Southern Ontario. *Forensic Science International* 178:16–23.

Johnson, E. (1985) Current developments in bone technology. In *Advances in Archaeological Method and Theory* (vol. 8) ed. M. B. Schiffer, pp. 157–235. Academic Press, Orlando, FL.

Karr, L. P. and A. K. Outram (2012a) Actualistic research into dynamic impact and its implications for understanding differential bone fragmentation and survivorship. *Journal of Archaeological Science* 39:3443–3449.

Karr, L. P. and A. K. Outram (2012b) Tracking changes in bone fracture morphology over time: Environment, taphonomy, and the archaeological record. *Journal of Archaeological Science* 39:555–559.

Keller, T. S., Z. Mao, and D. M. Spengler (1990) Young's Modulus bending strength and tissue physical properties of human compact bone. *Journal of Orthopaedic Research* 8:592–603.

Klepinger, L. L. (2006) Fundamentals of forensic anthropology. In *Foundation of Human Biology* eds. M. Cartmill and K. Brown, pp. 101–117. John Wiley, Hoboken, NJ.

Klippel, W. E. and J. A. Synstelien (2007) Rodents as taphonomic agents: Bone gnawing by brown rats and gray squirrels. *Journal of Forensic Sciences* 53:765–773.

Komar, D. and J. E. Buikstra (2008) *Forensic Anthropology: Contemporary Theory and Practice.* Oxford University Press, New York.

LaCroix, M. (2013) *A Study of the Impact of Weathering upon the Minimal Force Required to Fracture Bone.* Unpublished M.S. thesis, Boston University, Boston, MA.

Lee, P., T. B. Hunter, and M. Taljanovic (2004) Musculoskeletal colloquialisms: How did we come up with these names? *Radiographics* 24:1009–1027.

Low, J. and A. Reed (1996) *Basic Biomechanics Explained.* Reed Educational and Professional Publishing, Oxford, U.K.

Morlan, R. E. (1984) Toward the definition of criteria for the recognition of artificial bone alterations. *Quaternary Research* 22:160–171.

Nawrocki, S. P. (2009) Forensic taphonomy. In *Handbook of Forensic Anthropology and Archaeology* eds. S. Blau and D. H. Ubelaker, pp. 284–295. Left Coast Press, Walnut Creek, CA.

Nawrocki, S. P., J. E. Pless, D. A. Hawley, and S. A. Wagner (1997) Fluvial transport of human crania. In *Forensic Taphonomy: The Postmortem Fate of Human Remains* eds. W. D. Haglund and M. H. Sorg, pp. 529–548. CRC Press, Boca Raton, FL.

Özkaya, N. and M. Nordin (1999) *Fundamentals of Biomechanics: Equilibrium, Motion, and Deformation* (2nd edn.). Springer, New York.

Pechníková, M., D. Porta, and C. Cattaneo (2011) Distinguishing between perimortem and postmortem fractures: Are osteons of any help? *International Journal of Legal Medicine* 125:591–595.

Pierson, O. M. and D. E. Lieberman (2004) The aging of Wolff's law: Ontogeny and responses to mechanical loading in cortical bone. *American Journal of Physical Anthropology* 39:63–99.

Reilly, D. T. and A. H. Burstein (1974) The mechanical properties of cortical bone. *Journal of Bone and Joint Surgery* 56A:1001–1022.

Sauer, N. (1998) The timing of injuries and the manner of death: Distinguishing among antemortem, perimortem, and postmortem trauma. In *Forensic Osteology: Advances in the Identification of Human Remains* (2nd edn.) eds. K. J. Reichs, pp. 321–332. Charles C Thomas, Springfield, IL.

Shattuck, R. E. (2010) *Perimortem Fracture Patterns in South-Central Texas: A Preliminary Investigation into the Perimortem Interval.* Unpublished M.A. thesis, University of Texas, San Marcos, TX.

Simon, S. R., E. L. Radin, I. L. Paul, and R. M. Rose (1972) The response of joints to impact loading. II. in vivo behaviour of subchondral bone. *Journal of Biomechanics* 5:267–272.

Smith, O. C., H. E. Berryman, and C. H. Lahern (1987) Cranial fracture patterns and estimate of direction of low velocity gunshot wounds. *Journal of Forensic Sciences* 32:1416–1421.

Swanson, S. A. V. and M. A. R. Freeman (1966) Is bone hydraulically strengthened? *Medical and Biological Engineering* 4:433–438.

Symes, S. A., E. N. L'Abbé, E. N. Chapman, I. Wolff, and D. C. Dirkmaat (2012) Interpreting traumatic injury from bone in medicolegal investigations. In *A Companion to Forensic Anthropology* ed. D. C. Dirkmaat, pp. 340–389. Wiley-Blackwell, London, U.K.

Symes, S. A., E. N. L'Abbé, K. E. Stull, I. Wolff, and D. E. Raymond (2013) A return to the basic principles of biomechanics to interpret blunt force trauma in long bones. *Proceedings of the American Academy of Forensic Sciences* 19:409–410.

Symes, S. A., O. C. Smith, H. E. Berryman, C. E. Peters, L. A. Rockhold, S. J. Haun, J. T. Francisco, and T. P. Sutton (1996) *Bones: Bullets, Burns, Bludgeons, Blunderers, and Why.* Workshop conducted at the *48th Annual Meeting of the American Academy of Forensic Sciences*, Nashville, TN.

Tencer, A. F. (2006) Biomechanics of fixation and fractures. In *Rockwood and Green's Fractures in Adults* (6th edn.) eds. C.A. Rockwood, D. P. Green, R. W. Bucholz, and J. D. Heckman, pp. 3–42. Lippincott-Raven, Philadelphia, PA.

Thornton, J. I. and P. J. Cashman (1986) Glass fracture mechanism—A rethinking. *Journal of Forensic Sciences* 31:818–824.

Ubelaker, D. H. and B. J. Adams (1995) Differentiation of perimortem and postmortem trauma using taphonomic indicators. *Journal of Forensic Sciences* 40:509–512.

Villa, P. and E. Mahieu (1992) Breakage patterns of human long bones. *Journal of Human Evolution* 21:27–48.

Wheatley, B. P. (2008) Perimortem or postmortem bone fractures? An experimental study of fracture patterns in deer femora. *Journal of Forensic Sciences* 53:69–72.

Wieberg, D. A. M. and D. J. Wescott (2008) Estimating the time of long bone fractures: Correlation between postmortem interval, bone moisture content, and blunt force trauma fracture characteristics. *Journal of Forensic Sciences* 53:1028–1034.

Zioupos, P., U. Hansen, and J. D. Currey (2008) Microcracking damage and the fracture process in relation to strain rate in human cortical bone tensile failure. *Journal of Biomechanics* 41:2932–2939.

Thermal Alteration to Bone

14

STEVEN A. SYMES
ERICKA N. L'ABBÉ
JAMES T. POKINES
TAYLOR YUZWA
DIANA MESSER
AMY STROMQUIST
NATALIE KEOUGH

Contents

In a dry ditch on the slightly elevated river bank, a shallow grave was dug with bushveld wood and tyres. The two corpses were lifted onto the pyre and as the sun set over the Eastern Transvaal bushveld, two fires were lit, one to burn the bodies to ashes, the other for the security policemen to sit around, drinking and grilling meat….It was another job to be done. In the beginning it smells like a meat braai, in the end like the burning of bones. It takes about seven to nine hours to burn the bodies to ashes. We would have our own little braai and keep on drinking. Every hour or so, one of the policemen had to add a new pile of wood to the fire and turn the bodies over. Early the next morning their remains were dropped into the river.

—**Pauw,** *Into the Heart of Darkness: Confessions of Apartheid's Assassins* **(1997:154)**

Introduction

Few taphonomic alterations to bone are as destructive, rapid, and common in forensic settings as combustion of whole, fleshed bodies or isolated remains (Bass 1984; Fairgrieve 2008; Heglar 1984; Mayne Correia 1997; Mincer et al. 1990; Ubelaker 2009), especially when commercial cremation and subsequent processing are involved (Warren and Schultz 2002). Thermal destruction of bone usually results from continued combustion of an intact body and is associated with an endless array of possibilities, such as house fires, fatal car crashes, airplane accidents, explosions, or "necklacing" (a type of homicide) (Symes et al. 2008, 2012). Thermal destruction also occurs when a perpetrator deliberately destroys a body or other evidence of criminal activity (Baker 2004; Herrmann and Bennett 1999; Owsley 1993; Owsley et al. 1993; Pope and Smith 2004; Symes et al. 2008), so the effects of fire on perimortem and postmortem trauma must be examined and considered. Boiling and cooking also are destructive to bone, albeit less common in a forensic setting than combustion of intact bodies, unless one includes the effects of deliberate maceration of skeletal remains (Fenton et al. 2003; Rennick et al. 2005; see Chapter 15, this volume).

Standard commercial (funerary) cremation practices also pose a challenge to forensic anthropologists. For example, an expert may be asked whether a set of cremains found outdoors represents the scattering of funeral ashes or an attempt to conceal a crime (Baker 2004). More often, forensic anthropologists are requested to determine whether a funeral home presented the correct cremains to the next of kin and not those of another person or an inorganic substance. The most prominent incident of "false cremains" was at the Tri-State Crematory in Georgia with several other incidents also occurring in the United States. The gross negligence associated with false cremains was attributed to a lack of formal government inspections on the funerary institutions (Brooks et al. 2006; Kennedy 1996; Murray and Rose 1993; Rosen 2004; Ubelaker 2009; Warren and Schultz 2002). While standard osseous analytical techniques and chemical testing are often necessary to answer questions regarding who or what is contained in the purported cremains (Schultz et al. 2008), the increase in cremations for both human and nonhuman remains and the increase in fraudulent claims surrounding cremated bodies require that forensic anthropologists also understand the processes and taphonomic effects of commercial cremations.

The aim of this chapter is to describe thermal alteration to intact bodies and skeletal elements within a combustion spectrum that includes thermally induced alterations (house fires, criminal activity, motor vehicle accidents, etc.), cooking (maceration, consumption, etc.), and formal cremations (cremains, etc.). Burned bone fracture characteristics are discussed as a possible means to evaluate the condition of the remains prior to burning, such as fleshed/wet and dry and to differentiate burned bone fractures from prior perimortem injury—sharp, blunt, and ballistic trauma.

Fire Modification of Bodies and Bones

Anyone with practical experience in cooking meat on a fire knows that exposure to high temperatures can char the outside of a piece of meat, including skin, connective, and muscle tissues, while protecting for some time the inner tissues from cooking, scorching, and further fire modification (Roberts et al. 2002). The process of cooking and charring of soft tissue (meat) as well as calcination of bone also occurs when burning a human body. Due to the protective and insulative effects of soft tissue, different burning processes occur to a whole body, to different parts of a whole body, and to individual bones. Since the skeleton is the body's core support structure, bones are usually positioned at the center of a mass of several layers of tissue: muscle, connective, adipose (subcutaneous fat), and epithelium (skin) as well as clothing (Bohnert et al. 1998; Pope 2007; Symes et al. 2008; Thompson 2004, 2005).

Four research areas into fire modification that are discussed in this chapter and are most pertinent to forensic anthropologists include (1) the visual classification and identification of bone from color changes due to carbonization and calcination, (2) experimental research into whole body burn patterns, (3) trauma interpretation, and (4) historical and modern cremations (Symes et al. 2008).

Color Changes

During combustion and with increasing damage to soft tissue and bone, a full spectrum of color changes are observed and range from natural beige, to carbonized (black), gray with blue tints, gray, and then to white, with the last color representing full calcination (Mayne Correia 1997; Mayne Correia and Beattie 2002; Symes et al. 2008).

Burned bone undergoes various color changes that camouflage the material with surrounding burned objects; a situation that can impede complete recovery of fragmented remains (Devlin and Herrmann 2008; Ubelaker et al. 1995; Walker and Miller 2005; Walker et al. 2008; see also Chapter 17, this volume). In car accidents, airplane crashes, and other burning events involving people and nonorganic remains, burned bone often has substances melted onto it. These may derive from artificial fiber clothing, shoe portions, or the interior objects of automobiles, aircraft, or buildings, and the substances involved may include nylon, polyester, or a variety of plastic types. Each of these melts as it burns and can create a mass of partially carbonized residue that is fluid and can conform over surfaces, including bone. These melted artificial substances can also superficially mimic the structure of bone (Figure 14.1). This is especially true of plastic materials that emit gases when combusting, which bubble through the molten plastic or other material and leave behind air spaces when the carbonized substance cools.

Teeth experience color changes that do not exactly parallel those of bones. Even though tooth enamel and dentine have a much lower organic content than bones, the same gradual breakdown of the organic molecules into carbon followed by a loss of carbon occurs (Beach et al. 2008; Schmidt 2008). Beach et al. (2008), in their experimental study, heated dental specimens in a muffle furnace to temperatures ranging from 400°C to 1000°C for 30 or 60 min. During intermediate heating stages, the enamel became translucent, and the teeth took on a red-brown color as the dentin increased in visibility. With additional exposure temperature/duration, enamel turned a dark, metallic gray and retained a glossy texture. Crowns became light gray and were very friable, sometimes disintegrating into multiple fragments. The color of tooth roots, which are within the alveolar bone and are more protected than crowns, advanced from the original beige/yellow of unaltered dentin, to carbonized, brown/olive, gray, then calcined with some loss of structural integrity. These thermal changes were generally more consistently observable in roots, as crowns tended to disintegrate at the

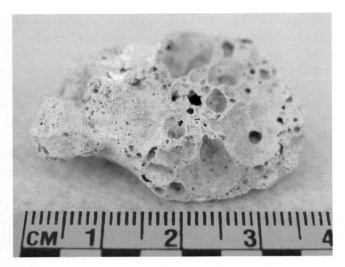

Figure 14.1 Melted plastic that provides the illusion of spongy bone. Note the irregular structure to the porous spaces, formed by bubbling gases.

higher temperatures used. In an experiment using the teeth of domestic pigs (*Sus scrofa*), Hughes and White (2009) found that fracture propagation in dental enamel was similar to that of bone. They observed longitudinal and transverse heat-induced cracks contoured around dental enamel with dentin presenting greater shrinking and deformation than the less organic enamel.

Essentially, color changes on thermally altered bone represent a gradient of burn intensity and duration from the outside to the inside of a bone (Beach et al. 2008; Buikstra and Swegle 1989; Devlin and Herrmann 2008; Dunlop 1978; Gilchrist and Mytum 1986; Schmidt 2008; Shipman et al. 1984; Stiner et al. 1995; Symes et al. 2008; Walker and Miller 2005; Walker et al. 2008). Color is also used as a criterion to assess unburned areas and to determine the probable location/position of the body in the fire (Symes et al. 2012). Visual color classifications for bones and teeth, as discussed earlier, are attributed to two main processes, carbonization and calcination.

Carbonization

Organic substances contain high proportions of carbon atoms and experience *carbonization* when subject to intense heat. As the complex organic molecules are broken down and other elements including oxygen and hydrogen become volatile and are either liberated into the atmosphere or combine with other elements, carbon remains behind. Naturally occurring carbon is black in color and is used as a darkening pigment suspended in oil paints. Therefore, carbonized (also referred to as *charred* or *smoked*) bone is black in color and is likely to have had direct contact with an intense heat source (such as an electrical heating element), burning soft tissue, or flames (Symes et al. 2008).

Other natural (see Chapter 12, this volume) and artificial (Chapter 8) processes may stain bone black, so this coloration alone is not a clear indicator of carbonization. In particular, some manganese and/or iron oxides stains bone in a manner that mimics carbonization (Marín Arroyo et al. 2008; Shahack-Gross et al. 1997). Mineral staining tends to be superficial, while carbonization may either affect the entire thickness of the bone (Symes et al. 2008) or integrate with areas of other color changes, including those resulting from calcination.

Carbonized bone is most similar to dry bone because the organic component (collagen) is largely destroyed; both dry bone and carbonized bone are less durable than unburned bone. Similarly, burned and dry bone is less able to withstand tensile and compressive strain deformation than unburned bone (e.g., Currey 2002; Reilly and Burnstein 1974). Carbonized bones are still identifiable, but, unlike dry bone, measurements cannot be taken accurately from this material (Thompson 2004, 2005). With continuous loss of moisture and organic content due to prolonged combustion, bone undergoes significant shrinkage and deformation (Buikstra and Swegle 1989; Thompson 2004, 2005). The rate of moisture loss and bone shrinkage is dependent on a myriad factors including condition of the body (flesh or decomposed), condition of the bone (wet or dry), type and location of material (bone or teeth; spongy vs. cortical bone), and the duration of the burn event (DeHaan 2008, 2012; Symes et al. 2008, 2012). Because of the complexity of bone shrinkage in thermal destruction, the amount of shrinkage is still debated and likely dependent upon multiple factors.

Calcination

Calcination is a continuation of the bone combustion process where the liberated carbon from organic molecules combines with oxygen to form carbon dioxide (CO_2) or carbon monoxide (CO) and is freed into the atmosphere (to global detrimental effect). The remaining bone material is comprised of the original inorganic component (hydroxyapatite), consisting of fused bone salts (Mayne Correia 1997; Mayne Correia and Beattie 2002; Thompson 2004, 2005). The color therefore shifts from black of carbonized bone to white, the natural color of hydroxyapatite, with many possible intermediate color stages (mentioned earlier) between the two states (Figure 14.2).

Calcined bone is extremely fragile and has an even greater loss of strength than carbonized bone. Heglar (1984:149) describes calcined bone fragments as having a fine-pottery appearance, including feel, mass, and sound (when fragments are clinked together). As bone is heated above 500°C, some hydroxyapatite recrystallization occurs. The average crystal size increases (Hiller et al. 2003) as the temperature increases

Figure 14.2 Gray–blue discoloration of calcined bone with longitudinal fractures and charring. Patina fractures are noted on the surface. (Photograph courtesy of Natalie Keough, University of Pretoria, Pretoria, South Africa.)

up to 900°C, ultimately making the overall bone structure more brittle (Stiner et al. 1995). Arc-shaped fragments of cortical bone, such as from long bones or metapodial shafts, easily snap when little pressure is applied. Fracture, shrinkage, and deformation accompany calcination and further weaken the bone structure and integrity. Damage makes skeletal element identification of a calcined bone much more difficult. As a rule, bone altered to this degree cannot be measured as a part of skeletal analyses, and the potential for DNA recovery has been reduced or obliterated (Schwark et al. 2011; Thompson 2004, 2005). Commingling of heavily calcined individuals also becomes extremely difficult to resolve, as many analytical methods (DNA, refitting, pair-matching, or articulation) are no longer possible. However, substantial information on the biological profile may be obtained from calcined remains as long as careful handling and reconstruction are employed (Grévin et al. 1998).

Archaeologists have noted that calcined bone may prove more resistant to subsequent diagenetic breakdown in the soil (Gilchrist and Mytum 1986), particularly in acidic substrates which typically destroy bone integrity over time (see Chapter 5, this volume). This differential preservation potential has neither been tested nor shown to affect remains detectably over shorter forensic intervals.

Effects of Cooking on Bone

Another type of thermal alteration to bone is cooking, various heating techniques designed to raise the temperature of soft tissue and bone which usually occur without actual combustion. These methods include roasting and boiling, the former of which is similar in its effects to the interior tissue of a body exposed to direct flames. Since the taphonomic changes brought about by boiling do bear upon the overall structural degradation of heated bone, possible changes to bone and differentiated cooked and uncooked bone are addressed.

Boiling of bone (which occurs at 100°C at sea level) is relevant to forensics in two contexts: in rare cases of cannibalism involving cooking and as part of the taphonomic suite of alterations common to animal bones which may aid in the determination of their nonhuman origin when morphological analysis is insufficient. Long periods of boiling makes bone smoother, lighter in color, and more translucent than fresh, uncooked bone (Bosch et al. 2011; Lupo and Schmitt 1997; Roberts et al. 2002), with more subtle changes at lower intervals and temperatures (Koon et al. 2010). Additionally, some of the bone collagen may convert into gelatin which leaches from the bones (Roberts et al. 2002). This method is purposefully employed on a large scale in some food manufacturing processes. A weakening of the overall bone structure due to loss of collagen content and integrity also occurs (Roberts et al. 2002). Using SEM analysis, Bosch et al. (2011) and Trujillo-Mederos et al. (2012) noted progressive smoothing of surfaces by the buildup of residues as the boiling interval increased from 2 to 6 h, although noncrystalline crusts may appear after extended boiling. Bleaching also occurs as the bone is boiled and organic content is leached out (Figure 14.3).

Cooking as a part of cannibalism occurs rarely in forensic cases, but this taphonomic process is found much more frequently in archaeology/ethnography. Multiple researchers have provided a suite of taphonomic characteristics for human remains from archaeological sites which may be used as indicators of cannibalism (Degusta 2000; Flinn et al. 1976;

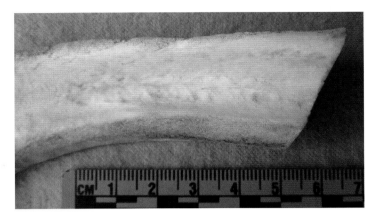

Figure 14.3 Nonhuman rib, boiled for approximately 12 h. Note evidence of bleaching.

Graver et al. 2002; Hurlbut 2000; Turner and Turner 1992, 1999; White 1992) versus other behavior, including secondary mortuary treatment or trophy-taking.

Commercial Cremation

Dr. Julius LeMoyne established the first U.S. commercial crematory in the town of Washington, PA in 1876, after multiple attempts in Europe had been unsuccessful. The event was widely reported in various popular and scientific articles of the time (Rosen 2004). This novel treatment of the dead was in stark contrast to and in many cases much cheaper than the elaborate coffins, monuments, and funerals that pervaded nineteenth-century American culture (see Chapter 5, this volume). Since then, the prevalence of cremation as a funerary option has greatly increased. From 1876 to 1884, only 41 cremations were performed in the United States; in 2001, this increased to 651,176 (out of 2,409,000 deaths or a rate of 27%). In 2010, an estimated 40% of all U.S. deceased were cremated (Rosen 2004).

The practice of cremation is fundamental to Hindu funeral treatment and many other worldwide religions. In addition, some religions prohibit the practice, as in the case of Orthodox or Conservative Jews and Muslims. Only in 1963 did the Second Vatican Council reverse an earlier (1886) ban on cremation for Catholics (Rosen 2004), so some portions of the U.S. population are not represented in the total produced cremains. In tandem with this trend, increasing popularity of pet cremation (U.S. Cremation Equipment 2012) in the United States likely will cause more cases of potential commingling or misidentification in the future. Furthermore, popularity has increased for the use of both human and nonhuman cremains to create synthetic diamonds and moissanite gems along with the purchasing of "cremains jewelry" which is the fashioning of ashes into charms, bracelets, lockets, etc. As expected, the fashion of wearing and collecting cremains will affect the biological information that can, if any, be obtained from cremains cases in the future.

Standard Cremation Procedures

Modern cremations proceed in gas-fired ovens, and the main chamber (the retort) is lined with heat-resistant refractory bricks (Davies and Mates 2005; Ubelaker 2009). The body is placed into the retort and cremated in a container ranging from a body bag, a simple stapled cardboard box, to a wooden casket (Bass and Jantz 2004). The heat of cremation typically is 1600°F–1800°F (870°C–980°C), with an average time of 2–2.5 h necessary (Rosen 2004). The duration of heat necessary for a full cremation varies primarily with body mass such that larger individuals take longer to fully reduce into ash. The cleaning of the oven between runs is accomplished by sweeping the retort contents into a steel cooling pan. The likelihood of a slow intermixing of residual ashes among individuals cremated in the same retort does exist, but larger and more visible bone fragments are less likely to be left behind between successive retort runs.

Post-Cremation Processing

To render remains fully unidentifiable through normal analytical means, cremains are deliberately pulverized after being removed from the retort. Numerous reasons exist for the implementation of this standardized method, but it also reduces the likelihood of civil litigations against the crematorium due to the reduced ability to determine when one set of cremains has been mixed for or with another (Warren and Schultz 2002). While hand methods of pulverization of large bone fragments using mallet-like implements were once common, newer electrical devices dubbed *cremulators* are now frequently used. A cremulator is basically a ball or hammer mill utilized within a rotating drum pierced with 4 mm holes. The cremains are placed inside and are rotated with tumbling metal cylinders or balls to cause crushing. Fragments pass through the drum when they are smaller than the 4 mm outlet holes (Warren and Schultz 2002). The machine tends to produce long slivers of bone along with smaller fragments and dust. The most common type of cremulator uses rotating blades and largely functions like a food processor to produce tiny fragments rapidly (Warren and Schultz 2002). Little diagnostic bone survives this procedure.

Mass of Cremated Human Remains

Burning also results in a loss of bone mass, through the volatilization of moisture, the breakdown and oxidation of organic molecules, and the combustion of fats (Grupe and Hummel 1991; Thompson 2004, 2005). Hiller et al. (2003) reported an overall bone mass loss of 30%–55% with samples of calcined cortical bone. Whole bones are likely to lose a greater proportion of mass due to the large amount of soft tissue (primarily fat contained in marrow cavities and cancellous bone) contributing to their initial, unheated mass. Warren and Maples (1997) found that cremains had a mass approximately 3.5% of pre-cremation adult body mass, and this amount dropped to 2.5% for children and 1% for fetuses. Clearly, bone mineral component is the major contributor to the mass of cremains. The percentage of cremated mass remaining after long bones were defleshed and defatted ranged from 64.8% to 66.9% (Trotter and Peterson 1955). Bass and Jantz (2004) measured the average mass of adult cremains obtained from typical commercial cremations (151 males and 155 females) in east Tennessee, USA. The contents of each cremation included the body and usually some kind of container, including body bags, cardboard boxes, and wooden caskets. The cooled oven contents were removed, with any visible large pieces of container or other large artificial objects removed along with ferrous object removal (carton staples, etc.) using a magnet. Masses were determined after extraneous object removal, but some of the ash content must have derived from burial container and/or clothing. Bass and Jantz

(2004) found that the male mean was 3380 g (range: 1865–5379 g) and the female mean was 2350 g (range: 1050–4000 g). Warren and Maples (1997) obtained similar results, notably with adult male and female means separated by 1053 g, while the difference in adult male and female means in the Bass and Jantz (2004) sample was 1030 g. Warren and Maples (1997) also found in their adult sample ($n = 91$) that all cremains masses above 2750 g were male and all below 1887 g were female; notably, their sample uniformly was cremated in cardboard containers.

These masses likely represent a higher degree of incineration and overall body mass loss than would be obtained through most common means attempted for criminal body disposal and also lack soft tissue and significant amounts of carbonized bone (Ubelaker 2009). After removal of all artifacts, all large pieces of bones are crushed. The lack of large fragments of bone also would distinguish a commercial cremation from most criminal cremations (Baker 2004).

Surgical Implants and Dental Restorations Surviving Cremation

Fortunately for forensic investigations, multiple types of items implanted into human bodies survive both accidental and deliberate cremation and in many cases can be used for positive identification. This is especially true where individual serial numbers have been engraved into the object, which is required of all such devices of sufficient size since 1993 in the United States and with at least a manufacturer's mark on smaller devices such as screws (Ubelaker and Jacobs 1995). Figure 14.4 shows multiple titanium alloy

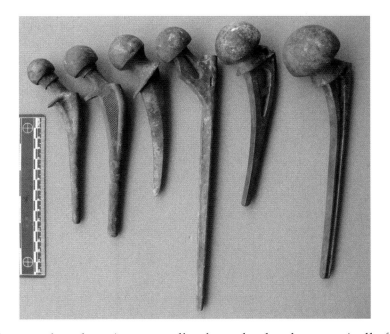

Figure 14.4 Surgical implants (titanium alloy femur head replacements), all of which have survived commercial cremation in excellent condition. Scale is in centimeter. (Photographed materials courtesy of Ranald Donaldson, University of Victoria, Saanich, British Columbia, Canada.)

femoral head implants of various manufacturers and configurations, all of which survived the intense heat of commercial cremation completely intact except for surface color change. Warren and Schultz (2002) noted that while large, obvious devices such as these are normally removed (in recent years) from cremains prior to their handover to next of kin, smaller surgical implants including surgical staples used for skin closure, vascular clips, sternotomy sutures, pacemakers leads, and sometimes other pacemaker components are noted, despite crematories recommending their removal prior to cremation (Ubelaker 2009).

The degrees to which dental restorations and fixtures survive both accidental/criminal and commercial cremation is less known due to the multiple types of materials currently used for these objects, including gold, silver amalgam, composite resins, acrylic, and ceramic. Metallic dental implants which may survive cremation include crowns, posts, and bridgework (Warren and Schultz 2002) and orthodontic braces.

Distinguishing Cremated Nonhuman from Human Bone

A particular problem when examining cremains is the potential for commingling with animal bones (Whyte 2001). The ability to differentiate human from nonhuman skeletal elements is directly dependent on the condition of the remains on the combustion spectrum. Large fragments, especially epiphyses, can be diagnostic at the species level. However, this becomes more difficult when the skeletal structure has been reduced to ash or unidentifiable fragments. This is particularly true of certain depositional settings, such as outdoor burn pits, chimneys, incinerators, or certain accident scenes, such as vehicles carrying humans and animals together (aircraft, personal vehicles, or commercial transport of animal parts). Analysis of accidental/criminal or commercial cremains may include assessing the minimum number of individuals (if possible) and identification such as pet tags, surgical implantations, and other nonperishable devices (Ubelaker 2009). Under these circumstances, no clear methodology is available in which to address the separation of commingled remains that have been reduced in many cases to calcined fragments which are devoid of morphological indicators of species origin. Brooks et al. (2006) suggested that elemental analysis can be performed, but this is more to examine the difference between organic and inorganic components. If bone has diagnostic features and surviving cortical bone, then both morphological characteristics definitive of a particular species and the microstructural layout of cortical bone (histology) are options for distinguishing human and nonhuman fragmentary remains (Hillier and Bell 2007).

Combustion of Whole Bodies: Tissue Shielding and Burned Bone Fracture Characteristics

The rate of destruction of a bone with combustion is dependent on the size of the body or body part, the differential distribution of soft tissue on the body, the position of the body in the fire, and the biomechanics of burned bone (Symes et al. 2008). Therefore, bone with little tissue thickness and direct exposure to fire, such as the frontal bone (forehead), anterior mandible and teeth, and the dorsal surface of the metacarpals, experience greater thermal alteration over the same period than bones surrounded by more tissue, such as the head of the femur. The differential burning of a human body is conditional on the body entering *pugilistic posture*, a position that is based on the contraction of strong, flexor muscles due to rapid dehydration of muscular tissue (Symes et al. 1999, 2001, 2008) (Figure 14.5).

Patterned Thermal Destruction

Combustion of a body has been shown to occur in a uniform, recognizable, and predictable pattern (Adelson 1955; Bass 1984; Bohnert et al. 1998; DeHaan 2012; Icove

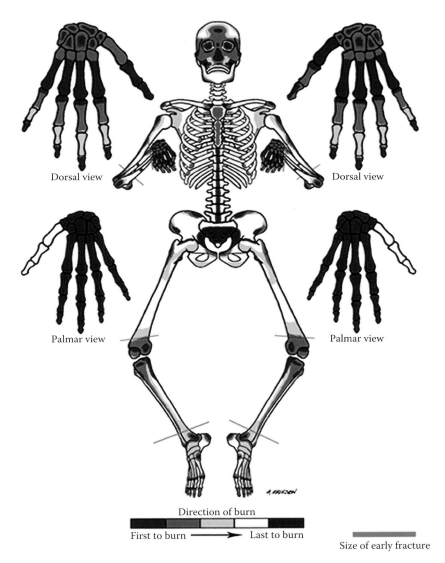

Dorsal view   Dorsal view

Palmar view   Palmar view

Direction of burn

First to burn ⟶ Last to burn

Size of early fracture

Figure 14.5 Pattern of thermal destruction of a skeleton indicating the initial, secondary, and final areas to express burning on bone, both anterior and posterior. (From Symes et al., 2008, Patterned thermal destruction of human remains in a forensic setting, In *The Analysis of Burned Human Remains* eds. C.W. Schmidt and S.A. Symes, pp. 15–54. Academic Press, Amsterdam, the Netherlands; 32–33.) (Image reprinted with permission of Academic Press, Amsterdam, the Netherlands.)

(continued)

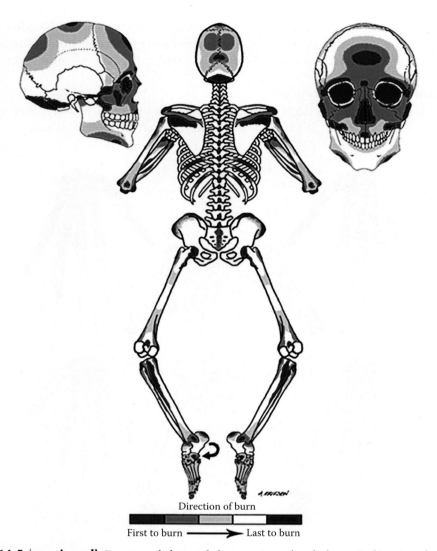

Direction of burn

First to burn ⟶ Last to burn

Figure 14.5 (continued) Pattern of thermal destruction of a skeleton indicating the initial, secondary, and final areas to express burning on bone, both anterior and posterior. (From Symes et al., 2008, Patterned thermal destruction of human remains in a forensic setting, In *The Analysis of Burned Human Remains* eds. C.W. Schmidt and S.A. Symes, pp. 15–54. Academic Press, Amsterdam, the Netherlands; 32–33.) (Image reprinted with permission of Academic Press, Amsterdam, the Netherlands.)

and DeHaan 2003; Pope 2007; Spitz 1993; Symes et al. 2008). However, the location and position of the body; the presence of broken bones, dismemberment, restraints, or confinement; the condition of the body (fleshed or decomposed); and the duration of exposure to fire can alter this pattern, thus rendering it abnormal (Fojas et al. 2011; Symes et al. 1999, 2008). When assessed within the scene context, an abnormal burn pattern may provide information as to the condition, location, and position of the body prior to the burn event.

An unconfined body can transform from a supine to a pugilistic posture within 10 min of exposure to fire (Crow and Glassman 1996). This postural change is the result

Figure 14.6 Postmortem fracture of the distal metacarpals and proximal phalanges from burning of the knuckles in a pugilistic fist. With the joint destroyed, release of the postured fingers are relaxed and the distal phalanges are exposed to fire. This represents a normal burn pattern where the distal phalanx of the four fingers is the last to burn.

of rapid moisture loss in soft tissues with subsequent contractions of what are the stronger antagonist flexor muscles over the weaker extensor muscles (Adelson 1955; Symes et al. 2008). With continual combustion, the pugilistic posture provides differential protection across the body; a situation which contributes to the manifestation of a normal burn pattern (Symes et al. 1999, 2001, 2008).

As the antagonist muscles contract, flexion of the appendicular skeleton occurs (Symes et al. 2008). In the upper limbs, the humerus medially rotates and adducts, the elbow joint hyperflexes, the forearm pronates, the wrist flexes (toward the forearm), and the phalanges curl into a fist. In this position, the dorsal surface of the hand, wrists, and elbows are the least protected joints from thermal damage, whereas the anterior distal humerus and anterior proximal ulna and radius are joints protected longer from destruction (Symes et al. 1999, 2008). Figure 14.6 illustrates the pugilistic posture of the hand making a fist, and eventually losing the posture due to the destruction of the bone joint.

Joint shielding indicates that two joints were articulated and that the area of articulation protected the surfaces from burning. This phenomenon can be noted anywhere on the skeleton but is not observed in bodies disarticulated prior to burning. Figure 14.7 illustrates an abnormal burn pattern, where the skull base is the area of initial burning due to its disarticulated position in the South African veldt. Despite advanced decomposition, the burn pattern reveals the presence of the mandibular condyle during the fire.

In the lower limbs, the thigh flexes, such that the anterior knee is exposed, but the posterior popliteal fossa (behind the knee) is protected. The ankle plantar flexes, the foot inverts, and the phalanges flex (Symes et al. 2008). Thermally induced damage progresses generally from distal to proximal on the lower limbs with the dorsal surface of the foot, ankle, medial malleolus and anterior shaft of the tibia, tibial tuberosity, patella, distal femur, and eventually the hip (acetabulum) being destroyed. The first area to be completely compromised is the ankle, followed by the distal femur, just above the knee. The posterior knee is protected in the popliteal region on account of the pugilistic flexing posture (Figure 14.5).

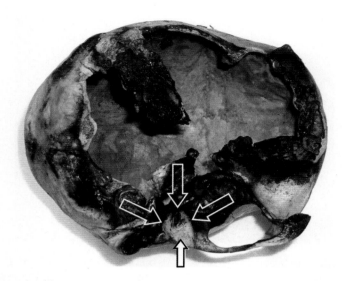

Figure 14.7 Joint shielding represented in a decomposed skeleton discovered in the South African veldt. While the burn pattern is abnormal, the mandible was articulated at the time of burning. (Photograph courtesy of Marius Loots, University of Pretoria, Pretoria, South Africa.)

With regard to the axial skeleton (head and trunk), the head and neck is hyperextended due to contraction of the nuchal muscles (Symes et al. 2008). The face and mandible are consequently exposed to fire, but the area around the occipital bone and neck proper are protected. Since the forehead and facial bones are thinly lined with soft tissue and muscle, thermal destruction is initiated at the frontal bone, followed by projecting bones of the face, anterior teeth, and lateral margins of the external mandible. Even though the cheek bones and lateral mandible char early, the face is comparably higher in moisture and is more resistant to burning than either the forehead or the vault. Total destruction of the forehead and apex skull occurs prior to severe burning destruction of the face (Symes et al. 1999, 2008).

Contrary to popular opinion, the cranium does not explode when exposed to continual combustion (Pope and Smith 2004; Symes et al. 1999, 2001, 2008). Once the calvaria is exposed, sutures separate, and darkish brown coagulated masses of boiled (or boiling) blood and fluids often form between the dura mater and the skull (*heat hematoma*). Since this is a normal process of thermal destruction, the appearance of dried or cooked blood on both parietals should not be immediately associated with perimortem trauma or injury. The skull often presents with differential areas of charred and calcined bone, and the differences can often be recognized as relating to soft tissues and body fluid protection (Symes et al. 2008:40–41). According to Symes et al. (2008), the differential distribution of color associated with charred and calcined bone in a single skull is due to the various areas of this structure simultaneously experiencing different degrees and duration of heat. In other words, a heterogeneous burn pattern is noted with fleshed remains with differential burning patterns also being observed on other areas of the skeleton. Under these circumstances, color changes indicate the duration and gradient of burning.

The trunk and parts of the appendicular body closely associated with the trunk (clavicles, scapulae, ribs, sternum, vertebrae, and pelvis) consist of the largest and heaviest part of the body and tend to survive burning for longer than the head and the rest of the appendicular skeleton. In the pugilistic posture, the shoulders and arms adduct, and the vertebral column hyperextends. The first areas to burn are the sternal ends and midshafts of the external clavicles, the acromion process of the scapulae, the sternum, the anterior ends and lower, posterior external surface of the ribs, and the vertebral spinous processes. The anterior vertebral column and a small area inferior to the scapular spine (infraspinous fossa) are the last to burn. In the pelvis, thermal damage appears on the superior anterior iliac crests followed by the anterior surfaces of the pubic bones (Figure 14.5).

Interpretations of Traumatic Injury from Burned Bone

As discussed in Chapter 13, an anthropologist's knowledge as to the timing of a traumatic injury is paramount for the accurate interpretation of that injury. The potential for perimortem trauma to be concealed through burning requires the forensic anthropologist to understand the dynamics of burning bodies as well as the context of the remains and to distinguish between defects inflicted *prior* to thermal alteration and those occurring *as a result* of burning (de Gruchy and Rogers 2002; Herrmann and Bennett 1999; Pope and Smith 2004; Symes et al. 2008). The context and condition of the bone and body at the time of burning contribute to the complex questions associated with burning. This section addresses observable fracture patterns on wet and dry bone, the biomechanics of wet and dry bone, and the complexity of perimortem and postmortem terminology when addressing burned remains.

Fracture Patterns on Burned Bone

Despite common misconceptions, bone does not combust in a uniform manner, even on the same bone. Just as a piece of wood often burns in stages, with some portions reduced to ash, some portions carbonized, and some portions unburned at any given moment, so too does bone. The insulative properties of soft tissue increase this effect. Thermal alteration might be observed only on a small, exposed area of bone and consist only of a *heat-altered border*, where the soft tissue has been burned away to that point (Symes et al. 2008). The exposed border of the bone is visibly affected, but the bone not visibly affected also has undergone some dehydration and molecular alteration. Visible damage associated with the heat-altered border may include heat shrinkage fractures and flaking or distortion of the outer cortical layers (Symes et al. 1999, 2008). In addition, a *heat line* is occasionally found adjacent to the heat-altered border and at the junction between unburned and burned bone (Symes et al. 2008). The heat line is generally narrower than the width of the border and appears as a transitional zone between the two (Figure 14.8). Heat-altered bone is usually opaque, while unburned fresh bone is more translucent (Symes et al. 2005, 2008). Recognition of heat-altered borders in bones, which have subsequently been skeletonized, is often difficult.

The condition of a body, such as fleshed, decomposed, or skeletonized, and the organic composition of the respective skeletal structure prior to burning contributes to the burn morphology and fracture characteristics (e.g., Baby 1954; Binford 1963; Keough et al. 2012; Symes et al. 1999, 2008; Thurman and Wilmore 1980–81). With fleshed remains, soft tissue destruction starts at the skin, advances through fat, muscle, and cartilage, and eventually reaches bone. Consequently, skeletal elements present with shielding, a greasy appearance, a white heat-altered border with predictable cracking at the heat line, and

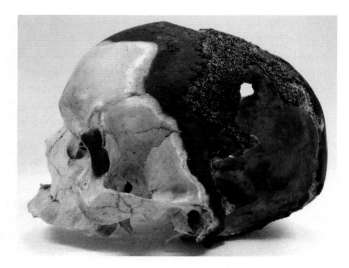

Figure 14.8 White heat line, heat border, charring, and delamination observed in a case of "necklacing" from Kimberley, South Africa. The abnormal burn pattern is possibly due to perimortem injuries on the face and mandible as well as location of the tires. Necklacing is a type of execution that originated as a form of vigilante justice against Apartheid conspirators in the townships in the mid-1980s. Two or more tires (filled with gasoline) are placed around a victim's chest and arms, and the person is set on fire (From Bornman et al. (eds.), *Violence in South Africa: A Variety of Perspectives. Human Sciences Research Council*, Pretoria, South Africa, 1998.) (Photograph courtesy of Natalie Keough, University of Pretoria, Pretoria, South Africa.)

various heat-induced fractures such as deep longitudinal and transverse splits as well as curved transverse fractures (Curtin 2008; Keough et al. 2012; Symes et al. 1999, 2008) (Figures 14.7 through 14.9).

Curved transverse fractures result from heating and cracking of wet bone as kinetically charged protective soft tissues (muscles) and periosteum shrink away from

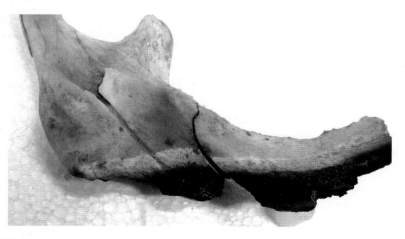

Figure 14.9 Heat line, heat-altered border and predictable cracking within this border, and charring are observed on the mandible associated with a case of "necklacing" from Kimberley, South Africa (see Figure 14.8). Note perimortem injury that traverses the unburned and burned areas. (Photograph courtesy of Natalie Keough, University of Pretoria, Pretoria, South Africa.)

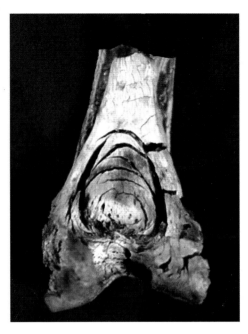

Figure 14.10 Curved transverse fracture noted on a distal femur shaft. The concentric fractures along the bone are an indication of the direction of burning. This pattern represents the last bastion of soft tissue to succumb to heat destruction.

their attachments and expose a new surface to direct heat. The curved defect reflects the partially destroyed end of a muscle or other tissues as they shrink toward the unburned end (Symes et al. 1999, 2008). However, shrinking muscles that appear to create these "trailing" fractures do not necessarily create a curved shape, especially if wide muscles, like the nuchal muscles, are being destroyed (Symes et al. 2008:45–46).

Less commonly, the curved transverse fractures appear as concentric rings in fossae or simply areas of concentrated tissues, such as the popliteal region of the femur (Figure 14.10). This type of fracture is the result of a combination of factors such as cortical bone thickness, bone shape, articulation, and soft tissue obstruction, as well as gradual muscle retraction. Concentric rings can also form in flat joints, where little soft tissue exists. As distorting tissues further strain joints (that are subjected to heat, joint manipulation, and gradual movement of the bones) out of articulation, concentric fracture rings are suggested to occur. Figure 14.11 illustrates the first proximal foot phalanx joint with curved transverse fractures illustrating a burn pattern of slow encroachment into the joint. Encroachment is dependent upon the distal metatarsal and proximal phalanx's slow separation due to soft tissue shrinkage.

In long bones, curved transverse fractures commonly result in *coning*, where the fractured diaphysis appears arched at the fracture margin. However, in recent research Gonçalves et al. (2011) did not exclusively observe curved transverse fractures, or thumbnail fractures, on fleshed or wet bone and in fact observed warping and curved transverse fractures in bones that had been buried for years. Therefore, they suggest that this variable should not be exclusively used to distinguish whether the body was fleshed, wet, or dry prior to the burn event. However, the first author (SAS) contends that curved transverse, and any by-product or variant of curved transverse (see above), appears only in fleshed

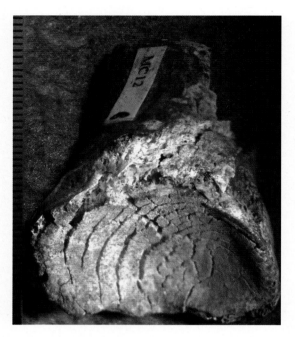

Figure 14.11 The first proximal foot phalanx joint with curved transverse fractures and illustrates a burn pattern of slow encroachment into the joint.

remains. The number of exceptions in their sample were few and far between but, nonetheless, some curved fractures appeared on buried and possibly dried remains. The authors have to agree with Gonçalves et al. (2011) that a more in-depth study is needed.

With less organic material and soft tissue protection, dry and wet bones have been shown to burn as a more homogeneous unit. Unfleshed bone chars and becomes calcined more quickly than fleshed bone and presents with a brownish to beige heat border with minimal heat-altered cracking (Figure 14.12), a brown heat line or no visible delineation between the altered and unaltered areas (Figures 14.13 and 14.14), and no curved transverse fractures (Keough et al. 2012; Symes et al. 1999, 2001). According to Keough et al. (2012), burned dry bone becomes discolored and presents as burned brown or black bone

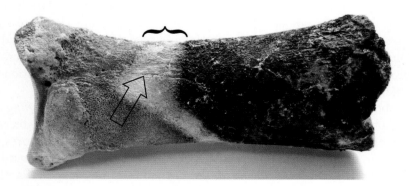

Figure 14.12 Minimal heat-altered cracking (black arrow) in the heat-altered border of a mostly dry burned bone of a domestic pig (*Sus scrofa*). (Photograph courtesy of Natalie Keough, University of Pretoria, Pretoria, South Africa).

Figure 14.13 Brown heat line (arrows) noted on the proximal humerus of skeletal remains of a domestic pig (*Sus scrofa*). (Photograph courtesy of Natalie Keough, University of Pretoria, Pretoria, South Africa.)

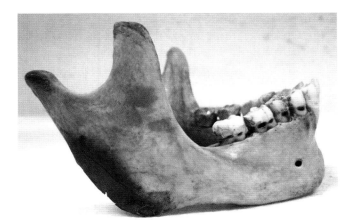

Figure 14.14 Irregular charring, longitudinal fractures, and absence of a heat line on wet/dry skeletal remains discovered in the South African veldt, with an abnormal burn pattern. (Photograph courtesy of Natalie Keough, University of Pretoria, Pretoria, South Africa.)

(Figure 14.15). The burning on dry or decomposition-stained bone is often associated with minimal to no heat-altered cracking or heat lines or warping. If charring is absent, it is most likely due to the duration of the fire or the condition of the bone though many other factors are involved. Despite disparities in definitions and applications, the conclusions of Keough et al. (2012) are comparable to previous observational and experimental studies on burned fleshed and wet/dry bone (e.g., Baby 1954; Binford 1972; Krogman 1943a,b; Symes et al. 2008; Thurman and Willmore 1980–81).

The differences in fracture morphology between fleshed and dry/wet bone are associated with differences in the biomechanical properties of the bone prior to and

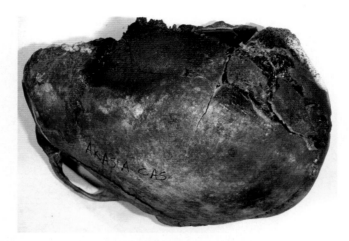

Figure 14.15 Charring, minimal heat-induced fracture and absence of both a heat line or heat-altered border on dry skeletal remains with decomposition staining discovered in the South African veldt. (Photograph courtesy of Marius Loots, University of Pretoria, Pretoria, South Africa.)

during burning. Fleshed bone shrinks and warps due to a loss of moisture and collagen; the same process occurs in semi-wet to dry bone but to a lesser extent. Because the process of a bone losing moisture—or switching from a wet to dry state—is a continuous process, fracture differences between wet (unfleshed) and dry bone may be difficult to decipher (see Chapter 13). Contrarily, a fleshed body presents with a pattern as various soft tissues need to be destroyed along with bone, a situation that presents a unique sequence to the burning event. While knowledge of these differences may inform forensic investigators of the postmortem chain of events and to the possible timing of a burn event, further experimental studies are needed.

Other thermally induced fracture characteristics noted in all bones, regardless of prior burn conditions, include longitudinal, transverse, step, and patina fractures and delamination (Symes et al. 2008; see Figures 14.2 and 14.8). Longitudinal fractures are found in long bones and are considered common due to the fact that longitudinal failure is expected with the rapid shrinking of a tube-like shape. This is similar to burned skin patterns on the arms of fire victims. When the bone heats to the point of evaporation and protein denaturation, the matrix shrinks, structural failure occurs and often follows the grain of the bone. While this failure is often parallel to the Haversian canals, longitudinal fractures also may spiral helically down the long axis of the bone. These fractures occur superficially in trabecular bone due to a completely different biomechanical response to shrinkage.

Transverse fractures are commonly a product of tissue shielding: as fire and heat progress up the bone shaft, the area rapidly shrinks along the line of retreating tissues. Transverse fractures accompany longitudinal fractures and transect Haversian canals. These fractures should not be confused for perimortem sharp trauma if examined under a microscope. With magnification, tension shrinkage fractures are visible as opposed to incised wounds.

Both longitudinal and transverse fractures may make up step fractures, which extend from one margin of a longitudinal fracture transversely across the bone shaft until they terminate in another longitudinal fracture. Lastly, patina fractures appear as a fine mesh

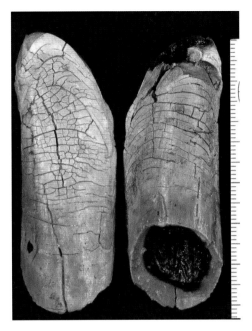

Figure 14.16 A burned humeral shaft, back (left) and front (right). Note the posterior patina pattern mixed with transverse and longitudinal as well as curved transverse fractures. Distal end (top) represents coning while the proximal shaft (bottom) reveals negative coning, indicating a normal burn pattern.

of uniformly patterned superficial cracks similar to those seen in old china or an aged painting (Herrmann and Bennett 1999; Krogman 1943a,b) (Figure 14.16). They are often observed on flat areas of postcranial bones and may be the result of a broad area receiving uniform amounts of heat. Others have suggested that this pattern is due to the incineration of thin protective soft tissue. Delamination and bone splintering are also common and are characterized with the splitting away of cortical bone layers from cancellous bones, the separation of the inner and outer tables of cranial bone exposing the diploë (see Figure 14.8), or the exposure of cancellous bone on epiphyses.

Figure 14.16 epitomizes classic thermal destruction to fleshed bone. The distal humerus is exposed and is the initial area to burn on this bone. This example shows a distal third of the shaft from a front and back view. This bone has more thermal damage distally as opposed to proximally, as indicated by color. The distal humerus burns first and then slowly burns up the shaft of the arm. The curved transverse fractures indicate the direction of burn and failed curved transverse fractures reveal coning, where the bevel indicates the direction of the burn as well. The beveling indicates direction due to the external burning of bone first and internal burning last. In addition, the external calcined and internal charred color indicates that the bone was intact and burning from the outside in as well as distal to proximal.

Thermal Destruction of Remains in a Brushfire/Grassfire

In cases of remains recovered outdoors, both normal and abnormal burn patterns can be present on one individual. This is due to body decomposition and the complete unpredictability of the fire which is based on the environmental diversity of the area and the climate. This makes analysis of remains recovered from a brushland or grassland difficult and often confusing to the analyst.

The nature of the fire is dependent on the surrounding vegetation and climatic conditions. For example, vegetation that is dry is often highly flammable and will result in a hot fire but the duration is shortened due to the fast fuel consumption. A fire that is fuelled by oilier vegetation may take time to ignite, but the duration is prolonged due to the increased source of fuel from the plant substance. In contrasts to oily plants, if vegetation is lush and wet a fire may not even ignite. A strong relationship is seen between fuel source and duration of the burn event such that if fuel source is limited the duration of the fire is reduced. Climate will also affect the duration of the fire. In windy conditions, a fire may spread over a large area in a short period, minimally affecting remains. Non-windy conditions do not accelerate the spread of fire, thus areas may be exposed for longer durations. Similarly, a body may be exposed to the fire longer. The same patterns are true for the environments that are dry versus wet and rainy.

As stated earlier, the condition of the body plays a major role in the manifestation of the burn pattern. Decomposing bodies may not have the ability to assume the pugilistic posture. As soft tissue starts to degrade and tendons and ligaments no longer form strong attachments over joint surfaces, thermal alterations may appear abnormal. For example, elements that normally would be exposed last to fire when following a normal burn pattern (i.e., the head of the femur) may be burned simultaneously to areas which are usually burned first, depending on the stage of decomposition. In addition, body positioning is still an important factor to consider in brushlands. Areas of the body that are in direct contact with the ground may not display any signs of fire damage, thus rendering an abnormal burn pattern. However, the opposite body surface (that is exposed to the fire) will undergo thermal alteration. Understanding the context of the remains and the environmental conditions may assist in interpreting burn patterns. The variables noted earlier should be taken into consideration when analyzing skeletal remains that have been recovered from outdoor contexts.

Perimortem and Postmortem: Thermal Fracture Characteristics

As stated in Chapter 13 of this volume, forensic anthropologists and pathologists differ in their use of perimortem and postmortem terminology in bone trauma analysis, which also includes thermal destruction to bone (see Symes et al. 2012). While medical examiners are primarily concerned with changes occurring to soft tissues, forensic anthropologists are limited to defining changes to the condition of bone with or without the influence of other tissues. The fact that the physical condition of bone changes at a different rate than that of the soft tissues of the body further complicates the issue of trauma analysis, with forensic anthropologists assessing the condition of the bone, such as fresh, wet, dry, or degraded, at the time that the defect occurred, which may or may not coincide with the death event (Nawrocki 2009; Symes et al. 2008). From the anthropological perspective, the perimortem period may extend as long as the condition of the bone remains moist and retains its viscoelastic properties; this sharply contrasts the medico-legal definition, which is mainly limited to the death event (Chapter 13).

The consequence of discussing perimortem and postmortem in terms of a physical condition is the reliance on the intrinsic biomechanical properties of bone. No set period exists in which a bone loses organic content, as the context of the deposition largely determines the rate of interaction between the bones and the environment. As bone decays its organic content diminishes, and the accompanying reduction of its elastic properties results in a continuous transition of biomechanical behavior from viscoelastic (fresh) to brittle (dry) (e.g., Currey 2002; Reilly and Burnstein 1974; see Chapter 13). However, attempting to divide a continuous measure such as organic decay into discrete categories, such as fresh, wet, and dry, is a source of inconsistency among various disciplines. Further complications arise from the necessity of relating a physical condition to a temporal period. Consequently, forensic anthropologists have distinguished perimortem and postmortem periods in terms of a relative sequence of events irrespective of chronological time (Haglund and Sorg 1997, 2002). Unfortunately, the forensic anthropologist's definition of perimortem may conflict with that of the medical examiner and law enforcement, and as such forensic anthropologists perpetually attempt to create a systematic association between the condition of bone and its temporal context (Chapter 13). One quickly formulates the impression that the anthropological concept of perimortem has little to do with the chronology of cause of death.

Thermal modification to bone provides another layer of complexity as the normal transition in biomechanical properties from viscoelastic to brittle is accelerated. The accelerated loss of organic content in bone under thermal alteration results in a unique distinction of perimortem and postmortem definitions. The response of thermally modified bone to stress is entirely different from the viscoelastic response of fresh bone. Fractures due to the drying of bone under intense heat are *biomechanically* postmortem, as they occur in bone that is, or is almost, devoid of organic content (Symes et al. 2008), where the structure fracturing is not viscoelastic bone. Heat-treated bone is a different material than fresh bone. Furthermore, in contrast to normal decomposition, soft tissue plays an active role in the prolonging of bone modification during burning.

Now that burned bone has been identified essentially as a nonliving, nonviable "non-bone," the authors would be negligent in their discussion without pointing out the drawback of labeling all thermally altered bone fractures as postmortem. Labeling burned bone fractures in a fatal house fire as postmortem neglects the observable conditions of the bone prior to burning. If all burned bone fractures are termed "postmortem," this description ignores details of the burned specimen that relate back to the circumstances of the victim at the time of the fire.

For example, imagine a hypothetical fire that destroys a small county morgue. All employees evacuate the building, but a fleshed body remained on the autopsy table after evacuation. After a major fire destroys the morgue, anthropologists are called in to recover all deceased victims housed in the morgue prior to the fire. Only two bodies are known to be in the morgue that day, the one left on the autopsy table and one dry skeleton laid out in anatomical position on a gurney. The bones belonged to a single human collected from a construction site that accidently disturbed a grave within a historic cemetery.

The recovery is simple; the anthropologists systematically remove the extensively burned fresh body on the autopsy table, being careful to get all visible fragments of calcined bone. They also recover a dry burned skeleton on a badly burned gurney. Anthropologists should be able to separate the skeleton from the fresh body. If we assume heat-induced fractures are present on each skeleton, we can probably recognize differences in fresh and dry skeletal remains (as discussed earlier).

The anthropologists recognize features on the fresh body, curved transverse fractures, coning (curved transverse fractures that are separated in fracture), heat lines, border, charred, and calcined bones. The features create expected patterns that suggest the body conformed to the pugilistic posture and burned, in this case, in a typical fashion. These patterns are strong indicators that the body was fleshed when it burned, not to mention that a bit of torso (flesh) survived the fire. Everything is as expected. Examination of the dry bones reveals different fracture patterns. The bones are not severely fractured; warpage is reduced and curved transverse or coning patterns are less likely to be present. Furthermore, the bone is a different color than the fresh burned bone, as brown soil staining persists, even after the bone is burned.

Obviously, bone chars and calcines in intense heat, no matter the prior burn condition, but the dry bones in this example appear to be the product of a postmortem event. Under a microscope, heat damage causes the bone to fracture, although their reaction is different than that of fresh bone and they convey the idea of dry brittle bone.

While fractures on the fleshed body and dry skeleton are classified as originating from a postmortem (after death) fire event, the dry bones are altered only after they had dried. On the other hand, the fresh body, when considered as a whole, obviously presents characteristics of perimortem destruction, where features of tissue destruction, shrinkage, and organic tissue removal from bone which quite obviously passed through a fresh stage and ended, in some areas, as calcined bone. This was a perimortem event, and our classification of perimortem burning indicated not only fresh bone but that a fleshed body was present before the fire. The senior author (SAS) opines that anthropologists are remiss to label a fresh burned body as postmortem. No one will argue with a "postmortem" as a label when dry bones are exposed to a fire.

While the aforementioned characteristics are helpful in describing postmortem changes to thermally altered bone, the potential for fire to disguise or create "evidence" is of critical importance in evaluating the cause or manner of death and can be elucidated if the forensic anthropologist understands the dynamics of burning bodies. A crucial element to distinguishing the timing or sequence of fractures in thermally altered remains is the identification of specific morphological features that differ between perimortem and thermal fractures. Fire has such destructive properties that it can mask or destroy perimortem trauma; or worse, it may create trauma that experts mistake for perimortem (before fire) damage to bone. The repercussions of testifying in court with postmortem trauma portrayed as perimortem trauma are enormous.

The senior author (SAS) recently examined a case that exemplifies the issue of distinguishing perimortem versus postmortem trauma. In this case, three areas of fracture morphology, fracture initiation/termination, and overall "texture" of the exposed surfaces were essential in determining a perimortem insult. This same approach can be used when interpreting trauma after the taphonomic influence of fire.

Case Study: Perimortem versus Postmortem in Thermal Modification

A burned-out car was discovered near a small river in the southern United States. The vehicle was eventually traced to a young female who had been missing for several months. A search of the area around the car ensued, only to find a burn pit with debris that consisted of small fragments of human bone, remnants of charcoal, and a burned tire. The scattered remains were eventually identified as belonging to the owner of the car.

Cause and manner of death were unknown in this case but foul play was obviously suspected. While not much of the skull was recovered, a fragment of the right parietal displayed a fairly straight fractured edge with bevel. The suspicious skull fractures and attempts to disfigure and hide the body and car were suspected to indicate a violent cause and manner of death. These issues were presented to the chief medical examiner. The complexity of the scene and paucity of the remains prompted the forensic pathologist to defer this case to an anthropologist for an additional opinion.

Upon receipt of the evidence, the anthropologist realized the daunting task of sorting remains that were extremely fragmented and all, to some extent, thermally altered. Many of these bones, including the aforementioned parietal, were charred and calcined, indicating a long-period and/or high-temperature burning. Burned and decayed muscle tissue also was observed with the skeletal remains.

As seen in Figure 14.17, many areas of the skeleton are absent. While the bones are sorted anatomically, burn and fracture patterns are difficult to visualize in extremely

Figure 14.17 Photographic representation of the skeletal remains of the victim, case study. Note the extreme fragmentation of the bones and, while varying in degree, all bones are thermally altered. Many bones are charred or calcined, indicating a long period and/or high temperature burning.

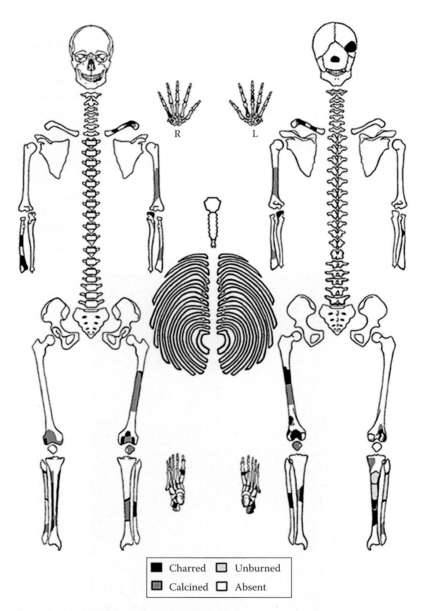

Figure 14.18 A skeletal homunculus is used to demonstrate the location of the bone fragments in the skeleton and to illustrate the degree of burning, case study: no burn (beige); charred (black); and calcined (gray). If the bone is absent, then no color is given. Note the complete absence of bones associated with the torso.

fragmented remains. To assist this pattern recognition, Figure 14.18 illustrates the location of identifiable fragments in the body. The core of the body is minimally represented with a few damaged pieces of bone.

With the sparse representation of bones from the axial skeleton—neck, proximal limbs, abdomen, and pelvis—one must consider two possible scenarios. The torso contains the densest area of soft tissue and fluids in the body and is the most difficult area to burn. With little evidence of these bones at the scene, the torso may not have burned effectively and the perpetrator may have removed it from the scene and dumped in another location or in the river. Alternatively, it is possible that the body was located on a large amount of fuel and accelerants such that the torso was burned beyond recognition, and the outlying areas of the head, arms, and legs were outside the hottest source of fuel and accelerants, were slower to burn, and remained recognizable.

The latter scenario seems unlikely in that almost no bones were found from the core part of the body. Admittedly, a professional osteologist/archaeologist did not perform the recovery, but no representation of these bones seems impossible, especially with a low "campfire" approach to burning a body. The first scenario is most likely to be accurate in that an inexperienced perpetrator attempted to burn a fresh body. Initial attempts severely damaged the top of the head but with enough of the core present to be identifiable as human, the perpetrator likely removed it and dumped it remotely.

The anthropologist's findings were summarized in a report as shown in Table 14.1. The different terminology among experts is of note. Most experts involved before the anthropologist considered the burning event to be postmortem. Obviously, law-enforcement recognizes the fire as an attempt to hide or destroy evidence after a suspected homicide. The medical examiner recognizes a body completely burned and knows physiologically that this is a postmortem event. However, as indicated in Table 14.1, the anthropologist immediately refers to the burning of the body as "perimortem trauma." While investigators and medical personnel realize that the fire likely occurred after death, anthropologists are tied to their medium (i.e., the human body or in this case the remaining fragmentary bones), the burn patterns on this body are indicative of a severely burned fresh body with fragmentary damage to all limbs and the top of the head. Unrelated processes like burning and weathering dehydrate bone at different rates and eventually damage bone. Fractures due to weathering are considered postmortem. Thus, Table 14.1 also summarizes postmortem influences on the body.

Most of the recovered skeletal material shows perimortem burn characteristics as evidenced in wet bone color changes that occurred before the bone dried, evidence of grease in the lesser-burned bones and a normal pattern of thermal bone destruction (Symes et al. 2008). Figure 14.19 shows the distal left humerus shaft. As expected, the curved transverse

Table 14.1 Summary of the Examination of Fragmented Bones Associated with Burned Remains Case Study

Summary Examination of Burned Bone	
Human skeletal remains found in suspicious circumstances; burned, scattered, and associated with a burned car and tire	Perimortem trauma
	1. Thermal alteration to tissues
	2. Burning occurred to fleshed bone
	Postmortem trauma to skull
	1. Deterioration of bone due to extreme heat including
	a Fracturing and fragmentation
	b Exposure of trabecular bone
	c Delamination
	d Discoloration of all features of perimortem thermal destruction
	Overall appearances and inventory
	1. Deterioration of bone due to weathering
	2. Body core appears to be missing

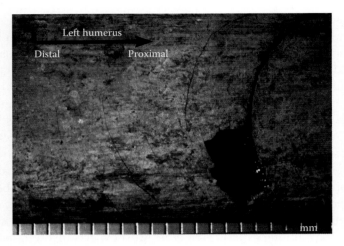

Figure 14.19 Curved transverse fractures from the distal left humerus shaft, case study. The black arrow indicates the direction of burn from distal to proximal. As expected, the curved transverse fractures progressed up the shaft where the elbow (distal) was exposed early, and the shoulder (proximal) was exposed last.

fractures progressed up the shaft where the elbow was exposed early and the shoulder was exposed last. This is one example of soft-tissue-related fractures that sequentially burn and fracture bone as expected in a normal pugilistic posture, although some (Gonçalves et al. 2011) oppose these theories associated with curved transverse fractures.

The anthropologist's report summary suggests that features and characteristics on the bone indicate a fleshed body in a fire, but the question remains as to whether perimortem fractures can be attributed to trauma that occurred before the fire, and, if so, do the features contribute to the cause and manner of death? Figure 14.20 illustrates the parietal that was suspected to reflect characteristics of blunt trauma due to a beveled straight-edged fracture (notice in Chapter 13, a fracture similar to this enabled a homicide investigation). With a closer examination and with comparable exemplar material, the parietal fragment

Figure 14.20 Fragment of the right parietal bone of the victim, case study; black arrows reveal a beveled surface.

Figure 14.21 Fragment of the right parietal (internal) shows a scalloped fracture surface, indicating brittle external cortical bone fire modification or flaking off as opposed to beveling from bending a viscoelastic material (case study).

does not appear to contribute to cause and manner of death. Several characteristics determined this:

- The texture and morphology of the beveled, sloping surface is undulating and is consistent with brittle, rather than viscoelastic, flaking (Figure 14.20).
- The internal fracture surface is scalloped and indicates brittle external cortical bone fire modification or flaking off as opposed to beveling due to bending, viscoelastic material (Figures 14.21). Unfortunately, this feature is not definitive enough to rule out trauma before the fire.

However, fire and heat are opportunistic: once soft tissues are destroyed, initial thermal damage to bone is always external. Certain areas of the skeleton, including the skull, exhibit particular patterns of thermal destruction. The cranial vault has two layers of cortical bone separated by spongy bone. If you combine this anatomical feature with the fact that external bone heats up first, the separation of external and internal layers (delamination) is inevitable. Even though the integrity of the internal skull is eventually compromised, the external skull continues to receive the brunt of the heat, so even with an open skull, beveling may occur with the gradient of temperatures. Closer examination of the parietal bone confirms beveling due to differential bone layer shrinkage as opposed to bending.

To confirm this pattern of delamination, an exemplar burned skull was examined and compared. Figure 14.22 is a close-up of that exemplar burned skull examined in a similar area of the cranial vault. The bevel is labeled with a double black arrow and the area that is cracked and about to delaminate is labeled in the blue arrows with a white arrow indicating the direction of heat-related delamination. This example shows a gradient from unburned, to border, to charred, and eventually more beveled. Figure 14.23 is a close-up of the victim's right parietal fragment. Close examination reveals an identical pattern where the white arrow indicates the direction of failure of the cortical bone, and the encircled area is the cortical bone that is about to fail and flake off, leaving a longer beveled surface. If this had been blunt impact to an unburned bone, there would not be generations of flaking bone,

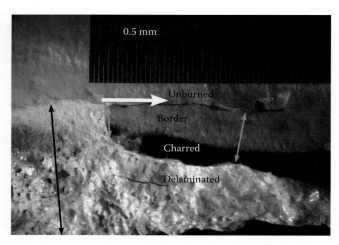

Figure 14.22 Exemplar of the outer table of a burned parietal (unrelated to this case study). The bone burns while fleshed or as the flesh recedes. Beveling can be observed between the black double-pointed arrows. Above this area, more bone is in the process of further heat alteration and is shrinking, breaking, and creating beveling (white arrow).

Figure 14.23 Close-up of the fragment of the right parietal of the victim, case study; white arrow above the beveled area shows the progress of additional burn fractures.

and blunt trauma fractures would not be following thermal heat lines. Finally, the investigation recovered no skull bones definitively indicative of blunt force or any other force for that matter. The separation of the inner and outer tables of cranial bone (Figure 14.8) is common in cases of thermal alteration (Symes et al. 2008). The fractured area in the parietal is no different and therefore appears to be fire-related. The fracture terminated in a way that indicated that the process of flaking would continue with further fire modification. In this case, the parietal fragment exhibits fracture characteristics associated with bone that rapidly dried and, due to heat shrinkage, fractured. The senior author (SAS) ascertained that the damage was consistent with a postmortem fracture.

This examination illustrates how a case referred to the anthropologist as a second opinion, produced, after many hours of the examination, no results that contributed to the cause of death. How the victim died still remains a mystery. Despite the frustration of hours of examination for no immediately relevant results, this is a typical case for an anthropologist to confront. The analysis was not of a victim from 500 years ago, or even 50 years ago, but of a recent death, so repercussions of inaccuracy are severe. The evidence deserves an adequate investigation, examination, and interpretation. While the medical examiner and coroner must assess all situations of a recent death, anthropologists have no such obligation. If there is no accurate assessment to report, no appraisal should be reported. Since this is a suspected homicide, there is no place for conjecture or hypothetical scenarios. An anthropologist's interpretation must stand up to scrutiny and accuracy in court. In this case, a suspicious bone was shown to be a product of burning not a beating before the fire. These results, although mundane in appearance, are relevant and useful to the courts. This case, however, never went to trial due to an eventual guilty plea.

Conclusions

Thermal alteration of remains is a pervasive taphonomic process in forensic cases and may be associated with a cause of death, an immediate circumstance after death, multiple accidental scenarios, or a deliberate means to destroy evidence of a homicide victim's remains. Mayne Correia (1997) beautifully illustrated the 50-year debate and lack of consensus regarding the interpretation of burned skeletal remains. Interestingly enough, despite our observations and research, few issues have been concluded. This debate will continue.

Within complete cremations, various techniques can be used to estimate the biological profile (Grévin et al. 1998), interpret perimortem from postmortem burn injuries, and to distinguish human or nonhuman bone. According to Thompson (2004), the most influential variable with regard to heat-induced change is the removal of the organic components in bone and replacing/restricting them with inorganic material. This process affects the size, shape, and appearance of the bone as well as its histological components (Bradtmiller and Buikstra 1984; Thompson 2005). Most importantly, the rapid dehydration, shrinking, and warping of burnt bone creates dry bone fractures superficially consistent with but more extreme than subaerial weathering (Chapter 11) that may obscure prior antemortem injuries.

In evaluating a burned body or burned skeletal elements, a forensic anthropologist needs to use knowledge of the pugilistic postural changes, biomechanics of burned bone, and fracture morphology to ascertain a normal or abnormal burn pattern, perimortem and postmortem bone injuries, and the possible condition of the body (fleshed or wet/dry) prior to the burn event. However, a forensic anthropologist can only recognize perimortem burned trauma with insight into patterned thermal destruction to both soft tissue and bone. Additionally, knowledge regarding the biomechanics of bone is necessary to distinguish perimortem fractures (impact site, bending of bone, and energy) and postmortem heat-induced damage (splitting of bone, cracking within burned areas but lacking energy to travel further than the burned area). Lastly, for an accurate analysis one also needs to have knowledge of the context in which the material was recovered (Dirkmaat et al. 2012). Anthropological "perimortem" may not focus as much on the death event itself, as much as simply describing the condition of bone, but it is the accurate analysis of the condition of bone that allows anthropologists to be forensic anthropologists.

Acknowledgments

The authors thank Erin N. Chapman, Ranald Donaldson, and Marius Loots for their generous access to materials, illustrations, and photographs. The authors also thank Brianne Charles and Clarisa Sutherland for their kind editorial assistance. And finally, many thanks to Dr. Mark M. LeVaughn, Chief Medical Examiner, State of Mississippi, and T. H. Jones, Esq., Assistant District Attorney, Leflore County District, Mississippi.

Grant Funding No. 2008-DN-BX-K131. NIJ, U.S. Department of Justice. *Recovery and Interpretation of Burned Human Remains*. Coauthors D. Dirkmaat, S. Ousley, E. N. Chapman, and L. Cabo.

References

Adelson, L. (1955) Role of the pathologist in arson investigation. *The Journal of Criminal Law, Criminology, and Police Science* 45:760–768.

Baby, R. S. (1954) Hopewell cremation practices. *The Ohio Historical Society Papers in Archaeology* 1:1–7.

Baker, A. J. (2004) *A Taphonomic Analysis of Human Cremains from the Fox Hollow Farm Serial Homicide Site*. Unpublished M.A. Thesis, University of Indianapolis, Indianapolis, IN.

Bass, W. M. (1984) Is it possible to consume a body completely in a fire? In *Human Identification: Case Studies in Forensic Anthropology* eds. T. Rathbun and J. Buikstra, pp. 159–167. Charles C Thomas, Springfield, IL.

Bass, W. M. and R. L. Jantz (2004) Cremation weights in east Tennessee. *Journal of Forensic Sciences* 49:901–904.

Beach, J. J., N. V. Passalacqua, and E. N. Chapman (2008) Tooth color: Temperature versus duration of exposure. In *The Analysis of Burned Human Remains* eds. C. W. Schmidt and S. A. Symes, pp. 137–144. Academic Press, Amsterdam, the Netherlands.

Binford, L. R. (1963) An analysis of cremations from three Michigan sites. *Wisconsin Archaeologist* 44:98–110.

Binford, L. R. (1972) *An Archaeological Perspective*. Seminar Press, New York.

Bohnert, M., T. Rost, and S. Pollak (1998) The degree of destruction of human bodies in relation to the duration of the fire. *Forensic Science International* 95:11–21.

Bornman, E., R. van Eeden, and M. Wentzel (eds.) (1998) *Violence in South Africa: A Variety of Perspectives*. Human Sciences Research Council, Pretoria, South Africa.

Bosch, P., I. Alemán, C. Moreno-Castilla, and M. Botella (2011) Boiled versus unboiled: A study on Neolithic and contemporary human bones. *Journal of Archaeological Science* 38:2561–2570.

Bradtmiller, B. and J. E. Buikstra (1984) The effects of burning on human bone microstructure: A preliminary study. *Journal of Forensic Sciences* 29:535–540.

Brooks, T. R., T. E. Bodkin, G. E. Potts, and S. A. Smullen (2006) Elemental analysis of human cremains using ICP-OES to classify legitimate and contaminated cremains. *Journal of Forensic Sciences* 51:967–973.

Buikstra, J. and M. Swegle (1989) Bone modification due to burning: Experimental evidence. In *Bone Modification* eds. R. Bonnichsen and M. H. Sorg. Center for Study of the First Americans, Orono, ME.

Crow, D. M. and R. M. Glassman (1996) Standardization model for describing the extent of burn injury to human remains. *Journal of Forensic Sciences* 41:152–154.

Currey, J. D. (2002) *Bones: Structure and Mechanics* (2nd edn.). Princeton University Press, Princeton, NJ.

Curtin, A. J. (2008) Putting together the pieces: Reconstructing mortuary practices from commingled ossuary cremains. In *The Analysis of Burned Human Remains* eds. C. W. Schmidt and S. A. Symes, pp. 201–209. Academic Press, Amsterdam, the Netherlands.

Davies, D. J. and L. H. Mates (eds.) (2005) *The Encyclopedia of Cremation*. Ashgate, Aldershot, U.K.

de Gruchy, S. and T. L. Rogers (2002) Identifying chop marks on cremated bone: A preliminary study. *Journal of Forensic Sciences* 47:933–936.

Degusta, D. (2000) Fijian cannibalism and mortuary ritual: Bioarchaeological evidence from Vunda. *International Journal of Osteoarchaeology* 10:76–92.

DeHaan, J. D. (2008) Fire and bodies. In *The Analysis of Burned Human Remains* eds. C. W. Schmidt and S. A. Symes, pp. 1–13. Academic Press, Amsterdam, the Netherlands.

DeHaan, J. D. (2012) Sustained combustion of bodies: Some observations. *Journal of Forensic Sciences* 57:1578–1584.

Devlin, J. B. and N. P. Herrmann (2008) Bone color as an interpretive tool of the depositional history of archaeological cremains. In *The Analysis of Burned Human Remains* eds. C. W. Schmidt and S. A. Symes, pp. 109–128. Academic Press, Amsterdam, the Netherlands.

Dirkmaat, D. C., G. O. Olson, A. R. Klales, and S. Getz (2012) The role of forensic anthropology in the recovery and interpretation of the fatal-fire victim. In *A Companion to Forensic Anthropology* eds. D. C. Dirkmaat, pp. 113–135. Wiley-Blackwell, Chichester, U.K.

Dunlop, J. (1978) Traffic light discoloration in cremated bones. *Medicine, Science and the Law* 18:163–173.

Fairgrieve, S. I. (2008) *Forensic Cremation: Recovery and Analysis*. CRC Press, Boca Raton, FL.

Fenton, T. W., W. H. Birkby, and J. Cornelison (2003) A fast and safe non-bleaching method for forensic skeletal preparation. *Journal of Forensic Sciences* 48:274–276.

Flinn, L., C. G. Turner, and A. Brew (1976) Additional evidence for cannibalism in the Southwest: The case of LA 4528. *American Antiquity* 41:308–318.

Fojas, C, C. W. Rainwater, and S. A. Symes (2011) Using spatial analysis to recognize normal and abnormal patterns in burned bodies. *Proceedings of the American Academy of Forensic Sciences* 17:367–368.

Gilchrist, M. and H. Mytum (1986) Experimental archaeology and burnt animal bone from archaeological sites. *Circaea* 4:29–38.

Gonçalves, D., T. J. U. Thompson, and E. Cunha (2011) Implication of heat-induced changes in bone on the interpretation of funerary behavior and practice. *Journal of Archaeological Science* 38:1308–1313.

Graver, S., K. D. Sobolik, and J. Whittaker (2002) Cannibalism or violent death alone? Human remains at a small Anasazi site. In *Advances in Forensic Taphonomy: Method, Theory, and Archaeological Perspectives* eds. W. D. Haglund and M. H. Sorg, pp. 309–320. CRC Press, Boca Raton, FL.

Grévin, G., P. Bailet, G. Quatrehomme, and A. Ollier (1998) Anatomical reconstruction of fragments of burned human bones: A necessary means for forensic identification. *Forensic Science International* 96:129–134.

Grupe, G. and S. Hummel (1991) Trace element studies on experimentally cremated bone. I. Alteration of the chemical composition at high temperatures. *Journal of Archaeological Science* 18:177–186.

Haglund, W. D. and M. H. Sorg (eds.) (1997) *Forensic Taphonomy: The Postmortem Fate of Human Remains*. CRC Press, Boca Raton, FL.

Haglund, W. D. and M. H. Sorg (eds.) (2002) *Advances in Forensic Taphonomy: Method, Theory, and Archaeological Perspectives*. CRC Press, Boca Raton, FL.

Heglar, R. (1984) Burned remains. In *Human Identification: Case Studies in Forensic Anthropology* eds. T. Rathbun and J. E. Buikstra, pp. 148–158. Charles C Thomas, Springfield, IL.

Herrmann, N. P. and J. L. Bennett (1999) The differentiation of traumatic and heat-related fractures in burned bone. *Journal of Forensic Sciences* 44:461–469.

Hiller, J. T., J. U. Thompson, M. P. Evison, A. T. Chamberlain, and T. J. Weiss (2003) Bone mineral change during experimental heating: An X-ray scattering investigation. *Biomaterials* 24:5091–5097.

Hillier, M. L. and L. S. Bell (2007) Differentiating human bone from animal bone: A review of histological methods. *Journal of Forensic Sciences* 52:249–263.

Hughes, C. E. and C. A. White (2009) Crack propagation in teeth: A comparison of perimortem and postmortem behavior of dental materials and cracks. *Journal of Forensic Sciences* 54:263–266.

Hurlbut, S. A. (2000) The taphonomy of cannibalism: A review of anthropogenic bone modification in the American Southwest. *International Journal of Osteoarchaeology* 10:4–26.

Icove, D. J. and J. D. DeHaan (2003) *Forensic Fire Scene Reconstruction*. Prentice Hall, New York.

Kennedy, K. A. R. (1996) The wrong urn: Commingling of cremains in mortuary practices. *Journal of Forensic Sciences* 41:689–692.

Keough, N., K. Colman, E. N. L'Abbé, S. A. Symes, and L. Cabo (2012) Distinguishing features of thermal destruction on fleshed, wet and dry remains. *Proceedings of the American Academy of Forensic Sciences* 18:386.

Koon, H. E. C., T. P. O'Connor, and M. J. Collins (2010) Sorting the butchered from the boiled. *Journal of Archaeological Science* 37:62–69.

Krogman, W. M. (1943a) Role of the physical anthropologist in the identification of human skeletal remains, Part I. *FBI Law Enforcement Bulletin* 12(4):17–40.

Krogman, W. M. (1943b) Role of the physical anthropologist in the identification of human skeletal remains, Part II. *FBI Law Enforcement Bulletin* 12(5):12–28.

Lupo, K. D. and D. N. Schmitt (1997) Experiments in bone boiling: Nutritional returns and archaeological reflections. *Anthropozoologica* 25–26:137–144.

Marín Arroyo, A. B., M. D. Landete Ruiz, G. Vidal Bernabeu, R. Seva Román, M. R. González Morales, and L. G. Straus (2008) Archaeological implications of human-derived manganese coatings: A study of blackened bones in El Mirón Cave, Cantabrian Spain. *Journal of Archaeological Science* 35:801–813.

Mayne Correia, P. M. (1997) Fire modification of bone: A review of the literature. In *Forensic Taphonomy: The Postmortem Fate of Human Remains* eds. W. D. Haglund and M. H. Sorg, pp. 275–293. CRC Press, Boca Raton, FL.

Mayne Correia, P. M. and O. Beattie (2002) A critical look at methods for recovering, evaluating, and interpreting cremated human remains. In *Advances in Forensic Taphonomy: Method, Theory, and Archaeological Perspectives* eds. W. D. Haglund and M. H. Sorg, pp. 435–450. CRC Press, Boca Raton, FL.

Mincer, H. H., H. E. Berryman, G. A. Murray, and R. L. Dickens (1990) Methods for physical stabilization of ashed teeth in incinerated remains. *Journal of Forensic Sciences* 35:971–974.

Murray, K. A. and J. C. Rose (1993) The analysis of cremains: A case study involving the inappropriate disposal of mortuary remains. *Journal of Forensic Sciences* 38:98–103.

Nawrocki, S. P. (2009) Forensic taphonomy. In *Handbook of Forensic Anthropology and Archaeology* eds. S. Blau and D. H. Ubelaker, pp. 284–294. Left Coast Press, Walnut Creek, CA.

Owsley, D. W. (1993) Identification of the fragmentary, burned remains of two U.S. journalists seven years after their disappearance in Guatemala. *Journal of Forensic Sciences* 38:1372–1382.

Owsley, D. W., R. W. Mann, R. E. Chapman, E. Moore, and W. A. Cox (1993) Positive identification in a case of intentional extreme fragmentation. *Journal of Forensic Sciences* 38:985–996.

Pauw, J. (1997) *Into the Heart of Darkness: Confessions of Apartheid's Assassins*. Johnathan Ball, Johannesburg, South Africa.

Pope, E. J. (2007) *The Effects of Fire on Human Remains: Characteristics of Taphonomy and Trauma*. Unpublished Ph.D. Dissertation, University of Arkansas, Fayetteville, AR.

Pope, E. J. and O. C. Smith (2004) Identification of traumatic injury in burned cranial bone: An experimental approach. *Journal of Forensic Sciences* 49:431–440.

Reilly, D. T. and A. H. Burstein (1974) The mechanical properties of cortical bone. *Journal of Bone and Joint Surgery* 56A:1001–1022.

Rennick, S. L., T. W. Fenton, and D. R. Foran (2005) The effects of skeletal preparation techniques on DNA from human and non-human bone. *Journal of Forensic Sciences* 50:1016–1019.

Roberts, S. J., C. I. Smith, A. Millard, and M. J. Collins (2002) The taphonomy of cooked bone: Characterizing boiling and its physico-chemical effects. *Archaeometry* 44:485–494.

Rosen, F. (2004) *Cremation in America*. Prometheus Books, Amherst, NY.

Schmidt, C. W. (2008) The recovery and study of burned human teeth. In *The Analysis of Burned Human Remains* eds. C. W. Schmidt and S. A. Symes, pp. 55–74. Academic Press, Amsterdam, the Netherlands.

Schultz, J. J., M. W. Warren, and J. S. Krigbaum (2008) Analysis of human cremains: Gross and chemical methods. In *The Analysis of Burned Human Remains* eds. C. W. Schmidt and S. A. Symes, pp. 75–94. Academic Press, Amsterdam, the Netherlands.

Schwark T., A. Heinrich, A. Preuße-Prange and N. von Wurmb-Schwark (2011) Reliable genetic identification of burnt human remains. *Forensic Science International: Genetics* 5:393–399.

Shahack-Gross, R. O. Bar-Yosef, and S. Weiner (1997) Black-colored bones in Hayonim Cave, Israel: Differentiating between burning and oxide staining. *Journal of Archaeological Science* 24:439–446.

Shipman, P., G. Foster, and M. Schoeninger (1984) Burnt bones and teeth: An experimental study of color, morphology, crystal structure and shrinkage. *Journal of Archaeological Science* 11:307–325.

Spitz, W. U. (1993) Thermal injuries. In *Spitz and Fisher's Medicolegal Investigation of Death: Guidelines for the Application of Pathology to Crime Investigation* (3rd edn.) ed. W. U. Spitz, pp. 413–443. Charles C Thomas, Springfield, IL.

Stiner, M. C., S. L. Kuhn, and O. Bar-Yosef (1995) Differential burning, recrystallization, and fragmentation of archaeological bone. *Journal of Archaeological Science* 22:223–237.

Symes, S. A., A. M. Kroman, C. W. Rainwater, and A. L. Piper (2005) Bone biomechanical considerations in perimortem vs. postmortem thermal bone fractures: Fracture analyses on victims of suspicious fire scenes. Poster presented at the *104th Annual Meeting of the American Association of Physical Anthropology*, 8th April 2005, Milwaukee, WI.

Symes S. A., E. N. L'Abbé, E. N. Chapman, I. Wolff, and D. C. Dirkmaat (2012) Interpreting traumatic injury from bone in medico-legal investigations. In *Companion to Forensic Anthropology* ed. D. C. Dirkmaat, pp. 340–389. Wiley-Blackwell, London, U.K.

Symes, S. A., E. J. Pope, O. C. Smith, C. D. Gardner, and L. A. Zephro (2001) Burning observations III: Analysis of fracture patterns in burned human remains. *Proceedings of the American Academy of Forensic Sciences* 7:278.

Symes, S. A., C. W. Rainwater, E. N. Chapman, D. R. Gipson, and A. L. Piper (2008) Patterned thermal destruction of human remains in a forensic setting. In *The Analysis of Burned Human Remains* eds. C. W. Schmidt and S. A. Symes, pp. 15–54. Academic Press, Amsterdam, the Netherlands.

Symes, S. A., O. C. Smith, H. Berryman, and E. J. Pope (1999) Patterned thermal destruction of human remains. Paper presented to the *30th Anniversary of the T. D. Stewart Personal Identification in Mass Disasters*, Central Identification Laboratory, Honolulu, Hawaii.

Thompson, T. J. U. (2004) Recent advances in the study of burned bone and their implications for forensic anthropology. *Forensic Science International* 146:203–205.

Thompson, T. J. U. (2005) Heat-induced dimensional changes in bone and their consequences for forensic anthropology. *Journal of Forensic Sciences* 50:1008–1015.

Thurman, M. and L. J. Willmore (1980–1981) A replicative cremation experiment. *North American Archaeologist* 2:275–283.

Trotter, M. and R. R. Peterson (1955) Ash weight of human skeletons in per cent of their dry, fat-free weight. *The Anatomical Record* 123:341–358.

Trujillo-Mederos, A., I. Alemán, M. Botella, and P. Bosch (2012) Changes in human bones boiled in seawater. *Journal of Archaeological Science* 39:1072–1079.

Turner, C. G. and J. A. Turner (1992) The first claim for cannibalism in the Southwest: Walter Hough's 1901 discovery at Canyon Butte Ruin 3, Northeastern Arizona. *American Antiquity* 57:661–682.

Turner, C. G. and J. A. Turner (1999) *Man Corn: Cannibalism and Violence in the Prehistoric American Southwest*. University of Utah Press, Salt Lake City, UT.

Ubelaker, D. H. (2009) The forensic evaluation of burned skeletal remains: A synthesis. *Forensic Science International* 183:1–5.

Ubelaker, D. H. and C. H. Jacobs (1995) Identification of orthopedic device manufacturer. *Journal of Forensic Sciences* 40:168–170.

Ubelaker, D. H., D. W. Owsley, M. M. Houck, E. Craig, W. Grant, T. Woltanski, R. Fram, K. Sandness, and N. Peerwani (1995) The role of forensic anthropology in the recovery and analysis of Branch Davidian compound victims: Recovery procedures and characteristics of the victims. *Journal of Forensic Sciences* 40:335–340.

U.S. Cremation Equipment (2012) Animal cremation equipment. Electronic document, http://uscremationequipment.com//index8f4d.html?option=com_content&view=article&id=47&Itemid=53 (accessed December 27, 2012).

Walker, P. L. and K. P. Miller (2005) Time, temperature, and oxygen availability: An experimental study of the effects of environmental conditions on the color and organic content of cremated bone. Poster presented at the *104th Annual Meeting of the American Association of Physical Anthropologists*, 8th April 2005, Milwaukee, WI.

Walker, P. L., K. W. P. Miller, and R. Richman (2008) Time, temperature, and oxygen availability: An experimental study of the effects of environmental conditions on the color and organic content of cremated bone. In *The Analysis of Burned Human Remains* eds. C. W. Schmidt and S. A. Symes, pp. 129–135. Academic Press, Amsterdam, the Netherlands.

Warren, M. W. and W. R. Maples (1997) The anthropometry of contemporary commercial cremation. *Journal of Forensic Sciences* 42:417–423.

Warren, M. W. and J. J. Schultz (2002) Post-cremation taphonomy and artifact preservation. *Journal of Forensic Sciences* 47:656–659.

White, T. D. (1992) *Prehistoric Cannibalism at Mancos 5Mtumr-2346*. Princeton University Press, Princeton, NJ.

Whyte, T. R. (2001) Distinguishing remains of human cremations from burned animal bones. *Journal of Field Archaeology* 28:437–448.

DNA Survivability in Skeletal Remains

15

KRISTA E. LATHAM
MEGAN E. MADONNA

Contents

Oh! Mr. DNA! Where did you come from?

—**John Hammond, *Jurassic Park***

Introduction

The analysis of DNA from skeletal remains has numerous applications in archeological and forensic contexts. In archeological settings, bones and teeth represent the most numerous human biological materials to survive from the past, and morphological or genetic analyses of these hard tissues can provide invaluable insight into deceased individuals and past populations. In a forensic context, identification may be difficult once all soft tissues have decomposed beyond recognition, and the analysis of skeletal remains is often the only means to gather forensically significant information long after the death of the individual.

Bones encountered by the analyst will vary in their degree of degradation, as will the DNA contained within the hard tissues. The low copy numbers of template DNA and the DNA modifications accrued during the decomposition process can potentially pose complications for subsequent genetic analyses. However, progress has been made in the specific analytical techniques employed when analyzing DNA isolated from skeletal remains when more optimal DNA samples are not available for investigation. In addition, certain genetic loci have been shown to be more useful in terms of analysis when working with skeletal DNA. It is important not only to recognize such possible difficulties, but also to have a basic understanding of what is happening to the DNA contained within the human body after cell death.

DNA and Human Identification

Genetic analysis has established itself as a fundamental tool in the positive identification of human skeletal remains. The various genetic techniques employed in positive identification involve the comparison of a DNA profile obtained from unidentified remains to a DNA profile known to have originated from the missing person or close relative. Current techniques rely upon the ability to make many copies of the regions of the genome analyzed for identification purposes using a process called *polymerase chain reaction* (PCR). The PCR process is essentially a "molecular copy machine" that enables analysts to produce sufficient copies of the DNA region of interest to be detected and analyzed.

PCR employs enzymes (*DNA polymerases*) that selectively amplify a DNA segment delineated by synthetically produced single-stranded DNA primers (*synthetic oligonucleotide primers*). The target DNA is heated to denature the double-stranded molecule into single strands and then cooled to allow the single-stranded primers to hybridize to complementary regions in the genome defining the region of interest. The enzymes then construct complimentary copies of the target DNA by incorporating free nucleotides (*deoxynucleotide triphosphates*) into a newly constructed DNA molecule. This process is repeated until millions of copies (*amplicons*) of the original target DNA are produced.

An advantage of PCR-based genetic analysis is that it is often sensitive enough to replicate the suboptimal DNA samples recovered from skeletonized remains in order to produce a genetic profile. Current technologies allow for the generation of DNA profiles from samples containing 100 picograms (pg) or less of template DNA. This process is referred to as *low copy number* (LCN) DNA testing. However, research has shown that interpretations from LCN samples should be approached with caution, because the increased sensitivity used for the generation of LCN profiles also allows for the detection of low levels of contaminant DNA (Alonso et al. 2004; Gill et al. 2000).

While the PCR process is essential for genetic analyses, it also has its limitations. PCR requires that the DNA be sufficiently preserved to serve as a template for the DNA polymerases. If the enzymes encounter lesions or other modifications of the template DNA, they are unable to continue copying the DNA molecule. Unlike the process of DNA replication in the human body, PCR does not have proofreading abilities, so analysts must be cautious of the possibility of misincorporated bases. This is especially problematic if the template DNA is damaged or degraded. Additionally, the DNA sample must be free of co-purified substances that act as inhibitors to the PCR process (Geigl 2002; Hagelberg et al. 1991; Kalmár et al. 2000; Rogan and Salvo 1990).

The human genome consists of *nuclear DNA* (nucDNA) and *mitochondrial DNA* (mtDNA). The human nuclear genome is most often employed in forensic investigations and is comprised of approximately six billion base pairs (bp) per diploid cell. Forensic genetic analyses rely on regions of the genome that are highly polymorphic within the population at large. Employing loci that exhibit a wide range of variability across the human population increases the probability that the genetic profiles generated from two unrelated individuals will be different and therefore individualizing. For identification purposes, this allows for two samples to be compared and either exclusions be made if the DNA profiles do not match or statistical probabilities of a match be calculated if the two DNA profiles are consistent.

Nuclear DNA

Nuclear DNA is wrapped around proteins to form chromatin, which is packaged into chromosome structures contained within the cell nucleus. The 46 human chromosomes are arranged into 22 homologous pairs (*autosomal chromosomes*) and one pair of sex chromosomes, from which individuals inherit one copy of one half of the pair from their mother and one copy of one half of the pair from their father, creating a biparental inheritance pattern. Thus, nucDNA is a representation of all an individual's ancestors' DNA. Genetic recombination between the homologous chromosomes creates a situation where the DNA is continually mixed and shuffled from generation to generation, and this inheritance pattern produces a unique genetic profile for each individual (except, in most cases, identical twins).

The loci most commonly utilized in forensic genetic analyses are *nuclear short tandem repeats* (STRs), which are DNA sequences comprised of tandem repeats with a core repeating unit of two to six nucleotides. STRs are noncoding regions of the genome, meaning they do not code for proteins that contribute to the body's phenotype. Of these, the tetranucleotide repeats, which contain a core repeating unit four nucleotides in length, are most often employed in forensic investigations. The number of tandem repeats varies per individual, and therefore STRs have a high degree of discrimination. Because it is a PCR-based technique and targets small DNA markers ranging in size from approximately 100 to 400 base pairs, there is a greater likelihood of producing a genetic profile from degraded DNA samples when the PCR target is small due to the fact that the longer stretches of the genome are broken apart during the degradation process.

The forensic community in the United States relies upon a standardized set of 13 STR loci for forensic genetic analyses, which are available in commercial multiplex kits. The standardization of this process allows a direct comparison of genetic profile results between various U.S. laboratories and law enforcement agencies (Anđelinović et al. 2005;

Butler 2007; Foran 2006a; Schneider 2007). However, there are currently no international standards for genetic investigations. The development of universal standards could benefit both individual investigations and the identification of mass disaster victims.

Mitochondrial DNA

Mitochondrial DNA is located outside the cell nucleus within cytoplasmic organelles called mitochondria. Each mitochondrion may contain multiple identical copies of the mitochondrial genome (an average 2.6 mtDNA molecules per mammalian cell), and cells may contain multiple mitochondria (variation in values between cell types and also temporally within a single cell based on energy requirements), creating a situation where the mtDNA exists in hundreds to thousands of copies within each cell (Robin and Wong 1988). Therefore, there is a higher probability of obtaining analyzable mtDNA than nucDNA from degraded biological samples. Due to its unique inheritance pattern in comparison to the autosomal chromosomes, mtDNA is extensively employed in population-level analyses investigating anthropological questions such as population movement and population relationships. The mitochondrial genome displays uniparental inheritance, follows the maternal lineage, and does not participate in the process of genetic recombination (shuffling) as seen in the autosomal chromosomes. In other words, an individual's mtDNA will be the same as all of his or her consanguineous maternal relatives. In addition, the entire sequence (16,569 base pairs) of the mitochondrial genome is well-understood and has been extensively studied for population variability. Population-level studies have revealed that due to its high mutation rate, the mtDNA sequence is often geographically specific (Anderson et al. 1981; Cavalli-Sforza 1998; Giles et al. 1980; Kaestle and Horsburgh 2002; Mulligan 2006; von Haeseler et al. 1995).

Mitochondrial DNA sequence analysis is also important in forensic investigations when nuclear analysis is not possible or to supplement profiles generated from regions of the nuclear genome (Alaeddini et al. 2010; Butler and Levin 1998; Coble et al. 2009; Leney 2006). Similar to forensic nucDNA analyses, investigations of the mtDNA for forensic applications also focuses on noncoding regions because areas of the genome that do not code for proteins are more polymorphic among individuals. While forensic nucDNA analysis involves a comparison of different-sized STR amplicons (length polymorphisms), mtDNA analysis is more time-consuming, as it involves a direct sequence comparison of portions of the mitochondrial genome (sequence polymorphisms). Specifically, a segment of the mitochondrial genome is PCR-amplified, sequenced, and compared to the corresponding sequence of a missing person or a (usually) close maternal relative. Since the mitochondrial genome is shared by all relatives within a consanguineous maternal lineage, it can only provide a circumstantial identification. In other words, it is not individualizing to the point that it can provide a positive identification, as it cannot distinguish between the mitochondrial genome of mothers and their offspring or maternal aunts and maternal grandmothers (Alaeddini et al. 2010; Butler and Levin 1998; Harvey and King 2002). In addition, other members of the population at large may share a common mtDNA sequence due to very ancient common ancestry. For example, around 50% of individuals of Western European descent share a common mtDNA sequence called haplogroup H. This same sequence is found in frequencies of 25%–30% in the Near East and up to 61% in some North African populations (Ottoni et al. 2010; Richards et al. 2002).

Y-Chromosome DNA

The Y-chromosome is part of the nuclear genome, yet its uniparental inheritance pattern enables it to be employed in population analyses in ways similar to mtDNA. The Y-chromosome is the smallest human chromosome, and 95% of its structure consists of a nonrecombining sequence block referred to as the NRY (*nonrecombining portion of the Y-chromosome*) (Jobling and Tyler-Smith 2003). Since the NRY is passed relatively unchanged through the paternal lineage, it can be used to address questions regarding population variability and population movement (Hammer et al. 2001; Scheinfeldt et al. 2006; Underhill et al. 2000).

While not as frequently utilized as traditional nucDNA STR analyses in forensic situations, the Y-chromosome could be useful in male-specific identifications. Y-chromosome specific STRs are the most frequently used markers for identification purposes involving Y-chromosome DNA (Jobling et al. 1997; von Wurmb-Schwark et al. 2003). However, the same NRY sequence is shared by all relatives within a consanguineous paternal lineage and can only provide a circumstantial identification.

Molecular Diagenesis

Molecular diagenesis refers to changes that accumulate in a molecule, like DNA, as the result of degradation, modification, and interaction with the exogenous environment. It is intimately linked to the chemical processes involved in cell death and postmortem decomposition. Cell death may proceed via *apoptosis, necrobiosis*, or *autolysis* depending on various intrinsic and extrinsic signals (see Chapter 3, this volume). Apoptosis is an enzymatically dependent programmed cell death that removes damaged or diseased cells from the body. Necrobiosis is natural cell death that provides a mechanism for the replacement of cells that are no longer functioning properly. Apoptosis and necrobiosis do not play a major factor in human decomposition because these processes refer to cell death in the living body. Autolysis is cell death due to the rupture of the cellular membranes and a release of enzymes liberated from membrane-bound cellular organelles called lysosomes. This process occurs in response to the lack of oxygen needed to generate cellular energy (ATP) as the cell is no longer in contact with circulating blood. ATP is essential in the operation of membrane pumps, which maintain concentration gradients within the cell, and the synthesis of intercellular molecules. In the absence of oxygen, the cell will switch to anaerobic respiration to produce ATP, which ultimately lowers the pH of the cell. These cellular changes result in the rupture of cellular membranes and the release of enzymes that will degrade the cellular structures including the DNA (Alaeddini et al. 2010; Gill-King 1997).

The DNA contained within a cell begins to degrade immediately following cell death, as it is no longer protected by the repair mechanisms that counteract in vivo DNA damage. DNA degradation results from strand breakage, chemical modifications, and microbial attack. These degradative processes reduce the yield of high molecular mass DNA molecules and increase the chance of subsequent PCR failure (Alaeddini et al. 2010; Bär et al. 1988; Binladen et al. 2006; Eglinton et al. 1991; Handt et al. 1994; Höss et al. 1996; Richter et al. 1988; Rogan and Salvo 1990). Much of what is known about DNA degradation has been investigated in vitro, and it is assumed that the chemical processes occur the same way in cells that are not being studied in controlled laboratory settings (Lindahl 1993; Lindahl and Andersson 1972; Lindahl and Nyberg 1972, 1974). However, a thorough understanding of molecular diagenesis remains daunting due to the high number of variables influencing postmortem DNA degradation in tissues.

A major complicating factor in retrieving analyzable DNA from older tissues is the reduced size of template molecules. Strand breakage reduces the DNA molecules to, on average, under 200 base pairs in length in older soft tissues and skeletal remains (Foran 2006a; Höss et al. 1996). A large portion of strand breakage is caused by autolytic processes that occur soon after cell death as the molecules are digested by the enzymes liberated from lysosomes. As the nuclear membrane degrades, the nucDNA located within becomes vulnerable to attack from these enzymes. The DNA is digested by *nucleases*, a category of enzymes capable of cleaving the phosphodiester bonds holding adjoining nucleotides together along the DNA molecule. *Endonucleases* act to cleave the DNA molecules into smaller pieces, while *exonucleases* detach nucleotides from the terminal ends of the DNA molecule and gradually reduce it into smaller pieces (Bär et al. 1988; Child 1995; Lynnerup 2007; Rogan and Salvo 1990; Thomas and Pääbo 1993). This process usually begins with the degradation of easily accessible DNA into high molecular weight fragments. As the histone proteins that participate in DNA folding are digested by other liberated enzymes called proteases, the DNA is vulnerable to random fragmentation by endonucleases (Alaeddini et al. 2010).

In addition to endogenous enzymes, microbes contribute significantly to decomposition (Lynnerup 2007). Autolysis is followed by putrefaction, where anaerobic bacteria decompose the macromolecules of the body, such as the lipids, carbohydrates, proteins, and nucleic acids. The ruptured cells release nutrient-rich fluids that further encourage microbial growth. The putrefaction phase is followed by a longer phase of aerobic and anaerobic microbial decomposition of organic material. The complex process of decomposition by microbes occurs as the decomposers release enzymes that degrade macromolecules like DNA into smaller pieces (Alaeddini et al. 2010; Bär et al. 1988; Rogan and Salvo 1990). For a more detailed discussion of microbial alteration of bone, refer to Chapter 2, this volume.

Chemical modifications that occur over long periods can be equally problematic for subsequent DNA analysis, and those molecules that survive the initial autolytic actions are subject to damage via *hydrolysis* and *oxidation*. Hydrolysis is the addition of water to a chemical bond, and results in the cleavage of the N-glycosyl bond holding the nitrogenous base to the deoxyribose sugar in the DNA nucleotide and breakage of the phosphodiester bonds in the DNA backbone. Oxidative damage results in modified bases that block the extension of the DNA polymerase during the PCR process or result in loss of ability to incorporate the appropriate complimentary base during PCR replication, as well as cleavage of the sugar and phosphate backbone (Eglinton et al. 1991; Höss et al. 1996; Lindahl 1993). Other chemical reactions that may complicate later analysis include DNA concatemerization, whereby DNA molecules form cross-links with proteins or other DNA molecules (Alaeddini et al. 2010).

In a living cell, each DNA nucleotide forms a chemical bond with eight to ten water molecules, making it highly reactive and the target for multiple chemical reactions (Alaeddini et al. 2010). This affinity of DNA for water molecules makes it vulnerable to hydrolysis. In the living cell, the DNA is maintained by continuous DNA repair. In dead tissues, the DNA will continue to attract water molecules, even in dry microenvironments, and is thus a target for hydrolytic damage. Hydrolytic damage results in *deamination* (loss of an amine group) of bases, as well as *depurination* (loss of adenine and guanine) and *depyrimidination* (loss of thymine and cytosine). Such modifications will halt or inhibit the PCR process. In addition, apurinic sites can further contribute to strand breakage by leading to the cleavage of the phosphodiester bonds along the backbone of the DNA molecule. Therefore, over long periods depurination will lead to short DNA fragments (Bada et al. 1999; Burger et al. 1999; Handt et al. 1994; Lindahl 1993).

The DNA located within a human cell is continually exposed to oxygen and therefore susceptible to oxidative stress. However, there are elaborate repair mechanisms that function to protect the DNA from mutagenesis during the lifetime of the cell that are not present after the death of the cell. In addition to intracellular oxygen radicals produced by the mitochondria, oxygen radicals are ubiquitous in the environment and can extensively damage DNA molecules. Oxidative damage results in modified bases and the misincorporation of bases during replication events, such as during PCR amplification. Oxidation acts to remove the 3′ hydroxyl group that serves as a primer for the DNA polymerase enzyme that participates in chain elongation. In addition, oxidation can result in base lesions whereby the nucleotides lose their ring structure, and cause helical distortion that can interfere with subsequent genetic analyses (Lindahl 1993; Richter et al. 1988; Rogan and Salvo 1990).

Skeletal DNA

The preservation of the skeleton and skeletal DNA is variable from case to case, and significant variability is even witnessed among remains from a single archeological site (Bell et al. 1996; Hagelberg et al. 1991; Haynes et al. 2002; Hedges 2002; Hedges and Millard 1995; Parsons and Weedn 1997; Ricaut et al. 2005). The extent of skeletal DNA degradation is, in part, related to gross bone degradation. Bone is a complex tissue consisting of inorganic calcium phosphate (mostly hydroxyapatite) and organic collagen protein components. As the bone degrades, the ratio of the inorganic to organic portions changes while the bone exchanges chemical constituents with the depositional environment. The rate of *bone diagenesis*, the complex process of degradation and modification to the chemical and/or structural properties of bone, is based on the leaching of the various inorganic and organic components of the osseous tissue, whose rate of loss is heavily dependent upon depositional environment and intrinsic bone factors. Studies suggest that as the inorganic portion of bone degrades so does the skeletal DNA (Götherström et al. 2002; Vass 2001; Von Endt and Ortner 1984; White and Hannus 1983).

Analyzable DNA often persists within hard tissues for much longer periods than in soft tissues, as conditions within the bone may provide some protection against DNA degradation (Lassen et al. 1994). Bone has a low water and degradative enzyme content, which may shield against some of the hydrolytic damage and other chemical damage experienced by DNA contained within soft tissues. Bone also acts as a physical barrier that can protect the DNA from ultraviolet (UV) light, which is a major cause of the dimerization of bases and interstrand/intrastrand cross-links, and can prevent some larger enzymes or microbes from gaining access to the molecular material (Child 1995; Parsons and Weedn 1997; Rogan and Salvo 1990). Since UV light damages DNA molecules through thymine–thymine dimerization, it is often used as a sterilizing agent in laboratory settings (Aslanzadeh 2004).

Skeletal DNA becomes bound to the hydroxyapatite portion of bone as the negatively charged phosphate groups in the DNA molecules become attracted to the positively charged calcium ions of the hydroxyapatite (Götherström et al. 2002). This process stabilizes the DNA and provides some protection against the most common chemical and environmental factors acting to degrade the DNA molecules. For example, adsorption of the DNA molecules to the hydroxyapatite portion of bone results in a twofold reduction in depurination rates. Depurination is a major factor contributing to DNA degradation and reduced template size. The relationship between the skeletal DNA and hydroxyapatite may be one factor contributing to the preservation of DNA in skeletal tissues for long periods. In addition to the structural stability provided by adsorption of the DNA to the hydroxyapatite, this process might render the DNA physically inaccessible to larger enzymes that act to degrade the DNA molecules (Geigl 2002; Hedges and Millard 1995; Lindahl 1993).

Molecular Taphonomy

Molecular taphonomy is the study of those factors that influence molecular diagenesis and explores the impact of the various intrinsic and extrinsic forces influencing molecular integrity. Different molecules will degrade at different rates and are dependent upon the particular local environment, making a full understanding of the molecular diagenesis of DNA over long periods difficult due to the complexity and number of variables involved. While several variables have been identified as instrumental in the preservation or degradation of biological molecules, these variables do not work in isolation but rather within a complex web of interactions (discussed subsequently). In addition, as mentioned previously, DNA degradation is influenced by the rate and level of bone degradation, since the skeletal DNA binds to the hydroxyapatite. As the inorganic component of the bone degrades, the DNA is released from the hydroxyapatite and is no longer stabilized or protected.

Postmortem Interval (PMI)

Multiple studies have demonstrated that depositional environment is a more important factor in DNA preservation than the absolute age of the DNA sample (Dobberstein et al. 2008; Hagelberg and Clegg 1991; Haynes et al. 2002; Hochmeister et al. 1991; Latham 2003; Leney 2006; Meyer et al. 2000). A study by Perry et al. (1988) attempted to use the degradation rate of DNA isolated from human ribs obtained at autopsy to estimate the PMI. They incubated the bones at either high or low humidity at room temperature and took samples for DNA analysis at selected time intervals. They found variation in the amount of degradation for samples that were collected at the same time interval, suggesting that DNA does not follow a specific degradation trajectory that can be used to predict time since death. They did find, however, that humidity had a more profound impact on DNA degradation, as the samples incubated at low humidity were much less degraded than those incubated at high humidity.

Hagelberg et al. (1991) investigated the relationship between gross bone preservation, histological preservation, and DNA recovery in human bone and found that their thirteenth-century bone samples had consistently produced better PCR amplification results than their seventeenth-century bone samples. They analyzed skeletal DNA isolated from human femora and found gross, microscopic, and molecular preservation to be better in the older skeletal remains. The authors suggested that this may be due to soil geochemistry or burial depth, supporting the observation that DNA preservation is not directly related to the time since death of the individual.

Depositional Environment

Temperature

Temperature influences both gross bone and DNA preservation. This relationship is due to the fact that degradation at both the macroscopic and microscopic levels is the result of a complicated series of chemical reactions and all chemical reactions are greatly influenced by temperature. Initial decomposition processes like autolysis and putrefaction display a maximum chemical activity at 34°C–40°C, and there is a two- to threefold decrease in the reaction rate for simple chemical processes for each 10°C decrease in temperature (Bär et al. 1988; Lindahl 1993). For example, depurination is a major contributor to DNA degradation, and the activation energy for this chemical reaction is highly temperature-dependent (Götherström et al. 2002). Thus, the chemistry of biological degradation is slowed at lower temperatures.

Temperature is one of the most important factors governing microbial growth and therefore one of the most important factors governing the rate and extent of microbial attack on biological material. In general, microbial activity associated with decomposition is greater at warmer temperatures. Microorganisms have a profound impact on gross bone diagenesis by leading to collagen loss and increased bone porosity. The microbes that participate in the decomposition of bone produce enzymes called collagenases that allow them to digest mineralized collagen. Since the hydroxyapatite crystals of bone are surrounded by collagen, the loss of collagen weakens the mineral component of bone and makes it more vulnerable to degradation. Some decomposers have the ability to participate in a specialized form of degradation called *microscopic focal destructions* (MFD). MFDs are small tunnels in the bone mediated by microbial dissolution of the mineral component of bone (Child 1995; Collins et al. 2002; Hedges 2002; and Chapter 2, this volume). On the molecular scale, invading decomposers release enzymes that degrade molecules like DNA into smaller pieces and therefore reduce overall DNA quantity and quality. Thus, decomposer activity as well as chemical degradation are slowed at cooler temperatures. This relationship is supported by studies that have found that DNA retrieved from bones deposited in cooler environments are better preserved than DNA retrieved from bones deposited in warmer environments (Burger et al. 1999; Höss et al. 1996; Smith et al. 2003).

However, there are also circumstances where mild heating has been found to be beneficial to obtaining high quantities of skeletal DNA. For example, mild heating may accelerate the loss of in situ water from bone and reduce hydrolytic damage (Geigl 2002). In addition, bones subjected to warm temperatures are more friable and may more easily release the DNA bound to their mineral phase. Reidy et al. (2009) compared ease of DNA isolation from an 800-year-old skeleton recovered from a subterranean cave in southern Mongolia and a recently deceased individual from the United States. She encountered difficulty in extracting skeletal DNA from the modern individual and relative ease in isolating DNA from the 800-year-old skeleton. This inspired her to bake a bone sample from the modern individual to mimic the mummification process and environmental conditions of the Mongolian cave. After the bone baking process (100.0°C for 72 h), she was able to isolate analyzable DNA from the modern sample and suggested that bones exposed to heat and extreme drying more readily release the DNA bound to the hydroxyapatite, making the probability of subsequent genetic analysis more likely.

Geochemistry

The geochemistry of the depositional environment is an important extrinsic factor impacting biological diagenesis. The presence of groundwater in soil has a profound influence on bone diagenesis that can also affect DNA preservation. It participates in many of the chemical reactions that occur during decomposition, such as diffusion and hydrolysis (Eglinton et al. 1991). Groundwater enters and percolates through bone, depending upon the available free energy required to move the water from the soil into the bone matrix. The free energy is determined mostly by the size of the pores in the bone; therefore, the pore structure for any given bone will dictate how it interacts with groundwater. As bone dissolution progresses, the pores become larger and act as channels for hydraulic flow, leading to a greater loss of bone mineral (Hedges 2002; Hedges and Millard 1995; Roberts et al. 2002). The greater the dissolution of the inorganic component of the bone, the greater the chance of DNA loss as the DNA molecules dissociate from the protection of the hydroxyapatite.

At the microscopic level, moisture content impacts initial autolytic processes that can damage DNA (Carter et al. 2010). Initial rapid desiccation of tissues tends to limit early hydrolytic damage of the DNA, while aqueous environments favor hydrolytic reactions that fragment DNA molecules and cause the loss of purine bases from the nucleotides (Eglinton et al. 1991; Poinar and Stankiewicz 1999). The profound impact of moisture is likely a factor as to why soft tissues, with a high water content, are more readily decomposed and have poorer DNA preservation than osseous tissues. In addition, microbial activity is reduced at the extreme ends of moisture content (in more aqueous and extremely dry environments), and microbes have a profound effect on degradation, as previously discussed (Lynnerup 2007).

The chemical composition of the depositional environment influences the rate and extent of mineral leaching from the bone and the uptake of different solutes from the soil. In the majority of cases, the osseous tissue is not in complete chemical equilibrium with the depositional environment and will begin to degrade as mineral is leached from the bone (Collins et al. 2002). Additionally, bone crystallinity (the degree of order within the crystal lattice) increases over time as exogenous materials from the depositional environment are incorporated into the mineral component of bone. Living bone displays irregularities in the hydroxyapatite matrix, and after death a net increase in hydroxyapatite crystallinity is observed over time. The exact mechanisms are poorly understood, yet it appears that this process (called *recrystallization*) may involve the dissolution and re-precipitation of the smallest hydroxyapatite crystals (Hedges 2002; Hedges and Millard 1995; Pate and Hutton 1988; Surovell and Stiner 2001; Roberts et al. 2002; Tuross et al. 1989). Since skeletal DNA is tightly bound to the hydroxyapatite, chemical changes regarding the hydroxyapatite have an influence on DNA preservation in the bone, with a negative correlation being found between hydroxyapatite crystallinity and DNA preservation. This occurs because the process of dissolution and re-precipitation releases the DNA from the hydroxyapatite, leaving it vulnerable to further degradation (Götherström et al. 2002). The interaction of soil minerals and bone is a complex process, and a more in-depth discussion can be found by referring to Chapters 5 and 12, this volume.

In addition, solutes may be incorporated into the bone that are later co-purified with the extracted skeletal DNA and serve as PCR inhibitors that limit subsequent genetic analyses (Kemp et al. 2006; Tuross 1994). Such PCR inhibitors act to block the enzymatic reactions during the PCR process. The hydroxyapatite crystal lattice gains an affinity for acidic molecules as the collagen component is lost from the bone. An example is the humic acid group of molecules, which are produced as a by-product during microbial digestion of organic material. Humic acid is a known PCR inhibitor and is ubiquitous in soil. The uptake of humic acids by osseous materials is recognized by a brown staining on bones that have been in contact with soils or decaying organic materials (Burger et al. 1999; Hedges 2002; see also Chapter 5, this volume). The presence and abundance of particular elements in bone also may provide clues as to the original depositional environment. For example, the uptake of iron and manganese indicates an oxidizing environment, which promotes DNA degradation (Elliott and Grime 1993).

Soil chemistry also heavily influences microbial activity. The appropriate nutrients and ions must be available to the decomposers living in the soil and the substances that are toxic to them must be absent. The two major processes involved in microbial decomposition of bone are the production of inorganic ions from the oxidation of organic compounds (mineralization) and the incorporation of inorganic molecules into the microbial protoplasm (immobilization). These processes are highly dependent upon the cycling of nitrogen and calcium in that particular position of the ecosystem. Furthermore, different depositional environments will be home to different decomposer communities that will produce different decay processes. This may refer to different geographical locations or different burial depths within a single geographic location, as the top several feet of soil will have a different microbial community than that found at deeper depths (Child 1995; Eglinton et al. 1991).

Bone dissolution and DNA degradation are highly influenced by soil and groundwater pH (Hedges and Millard 1995). Since most of the living human body is near neutral pH, tissues and DNA are better preserved in neutral or slightly alkaline environments (Burger et al. 1999). Soil that has a neutral pH tends to have calcium and phosphate concentrations similar to those found in bone and leads to a slower rate of bone degradation. Soil that has a low pH tends to have lower calcium and phosphate concentrations in comparison to bone and will lead to a faster rate of bone degradation as H^+ ions from the soil replace the calcium ions of the bone (Foran 2006a; Hedges 2002; White and Hannus 1983). The pH of the immediate bone environment also can be altered by microorganism activity. Microbes will produce acids as they decompose collagen. The H^+ ions from these acids can then replace the calcium in the hydroxyapatite of the bone and contribute to the chemical weathering of the bone (White and Hannus 1983).

The rate of recrystallization of hydroxyapatite is also influenced by pH. This rearrangement of the mineral component of the bone leads to problems with gross structural integrity such as cracking and the dissolution of osteons (Piepenbrink 1989). Such alterations of bone mineral content can increase bone dissolution and impact the DNA located within the bone by accelerating DNA degradation. However, the greatest damage to skeletal DNA occurs at pH extremes, as bone provides some buffering effect against pH-induced damage from surrounding acidic or alkaline soils (Smith et al. 2003).

While a neutral or slightly alkaline pH tends to produce better-preserved bones, it also provides an optimal environment for microbial activity. The majority of known microorganisms grow optimally at or around neutral pH, as cell chemistry is especially sensitive to pH changes. The internal cellular proteins of the microbes are destroyed if the cytoplasm becomes too acidic or too alkaline (Collins et al. 2002). Thus, environmental pH influences both chemical and microbial digestion of biological material.

Processing Techniques

Different processing techniques for soft tissue removal employed by forensic anthropologists may also influence DNA quantity and quality. Several studies over the past 10 years have tested the relationship between various maceration techniques and the success of subsequent genetic analyses. There is general agreement that some soft tissue removal procedures are more detrimental to subsequent DNA analysis than others.

Arismendi et al. (2004) assessed the influence of five maceration procedures on subsequent nuclear STR and amelogenin amplification success. Rennick et al. (2005) analyzed the effects of three processing techniques on subsequent mtDNA amplification success. Steadman et al. (2006) analyzed the relationship between 10 heat and chemical maceration techniques and PCR amplification success using both nucDNA and mtDNA primers. Lee et al. (2010) tested the impact of nine different processing techniques on subsequent nuclear STR analysis in human bone samples. All of these studies found techniques that use heat for short periods to be the most effective in terms of cleaning the bones and yielding successful genetic analyses, and that boiling for long periods or the use of large volumes of chemicals like bleach were detrimental to DNA integrity and analysis. Long-term exposure to heat can denature and degrade the DNA molecules, and cleaning chemicals like household bleach (NaClO) are oxidizing agents that can promote DNA damage. Exposing the DNA molecules to bleach will cause oxidative damage such as base modifications and chlorinated base products, and will inhibit the PCR process. In fact, high concentrations of bleach are often employed to destroy contaminating surface DNA from biological samples (like bone) and laboratory equipment (Kemp and Smith 2005).

Embalming may also influence subsequent genetic analysis. Chemical mortuary treatments can enhance DNA degradation or modify the DNA molecules and thus complicate PCR analysis. Embalming fluids like formaldehyde (CH_2O) act to concatemerize the DNA molecules and inhibit PCR amplification by preventing denaturation of the double-stranded DNA. Sterilizing agents like lime (CaO) increase the rate of alkaline hydrolysis and accelerate DNA damage. While mortuary practices may not be a significant factor in the majority of forensic cases, it is a potential complicating factor when bodies need to be exhumed for genetic testing (Koon et al. 2008).

Skeletal Element

At the macroscopic level, small bones are generally not as well-preserved as large bones in the archeological record (Grupe 1988; Von Endt and Ortner 1984; see also Chapter 4, this volume). Since DNA preservation is influenced by gross bone preservation, this suggests that smaller bones may not be as reliable as large bones in producing DNA profiles. However, there are studies that indicate analyzable DNA can be isolated from even poorly preserved bones and suggest that in situations where a large number of bones are available for analysis, it is better to choose samples from bones with better gross preservation

(Haynes et al. 2002; Richards et al. 1995). On the other hand, several studies found that more weathered bones produced higher quantities of analyzable DNA due to bone friability (Foran 2006b; Misner et al. 2009). This observation is similar to those studies that found bones subjected to warm temperatures produce better quantity DNA (as discussed previously). The studies by Foran (2006b) and Misner et al. (2009) analyzed human skeletal remains from an historic cemetery located in Pennsylvania, USA and a Late Bronze Age/Early Iron Age burial mound located in eastern Albania. Each bone in the study was given an overall weathering score ranging from 0 to 5 based on gross bone preservation (Behrensmeyer 1978). These scores were then compared to the amount of extracted skeletal DNA and mtDNA amplification success. The bones with the higher weathering scores (stages 4 and 5) produced greater quantities of analyzable DNA and had higher PCR amplification success rates.

In addition, several studies have indicated that bone type influences the quantity of recoverable DNA isolated from skeletal remains. In general, compact bone tends to yield a greater quantity of extracted DNA than spongy bone. Compact bone contains approximately 20,000 osteocytes per cubic mm and can yield up to 3–10 ng/mg of DNA. Differential yield between compact and spongy bone may be due to: (1) the higher moisture content of spongy bone leading to increased hydrolytic damage, (2) the increased rigidity of the cortical bone due to tightly packed hydroxyapatite crystals and the greater binding affinity of DNA molecules, (3) the more porous nature of spongy bone leading to an increased rate of leaching of the mineral matrix and greater exposure of the DNA molecules to destructive enzymes, or (4) that cortical bone tends to protect trapped osteocytes and other cells better than spongy bone and therefore provides better protection of the cellular DNA (Foran 2006b; Leney 2006; Parsons and Weedn 1997; White and Hannus 1983). Miloš et al. (2007) found the highest success rates for subsequent genetic analyses on samples taken from long bone shafts and virgin teeth, with lower PCR success displayed by samples from the vertebrae, ilium, and cranium. Their study was based on a large sample of over 25,000 human skeletal elements from the former Yugoslavia that were subjected to nuclear STR analysis. In addition, they found differences in PCR success rates between the compact long bones of the legs (femur at 86.9%, tibia at 75.9%, and fibula at 62.5%) and arms (humerus at 46.2%, radius at 24.5%, and ulna at 22.8%), which is a pattern found by other investigations with smaller sample sizes investigating various sampling loci including mtDNA (Edson et al. 2004; Foran 2006b; Leney 2006; Mundorff et al. 2009).

Virgin teeth have been found to be excellent reservoirs for DNA (Dobberstein et al. 2008; Kaestle and Horsburgh 2002; Ricaut et al. 2005). Enamel, dentin, and cementum are the three main tissues found in human teeth. Enamel covers the crown surface and contains an organic and inorganic fluorapatite component similar to bone. While both bone and teeth are mineralized tissues, their morphology and biochemistry are different and lead to different decay processes. Bone is more porous than enamel and degrades more rapidly as pore number and size influences the interaction of the particular biological element (bone or tooth) with available groundwater and access of enzymes to the DNA. In addition, enamel is more mineralized than bone. Enamel consists of 95% inorganic fluorapatite while only 65% of adult bone consists of inorganic matrix, suggesting even greater protection to the DNA bound to the inorganic portion of the tooth (Dobberstein et al. 2008; Lambert et al. 1985; Marieb and Hoehn 2010; Schwartz et al. 1991; Woelfel and Scheid 1997).

Area of the Genome

In addition to the different inheritance patterns of nucDNA versus mtDNA, the two regions of the genome also have different biological properties. The two types of human DNA have different cellular locations, with the nucDNA found within the cell nucleus and the mtDNA contained within extranuclear organelles. There are two copies of nucDNA per cell, one maternal and one paternal copy. In other words, an individual inherits one chromosome one to twenty-three from their mother and one chromosome one to twenty-three from their father. On the other hand, the mtDNA is present in multiple identical copies per cell, because each mitochondrion contains multiple copies of the mitochondrial genome, and most human cells contain multiple mitochondria. The higher copy number of the mtDNA per cell results in a greater probability that analyzable segments of the mtDNA will be recovered versus the nucDNA genome (Foran 2006a; Kaestle and Horsburgh 2002). Schwarz et al. (2009) determined the ratio of nucDNA to mtDNA in six mammoth bone samples using quantitative PCR. While the numbers were variable, all six bones displayed a preferential preservation of mitochondrial over nucDNA, with ratios ranging from 245:1 to 17,369:1, suggesting that targeting the mitochondrial genome for genetic analysis of old skeletal remains may prove more fruitful than targeting the nuclear genome. However, while the mtDNA may be easier to obtain from degraded samples, it does not contain as much individualizing information as the nuclear genome.

The small size of the mitochondrial genome in terms of bp and the circular structure of the mtDNA might make it less susceptible to enzymatic modification than nucDNA (Alaeddini et al. 2010; Foran 2006a; Hagelberg et al. 1991). In addition, the mtDNA is enclosed within the double membrane of the mitochondrion. The compartmentalization of the mitochondrion due to an inner and outer membrane is essential in creating cellular energy via the electron transport chain. This compartmentalization may provide more protection to the mtDNA. There are other explanations for the preferential preservation of the mtDNA over the nucDNA, including a negative influence of the chromatin folding structure of the nucDNA (Collins et al. 2002; Foran 2006a; Schwarz et al. 2009).

It is important to understand that nucDNA is more vulnerable to degradation, as this may influence the choice of genetic analytical techniques and the interpretation of genetic data from skeletal remains. The nucDNA may be degraded beyond the point at which it is detectable using PCR-based analyses, making mtDNA sequence analysis the only option. However, many forensic DNA laboratories will try to amplify a nucDNA profile first, as it is more individualizing. In addition, degraded nucDNA may produce incomplete STR profiles due to stochastic fluctuations like allelic dropout. In cases of positive identification, the ability to compare a complete genetic profile from the unknown remains to a known sample originating from the missing individual or a close family member increases the statistical strength in the identification. Therefore, an analyst may choose to sequence a portion of the mitochondrial genome, or, reduce the size of the nuclear STR amplicon by moving the primers closer to the STR repeat region (Butler et al. 2003).

Concluding Remarks

The analysis of DNA extracted from skeletal remains requires destructive sampling of the skeleton. Therefore, it is important that the analyst understand those environments that are most favorable for DNA preservation, those areas of the skeleton that are most successful in producing PCR amplifiable DNA for subsequent genetic analysis, and the appropriate genetic tests to employ to address their particular research or forensic questions. General scientific literacy regarding DNA survivability in skeletal remains can reduce the amount of human skeletal material destroyed for subsequent genetic testing in potentially futile situations.

Recommendations

Depositional Environment

A variety of environmental factors act collectively to influence the rate and extent of DNA damage. Therefore, knowledge of the depositional environment is important in predicting the probability of successful genetic testing. Genetic analysis has been successful from skeletal remains recovered in both indoor and outdoor contexts, including for the latter both burials and surface scatters. However, individual variation in the production of a successful DNA profile can be related partly to differences in the depositional environments of individual cases and even to variations between microenvironments within the same skeleton. Furthermore, processing techniques produce an artificial environment that can influence the ability to generate a usable DNA profile.

Temperature

The chemical reactions that contribute to DNA degradation occur at a faster rate in higher temperatures. Thus, cooler depositional environments will favor DNA preservation. However, recent studies suggest that mild heating may lead to increased DNA yields, as it makes the bones more brittle and better able to release the bound skeletal DNA.

Moisture Levels

Hydrolytic reactions are a major contributor to DNA damage. These chemical reactions require water molecules and result in the loss of DNA bases and strand breakage. Such modifications can complicate later PCR-based genetic analyses. DNA has an affinity for water molecules, and therefore the more groundwater or humidity that is present in the depositional environment, the greater the probability of DNA damage.

Oxygen Levels

Oxidative reactions result in modified DNA bases, as electrons are lost to oxygen molecules. The DNA base modifications or lesions interfere with the ability of the DNA polymerase to copy the target DNA template during the PCR process. Therefore, oxygen-rich environments will contribute to greater DNA damage and potential complications with later genetic analysis.

Exposure to Microorganisms

Both endogenous and exogenous microorganisms contribute to the decomposition of biological material. Microbes digest mineralized collagen, which makes the mineral portion of bone and the DNA bound to it more prone to damage. In addition, decomposing microorganisms release enzymes that fragment DNA molecules. The more access microbes have to the decomposing body, the greater the probability of DNA degradation.

Chemical Composition of the Soil

The chemical composition of the soil of the depositional environment has an impact on bone crystallinity. There is a correlation between crystallinity and the ability to PCR-amplify successfully extracted skeletal DNA, with the higher the crystallinity, the lower the PCR amplification success rate. Additionally, the soil might contain solutes that co-purify with the DNA and inhibit the PCR amplification process. Thus, knowledge of the chemical composition of the soil of the depositional environment can be informative in understanding failed PCR amplification attempts.

pH

The human body is near neutral pH. Thus, DNA is less prone to damage in environments consisting of soil and groundwater at near neutral pH. Environments of extreme pH (very acidic or very alkaline) encourage the disruption of cellular membranes and the denaturation of the DNA molecules.

Bone Type

DNA degrades more rapidly in soft tissue than in skeletal elements. Therefore, skeletal material should be given preference over decomposed or mummified soft tissues for subsequent PCR-based genetic analyses. The sampling of skeletal remains for genetic analysis should not be based on convenience but on an understanding of those skeletal elements likely to yield successful genetic analyses. Multiple lines of independent research have demonstrated that the cortical portions of the bones of the lower limb or the teeth are the most successful in generating a DNA profile. The teeth, femora shafts, and tibiae shafts consistently produce high success rates. In addition, the metatarsals and pedal phalanges have shown to be very reliable in recent investigations. Success rates for the cranium (in particular, the petrous portion of the temporal bone) and other areas of the skeleton vary widely from study to study and among laboratory facilities.

Sampling Strategy

Forensic anthropologists employ a variety of processing techniques to remove soft tissues from the skeletal elements. The removal of a bone for genetic testing before or after processing is often the decision of the individual laboratory facility. The effects of different processing techniques on subsequent DNA quality and quantity have been thoroughly investigated, and some processing procedures have been demonstrated to be more detrimental to subsequent genetic testing than others. In general, those methods that employ heat for shorter periods of time and without caustic chemicals tend to be the most effective in cleaning the bones while producing subsequently successful DNA analyses.

The decision to provide a tooth, bone, or portion of a bone to a DNA laboratory for genetic analyses varies widely among forensic facilities. This is a decision that should be made in close consultation between the forensic anthropologist and the DNA analyst. Some DNA laboratories prefer to isolate DNA from teeth and others from bone. If choosing a bone for analysis, the decision must be made whether to cut a portion to be sent for genetic testing or send an entire bone. The process of isolating DNA from skeletal tissue is a destructive process. DNA extraction techniques vary across laboratories and, based upon the procedure employed, typically require a minimum of 0.2–2.0 g of skeletal material. Laboratories often require more bone than employed in a single extraction due to the removal of outer layers that may contain contaminating DNA or

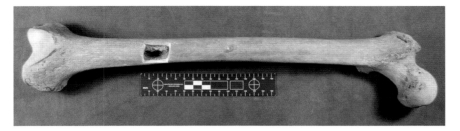

Figure 15.1 Right femur sampled for subsequent genetic analysis.

the possibility of additional extractions if the first attempt fails. If sending a whole bone, all observations, measurements, and photographs must be completed prior to genetic testing, with the assumption that some or all of the bone will be consumed during the DNA extraction process. If cutting a bone, strict cross-contamination precautions must be employed to prevent questioning of the DNA results by opposing counsel. In addition, cutting should be done in areas that do not destroy important landmarks used in osteological analyses (Figure 15.1).

Appropriate Genetic Tests

Choosing the appropriate genetic test to perform on the unidentified individual is dependent upon the question that needs to be addressed, the ability to obtain a reference sample, and the condition of the DNA-yielding tissue. The majority of forensic situations necessitate positive identification of the unknown skeletal remains, and thus nucDNA analysis. However, nucDNA is more prone to degradation, and such analyses may not be feasible. In such situations, mtDNA analysis may contribute to a collection of circumstantial information strong enough to identify the individual.

In other situations, mtDNA is the most appropriate target for analysis. Questions regarding familial relationships within a cemetery population, population movement across geographic space, or population relationships extensively utilize mtDNA analysis due to its unique inheritance pattern and geographic specificity. In addition, ancient DNA studies extensively rely on mtDNA analysis, because it is less susceptible to degradation than nucDNA.

Thermal Alterations to Bone

Thermally altered bone is frequently encountered in a forensic setting and may be the major contributor to the destruction of recognizable soft tissue features that would have allowed identification of the individual without forensic anthropological analysis. In some more extreme situations osseous identifiers may no longer exist, necessitating the need for another means of identification, namely the generation of a DNA profile. The successful generation of a DNA profile from burned bone varies across studies and is dependent upon the degree of thermal destruction, as well as the extraction and amplification procedures used by the DNA laboratory. Several studies have reported the ability to generate genetic information from bones ranging from charred to cremated at temperatures up to 600°C (Schwark et al. 2011; Ubelaker 2009).

In reality, the skeletonized cases encountered by a forensic scientist will be less than pristine in terms of available elements and condition. The bones and teeth will be scattered, fragmented, buried, burned, damaged by carnivores and other living organisms in the environment, sun-bleached, and handled by crime scene technicians, to name just a few possibilities. In many situations, the need for a positive identification is so great that any available biological element will be processed in hopes of obtaining a DNA profile. The recommendations in this chapter are just that: general recommendations aimed at saving time, money, and the unwarranted destruction of skeletal material.

Different DNA laboratories use different DNA extraction techniques, which greatly influences subsequent DNA yield regardless of the area of the skeleton sampled for DNA testing. Different DNA laboratories are optimized for different loci and use slightly different PCR parameters, again influencing DNA typing success regardless of skeletal element. Additionally, technological advances regarding low-quality and low-quantity DNA are increasing rapidly in their ability to extract and successfully generate DNA profiles. However, many DNA laboratories lag behind cutting-edge technology, as optimization and the creation of new standard operating procedures are timely and costly. Thus, a basic working knowledge of DNA survivability in skeletal remains is essential when working in fields that aim at identifying unknown individuals.

Acknowledgments

The authors would like to thank Dr. James Pokines and Dr. Steven Symes for organizing and editing this volume. The authors would also like to thank Dr. Harrell Gill-King, Dr. Lori Baker, Dr. Stephen Nawrocki, and Dr. Angie Embers for reviewing drafts of this chapter and providing invaluable feedback. Feedback was also provided by two anonymous reviewers, and the authors thank them for their comments.

References

Alaeddini, R., S. J. Walsh, and A. Abbas (2010) Forensic implications of genetic analyses from degraded DNA—A review. *Forensic Science International: Genetics* 4:148–157.

Alonso, A., P. Martín, C. Albarrán, P. García, O. García, L. F. de Simón, J. García-Hirschfeld, M. Sancho, C. de la Rúa, and J. Fernández-Piqueras (2004) Real-time PCR designs to estimate nuclear and mitochondrial DNA copy number in forensic and ancient DNA studies. *Forensic Science International* 139:141–149.

Anđelinović, S., D. Sutlović, I. E. Ivkosić, V. Skaro, A. Ivkosić, F. Paić, B. Rezić, M. Definis-Gojanović, and D. Primorac (2005) Twelve-year experience of skeletal remains from mass graves. *Croatian Medical Journal* 46:530–539.

Anderson, S., A. T. Bankier, B. G. Barrell, M. H. L. de Bruijn, A. R. Coulson, J. Drouin, I. C. Eperon et al. (1981) Sequence and organization of the human mitochondrial genome. *Nature* 290:457–465.

Arismendi, J. L., L. E. Baker, and K. J. Matteson (2004) Effects of processing techniques on the forensic DNA analysis of human skeletal remains. *Journal of Forensic Sciences* 49:930–934.

Aslanzadeh, J. (2004) Preventing PCR amplification carryover contamination in a clinical laboratory. *Annals of Clinical and Laboratory Science* 34:389–396.

Bada, J. L., X. S. Wang, and H. Hamilton (1999) Preservation of key biomolecules in the fossil record: Current knowledge and future challenges. *Philosophical Transactions of the Royal Society of London. Series B: Biological Sciences* 354:77–87.

Bär, W., A. Kratzer, M. Machler, and W. Schmid (1988) Postmortem stability of DNA. *Forensic Science International* 39:59–70.

Bell, L. S., M. F. Skinner, and S. J. Jones (1996) The speed of post mortem change to the human skeleton and its taphonomic significance. *Forensic Science International* 82:129–140.

Behrensmeyer, A. K. (1978) Taphonomic and ecologic information from bone weathering. *Paleobiology* 4:150–162.

Binladen, J., C. Wiuf, M. T. Gilbert, M. Bunce, R. Barnett, G. Larson, A. D. Greenwood, J. Haile, S. Y. Ho, A. J. Hansen, and E. Willerslev (2006) Assessing the fidelity of ancient DNA sequences amplified from nuclear genes. *Genetics* 172:733–741.

Burger, J., S. Hummel, B. Herrmann, and W. Henke (1999) DNA preservation: A microsatellite-DNA study on ancient skeletal remains. *Electrophoresis* 20:1722–1728.

Butler, J. M. (2007) Short tandem repeat typing technologies used in human identity testing. *Biotechniques* 43:2–5.

Butler, J. M. and C. L. Levin (1998) Forensic applications of mitochondrial DNA. *Trends in Biotechnology* 16:158–162.

Butler, J. M., Y. Shen, and B. R. McCord (2003) The development of reduced size STR amplicons as tools for analysis of degraded DNA. *Journal of Forensic Sciences* 48:1054–1064.

Carter, D. O., D. Yellowlees, and M. Tibbett (2010) Moisture can be the dominant environmental parameter governing cadaver decomposition in soil. *Forensic Science International* 200:60–66.

Cavalli-Sforza, L. L. (1998) The DNA revolution in population genetics. *Trends in Genetics* 14:60–65.

Child, A. M. (1995) Towards an understanding of the microbial decomposition of archaeological bone in the burial environment. *Journal of Archaeological Science* 22:165–174.

Coble, M. D., O. M. Loreille, M. J. Wadhams, S. M. Edson, K. Maynard, C. E. Meyer, H. Niederstatter et al. (2009) Mystery solved: The identification of the two missing Romanov children using DNA analysis. *PLoS ONE* 4:1–9.

Collins, M. J., C. M. Nielsen-Marsh, J. Hiller, C. I. Smith, J. P. Roberts, R. V. Prigodich, T. J. Wess, J. Csapo, A. R. Millard, and G. Turner-Walker (2002) The survival of organic matter in bone: A review. *Archaeometry* 44:383–394.

Dobberstein, R. C., J. Huppertz, N. von Wurmb-Schwark, and S. Ritz-Timme (2008) Degradation of biomolecules in artificially and naturally aged teeth: Implications for age estimation based on aspartic acid racemization and DNA analysis. *Forensic Science International* 179:181–191.

Edson, S. M., J. P. Ross, M. D. Coble, T. J. Parsons, and S. M. Barritt (2004) Naming the dead—Confronting the realities of rapid identification of degraded skeletal remains. *Forensic Science Review* 16:1–90.

Eglinton, G., G. A. Logan, R. P. Ambler, J. J. Boon, and W. R. K. Perizonius (1991) Molecular preservation [and Discussion]. *Philosophical Transactions of the Royal Society of London. Series B: Biological Sciences* 333:315–328.

Elliott, T. A. and G. W. Grime (1993) Examining the diagenetic alteration of human bone material from a range of archaeological burial sites using nuclear microscopy. *Nuclear Instruments and Methods in Physics Research Section B: Beam Interactions with Materials and Atoms* 77:537–547.

Foran, D. R. (2006a) *Final Report Increasing the Predictability and Success Rate of Skeletal Evidence Typing: Using Physical Characteristics of Bone as a Metric for DNA Quality and Quantity*. NIJ Grant # 2002-IJ-CX-K016. Michigan State University, East Lansing, MI.

Foran, D. R. (2006b) Relative degradation of nuclear and mitochondrial DNA: An experimental approach. *Journal of Forensic Sciences* 51:766–770.

Geigl, E. M. (2002) On the circumstances surrounding the preservation and analysis of very old DNA. *Archaeometry* 44:337–342.

Giles, R. E., H. Blanc, H. M. Cann, and D. C. Wallace (1980) Maternal inheritance of human mitochondrial DNA. *Proceedings from the National Academy of Science* 77:6715–6719.

Gill, P., J. Whitaker, C. Flaxman, N. Brown, and J. Buckelton (2000) An investigation of the rigor of interpretation rules for STRs derived from less than 100 pg of DNA. *Forensic Science International* 112:17–40.

Gill-King, H. (1997) Chemical and ultrastructural aspects of decomposition. In *Forensic Taphonomy: The Postmortem Fate of Human Remains* eds. W. D. Haglund and M. H. Sorg, pp. 109–126. CRC Press, Boca Raton, FL.

Götherström, A., M. J. Collins, A. Angerbjörn, and K. Lidén (2002) Bone preservation and DNA amplification. *Archaeometry* 44:395–404.

Grupe, G. (1988) Impact of the choice of bone samples on trace element data in excavated human skeletons. *Journal of Archaeological Science* 15:123–129.

Hammer, M. F., T. M. Karafet, A. J. Redd, H. Jarjanazi, S. Santachiara-Benercetti, H. Soodyall, and S. L. Zegura (2001) Hierarchical patterns of global Y-chromosome diversity. *Molecular Biology and Evolution* 18:1189–1203.

Hagelberg, E., L. S. Bell, T. Allen, A. Boyde, S. J. Jones, and J. B. Clegg (1991) Analysis of ancient bone DNA: Techniques and applications. *Philosophical Transactions of the Royal Society of London, Series B: Biological Sciences* 333:399–407.

Hagelberg, E. and J. B. Clegg (1991) Isolation and characterization of DNA from archaeological bone. *Proceedings of the Royal Society of London. Series B: Biological Sciences* 244:45–50.

Handt, O., M. Höss, M. Krings, and S. Pääbo (1994) Ancient DNA: Methodological challenges. *Cellular and Molecular Life Sciences* 50:524–529.

Harvey, M. and M. King (2002) The use of DNA in the identification of postmortem remains. In *Advances in Forensic Taphonomy: Method, Theory, and Archeological Perspectives* eds. W. D. Haglund and M. H. Sorg, pp. 473–486. CRC Press, Boca Raton, FL.

Haynes, S., J. B. Searle, A. Britman, and K. M. Dobney (2002) Bone preservation and ancient DNA: The application of screening methods for predicting DNA survival. *Journal of Archaeological Science* 29:585–592.

Hedges, R. E. (2002) Bone diagenesis: An overview of processes. *Archaeometry* 44:319–328.

Hedges, R. E. and A. R. Millard (1995) Bones and groundwater: Towards the modeling of diagenetic processes. *Journal of Archaeological Science* 22:155–164.

Hochmeister, M. N., B. Budowle, U. V. Borer, U. Eggmann, C. T. Comey, and R. Dirnhofer (1991) Typing of deoxyribonucleic acid (DNA) extracted from compact bone from human remains. *Journal of Forensic Sciences* 36:1649–1661.

Höss, M., P. Jaruga, T. H. Zastawny, M. Dizdaroglu, and S. Pääbo (1996) DNA damage and DNA sequence retrieval from ancient tissues. *Nucleic Acids Research* 24:1304–1307.

Jobling, M. A., A. Pandya, and C. Tyler-Smith (1997) The Y chromosome in forensic analyses and paternity testing. *International Journal of Legal Medicine* 110:118–124.

Jobling, M. and C. Tyler-Smith (2003) The human Y chromosome: An evolutionary marker comes of age. *Nature Reviews Genetics* 4:598–612.

Kaestle, F. A. and K. A. Horsburgh (2002) Ancient DNA in anthropology: Methods, applications and ethics. *Yearbook of Physical Anthropology* 45:92–130.

Kalmár, T., C. Z. Bachrati, A. Marcsik, and I. Raskó (2000) A simple and efficient method for PCR amplifiable DNA extraction from ancient bones. *Nucleic Acids Research* 28:1–4.

Kemp, B. M., C. Monroe, and D. G. Smith (2006) Repeat silica extraction: A simple technique for the removal of PCR inhibitors from DNA extracts. *Journal of Archaeological Science* 33:1680–1689.

Kemp, B. M. and D. G. Smith (2005) Use of bleach to eliminate contaminating DNA from the surface of bones and teeth. *Forensic Science International* 154:53–61.

Koon, H. E. C., O. M. Loreille, A. D. Covington, A. F. Christensen, T. J. Parsons, and M. J. Collins (2008) Diagnosing post-mortem treatments which inhibit DNA amplification from US MIAs buried at the Punchbowl. *Forensic Science International* 178:171–177.

Lambert, J. B., S. Vlasak Simpson, C. B. Szpunar, and J. E. Buikstra (1985) Bone diagenesis and dietary analysis. *Journal of Human Evolution* 14:477–482.

Lassen, C., S. Hummel, and B. Herrmann (1994) Comparison of DNA extraction and amplification from ancient human bone and mummified soft tissue. *International Journal of Legal Medicine* 107:152–155.

Latham, K. (2003) The relationship between bone condition and DNA preservation, Unpublished Master's Thesis. University of Indianapolis Archeology & Forensics Laboratory (http://archlab. uindy.edu).

Lee, E. J., J. G. Luedtke, J. L. Allison, C. E. Arber, D. A. Merriwether, and D. W. Steadman (2010) The effects of different maceration techniques on nuclear DNA amplification using human bone. *Journal of Forensic Sciences* 55:1032–1038.

Leney, M. D. (2006) Sampling skeletal remains for ancient DNA (aDNA): A measure of success. *Historical Archaeology* 40:31–49.

Lindahl, T. (1993) Instability and decay of the primary structure of DNA. *Nature* 362:709–715.

Lindahl, T. and A. Andersson (1972) Rate of chain breakage at apurinic sites in double-stranded deoxyribonucleic acid. *Biochemistry* 11:3618–3623.

Lindahl, T. and B. Nyberg (1972) Rate of depurination of native deoxyribonucleic acid. *Biochemistry* 11:3610–3618.

Lindahl, T. and B. Nyberg (1974) Heat-induced deamination of cytosine residues in deoxyribonucleic acid. *Biochemistry* 13:3405–3411.

Lynnerup, N. (2007) Mummies. *Yearbook of Physical Anthropology* 50:162–190.

Marieb, E. N. and K. Hoehn (2010) *Human Anatomy and Physiology*. Benjamin Cummings, San Francisco, CA.

Meyer, E., M. Wiese, H. Bruchhaus, M. Claussen, and A. Klein (2000) Extraction and amplification of authentic DNA from ancient human remains. *Forensic Science International* 113:87–90.

Miloš, A., A. Selmanović, L. Smajlović, R. L. Huel, C. Katzmarzyk, A. Rizvić, and T. J. Parsons (2007) Success rates of nuclear short tandem repeat typing from different skeletal elements. *Croatian Medical Journal* 48:486–493.

Misner, L. M., A. C. Halvorson, J. L. Dreier, D. H. Ubelaker, and D. R. Foran (2009) The correlation between skeletal weathering and DNA quality and quantity. *Journal of Forensic Sciences* 54:822–828.

Mulligan, C. J. (2006) Anthropological applications of ancient DNA: Problems and prospects. *American Antiquity* 71:365–380.

Mundorff, A. Z., E. J. Bartelink, and E. Mar-Cash (2009) DNA preservation in skeletal elements from the World Trade Center disaster: Recommendations for mass fatality management. *Journal of Forensic Sciences* 54:739–745.

Ottoni, C., G. Primativo, B. Hooshiar Kashani, A. Achilli, C. Martínez-Labarga, G. Biondi, A. Torroni, and O. Rickards (2010) Mitochondrial haplogroup H1 in North Africa: An early Holocene arrival from Iberia. *PLoS ONE* 5(10):e13378.

Parsons, T. J. and V. W. Weedn (1997) Preservation and recovery of DNA in postmortem specimens and trace samples. In *Forensic Taphonomy: The Postmortem Fate of Human Remains* eds. W. D. Haglund and M. H. Sorg, pp. 109–126. CRC Press, Boca Raton, FL.

Pate, F. D. and J. T. Hutton (1988) The use of soil chemistry data to address post-mortem diagenesis in bone mineral. *Journal of Archaeological Science* 15:729–739.

Perry, W. L., W. M. Bass, W. S. Riggsby, and K. Sirotkin (1988) The autodegradation of deoxyribonucleic acid (DNA) in human rib bone and its relationship to the time interval since death. *Journal of Forensic Science* 33:144–153.

Piepenbrink, H. (1989) Examples of chemical changes during fossilization. *Applied Geochemistry* 4:273–280.

Poinar, H. N. and B. A. Stankiewicz (1999) Protein preservation and DNA retrieval from ancient tissues. *Proceedings of the National Academy of Sciences of the United States of America* 96:8426–8431.

Reidy, K. M., A. Gareis, D. Sun, R. AuClair, T. Wong, R. Lang, H. Meng, H. M. Coyle, H. C. Lee, and A. B. Harper (2009) Gender identification differences observed for DNA quantification versus STR genotyping of mummified human remains—How it relates to human identifications in forensic science. *Investigative Sciences Journal* 1:1–10.

Rennick, S. L., T. W. Fenton, and D. R. Foran (2005) The effects of skeletal preparation techniques on DNA from human and non-human bone. *Journal of Forensic Sciences* 50:1016–1019.

Ricaut, F. X., C. Keyser-Tracqui, E. Crubézy, and B. Ludes (2005) STR-genotyping from human medieval tooth and bone samples. *Forensic Science International* 151:31–35.

Richards, M., V. Macaulay, A. Torroni, and H. Bendelt (2002) In search of geographical patterns in European mitochondrial DNA. *American Journal of Human Genetics* 71:1168–1174.

Richards, M. B., B. C. Sykes, and R. E. M. Hedges (1995) Authenticating DNA extracted from ancient skeletal remains. *Journal of Archaeological Science* 22:291–299.

Richter, C., J. W. Park, and B. N. Ames (1988) Normal oxidative damage to mitochondrial and nuclear DNA is extensive. *Proceedings of the National Academy of Sciences of the United States of America* 85:6465–6467.

Roberts, S. J., C. I. Smith, A. Millard, and M. J. Collins (2002) The taphonomy of cooked bone: Characterizing boiling and its physico-chemical effects. *Archaeometry* 44:485–494.

Robin, E. D. and R. Wong (1988) Mitochondrial DNA molecules and virtual number of mitochondria per cell in mammalian cells. *Journal of Cellular Physiology* 136:507–513.

Rogan, P. K. and J. J. Salvo (1990) Study of nucleic acids isolated from ancient remains. *American Journal of Physical Anthropology* 33:195–214.

Scheinfeldt, L., F. Friedlaender, J. Friedlaender, K. Latham, G. Koki, T. Karafet, M. Hammer, and J. Lorenz (2006) Unexpected NRY chromosome variation in Northern Island Melanesia. *Molecular Biology and Evolution* 23:1628–1641.

Schneider, P. M. (2007) Scientific standards for studies in forensic genetics. *Forensic Science International* 165:238–243.

Schwark, T., A. Heinrich, A. Preuße-Prange, and N. von Wurmb-Schwark (2011) Reliable genetic identification of burnt human remains. *Forensic Science International: Genetics* 5:393–399.

Schwartz, T. R., E. A. Schwartz, L. Mierszerski, L. McNally, and L. Kobilinsky (1991) Characterization of deoxyribonucleic acid (DNA) obtained from teeth subjected to various environmental conditions. *Journal of Forensic Sciences* 36:979–990.

Schwarz, C., R. Debruyne, M. Kuch, E. McNally, H. Schwarcz, A. D. Aubrey, J. Bada, and H. Poinar (2009) New insights from old bones: DNA preservation and degradation in permafrost preserved mammoth remains. *Nucleic Acids Research* 37:1–15.

Smith, C. I., A. T. Chamberlain, M. S. Riley, C. Stringer, and M. J. Collins (2003) The thermal history of human fossils and the likelihood of successful DNA amplification. *Journal of Human Evolution* 45:203–217.

Steadman, D. W., L. L. DiAntonio, J. J. Wilson, K. E. Sheridan, and S. P. Tammariello (2006) The effects of chemical and heat maceration techniques on the recovery of nuclear and mitochondrial DNA from bone. *Journal of Forensic Sciences* 51:11–17.

Surovell, T. A. and M. C. Stiner (2001) Standardizing infra-red measures of bone mineral crystallinity: An experimental approach. *Journal of Archeological Science* 28:633–642.

Thomas, K. and S. Pääbo (1993) DNA sequences from old tissue remains. *Methods in Enzymology* 224:406–419.

Tuross, N. (1994) The biochemistry of ancient DNA in bone. *Experientia* 50:530–535.

Tuross, N., A. K. Behrensmeyer, E. D. Eanes, L. W. Fisher and P. E. Hare (1989) Molecular preservation and crystallographic alterations in a weathering sequence of wildebeest bones. *Applied Geochemistry* 4:261–270.

Ubelaker, D. H. (2009) The forensic evaluation of burned skeletal remains: A synthesis. *Forensic Science International* 183:1–5.

Underhill, P. A., P. Shen, A. A. Lin, L. Jin, G. Passarino, W. Yang, E. Kauffman et al. (2000) Y chromosome sequence variation and the history of human populations. *Nature Genetics* 26:358–361.

Vass, A. A. (2001) Beyond the grave—Understanding human decomposition. *Microbiology Today* 28:190–192.

Von Endt, D. W. and D. J. Ortner (1984) Experimental effects of bone size and temperature on bone diagenesis. *Journal of Archaeological Science* 11:247–253.

von Haeseler, A., A. Sajantila, and S. Pääbo (1995) The genetical archaeology of the human genome. *Nature Genetics* 14:135–140.

von Wurmb-Schwark, N., S. Petermann, and R. Wegener (2003) Y-STR typing in forensic analysis. *International Congress Series* 1239:487–490.

White, E. M. and L. A. Hannus (1983) Chemical weathering of bone in archaeological soils. *American Antiquity* 48:316–322.

Woelfel, J. B. and R. C. Scheid (1997) *Dental Anatomy: Its Relevance to Dentistry*. Williams & Williams, Baltimore, MD.

Avian Taphonomy

16

JAMES T. POKINES
STEPHANIE E. BAKER

Contents

> There is another practice, however, concerning the burial of the dead, which is not spoken of openly and is something of a mystery: it is that a male Persian is never buried until the body has been torn a bird or a dog.
>
> —**Herodotus, *The Histories, Book I*, translation by A. de Sélincourt**

Introduction

The effect of birds upon osseous remains is one of the earliest taphonomic topics speculated on prior to formalization of this field, in terms of how various types of birds might concentrate the bones of their small prey in favored feeding locations (Buckland 1823). This early interest and subsequent research into this topic may have been driven by its visibility and ubiquity: many raptor (predatory) bird species roost in the same location continuously for a large portion of a year, often raising a brood at that time. Their energy requirements are such that many trips per day with fresh prey to feed their young and themselves are necessary. The remains of these meals can build up substantial osseous assemblages in and under roosting sites, and many such roosts are reoccupied over multiple years, sometimes by different species in succession. Feeding often proceeds in a dramatic fashion, with whole prey gobbled up or torn into pieces for nestlings. These rather striking ecological proceedings (often occurring in urban/commensal settings as large raptors are reintroduced into these environments) may have spurred interest in the hunting and feeding habits of these charismatic species as determined from the remains of their feeding. Adding to this potential interest by humans into raptor activities may be the regurgitation of pellets, the undigested concentrated balls of fur, feathers, connective tissue, and bone, which also accumulate in and under raptor roosts in large quantities (Bunn et al. 1982). These are egested by many raptor species (Glue 1970), not just owls (Order Strigiformes). Pellets often protect their contained osseous remains exceedingly well until their incorporation into sediments (Lyman et al. 2003). Raptors therefore are likely the fastest concentrators of osseous remains (as measured by element counts) in the animal world, outpacing such taxa as hyaenids and canids. As such, their behavior relevant to small vertebrate taphonomy has been widely researched (Andrews 1990; Bochenski and Tornberg 2003; Pokines 1998; Pokines and Kerbis Peterhans 1998; Pokines et al. 2011).

Osseous accumulations by birds were recognized early as a boon to paleoecological reconstruction (Davis 1959; Southern 1954), as well as studies of extant ecosystems (Glading et al. 1943; Lovari et al. 1976; Moon 1940; Reed 1957). Many species of generalist avian predators are highly adept at sampling the small vertebrate community within their hunting radius, thus providing a relatively unpixelated snapshot of these species living in that area at that time. These remains also tend to be very undamaged and identifiable, depending upon the species of raptor (Andrews 1990; Mayhew 1977). Later research examined the taphonomic characteristics left behind on osseous remains relative to the accumulating agent, in order to identify and potentially control for the biases caused in species and body part representation (Cummings et al. 1976; Dodson and Wexlar 1979; Duke et al. 1975; Korth 1979; Levinson 1982; Mayhew 1977). This research has expanded to many species of raptors worldwide and the potentially unique taphonomic characteristics that they may leave on bone (Bochenski et al. 2009; Marín-Arroyo and Margalida 2011; Reed 2005; Robert and Vigne 2002; Sanders et al. 2003; Stewart et al. 1999; Terry 2010).

The taphonomic effects of large scavenging bird species upon large mammals are less well known, likely due to their lesser ability to transport large bones and concentrate them in easily analyzable samples. Remains are thus largely left at the initial death scene and not reconcentrated in a different location, potentially to become part of the fossil record. Remains left behind in surface scatters therefore are of lesser interest to paleoecological studies, but they are of course central to forensic anthropological sites where human remains have been deposited outdoors. The continued analysis of avian interaction with human remains is necessary in order to understand the physical alteration and movement of bone. Determination of these patterns may allow the separation of this source of taphonomic alteration from others of more direct forensic interest, including perimortem trauma, dismemberment, and loss of elements. The scavenging of soft tissue by birds or terrestrial scavengers also has the potential to alter the conclusions that may be drawn about postmortem interval (PMI) from patterns of decomposition and eventual skeletonization, since analysis of these relies in part upon observations of the degree of soft tissue loss (Megyesi et al. 2005). Scavenging birds also are capable of accessing some vertebrate remains that terrestrial scavengers cannot, including human remains suspended in the air due to hanging (Komar and Beattie 1998) or in some indoor settings (Dettling et al. 2001).

Raptor Predation upon Primates

Diurnal and nocturnal raptors are known to prey upon multiple extant species of nonhuman primates. Hart (2000) and Hart and Sussman (2008) note that 81 species of raptors are known or suspected primate predators, out of a total of 176 predatory species of all kinds (including mammals, reptiles, etc.) known or suspected to exploit this food source. Some species, including the large, powerful African crowned eagle (*Stephanoaetus coronatus*), are primate specialists over at least part of their range and hunt in forest canopies for multiple species of large monkey (McGraw et al. 2006; Sanders et al. 2003). Predation is more prevalent where the raptors have the size advantage, but some species are known to kill and transport primates heavier than themselves (Hart 2000). Hart and Sussman (2008:138) tabulated that 46% of published eyewitness accounts of instances of primate predation involved raptors. This number may be inflated by the ability of raptors to arrive on a scene and swiftly depart despite the presence of witnessing humans to their predatory activity, and the availability of primates within tree canopies where both they and their predators can be observed.

No known extant raptor species has been documented to prey upon adult humans, although the latter frequently is subject to attack in defense of self or nesting site (Parker 1999). Some instances of attacks by predatory birds upon children also are known, although a natural tendency to exaggeration of these events makes many claims suspect (Hart and Sussman 2008). Even large species such as golden eagles (*Aquila chrysaetos*) are limited in the size of their prey, which can include domestic calves (Phillips et al. 1996). Among North American taxa, Golden eagles can, however, lift prey items heavier than their own body mass (Sørensen et al. 2008) and conceivably could transport juvenile human remains. Bald eagles (*Haliaeetus leucocephalus*) also fall into this range. In the Old World, multiple species have the ability to transport juvenile humans, including crowned eagles (*Stephanoaetus coronatus*), Verreaux's eagles (*Aquila verreauxii*), martial eagles (*Polemaetus bellicosus*), and in South America, harpy eagles (*Harpia harpyja*) (Gargett 1990; Gilbert et al. 2009; and pers. obs.). Larger species of extinct raptors had the potential to include humans more regularly as prey items (Scofield and Ashwell 2009). Only very large, flightless species (ostrich, *Struthio camelus*, and cassowary, *Casuarius* spp.) have been known to inflict fatal harm upon adult humans through direct physical attack (Kofron 1999). These rare instances do not result in feeding and further taphonomic alteration of human remains. Such interactions with human remains are primarily in the realm of scavenging bird species, discussed in the following text.

Raptor predation is also relevant to extinct taxa of hominins and how their remains might have been incorporated into the fossil record. It has been posited that the type specimen for *Australopithecus africanus*, the Taung Child, was killed by a large eagle species and transported to its final deposition site (Berger 2006; Berger and Clarke 1995; Berger and McGraw 2007; De Ruiter et al. 2010; McGraw et al. 2006; Sanders et al. 2003). The estimated age at death is 3–4 years. The Taung site in South Africa is a large tufa accretion that encompasses over 24 fossil deposits of varying ages and accumulation mechanisms. The two limestone caverns that are most closely associated with the hypothesized provenience of the *A. africanus* skull are the Dart and Hrdlička Pinnacles, which also have yielded the remains of primarily smaller vertebrate fauna. These species are dominated by extinct baboon, rodents, hares, bats, birds, small antelopes, and hyraxes, all conforming in size to typical large eagle prey, with the majority of taxa having a body mass of less than 20 kg (Berger and Clarke 1995). These fauna also included multiple types of taphonomic damage typically caused by large birds of prey (Berger and Clarke 1995:280): depression fractures and puncture marks caused by talons; damage to the basicranium and crushing of the vault and facial bones to access cranial tissue; and V-shaped nicks in bone surfaces caused by beaks. Damage from eagle feeding also may take the form of gouges and scratches around the eye orbits (Berger and McGraw 2007). The scratch marks often appear in semiparallel clusters and may result from gripping and manipulation of the skull by talons. Damage also may appear to the orbital floors (Berger 2006), which likely result from talon gripping around the more durable orbital margins (McGraw et al. 2006).

Scavenging Birds

Scavenging Birds and Human Remains

Many extant species of scavenging bird are known to feed upon human remains, among the many other large vertebrates that comprise their diet. Scavengers, by their very nature, have non-discriminating feeding habits, and the low levels of humans in their diets have more to do with human than scavenger behavior. Most human death preparation involves scavenger exclusion from remains as quickly as possible, but human remains deliberately left in outdoor situations or those from remote suicides or accidents are subject to scavenging birds. Some human body disposal practices deliberately expose human remains (often left on platforms, high rock outcrops, or in specially built towers with open roofs, thereby largely excluding terrestrial scavengers) to decompose and be consumed by scavenging birds. This process is termed *sky burial* and was practiced historically by groups on the Himalayan plateau, Zoroastrians in Persia and later in India, and possibly by some Native American tribes and groups in northern Asia, Thailand, and Korea (van Dooren 2011; Martin 1996). This practice by the Zoroastrians was well known in the ancient world and was documented by many writers in antiquity, including Herodotus (Trinkaus 1984). This practice has also been depicted in artwork at the Neolithic urban site of Çatal Hüyük in Anatolia (Turkey), dating to ca. 7000 BC (van Dooren 2011). Less formally, in the Roman Empire, bodies of the poor were sometimes disposed of on rubbish heaps (Nock 1932), presumably with subsequent feeding by vultures and other scavengers occurring. In modern and historical times in the Himalayas, the express purpose of this type of body disposal was dismemberment and leaving it exposed to be consumed, primarily by scavenging birds. Multiple edicts attempted to ban this practice, with apparently little effect until recent decades (Hamilton and Spradley 2011; Martin 1996). That human mortuary ritual treatment in multiple parts of the world relied upon the repeated actions of scavenging birds (and other taxa) in the disposal of their dead indicates the pervasive taphonomic influence that birds have had upon exposed human remains, whether these remains were exposed through deliberate action or through other means. This strong association with death and the afterlife is likely why vultures appear in the artwork of so many cultures, including extensively in ancient Egypt (Houlihan and Goodman 1986), and the common presence of vulture remains in human sites in early Neolithic contexts in the Near East (Gourichon 2002).

Vultures

New World vultures and condors (Family Cathartidae) inhabit the tropical to temperate zones of North and South America (Table 16.1) and are most closely related to storks and herons (Ciconiiformes). Their fossil history dates back to the Eocene, 40–50 million years ago (Houston 2001). These species were more diverse during the Pleistocene (Stager 1964), and multiple extinctions may be traced to the loss of many species of mammalian

Table 16.1   New World (Family Cathartidae) Vulture Species

Taxon	Common Name	Current Range (Houston 2001)
Cathartes aura	Turkey vulture	Southern Canada through all of South America
Cathartes burrovianus	Lesser yellow-headed vulture	Northern South America into Central America
Cathartes melambrotus	Greater yellow-headed vulture	Northern South America
Coragyps atratus	Black vulture	United States through most of South America
Gymnogyps californianus	California condor	California (USA) and surrounding area
Sarcoramphus papa	King vulture	Northern South America into Central America
Vultur gryphus	Andean condor	Andes mountain range, South America

megafauna from the New World at that time and the loss of this scavenging food resource. New World vultures have a distinct evolutionary history from Old World vultures (Subfamily Aegypiinae), which include the bearded vulture (*Gypaetus barbatus*) and griffon vulture (*Gyps fulvus*) and are related to common raptor species such as eagles and falcons (Houston 2001). The similarities in scavenging lifestyle among the two major vulture lineages worldwide therefore are due to evolutionary convergence. Most Old World vultures, like their New World vulture counterparts, are obligate scavengers for sustenance and do not hunt live prey for a significant portion of their diet (Ogada et al. 2012). Unlike some New World vultures, Old World vultures do not have a highly advanced olfactory sense and locate the carcasses upon which they feed primarily through sight. Some species of New World vultures (*Cathartes* spp.) locate the carcasses upon which they feed primarily through an acute sense of smell (Stager 1964), so some delay between death and the onset of carcass discovery and feeding is typical. Other adaptations to an obligate scavenging lifestyle (Houston 2001; van Dooren 2011) include large wing areas relative to body mass, designed for gliding long distances with lesser energy expenditure (i.e., soaring flight as opposed to powered flight) while in search of food; large home ranges; large fat reserves to allow storage of energy between feeding bouts; the ability to consume over 20% of their own body mass at once; long, thin necks and long, hooked beaks evolved to reach into narrow spaces around bones for feeding; and a general lack of feathers on the head and upper neck also to facilitate feeding in narrow spaces.

Turkey Vultures (Cathartes aura)

Turkey vultures are easily distinguishable by their bright red head and dark plumage. Their adult body mass is around 850–2000 g, and their wingspan is around 180–200 cm (Houston 2001). This species is widespread, from southern Canada through South America, and its breeding range is expanding into southern Canada (Houston et al. 2011; Prior and Weatherhead 1991; Rabenold and Decker 1989). It tends to settle in communal roosting trees and foray out over a large home range in search of food. Coleman and Fraser (1989) found that the turkey vultures they studied in western Pennsylvania, USA, spent from 33% to 27% of the day (varying seasonally) on the wing, primarily searching for food. Up to 15 km were covered in 1 day. The size of home ranges likely increases in environments where food resources are sparser. Thomaides et al. (1989) detected movement of up to 74 km from a home roost in west Texas based upon the availability of a distant food resource showing up in the diet. Coleman and Fraser (1989) measured average home ranges of turkey vultures in southern Pennsylvania and northern Maryland, USA, as 37,072 ha (143 miles^2). In addition to normal movement over their home ranges, turkey vultures are also seasonally migratory (Mandel et al. 2008; Rabenold and Decker 1989) between northerly and southerly portions of their ranges to ameliorate winter food scarcity and temperature extremes. Some individuals, however, over-winter in the northern portions of their range.

Movement within the home range is frequent. Roost locations often circulate among multiple reused sites with many single-use locations within the home range. Roosts may serve as centers for information exchange among individuals returning to it at night, regarding food sources located that day and still viable the next day (Prior and Weatherhead 1991; Rabenold 1987). Foraging usually is singular or in small groups of only a few individuals (Stewart 1978), but larger foraging groups numbering up to 21 individuals have been noted (summarized in Prior 1990). Feeding, however, often involves agonistic displays, with more dominant turkey vultures feeding before subordinate individuals (Prior and Weatherhead 1991). This subordination extends both ways in interspecies interactions: turkey vultures are subordinate to, for example, larger species of vultures and red-tailed hawks, but crows are subordinate to turkey vultures and usually are driven away from carcasses that the crows locate first (Prior and Weatherhead 1991; Wallace and Temple 1987). This successive use of the same carcass also may benefit the smaller species, in that the larger species are more able to open up larger carcasses so that it can be exploited more fully by (generally) smaller species feeding later (Wallace and Temple 1987).

Habitat use by turkey vultures often includes forested areas (Coleman and Fraser 1989). Reports of the exploitation of road kills are variable, with some researchers noting the importance of the resource (Yahner et al. 1990) and others noting its lack (Coleman and Fraser 1989), despite its presumed availability. Turkey vulture diet, being based upon the availability of fresh, scavengeable carcasses within their home range, naturally tends to reflect the abundances of species within that environment. Dietary analysis frequently is achieved by the identification of hairs and feathers within egested pellets collected under home roosts, as the bone fragments contained within are usually too small to identify from large food species (Hiraldo et al. 1991). Thomaides et al. (1989) found that turkey vulture diet in west Texas, USA, reflected the abundance of smaller taxa in their environment. Mammals (including abundant leporid remains) were detected in all pellets ($n = 91$) examined, reptiles in 83.5%, and birds in 44%. Hiraldo et al. (1991) noted a similar propensity for smaller mammal species in turkey vulture diet in northern Mexico and attributed it to competitive exclusion by the larger black vultures from larger carcasses. Prior (1990) found similar reliance upon smaller scavenged species for turkey vultures in southern Canada in an environment lacking any other species of competing vulture, so turkey vultures may focus upon smaller carrion as an evolutionary adaptation rather than competitive exclusion by larger scavenging birds. Their diet (Prior 1990:709) also included many large species, such as dog (*Canis familiaris*), horse (*Equus caballus*), cattle (*Bos taurus*), pig (*Sus scrofa*), bison (*Bison bison*), and sheep (*Ovis aries*), but smaller mammals dominated in the number of taxa exploited and the frequency with which they were detected among pellets.

Unlike other species of New World and Old World vultures, turkey vultures and the other species within the genus *Cathartes* have a highly developed sense of smell, which they use to detect their food sources (Stager 1964). Houston (1986) found that the turkey vultures he studied in Panama rely almost entirely upon their sense of smell to locate food. Recently dead carcasses were not easily located by them, with 1 day old carcasses much more efficiently located. Four-day old carcasses with more advanced putrescence likely were just as locatable by the turkey vultures but generally rejected as a food source.

The onset of putrescence in this tropical environment is faster than that in the temperate zone, so the available window of opportunity between a carcass being locatable by decomposition smell and its too-far advancement into decay is wider in colder climates. No significant differences were noted between the amount of time necessary to locate carcasses that were exposed on the forest floor vs. those covered with a layer of leaves and were essentially invisible from the air. Stager (1964) also found that turkey vultures could locate hidden food baits and that they were not attracted to decoy (non-food) baits meant to evoke a visual response. The preference for fresher over actively decomposing meat was confirmed using side-by-side baiting scenarios (Houston 1986). The turkey vultures were also highly efficient at locating 1 day old carcasses, with 80% of $n = 24$ 1 day old carcasses located in the first 12 h after placement and the remainder located the next day. Of a total of 74 baits of all types used in the study, 71 were located by the turkey vultures within 3 days of placement, with the remaining three being carcasses that were older at the time of placement. Excluding older carcasses, over 90% of the original bait mass (in this case domestic chickens, *Gallus gallus*) was consumed by vultures.

Black Vultures (Coragyps atratus)

Black vultures have black head and plumage coloration and therefore are easily distinguished from turkey vultures at close range or when viewed using remote cameras at experimental feeding stations. They overlap in size with turkey vultures and have an adult body mass around 1100–1900 g and a wingspan around 137–150 cm (Houston 2001). Black vultures range from the southern United States, wintering at least as far north as Pennsylvania, and through most of South America. In recent years, their summer range has been expanding farther north, including New England (Rabenold and Decker 1989), possibly in response to climate change, new sources of food/reduced competition, or reestablishment of a prior range. Coleman and Fraser (1989) measured average home ranges of black vultures in southern Pennsylvania and northern Maryland, USA, at 14,881 ha (57.5 miles²). Coleman and Fraser (1989) found that the black vultures they studies in western Pennsylvania, USA, spent from 9% to 12% of the day (varying seasonally) on the wing, significantly less than the turkey vultures in the same study. While almost entirely a scavenger, this species is also known to prey upon live small vertebrates on occasion (Stager 1964).

Black vultures are more aggressive than turkey vultures and tend to dominate turkey vultures where the two feed together (Buckley 1996; Stolen 2000; Wallace and Temple 1987), but they also tend to exploit carcasses of larger species more frequently than turkey vultures (Stewart 1978). This may account for why black vultures spend less time in flight, visually searching for food, since they usually exploit larger individual carcasses once located. They also tend to fly at higher altitudes in search of food (Stolen 2000), perhaps because they rely upon sight rather than upon scent to locate food (Stager 1964) and do not have highly developed olfactory structures. Black vultures also may rely upon turkey vultures to locate food for them and follow this species to a carcass, where they then displace the less dominant turkey vultures (Stewart 1978; Wallace and Temple 1987). Black vultures may live closely with turkey vultures and often share the same roosting areas, with no segregation among the species (Yahner et al. 1990) and with overlapping home ranges (Coleman and Fraser 1989). This sympatric behavior makes dietary analysis difficult from pellet analysis, as data must often be pooled between the two species when utilizing this source of data.

The dietary niche of black vultures is to exploit larger vertebrate carcasses on average than are typical of turkey vultures, although a great deal of overlap occurs (Houston 2001; Kelly et al. 2007; van Dooren 2011). Stewart (1978) recorded multiple instances of cattle carcasses being fed upon by black vultures, with turkey vultures spotted in the area but never alighting on the carcasses. Reeves (2009) also recorded black vultures dominating feeding at large carcasses.

Roosting groups of black vultures can be quite large throughout the year, but nesting tends to take place in isolation. Rabenold (1987) noted a 10 day average of 238.8 individual black vultures sharing the same roosting area during winter in North Carolina, USA. When feeding, large flocks of black vultures may exploit the same resource. Stewart (1978) noted up to 60 black vultures congregating daily at a chicken farm, which could supply a large and reliable source of carcasses to support such a large group at once. Wallace and Temple (1987:294) noted groups of over 50 black vultures feeding at the same large carcasses at sites in Peru, with the largest group ever noted including 230–240 individuals of this species. Reeves (2009) noted peaks of around 30 individuals feeding on single carcasses in Texas, most of which were black vultures, and Spradley et al. (2012) noted similar amounts feeding upon a single human body in Texas.

Other North American (Nearctic) Scavenging Bird Species

Multiple other avian taxa with ranges including portions of North America are common scavengers of vertebrate remains. These include crows (*Corvus* spp.), hawks and buzzards (*Buteo* spp.), some falcons (Falconidae), gulls (Family Laridae), and even blue jays (*Cyanocitta cristata*) and chickadees (Paridae) (Flint et al. 2010; Jennelle et al. 2009; Komar and Beattie 1998; Montalvo and Tallade 2009; Prior and Weatherhead 1991; Roen and Yahner 2005; Selva et al. 2005; Sorg et al. 2012). Most of these taxa are smaller than vultures and have a lesser potential to cause taphonomic alterations to large vertebrate skeletal remains, due to their lower biting force, lower daily food intakes, and decreased ability to disperse remains around their point of initial deposition, three factors that are also important in the scale of taphonomic effects of terrestrial scavengers (see Chapter 9, this volume). While some of these species also feed in large groups (Restani et al. 2001), some are less gregarious than vultures and feed in smaller groups or singly (Dall and Wright 2009), further reducing their potential overall effect. The social dominance of vultures also may reduce the taphonomic effect of these other species if they are displaced from feeding at the same carcass.

The Family Corvidae includes the genus *Corvus* (crows, rooks, ravens, and jackdaws), which includes approximately 40 species worldwide. These include American crow (*C. brachyrhynchos*) and the common raven (*C. corax*). Blue jays are also members of the Family Corvidae and consume carrion. Crows are broad omnivores who prey upon small species (Dall and Wright 2009; Frame 2010; Komar and Beattie 1998). They are known to eat almost anything, including garbage at landfill sites, where they are frequent pests (Baxter and Robinson 2007; Restani et al. 2001). They often include large vertebrate carrion in their diet (Jennelle et al. 2009). Common ravens are known to follow predatory species, including wolves (*Canis lupus*), to feed on the leftovers of their kills (Selva et al. 2005; Stahler et al. 2002). Such behavior (kleptoparasitic foraging) would allow them to arrive at carcasses on average prior to vultures and other species and gain a feeding advantage prior to being displaced by more dominant scavengers. Wolf feeding also allows entry through thick-skinned prey species that the ravens could not open themselves (Stahler et al. 2002). Ravens also will feed on discarded prey remains from other predatory species, including seabirds, bears, and humans (Matley et al. 2012; Restani et al. 2001). A general lack of fear of humans including an increasing reliance upon human-derived scavenged food sources (Restani et al. 2001) throughout their range also may favor corvids to be one of the earliest vertebrate scavenging species to show up at human remains left in outdoor settings. While corvids do not have highly developed olfactory apparati and generally rely upon sight to forage for food, ravens have been demonstrated (Harriman and Berger 1986) to use smell to some degree to locate food, at least over short distances.

The specific roles that these species play in the scavenging of human remains has been little researched. Komar and Beattie (1998) noted that crows and magpies were frequent scavengers of the experimental pigs they analyzed in an outdoor setting in Saskatchewan, Canada. Damage to soft tissue usually included triangular lesions from the beaks, and large amounts of soft tissue were consumed by these species alone. Edges of flesh exposed by feeding activity often had a cut appearance as if sliced by human action. Komar and Beattie (1998) also noted that feeding often began in areas of a carcass where soft tissue trauma had occurred, so the subsequent actions of the birds might obscure these areas of forensic interest. Asamura et al. (2004) attributed two cases of postmortem scavenging of human remains in Japan to *Corvus* through multiple lines of circumstantial evidence, including triangular defects left at the edges of feeding on soft tissue, crow footprints, and droppings nearby, sightings of large numbers of these birds in the immediate vicinity, and possible exclusion of other scavengers due to setting. Asamura et al. (2004) found that strands of more resilient tissues (nerve fibers, tendons, and ligaments) still attached to bones often had become frayed and "fluffy," likely due to the crows' inability to detach these types of strongly attached tissue while feeding on more easily removed portions. In both of their cases, soft tissue loss overall was massive, although in both cases, the individual had died outdoors from burning, and other sources of postmortem tissue loss are likely.

Additional research also is required on the feeding by small birds, including song birds (passerines). Dettling et al. (2011) describe a case of postmortem epidermal skin lesions on a recently deceased individual, where the most likely culprit was a pet finch (cf. Estrildidae) in the same household. They note that the damage accrued to the skin fit with the known pecking behavior of small birds attempting to gain moisture. Taphonomic alteration in this case was confined to superficial soft tissue damage and was not found on a second deceased individual in the same house.

Direct Damage to Bone by Large Scavenging Birds

Scavenging birds also may leave distinctive damage patterns upon bone while manipulating and consuming associated soft tissue (Hamilton and Spradley 2011; Reeves 2009; Spradley et al. 2012). Vultures have powerful beaks used to flense soft tissue from bone (i.e., strip the meat away while leaving the bones behind). Studies involving extant birds species scavenging humans and other large vertebrates confirm this pattern (Domínguez-Solera and Domínguez-Rodrigo 2011; Reeves 2009). Reeves (2009) found two types of markings left behind on pig and goat carcasses from (primarily black) vulture feeding: relatively shallow, irregular linear scratches up to 4 cm in length found most frequently on the skulls and less frequently on scapulae, ribs, long bones, and vertebrae, and very

Figure 16.1 Surface striations to cattle (*Bos taurus*) long bone caused by captive, rehabilitating female bald eagle (*Haliaeetus leucocephalus*) feeding. The scoring penetrates through the adhering soft tissue (left arrow) and into the bone surface (right arrow). (Data and image courtesy of Jessie Paolello, Conservancy of Southwest Florida, Naples, FL.)

shallow surface scratches mostly visible as a color change on the bone surface. Scratches of the latter type were ephemeral and may be lost easily through further manipulation or environmental factors. These scratches may have been caused by beaks directly during feeding or by talons while holding food for feeding. Other large raptor species leave similar marks (Figure 16.1). Reeves (2009) noted that more telling direct signs of vulture feeding include their droppings on and around the skeletal remains, trampling of grass, and feathers left behind.

Large raptors typically hunt their own prey items rather than scavenge, but there are cases where they have opted for the latter (Gargett 1990). In cases where the raptor has overestimated the mass of its chosen prey, it will disarticulate choice elements such as the skull or a hind limb for transport back to the nest or feeding perch (Baker 2012; Berger and Clarke 1995; Gargett 1990; MacGraw et al. 2006). In cases of predatory raptor feeding, puncture damage to bone (Figure 16.2) also has been noted (Baker 2012; Bochenski et al. 2009; Bochenski and Tornberg 2003), especially on prey taxa that are too large to be consumed whole and must be dismembered and/or flensed. Damage to large mammal skeletons often is confined to areas of thin bone cortex, including portions of the face, scapula blades, and long bone diaphyses (McGraw et al. 2006). Typical skull damage on primates (Figure 16.3) are scratches around the orbits, circular talon punctures through eye orbits (to access the eye), V-shaped punctures from the beak along the cranial vault resulting from removal of the scalp, and breaks through the zygomatic arch and respective maxillary to access the tongue. Sometimes, the occipital is removed in order to gain access to the brain case. Komar and Beattie (1998) found that even scavenging corvids can puncture thin cortical bone and leave behind conical-shaped marks in the cancellous bone of large vertebrate bones. This type of feeding may have been to access maggots feeding in these areas.

More taphonomically exotic are the actions of bearded vultures (*Gypaetus barbatus*) upon bone. This Old World species carries bones into the air to drop them on rocks far below in order to break them open to feed on the bone fragments and marrow contents (Margalida and Bertran 2001), especially the fat reserves of adult mammals (Margalida 2008). It also swallows bone fragments, and its digestive system may cause surface

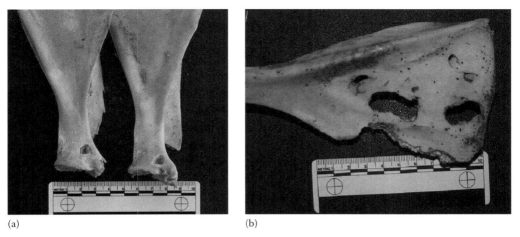

(a)   (b)

Figure 16.2 (a) Characteristic punctate depressions on the medial surface of two bovid scapulae left by an African tawny eagle (*Aquila rapax*). Note that the punctures are through the denser section of the bone, illustrating the ability of the large raptors to modify mammal skeletons larger than humans. Also note the characteristic triangular puncture left by beak piercings. (b) Composite raptor activity on a bovid scapula blade showing V-shaped nicks, scratches, and beak punctures. The scales are in cm.

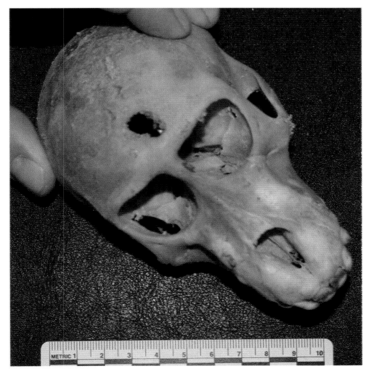

Figure 16.3 A vervet monkey (*Chlorocebus pygerythrus*) cranium showing a circular puncture, possibly from a talon pressing though the skull, along with punctures of the right orbit floor. Large raptors have the potential to produce similar damage to human crania. The scale is in cm.

alterations to bone (Houston and Copsey 1994; Margalida 2008; Margalida and Bertran 2001; Marín Arroyo and Margalida 2011; Robert and Vigne 2002). This adaptation may allow it to exist in higher altitude environments with more dispersed food resources, since bones and their digestible components (protein and fat) can survive for months or longer in a usable state, longer after exterior soft tissue has been consumed or decomposed. They also may be responsible for some archaeological accumulations across their formerly much broader Old World range (Marín Arroyo et al. 2009; Robert and Vigne 2002).

Potential Estimation of the PMI

Feeding rates of large numbers of scavenging birds potentially may allow an estimate of the PMI, provided that it is known that they were the primary scavenging species involved with soft tissue consumption. A relative paucity of competing terrestrial scavengers that might disperse remains or reduce the amount of soft tissue more quickly therefore is necessary for meaningful PMI estimates, as well as an arid or semiarid (i.e., desiccating) or freezing environment that would limit the amount of tissue loss to maggot consumption. In practical terms, these factors may limit application to outdoor cases early in the PMI. The amount of time necessary for scavenging birds to locate a set of remains also must be considered, as must be the time of day that a body is introduced to the environment. Vultures are diurnal and stop feeding at darkness until the next morning, when they often return to the same food source from the previous day. An understanding of the potential involvement of scavenging birds (and other species) in the skeletonization process of human remains must be known if the overall rate of skeletonization (presumably from maggot and other invertebrate feeding alone) is to be used to estimate the PMI (Megyesi et al. 2005) in a given environment. Losses of large amounts of soft tissue from unknown amounts of vertebrate scavenging would greatly increase the apparent PMI estimate if it were assumed that the bulk of soft tissue loss were due to the actions of invertebrates alone.

Reeves (2009), in her experiments exposing pig and goat carcasses to vulture feeding in an enclosed area that prevented large terrestrial scavenger access, noted a typical interval of over 24 h after the time of death of the individual before the arrival of the first vultures. The amount of time between death and placement of the carcass outdoors included 2, 18 and 24 h delays, and the time of day of placement also varied. The first vultures located the carcasses in as little as 7.5 h after placement (for a carcass dead 24 h already). Other trials required 8.5 h after placement (for a carcass dead 18 h already), 24 h (dead 2 h already), and 36 h (dead 2 h already). It is unknown if the vultures would eventually reduce their carcass location time if continually baited in the same location, but other habitual artificial food sources are known to receive more constant vulture attention (Hamilton and Spradley 2011; Stewart 1978). As indicated earlier, a certain delay in finding food by turkey vultures is to be expected, given their reliance upon smell to locate decaying remains. Even where black vultures first descend upon a carcass, they in some cases may be following the locating behavior of turkey vultures. The results of Reeves (2009) follow closely those of Houston (1986) (described earlier) for turkey vultures to locate carcass baits placed outdoors in Panama, where an initial decomposition period of 24 h was necessary for olfactory reasons. The amount of time necessary for vultures to locate a carcass, however, included a very long delay in the experiment performed by Spradley et al. (2012) using a human cadaver in the same environment in Texas used by Reeves (2009). A single unclothed female body was not fed upon by black vultures until during the first week after placement, with only minor damage to soft tissue accrued at that time. Feeding in earnest did not ensue until 37 days after placement, then proceeded rapidly. Areas with winter snow preserving and hiding bodies also may include delays between body deposition and active feeding. Given the large differences in the time of feeding onset between these two experiments, additional research may elucidate clearer patterns in vulture behavior.

Vultures skeletonizing a set of remains, once these are located and a large number of feeding birds has arrived, may proceed very rapidly (Figure 16.4). Reeves (2009) noted typical flocks of 30 vultures skeletonizing her test carcasses (ranging in mass from

Figure 16.4 Black vultures (*Coragyps atratus*; all dark plumage) with some intermixed turkey vultures (*Cathartes aura*; paler head plumage) feeding on a large pig (*Sus scrofa*) carcass. The second image was taken 25 min after the first, and the third image was taken 43 min after the second. Note the rapidity of soft tissue loss. (From Reeves, N. M., J. *Forensic Sci.*, 54, 523, 2009.) (Data and images courtesy of Nicole Reeves.)

27 to 63 kg) within 48–96 h after death. The time spent actively feeding, however, was much less than these amounts: the amount of active feeding time necessary to skeletonize remains ranged from 2 h and 39 min to 26 h and 45 min. In contrast, an enclosed (i.e., eliminating vulture access) 45-kg pig control carcass took over 2 weeks to skeletonize in the same environment during a trial run concurrently with a vulture feeding trial. The drying and hardening of skin may decrease the ease of vulture access and increase the amount of time necessary to skeletonize a set of remains. Spradley et al. (2012) noted that their human test cadaver, once located, was skeletonized over a 24 h period that included around 5 h of active vulture feeding. Other researchers similarly have noted the rapidity at which vultures can feed (van Dooren 2011; Houston 1986, 2001; Prior and Weatherhead 1991; Roen and Yahner 2005). The rapidity may increase in regions where multiple species of vulture are in competition over the same food sources (Wallace and Temple 1987). Since vulture species are in decline in some portions of the world due to losses of habitat, suitable food sources, and accidental ingestion of poisonous substances fed or injected into livestock (van Dooren 2011), estimates of feeding rates must take into account local population densities (Ogada et al. 2012).

Feeding rates for other scavenging bird taxa are less well known. Komar and Beattie (1998) noted that the hindquarters of an 80 kg experimentally deposited pig were consumed by the feeding of magpies alone, over the course of 1 week, with scavenging continuing over the course of a month. In this case, colder autumn weather subdued maggot activity and allowed continued access to remains.

Dispersal of Human Remains by Large Scavenging Birds

The feeding behavior of large scavenging birds also may disperse human remains around the site of deposition, especially due to the large number of birds that often feed simultaneously and the interspecies and intraspecies competition. These factors are known to increase the amount of osseous dispersal caused by terrestrial scavengers (see Chapter 9, this volume). Less dominant individuals may have no choice other than to grab edible portions and retreat a safe distance from the main food concentration or risk losing this food to more dominant individuals of their own or other species. Separating soft tissue from bones also may alter their original positions, as will the burrowing into a body to access easier to feed upon portions, especially where desiccated skin impedes feeding on soft tissue closer to the surface. Given the scavenging birds' ability to reach tight spots within and between bones with their long, sharp beaks, it is not surprising that a great deal of skeletal element manipulation and movement is typical as soft tissue is exploited more fully than that is possible without direct damage to the bones (as is typical of scavenging carnivores: see Chapter 9, this volume). Once separated, individual elements may be acted upon by precipitation and gravity and dispersed even further around the area of initial deposition. Birds, regardless of their small size, should not be ignored as a potential source of osseous dispersal even among large vertebrate food sources.

Reeves (2009) noted the ability of black vultures to carry small skeletal elements in their beaks, including elements at least as large as adult goat scapulae. Other elements were observed to be carried short distances, including pig vertebrae, and displacement outside of the fenced area included a pig scapula, radius, and ulna. Other localized dispersal of elements was found to be routine in her experimentation with large vertebrate carcasses.

The mandible often was detached first, followed in order by the cranium, the front limb elements, and the hind limb elements. Spradley et al. (2012) specifically examined the spatial patterning over time of human remains scavenged primarily by black vultures. They found a maximum linear displacement between body parts of 15.8 m, with a total area of dispersal of 83.6 m². Terrain effects may account for some of this dispersal, as minor variations in local topography were noted. Much skeletal element movement was detected in between mapping dates, so continued feeding even after the main bout of skeletonization has occurred can continue to displace elements around the deposition area. Komar and Beattie (1998) found that corvids were capable of dispersing small bones or fragments around a carcass feeding site and that some small bones including a pig metatarsal (comparable in size to a human metacarpal or metatarsal) was transported to a magpie nest 600 m distant.

The ability of birds to reach a carcass by air, with no passage over the ground leaving visible marks leading up to the carcass nor a large body mass in some cases to leave footprints or other traces upon landing, may account for the small amount of skeletal dispersal encountered on remains that bear no signs of terrestrial scavengers (see Chapter 9, this volume). Shed feathers and droppings may indicate the previous presence of avian scavengers (Asamura et al. 2004; Reeves 2009). The minor amounts of osseous dispersal caused by the migration of the maggot mass during advanced decomposition also account for the movement of smaller elements short distances (pers. obs.). Stolen (2003) also notes instances of turkey vultures transporting small scavenged food items in their beaks for up to 100 m before alighting to continue feeding. This behavior has the potential to disperse smaller human remains far past the immediate feeding area, where they are unlikely to be located later even with intensive searches. Turkey vultures have even been noted to exhume shallowly buried mammal remains for consumption, apparently detecting them through their decomposition scent alone (Smith et al. 2002). Small disturbances to recent, shallow human burials therefore cannot be assumed to be the result of terrestrial scavengers alone. Since vulture species also regurgitate pellets with the indigestible remnants of prey (Kelly et al. 2007), small consumed bones or fragments could be dispersed from the point of feeding in this manner. Since turkey vultures and black vultures congregate in communal roosts, it is possible though largely uninvestigated that highly fragmentary, digestively eroded (Houston and Copsey 1994) osseous remains could be concentrated in these areas (Thomaides et al. 1989; Yahner et al. 1990). Multiple species of Old World vulture frequently reconcentrate bones at their roosting sites to a far greater degree and in a more identifiable state (Plug 1978), sometimes as a result of provisioning juveniles (Mundy and Ledger 1976). Multiple crow species also *cache* food, removing it from its source and hiding it in other locations for later consumption (Bugnyar et al. 2007; Heinrich and Pepper 1998). Caching is also practiced among some species of terrestrial carnivore (see Chapter 9, this volume). This behavior among crows has the potential to disperse small human bones or fragments thereof away from their place of initial deposition, and they are unlikely to be recovered once removed and hidden in this manner.

Conclusions

While taphonomic alteration of primate remains by large raptor predation is common, including extant monkey taxa and in at least one case (the Taung Child) the extinct hominin species *Australopithecus africanus*, such alteration to modern human remains is generally not a factor in forensic investigations. While large raptors do damage bone during predation, feeding, and transport, far more likely is the taphonomic alteration of human remains by avian scavengers, which feed on a wide range of vertebrate carcasses. In North America, the most ubiquitous of these are the turkey vulture and black vulture, two wide-ranging and common species that evolved to exploit carrion efficiently. Their adaptations include the ability to locate fresh remains within their home ranges and feeding apparati to exploit these food sources when encountered. The introduction of human remains into their environment represents an important food source, and feeding upon these remains can leave distinctive direct alterations to bone surfaces and cause the dispersal of bone away from the point of initial deposition. While not as overall destructive and dispersive as some of the large terrestrial scavengers inhabiting North America (see Chapter 9, this volume), the potential for feeding by vultures and smaller avian scavengers (including crows and blue jays) is an important taphonomic consideration that cannot be overlooked in rural, outdoor crime scenes. Such feeding may occur in suburban areas close to human habitations as well (pers. obs.). Avian scavengers also have access to locations that exclude large terrestrial scavengers, sometimes by specific design as in the case of fenced outdoor decomposition facilities designed for forensic taphonomic experimentation (Reeves 2009; Ricketts 2012). Recent advances in our knowledge of the taphonomic effects these taxa have upon large vertebrates in the New World (Hamilton and Spradley 2011; Komar and Beattie 1998; Reeves 2009; Spradley et al. 2012) and Old World (De Ruiter et al. 2010; Domínguez-Solera and Domínguez-Rodrigo 2011; Margalida 2008; Margalida and Bertran 2001; Marín Arroyo and Margalida 2011) are important steps that should be followed up with additional research programs geared toward these species.

Acknowledgments

The senior author thanks the staff of the Division of Mammals and Division of Birds, Field Museum, Chicago, for their decades of assistance, access to comparative collections, and collaboration on avian taphonomy and many other topics. Some images and data were kindly provided by Nicole Reeves and Jessie Paolello. The junior author thanks Dr. Brian F. Kuhn for his help as a thesis supervisor. Thanks also go to Brianne Charles for her editorial assistance.

References

Andrews, P. (1990) *Owls, Caves and Fossils*. University of Chicago Press, Chicago, IL.
Asamura, H., K. Takayanagi, M. Ota, K. Kobayashi, and H. Fukushima (2004) Unusual characteristic patterns of postmortem injuries. *Journal of Forensic Sciences* 49:592–594.
Baker, S. E. (2012) *Accumulation Behaviours and Taphonomic Signatures of Extant Verreaux's Eagles, Aquila verreauxii, in Southern Africa*. Unpublished M.A. dissertation, University of the Witwatersrand, Johannesburg, South Africa.
Baxter, A. T. and A. P. Robinson (2007) A comparison of scavenging bird deterrence techniques at UK landfill sites. *International Journal of Pest Management* 53:347–356.
Berger, L. R. (2006) Predatory bird damage to the Taung type-skull of *Australopithecus africanus* Dart 1925. *American Journal of Physical Anthropology* 131:166–168.
Berger, L. R. and R. J. Clarke (1995) Eagle involvement in accumulation of the Taung child fauna. *Journal of Human Evolution* 29:275–299.

Berger, L. R. and W. S. McGraw (2007) Further evidence for eagle predation of, and feeding damage on, the Taung child. *South African Journal of Science* 103:496–498.

Bochenski, Z. M., T. Tomek, R. Tornberg, and K. Wertz (2009) Distinguishing nonhuman predation on birds: Pattern of damage done by the white-tailed eagle *Haliaetus albicilla*, with comments on the punctures made by the golden eagle *Aquila chrysaetos*. *Journal of Archaeological Science* 36:122–129.

Bochenski, Z. M. and R. Tornberg (2003) Fragmentation and preservation of bird bones in uneaten food remains of the Gyrfalcon *Falco rusticolus*. *Journal of Archaeological Science* 30:1665–1671.

Buckland, W. (1823) *Reliquiae Diluvianae, or, Observations on the Organic Remains Contained in Caves, Fissures, and Diluvial Gravel, and on Other Geological Phenomena, Attesting to the Action of an Universal Deluge*. John Murray, London, U.K.

Buckley, N. J. (1996) Food finding and the influence of information, local enhancement, and communal roosting on foraging success of North American vultures. *The Auk* 113:473–488.

Bugnyar, T., M. Stöwe, and B. Heinrich (2007) The ontogeny of caching in ravens, *Corvus corax*. *Animal Behaviour* 74:757–767.

Bunn, D. S., A. B. Warburton, and R. D. S. Wilson (1982) *The Barn Owl*. Buteo Books, Vermillion, SD.

Coleman, J. S. and J. D. Fraser (1989) Habitat use and home ranges of black and turkey vultures. *Journal of Wildlife Management* 53:782–792.

Cummings, J. H., G. E. Duke, and A. A. Jegers (1976) Corrosion of bone by solutions simulating raptor gastric juice. *Journal of Raptor Research* 10:55–57.

Dall, S. R. X. and J. Wright (2009) Rich pickings near large communal roosts favor 'gang' foraging by juvenile common ravens, *Corvus corax*. *PLoS ONE* 4:1–7. DOI: 10.1371/journal.pone.0004530.

Davis, D. H. S. (1959) The barn owl's contribution to ecology and palaeoecology. In *Proceedings of the First Pan-African Ornithological Conference,* ed. M. K. Rowan, pp. 143–153. *Ostrich*, Supplement No. 3.

De Ruiter, D. J., S. R Copeland, J. Lee-Thorp, and M. Sponheimer (2010) Investigating the role of eagles as accumulating agents in the dolomitic cave infills of South Africa. *Journal of Taphonomy* 8:129–154.

Dettling, A., P. Strohbeck-Kühner, G. Schmitt, and H. T. Haffner (2001) Tierfraß durch einen Singvogel? *Archiv für Kriminologie* 208:48–53.

Dodson, P. and D. Wexlar (1979) Taphonomic investigations of owl pellets. *Paleobiology* 3:275–284.

Domínguez-Solera, S. and M. Domínguez-Rodrigo (2011) A taphonomic study of a carcass consumed by griffon vultures (*Gyps fulvus*) and its relevance for the interpretation of bone surface modifications. *Archaeological and Anthropological Sciences* 3:385–392.

van Dooren, T. (2011) *Vulture*. Reaktion Books, London, U.K.

Duke, G. E., A. A. Jegers, G. Loff, and O. A. Evanson (1975) Gastric digestion in some raptors. *Comparative Biochemistry and Physiology* 50A:649–656.

Flint, P. L., E. W. Lance, K. M. Sowl, and T. F. Donnelly (2010) Estimating carcass persistence and scavenging bias in a human-influenced landscape in western Alaska. *Journal of Field Ornithology* 81:206–214.

Frame, P. F. (2010) Observations of a possible foraging tool used by common ravens. *The Wilson Journal of Ornithology* 122:181–182.

Gargett, V. (1990) *The Black Eagle: A Study*. Acorn Books and Russel Friedman Books, Randburg, South Africa.

Gilbert, C. C., W. S. McGraw, E. and Delson (2009) Plio-Pleistocene eagle predation on fossil Cercopithecids from the Humptata Plateau, southern Angola. *American Journal of Physical Anthropology* 139:421–429.

Glading, B., D. F. Tillotson, and D. M. Selleck (1943) Raptor pellets as indicators of food habits. *California Fish and Game* 29:92–121.

Glue, D. E. (1970) Avian predator pellet analysis and the mammalogist. *Mammal Review* 1:53–62.

Gourichon, L. (2002) Bird remains from Jerf El Ahmar a PPNA site in northern Syria with special reference to the griffon vulture (*Gyps fulvus*). In *Archaeozoology of the Near East, V* eds. H. Buitenhuis, A. M. Choyke, M. Mashkour, and A. H. Al-Shiyab, pp. 138–152. ARC-Publicaties 62, Groningen, the Netherlands.

Harriman, A. E. and R. H. Berger (1986) Olfactory acuity in the common raven (*Corvus corax*). *Physiology & Behavior* 36:257–262.

Hart, D. L. (2000) *Primates as Prey: Ecological, Morphological, and Behavioral Relationships between Primate Species and Their Predators*. Unpublished PhD Dissertation. Washington University, St. Louis, MO.

Hart, D. L. and R. W. Sussman (2008) *Man the Hunted: Primates, Predators, and Human Evolution* (rev. edn.). Westview Press, Cambridge, MA.

Hamilton, M. D. and M. K. Spradley (2011) Purported drug cartel use of vultures as a method for body disposal. *Journal of Forensic Identification* 61:425–429.

Heinrich, B. and J. W. Pepper (1998) Influence of competitors on caching behaviour in the common raven, *Corvus corax*. *Animal Behaviour* 56:1083–1090.

Hiraldo, F., M. Delibes, and J. A. Donazar (1991) Comparison of diets of turkey vultures in three regions of northern Mexico. *Journal of Field Ornithology* 62:319–324.

Houlihan, P. F. and S. M. Goodman (1986) *The Birds of Ancient Egypt*. The Natural History of Egypt, Vol. 1. Aris & Phillips, Warminster, U.K.

Houston, D. C. (1986) Scavenging efficiency of turkey vultures in tropical forest. *The Condor* 88:318–323.

Houston, D. C. (2001) *Condors and Vultures*. Voyager Press, Stillwater, MN.

Houston, D. C. and J. A. Copsey (1994) Bone digestion and intestinal morphology of the bearded vulture. *Journal of Raptor Research* 28:73–78.

Houston, C. S., P. D. McLoughlin, J. T. Mandel, M. J. Bechard, M. J. Stoffel, D, R. Barber, and K. L. Bildstein (2011) Breeding home ranges of migratory turkey vultures near their northern limit. *The Wilson Journal of Ornithology* 123:472–478.

Jennelle, C. S., M. D. Samuel, C. A. Nolden, and E. A. Berkley (2009) Deer carcass decomposition and potential scavenger exposure to chronic wasting disease. *Journal of Wildlife Management* 73:655–662.

Kelly, N. E., D. W. Sparks, T. L. DeVault, and O. E. Rhodes, Jr. (2007) Diet of black and turkey vultures in a forested landscape. *The Wilson Journal of Ornithology* 119:267–270.

Kofron, C. P. (1999) Attacks to humans and domestic animals by the southern cassowary (*Casuarius casuarius johnsonii*) in Queensland, Australia. *Journal of Zoology (London)* 249:375–381.

Komar, D. and O. Beattie (1998) Identifying bird scavenging in fleshed and dry remains. *Canadian Society of Forensic Science Journal* 31:177–188.

Korth, W. W. (1979) Taphonomy of microvertebrate fossil assemblages. *Annals of the Carnegie Museum* 48:235–285.

Levinson, M. (1982) Taphonomy of microvertebrates from owl pellets to cave breccia. *Annals of the Transvaal Museum* 33:115–120.

Lovari, S., A. Renzoni, and R. Fondi (1976) The predatory habits of the barn owl (*Tyto alba* Scopoli) in relation to the vegetation cover. *Bollettino de Zoologia* 43:173–191.

Lyman, R. L., E. Power, and R. J. Lyman (2003) Quantification and sampling of faunal remains in owl pellets. *Journal of Taphonomy* 1:3–14.

Mandel, J. T., K. L. Bildstein, G. Bohrer, and D. W. Winkler (2008) Movement ecology of migration in turkey vultures. *Proceedings of the National Academy of Sciences* 105:19102–19107.

Margalida, A. (2008) Bearded vultures (*Gypaetus barbatus*) prefer fatty bones. *Behavioral Ecology and Sociobiology* 63:187–193.

Margalida, A. and J. Bertran (2001) Function and temporal variation in the use of ossuaries by the bearded vulture (*Gypaetus barbatus*) during the nestling period. *The Auk* 118:785–789.

Marín Arroyo, A. B. and A. Margalida (2011) Distinguishing bearded vulture activities within archaeological contexts: Identification guidelines. *International Journal of Osteoarchaeology.* DOI: 10.1002/oa.1279.

Martin, D. (1996) On the cultural ecology of sky burial on the Himalayan Plateau. *East and West* 46:353–370.

Matley, J. K., R. E. Crawford, and T. A. Dick (2012) Observation of common raven (*Corvus corax*) scavenging Arctic cod (*Boreogadus saida*) from seabirds in the Canadian High Arctic. *Polar Biology* 35:1119–1122.

Mayhew, D. F. (1977) Avian predators as accumulators of fossil mammal material. *Boreas* 6:25–31.

McGraw, W. S., C. Cooke, and S. Shultz (2006) Primate remains from African crowned eagle (*Stephanoaetus coronatus*) nests in Ivory Coast's Tai Forest: Implications for primate predation and early hominid taphonomy in South Africa. *American Journal of Physical Anthropology* 131:151–165.

Megyesi, M. S., S. P. Nawrocki, and N. H. Haskell (2005) Using accumulated degree-days to estimate the postmortem interval from decomposed human remains. *Journal of Forensic Sciences* 50:618–626.

Montalvo, C. I. and P. O. Tallade (2009) Taphonomy of the accumulations produced by *Caracara plancus* (Falconidae). Analysis of prey remains and pellets. *Journal of Taphonomy* 7:235–248.

Moon, E. L. (1940) Notes on hawk and owl pellet formation and identification. *Transactions of the Kansas Academy of Science* 43:457–466.

Mundy, P. J. and J. A. Ledger (1976) Griffon vultures, carnivores and bones. *South African Journal of Science* 72:106–110.

Nock, D. B. (1932) Cremation and burial in the Roman empire. *Harvard Theological Review* 25:321–359.

Ogada, D. L., M. E. Torchin, M. F. Kinnaird, and V. O. Ezenwa (2012) Effects of vulture declines on facultative scavengers and potential implications for mammalian disease transmission. *Conservation Biology* 26:453–460.

Parker, J. W. (1999) Raptor attacks on people. *Journal of Raptor Research* 33:63–66.

Phillips, R. L., J. L. Cummings, G. Notah, and C. Mullis (1996) Golden eagle predation on domestic calves. *Wildlife Society Bulletin* 24:468–470.

Pokines, J. T. (1998) *Paleoecology of Lower Magdalenian Cantabrian Spain.* British Archaeological Reports, International Series S713, Oxford, U.K.

Pokines, J. T. and J. Kerbis Peterhans (1998) Barn owl (*Tyto alba*) taphonomy in the Negev Desert, Israel. *Israel Journal of Zoology* 44:19–27.

Pokines, J. T., A. Nowell, M. S. Bisson, C. E. Cordova, and C. J. H. Ames (2011) The functioning of a natural faunal trap in a semi-arid environment: Preliminary investigations of WZM-1, a limestone sinkhole site near Wadi Zarqa Ma'in, Hashemite Kingdom of Jordan. *Journal of Taphonomy* 9:89–115.

Plug, I. (1978) Collecting patterns of six species of vultures (Aves: Accipitridae). *Annals of the Transvaal Museum* 31:51–63.

Prior, K. A. (1990) Turkey vulture food habits in southern Ontario. *The Wilson Bulletin* 102:706–710.

Prior, K. A. and P. J. Weatherhead (1991) Competition at the carcass: Opportunities for social foraging by turkey vultures in southern Ontario. *Canadian Journal of Zoology* 69:1550–1556.

Rabenold, P. P. (1987) Roost attendance and aggression in black vultures. *The Auk* 104:647–653.

Rabenold, P. P. and M. D. Decker (1989) Black and turkey vultures expand their ranges northward. *Eyas* 2:11–15.

Reed, E. B. (1957) Mammal remains in pellets of Colorado barn owls. *Journal of Mammalogy* 38:135–136.

Reed, D. N. (2005) Taphonomic implications of roosting behavior and trophic habits in two species of African owl. *Journal of Archaeological Science* 32:1669–1676.

Reeves, N. M. (2009) Taphonomic effects of vulture scavenging. *Journal of Forensic Sciences* 54:523–528.

Restani, M., J. M. Marzluff, and R. E. Yates (2001) Effects of anthropogenic food sources on movements, survivorship and sociality of common ravens in the Arctic. *Condor* 103:399–404.

Ricketts, D. R. (2012) *Scavenging Effects and Scattering Patterns on Porcine Carcasses in Eastern Massachusetts*. Unpublished M.S. Thesis, Boston University School of Medicine, Boston, MA.

Robert, I. and J. D. Vigne (2002) The bearded vulture (*Gypaetus barbatus*) as an accumulator of archaeological bones: Late glacial assemblages and present-day reference data in Corsica (Western Mediterranean). *Journal of Archaeological Science* 29:763–777.

Roen, K. T. and R. H. Yahner (2005) Behavioral responses of avian scavengers in different habitats. *Northeastern Naturalist* 12:103–112.

Sanders, W. J., J. Trapania, and J. C. Mitanic (2003) Taphonomic aspects crowned hawk-eagle predation on monkeys. *Journal of Human Evolution* 44:87–105.

Scofield, R. P. and K. W. S. Ashwell (2009) Rapid somatic expansion causes the brain to lag behind: The case of the brain and behavior of New Zealand's Haast eagle (*Harpagornis moorei*). *Journal of Vertebrate Paleontology* 29:637–649.

Selva, N., B. Jędrzejewska, W. Jędrzejewski, and A. Wajrak (2005) Factors affecting carcass use by a guild of scavengers in European temperate woodland. *Canadian Journal of Zoology* 83:1590–1601.

Smith, H. R., R. M. DeGraaf, and R. S. Miller (2002) Exhumation of food by the turkey vulture. *Journal of Raptor Research* 36:144–145.

Sørensen, O. J., M. Totsås, T. Solstad, and R. Rigg (2008) Predation by a golden eagle on a brown bear cub. *Ursus* 19:190–193.

Sorg, M. H., W. D. Haglund, J. A. Wren, and A. Collar (2012) Taphonomic impacts of small and medium-sized scavengers in northern New England. *Proceedings of the American Academy of Forensic Sciences* 18:400.

Southern, H. N. (1954) Tawny owls and their prey. *Ibis* 96:384–410.

Spradley, M. K., M. D. Hamilton, and A. Giordano (2012) Spatial patterning of vulture scavenged human remains. *Forensic Science International* 219:57–63.

Stager, K. E. (1964) *The Role of the Olfaction in Food Location by the Turkey Vulture* (Cathartes aura). Los Angeles County Museum Contributions to Science, No. 18.

Stahler, D., B. Heinrich, and D. Smith (2002) Common ravens, *Corvus corax*, preferentially associate with grey wolves, *Canis lupus*, as a foraging strategy in winter. *Animal Behaviour* 64:283–290.

Stewart, P. A. (1978) Behavioral interactions and niche separation in the black and turkey vultures. *Living Bird* 17:79–84.

Stewart, K. M., L. Leblanc, D. P. Matthiesen, and J. West (1999) Microfaunal remains from a modern east African raptor roost: Patterning and implications for fossil bone scatters. *Paleobiology* 25:483–503.

Stolen, E. D. (2000) Foraging behavior of vultures in central Florida. *Florida Field Naturalist* 28:173–181.

Stolen, E. D. (2003) Turkey vultures carrying carrion. *Florida Field Naturalist* 31:2.

Terry, R. C. (2010) On raptors and rodents: Testing the ecological fidelity and spatiotemporal resolution of cave death assemblages. *Paleobiology* 36:137–160.

Thomaides, C., R. Valdex, W. H. Reid, and R. J. Raitt (1989) Food habits of turkey vultures in west Texas. *Journal of Raptor Research* 23:42–44.

Trinkaus, K. M. (1984) Mortuary ritual and mortuary remains. *Current Anthropology* 25:674–679.

Wallace, M. P. and S. A. Temple (1987) Competitive interactions within and between species in a guild of avian scavengers. *The Auk* 104:190–295.

Yahner, R. H., G. L. Storm, and W. L. Thompson (1990) Winter diets of vultures in Pennsylvania and Maryland. *The Wilson Bulletin* 102:320–325.

Effects of Recovery Methods

17

JAMES T. POKINES
JOAN E. BAKER

Contents

Cast the net on the right side of the boat, and ye shall find.

—**John 21:6**

Let your hook be always cast. In the pool where you least expect it, will be fish.

—**Ovid**

Introduction

Before drawing conclusions about the overall pattern of recovery from an incomplete skeleton, the question must be addressed of whether individual bones or portions thereof are missing because they (1) were destroyed and/or dispersed away prior to excavation/ surface recovery or (2) the searching/excavation methods or the execution thereof failed in fully recovering the remains (Bunch 2010; Cannon 1999; Dupras et al. 2011; Freeman et al. 1998; Haglund and Reay 1993; Lyman 2008, 2012; Mays et al. 2012; Ozbun 2011; Payne 1972; Pokines 2000; Quitmyer 2004; Shaffer and Sanchez 1994). Natural taphonomic processes that may destroy bones include breakdown and dissolution while buried (Chapters 2 and 5, this volume), gnawing and consumption by animal species (Chapters 7, 9, and 16), advanced subaerial weathering (Chapter 11), and thermal alteration (Chapter 14).

447

The inherent differences in survivability relating to bone density and structure also affect recovery (Chapter 4), as does developmental state (juvenile vs. adult). Natural taphonomic processes that may disperse bones away from an area that reasonably can be excavated or searched include water (Chapters 6 and 7) and large scavengers (Chapters 7, 9, and 16). Before a natural or criminal agency of bone loss can be surmised, the effects of the overall recovery system first must be ruled out. Failure to understand the potential of a search/ excavation system to be unsuccessful in its main function of osseous and other evidence recovery may lead to erroneous conclusions, such as ascribing missing items to natural taphonomic forces or perimortem trauma and incorrectly interpreting forensic context and postmortem history (Ball and Bobrowsky 1987).

Clearly, the goals of a given recovery shape the meaning of recovery bias, and these goals are shaped by many practical time and resource considerations. The forensic archaeologist must decide, prior to excavation or surface search, how to secure the required amount of evidence to process the scene in accordance with established professional standards (e.g., SWGANTH 2012). The acceptable minimum must be addressed along with the practical maximum: it is entirely possible to gather too much evidence, beyond the possible storage and processing capabilities of one's agency/institution and which will never be required to prosecute a case or identify a missing individual. Human remains in forensic settings pose a special problem. While maximum recovery of all surviving remains is expected (i.e., representative sampling is not the goal the way it might be in the archaeological recovery of an ancient cemetery, settlement, or cave site), the fineness of the metaphorical net cast to recover these remains is subject to change based on optimizing resources relative to constraints in light of the goals of recovery and ensuing analysis.

For example, in cases where time for search or recovery is limited, the modalities of identification may be an important consideration in developing a strategy, as prioritization of some aspect of the process may be required. Political or other pressures also may call for a focus on conclusively identifying the most individuals in the least amount of time rather than complete recovery of the remains for each individual (Sledzik et al. 2009:291). In cases of extreme fragmentation, DNA may be the primary method for individual identification (Sledzik et al. 2009:290), and precise spatial relationships may be less critical, allowing more focus on bulk recovery. If isotopic analysis or dental identifications are particularly important in a given recovery situation or if the burial environment is such that only teeth are expected to be recovered, then a finer screening protocol may be desirable in order to maximize the recovery of teeth (Mays et al. 2012). In mass graves, bone articulations may provide the best linkages between elements, so a clear understanding of anatomy and documentation of spatial relationships are crucial for expediting the identification process. If circumstances allow, fill from an excavation may be transported to another location for processing (Fairgrieve 2008; Sledzik et al. 2009). Thus, the circumstances of deposition, ultimate goals of the recovery, and methods to be used in analysis are critical to developing an appropriate recovery strategy.

Recovery system design, therefore, will be influenced by multiple factors including available overall time, budget, prepositioning of recovery equipment, the necessity for proper documentation of finds, availability of other specialists (including handlers with cadaver dogs, heavy machinery operators, and pilots), impending poor weather or darkness, trained recovery personnel (balanced with the simultaneous need to train additional recovery personnel for future operations), other law enforcement agencies, the needs of private citizens (landowners, etc.), and the need for a safe and functioning infrastructure by the community at large (including the need to return airport runways to operational use as soon as possible after an air crash or to demolish an unsafe building after it has been largely destroyed by a fire). Forensic archaeology also has, unlike most other types of archaeology, a built-in countdown to recover remains before additional decomposition can set in, making working conditions far less pleasant and subsequent identification less possible, especially in the case of mass disasters (Randall 1991; Sledzik et al. 2009; Ubelaker et al. 1995). Forensic archaeologists in general long for more time to process their sites and must have practical systems in place for the inevitable logistical compromises that must be made (Ball and Bobrowsky 1987; Menez 2005). Mistaken interpretations of the results of these compromises as the cause of certain missing skeletal remains can be mitigated through a thorough understanding of the limitations of the recovery methods employed.

Effects of Search and Recovery Methods

Field methods for recovering human remains from terrestrial environments are split into two main categories: (1) those used to search for and recover remains on the ground surface and (2) those used to locate and recover underground remains. The problems with each are different, but both involve difficulties in *seeing* osseous remains. Surface search and recovery often require some screening of the surface decomposing humus layer and frequently are hindered by the challenges associated with finding osseous remains and associated artifacts (clothing, identification media, bullets, etc.) dispersed over a large area in potentially difficult terrain with natural obstacles (live foliage, streams, etc.). The color of bone can be a significant impediment, as its natural beige color can match the color of dried leaf litter, or subsequent algae formation may turn it green, matching the color of foliage (Huculak and Rogers 2009; see also Chapter 12, this volume). This camouflage effect decreases when bones have been bleached naturally through long-term sun exposure (Chapter 11), which tends to increase the amount of contrast between bones and the ground surface. Highly fragmentary remains or those covered by snow, foliage, or other types of plant litter will be more difficult to locate. Similarly, the main problems with locating remains during excavation arise from seeing the osseous remains, which are often stained in colors similar to the surrounding sediments (see Chapter 12, this volume). Of course, some cases may have aspects of surface search and recovery as well as excavation, such as when buried remains have been partly exhumed by scavengers, plowing, etc., and dispersed on the surface, thus marking the burial location with a surface scatter of bones. In all cases, certain procedures and equipment may help the forensic archaeologist to "see" better, and these are discussed later.

Surface Search Methods

Visual searches are by their nature reliant on the ability of the searchers to recognize human remains as they walk through an area (Fairgrieve 2008:62), and as such they are partially dependent upon the individual ability levels of search team members to spot bone while walking. All effective surface search methods must have in common the following components: (1) searchers must be spaced appropriately for the terrain and surface conditions so that they can cover all ground visually on a sweep without gaps between searchers; (2) a method of marking swept areas must be devised to prevent gaps; and (3) the search area must contain all of the surface remains that can be found. The last component may be easy to determine in some cases, such as when a partial skeleton is found and searches in the surrounding area continue until all missing elements are located. The full extent of a search area only can be estimated in other cases, since the forensic anthropologist may have to presume that any missing skeletal material was consumed or dispersed beyond any reasonable search area. Agents of dispersal may include vertebrate scavengers, such as ursids, canids, and birds (see Chapters 9 and 16, this volume), especially where remains have traces of large carnivore gnawing or bird beak/talon marks), as well as agricultural practices and criminal activities. The question still may exist regarding the searched area being large and/or searched thoroughly enough, and the final decision regarding cessation of search efforts will rest with the forensic archaeologist and law enforcement personnel.

Strip/line searches, grid searches, and circular searches (Figure 17.1) are all variations of surface survey, with the goal of maximizing the amount of ground searched visually while minimizing personnel and time (Dupras et al. 2011). Strip/line searches use multiple passes through a predetermined area. Strips or paths of travel may be individually measured off and marked to facilitate the arrangement of ground search personnel and to supply provenience for material evidence. Grid searches are similar to strip/line searches, except after the initial parallel swaths through an area, the course is reversed 90°, and the same area is covered again. This method provides redundancy of areal coverage, places different sets of eyes over the same pieces of ground if multiple personnel are used, and further provides the advantage of looking for evidence from different angles, maximizing shifts in lighting or surface cover that may affect visibility. Both of the first two methods are amenable to area control, as successive large rectilinear areas can be measured adjacent to each other and searched, spreading outward from core areas to more peripheral ones. Corners can be marked temporarily and recorded using a GPS unit within acceptable limits of accuracy. Circular searches are the most problematic, as it is inherently more difficult to guide the path of an expanding Archimedes spiral without overlapping previous rotations or straying too far outward and leaving gaps. This type of search may be used as an

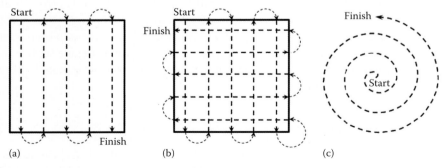

Figure 17.1 Types of search patterns: (a) strip or line, (b) grid, and (c) circular. (Redrawn after Dupras, T. L. et al., *Forensic Recovery of Human Remains: Archaeological Approaches*, 2nd edn., CRC Press, Boca Raton, FL, 2011.)

initial reconnaissance of an area, moving outward from a centralized bone concentration or other starting point in order to plan more thorough strip/line or grid searches covering the same ground. Items found on the initial search can be marked with pin flags for later mapping and retrieval. Combination search methods such as these make a fuller recovery more likely and allow the forensic anthropologist to assess the reason for any missing remains more reliably.

Special methods may augment the success of human search teams. Most obvious is the use of trained cadaver dog teams (Lasseter et al. 2003), which may be particularly useful not just for the initial discovery of bone concentrations and burials but also to detect widely dispersed remains, such as those dispersed along game trails by large scavengers or reconcentrated in carnivore dens (Chapter 9). Cadaver dogs, utilizing their acute sense of smell, have parallel limitations to the use of sight by searching humans. Environmental effects will alter how the scent is transmitted in the air, with such factors as wind direction and intensity, ambient temperature, and precipitation all crucial to the individual dog's success. Handler experience and fatigue of the dogs are also factors that can affect success (Lit et al. 2011). While dogs searching an area may locate scattered remains in multiple locations, one cannot say for certain that the searched areas that yielded no hits by the dogs perforce contained zero remains any more than a negative visual search by humans in a forest covered with leaf litter indicates that no remains can be present. Other special methods of searching are geared toward finding burials and not scattered surface remains. These include probing (Owsley 1995), ground penetrating radar (Pringle et al. 2012; Schultz 2008), metal detection for associated objects (Rezos et al. 2011), and other geophysical methods (Dupras et al. 2011). Of these, metal detection is the most useful in surface searches in that it is noninvasive and may locate metal objects (rings, watches, coins, zippers, snaps, projectiles, etc.) associated with not-yet visible skeletal remains, especially those lightly buried within the surface layer of decomposing leaf litter.

Failure to recover remains may lead to other issues besides false interpretations of taphonomic history. Elements missed during the initial recovery of surface remains may be discovered after the case already has been resolved and after the previously recovered remains have been buried by next of kin. The recovery of additional remains may place an emotional burden upon surviving relatives if they have assumed closure in the aftermath of losing a loved one. Additional remains also create a resource burden for the anthropologist who likely must search the original area again, generate additional reports, and expend limited resources for DNA testing, even if no change in the previous overall analytical conclusions is necessitated by the new remains. Such issues can be avoided if a full recovery is made during the initial fieldwork.

Burned remains may be particularly difficult to locate due to heat-related changes in color, shape, and overall appearance. In general, burned bones in a human body will remain in the same relative (anatomical) position when burned unless another agent acts before, during, or after the fire to disturb the remains (Dirkmaat 2002; Fairgrieve 2008:72; Ubelaker et al. 1995; and pers. obs.). Such actors may include criminal agents as well as fire suppression and rescue personnel. In addition, vehicle and building fires frequently contain nonorganic materials that may be confused with human remains due to heat-related damage: plastics, plaster, foam, and insulation can all melt, warp, and discolor in ways that resemble bone (see Chapter 14, this volume). Best practice requires recovery of any items suspected as being bone, burned or unburned, with the final determination made under a binocular microscope in the laboratory.

Excavation Methods

Multiple resources exist for training in the archaeology of skeletal recovery (Barker 1993; Blau and Ubelaker 2009; Ferllini 2007; Ubelaker 1999), and an extensive review of methods is not possible here. The methods selected may have to be modified due to resource availability, as discussed earlier. In addition, forensic archaeologists must choose not only the area and depth where they are excavating (the volume of sediments to be examined) but also the size of excavation grid units that will be used. In so doing, forensic archaeologists are in effect choosing the level of resolution within the site. If four-meter grid units are used, for example, and no finer control is implemented within that unit, the provenience of any object found is limited to that 16 m² area and within the depth range chosen. Excavators are free to subdivide larger units, at least temporarily, such as by digging this same 16 m² unit in sixteen 1 m² subunits and recording the subunit of evidentiary items. (This process is analogous to decreasing the amount of pixilation in a digital image.) Similarly, burial features are usually broken down by grid unit, and individual sediment lots are often tracked for screening with such designations as "area of right foot," "area of left hand," and "superior thoracic area," so that finds too small to be noted while excavating can be traced to a general location within the grave, relative to the skeleton. This procedure may save substantial time later in the laboratory where the identification and/or siding of degraded small elements or fragments can be expedited.

Underwater Search and Recovery

Underwater search and recovery operations have their own set of challenges and procedures (Green 2004). Such operations are restricted to certified dive masters with specific training in body and evidence recovery, and, in the case of disposal of fragmented or cremated remains, minimizing silt disturbance (Fairgrieve 2008). Audio and video communications to the surface with experts trained in bone recognition are essential in these operations (Fox 2003), as is the monitoring of any siphoned output for skeletal remains by trained osteologists.

The remains recovered from marine and freshwater environments in forensic cases are often fleshed, since soft tissue tends to decompose significantly more slowly underwater (Anderson 2008; Anderson and Hobischak 2002), and a large mass of fleshed remains is a much larger visual search target than individual remains. Submerged remains frequently float due to decomposition-related gas bloating (see Chapters 6 and 7, this volume). Individual skeletal elements from floating remains, as they become exposed through soft tissue decomposition and scavenger feeding, frequently drop off and are dispersed, making the recovery of these isolated elements rare from any large body of water, especially the ocean. The recovery of individual skeletonized elements in underwater environments away from shipwrecks, air crashes, and other vehicles therefore is rare in forensic contexts due to the difficulty in locating them once detached from the main body of remains. Despite the obvious differences in operational environment, the same basic problems apply as on land: (1) visibility of skeletal elements and associated artifacts when performing underwater survey and (2) the mesh size of the screening system being sufficient to collect the remains without significant loss of elements.

Effects of Screen Mesh Size

The trade-off involved in the data gained through recovery of smaller elements with finer mesh sizes versus the greater time needed to process the sediments is one of the most fundamental methodological decisions to make on any archaeological excavation (Ball and Bobrowsky 1987). Much research exists on the effects of screen size upon bone recovery, with size classes of taxa spanning microfauna (rodents, etc.) through megafauna (cattle, horses, goats, etc.) (Cannon 1999; Freeman et al. 1998; Mays et al. 2012; Payne 1972; Pokines 2000; Shaffer and Sanchez 1994), and the effects of variable wet-screening procedures employed within the same site have been examined for macrobotanical recovery (Hosch and Zibulski 2003). Mays et al. (2012) found that by mass, a third of the remains (including bones and teeth) recovered in a series of poorly preserved inhumations were found in 4 and 8 mm screens; notably, none of the bone or dental fragments found in the 2 mm screens could be identified to element. Significantly, in these poorly preserved burials, almost 23% of the graves yielded identifiable remains only in the screened sediments (i.e., no identifiable remains were recovered in the hand-excavated sediments). Furthermore, screening of grave sediments increased recovery of human skeletal remains by 53% versus the remains recovered solely from hand excavation (Mays et al. 2012). Considering the DNA identification potential in a single tooth or bone fragment in decades-old forensic cases (Leney 2006) and the rapidity with which acidic soil can break down remains in recent contexts (Casallas and Moore 2012), screening all burial sediments is the best option, especially in contexts where bone quality is expected to be poor.

There is, however, little consensus on what constitutes a current "industry standard" for archaeological mesh size across all sites and recovery systems. Lyman (2012) notes that many authors examining osseous recovery rates based on mesh size assumed that 1/4 in. (6.35 mm) is the most popular mesh employed in large parts of the world and then compared 1/4 in. screen recovery rates with finer mesh sizes. In a sample of 25 screening method studies, 22 (88%) examined 1/4 in. mesh, 20 (80%) examined 1/8 in. (3.2 mm) mesh, and 7 (28%) examined 1/16 in. (1.6 mm) mesh. Ozbun (2011) noted the general inadequacy of 1/4 in. mesh to capture fine lithic debris and recommended 1/8 in. James (1997) noted the prevalence of 1/4 in. screens among archaeological excavations throughout the American Southwest and Great Plains and in Mesoamerica. Forensic archaeologists receiving large parts of their broader training engaging in other types of archaeology are likely to transfer these methods to forensic settings. In the more specific world of forensic recoveries, 1/4 in. mesh is standard for all Joint POW/MIA Accounting Command (JPAC) recovery operations (Pokines 2009), and Dupras et al. (2011) also recommended 1/4 in. mesh for the bulk of forensic recoveries, with finer mesh employed for special situations such as fetal remains. Without actual polling data from archaeologists, published professional standards for forensic archaeology (SWGANTH 2012), data culled from a suitable sample of grant reports, or sales data from archaeological mesh suppliers, the assumption that 1/4 in. mesh is employed across a large proportion of current excavations is plausible but unproven.

Figure 17.2 Examples of nesting geological screens of 2 and 1 mm mesh useful for screening special contexts such as pelvic areas of adult female skeletons when searching for fetal remains. Scale is in cm.

Very fine screening systems also have been explored. For example, Freeman et al. (1998) explored wet-screening and flotation recoveries using nested screens, with the ultra-fine (nylon) mesh size at 0.25 mm, which allowed for the recovery of artifacts as small as broken bone needle tips and eyelets in large amounts from a 14,000 year old Paleolithic cave site (Freeman et al. 1998). The time cost involved in this type of intensive screening is high, with the time to process the sediments taking on average longer than the time to excavate them. The size of sediment lots also is a factor, as fine-screening normally involves processing of smaller individual sediment lots.

Finer mesh sizes, however, do not always translate into higher recovery rates, as finer meshes also trap larger amounts of sediment and other debris that are not relevant to the investigation (pers. obs.). If this trapped sediment obscures small bones in the screen, the finer mesh actually decreases overall osseous recovery. The authors recommend no finer mesh than 1 mm for wet screening and 2 mm for dry screening in most forensic situations, even of fetal remains (see later). A variety of high-durability, metal-construction, nesting geological screens are available commercially (Figure 17.2) and can be used in conjunction with traditional wooden box screens with a coarser mesh for bulk processing of sediments. Wet screening is recommended for wet sediments of any kind, although the option exists with delayed processing methods to dry the sediments and then dry-screen them. This expedient solution is particularly useful where sites are far from water sources, where wet-screening equipment or trained personnel in wet-screening operations are lacking, or where insufficient time exists in the field to process burial sediments on-site. Sediments high in clay also pose a special problem in that clay adheres to bone surfaces and reduces bone visibility during sorting the contents of a screen, so wet screening in these cases may yield higher recovery rates.

Element Size

Individual element size also is correlated with the likelihood of recovery. Due to their small size, carpals, tarsals, hand and foot sesamoids, teeth (particularly incisors or any tooth fragments), epiphyses, and fetal or infant elements are perhaps some of the least likely elements to be noticed by untrained observers as well as the most likely to be overlooked during

Table 17.1   Screening Loss, Sample of Modern Permanent Human Teeth Passed through 1/4 in. (6.35 mm) Wire Mesh

Tooth Type	n	Number Lost through Screen	% Lost
Molar	43	0	0
Premolar	48	0	0
Canine	26	0	0
Incisor	60	15	25

recovery. This is particularly true if the remains are not in anatomical order as in a primary burial. The results of a practical dry-screening experiment using a sample (n = 177) of modern human teeth are depicted in Table 17.1. Two common mesh sizes, 1/4 in. (6.35 mm) and 1/8 in. (3.2 mm), were used to screen mixed, loose, undamaged, permanent upper and lower dentition. In order to protect the remains from damage, neither agitation nor sediment matrix was used. The purpose of screen agitation is to cause each object in the screen to present multiple aspects to the mesh openings, so that smaller objects will pass through. This can occur even if the object is only small enough in two dimensions to fit through the mesh, while the third dimension is larger (Ozbun 2011). Thus, a rib theoretically could pass through a mesh opening if its width and thickness were sufficiently small, despite its long length. Each element in the experiment was manipulated with fine forceps to determine which could pass through the mesh at any angle. This method likely overestimates the number of intact elements that would pass through the mesh during real screening operations, since several of the elements that did fit through (see later) could only do so in one orientation. These therefore might get captured by the screen mesh, especially with any sediments adhering. No teeth passed through the 1/8 in. mesh. The 1/4 in. mesh did not allow any of the molars, premolars, or canines to pass through, but 15 of 60 incisors (25%) could fit through. None of the incisors that passed through were maxillary central incisors. Fragments from any type of permanent tooth likely could pass through a 1/4 in. mesh, and the effects of screen mesh size on deciduous dentition or partially formed permanent tooth recovery are likely to be much greater.

Juvenile Remains

Few comparative experimental data exist for the relative recovery rates of adult versus juvenile human skeletal elements, but findings may be extrapolated from experiments with faunal remains. Shaffer (1992) and Shaffer and Sanchez (1994) found that the highest potential for recovery was with mammalian taxa above 4500 g (approximately 10 lbs.) adult body mass and that finer mesh sizes (1/8 in.) significantly increased recovery rates of smaller bones. As taxon (and therefore skeletal element) body size decreased, so did relative recovery. While Mays et al. (2012) caution against extrapolating from animal remains recovery studies, the same principle holds true within a single species: remains from adult humans are much more likely to be recovered than those of human fetuses or infants (Scott 1999; Walker et al. 1988). In forensic contexts, the field recovery of fetal remains is more likely to occur in conjunction within the abdominal/pelvic area of the skeletal remains of the mother than if they occur in isolation. Alternately, juvenile remains recovery can be situational, with fetal or infant remains sometimes recovered in abundance in archaeological sites where they have been concentrated by cultural practices, such as via infanticide at the Roman site of Ashkelon in Israel (Faerman et al. 1998; Smith and Avishai 2005) or Hambleden Roman villa in England (Mays and Eyers 2011).

A brief experiment addressing the recoverability of fetal remains was performed in order to determine which portions of intact skeletons of known gestation age would pass through mesh screens of 2.0 mm (maximum diagonal opening, 2.83 mm) and 1.0 mm (maximum diagonal opening, 1.41 mm). The gestational age for these fetal remains was estimated from measurements of the maximum length of the femur diaphysis, following Fazekas and Kósa (1978). Two sets of fetal remains were used: the younger individual was estimated at 28–30 weeks, and the older individual was estimated at 36 weeks (or near full term). The basic methods followed those for the adult tooth screening experiment described earlier. This experiment did not address fragmentary fetal remains, which are likely to be encountered in the field. For example, intact tympanic rings of the older fetal skeleton were far too large to pass through the 2.0 mm mesh, but if broken, portions of them could fit through. Each skeleton was largely complete, except where noted. No dental remains (partially formed tooth crowns) were tested.

The screening results are presented in Table 17.2. None of the available intact ossified elements passed through the 1.0 mm mesh for either fetal skeleton, and only small, nondiagnostic elements passed through the 2.0 mm mesh. These included distal row manual and pedal phalanges, 9th through 12th ribs, lateral portions of the sacral vertebrae, and one of the auditory ossicles (the malleus). Naturally, the presence of such small elements is highly dependent upon the gestational age and the overall degree of skeletal ossification. Any element undergoing initial ossification that could pass through a 1.0 mm mesh is unlikely to be identifiable under normal conditions, but recovery personnel should be aware that small amounts of fetal bone loss may occur with 2.0 mm screens.

Table 17.2 Screening Loss, Sample of Human Fetal Remains, Gestation Age 28–30 Weeks and 36 Weeks Passed through 2.0 mm Wire Mesh

Gestation Age (Weeks)	Elements That Passed through 2.0 mm Mesh	Comments
36	Manual distal row phalanges, ray II–V	Seven of seven present passed; all other phalanges present except for 1 medial row phalanx
36	Medial and distal row pedal phalanges, ray II–IV	Two of two present passed; all proximal row phalanges present and did not pass
36	12th rib	One of two passed
36	Malleus	Left and right; other ossicles captured
36	Fourth sacral segment lateral portion	Only one present
28–30	Malleus	One of two passed
28–30	11th rib	Only one present; 12th ribs not present
28–30	10th ribs	Left and right
28–30	Ninth ribs	One of two passed
28–30	Third sacral segment lateral portions	Fourth not present
28–30	Manual distal row phalanx, ray II–V	Only one present
28–30	Left/right pedal proximal row phalanges	4 of 10 passed
28–30	Left pedal I distal row phalanx	Right not present; no additional pedal phalanges present/ossified

Note: All elements passing through the 2.0 mm mesh were captured by the 1.0 mm mesh.

Burned Remains

Additional taphonomic events, such as burning or fragmentation, may accentuate the effect of size on recovery (Dirkmaat 2002). For example, burned teeth may shrink between 10% and 15% (Buikstra and Swegle 1989; Shipman et al. 1984). Burning also can affect recognition of skeletal material due to changes in color and/or heat-related fragmentation. Teeth may be particularly susceptible to these changes, with burning sometimes causing shattering of the enamel or complete separation of the crown from the root. If the enamel falls off of the tooth due to thermal alteration, the dentin may retain most or all of its original relief, potentially allowing identification of the tooth type, position, and size (Schmidt 2008:65). Incompletely formed teeth and mature decid-uous teeth may be more susceptible to heat damage (e.g., color change and fragmenta-tion) than mature, erupted permanent teeth, particularly if they have fallen out of their sockets (Schmidt 2008). In cases where burned remains are expected, Schmidt (2008:71) recommended screening sediment with a 1/8 in. or finer screen to ensure that all teeth and tooth fragments are recovered.

Value of Small Elements

Apart from the professional and ethical obligation to turn over as a complete set of remains as possible to the next of kin, many easily overlooked skeletal elements have analytical value. As indicated earlier, teeth may provide DNA for identification as well as an avenue for individualization through morphology and restoration patterns; they also record valuable biological profile information including ancestry, age, sex, and childhood health. Stable isotope analysis, even of burned teeth, also may reveal the location in which an individual lived when the enamel was being formed (Knudson 2008; Knudson and Buikstra 2007). Even the fragmentary partial crowns of perinatal remains may be analyzed for the presence of the neonatal line in order to determine if the remains are full-term fetal or post-natal (Smith and Avishai 2005), which may have important implications in forensic analyses and legal proceedings. Ríos et al. (2011) noted several of the important data that can be gathered from small skeletal elements that are frequently overlooked in situations lacking adequate screening or searching. In their excavations of a prison cemetery from the Spanish Civil War, they were able to recover large amounts of laryngeal cartilage, manual and pedal sesamoids, and medial clavicle epiphyses *in situ*. Laryngeal cartilage and sesamoids yielded information regard-ing relative age, perimortem trauma, and degenerative changes, while the presence of detached medial clavicle epiphyses has important implications for aging a young adult skeleton (Webb and Suchey 1985). Similarly, the easily overlooked hyoid may preserve traces of perimortem strangulation trauma (Pollanen and Chiasson 1996). Small bone fragments created during a perimortem trauma event (gunshot wound, blunt force, etc.) are especially relevant to reconstructions of the events, which may have caused their fragmentation.

   Field archaeologists excavating a mostly undisturbed depositional context fre-quently blame missing elements on the actions of small species such as rodents rather than the recovery method or lack of recognition of remains as human instead of non-human mammal (pers. obs.). While fossorial rodents have a high potential to disturb elements (Bocek 1992), their presence in a site normally is accompanied by traces of burrows, some of which may contain their complete skeletons resulting from in-burrow mortality. Rodents do not preferentially target the smallest human skeletal elements in each hand and foot or unfused epiphyses, so lacking direct evidence of rodent involvement, the loss of these small elements is more likely to be due to excavation/screening loss or through degradation in acidic soil (Chapter 5). In addition, burrowing rodents normally displace small elements rather than destroy them, so these elements would still be present within the burial fill.

Effects of Recovery Personnel

An attentive, motivated, trained, and well-rested technician will recover more than one who is lacking in these aspects. Without personnel who can recognize, preserve, and document evidence properly, recovery efforts may be compromised or even unsuccessful (Fairgrieve 2008:61). In some international archaeological and forensic settings, local people supply much of the required field labor, including excavation and screening. Communication during training and field operations may be complicated by the fact that excavation organizers and local laborers speak different languages. In some cases, training, particularly in terms of recognition of bone and other relevant materials, may be perfunctory. For example, labor at a forensic recovery site may be supplied by individuals with varying amounts of training in recognizing skeletal material, such as sheriff's deputies, death investigators, other law enforcement personnel, morgue technicians, or forensic laboratory personnel (Fairgrieve 2008:61; Sledzik et al. 2009:294). Training level is a particular issue when the skeletal material is isolated and fragmented (i.e., not an articulated burial). This situation can be exacerbated in mass grave situations, where a clear understanding of skeletal variation, maturation, and anatomy is crucial to segregating individuals from one another as they are recovered.

Although rarely acknowledged in the literature, fatigue is an important consideration in fieldwork in that workers who are tired are unlikely to maximize their own potential for spotting relevant items either *in situ* or in a screen mesh. Fatigue may be situational or cumulative in that it may be related to performing a single repetitive task requiring precise focus for many hours in a single day, or it may be related to exhaustion brought on by many days of such effort. Workers in mass disaster situations, such as the World Trade Center or Pentagon recoveries, or long-term recovery efforts in stressful environments, such as mass grave excavations in wartime Iraq, may be particularly prone to cumulative fatigue (Fairgrieve 2008; Sledzik et al. 2009). Emotional stress, whether personal or related to the recovery situation, and climatic conditions may exacerbate fatigue-related recovery bias. Additional factors in fatigue may be physical in origin and not directly related to the fieldwork (e.g., illness, jet lag, or drug or alcohol use).

Some studies have been performed on interobserver effects during archaeological survey. Hawkins et al. (2003) measured the success rates of multiple observers during surface survey for lithic concentrations in Cyprus and Egypt. This included analyses of the rate of lithic scatters located per hour by individual surveyors, with variations in this rate suggesting bias. In addition, linear patterns in site density were noted in Egypt, where lines of increased site density corresponded not to natural or manmade features such as rivers or settlements but rather to transects walked by individual surveyors (Hawkins et al. 2003:1505–1506). Only a weak correlation was found regarding surveyors' experience levels, and some correlation was found with specific experience in lithics. Interestingly, individual motivation may have been a factor in recovery (e.g., someone without the most experience but with a vested personal interest, such as collecting data for a doctoral dissertation, may have a higher success rate).

Effects of Recovery Setting

The environment in which recovery is conducted necessarily affects completeness of recovery. Relevant factors may include weather, lighting, and soil type. Precipitation may cause evidence to be lost through erosion or tracking of wet sediments and associated evidence away from the recovery site on workers' shoes and boots. The former may be mitigated through the use of sandbag walls or other structures to block sediment loss. The latter may be of lesser concern due to the minimal amounts of sediment typically involved, but such concerns can be addressed through setting aside a separate area for workers to collect sediment as they clean their footwear prior to leaving the site.

Lighting may play an important, but little acknowledged, role in successful recovery of evidence. In situations where sediments may be transported from the site to a separate indoor location for processing, bright lighting may not be an issue. However, where the sole or primary location of recovery is in the field, natural lighting may influence recovery potential. Locales with high heat indices are often accompanied by bright natural lighting, but shaded processing areas are required to protect workers from heat injury. While no studies have been done to quantify the effects of lighting on recovery, common sense dictates that such considerations may play an important role in recovering skeletal remains and associated materials.

The choice of material used to provide the shade can affect visibility of evidence. For example, heat injury is a serious issue for recovery teams excavating sites in pursuit of missing U.S. servicemembers in Southeast Asia, such as those conducted by the former Central Identification Laboratory-Hawaii, now known as the JPAC (Moore et al. 2002; Webster 1998). During the authors' tenure at these organizations, temporary shade structures were often constructed over sediment processing areas using heavy plastic tarps, usually bright blue in color. These tarps provided some relief from heat and sunlight but decreased the ambient lighting by a significant degree and often blocked any incipient breezes. The blue-tinted light also made it more difficult to see bone and other objects that had been stained red in tropical clay soil. In an attempt to moderate the amount of available lighting while maintaining air circulation, some recovery teams began using black "gardener's cloth," a type of shade netting comprising woven strips of plastic, to cover screening stations. While the strips allow both light and air through, the resulting illumination is mottled, making it difficult to discern subtle distinctions in color and shape that allow workers to distinguish evidence from organic debris and sediment. Naturally shaded areas (e.g., those located under tree cover) may present similar visibility challenges. Clearly, the question of how best to protect personnel health while maintaining maximum recovery is a complex one that deserves consideration when devising site protocols, since the very real danger of heat stroke exists under certain climatic conditions.

The effects of recovery setting may be mitigated by the transfer of sediments from a difficult field setting to a laboratory setting where sediments are screened. For example, Bunch (2010) described a process for wet-screening recovery of three sets of exhumed child remains (ages 18 months, 3 years, and 5 years) in a laboratory, where the environment and time expended could be controlled. Poor wooden coffin preservation combined with cold and rain made field conditions for recovery less than optimal. The entire coffins were removed and returned to the laboratory, and the contents underwent additional excavation and provenience recording. The two more poorly preserved sets of remains (recovered initially from a house fire) were processed with very low-pressure water and without screen agitation over 1/4 in. (6.35 mm) mesh. This gentle technique allowed the recovery of remains with signs of previous trauma, despite their delicate nature, subsequent thermal damage, and the suboptimal depositional environment. This procedure is particularly suited for forensic recoveries from coffin exhumations, where there is no real question within these sealed contexts about containment of remains and where the spatial context of individual elements is no longer critical to analysis (since these elements were not placed there as a criminal act but subsequent to any such actions). In cases where single individuals (making provenience less important) have been cremated in intense vehicle fires and where the initial recovery by law enforcement personnel lacked screening, significant additional remains may be recovered by removing the ashen debris from the vehicle interior and subsequent wet screening in a laboratory setting (pers. obs.). Burned interior components (melted plastic, foam rubber, etc.) make bone recognition in the field very difficult. Excavators also have the option to remove very delicate remains in the field *en bloc* (i.e., with the mass of sediments and associated artifacts attached) so that careful, controlled recovery may occur in a laboratory setting.

Effects of Handling Procedures

Once remains have been recognized in the field, appropriate handling is essential to mitigate additional taphonomic damage (Cronyn 1990). Damp remains may be fragile and easily damaged, and mold and mildew may obscure evidence and degrade the DNA recovery potential of osseous remains. Whenever possible, remains recovered from damp settings, including many (if not most) buried remains, should be transported and stored in containers that allow moisture to evaporate. Paper bags or boxes may be used for short-term transport and storage, or desiccant packets can be used to mitigate possible damage if plastic bags are required. Further damage of burned remains during transport, storage, or analysis may reduce the identifiability of dental elements, which are especially critical to positive identification in cases where DNA potential has been destroyed by thermal alteration. Very fragile or friable remains, such as burned bone fragments or teeth, should be wrapped in cotton, tissue paper, or other soft materials to prevent damage. These items should then be placed in small hard-sided containers, such as plastic medicine bottles or film canisters, to protect them further (Fairgrieve 2008:83).

The effects of poor transport and storage procedures are akin to other destructive taphonomic processes. Bones stored in a hard container with inadequate cushioning may become crushed or fragmented, thus reducing their identifiability and obscuring their previous postmortem history. Postmortem breakage also will reduce the amount of information in a biological profile through the loss of intact surface morphology and the number of measurements that can be taken for metric estimates of sex, age, stature, and ancestry. The destruction of a single fragile pubic bone, for example, may greatly reduce the more reliable options for sexing and aging an adult individual. In some circumstances, postmortem storage and transport damage also may be mistaken for perimortem trauma (see Chapter 13, this volume), so minimizing this type of damage may prevent incorrect interpretations about perimortem events.

Direct Effects of Excavation upon Osseous Remains

The processes of excavation themselves may damage osseous remains in ways that mimic other taphonomic processes, including perimortem trauma. The need to move large amounts of sediment rapidly, such as in hand or mechanical trenching operations while searching for a buried body, often means that the initial discovery of remains is rather abrupt. Excavation (tool) damage is especially well known to those who have worked with skeletal remains recovered by avocational/amateur archaeologists, Works Progress Administration projects, and/or construction crews. Buried remains are often encountered accidentally by local citizens through construction work, farming activities, gardening, or digging by pets. Large amounts of damage to a skeleton may be caused at this point, especially if remains go unnoticed while the digging proceeds and are only later recognized as significant. Recovery-related damage may result from heavy machinery such as backhoes and graders or from hand tools such as picks, shovels, and trowels even among professional archaeologists. An example of postmortem excavation damage from a heavy tool is shown in Figure 17.3. More delicate hand operations usually follow initial discovery and are less likely to damage remains, although poorly visualized remains are still susceptible to damage from trowels. The wood and plastic implements often used during hand excavation typically cause less damage to bone surfaces than metal ones. If the bone has become friable due to loss of organic content, a blow from a shovel can leave a deep gouge typically a few millimeters wide and exposing underlying lighter-colored bone (see Chapter 13, this volume). Friable bone also may crack at this impact site. If the gouge is large enough, the arc shape of the shovel may be visible in the gouge, leaving little doubt as to the source of the damage. These marks also may appear as lighter-colored scratches, gouges, or jagged and blocky postmortem fractures.

Figure 17.3 Nonhuman (cattle, *Bos taurus*) rib showing postmortem excavation damage to one margin. Note the width of the gouge, cracking at its base, and associated margin flaking exposing lighter-colored underlying bone. Scale is in cm. (Photograph by Jade De La Paz and Amanda Yano-Litwin.)

Conclusions

A great deal of information gleaned from a site is gained not through immediate identification of objects *in situ* but through the recovery of objects by screening individual
lots of sediments. Acuity in this sense therefore is increased through improvements
in screening operations, including (where needed) finer mesh sizes, wet screening of
adherent sediments, and transfer of block sediments or whole exhumed coffins to a laboratory setting for processing. Training, motivation, and fatigue among recovery personnel may alter the recovery rates of remains and therefore the analytical conclusions
drawn from them. Recovery rates may be improved through changes in the working
environment, including protecting teams from sun exposure or precipitation and controlling ambient lighting to maximize the visibility of osseous remains and other evidence. Exacting recovery procedures minimize evidence loss, which in turn increases
skeletal representation, completeness of biological profiles, and the identifiability of
remains. Strict attention to the potential for bone loss due to possible gaps in the recovery system will prevent the assumption that natural taphonomic processes, including
consumption or dispersal by large vertebrate scavengers, dissolution in acidic soil, water
transport, or weathering, must have been the cause. Since the postdepositional history
of skeletal remains can be recorded in many cases through their taphonomic alterations, it is incumbent upon investigators not to introduce artificial (recovery-caused)
taphonomic alterations of their own. If the sources of taphonomic alterations to remains
can be determined securely, the investigator may more clearly assess those that may be
criminal in origin.

Acknowledgments

The authors thank Donald Siwek for his loan of experimental skeletal materials and thank
Jonathan Bethard for his loan of experimental skeletal materials and for reviewing an
earlier version of this chapter. Thanks also go to Brianne Charles for her kind editorial
assistance.

DoD Employee Statement

Dr. Baker has more than 20 years of field experience in academic, federal government, and
cultural resource management areas, including field investigations and/or excavations in
Vietnam, Laos, Cambodia, South Korea, France, Italy, Fiji, Jamaica, Texas, and New York.
She also has worked on mass graves excavation and forensic analysis of remains in Iraq.
Dr. Baker has three degrees in anthropology (B.A., M.A., and Ph.D.) from the University
of Nebraska-Lincoln, Syracuse University, and Texas A&M University, respectively. Her
work experience includes her current position as Scientific Advisor at the Defense Prisoner
of War/Missing Personnel Office, as well as serving as a forensic anthropologist and laboratory manager at the Joint POW/MIA Accounting Command, Central Identification
Laboratory and as a project archaeologist and osteologist for Prewitt and Associates,
Inc. and Espey-Houston and Associates. This chapter was written in the author's personal capacity and does not set forth any official positions, policies, or decisions of the
Department of Defense or the U.S. Government.

References

Anderson, G. (2008) *Determination of Elapsed Time Since Death in Homicide Victims Disposed of in the Ocean*. Canadian Police Research Centre, Technical Report TR-102008, Ottawa, Ontario, Canada.

Anderson, G. and N. Hobischak (2002) *Determination of Time of Death for Humans Discovered in Saltwater Using Aquatic Organism Succession and Decomposition Rates*. Canadian Police Research Centre, Technical Report TR-09-2002, Ottawa, Ontario, Canada.

Ball, B. F. and P. T. Bobrowsky (1987) Cost effectiveness and time management evaluation of intensive recovery techniques. *Canadian Journal of Archaeology* 11:75–97.

Barker, P. (1993) *Techniques of Archeological Excavation* (3rd edn.). B. T. Batsford, London, U.K.

Blau, S. and D. H. Ubelaker (eds.) (2009) *Handbook of Forensic and Anthropology and Archaeology*. Left Coast Press, Walnut Creek, CA.

Bocek, B. (1992) The Jasper Ridge reexcavation experiment: Rates of artifact mixing by rodents. *American Antiquity* 57:261–269.

Buikstra, J. and M. Swegle (1989) Bone modification due to burning: Experimental evidence. In *Bone Modification* eds. R. Bonnichsen and M. H. Sorg, pp. 247–258. Center for Study of the First Americans, Orono, ME.

Bunch, A. W. (2010) Indoor wet screening of exhumed skeletal remains: A suggested procedure for the preparation of fragile evidence for anthropological analysis. *Journal of Forensic Sciences* 55:1102–1104.

Cannon, M. D. (1999) A mathematical model of the effects of screen size on zooarchaeological relative abundance measures. *Journal of Archaeological Science* 26:205–214.

Casallas, D. A. and M. K. Moore (2012) High soil acidity associated with near complete mineral dissolution of recently buried human remains. *Proceedings of the American Academy of Forensic Sciences* 18:400–401.

Cronyn, J. M. (1990) *The Elements of Archaeological Conservation*. Routledge, London, U.K.

Dirkmaat, D. C. (2002) Recovery and interpretation of the fatal fire victim: The role of forensic anthropology. In *Advances in Forensic Taphonomy: Method, Theory, and Archaeological Perspectives* eds. W. D. Haglund and M. H. Sorg, pp. 451–472. CRC Press, Boca Raton, FL.

Dupras, T. L., J. J. Schultz, S. M. Wheeler, and L. J. Williams (2011) *Forensic Recovery of Human Remains: Archaeological Approaches* (2nd edn.). CRC Press, Boca Raton, FL.

Faerman, M., G. Kahila Bar-Gal, D. Filon, C. L. Greenblatt, L. Stager, A. Oppenheim, and P. Smith (1998) Determining the sex of infanticide victims from the Late Roman era through ancient DNA analysis. *Journal of Archaeological Science* 25:861–865.

Fairgrieve, S. I. (2008) *Forensic Cremation: Recovery and Analysis*. CRC Press, Boca Raton, FL.

Fazekas, I. G. and F. Kósa (1978) *Forensic Fetal Osteology*. Akadémiai Kiadó, Budapest, Hungary.

Ferllini, R. (2007) *Forensic Archaeology and Human Rights Violations*. Charles C Thomas, Springfield, IL.

Fox, M. (2003) Turret excavation reveals insights into ship's sinking. *Cheesebox* 13:8–11.

Freeman, L. G., J. González Echegaray, J. Pokines, H. Stettler, and M. Krupa (1998) Tamisage ultra fin et récupération de l'outillage: Observations réalisées a El Juyo (Espagne Cantabrique). *L'Anthropologie (Paris)* 102:35–44.

Green, J. (2004) *Maritime Archaeology: A Technical Handbook* (2nd edn.). Elsevier, San Diego, CA.

Haglund, W. D. and D. T. Reay (1993) Problems of recovering partial human remains at different times and locations: Concerns for death investigators. *Journal of Forensic Sciences* 38:69–80.

Hawkins, A. L., S. T. Stewart, and E. B. Banning (2003) Interobserver bias in enumerated data from archaeological survey. *Journal of Archaeological Science* 30:1503–1512.

Hosch, S. and P. Zibulski (2003) The influence of inconsistent wet-sieving procedures on the macro-remain concentration in waterlogged sediments. *Journal of Archaeological Science* 30:849–857.

Huculak, M. A. and T. L. Rogers (2009) Reconstructing the sequence of events surrounding body disposition based on color staining of bone. *Journal of Forensic Sciences* 54:979–984.

James, S. R. (1997) Methodological issues concerning screen size recovery rates and their effects on archaeofaunal interpretations. *Journal of Archaeological Science* 24:385–397.

Knudson, K. J. (2008) Tiwanaku influence in the South Central Andes: Strontium isotope analysis and Middle Horizon migration. *Latin American Antiquity* 19:3–23.

Knudson, K. J. and J. E. Buikstra (2007) Residential mobility and resource use in the Chiribaya polity of southern Peru: Strontium isotope analysis of archaeological tooth enamel and bone. *International Journal of Osteoarchaeology* 17:563–580.

Lasseter, A. E., K. P. Jacobi, R. Farley, and L. Hensel (2003) Cadaver dog and handler team capabilities in the recovery of buried human remains in the Southeastern United States. *Journal of Forensic Sciences* 48:617–621.

Leney, M. D. (2006) Sampling skeletal remains for ancient DNA (aDNA): A measure of success. *Historical Archaeology* 40:31–49.

Lit, L., J. B. Schweitzer, and A. M. Oberbauer (2011) Handler beliefs affect scent detection dog outcomes. *Animal Cognition* 14:387–394.

Lyman, R. L. (2008) *Quantitative Paleozoology*. Cambridge University Press, Cambridge, U.K.

Lyman, R. L. (2012) The influence of screen mesh size, and size and shape of rodent teeth on recovery. *Journal of Archaeological Science* 39:1854–1861.

Mays, S. and J. Eyers (2011) Perinatal infant death at the Roman villa site at Hambleden, Buckinghamshire, England. *Journal of Archaeological Science* 38:1931–1938.

Mays, S., S. Vincent, and G. Campbell (2012) The value of sieving of grave soil in the recovery of human remains: An experimental study of poorly preserved archaeological inhumations. *Journal of Archaeological Science* 39:3248–3254.

Menez, L. L. (2005) The place of a forensic archaeologist at a crime scene involving a buried body. *Forensic Science International* 152:311–315.

Moore, C. E., II, B. D. Davis, and M. D. Leney (2002) Analysis of pilot-related equipment and archaeological strategy in the recovery of aircrew losses from the Vietnam War. *Journal of Forensic Sciences* 47:1210–1214.

Owsley, D. W. (1995) Techniques for locating burials, with emphasis on the probe. *Journal of Forensic Sciences* 40:735–740.

Ozbun, T. L. (2011) The inadequacy of the 1/4 inch mesh screen in archaeology. *Journal of Northwest Anthropology* 45:235–242.

Payne, S. (1972) Partial recovery and sample bias: The results of some sieving experiments. In: *Papers in Economic Prehistory* ed. E. S. Higgs, pp. 49–64. Cambridge University Press, Cambridge, U.K.

Pokines, J. T. (2000) Microfaunal research design in the Cantabrian Spanish Paleolithic. *Journal of Anthropological Research* 56:95–112.

Pokines, J. T. (2009) Forensic recoveries of U.S. war dead and the effects of taphonomy and other site-altering processes. In *Hard Evidence: Case Studies in Forensic Anthropology* (2nd edn.) ed. D. W. Steadman, pp. 141–154. Prentice Hall, Upper Saddle River, NJ.

Pollanen, M. S. and D. A. Chiasson (1996) Fracture of the hyoid bone in strangulation: Comparison of fractured and unfractured hyoids from victims of strangulation. *Journal of Forensic Sciences* 41:110–113.

Pringle, J. K., J. R. Jervis, J. D. Hansen, G. M. Jones, N. J. Cassidy, and J. P. Cassella (2012) Geophysical monitoring of simulated clandestine graves using electrical and ground-penetrating radar methods: 0–3 years after burial. *Journal of Forensic Sciences* 57:1467–1486.

Quitmyer, I. R. (2004) What kind of data are in the back dirt? An experiment on the influence of screen size on optimal data recovery. *Archaeofauna* 13:109–129.

Randall, B. (1991) Body retrieval and morgue operation at the crash of United Flight 232. *Journal of Forensic Sciences* 36:403–409.

Rezos, M. M., J. J. Schultz, R. A. Murdock II, and S. A. Smith (2011) Utilizing a magnetic locator to search for buried firearms and miscellaneous weapons at a controlled research site. *Journal of Forensic Sciences* 56:1289–1295.

Ríos, L., A. García-Rubio, B. Martínez, C. Coch, and S. Llidó (2011) Field recovery and potential information value of small elements of the skeleton. *Homo* 62:270–279.

Schmidt, C. W. (2008) The recovery and study of burned human teeth. In *The Analysis of Burned Human Remains* eds. C. W. Schmidt and S. Symes, pp. 55–74. Elsevier, Amsterdam, the Netherlands.

Schultz, J. J. (2008) Sequential monitoring of burials containing small pig cadavers using ground penetrating radar. *Journal of Forensic Sciences* 53:279–287.

Scientific Working Group for Forensic Anthropology (SWGANTH) (2012) Electronic document, http://www.swganth.org/.

Scott, E. (1999) *The Archaeology of Infancy and Infant Death*. BAR International Series 819, Archaeopress, Oxford, U.K.

Shaffer, B. S. (1992) Quarter-inch screening: Understanding biases in recovery of vertebrate faunal remains. *American Antiquity* 57:129–136.

Shaffer, B. S. and J. L. J. Sanchez (1994) Comparison of 1/8"- and 1/4"-mesh recovery of controlled samples of small-to-medium-sized mammals. *American Antiquity* 59:525–530.

Shipman, P., G. Foster, and M. Schoeninger (1984) Burnt bones and teeth: An experimental study of color, morphology, crystal structure and shrinkage. *Journal of Archaeological Science* 11:307–325.

Sledzik, P. S., D. Dirkmaat, R. W. Mann, T. D. Holland, A. Z. Mundorff, B. J. Adams, C. M. Crowder, and F. DePaolo (2009) Disaster victim recovery and education: Forensic anthropology in the aftermath of September 11. In *Hard Evidence: Case Studies in Forensic Anthropology* (2nd edn.) ed. D. W. Steadman, pp. 289–302. Prentice Hall, Upper Saddle River, NJ.

Smith, P. and G. Avishai (2005) The use of dental criteria for estimating postnatal survival in skeletal remains of infants. *Journal of Archaeological Science* 32:83–89.

Ubelaker, D. H. (1999) *Human Skeletal Remains: Excavation, Analysis, Interpretation* (3rd edn.). Taraxacum, Washington, DC.

Ubelaker, D. H., D. W. Owsley, M. M. Houck, E. Craig, W. Grant, T. Woltanski, R. Fram, K. Sandness, and N. Peerwani (1995) The role of forensic anthropology in the recovery and analysis of Branch Davidian compound victims: Recovery procedures and characteristics of the victims. *Journal of Forensic Sciences* 40:335–340.

Walker, P. L., J. R. Johnson, and P. M. Lambert (1988) Age and sex biases in the preservation of human skeletal remains. *American Journal of Physical Anthropology* 76:183–188.

Webb, P. A. and J. M. Suchey (1985) Epiphyseal union of the anterior iliac crest and medial clavicle in a modern multiracial sample of American males and females. *American Journal of Physical Anthropology* 68:457–466.

Webster, A. D. (1998) Excavation of a Vietnam-era aircraft crash site: Use of cross-cultural understanding and dual forensic recovery methods. *Journal of Forensic Sciences* 43:277–283.

Appendix A

JAMES T. POKINES

Macroscopic Osseous Taphonomy Checklist

Preservational

General state of remains (excellent, good, fair, or poor)
Cortical erosion/exposure of cancellous bone
Cortical exfoliation (bone loss in thin, spalling layers)
Postmortem breakage
Perimortem breakage/fragmentation or trauma
Rounding (erosion/tumbling in an abrasive environment)
Decalcified
Postmortem cracking of desiccated tooth enamel
Incidental surface striations/scratches

Decompositional

Adhering soft tissue, including hair
Adhering adipocere
Marrow present
Retained decomposition odor
Retained grease texture
Decompositional insect casings/other remains present

Surface exposure

Surface cracking/longitudinal splitting from drying of waterlogged bone
Subaerial weathering

Thermal alteration

Cooking (translucence, loss of hardness, pot polish, etc.)
Carbonization
Calcination
Cracking patterns from the burning of dry or green bone
Soot accumulation
Melted materials on bone (plastic, etc.)

Mineral

Copper (green), iron (red), calcium (white), manganese (black), or other mineral oxide staining
Vivianite formation
Subfossilization
Fossilization

Concretion

Salt crystal damage (drying of remains from saline environments)

Water staining (presence of a water line from calcium mineral deposits, color differential line)

Mechanical

Excavation damage (tool gouges, chatter marks, punctures, etc.)

Plowing damage (deep gouges)

Microabrasion (small irregular striations)

Residual artifactual

Boot portions/similar adhering

Metal oxidized onto bone

Adhering fabric/other

Adhering oil/other similar

Soil/burial substrate

General soil staining

Warping/flattening of elements (especially the cranial vault)

Crushing/compaction from overburden

Adhering/infiltrating sediments

Plant/fungal/protozoan/bacterial

Algal presence/staining

Mold presence/staining

Bacterial presence/staining

Dark brown staining from tannins (from leaves or wood, including wooden coffins)

Plant root damage on surfaces

Plant roots still infiltrating/adhering

Accumulation of decomposing leaf litter (humus) within/upon skeletal elements

Other adhering plant taxa (moss, etc.)

Analytical

Previous writing, labeling, other marking, gluing, taping, or other adhering non-biological (packaging material, preservative, etc.)

Previous analyst reconstruction or other alteration (labeling, gluing, waxing, taping, etc.)

DNA or histological analysis cuts

Faunal

Adhering fauna (mollusks, barnacles, etc.)

Carnivore gnawing (tooth punctures, gnawing wear on exposed margins, tooth pits, and gripping marks)

Marine organism boring

Gastric corrosion, winnowing, or windowing of bone

Rodent gnawing

Termite or other insect damage

Elemental patterning

Missing elements (postmortem tooth loss, etc.)

Spatial distribution of elements/articulation

Storage of smaller elements within the cranium (indicating reburial or postburial movement)

Previous/current commingling

Relationship of field recovery methods (surface survey only, lack of screening, screen mesh size, etc.) to patterning of non-recovered elements

Curational/personal display

Curation damage/alteration (polish developed from repeated handling, positional wear surfaces or "shelf wear," etc.)

Mounting hardware (screws, pedestal, etc.) or related alteration

Accumulation of dust

Accumulation of candle wax

Accumulation of non-decompositional arthropods (arachnids, ants, hornets, etc.) or other taxa

Specimen labeling

Other cultural modification

Alteration into an implement or other cultural signifier (bone awl, suspension for jewelry, etc.)

Alteration by autopsy (surgical saw marks in typical autopsy locations)

Painting, oiling, smoking, etc.

Bleaching, as in specimen preparation for an anatomical collection

Presence of embalming chemical residue (formalin, etc.)

Machine cutting from butchery (most likely indicating faunal rather than human remains)

Chemical acidic corrosion

Other

Any alteration not listed above

Abbreviated Macroscopic Osseous Taphonomy Checklist

General state of remains (excellent, good, fair, or poor)
Green (copper), red (iron), white (calcium), or other mineral staining
Algal staining
General (soil) staining
Retained grease texture
Adhering dried soft tissue, including marrow or adipocere
Surface cracking from drying of waterlogged bone
Subaerial weathering
Thermal alteration (carbonization, calcination, and cracking)
Plant root damage/plant roots still adhering or infiltrating
Other adhering taxa (mold, moss, molluscs, etc.)
Adhering or infiltrating sediments and type (clay, silt, sand, or larger)
Postmortem breakage
Excavation damage (tool marks)
Cortical erosion due to acidic substrate
Cortical exfoliation (bone loss in thin layers)
Marine coastal alteration (rounding and bleaching)
Writing, labeling, other marking; gluing, taping, packaging, or other adhering nonbiological
Curation damage/alteration
Carnivore damage
Rodent damage
Other

Appendix B

MIRANDA M.E. JANS

Microscopic Osseous Taphonomy Checklist

Microstructure

Histological index
Generalized destruction
Bacterial alteration
Bacterial alteration type
Fungal alteration
Fungal alteration type
Cracking
Birefringence

Thermal alteration

Color
Color distribution in bone
Cracking (haversian canals)
Carbon deposits
Crisscross cracking
Enlarged osteocyte lacunae

Inclusion and staining

Copper (green), iron (red), or other mineral staining
Vivianite, (framboidal) pyrite, calcite, gypsum, or other crystal formation
Adipocere, other soft tissue remains
Humic acid
Soil material (sand, clay, etc.) adhering or included in pores
Plant roots (adhering/penetrating)
Fungi, bacteria (adhering, penetrating)

Other

Any alteration not listed above

Index

Tonight
- Email Styers
- Email group ✓

- Study Anth. 341 Test 3
- Start Anth 362 book
- Call for appointment w/ Walk ✓ Tomorrow 8am Sharp !

Tomorrow
- Continue Anth. 362 book
    - write/Type (~5 pages)

- Study Anth. 341 Test 4

- Read Anth. 341 Article (If time)

Friday ?

- Read/Type Anth 341 essay OR...